THE ACHILLE LAURO HIJACKING

Also by MICHAEL K. BOHN

Nerve Center: Inside the White House Situation Room

THE ACHILLE LAURO HIJACKING

LESSONS IN THE POLITICS AND PREJUDICE OF TERRORISM

MICHAEL K. BOHN

Brassey's, Inc.
Washington, D.C.

Library of Congress Cataloging-in-Publication Data

Bohn, Michael K.
  The Achille Lauro hijacking : lessons in the politics and prejudice of terrorism / Michael K. Bohn.—1st ed.
    p.   cm.
  Includes bibliographical references and index.
  ISBN 1-57488-779-3 (alk. paper)
    1. Achille Lauro Hijacking Incident, 1985   2. Terrorism—Mediterranean Region—Case studies.   3. Italy—Politics and government—1976–1994.   I. Title.
HV6433.M4B65   2004
364.15'4'0916387—dc22   2004006728

Printed in the United States of America on acid-free paper that meets the American National Standards Institute Z39-48 Standard.

Brassey's, Inc.
22841 Quicksilver Drive
Dulles, Virginia 20166

First Edition

10 9 8 7 6 5 4 3 2 1

To the families of
Alex Odeh and Leon Klinghoffer

CONTENTS

ACKNOWLEDGMENTS

THE idea of writing this book came from my friend Gene Gibbons, the long-time White House correspondent for UPI, then later *Reuters*. Gene covered the White House when I served on the National Security Council staff as the director of the White House Situation Room during the Reagan administration.

I am indebted to Sarah Flynn for her inspired editorial guidance, and clear strategy for the structure and tone of the book. Thanks also to Rick Russell and Sam Dorrance at Brassey's, Inc.

I want to thank a unique group of Naval officers who not only helped capture the *Achille Lauro* hijackers, but also took the time to recall their memories of the incident: John Poindexter and Jim Stark, who were at the White House at the time of the hijacking, and Ralph Zia, Skid Massey, and Steve Weatherspoon, pilots who were on board USS *Saratoga*.

In addition, thanks to several people who contributed time to the project—Nick Veliotes, Rodney Gould, Peter Kohler, Bob Collins, Buck Revell, Alberto Negrin, and Jack Shaheen.

I am grateful for the help from Sami Odeh, brother of the late Alex Odeh, and Lisa and Ilsa Klinghoffer for their thoroughgoing assistance. May God bless Alex Odeh and Leon Klinghoffer. Finally, thanks to my wife Elin for her love and support.

PROLOGUE

ON November 1, 2001, the United States was still reeling from the extraordinary terrorist attack on America fifty days earlier. Smoke and steam continued to rise from the smoldering heap of rubble that was once the twin towers of the World Trade Center in New York City. At the Pentagon in Washington, DC, Department of Defense personnel were back at work, with many still haunted by memories of the blast, fire, and smoke. At nearby Reagan National Airport, flight operations remained suspended.

U.S. military forces were attacking the Taliban in Afghanistan in retaliation for its support of Osama bin Laden and his Al Qaeda terrorist organization. Americans were worrying about biological warfare as a fourth person died from exposure to anthrax in the postal system. The Justice Department held dozens of people who appeared to have connections to past and future terrorist attacks. Olympic officials were considering enhanced security at the Winter Games scheduled for the following February in Salt Lake City, Utah.

On the first day of November, Americans still seemed to be in withdrawal from their lives before 9-11, a retreat to the basics—family, friends, jobs—at the expense of leisure activities, travel, and entertainment that just felt inappropriate at that time. That withdrawal triggered aftershocks throughout the social and economic fabric of the country. One area, the entertainment industry and the arts, reflected the public's retreat to comfort zones.

Viewers could not retreat from terrorism on television—that's where the attacks took place—but in theater, Ground Zero seemed to reach all the way to Broadway in New York City. Hollywood producers and studios reassessed the appropriateness of both future production and finished films about to be released. People within the industry were questioning not only the propriety of traditional movie subjects such as romantic comedies set in Manhattan and police thrillers, but flat out cancelling anything connected to terrorism. Producers delayed indefinitely the release of a film titled *Big Trouble*, which includes the concealment of a nuclear weapon aboard an airliner. *Collateral Damage*, Arnold Schwarzenegger's new movie about a fireman avenging the killing of his family by terrorists, went immediately back in the can, to be released in 2002 as Hollywood gradually recovered.

Mark Volpe, the managing director of the Boston Symphony Orchestra, announced on November 1 that he had cancelled the scheduled performance of the choruses drawn from the opera *The Death of Klinghoffer*. Volpe cited "the proximity of the events of 9-11" as the reason for the decision. Robert Spano, who was scheduled to conduct the cancelled performance, said that it was "inappropriate to perform excerpts from an opera about a terrorist act right now."

Superficially, that reasoning seemed consistent with delaying the release of movies with terrorist themes. Composed by John Adams and written by librettist Alice Goodman, the opera tells the story of the 1985 hijacking of an Italian cruise ship, *Achille Lauro*, by four young Palestinian men. They brutally murdered one of the passengers, a Jewish-American named Leon Klinghoffer, while his wife and other hostages were held at gunpoint. But that was not the only reason for the cancellation.

The opera did not demonize the hijackers. In an extraordinary shift from American social and entertainment norms, *The Death of Klinghoffer* featured choruses and arias that focused on the other side of a violent act. The performers in the hijackers' roles sang of their feelings, their dreams, and their yearning for a free Palestine. Filled with rage over the horrific 9-11 attacks, few Americans were interested in any work of art that treated terrorists as anything other than despicable murderers. The Boston Symphony seemed to think that, too, but others disagreed. The debate over the politics of the opera took center stage.

"Adams and Goodman did not present this story as a simple matter of good vs. evil," wrote Richard Dyer in the *Boston Globe* after the performance was cancelled. "The opera does not condone terrorism—far from it. But it does say that terrorists are real people with inner lives, and that they are the result of the convergence of a specific set of historical and personal circumstances, just as the rest of us are."

Six opera companies collectively commissioned the opera in 1989: San Francisco Opera, Los Angeles Festival, Brooklyn Academy of Music, Theatre Royale de la Monnaie, Opera de Lyon, and Glyndebourne (UK) Festival. The work debuted in Brussels to mixed reviews, then played in Lyon and Vienna, before opening in Brooklyn. Several music critics hailed the brilliance of the composition, comparing it favorably to Adams's previous opera, *Nixon in China*, another adaptation of a political event to the operatic stage. Others panned the music, one calling the opera "pompous, turgid, derivative, and hopelessly confused." Other critics skipped artistic matters and declared Adams, Goodman, and director Peter Sellars to be prejudiced against Jews.

"Surely there is nothing in the libretto in an anti-Arab vein to match the repulsive anti-Semitism that drools from the mouth of a character called 'Rambo,'" wrote Raymond Sokolov of the *Wall Street Journal*. He saw no balance in the production and found the opera's portrayal of Jews and Palestinians to be "obnoxious," characterizations that cast the Klinghoffers as trivial suburbanites, while the assassins acted out the "righteous anger of their oppressed brethren."

Adams voiced anger when news of the cancellation became public, disagreeing with the Boston Symphony's assumption that audiences "only want comfort and familiarity during these difficult times." A month later, Adams reacted to the charges of anti-Semitism: "In this country, there is almost no option for the other side, no space for the presentation of the Palestinian point of view in a work of art."

"*The Death of Klinghoffer* is not only about a brief, violent incident from the recent news," Adams said in another interview. "It is about religious and social intolerance, about a struggle over land that is as old a story as the first pages of written history."

Adams is right. Terrorism is not a simple phenomenon. Terrorism is about power, politics, and prejudice.

As the director of the White House Situation Room during the second administration of Ronald Reagan, I spent my days and nights with my staff monitoring terrorist incidents around the world. We wrote daily memos to the President about plane hijackings, airport bombings, and hostage-taking that happened at an infuriating frequency. The hijacking of *Achille Lauro* was one of those incidents, and one of the few terrorist acts to which the U.S. government found a way to aggressively react during those years. In most other situations, such as the seizure of Westerners in Lebanon, the United States could not even find hostages, much less bring the kidnappers to justice.

Unable to rescue or otherwise liberate American hostages held by Arab guerrillas in Beirut, a frustrated President Reagan asked Iran, which had considerable influence over the groups that had kidnapped those persons, to intervene and hopefully broker the hostages' release. That initiative, which involved the illicit sale of arms to Iran in return for its help, later led to the Iran-Contra scandal of 1986, a crisis that almost destroyed Reagan's presidency. Two of my bosses at the National Security Council—Bud McFarlane and John Poindexter— knew that there were no simple solutions to international terrorism, so they undertook a risky plan to gain freedom for the hostages through political maneuvering and international intrigue.

The exposure of my colleague Marine Lieutenant Colonel Oliver North's enterprise, one that sent money produced by the sale of arms to Iran to rebels fighting Nicaragua's Marxist dictator, cast an unfavorable light on the White House's complex solution to what many Americans view as a simple, criminal problem. Just as sheriffs and marshals did in countless Hollywood Westerns, many Americans thought that all we had to do was send either cops or soldiers to capture the evildoers. My experiences in the 1980s, coupled with my study of the *Achille Lauro* incident, tell me that preventing terrorism, living with it, or even reacting successfully to it, is a far more complex endeavor.

Yet many have attempted to reduce international terrorism to simplistic terms—a battle between good and evil, for example. One of those with that view, President George W. Bush, talks straightforwardly about America's war against the "axis of evil," and issued a black-and-white challenge to the world: "Are you with us or against us?"

The reasons that Americans increasingly have become subjects of terrorism in the last twenty-five years are far too complex to be described by oversimplified jingoisms. Terrorism is not just about crime and punishment. Terrorism is about violence, power politics, prejudice, hatred, land, religion, greed, money, and a host of venal factors that all influence human society. All of these forces are present in the *Achille Lauro* hijacking and its aftermath. The very definition of terrorism should remind everyone of the powerful dynamics behind the phenomenon: "The unlawful use of force or violence against per-

sons or property to intimidate or coerce a government, the civilian population, or any segment thereof, in furtherance of political or social
objectives." These last few words—"political or social objectives"—
immediately bring to mind discussion, disagreement, and discord
among peoples. No society, much less a world of societies, can agree
on the same political and social objectives. The world is too complicated for consensus. The *Achille Lauro* hijacking, seemingly a simple
confrontation of good and evil, really is a case study in the complex
forces that shape both terrorism and the responses that it triggers.

The *Achille Lauro* hijackers, one only seventeen years old, surrendered to the Egyptian government after holding the passengers for fifty-
one hours. The Egyptians secretly put them on an EgyptAir jet bound
for Tunis. Through timely intelligence, U.S. Navy aircraft located and
intercepted the airliner, forcing it to land in Italy. Although the Italian
government detained the four men who actually hijacked the ship,
they allowed the leader of the scheme—Mohammed Abbas, who used
nom de guerre, Abu Abbas—to escape to Yugoslavia despite a personal
appeal to hold him by President Reagan. Abbas was the head of one
part of the Palestine Liberation Front (PLF), one of the eight constituent groups that originally formed the PLO under Yasser Arafat's chair-
manship. The PLF consisted of three factions: the first, headed by
Taalat Yacoub, an anti-Arafat Palestinian supported by Syria, who
immediately denounced the hijacking; Abd al-Fatah Ghanim, also
opposing Arafat, led the second; Abbas headed the third PLF faction,
was loyal to Arafat, and also sat on the PLO Executive Committee. His
part of the PLF had carried out a series of armed raids in Israel and the
West Bank starting in the late 1970s. (From this point on, any mention
of the PLF refers to the Abbas faction.)

Regardless of the extraordinarily deft capture of the hijackers, the
horrendous terrorist attacks of 9-11 appear to make the hijacking of
Achille Lauro a minor battle in the prolonged war between terrorists
and America. The *Achille Lauro* incident, however, showed that most
governments don't treat terrorism as a problem of crime and punishment. Nations will ignore international protocols and legalisms when
their national interests are at stake or domestic politics demand, just
as the United States did when it "hijacked the hijackers," as foreign
critics characterized the operation. Reagan, cheered at home for his
bold move to capture the hijackers, told the terrorists, "You can run,
but you can't hide." Egyptian President Hosni Mubarak denounced

Reagan for intercepting his country's plane, but then Mubarak publicly lied to the world to get himself out of an untenable international predicament. Italy thought maintaining good relations with Arafat's Palestine Liberation Organization and Middle Eastern Arab states was more important than jailing Abu Abbas. Italy chose a politically palatable solution, one acceptable both at home and in the Middle East; it didn't see a conflict of good and evil, just a political problem.

A common slogan claims that "one man's terrorist is another man's freedom fighter." The hijackers claimed that they were fighting for Palestine's freedom both during the hijacking and after they were arrested. I saw them as murderers, finding it hard to determine if they were speaking truthfully, or just acting out a courtroom dodge to escape punishment. An Italian court in 1986, however, accepted their argument, calling them "soldiers fighting for their ideals," not terrorists. The court ordered only a thirty-year sentence for Youssef Majed Molqi, the hijacker who shot Klinghoffer. The judges cited his depraved childhood, spent in Palestinian refugee camps surrounded by violence, as a mitigating circumstance.

The same court also convicted Abu Abbas *in absentia* of planning the hijacking, sentencing him to life in prison.

The U.S. dropped its arrest warrant for Abu Abbas in 1987, deferring to his Italian conviction. Italy made no serious, overt attempt to capture Abbas and enforce the sentence, apparently not wanting to open old wounds with the PLO. In the 1980s Libya and Iraq provided both financial and political support to Abbas and his organization. Libya, however, withdrew that support in 1990, leaving Baghdad as Abu Abbas's only location for his headquarters. After Israel and the PLO signed the 1995 Interim Agreement, which followed the 1993 Oslo Peace Accords, Israel promised not to arrest Palestinians for violent actions prior to September 1993. Abu Abbas was one of those "pardoned," if you will. Born in a Palestinian refugee camp in Syria, Abbas made his first trip to the West Bank and Gaza in 1996.

The news media lusted after Abu Abbas, a scheming, manipulative man who never met a microphone he didn't like. For someone given a life sentence for the hijacking, he found it remarkably easy to grant dozens of interviews since 1985. In one spectacular instance of discarding ethics for ratings, NBC News broadcast an interview with Abbas that a reporter garnered clandestinely while the United States had an active warrant for his arrest. The U.S. State Department called NBC

TV an accomplice to terrorism, but the network chided the government for not doing what their reporter had done—find Abbas. The marriage between the press and Abbas was certainly one of convenience—reporters got great sound bites from Abbas; he got to spin the media about his importance in the Palestinian fight for freedom. If terrorism were indeed a fight between good and evil, then Abbas was an evilly good interview.

During the second half of the 1990s, until the start of the second intifada in September 2000, Abbas talked and acted like a reformed terrorist, even doing lunch with Palestinian politicians. He moved safely back and forth to Baghdad because of the Israeli forgiveness of past sins that was central to continued dialogue with the PLO. Yet during that period, Abbas secretly recruited more West Bank Palestinians to join his organization, even as he declared to the news media that he was a man of peace, claiming the *Achille Lauro* was an "accident." The Israelis caught two of the cells he recruited and trained after they killed an Israeli teenager in 2001.

As President Bush prepared both American citizens and other nations for his invasion of Iraq in 2003, he and his advisors often cited Abu Abbas's presence in Baghdad as evidence of Saddam Hussein's support for known terrorists. But Abbas and his followers have not been major forces in the Arab-Israeli conflict. The novelty of his raids on Israel—hang gliders, hot-air balloons, and speedboats—far exceeded their results; he staged some simply to upset Yasser Arafat's negotiations with the Israelis. There is no scale to measure a man's worth as a terrorist; that's a moribund, if not a callous objective. But Abu Abbas exerted more effort talking about terrorism than he did actually killing people.

Abbas told a reporter from the *New York Times* in November 2002 that he was unafraid of the threatened U.S. invasion of Iraq. Perhaps he was calm, then, when U.S. special forces busted open the door of his house and apprehended him on April 15, 2003.

The Bush administration crowed about his capture as if they had found Osama bin Laden, not a petty thug, however articulate he might be. Repeating Reagan's line from eighteen years before, a spokesman said, "They can run but they cannot hide. We will hunt them down. We will find them. No matter how long it takes, we will bring them to justice."

Nothing in Washington is devoid of politics and certainly not terrorism. The U.S. government had done nothing since 1987 to apprehend Abbas, despite the frequent urging from Klinghoffer's two daughters, Lisa and Ilsa. Reporters were the only people who sought out Abbas, and their ease in contacting him tells me that the mechanics of finding the man did not inhibit government action. A reporter walked up to Abbas in a Baghdad hotel a few months before the start of the U.S. invasion and made an appointment for an interview. The administration, however, saw the political value of trumpeting Abbas's capture, especially as the specter of finding no weapons of mass destruction began to rise.

Senseless biases, and racial and religious stereotyping, influenced both the hijacking and its aftermath. Two days after the hijacking, Alex Odeh, a Palestinian-American, defended on television Arafat's apparent attempt to defuse the incident. He died the next day when a bomb exploded at his Santa Ana, California office. Odeh, a Catholic, was a poet, college instructor, and head of the local American-Arab Anti-Discrimination Committee. A Palestinian shot Klinghoffer because he was Jewish; someone killed Odeh because he was Palestinian.

Both the family of Alex Odeh and the Anti-Discrimination Committee have felt that the U.S. government has not aggressively pursued Odeh's murderer, despite protestations to the contrary by the U.S. Federal Bureau of Investigation. "For a case that has been a priority for over seventeen years now," Odeh's brother Sami said to me in 2002, "one has to conclude that either the FBI is incompetent, or they do not want to press charges for some reason, most likely political." Further, a leaked internal FBI memo described Israel's obstruction of the investigation—three suspects sought protection in Israel—that also slowed FBI progress.

Two movies were made about the death of Klinghoffer. One, produced for NBC TV, portrayed the hijackers as terrorists and evil men. A joint American-Italian team produced the second, representing the hijackers as more complex characters—young men with feelings, according to the film's Italian writer and director, Alberto Negrin. He also focused on the political underpinnings of the event and attempted a degree of what Negrin termed even-handedness in telling the story. The composer of the opera also tried to present what he described as a balanced treatment of the hijacking, even examining the sources of both Jewish and Palestinian hatred.

Understanding the *Achille Lauro* incident, and its aftermath, will help America understand its complicated involvement with international terrorism, especially that arising from the Arab-Israeli conflict. Read about what happened during the hijacking, the arrest and trial of the hijackers, follow the parallel stories of the search for Alex Odeh's murderer and the Klinghoffer family's crusade to get Abbas, and understand how films, opera, and the news media viewed the events. As more recent victims seek legal redress against terrorists, the Klinghoffer family's lawsuit against the PLO—and its unanticipated outcome—provides a valuable lesson. Read also about *Achille Lauro* herself, the "ship of death," and its jinxed life that brought sorrow to so many.

CHAPTER

1

Murder on the High Seas

SEYMOUR and Viola Meskin, passengers aboard a cruise ship off the coast of Egypt, had just finished their lunch when they heard the first shots.

Four men stormed into the ship's dining room, shooting over the heads of the passengers with automatic weapons and yelling unintelligible instructions. Viola and others echoed the gunmen's shouting with screams of their own as bullets sent shards of glass and splinters flying.

"I started to run toward a door, but a man with a gun got in front of me and I turned back," said Sophia Kubacki, on vacation with her husband, Stanley. Others panicked and ran to the kitchen, only to be followed by one of the hijackers who beat two of the kitchen staff to the floor. Anna Hoeranter, an Austrian passenger, ran to an exit and one of the hijackers pushed her down an adjacent flight of stairs. Stunned by the violence, most passengers cowered on the floor.

The ship's Captain, Gerardo de Rosa, was in his cabin when his executive officer told him that armed men were on board, shooting at the passengers. Captain De Rosa quickly descended through several decks toward the ship's stern, then heard an agitated voice on the ship's loudspeakers request that he come immediately to the bridge.

"As soon as I got there I faced the machine guns," said De Rosa.

"First they fired some shots at the deck, shouting in Arabic. Then they told to me to head for Tartus." A Syrian port, Tartus lay about 300 miles to the northeast.

It was October 7, 1985. Four Palestinian gunmen had just hijacked *Achille Lauro*.

Seven hundred and forty-eight passengers embarked on *Achille Lauro* in Genoa, Italy, on October 3, 1985 for an eleven-day cruise with ports of call in Naples, Italy, Alexandria and Port Said, Egypt, and Ashdod, Israel, before returning to Genoa. Among the passengers were a group of close friends from New York and New Jersey: Frank and Mildred Hodes, Neil and June Kantor, Leon and Marilyn Klinghoffer, Seymour and Viola Meskin, Sylvia Sherman, and Charlotte Spiegel.

"We called them the 'beach people' because they always vacationed together on the Jersey shore," Lisa Klinghoffer, Leon and Marilyn's daughter, told me during a 2002 conversation. "They all decided to take a cruise to celebrate my parents' thirty-sixth wedding anniversary, and my mother's fifty-eighth birthday."

Leon, 69, owned and operated a small appliance manufacturing firm. Marilyn worked as a personnel manager at a small publishing firm. The Klinghoffers had two daughters, Lisa, 34, an artist married to Jerry Abittier, and Ilsa, 28, a hospital administrator, who was engaged to Paul Dworin.

While the Klinghoffers looked forward to the trip and Leon said that he was anticipating "a relaxing cruise with my friends," the couple had serious health problems. Leon, paralyzed on his right side as a result of two strokes, walked occasionally with a cane, but generally moved about in a wheelchair. Described by his family as a determined man who fought hard to recover from the effects of the strokes, Leon still had a robust attitude. Marilyn had been suffering from colon cancer for almost two years. "Her cancer was in remission and the doctor told my mother that a cruise would be good for her," Lisa said. She also explained that the beach people chose *Achille Lauro* over other ships because it was wheelchair accessible.

Achille Lauro, at 631 feet long and displacing 23,600 tons, was a small cruise ship by today's standards. The Italian government owned the ship, leasing it first to Lauro Lines then Chandris Lines. In 1985, the ship offered inexpensive cruises throughout the Mediterranean.

The cruise line offered little more than passport checks as security measures in Genoa, despite a spate of terrorist incidents in Europe and the Middle East that year. There were bombings or shootings in Paris, Madrid, Athens, and Rome, and just four months earlier, Lebanese Shi-'ite gunmen hijacked a TWA flight from Athens to Rome, taking their hostages on a seventeen-day odyssey in the Middle East, killing one along the way. Passengers said that officials at Genoa did not check anyone's luggage and considering ship hijackings were unprecedented in those years, security procedures probably seemed normal at the time.

Achille Lauro called in Naples on Friday, October 4, then sailed eastward through the Straits of Messina, the waterway separating the Italian mainland from Sicily. The passengers enjoyed the warm fall days, lying in deck chaises and swimming in the two pools. Many remarked on the calmness of the Mediterranean. "It was like sailing on a lake," said Alan Knee of New York.

Perhaps wiser by benefit of hindsight, two passengers later told of events that they said were portentous of the activities to follow. A low, loud overflight by a fighter jet frightened Irving Goodman; Fernando Pedroso from Brazil recalled seeing two jets and a helicopter with U.S. Air Force markings fly over the ship. Pedroso said later that the incident was a premonition that the sailing would not always be as smooth as it was that day.

Some noticed other things that seemed odd. Cruise manager Max Fico told of several young men who suspiciously kept together, displaying none of the congenial friendliness common to most cruise guests. "I noticed four people who were always together in a strange way," said Fico later. Some passengers tried to start a conversation during a meal, but the men did not readily reply. "We are Argentineans," they said, trying to explain their reticence to chat. But they did not understand a thing when a woman speaking fluent Spanish wanted to speak with them. Having boarded the ship with passports from Portugal, Norway, and Argentina, perhaps they were trying to maintain the smallest shred of their cover story.

On Sunday, the Klinghoffers and their friends celebrated Marilyn's fifty-eighth birthday. The beach people were glad to see Leon enjoying himself, savoring the benefits of a good life.

Born in 1916, Leon was one of five children whose parents, Pinchas and Lena Klinghoffer, owned a hardware store in the Lower East Side of Manhattan. When their father died suddenly at age twenty-nine, Leon and his brother Albert took over the store. They eventually started manufacturing small appliances—fans and toaster ovens.

Leon met Marilyn Windemere at her home in New Jersey and the two seemed to have fallen in love immediately. They married in 1949 and their family said that the two were inseparable since then, especially now that Leon needed his wife's help in getting around.

Leon was not defeated by his physical condition, but rather taught himself to do everything with his left hand. He worked hard with his physical therapist to improve his stamina. According to family friend and fellow passenger Charlotte Spiegel, Leon wanted to walk well enough to escort Ilsa down the isle at her wedding.

Six hundred fifty-one of the passengers left the ship in Alexandria on Monday morning, October 7, for a bus tour of the pyramids. They planned to rendezvous with *Achille Lauro* fourteen hours later in Port Said, 150 miles to the east at the mouth of the Suez Canal.

Another curious event occurred that morning in Alexandria. Rene Sprecher stayed on board, watching with other passengers what appeared to be the filming of something involving the ship. As people ran on and off the ship firing guns with blanks, a camera crew recorded the activity. Then, according to Sprecher, a car arrived on the pier and a man took two wrapped packages from the car, then carried them on board the ship.

"Maybe that's how they got the guns aboard," said Sprecher.

After their shooting spree, the hijackers rounded up the remaining passengers, bringing them to the dining room. They missed one, however. Anna Hoeranter, pushed down a flight of stairs by a hijacker, entered the first open cabin, hiding in the bathroom. She remained in the cabin until the following Saturday, almost four days after her rough encounter with the gunman. The cleaning staff found her in the cabin the morning after the hijackers surrendered. "I found two apples and every day I ate half an apple and drank what ever water was available," she said later.

Through Captain De Rosa, the hijackers instructed the crewmembers to continue with their regular duties, but to remain clear of the group of hostages. They also told De Rosa that there were twenty hijackers on board the ship. That claim apparently neutralized a chance for the crew, which numbered about 450, to overpower the hijackers. Captain De Rosa and his officers later discovered that there were only four armed men.

In the dining room, perhaps thinking that a few rounds of automatic rifle fire might not be enough to sufficiently menace the hostages, the hijackers turned even more violent.

"That's when they started to threaten us and show their power," said Mrs. Meskin. "They constantly had their guns ready for shooting." Another passenger said that one of the hijackers with two machine guns raised one calling it his father, the other his mother.

Stanley Kubacki, a judge from Pennsylvania, said that the men pulled the safety pins from hand grenades, but kept the triggering lever depressed with their hands. They made Kubacki's wife Sophia and other women hold the grenades, forcing them to nervously keep a constant grip pressure to keep the grenades from detonating. "We had to sit very close so if one of these women fell asleep or fainted, we would all be blown up," said Kubacki.

But several passengers remarked about the erratic behavior of the hijackers, who alternated between comforting and terrorizing their captives. "If someone wanted a cup," said Mrs. Meskin, "they would go and wash it out and hand it to you. But when Mrs. Klinghoffer was on the floor, exhausted, one took the butt of his gun and hit her to get her up off the floor." Still in her wet bathing suit, Charlotte Knobloch asked if she could get dry clothes from her cabin. "He followed me with his rifle and said 'Four minutes,'" she said. "I brushed my teeth and dressed and he said 'Hey, four minutes.'"

The hijackers interrupted their mayhem occasionally to attempt some crude political proselytizing. "They kept saying 'Reagan no good, Arafat good,'" said Viola Meskin.

On that October Monday in 1985, I was the director of the White House Situation Room. The facility is the nerve center of the White House, manned twenty-fours hours a day by a team of duty officers since its creation in 1961. The Situation Room is not just a room. It is the President's intelligence and communications center, which also provides him and his most senior advisors a highly secure conference

room in which to meet both during peace and crisis. I was then a Commander in the U.S. Navy, supervising a staff of twenty-five people;
some were civilians on loan from the State Department, the CIA, and
other intelligence agencies, others active-duty military personnel.
America was still fighting the Cold War, but the uneasy balance
wrought by nuclear weapons was often overshadowed by terrorists
wielding handguns.

I arrived at my West Wing office at 6:15 A.M. As usual, the first thing
I did was review the leather-bound folder that my staff had prepared
overnight for the President. There were several papers for President
Reagan in the folder—the CIA's very sensitive report, the President's
Daily Brief, the daily State Department summary, and special items of
interest that I had designated the previous day for inclusion. They also
included the Situation Room Morning Summary, a brief overview of
world events that occurred during the past twelve hours.

Just after I closed the folder, the senior duty officer in the Situation
Room told me that the CIA Operations Center in nearby Langley, Virginia, had just received word that an unidentified cruise ship had sent
an SOS from somewhere in the Mediterranean Sea. A maritime radio
monitoring facility in Sweden picked up the ship's message, but the
only information available then was that Palestinians had seized an
Italian ship. I thought to myself, "Here we go again." In 1985, it
seemed that every week brought another terrorist incident. That trend
made for busy times in the Situation Room. I asked the duty officers to
contact President Reagan's national security advisor, Robert C. "Bud"
McFarlane. Bud then advised the President of the hijacking.

Later in the morning we received more information—the ship was
Achille Lauro and Americans were on board. (There is a seven-hour
time difference between Egypt and Washington. 11:00 A.M. at the
White House was 6:00 P.M. onboard *Achille Lauro*.) Armed with this
additional data, McFarlane's deputy, John M. Poindexter, an active
duty Navy vice admiral, initiated a series of predetermined counter-
terrorist procedures that had been established over the previous year to
deal with increasingly common incidents such as this hijacking. The
first step was to convene a meeting of designated government experts
on terrorism, the Terrorist Incident Working Group, to consider possible U.S. responses to the incident. John instructed the National Security Council staff member who sat on the working group, Marine
Lieutenant Colonel Oliver North, to organize the meeting. North, who

later became the central figure in the Iran-Contra scandal, had been a classmate of mine at the Naval War College and a former next-door neighbor. He called for an immediate meeting of the working group in the conference room of the Situation Room complex.

The group consisted of representatives from defense, intelligence, and law enforcement agencies, plus the State Department and the White House National Security Council staff. Among other measures, the working group agreed that the government should send a State Department Emergency Support Team to Rome to assist the U.S. embassy there, because the ship was Italian. Further, the group recommended that the Pentagon dispatch a team of special operations forces to Europe to be ready to seize the ship and rescue the hostages, if the need and opportunity to intervene arose.

The working group's recommendations floated up to the next higher level of committee deliberation, the Operational Sub-Group, chaired by Poindexter. The group also had representatives from all involved agencies, but at a higher rank than those in Ollie North's group. In this case, Poindexter's group agreed with the working group's proposals and soon the State and Defense Departments issued orders to deploy the Emergency Support Team and special operations forces.

By 1985, the defense department consolidated all of the special operations forces in the military into one command, headed by Major General Carl Stiner, U.S. Army. Late Monday night, October 7, Stiner gathered together two platoons from the Navy's counter-terrorism unit, SEAL Team Six, and Army commandos from the Delta Force, and boarded transport aircraft en route to Europe.

At the White House, as well as the whole government, we still had a big problem. We didn't know *Achille Lauro*'s location. The cruise ship disappeared after the hijacking. No one—Italy, Egypt, Israel, or the United States—could find it.

The ocean surveillance capabilities of the United States and her NATO allies were immense, especially in the Mediterranean Sea where the goings and comings of the Soviet Navy were of continuing interest. Yet that system was optimized for tracking warships, and merchant vessels which used their radios and transmitted regular position reports. Once the hijackers enforced radio silence on board the cruise ship as it steamed northward from Egypt, *Achille Lauro* was hard to find.

Not knowing the ship's exact location, Stiner's team needed a staging base in the Eastern Mediterranean in order to react quickly once the ship was found. "The Brits gave us permission to use their facilities at Akrotiri, Cyprus as a jumping off point for the special operations units," Poindexter recalled when he and I compared memories of the incident in 2002. "We hoped that we could find *Achille Lauro* in a position where we might board the ship with a minimum of casualties. It was clearly evident in the White House that we might be able to do something about the hijacking because it was a self-contained problem. While we were very concerned about casualties to the hostages, we thought an attempt at overtaking the ship was worth a try."

The State Department contacted several countries on the Mediterranean littoral, asking them to deny *Achille Lauro* access to their ports. Secretary of State George Shultz called U.S. ambassador to Cairo, Nicholas Veliotes, asking him to urge the Egyptians to keep the ship in international waters to facilitate any future attempt to regain control of the vessel. "He also wanted me to help the Egyptians keep the news media away from the ship," Veliotes recalled years later. "The news coverage of the hijacking of the TWA airliner the previous June played right into the hands of the terrorists. The media gave the hijackers a world-wide stage."

In Italy, the government launched a two-part reaction to the hijacking—military and political. Under the direct supervision of Defense Minister Giovanni Spadolini, the Italian military also sent sixty paratroopers, four helicopters, and experts on the ship's layout to the same British base at Akrotiri, Cyprus.

But Italy's Prime Minister Bettino Craxi's primary interest was to find a diplomatic solution to the hijacking. His government began a near-continuous dialogue with all of the countries involved, with emphasis on those nations who had citizens on board, and several Arab states—Egypt, Syria, Jordan, and Tunisia. The Italians also asked the Palestine Liberation Organization (PLO) to publicly declare if it had a role in the incident. In response, the head of the PLO, Yasser Arafat, denounced the hijacking and offered to help negotiate a peaceful end to the situation.

Arafat, claiming that he wanted to help resolve the matter, sent two men to Egypt to be part of a joint PLO, Italian, and Egyptian negotiating team—Hani al-Hassan, an advisor to Arafat and a member of the PLO executive committee, and Abu Abbas. Abbas and Hassan joined the PLO representative assigned to Cairo, Zohdi al-Qoudra, in Port Said, Egypt.

Probably unknown to Arafat at that time was the fact that members of Abu Abbas's PLF had hijacked the ship. If he did know, Arafat probably wanted Abbas to put an end to the incident.

Monday evening, about the same time that Ollie North was meeting with his Terrorist Incident Working Group in the Situation Room, the hijackers took all of the hostages up several decks to the Arazzi Lounge on the Promenade Deck where they spent the night. The hijackers gave their hostages blankets and asked the ship's kitchen to send up food. Yet at the same time, the hijackers placed containers of what they said was gasoline around the room. Presumably this tactic was to keep the ship's crew at bay, threatening to ignite the fuel if the crew attempted to overwhelm the hijackers. The passengers, though wary of the gas and grenades, attempted to sleep on the floor. Meanwhile, the ship steamed steadily toward Syria.

The tourists ashore reached Port Said that evening at 10:30, but the ship was not there. Cruise officials told the group that shipping traffic in the canal delayed the ship, but finally admitted at 1:30 A.M. that hijackers had seized control of *Achille Lauro* that afternoon. Frank Hodes, separated from his wife, Mildred, who had been ill and remained on board ship, began to worry.

On Tuesday morning, October 8, in the Eastern Mediterranean Sea, the hijackers began to separate the hostages. They looked for Jews and Americans, asking everyone to identify themselves, but no one responded. The hijackers collected and examined everyone's passports, quickly pulling aside twelve Americans, as well as six female British dancers who were on board to entertain the passengers in the very lounge in which they were now held as hostages. After examining the names of an elderly Austrian couple, the hijackers asked it they were Jewish. The man said yes and one of the gunmen knocked him to the floor, hitting him repeatedly with his gun butt.

The hijackers ordered these twenty people up a flight of stairs to the next deck. Marilyn Klinghoffer grabbed Leon's wheelchair. "I attempted to push my husband in his wheelchair in the direction of the staircase," she said later. "The terrorists ordered me to leave him. I told them I couldn't leave him and begged them to let me stay with him. They responded by putting a machine gun to my head and ordered me up the stairs." Another passenger, Anna Schneider, also asked to take Mr. Klinghoffer. "You go!" said a hijacker. "We will take care of him."

Once on the Lido Deck, located above the lounge and just below the bridge, the hijackers forced the hostages to lie on the deck. Again, they placed what they said were containers of fuel around the hostages and threatened to shoot the cans. Evelyn Weltman, from Illinois, said a hijacker told her if commandos tried to rescue the passengers, his group would shoot the hostages. By this time, the hostages and Captain De Rosa began to realize which one of the four hijackers was the leader—Youssef Majed Molqi.

Short, dark, and mustachioed, Molqi had a confident air, perhaps even a swagger, an attitude that remained after he later relinquished his Kalashnikov. It wasn't until later that the passengers and crew discovered that he was only twenty-three at the time of the hijacking. Molqi was born in a crowded Palestinian refugee camp in Jordan. Abbas had recruited Molqi as a teenager into the PLF, just as Abbas had attracted other angry young men in the camp.

Achille Lauro arrived off Tartus at 11:00 A.M., Tuesday. Breaking radio silence, Molqi asked Syrian authorities to allow the ship to dock in Tartus. He also demanded that Syria send British and American representatives, as well as someone from the International Red Cross, to the ship. He said that he and his team were members of the Palestine Liberation Front, then demanded that Syria contact Israel and request the release of fifty Palestinians held in Israeli jails. He identified one prisoner by name—Samir al-Qantari, who participated in an extraordinarily violent raid by the PLF in Israel in 1979. If the Israeli prisoners were not released, Molqi threatened to kill the hostages. "We will start executing at 3:00 P.M. sharp," Molqi said to the Syrians. Syria, in consultation with the U.S. and Italian governments, did not respond to his demands.

As it neared 3:00 P.M., the hijackers began to decide whom to kill by shuffling the passports of the U.S. and British hostages, plus the two Austrians. They selected Leon Klinghoffer to kill first, then Mildred Hodes.

Molqi ordered a nearby crewmember, Manuel De Souza, a Portuguese waiter, to push Klinghoffer outside onto the open deck. Accompanied by Molqi, De Souza took Klinghoffer back along the entire length of the ship to the stern. The hijacker directed De Souza to leave him alone with Klinghoffer and go back inside the ship. The other gunmen led the remaining hostages back down to the lounge. Marilyn realized that Leon was not where she had been forced to leave him and began to cry again. Viola Meskin said a hijacker told Marilyn that her husband was ill and in the ship's infirmary.

Molqi shot Leon Klinghoffer twice, once in the head, again in the chest. Dying instantly, Klinghoffer toppled face forward. Molqi found De Souza, ordering the man to throw the body over the side. When the waiter was unable to lift it over the life rail, Molqi located another crewmember to help: Ferruccio Alberti, the ship's Italian hairdresser. With Molqi pointing his gun at them, the two men threw Klinghoffer's body into the sea, then his wheelchair.

Molqi, his clothes splattered with Klinghoffer's blood, rejoined his comrades outside the lounge, saying, "I have killed the American." He and a second hijacker, Bassam al-Ashker, then went to the bridge. Molqi handed Klinghoffer's passport to Captain De Rosa, raised one finger, and said "boom, boom." He then handed Mrs. Hodes' passport to the captain and said, "This will be the second one." De Rosa was fully aware at that point that Klinghoffer was dead, a point that later became the basis for a serious diplomatic conflict.

"I was convinced they were going to kill more people," De Rosa recalled later. "I said that instead of killing everybody, they could kill just one person, me, the commander of the ship."

Peter Kohler, a writer and expert on merchant ships, especially passenger liners, came to know De Rosa well when he took a cruise aboard *Achille Lauro* only a few months after the hijacking. When Peter and I met in 2003, he described De Rosa as a sensitive, kind man who was intent on ensuring that no problem interfered with his passengers. "He was under immense pressure during the hijacking and I believe would have willingly given his life to prevent the death of any more hostages," Kohler said.

Molqi told the captain to mark the time of Klinghoffer's death—3:05 P.M.—then radioed the Syrians that they had killed one passenger and were prepared to kill another. The Syrian official responded by telling Molqi to "go back where you came from." Quickly giving up on Syria, Molqi ordered the captain to get underway for Libya.

Several hostages heard the shots and the splashes, including Marilyn. Still hoping that Leon was indeed in the ship's infirmary, she approached the hijackers. "I pleaded with the terrorists to allow me to see him in the hospital. They refused." Fearing the worst, yet hoping for the best, a tormented Marilyn sought solace from her friends.

◄◄ ►►

While *Achille Lauro* anchored off Tartus, Abu Abbas and Hassan attempted to contact the ship using Egyptian Naval communications. With the ship out of range of normal ship-to-shore channels, the Egyptian Navy sent a ship north in an unsuccessful attempt to contact the hijackers.

Abbas then called Radio Monte Carlo, an Arabic language station in Cyprus. He identified himself as "Abu Khaled," asking the station to broadcast a message to *Achille Lauro*. In the message, Abbas instructed the hijackers to return immediately to Port Said, treating the passengers "kindly."

That message got through to the ship. According to Captain De Rosa, Molqi was listening to the radio when he suddenly became "euphoric," then ordered the captain to change course to Port Said at 7:20 P.M., Tuesday.

Later that night Abbas, again calling himself Abu Khaled, made radio contact with the ship from Port Said.

ABU KHALED:	*Who is speaking? Is this Majed?*
MAJED *(Molqi)*:	*Right, right.*
ABU KHALED:	*How are you, Majed?*
MAJED:	*Good, thank God.*
ABU KHALED:	*Listen to me well. First of all, the passengers should be treated very well. In addition, you must apologize to them and the ship's crew, and to the captain, and tell them your objective was not to take control of the ship. Tell them what your main objective is. Can you hear me well?*
MAJED:	*Right. We talked to them, and we told them that our objective was not to take control of the ship. Roger?*
ABU KHALED:	*OK, tell the passengers, the captain, everyone, that our friendship with Italy is so important that it is unthinkable that any action would be taken against our European friends. Can you hear me?*

After a few more exchanges between Abbas and Molqi, Captain De Rosa began talking with Abbas:

DE ROSA: *I am the ship's captain. I am now on deck with my officers and we are all well.*

ABU KHALED: *How are you feeling?*

DE ROSA: *I am fine and very calm.*

ABU KHALED: *We are truly sorry, because we didn't intend to hijack you, but our situation was such that we had to assume control for several hours.*

DE ROSA: *I am familiar with your situation and I understand it well. We understand the Palestinians, we understand the Palestinian aspirations, and for that reason we are all with you.*

De Rosa's last remark to Abu Abbas was prescient of problems and issues that would arise later among Italy, the PLO, and the United States.

In the White House Situation Room, Molqi's radio conversation with the Syrians provided the first indication in thirty-six hours of the ship's location. We did not, however, have enough information to determine whether the hijackers were bluffing about killing hostages, but assumed the worst. Also, we speculated that the hijacking might be related to another incident the previous week.

On October 1, just two days before *Achille Lauro* departed Genoa, Israeli aircraft bombed PLO headquarters in Tunis, killing twelve Tunisians and sixty Palestinians. Several of the reports sent to the White House suggested that this attack, in turn, might have been in retaliation for the murder of three Israelis on board a yacht in Cyprus by two Palestinians and a British citizen on September 25.

Some of our questions were answered when Israeli officials gave Ollie North information regarding Abu Abbas's radio dialogue with Molqi. One was that Abu Abbas had organized and directed the operation. Then, as now, many were confused by the alphabet soup of Palestinian organizations—lots of fronts and groups, with all the P's, F's, and L's seeming to run together. It was a fine distinction, but a distinction nevertheless, that the PLF had hijacked the ship. Although the PLF was part of the greater PLO, Yasser Arafat did not directly control Abbas and his PLF activities.

Although the prospect of ending the hijacking improved with the ship headed to Port Said, its original destination, a huge question remained. Had the hijackers actually killed one or two as they told Syria? Captain De Rosa knew the answer, as did the waiter and hairdresser, and the other passengers heard shots and a splash. But no one off the ship knew for sure what had happened.

Most of us at the White House believed at that point that the hijackers had killed someone. We hoped that this event would not turn out to be like the TWA hijacking earlier that summer when the United States was powerless to intervene and free the hostages aboard the aircraft. McFarlane and Poindexter, along with other senior advisors to Reagan, were frustrated by their experiences during the TWA hijacking. Everyone wanted to take action, with or without the Italians, to prevent any further deaths. The Pentagon ordered Carl Stiner's special operations forces, by then staged on Cyprus, to prepare to board *Achille Lauro.*

At the State Department's request, U.S. ambassador to Rome Maxwell Rabb advised Prime Minister Craxi Tuesday afternoon of the U.S. intention to mount a military assault on the ship. Craxi did not endorse unilateral action by the United States, first because the ship was Italian and only Italy should act. Second, he said there was no confirmation of the killing of hostages and negotiations for the release of the ship seemed possible. Craxi had asked the Egyptians what they knew about possible deaths, with Egypt responding that no one had been killed.

Tuesday evening, the PLO began to maneuver for control of the hijackers should they surrender. Arafat told Craxi that the hijackers promised to release the passengers unharmed and drop demands for freeing Israeli prisoners, a promise presumably delivered via Abbas in Egypt. He also asked Egyptian President Hosni Mubarak to pledge to surrender the hijackers to the PLO in Tunis for prosecution.

About this time, the PLF issued a statement in Nicosia, Cyprus, in which the group apologized to the passengers for the hijacking. The statement read, in part: *"The aim of the operation was not to hijack the ship or its passengers, or any civilian of any nationality. The operation was likewise not aimed against states that are friendly to our people and their cause."* The statement also said that the mission was to *"travel on an ordinary sea journey to Ashdod harbor in occupied Palestine, from where our comrades were to proceed to a specified Israeli military target, as a reply to the war of extermination and terrorism against them and to avenge the martyrs of the Israeli raid on Tunis.*

Our comrades were compelled to take control of the ship before reaching the specified target. We wish to mention that the course toward Arab ports was the result of the situation and the confusion into which the squad fell."

Contemporaneous news reporting contained references to a cabin steward, who was assigned to the hijackers' stateroom, surprising the four Palestinians as they cleaned their weapons. The news accounts suggested that this untimely discovery panicked the men into hijacking the ship instead of following their plan to attack Ashdod, Israel. These stories jibed with the PLF statement, but later developments proved that the "stateroom surprise" has an unusual twist.

On Tuesday, October 8, the news media began reporting the hijacking. After discovering that Manhattan residents Leon and Marilyn Klinghoffer were on board the ship, the *New York Times* dispatched reporter Sara Rimer to interview the Klinghoffer family. It was a normal approach for a newspaper in the hometown of a terrorist hostage— get a local angle to go with the international developments. The *Times* had no idea at the time that Leon was already dead.

Rimer introduced Lisa and Ilsa Klinghoffer to the public and gathered their reactions to the incident. "I can't believe this is happening to us," Lisa said. "I feel so helpless." Both daughters told of their overnight anxiety about the fate of their parents and described to Rimer their father's illness. They gave Rimer a family photo of Leon and Marilyn that put at least two human faces on the hijacking.

Achille Lauro anchored off Port Said at 7:30 A.M., Wednesday, forty-two hours after the shooting started in the dining room. A small boat approached the ship and Molqi descended to talk with the visitors, Abu Abbas included. The hostages, including Marilyn Klinghoffer, still unaware of her husband's fate, remained in the lounge.

Acting with full support of the Italians, Egyptian officials, Abbas, and Hassan began talking with the hijackers. To the Egyptians, not knowing of Abbas's role in planning the hijacking, the talks must have appeared to be real negotiations. The session was really just a smoke-screen to allow Abbas to get his men off the ship. Nevertheless, the PLO took credit for ending the incident, citing successful "negotiations."

Hassan notified Arafat of the "deal," who in turn called Craxi midday Wednesday. The hijackers would release the hostages if Italy and Egypt met two "demands": the ambassadors from the United States, Italy, West Germany, and Great Britain visit the ship, then safe passage off the ship for the hijackers.

In response, Italian ambassador Giovanni Migliuolo approached his three colleagues in Cairo, asking them to join him on a helicopter flight to Port Said. "We met at the Italian ambassador's residence," Veliotes told me later. "Migliuolo told us that the hijackers wanted us to visit the ship and talk to them. I immediately argued that would give the hijackers the media platform they wanted. More importantly, I would not agree to a visit because my government did not negotiate with terrorists."

As the four diplomats were discussing the proposal, the Egyptian foreign minister telephoned the group, asking them to come at once to his office. "Abdel Meguid, a formal man, yet an effective minister, proposed a more sweeping solution to the hijacking," recalled Veliotes. "If the hijackers released the hostages and left the ship, would our four governments promise not to give chase to the terrorists? All of us told Meguid that we would not agree without consulting with our governments."

Rather than leave the Foreign Ministry to run the gauntlet of reporters outside, the Egyptians gave each ambassador an office and telephone. Meguid asked for their decisions in twenty minutes. The four men ignored that deadline and began discussions with their governments.

The four ambassadors soon reassembled in Foreign Minister Meguid's office to present their government's view of the proposed settlement with the hijackers. "The Italian agreed to the proposal, as did the German in vague terms," said Veliotes. "I said no to the deal, and the Brit said Mrs. Thatcher could not be disturbed in order to ask her if she wanted to change her policy of non-negotiation with terrorists."

While the diplomats were talking, the Pentagon was finishing up plans for Stiner's commandos to board *Achille Lauro* Wednesday evening. SEAL Team Six was embarked on board the amphibious assault ship USS *Iwo Jima* steaming toward Port Said, but the situation was clouded by *Achille Lauro*'s position in Egyptian territorial waters. John Poindexter and his colleagues at the Pentagon agreed that they should put the boarding operation on hold once the ship appeared to have entered Egyptian waters.

The day dragged on, but mid-afternoon brought a remarkable development. Captain De Rosa made an announcement on the ship-to-shore radio: "I am the captain. I am speaking from my office, and my officers and everybody is in good health." Those listening to De Rosa's false statement did not know at the time that Molqi was holding a gun to the captain's head.

The Egyptian foreign minister, meeting again with the four ambassadors, heard of Captain De Rosa's declaration. He urged the diplomats to agree to the hijackers' transfer to the PLO's control and not seek their arrest. Nick Veliotes refused, arguing that even if there had been no deaths, the men must be punished for the hijacking itself. The British ambassador also refused to sign such a proposal, the German offered general, but undefined support, and the Italian ambassador endorsed the agreement. The two yes votes were good enough for the Egyptian government, and Foreign Minister Meguid told Abbas and Hassan that the hijackers were free to leave the ship.

News that all of the hostages were reportedly safe quickly spread through the capitals of Europe and the U.S. In New York, *New York Times* reporter Sara Rimer was at the Klinghoffer home in Greenwich Village and witnessed the joy and relief felt by the daughters and their friends. All lifted glasses of champagne, toasting Leon and Marilyn's apparent safe deliverance. The State Department, using information from Nick Veliotes, called Lisa to confirm the news reports.

At the same time the Klinghoffer daughters began their celebrating—5:00 P.M. Egyptian time—the four Palestinian hijackers left the ship, with the Egyptians taking them ashore by boat. As they departed, the men waved at the passengers and, surprisingly, the former hostages applauded. Passenger Charlotte Knobloch thought the applause was a reaction to being free. "When they left, they passed by everybody and said goodbye and blew kisses," she said. "Oh, how we applauded. We were happy. Waiting for them to leave were the longest minutes I ever lived."

A crowd of Egyptians ashore saw the hijackers approaching the land and burst into cheers. "Fedayeen, fedayeen, Allah akbar!"—"The guerrillas, the guerrillas, God is great!"

Back on board ship, Captain De Rosa explained to the passengers that the hijackers told him they never intended to seize the ship. "They had an assignment to do something in Israel," said Paul Weltman. "They told the captain to apologize to us. They said they interrupted our trip accidentally."

To Marilyn Klinghoffer, the hijacking didn't look like an accident. After the hijackers departed, she rushed to the ship's infirmary, seeking her husband. He wasn't there and no one had seen him. The staff told her to go see the captain. Perhaps putting off the inevitable, Captain De Rosa stayed on the ship's bridge, while a distraught Marilyn Klinghoffer climbed the stairs from near the bottom of the ship to the top. Captain De Rosa told her of Leon's death. She collapsed into uncontrollable sobs.

After friends helped Marilyn to her cabin, Captain De Rosa received a call from Italian Foreign Minister Giulio Andreotti in Rome. De Rosa reported that he was again in command of his ship and the hijackers had surrendered. Inexplicably, De Rosa said that all the passengers were well. The pressure of the incident must have pushed him to the edge of rational thought.

Andreotti passed the apparent good news to Craxi, who was about to hold a news conference to announce the successful resolution of the crisis. Craxi, in a strange and largely unexplained move, reportedly thought that the issue of possible killings was worth double-checking and called De Rosa again. Finally, De Rosa admitted that the hijackers had shot Klinghoffer. Craxi changed his script, telling the news media and the world that Leon Klinghoffer was dead.

Sara Rimer was still at the Klinghoffer home, watching the family celebrate when a local New York City television station picked up the news of Craxi's statement. With the *New York Times* reporter looking on, the station called the Klinghoffer home with the bad news. Paul Dworin, Ilsa's fiancé, took the call and passed the information quietly to Lisa's husband, Jerry Arbitier. Rimer wrote what happened next: "Several minutes later, Mr. Dworin and Mr. Arbitier took the two daughters aside and told them that their father might be dead. Their screams, heartbreaking after so much jubilation, filled the living room, where their friends and relatives looked at each other in horror and disbelief."

"It was such a shock," Lisa recalled during our conversation in 2002. "Just two hours after we were told that everyone one was all right. To go that quickly from joy to devastation was horrible."

<+- +>

Why did the hijackers pick Leon Klinghoffer to kill?

Fellow hostage Rene Sprecher thought it might have had something

to do with one of the gunmen taking Klinghoffer's watch and cigarettes, giving them to another hijacker. Klinghoffer was upset, she said,
and even though a second gunman gave everything back, the invalid's
brusque behavior and slurred speech may have antagonized the hijackers. Another passenger spoke of an incident in which Klinghoffer allegedly bit one of the hijackers, but that proved false.

Captain De Rosa believed there were several reasons. First, Klinghoffer was Jewish and American, and second, he was in a wheelchair
and was not easily moved about the ship, further irritating the hijackers. Lastly, De Rosa suggested that the men wanted to kill him without
the others knowing it to prohibit a chain reaction. While there were
only four hijackers against 545 crew and passengers, De Rosa, at that
point, still believed there were more gunmen. The hijackers, however,
knew they were vastly outnumbered. After the hijacking ended, De
Rosa said that the hijackers were probably concerned that a public killing might provoke an attempt to overpower them. Since Klinghoffer
was separated from the others, they chose him.

"I and Bassam [al-Ashker] agreed that the first hostage to be killed
had to be an American," Molqi said later. "I chose Klinghoffer, an
invalid, so that they would know that we had no pity for anyone, just
as the Americans, arming Israel, do not take into consideration that
Israel kills women and children of our people."

After the hijackers departed, Nicholas Veliotes boarded *Achille
Lauro* to confirm Craxi's statement about Klinghoffer's death. "I went
to the bridge and found De Rosa distraught and thoroughly shaken,"
said Veliotes. "He explained about Molqi holding the gun to his head
and tearfully handed me Klinghoffer's passport."

Veliotes called his embassy over the ship-to-shore radio, giving his
staff the following instructions.

"Leon Klinghoffer was murdered by the terrorists off of Tartus when
they were trying to get the attention of the Syrians. In my name, I want
you to call the [Egyptian] foreign minister, tell him what we learned,
tell him the circumstances, tell him in view of this and the fact that
we—and presumably them—didn't have those facts, we insist that
they prosecute those sons of bitches."

With that demand the next act in the *Achille Lauro* drama burst
upon the international stage.

CHAPTER

2

"You Can Run, But You Can't Hide"

THEY have actually left Egypt. I do not know exactly where they have gone. Perhaps they have left for Tunisia."

On the day following the hijackers' surrender at Port Said, Egyptian President Hosni Mubarak uttered a bald-faced lie. Questioned by the news media about the whereabouts of the four men, Mubarak insisted that they had left the country within hours of departing *Achille Lauro*. Mubarak's Foreign Minister, Esmat Abdel Meguid, later reiterated the government position: "They left Egypt. I know where they are, but I am not going to tell you."

Why did the Egyptian government release four hijackers who murdered Leon Klinghoffer and why was Mubarak's statement a lie?

As an Egyptian tugboat ferried the hijackers ashore, Italy, the United States, the PLO, Israel, and Egypt began a three-day quarrel about what they should do about the four Palestinians.

Italy staked out its position immediately. Its government insisted that the four hijackers should be tried in Italy because the ship that they commandeered was Italian. The ship was Italian territory, they argued, and a murder aboard *Achille Lauro* was the same as a killing in Italy. Prime Minister Craxi declared his government's intention to seek extradition to Italy of the four hijackers.

Israel also had a straightforward demand—prosecute the hijackers. "Klinghoffer and his wife were singled out for one thing—because they were Jewish," said Benjamin Netanyahu, at that time an Israeli representative to the United Nations.

In Washington, the White House and the State Department dispatched a series of urgent messages to Cairo, all urging swift prosecution of the hijackers by either the United States or Italy. Ollie North and another National Security Council staff member, Jim Stark, drafted a personal message for President Reagan to send to Mubarak. Stark, a Navy captain, worked with North in the politico-military section of the staff; North had the added responsibility of coordinating counter-terrorism activities on the staff.

Reagan approved the draft message, which asked Mubarak to relinquish the hijackers to the United States, or at the very least, the Italians. My staff in the Situation Room handled these sensitive messages between the President and other heads of state, but we did not send it through the State Department and normal diplomatic communications circuits. We sent it directly to Ambassador Veliotes in Cairo. "I tried to pass the message to Mubarak, but he refused to see me," Veliotes told me later. "George Shultz also called Mubarak unsuccessfully." Was that because Mubarak did not want to lie to the U.S. government directly? "I suspect so," answered Veliotes.

The PLO continued to portray itself as a useful party to the incident, following the theme that Yasser Arafat established when he claimed that he sent Hassan and Abbas to Cairo to negotiate an end to the hijacking. Officials at PLO headquarters in Tunisia said that Egypt, at the time of the hijacker's surrender, gave the PLO forty-eight hours to take control of the four men. Arafat said that they needed time to find a country where the PLO could take the hijackers for trial. Further, according to the PLO officials, if the PLO could not find such a country, Egypt would release the men, or turn them over to Italy. In recognition of the complex political issues at work and a portent of things to come, the PLO said that Italy's assumption of control of the hijackers would be acceptable. "Italy is a friend of ours, so it's no problem," said a PLO official.

The PLO also claimed that the four hijackers were not PLO members, but rather part of the PLF. This distinction, however minor it might seem to a bystander, was always useful to Yasser Arafat when one of the PLO's constituent groups committed an act of violence. Arafat always claimed that the group, in this case the PLF, was off the reservation or were renegades that he could not control.

Finally, suggesting that there might not even be an issue, PLO official Farouk Kaddoumi said that Klinghoffer's alleged murder was "a big lie fabricated by the intelligence service of the United States." In New York for a United Nations meeting, Kaddoumi suggested to the UN Security Council that Klinghoffer could have died naturally. "Is there any evidence that those hijackers had killed that civilian? Where is the evidence?"

Egypt inherited this problem when Abbas ordered his four men to return the ship to Port Said, which had been its next port of call at the time of the hijacking. When the hijackers forced the ship's captain to radio Egyptian port officials that all aboard were well, Mubarak's foreign minister used that call to get agreement from Italy and West Germany to allow the hijackers to surrender without consequence.

Egypt was in a tight spot. Mubarak was attempting to maintain Egypt's peace treaty with Israel—the 1978 Camp David Accords—yet sustain good relations with other Arab states in the Middle East. The Israeli bombing of PLO headquarters in Tunis the previous week, in which many innocent Tunisians were killed and wounded, heightened pressures on him. Further exacerbating his predicament, according to one observer, was his continuing interest in billions of dollars in U.S. foreign aid, largess that might be jeopardized by acting against U.S. objectives.

Mubarak seemed to justify his efforts to get the hijackers out of Egypt quickly based on three issues. First, he said the United States "made no claims on the hijackers" of the TWA airliner earlier that summer, suggesting the United States would acquiesce this time, as well. Second, President Reagan told the news media that it would be "all right" if the PLO tried the hijackers. Bud McFarlane, realizing that a PLO trial would be an implicit U.S. recognition of the PLO, later corrected the President's statement. But Captain De Rosa's false report of no casualties was the main reason. Mubarak maintained that he sent the hijackers out of Egypt before receiving word that De Rosa had recanted, telling Italy's Prime Minister Craxi that Klinghoffer was indeed dead. The only way Mubarak could justify his actions was to falsely maintain that he had sent the hijackers out of Egypt before De Rosa corrected his first statement.

"If the captain had told us that a passenger had been killed, we would have changed our position toward the whole operation," Mubarak told the news media. "But when this [news of Klinghoffer's death] emerged, we already had sent the hijackers out of the country." Mubarak punctuated that claim with a gratuitous suggestion that perhaps no one died. "There is no body and no proof he has been murdered. Maybe the man is hiding or did not board the ship at all."

A few people in the U.S. government knew that Mubarak had lied. I was one of them. I held in my hand the intelligence reports that confirmed that the hijackers were still in Egypt.

The President, Bud McFarlane, John Poindexter, a few of us on the National Security Council staff, and several senior officials at State, CIA, and the Pentagon knew that the hijackers were still in Egypt on Thursday, October 10. The U.S. intelligence community produced this extraordinary bit of information, with important assistance from their Israeli counterparts.

The first indication that the hijackers had not immediately left Egypt, as Mubarak claimed, came from the Israelis. When Ollie North saw a report of Mubarak's statement Thursday morning, he called Major General Uri Simhoni, the military attaché at the Israeli embassy in Washington, requesting verification. Simhoni, who had been helpful in passing locating information on *Achille Lauro* during the hijacking, told North that the four men were at the Al Maza airfield near Cairo.

Later in the morning, we received corroborating reports from our own sources, information that provided additional insight into the hijackers' status. The Egyptians were planning to transport the men out of their country that night, late afternoon Washington time, probably to Tunis. The intelligence also indicated that the hijackers would be aboard a commercial EgyptAir jet. Jim Stark, North's officemate, began to consider what that news meant.

"If they were planning to fly to Tunis, the aircraft could not overfly Libya en route because Egypt and Libya were at each other's throat," Stark recalled years later. "They also could not fly south over Chad because of the hostilities between Chad and Libya. The aircraft had to

fly over the Mediterranean Sea. It was then that I thought about intercepting the Egyptian airliner with U.S. Navy fighters."

Stark continued, "I went in to Ollie's office and asked 'Do you
remember Yamamoto?'" Japanese Admiral Isoroku Yamamoto was in
charge of the Pearl Harbor raid and a key strategist in the Pacific war.
In 1943, American intelligence learned of Yamamoto's planned trip to
the Solomon Islands and U.S. fighters intercepted his transport plane
and shot it down. "Ollie was surprised at first, thinking I wanted to
shoot down the Egyptian airliner," said Stark. "As much as I would
have liked to, I told Ollie that we might intercept it and force it to land
somewhere. We ran over the places where the plane could land—Israel
and Cyprus presented too many political problems—then thought that
the NATO base in Sigonella, Italy, might work."

Stark and North then approached John Poindexter with the idea. "I
didn't remember Yamamoto, but I, too, was thinking about intercepting the Egyptian plane," Poindexter told me. "I called Bud, who was
traveling with President Reagan in Chicago, asking him to sound out
the President about the idea of intercepting the plane."

Poindexter, a brilliant nuclear engineer who graduated first in his
class at the Naval Academy, had enjoyed a stellar career in the Navy to
that point. The service sent him to the White House to help Presidential Counselor Ed Meese analyze the functioning of the Situation
Room during the assassination attempt on Ronald Reagan in 1981.
John's computer creativity lead to a major upgrade in Sit Room information systems. He later became McFarlane's deputy and worked in a
tiny West Wing office no larger than a walk-in clothes closet. John
trusted his own judgement and excelled in these sorts of situations.

Reagan, McFarlane, and the rest of the Presidential party were at
Chicago's Sara Lee Bakery where the President was speaking to the
company employees. McFarlane explained to Reagan the idea and
potential problems—finding the right aircraft, damaging relations with
Egypt and Italy. In what became known as the "Sara Lee decision,"
Reagan approved the operation in principle.

Reagan generally went along with his advisor's recommendations.
Usually, he stuck with the broad-brush issues and left the details to his
staff. While there was little time for significant Presidential involvement in this instance, his style generally left him detached from the
nitty-gritty of operations.

With the President's blessing, Poindexter asked North to maintain

contact with the Israeli Simhoni, then called Vice Admiral Art
Moreau, assistant to the Chairman of the Joint Chiefs of Staff, Admiral
William Crowe. "On behalf of the President, I asked Art to ask the
chairman to start the planning of the intercept mission," said Poindexter.

This sort of assertive action in response to terrorism had been an
elusive goal of the U.S. government. President Jimmy Carter probably
lost his bid for reelection in 1980 because of the long, drawn out hostage affair in Iran. On Sunday, November 4, 1979, three thousand Iranian student demonstrators swept over the wall surrounding the U.S.
embassy chancery in Tehran, trapping more than sixty Americans on
the second floor. Observers thought the seizure was in response to the
arrival of the Shah of Iran in the United States on October 22, 1979.
The Shah, who had abdicated his throne in the face of an Islamic revolution earlier in the year, had left his exile in Mexico to seek medical
treatment in New York.

Three Americans, including the embassy chargé d'affaires, Bruce
Laingen, were at the Iranian Foreign Ministry at the time of the seizure
and remained there as hostages until they joined the rest in January
1981. Fourteen of the original hostages were released early, leaving
fifty-two in prolonged captivity.

Diplomatic maneuvering yielded no movement to release the hostages. President Carter attempted to free them through a risky, secret
military mission. It failed and those hostages were not released until
minutes after Ronald Reagan was inaugurated President, fourteen
months later. The frustration rising out of Carter's rescue failure lin-
gered on into the Reagan administration. From my front row vantage
point in the White House Situation Room I saw that frustration. The
feeling that the U.S. government was powerless to either deter or
aggressively respond to terrorism was as strong in the West Wing as it
was in the minds of the public.

Most often, circumstances did not allow clear, decisive action. We
could not find Americans held hostage in Lebanon, despite covert CIA
searches, nor could we identify individuals who had kidnapped the victims. The circumstances of the TWA hijacking never allowed direct
U.S. intervention. We were winning the Cold War, but we were not
gaining even a step on terrorists.

In the *Achille Lauro* case, the neat package delivered to the White
House doorstep by extraordinary intelligence and brilliant thinking by

Jim Stark, gave us a chance to act firmly, simultaneously pushing aside the frustrations of the past six years. But was there time?

The vast, ponderous machinery within the Pentagon, at U.S. military headquarters in Europe, and the Navy's Sixth Fleet began to turn, and surprisingly quickly at that. These sorts of operations usually require more than just a few hours to conceive, plan, and execute. Even with the President's backing, the Pentagon still had to work out thorny details. How would the aircraft force the airliner to land? Could they fire their weapons to lend seriousness to their orders to land? (The aerial equivalent of firing across the bow of a ship.) But everything came together rapidly.

"We got this thing off the ground quickly because Cap Weinberger was out of town," Stark said to me in retrospect. "It seemed like every military operation we undertook in those days worked better when he wasn't around."

Crowe, on the job for only ten days, wrote in his 1993 memoir that Secretary of Defense Casper Weinberger, traveling in Ottawa, objected to an intercept of the aircraft. "That's a terrible idea," Weinberger told Crowe over the telephone. "I'm dead set against it, interfering with a civilian aircraft. We'll be castigated all over the world." Telling Crowe to "stop everything," Weinberger called President Reagan in Air Force One to argue against the plan. The secretary had earned a reputation for opposing "incidental" use of the armed forces, and many in the administration viewed his attitude as an impediment to unusual operations. True to form, Weinberger gave the President reasons for not attempting the intercept. The public learned of this later because he made the call on an open, unencrypted radio channel and a ham radio operator monitored the call.

According to explanations issued by spokesmen at the White House and the Pentagon, Weinberger placed the call from his plane to Air Force One. Due to time constraints, military communications technicians reportedly did not take the trouble to patch together incompatible secure voice systems, but rather just used a clear circuit. The ham radio buff who listened to the conversation told the news media that Reagan was not persuaded by his defense secretary's entreaties and told him to make it happen.

Reagan made the final decision to intercept the EgyptAir jet late in the afternoon of October 10 while he was returning to Washington on Air Force One. McFarlane called Poindexter, who relayed the decision to the Pentagon. Orders soon flashed across the Atlantic to the aircraft carrier USS *Saratoga*, and her aircraft made ready for a rendezvous with four hijackers above the dark waters of the Mediterranean Sea.

Saratoga was in the Mediterranean for a six-month deployment, and served as the flagship of a Sixth Fleet taskforce commanded by Rear Admiral David Jeremiah. The task force had just finished a NATO exercise at sea and was headed toward Dubrovnik, Yugoslavia. Late in the evening on Thursday, October 10, Vice Admiral Frank Kelso, commander of the Sixth Fleet, ordered *Saratoga* and her accompanying ships to reverse course.

Jeremiah not only had been following the *Achille Lauro* hijacking, but also dispatched aircraft in an attempt to locate the cruise ship after its seizure. But he was surprised when Kelso ordered him to send his aircraft out to locate and intercept a commercial jet carrying the hijackers out of Egypt. Missing some important details—where, when, which jet—Jeremiah sent two F-14 Tomcat fighters and an E-2C Hawkeye early-warning aircraft into the nighttime sky. The Hawkeye carried a special radar that allowed the crew to track all aircraft within hundreds of miles of the Hawkeye's location, and this seat-of-the-pants operation would only work if the Hawkeye's radar could find the Egyptian airliner.

"We knew we had a mission to intercept that airliner," Ralph Zia told me in 2002. Zia, the commanding officer of the group of Hawkeye aircraft aboard *Saratoga*, continued, "but we launched [catapulted the aircraft off the ship] our first without any location data or a timeline. We figured that by the time they got to their assigned stations, we would get more info."

Steve Weatherspoon, a Tomcat fighter pilot, was one of the first to take off. "I was ready to launch but the crew had to change the weapons on the aircraft," Weatherspoon told me. "We had to remove the radar-guided missiles which were standard for the Cold War and load simpler weapons, including tracer bullets."

About that time, Israeli intelligence agents discovered that the plane carrying the hijackers was an EgyptAir Boeing 737, flight 2843, as well as its tail number (a registration number painted on the airliner) and departure time. They passed that information to North, who called the Pentagon, which passed the details to Sixth Fleet and *Saratoga*. Armed with more information, Zia climbed aboard another Hawkeye and took off to help the fighters find the 737.

"At first we thought it was just another drill that would be called off when the adults woke up in Washington," said Weatherspoon. "But it was real."

Zia searched the designated airways that commercial jets use to safely traverse the area. Several of the routes converge south of Crete, sort of a choke point in the Eastern Mediterranean. His plan was to track radar contacts that were flying west on conventional routes out of Egypt, presumably en route to Tunis. Each time a radar contact seemed to fit this pattern, Zia sent a Tomcat to visually determine if a radar contact was an EgyptAir 737. Despite the fighter aircraft's sophisticated electronic systems, the pilot's eyes were the only sensor to confirm the exact identity of each radar blip.

"It wasn't a big deal," Weatherspoon said, describing a nighttime intercept. "We got a good radar picture which safely controlled the intercept, and pulled close enough to get a visual identification. As we slowly closed, either we illuminated the aircraft with the glow of our exterior position lights, or tried to make out a silhouette by starlight. If its shape was similar to a 737, we had to get closer to see the carrier or national markings."

The fighters checked on two radar blips headed west, discovering that they were U.S. Air Force transport planes flying without lights. Although unknown to the *Saratoga* fliers, they were loaded with the special operations troops, including their commander Carl Stiner, who had been ready to storm *Achille Lauro* to free the hostages. Art Moreau had called Stiner during the intercept planning and instructed him to fly from Cyprus to Sigonella and capture the hijackers should the Navy succeed in diverting the Egyptian airliner.

After approaching six or eight aircraft without finding the 737, Zia instructed Weatherspoon and the pilot of another Tomcat, William Roe "Skid" Massey, to approach the next contact. "Skid closed for the identification while I stayed behind the contact," said Weatherspoon. Massey eased up to the aircraft to determine if it was a 737. His Radar Intercept Officer in the back seat, Dennis "Doc" Plautz, saw the EgyptAir logo. Massey told Plautz to shine a flashlight on the fuselage and soon the two were able to see the tail number—"SU-AYK." Massey called Zia and *Saratoga*, confirming that they had the right plane.

Massey performed an extraordinary bit of airmanship in flying a

63,000 pound fighter close enough to an airliner to see its tail number with a flashlight, without either spooking the other pilot or having himself a mid-air collision. To paraphrase Tom Wolfe, Massey had the right stuff that night.

Finished with the easy part, Zia now had to orchestrate an event that the pilots had never practiced—safely forcing a civilian airliner to land.

In Washington, the National Security Council staff and the State Department busily tried to make arrangements with other governments to limit the Egyptian airliner's options if the Navy could not force it to land at Sigonella. We learned the value of minimizing an aircraft's landing choices during the TWA hijacking when the hijackers forced the pilot to fly from one airport to another. Stark and North drafted a cable for Reagan's signature that we sent to Tunisian President Habib Bourguiba requesting he deny landing rights to the 737. The State Department also sent similar requests to Athens and Beirut.

President Reagan insisted that the Navy aircraft not shoot down the EgyptAir jet if it did not cooperate. He would have rather seen the hijackers get away than kill innocent people on board the plane. The Pentagon issued these rules of engagement, as the military calls such instructions, to everyone concerned.

The Israelis produced another intelligence nugget about this time— Abu Abbas had joined his hijacking crew on board the Egyptian plane.

Rear Admiral Jeremiah instructed Zia and the Tomcat pilots to simply follow the 737 for the time being, since it was heading west, the right direction for Sigonella. But soon Zia, who was monitoring the airliner's communications, heard Tunis deny the airliner permission to land. Flight 2843 then called Athens, which also refused authorization to land. Orbiting south of Crete, the 737 contacted Cairo for instructions, and controllers there told the pilot to return to Egypt. When Zia heard this, he consulted with *Saratoga* and Jeremiah, who instructed him to make radio contact with the airliner.

"EgyptAir 2843, this is Tigertail 603, over," Zia radioed. English is the standard language between pilots of international flights, as well as ground-based air traffic controllers. Zia used the standard protocol in aircraft communications in which he said the name of the airline and the flight number first, followed by his call sign. "I knew the Egyptian pilot would not know who the heck 'Tigertail 603' was," Zia told me later, "but I didn't want to confuse the other Navy aircraft by using another call sign or name."

"The 737 didn't respond," Zia told me, "so I tried again with a sterner and louder voice, **'EgyptAir 2843, this is Tigertail 603, over.'** The Egyptian was confused and asked me to identify myself. I advised him that he was being escorted by U.S. Navy fighters and instructed him to proceed to Sigonella, Italy, giving him compass course to follow."

Two Tomcat fighters turned on their lights and pulled up close to the 737, quickly reinforcing Zia's instructions. As passengers on board the airliner looked out the windows, the Egyptian pilot responded, "I'm saying you are too close. I am following your orders. Don't be too close. Please."

The 737 pilot remained remarkably calm during these initial moments, according to a pilot of a nearby El Al plane. Flying from Israel to Madrid, the El Al pilot, Shabbetai Gilboa, listened in as the Egyptian told an Athens air controller that he had been intercepted by two jet fighters. Gilboa later told an Israeli newspaper that he had been amazed by the pilot's coolness as he briefed the more agitated Greek, then asked Athens to advise Cairo of the intercept.

"I was the only one who could talk with the 737 because the Tomcats did not have a radio with the right frequency," Zia said later. "I think the pilot thought I was in one of the fighters and I was not about to tell him that I was miles away." Zia told Flight 2843's pilot what direction to fly in order to get to Sigonella and what radio channels to use in contacting the airfield. Then the whole gaggle—Flight 2843, Zia and his Hawkeye radar aircraft, four Tomcats, including Weatherspoon's and Massey's—headed toward Sigonella. Two other aircraft soon joined the high altitude procession, the Air Force transports carrying U.S. special operations troops.

At the White House, John Poindexter was the point man for our activities. Bud McFarlane had gone to New Jersey after returning from Chicago with President Reagan. Reagan had sent Bud on a secret trip to visit with former President Richard Nixon and exchange views on international matters. Although my duty officers talked with him regularly on the phone, McFarlane had to leave most decisions to Poindexter.

Poindexter waited until after the Navy intercepted the Egyptian airliner to contact Italy and request permission for EgyptAir 2843 to land at Sigonella. There was concern that Italy, because of its good relations with Egypt and the PLO, might warn the Egyptians. Besides, Poindexter, North, and Stark reasoned, presenting Italy with a *fait accompli* might ensure better Italian cooperation. Although Sigonella was a NATO air base about fifteen miles from Catania on the east coast of Sicily with a U.S. Navy captain in charge of the U.S. side of the base, it was an Italian facility.

My staff attempted to get Prime Minister Craxi on the phone so that North and Stark could enlist his assistance, but neither the U.S. embassy personnel in Rome nor the Italians could find him. North remembered that a White House consultant, Michael Ledeen, knew Craxi and also spoke fluent Italian. Ollie called Ledeen at home and asked that he attempt to find Craxi and get him on the phone. Ledeen called via the Situation Room to Rome's Hotel Raphael, Craxi's residence, but one of the prime minister's assistants refused to cooperate.

"I identified myself and told him in Italian that I was calling from the White House because there was a serious crisis," wrote Ledeen later. "'Lives were at stake. If people die tonight because you refuse to let me talk to Craxi because he doesn't want to be disturbed, you will find your picture on the front page of every newspaper in the world tomorrow morning.'"

With that hyperbole Ledeen got through to Craxi. Ledeen described the situation, but Craxi asked why the United States chose Sigonella. Ledeen explained: "'Because,' I replied, hoping that a light-hearted approach was the most likely to gain a favorable response, 'no other place on earth can offer the unique combination of beautiful weather, cultural tradition, and magnificent cuisine that Sicily can provide these people.' Craxi laughed and said he would take care of it at once."

Ralph Zia maintained a continuous dialogue with Flight 2843 from his Hawkeye. Slower than the Tomcats and the Boeing 737, Ralph was lagging behind, but still in radio range. "About 150 miles out from

Sigonella, one of the Tomcats contacted the airfield control and advised them that Flight 2843 was inbound," said Zia.

The Italians refused Flight 2843's request to land, apparently because Craxi's approval had not yet reached Sicily. After repeated refusals, Zia told the Egyptian to declare a low fuel emergency, a move that guarantees authorization to land. Also, a U.S. Navy officer assigned to the NATO base reportedly grabbed the microphone from his Italian counterpart and gave Flight 2843 permission to land. With his first pass too low, the Egyptian pilot went around a second time and finally landed at 1:30 A.M. Italian time. The Navy aircraft returned to *Saratoga*.

As the 737 taxied to a stop, members of SEAL Team Six who Stiner had left behind earlier in the week drove out to the taxiway and surrounded the airliner. Within moments, Stiner's two darkened Air Force transports landed and parked on the main runway to block its use. Troops from the aircraft reinforced the perimeter around the airliner and snipers took positions with a clear view of the plane's doors.

Stiner called the Egyptian pilot on the radio and explained that U.S. forces had surrounded the airliner. The pilot explained that an Egyptian ambassador was on board and wanted to talk with the Americans.

Captain Bob Gormly, commanding officer of SEAL Team Six, waited as the airliner's crew lowered a ladder from the forward door. Soon the pilot, Captain Ahmed Moneeb, descended the ladder with a second man, Zeid Imad Hamed, an Egyptian diplomat. Hamed presented his credentials and an Egyptian diplomatic passport to Gormly. After a quick discussion with Stiner, Hamed went inside the base operations center to consult with Egyptian Foreign Minister Meguid by telephone. All others on the plane remained on board.

Stiner and one of Gormly's SEAL officers then entered the airliner. On board were the four young, easily recognizable hijackers, Abu Abbas, about ten armed members of Egypt's counter-terrorism unit, Force 777, and the rest of the aircraft crew. Another, unexpected man was on the plane—Ozzuddin Badrakkan, chief of PLF military operations. He must have either joined Abbas in Port Said or accompanied his leader from the start.

Stiner did not attempt to seize the six Palestinians, although that is what his orders specified. As he stood at the top of the boarding ladder, he realized that the Italians might have a different plan for the hijackers. His force of about 80 SEALs and other special operations troops circled the plane, but they were in turn surrounded by some 300 armed Italians, both soldiers and officers of the Italian national police force, the Carabinieri. Italian trucks blocked the runway.

Everything had gone perfectly up to this point. The intelligence agencies discovered the plan to ship the hijackers out of Egypt, Jim Stark hatched a great idea, the Pentagon moved quicker than ever, and the Navy pilots found the plane over the vast expanse of the Mediterranean. A little moxie got the hijackers on the ground at an airfield of a NATO ally. A question remained: What next?

The first thing the U.S. government did was place a barrage of phone calls to Italy. After Stiner and Gormly confirmed that the Italians were serious about preventing their departure with the hijackers, they notified the Pentagon of the standoff by satellite telephone. Knowing that centralized decision-making was not a strength of the Italian government, Secretary of State Shultz called the Italian foreign minister and Secretary of Defense Weinberger called his counterpart, both declaring the U.S. intention to take control of the hijackers.

Ledeen drove to the White House and called Craxi again, this time from the Situation Room. According to Ledeen, Craxi said that "If it were up to me, I'd turn them over in a minute, but it's not a political question, it's a legal matter." All of the senior Italian government officials, including Foreign Minister Giulio Andreotti, and Defense Minister Giovanni Spadolini, argued that the Italian judicial system controlled the situation. The hijackers committed a crime on Italian soil—*Achille Lauro*—and since those men were again in Italy—Sigonella airfield—there was no political solution to the problem. The Italians regretted the death of an American, but Italy's laws took precedence.

At Poindexter's direction, my staff in the Situation Room placed a call from President Reagan to Craxi at 3:30 A.M. in Rome (9:30 P.M. at the White House), with Ledeen acting as the interpreter. Reagan pressed Craxi to relinquish custody of the hijackers to the U.S. government, but the Italian held firm. Craxi did promise to apprehend the four hijackers, but there was a misunderstanding between the two leaders about the fate of Abu Abbas and Badrakkan. According to Ledeen, Reagan believed that Craxi promised to arrest all six. But Craxi said later that he only agreed to "obtain useful elements of the information from the Palestinian leaders." Reagan grudgingly accepted Craxi's argument, but told the Italian that the U.S. intended to request extradition of the hijackers.

Meanwhile, Stiner called the Pentagon and described his dilemma. He had the plane, the hijackers, and Abbas, but he was eyeball-to-eyeball with hundreds of armed Italians. "I am not worried about our situation," Stiner wrote later about his predicament at the time. "We have the firepower to prevail. But I am concerned about the immaturity of the Italian troops. . . . A backfire from a motorbike or a construction cart could precipitate a shooting incident that could lead to a lot of Italian casualties. And I don't believe that our beef is with our ally, the Italians, but rather with the terrorists."

With that news, Poindexter convened a secure conference call with Admiral Crowe, Secretary Weinberger, Stiner, and others. "We could get the hijackers," recalled Poindexter, "but we might not get them out of Italy. It was the general feeling of everyone not to try." At 4:00 A.M. Italian time, Crowe ordered Stiner to stand down and defuse the situation. Although tensions subsided, the debate over what to do with Abu Abbas was just beginning.

About the time I went home, a little after midnight, October 11, Washington time, the American public knew nothing yet of the Navy's heroics. What they knew was that Palestinians hijacked a ship, killed an American, then got away with murder. The public didn't care if the hijackers were members of the PLO, PLF, or XYZ. For those who did pay attention, they had no reason to reject PLO Chairman Yasser Arafat's claim that the PLO negotiated the surrender of the hijackers. Only insiders, government officials with access to classified information, knew that his claim, however technically correct it might have been, was really bogus.

Across the country, Alex Odeh, a Palestinian-American, voiced his outrage over the hijacking to his brother Sami. His reaction to the hijacking was much the same as the Jewish-American Klinghoffer daughters. Alex was the West Coast regional director of the American-Arab Anti-Discrimination Committee, the most prominent Arab advocacy group in the United States. Despite his support for the establishment of an independent Palestinian state, Odeh never felt that terrorism was a means to that end.

Alex and his brother were Catholics, born in the West Bank town of Jifna. Alex attended Bir Zeit University and Al-Najah University on the West Bank, as well as the University of Cairo. Moving to the United States in 1972, Alex earned a master's degree in political science, and became an American citizen in 1977. In 1985, Odeh was teaching Arabic at California State University, Fullerton, and Middle East history and politics at Coastline Community College. Odeh, 41, and his wife Norma, also from Jifna, lived in Orange County and had three daughters, Helena, 7; Samia, 5; and Susan, 2.

Odeh decided to speak out publicly about the hijacking. When he saw reports in which Arafat claimed to have ended the hostage-taking, Odeh arranged to make two appearances on television. The first was on CNN, which he taped in the afternoon of October 10; the segment aired that evening. He also taped a spot that aired on the 11:00 P.M. October 10 news program at KABC-TV in Los Angeles. It was just four hours after Carl Stiner and his men backed away from a confrontation with the Italians.

When KABC taped Odeh's remarks, he condemned the hijacking and terrorism in general. But in editing Odeh's segment for the newscast, the station reduced his statement to the following:

"I think the media mistakenly linked this incident with the PLO. As far as I know Arafat did an excellent job and we commend Arafat for his positive role in resolving this issue. The media ought to give the PLO and Arafat recognition, inform the public about the PLO and the political organization, and Arafat in particular, as chairman of the PLO, who is a man of peace."

Odeh's public support of the PLO and Arafat, shorn of his denunciation of the hijacking by a TV producer, proved to be an inflammatory position, at least to one person.

"We Bag the Bums," shouted the *New York Daily News'* headline. *Newsweek Magazine* wrote "the good guys finally won one." Up until this bold move, critics viewed the Reagan administration's actions against terrorism as more talk than action. When Reagan came to the White House Press Briefing Theater that morning, October 11, he defended his apparent inaction during past terrorist acts. ". . . in a number of incidents where, to retaliate would simply be an act of violence without any knowledge that you were striking the perpetrators of the deed, and you might be attacking many innocent people. This has been our great problem with terrorism. But here was a clear-cut case in which we could lay our hands on the terrorists."

Reagan also hailed the sterling efforts of the U.S. military, intelligence community, and Foreign Service. "These young Americans sent a message to terrorists everywhere, 'You can run, but you can't hide.'"

This catchy slogan first surfaced in 1946 when heavyweight champ Joe Louis coined the phrase before his fight with the elusive Billy Conn. John Poindexter told me later that he could not remember who drew the phrase from boxing history, but thought one of the President's speechwriters might have resurrected it.

When Poindexter entered the Oval Office earlier for Reagan's daily national security briefing, the President echoed the feeling of the country. "He rose from his chair, snapped his heels, raised his hand to his forehead, and said 'I salute you, Admiral,'" recalled Poindexter. "I thanked him, but told him that he ought to salute the Navy, not me. They deserved commendation for an impromptu plan and executing it flawlessly."

Secretary of Defense Weinberger, who lobbied against the intercept, was quick to jump on the bandwagon. "We had the planes, we had the intelligence, and we had the guts."

Alas, there were critics. Egypt claimed that America had "hijacked the hijackers" and insulted the country; Mubarak was furious that his lie was exposed. The American arrogance and unilateral military maneuvers stunned Italy. Saudi Arabia saw its friend the United States applying a double standard, and Arab news organizations decried the intercept as air piracy.

Yasser Arafat angrily denounced the intercept and called the basis for the action "cowboy logic." "There is no difference between a terrorist who hijacks an airplane with a pistol and a terrorist who hijacks a plane with a warplane," Arafat told the news media.

Perhaps some of that ill will was behind a rumor circulating around Europe and the Middle East that the intercept was the result of collusion among Italy, Egypt, the United States, and the PLO. While untrue, the New York Times reported that Egyptian officials told the Italians the specifics of the hijackers' flight from Cairo, information that allowed the successful intercept and force down. That allegation was false and Reagan denied the rumors, declaring at his press conference, "We did this all by our little selves."

Not everyone celebrated that morning.

◄+- -+►

Alex Odeh opened the door to his Santa Ana, California, office the next morning at 9:00, a scant ten hours after his taped appearance on KABC-TV the night before. A tripwire attached to the door exploded a bomb that shredded Odeh's lower body. He died in surgery two hours later.

The blast injured seven others and demolished the Los Angeles offices of the American-Arab Anti-Discrimination Committee. Six of the injured worked at an insurance company across the hall. A carpenter working next door helped evacuate the surviving victims. "I heard the explosion and ran to the window," said Linda Bullard who was in an adjacent building, "and there was just glass strewn across the street."

The FBI later described the triggering device on the bomb as sophisticated, with the timer only allowing the bomber one minute to place the bomb and close the door to set the tripwire. The explosive itself was a relatively simple pipe bomb.

Now there were two American families grieving as a result of the *Achille Lauro* hijacking, one Jewish, the second, Palestinian. "Violence only begets violence," Alex's brother Sami Odeh once said.

Through the Anti-Discrimination Committee, Odeh helped Arab residents in southern California with health, immigration, and discrimination problems. Additionally, he was a member of the Orange County Human Relations Commission and actively worked to set up meetings between Arab and Jewish community leaders. Richard Ayood, director of the National Association of Arab-Americans, said Odeh was "very committed to the idea of dialogue with the leading Jewish organizations. It would be hard for me to think anyone would harm a hair on his head."

His friends and family regarded Odeh as a man of peace and were surprised that the TV station edited out portions of his statement about the *Achille Lauro* hijacking. Los Angeles Anti-Discrimination Committee chapter president David Habib said that Odeh "condemned the hijacking of the ship, condemned terrorism around the world . . . yet they decided to broadcast a little part that seemed to show Alex Odeh and the Committee are a pro-Arafat organization." KABC declined to respond to Habib's allegation.

Odeh's wife, Norma, said at the time that Alex began receiving threats in 1980, often against his family. By 1984, the Odehs's phone rang almost daily with anonymous threats. "If they want to kill me, let them," Alex said to Norma. "I'm not afraid to die. I have never said anything to hurt anyone." After changing their home telephone number, the threats subsided. Despite the decrease in threats, a member of Odeh's family thought the interview might trigger an angry reaction; Odeh reportedly was not concerned. "He was a very quiet, very gentle man," said his brother Sami's wife, Lisa Odeh. "We had some fear that something might happen to him in Israel, but we never thought this would happen in the United States."

Some observers have raised the point that whomever planted the bomb did not have time to prepare the device, case the Committee office, and set the booby trap between the time of Odeh's TV appearance, 11:00 P.M., and the time of the detonation, 9:00 A.M. the next morning. Two things make it a plausible scenario. First, Alex Odeh had received numerous other threats, so it's possible that whomever set the bomb had already thought about how to target the Committee office. The TWA airliner hijacking triggered a wave of anti-Arab threats a few months earlier. It's not as if someone had yet to think about reprisals against Arab-Americans by October 9. Second, news of Klinghoffer's death reached the West Coast about 9:00 A.M. October 9, forty-eight hours before the bombing detonated. It's plausible for an experienced, vengeful person to act in two days.

There were news reports that Odeh normally did not open the office, a job usually left his secretary, and therefore was not the intended target. Perhaps so, but the bomb killed Alex Odeh, not his secretary.

Shortly after Reagan and Craxi talked on the phone about the fate of the hijackers, the Italian foreign ministry told Egypt's ambassador to Rome of their intention to arrest the hijackers and remove Abbas and Badrakkan from the plane for questioning. Egypt initially assented. As Stiner and his Italian counterparts disentangled their respective troops, the Italian base commander, Colonel Annicchiarico, boarded the airliner with the Egyptian diplomat, Hamed. They negotiated the removal and arrest of the hijackers, sending them to the air base jail. Abbas and Badrakkan refused the leave the aircraft, citing diplomatic immunity as representatives of the PLO and Yasser Arafat. Following Abbas's lead, Egypt reversed its position on the two Palestinians, now claiming that they were on board an Egyptian aircraft sent on a governmental mission, thus accruing extraterritorial rights. Further, Egypt asked the Italians to allow the plane and the men, who Egypt said America brought to Italy against their will, to depart Sicily.

Prime Minister Craxi held a press conference late in the afternoon that day, Friday, October 11. Pinched between the United States, which demanded he arrest Abbas and Badrakkan, and Egypt, which wanted the plane and the two "emissaries" released, Craxi chose his words carefully. He acknowledged that the two played a role in ending the hijacking, but invited them to furnish "useful testimony" about the incident. With respect to the future of Abbas and Badrakkan, Craxi shifted the problem to the Italian legal system. "We hope to resolve these residual problems in the coming hours, after which it will be up to the courts to judge those who are responsible for the crimes that have been committed."

Craxi earlier sent his personal foreign affairs advisor, Antonio Badini, to Sigonella to assess the situation. Badini boarded the airliner, speaking at length with Abbas. The prime minister's office released an account of that meeting and Abbas's version of his role in the incident was an audacious mixture of half-truths, posturing, and lies. Abbas thought Arafat chose him as a negotiator because "he [Abbas] knew how to behave in these circumstances and which persuasive arguments would be most useful." Abbas also suggested that "certain developments, still unknown to him, had intervened to create panic among the four hijackers, leading them to undertake a very harmful initiative." The decisive role in rescuing the passengers was his, Abbas said.

In the background of all this diplomatic and political maneuvering was the status of *Achille Lauro*. Egypt refused to let it get underway and the Italians detected a less than subtle Egyptian pressure for a quid-pro-quo. Let the airliner leave and we will allow the ship to sail.

After transferring the four hijackers from the airbase to a local prison, the public magistrate in Syracuse declared, late in the evening of the 11th, that his inquiries were complete. He said that EgyptAir 2843 could depart for Rome with Abbas and Badrakkan on board. Craxi saw moving the plane to Rome as a chance to keep it and Abbas in Italy a little longer as a courtesy to the United States. The Italian foreign ministry notified the U.S. embassy of the flight, explaining that Abbas and Badrakkan wanted to consult with the PLO office in Rome. Cynical U.S. officials viewed the development as a precursor to Abbas's release.

Stiner, still near the airliner, also felt that the 737 could fly anywhere once it left Sigonella, even to Cairo. Not wanting to lose touch with the airliner, he readied a T-39 Navy executive jet to follow the Boeing 737. Putting a team of his best men aboard, Stiner kept it ready for immediate takeoff.

At 10:00 P.M. EgyptAir 2843 taxied toward the main runway, with Italians blocking all other entrances to the main runway. As the airliner lifted off, Stiner ordered the T-39 to take off, too. Without access to the runway, the Navy aircraft used an adjacent taxiway to take off. The Italians reacted to the latest American act of bravado by launching their own fighter aircraft to escort the airliner to Rome. Pilots on board the U.S. and the Italian jets exchanged colorful epithets over the radio about their respective intentions, family heritage, and sexual preferences. Yet another strange formation of aircraft flew toward an Italian airfield.

As the 737, Italian jets, and the Navy aircraft approached Rome's Ciampino airport, Italian air controllers denied permission for the Navy jet to land. Using the proven "inflight emergency" ploy, the T-39 landed just after the Egyptian airliner. Pulling alongside the airliner on the ramp, Stiner's men watched the passengers disembark.

In Washington, Justice Department officials redoubled their efforts to generate an arrest warrant for Abbas that could be served while he was in Italy. Earlier U.S. actions aimed at arresting the four hijackers generally ceased when the Italians jailed them in Syracuse, Sicily. Now with the focus on Abbas, Justice had to deliver a warrant to Rome to meet the requirements of the U.S.–Italy extradition treaty. The treaty required Italy to hold a suspect for forty-five days once the United States produced an arrest warrant.

Justice and FBI representatives began assembling information that linked Abbas to the hijacking two days before, but the most telling evidence came from classified Israeli intelligence reports. Urgent discussions with the Israeli embassy in Washington and officials in Tel Aviv yielded declassified versions that were melded with U.S. information. Justice attorneys then petitioned Judge Charles R. Richey of the U.S.

District Court in Washington, DC, who issued the required warrants for both the hijackers and Abu Abbas.

The Situation Room transmitted a message from Reagan to Craxi, reminding the Italian of his country's extradition treaty obligations. Edwin Meese, who had become Attorney General after leaving the White House staff, called his Italian counterpart, Mino Martinazzoli, informing him of the arrest warrants. FBI officials notified Italian law enforcement agencies of the warrants, and U.S. ambassador to Rome Maxwell Rabb delivered the warrants to Salvatore Zhara Buda, of the Italian Ministry of Justice, at his home at 5:30 A.M. Saturday morning, October 12. The U.S. government felt this action would be enough for the Italians to hold Abbas.

Within a few hours of Rabb's early morning visit, Zhara Buda met with three judges from the Ministry of Justice to review the U.S. petition. After they completed their analysis, the group advised Prime Minister Craxi and Justice Minister Martinazzoli that the documents did not support a provisional arrest of Abu Abbas. Craxi later said that the U.S. request to hold Abbas "did not, in the Justice Minister's opinion, satisfy the factual and substantive requirements laid down by Italian law." This being so, there was no longer any legal basis, in Ministry's opinion, for detaining Abbas, since at the time he was on board an aircraft which enjoyed extraterritorial status.

This interpretation stunned everyone at the White House. Nicholas Veliotes in Cairo, however, was not surprised. "I received a copy of the document arguing for Abbas's arrest and I knew immediately that the Italians would be troubled by it," Veliotes said. "It read exactly like a Mossad document and anyone with Middle East experience would recognize its origins." Mossad is the Israeli intelligence agency that was the source of the reports of Abbas's involvement in the hijacking. "I am sure that the Italians instantly understood that Israel was instrumental in the attempt to arrest Abbas and that did not please them."

After receiving the judge's decision, Craxi convened a cabinet meeting at 1:30 P.M. Saturday to discuss his country's difficult situation. It was a dilemma that many countries face during terrorism crises. Some nations seek legal solutions to terrorist actions, declaring that such problems merit only black or white, good or evil arguments. Others consider political and diplomatic arrangements to be helpful, or a mix of policies, with a pinch of legalism and dash of old-fashioned *real politik*. All of these arguments found their way into Craxi's meeting.

The U.S. position in this matter was abundantly clear; in fact, Rabb interrupted the cabinet meeting with a personal plea from Reagan to hold Abbas. The U.S. wanted to bring these "sons-of-bitches," to quote Nick Veliotes, to the bar of justice. Italy knew that ignoring the senior member of NATO would have serious consequences to the Italian government.

Holding Abbas, however, would easily undermine Italy's relatively good relations throughout the Middle East, a priority for Craxi and Foreign Minister Andreotti. Egypt's Mubarak lashed out at American arrogance and Italy's role in the intercept of his aircraft. Egypt kept insisting that Italy return the plane and Abbas, appearing to hold *Achille Lauro* as ransom for the Boeing 737. The negative public reaction in Egypt to the American seizure of the airliner was loud and widespread. If the Italians relinquished custody of Abbas to the United States, anti-American demonstrators in Cairo might direct their wrath at Mubarak for acceding to U.S. and Italian pressures.

Italy had achieved a semblance of rapprochement with the PLO, thus keeping most Palestinian terrorists away from Italian citizens and interests. In fact, Italy and the PLO had a deal, made in 1973 after a PLO attack at the Rome airport, that the PLO would not target Italians in return for Italian acquiescence of PLO objectives. Apparently Arafat reminded Craxi of the arrangement by warning that "uncontrollable actions could result" if Abbas were surrendered to the United States.

Also, the Italian Ministry of Justice's ruling on the U.S. warrant for Abbas was not watertight. The provincial magistrates, who are part judge and part public prosecutor, normally are the first to adjudicate extradition requests. A judge in Rome and the Sicilian magistrate who was holding the hijackers faulted the ministry's premature judgment.

Lastly, Craxi faced divisions within his governing coalition. Defense Minister Spadolini and two other cabinet officers supported U.S. actions in the incident, but Spadolini was in Milan during the cabinet meeting. Although Craxi and Spadolini reportedly conversed by phone, Spadolini's opposition to releasing Abbas would have huge repercussions in Italy in the following weeks.

After considering all of these issues, the Craxi cabinet voted to permit Abbas's departure from Italy. The foreign ministry informed Rabb and Egypt's ambassador to Rome.

Earlier on Saturday, Italian police escorted Abbas and Badrakkan back to the EgyptAir 737. Wearing unidentified uniforms, the two boarded the plane. Zeid Imad Hamed, the Egyptian diplomat who accompanied the Palestinians from Cairo, arranged for the Yugoslav national airline—JAT—to transport the men from Rome's main airport, Fiumicino (now Leonardo da Vinci–Fiumicino) to Belgrade. EgyptAir flight 2843 flew its penultimate leg at 5:30 P.M., a ten-minute hop from Ciampino airport to Fiumicino. Abbas and Badrakkan exited the Egyptian airliner, walked across the ramp with Italian escorts, and embarked on the waiting Yugoslav aircraft. They departed Rome at 7:10 P.M., Saturday, October 12, 1985.

Politics in Italy and Egypt trumped crime and punishment. Mohammed Abbas was at large again and free to wage his war of terror.

The U.S. Navy's capture of the four *Achille Lauro* hijackers made this affair, at least to this point, seem like a morality play of good versus evil. Indeed, we caught some evil men, but look at everything else that happened, events that had nothing to do with crime and punishment, but rather power, politics, and prejudice.

Leon Klinghoffer was an innocent bystander in the war between Palestinians and Israelis. He died because of the hijacker's prejudices against Jews. Alex Odeh died because he defended Palestinians, but not terrorists. Was Odeh's killer as evil as Klinghoffer's?

The Italians didn't want the political problems, either domestic or international, associated with jailing Abu Abbas. They didn't even want the four hijackers, but we had dropped them in their lap. Craxi's government used some legal mumbo-jumbo to shroud what was really a political decision to release Abbas. Italy, along with some of their European neighbors, was learning that the root cause of much of terrorism, at least that arising from the Arab-Israeli conflict, is politics. And it was not just Italian politicians who understood that. Consider Captain De Rosa's comment to Abu Abbas on the radio during the hijacking: "I am familiar with your situation and I understand it well. We understand the Palestinians, we understand the Palestinian aspirations, and for that reason we are all with you." While De Rosa might have been trying to appease Abbas and not upset the equilibrium at that point aboard ship, I think De Rosa reflected the Italian view of Palestinian terrorism.

Egyptian Foreign Minister Meguid brokered a deal with Italy and West Germany to release the hijackers after their surrender. When the Egyptian government learned of Klinghoffer's murder, why didn't it simply throw the evildoers in jail? Why did President Mubarak lie about the hijacker's status? Politics. Political pressure within Egypt, from fellow Arab states, and from the PLO prevailed over the issues of right and wrong.

At the White House, Reagan's staff was spinning the press about how Reagan succeeded where Carter failed. America's military power prevailed. Egypt's Mubarak could complain all day, but he couldn't match Reagan's power. Get over it, Hosni, they seemed to think. Besides, the President's tough stance of not negotiating with terrorists, the spinmasters said, had finally worked.

Yet less than a month earlier Bud McFarlane and Ollie North arranged for Israel to secretly ship anti-tank missiles to Iran in return for that country's assistance in freeing American hostages in Lebanon. As a result, one of those kidnapped, Reverend Benjamin Weir, was released on September 15, 1985. The administration was speaking out of both sides of its mouth.

In the years since the hijacking Ollie North has taken credit for conceiving of the plan to intercept and force down the Egyptian 737. Jim Stark thought of the idea, not Ollie. During the Iran-Contra investigation a couple years later, the news media referred to Ollie's role in capturing the *Achille Lauro* hijackers as his finest hour. He clearly was a major reason for the success of the operation, but Stark, John Poindexter, Art Moreau, Ralph Zia, Skid Massey, and Steve Weatherspoon deserve credit as well.

Information concerning the departure of the hijackers from Cairo came from sensitive U.S. intelligence sources, as well as from the Israelis. During the investigation into the Iran-Contra scandal, North told a U.S. Congressional committee that he lied to Congress about his support of the Contras because he did not trust its members to keep a secret. The example that he gave to support his assertion was that congressmen had leaked sensitive intelligence regarding the *Achille Lauro* hijackers' departure from Egypt. That information, which North said compromised intelligence activities, found its way into the *Newsweek* account of the White House derring-do.

A few days after North's testimony, *Newsweek*, in its July 27, 1987, issue, wrote that no congressman passed sensitive intelligence to the magazine for its article on the intercept. Ollie North leaked that information, *Newsweek*'s editors stated. "Congress may be guilty of leaks, as North alleges," the article read. "But most come from the other end of Pennsylvania Avenue. . . . And on occasion they have come from the lips of Oliver North."

CHAPTER

3

Backlash (1985)

I SPIT in their faces," Marilyn Klinghoffer told President Ronald Reagan, describing her confrontation with the hijackers in a Sicilian jail just three days after they murdered her husband. Mrs. Klinghoffer was not the only person with strong emotions that day. Politicians from Washington to Tel Aviv were outraged, the former hostages and their families were still torn with grief, and the citizens in four countries were mad. The Jewish Defense League was mad as well, angered at the suggestion that it was responsible for Alex Odeh's murder.

After Ambassador Nick Veliotes delivered his profanely clear suggestion to Egypt about what it should do with the hijackers, he began combing the ship for American passengers in the early morning hours of Thursday, October 10. He found none in the public areas.

"I started knocking on cabin doors, shouting in the hallways that I was the American ambassador," said Veliotes when we met in 2002 to discuss the hijacking. "I yelled out that they were safe and that I had a doctor with me." The passengers cautiously emerged from their staterooms and Veliotes gently asked them for details of the hijacking.

Gradually Veliotes gathered the Americans together, but realized that Marilyn Klinghoffer remained in her room.

"She answered my knock on her door, distraught and in terrible shape," recalled Veliotes. "I told her that her friends would be having breakfast in an hour and they would not start without her. She agreed to attend, showing up later in a fresh dress, makeup on, and more composed than when I first saw her."

After his meeting and breakfast with the passengers, Veliotes said that one of them, a man who wanted his name withheld, rose to speak for the group. "He wanted me to know how the group reacted to the hijacking. 'They debased us, threatened us, humbled us, and even killed one of us,' he said quietly. 'But through it all, we never cracked, we never crawled, and we never forgot that we were Americans.'"

As Veliotes talked to the American passengers, *Achille Lauro* got underway from her anchorage and entered Port Said at dawn. Captain De Rosa had told the U.S. ambassador earlier that his superiors had ordered him to embark the passengers left behind in Egypt during the hijacking and resume the ship's planned itinerary. "I was appalled that the Italians were so callous about the schedule; besides, it was a crime scene," said Veliotes, "so I offered to find a reason for De Rosa to ignore the order. I approached the senior Egyptian military general on the scene, asking him to help find a way to hold the ship. He understood the situation and quickly announced to De Rosa that the Egyptian Defense Ministry was commandeering the ship." Veliotes's good intentions notwithstanding, the Egyptian government prohibited the ship from sailing until the Italians released the EgyptAir plane.

As the ship moored, hordes of news media representatives buzzed about the pier, desperately seeking interviews with the passengers and crew. Diplomats from every country that had citizens on board the ship scurried about, attempting to organize the paperwork required for passengers to leave the ship and forego the remainder of the cruise. Although the Egyptian government held the ship in port, it declared that individuals could depart.

Marilyn walked across the gangway to the pier, almost overwhelmed by reporters and cameramen. Pushed and shoved by journalists jostling for a story, she snapped at them, "Get away."

She found a phone and called her daughters in New York. "She told us not to worry and that she would be home soon," Lisa Klinghoffer said later. "Then she said, 'But first there is something I have to tell you. . . .' I interrupted her to say that we already knew about Daddy. She thought that she had to break the news to us."

President Reagan also called Lisa and Ilsa, expressing his condolences. Sympathetic strangers wrote comforting letters to the sisters, one of which read, "It could have been my father." "But it wasn't," Lisa said. "It was our father."

A group of seventeen American passengers, including Marilyn Klinghoffer, left Port Said Thursday evening on a three-hour bus ride to Cairo. Early the next morning they boarded a U.S. Air Force transport aircraft for a flight to Sigonella air base. The transport landed in Sicily soon after the EgyptAir 737 departed for Rome with Abu Abbas on board.

Carl Stiner, still at Sigonella after his standoff with the Italian Carabinieri over the hijackers' fate, wrote that he conceived of the idea of bringing the former hostages to Sicily to identify the four Palestinians. He accompanied Marilyn and four other passengers to the Sicilian jail in Catania, where an Italian magistrate arranged a lineup. According to Stiner, Marilyn not only spat in Molqi's face, she asked Stiner for his pistol. "I want to shoot him," she said.

Having firmly identified the four hijackers, the Americans reboarded the Air Force plane and flew to Rhein-Main Air Force Base in Frankfurt, Germany, for refueling. All but two of the seventeen then took off for the last leg of their journey home.

The aircraft landed at Newark airport in New Jersey at 12:50 P.M. on Saturday, October 12, five days after the hijackers seized control of *Achille Lauro.* Marilyn Klinghoffer stepped off the plane first, met by a phalanx of politicians: Senator Alfonse D'Amato and Representative Ted Weiss of New York, and New Jersey Senator Frank Lautenberg. While she did not speak to reporters, D'Amato and Lautenberg later told the news media what Marilyn said to them. "Thank God the President did something. I hope we're able to bring them [the hijackers] back to the United States to try them. But if we're not, I want to go over there and testify against them."

Government officials took the former passengers to a nearby hotel for reunions with their families. Marilyn met her daughters, son-in-law, and others in one room, while the rest of the group joined family and friends in another. One room was filled with grief, the other joy. "It was a bittersweet homecoming," Lisa said.

Vernon Walters, U.S. ambassador to the United Nations, spoke briefly with the group, carrying a message from President Reagan. Also, teams of FBI agents and State Department personnel debriefed each former hostage at the hotel. Marilyn and her family soon left for home, but others held a press conference to describe the hijacking and their reaction to the Navy's intercept of the hijackers.

President Reagan called Marilyn later that afternoon to offer his condolences and prayers. Reagan also told her of his administration's attempt to extradite the four hijackers.

"So many people called or came by to see my mother," Lisa recalled in 2002. "Simon Wiesenthal sent his regards, as did Benjamin Netanyahu. The mayor called; everyone wanted to reach out to her. But she didn't flinch because she had a story to tell—she wanted everyone to remember my father. It was not that different from the days after 9-11; it's all about families."

Leon Klinghoffer's body washed ashore in Syria on October 14, two days after Marilyn returned home. With the help of fingerprints and dental records, Syrian government physicians identified the body; the U.S. consul in Damascus, an FBI agent, and an independent Syrian pathologist observed the identification process. While an autopsy would be required to confirm the cause of death, White House spokesman Larry Speakes announced that the body had two gunshot wounds.

After sending the body to Rome for an examination by Italian magistrates preparing the case against the four Palestinian hijackers, the U.S. government arranged to fly Leon Klinghoffer's mortal remains to New York's Kennedy Airport.

The Klinghoffer family, accompanied by the usual knot of politicians who seemingly take advantage of grieving constituents, awaited the casket atop a rostrum at an isolated corner of the airport. A Pan American 747 discharged its passengers and baggage, then taxied to the group. An Army color guard from nearby Fort Hamilton saluted the flag-draped coffin as airline workers lowered it from the jetliner's cargo hold. Marilyn and her family struggled with their emotions.

New York Senator Daniel Patrick Moynihan called Leon "a symbol of righteousness in a world filled with evil and cruelty. He died because he was an American, because he was a Jew, and because he was a free man." Other officials offered similar tributes.

Escorted by her son-in-law, Jerry Arbittier, Marilyn kissed her hand then touched the coffin. The color guard presented her the flag from the coffin, ending the ceremony. Lisa later said that they sent the flag to the U.S. Military Academy at West Point, where it hangs in the Jewish chapel.

At Klinghoffer's funeral the next day at the reform Temple Shaaray Tefila in Manhattan, Rabbi Harvey Tattlebaum said that the murder was not God's will. It was, instead, "an act of an unjust and disordered world in which man's cruelty and stupidity are infinite." To the Klinghoffer family and a synagogue filled with 800 mourners, Rabbi Tattlebaum offered an old psalm that he suggested Leon might have spoken before his death. "Deliver me, O God, from the evil man; Preserve me from the violent man who devises evil things and every day stirs up wars."

The rabbi read a message from Israeli Prime Minister Menachem Begin. Others eulogized Klinghoffer, including Charlotte Spiegel, one of the "beach people," and his daughters. "The world knows you now as a hero," Ilsa said. "But you were always a hero to us."

After the end of the traditional Jewish shiva mourning period, which could not start until Leon's body was returned home, Marilyn met with President and Mrs. Reagan. In Manhattan to speak to the United Nations General Assembly, the Reagans postponed their return to Washington on October 25 to meet with the Klinghoffer family at the President's suite in the Waldorf-Astoria Hotel.

"It was wonderful," both Lisa and Ilsa recalled, "but it wasn't easy getting there. We had to send our Social Security numbers and everything to the Secret Service and go through metal detectors. Reporters and photographers were there and a social secretary led us to our seats. Once the Reagans entered the room, Mrs. Reagan seemed to take the lead."

President Reagan listened attentively to Marilyn's account of the hijacking and promised her that the terrorists would face consequences. Marilyn praised Reagan for his aggressive steps to capture the hijackers. "I'm so proud of you for that decision," she told Reagan.

Several days later, on October 28, Marilyn held a press conference in Manhattan, describing the hijacking, her attempts to stay with her husband, and the agonizing wait to find out what happened to him. She traveled to Washington the next day to appear before a House Foreign Affairs subcommittee. She endorsed a resolution to establish an international conference to discuss combating terrorism and told the congressmen, "I believe that my husband's death has made a difference in the way that people now perceive their vulnerability."

During this period, Marilyn worked hard to tell the story of her husband's death to as many people as possible. She had plenty of outlets for that story because the New York news media besieged her apartment. She and her family were not used to giving interviews; they had no experience with the spotlight. "I have to do everything that I can do and I hope you understand," she told her daughters. "I hope you understand, but if you don't, I still have to do it."

Ilsa and Lisa initially thought her aggressive efforts might draw too much attention to them, perhaps even turn them into targets of anti-Jewish zealots. "We were afraid to go outside at first," Lisa said, "but she insisted. She knew that she didn't have much time left."

From the news media's perspective, the hijacking was a near-perfect three-act play—a violent opening, the frustrating and mysterious disappearance of the killers, then a rousing and dramatic capture of the hijackers. It had tragedy, powerful characters, international intrigue and espionage, and derring-do by military heroes. Great stuff.

The news media, however, found themselves a step behind the events as they unfolded. The dramatic intercept of the Egyptian airliner, its forced landing at Sigonella, and the tense standoff between Carl Stiner's special forces and the Italian Carabinieri all happened away from TV cameras. Even if the Navy had embedded reporters like those in the 2003 U.S.–Iraqi War, they might not have caught much of this brief, nighttime action. The *Achille Lauro* incident was close to the preferred U.S. government model at the time—keep the press at bay until the incident is over. Because the news media did not get direct access to the drama's protagonists, reporters had to rely on statements from the governments of the United States, Italy, and Egypt, as well as boastful claims from the PLO. This situation gave politicians the chance to spin the story to their advantage. Reagan, Craxi, Mubarak, and Arafat had to share the stage with only one grieving family, so most of the news during the two-day hijacking and the one-day capture of the hijackers came not from TV's preferred sources, victims and families, but rather less ratings-worthy actors—government officials.

There was keen competition within the news media to tell the Klinghoffer story and reporters incessantly badgered family members. Never before in the public spotlight, the family, with help from friends, advisors, and a lawyer, established a comfortable relationship with the press. Spurning offers of money for exclusive interviews, the family or its spokeswoman, Letty Simon, a public relations consultant and friend, held periodic news conferences to feed the hungry media.

"Some other people might not have been accepted this way," Robert Squier told the news media. "It happens that this family is an extraordinarily attractive, interesting family," continued Squier, a political and media consultant. "This was the way the family would have been if a great fiction writer had written the story. Instead they're real." Squier also said that the press would go on to a new story at some point. "Then the family goes onto their real lives before the story."

Shortly after the news media learned of the hijacking of *Achille Lauro* and that American citizens were on board, editors, producers, and even the network TV anchors paused for a moment to consider how to cover the story. Not normally an institution to hesitate, the media had cause to ponder their strategy because of their uncontrolled exuberance during their coverage of the TWA hijacking the previous June. Understanding the journalistic circus that surrounded that incident helps put the *Achille Lauro* coverage in perspective.

Palestinian hijackers savagely beat to death U.S. Navy Petty Officer Robert Dean Stethem, a passenger on board TWA Flight 847, then pushed his body out the door of the aircraft onto the tarmac below. Yet images of his grieving parents, much less his name, do not linger in the memories of Americans like those of Leon and Marilyn Klinghoffer. The prolonged, exaggerated, and often bizarre news coverage of the TWA hijacking obscured Stethem's death. Conversely, the lack of media access to the *Achille Lauro* hijacking may have so focused press attention on the Klinghoffer family that the victim and his family transcended any other aspect of the incident. Say the names Leon Klinghoffer and Robert Dean Stethem to anyone over forty today (at least in Washington, DC, or New York) and they will easily remember the former. Saying "*Achille Lauro*" and "TWA 847" will yield the same results. Everyone would probably urge that both deaths should be mourned equally, but the news media has a way of creating imbalances in public reactions to terrorism.

Regardless of Stethem's name recognition, NBC News anchor Tom Brokaw said that the networks "probably overplayed" the TWA incident. "A kind of feeding frenzy developed," Brokaw said shortly after the airliner hijacking. He suggested that the news media overreacted to every development, however small, during the long incident, ignoring what he considers one of journalism's primary roles, acting as gate-keepers of information. "We left the gate open for the duration during the Beirut crisis."

Hostage-taking incidents are inherently rich situations for the news media. Reporting of the violent act is primary, but to sustain coverage and keep readers' and viewers' attention, reporters quickly turn to one of American journalism's basest proclivities—interviewing grief-stricken families of hostages. Some critics claim that sobbing wives and mothers are the story, but others question the ugly and insensitive intrusion into private lives, especially on the grand scale shown during the TWA incident.

"Pornography of grief" is how columnist and TV commentator George Will described the networks' indulgences.

Human interest angles aside, critics also faulted the news media for its unashamed transmission of the hijackers' message. "The terrorists seemed to be playing the networks like synthesizers," wrote the *Washington Post*'s Tom Shales. Steve Friedman, then the executive producer of NBC's *Today Show*, said, "I have a problem that any of this happened in the first place. The more coverage that something like this gets, the more somebody sitting out there watching says, 'You know, this is a good way to get on television.'" In what might have been this incident's clearest example of the symbiosis between terrorism and the news media, CBS televised a news conference given by two hijackers wearing hoods to protect their identities. Some journalists would defend that coverage as simple reporting, but critics view it as a crude debasement of the media, turning the drama into what one reporter called "the theater of the absurd."

"What the Shi'ite terrorists in Beirut achieved is spin control beyond the wildest dreams of any politician," wrote newspaper columnist Fred Barnes at the time. "The terrorists exploited the normal lust of the media—particularly TV—for breaking events of international impact, and for high drama and a human dimension to the news."

This was the state of the U.S. news media's coverage of terrorism in October 1985. The opportunities given to terrorists by a "lusting" media was assuredly not lost on Abu Abbas as he trained his crew to hijack *Achille Lauro*.

The *New York Times* led the way. Reporter Sara Rimer's chance connection to the Klinghoffer daughters during the hijacking gave the newspaper a scoop. For the next two weeks the *Times* ran pieces on the Klinghoffers, focusing on what became the dominant story of the hijacking—a widow's grief. Photographs and stories about Marilyn dominated the coverage, which peaked upon her return to New York, her meeting with President Reagan, the return of Leon's body, and his funeral. In the vernacular of newspaper reporters, the story had "legs"—long-lasting appeal. The story also had international, national, and local angles, the extraordinary human interest aspects that are fundamental to terrorist stories, and lasting images. Grief sells newspapers, even copies of the *Times*.

Most TV viewers don't want complicated stories about Palestinian hatred, years of fighting over land and religion in the Middle East, and political maneuvering and chicanery, accompanied by reasoned, even-handed analysis of the issues. They want a story about good and evil. During the *Achille Lauro* hijacking, that's all the news media gave them.

"There are millions of people saying 'Welcome, Abu Abbas,' and I am proud of that," Abbas told a reporter on October 14, 1985, just after he flew from Rome to Belgrade. For a former schoolteacher, he made a remarkable ascent to the front page of the *New York Times*, however infamous the journey. Perhaps he overstated his prominence in 1985, a common occurrence with Abbas over the years, but he did become a symbol of the Palestinian armed struggle against Israel.

Six feet, four inches tall, the ruggedly handsome Abbas rose from the ranks of foot soldiers in early guerrilla groups to the highest level of the Palestinian movement. He did that through a mixture of military skill, charisma, and energetic self-promotion. As the leader of a small group—his faction of the PLF never had more than a few hundred members—Abbas seemed to exert more influence within Arafat's PLO than those numbers might otherwise merit. Until the *Achille Lauro* hijacking, he was nothing more than what one terrorism expert called "a low-level thug" and a "mercenary gun-for-hire" with no real political program. But the extraordinary publicity surrounding the hijacking, the U.S. intercept of the Egyptian aircraft, and his release by the Italians elevated him to iconic status among many Palestinians.

Through his regular contacts with the Western news media, plus the ease with which he gave reporters good quotes, he tried to maintain that image. He was indeed a symbol, one emblematic of the confrontation between beliefs and goals in the Middle East. To the Israelis, many Westerners, and assuredly the Klinghoffer family, Abbas was a terrorist, a murderer. But he viewed himself as a freedom fighter, as did his followers and many in the Arab world.

The *Achille Lauro* hijacking was but one of hundreds of terrorist actions against Americans since the 1970s. Much of the political fuss surrounding this incident stems from the long-running relationship that Abu Abbas created with the news media. With timely help from Italian politicians, he made himself into a Palestinian symbol through shameless self-promotion.

Born Mohammed Zaidan in Afrin, Syria, in 1948, Abbas grew up in the Yarmouk Palestinian refugee camp near Damascus. His family, farmers in the Galilee, fled to Syria during the Israeli war of independence. He was described as an active child with a potential for leadership. "He was like a commander to his friends," said his eldest brother, Abu Ahmed, who operated a video-rental shop in Yarmouk during the mid-1980s. "I could tell from his childhood that he was a leader."

At Damascus University, Abbas participated in campus politics, and upon graduation with a degree in Arabic Literature, briefly taught school. He later married a daughter of a prominent Protestant Palestinian family in Beirut and had two children.

Captain Ahmad Jibril, a Palestinian officer in the Syrian Army, recruited Abbas to join the Palestine Liberation Front, a group Jibril founded in 1961. Jibril's group merged with two others in 1967—Heroes of the Return and The Youth of Revenge—to form the Popular Front for the Liberation of Palestine headed by George Habash. The Popular Front staged the first Palestinian hijacking of an airliner in 1968, taking over an Israeli El Al plane.

Jibril left the Popular Front in 1968 to start another organization, the Popular Front for the Liberation of Palestine—General Command (General Command for short) based in Jordan. These people did not know the value of distinctive brand names.

The General Command sent Abbas into Jordan to recruit among the young men of the refugee camps there. In September 1970, the Jordanian government attacked Palestinian guerrilla groups, forcing Jibril and the General Command to shift their base back to Syria. Abbas attended military training in the Soviet Union in 1973, then became the General Command's spokesman.

The General Command joined the fighting during the Lebanese civil war, drawing on the financial support of Libya. In 1975, Abbas assumed command of an elite group of General Command guerrillas, fighting Christian militia in downtown Beirut and destroying much of the old city in the process. The following year, Abbas and his group shifted allegiances, fighting alongside Arafat's PLO against the Syrians after that country entered the war. Jibril and the majority of the General Command supported Syria's intervention, so Jibril expelled Abbas and others from his group. The Palestinians fought amongst themselves for a period of time in the Palestinian areas of Lebanon.

Abbas and another former member of the General Command, Taalat Yacoub, re-established the PLF—Jabhat al-Tahir al-Filistiniyyah in transliterated Arabic—in 1977. Abbas served as deputy to Yacoub and operations chief of the new organization. The new PLF attempted cross-border attacks in northern Israel in its early years.

The PLF conducted their most notorious raid in 1979, a heinous attack on the Israeli beachside town of Nahariya. After coming ashore by boat, four PLF guerrillas burst into an apartment building. The residents scrambled to hide from the men. Smadar Haran, who was in that building, wrote later about what happened that night to her husband Danny and her two daughters, Einat, 4, and Yael, 2.

"Danny helped our neighbor climb into a crawl space above our bedroom; I went in behind her with Yael in my arms. Then Danny grabbed Einat and was dashing out the front door to take refuge in an underground shelter when the terrorists came crashing into our flat."

Some of the men took her husband and his older daughter outside while others searched the apartment for those in hiding. "I knew if Yael cried out, the terrorists would toss a grenade into the crawl space and we would be killed. So I kept my hand over her mouth, hoping she could breathe."

Another resident shot and killed one of the PLF men. In the ensuing shootout when the Israeli police arrived, the Israelis killed a second terrorist, but a third shot Danny in front of Einat, then smashed the girl's skull with his rifle butt. The officers arrested the assailant and the fourth man, then entered the building.

"By the time we were rescued from the crawl space, hours later, Yael, too, was dead. In trying to save all of our lives, I had smothered her."

Israel sentenced the two surviving Palestinians to life in prison. Israel exchanged one for Israeli POWs in 1985, but the second, Samir al-Qantari (Israelis spell his name Samir Kuntar), is serving five consecutive life terms in a Beershiva prison. The *Achille Lauro* hijackers demanded Qantari's release from Israel in return for the hostages on board the cruise liner.

Abbas sent two airborne raids into Israel in 1981 to attack a Haifa refinery; both failed. Observers were split into those who thought the raids were novel, yet ineffective, and those who viewed them as ludicrous ventures. The first took place in March, when two PLF fighters flew powered hang gliders toward Israel from south Lebanon. One crashed short of the border, while the second threw hand grenades at the ground before crash-landing and surrendering to the Israelis.

A month later, two units from the PLF hot-air balloon corps launched an attack on the same refinery. One snagged a power line on takeoff and the Israelis shot down the second. Except for the violence in their hearts, it was almost comical—the Palestinian version of the gang that couldn't shoot straight.

Ever-shifting alliances led to the breakup of the PLF in 1984. Abd al-Fatah Ghanim took one faction to Damascus, gathered support from Syria, and continued cross-border raids into Israel from south Lebanon. PLF general secretary Yacoub settled in Lebanon, generally keeping his group out of the friction between pro- and anti-Arafat forces. Yacoub's group disbanded after his death in 1988. Abbas headed the third faction and threw his support to Arafat. Abbas strengthened his ties to the PLO by divorcing his wife and marrying Reem al-Nimr, the sister-in-law of Farouk Kaddoumi, Arafat's chief political advisor.

In return, Arafat engineered Abbas's election to the PLO Executive Committee, a fifteen-member, high-level governing body that represents the interests of the PLO's constituent groups. Abbas was paid $900 a month for holding that position. Arafat also provided financial support to the PLF, the amount of which is unknown. The *Wall Street Journal*, however, estimated the PLO's annual budget to be about $200 million in the mid-1980s, so some money was available.

Abbas also arranged for Iraqi support for PLF activities, which included a Baghdad training camp, military aid, and the diplomatic passport that kept Abbas out of an Italian prison. In 1985, Abbas began to plan his first operation as head of a PLF faction, a mission that Abbas said was the infiltration of four gunmen into the Israeli seaport of Ashdod by having them pose as passengers on a cruise ship.

The Yugoslav airliner carrying Abbas and his assistant, Badrakkan, to Belgrade made a scheduled stop in Dubrovnik late on October 12. There, Abbas made his first attempt to add his spin to the hijacking story. Talking to reporters, he claimed that the U.S. fighter aircraft "fired warning shots and missiles on both sides of our plane. They appeared determined to shoot the plane down," he said. "What could we do?"

"They are the real terrorists," Abbas also said, indicting America for its actions. "We use handguns in our liberation struggle. They use fighter planes and aircraft carriers. But we will continue our struggle now more fiercely."

Abbas did not speak to the news media upon his arrival in Belgrade, but the Associated Press reported a conversation that he had with another person on the plane. The passenger said that Abbas identified himself by showing his Iraqi passport, and claimed that he was going to Belgrade "for a brief rest." "We shall continue our struggle to liberate our comrades from Israeli jails," the passenger quoted Abbas.

PLO representatives met Abbas and Badrakkan at the Belgrade airport and the Yugoslavs permitted them to sidestep customs. The officials escorted the men to the Belgrade PLO office, where Abbas stayed until his departure from Yugoslavia.

"If someone really died, which I doubt, then for sure it was a matter of a heart attack and the responsibility of the captain," Abbas said the next day, speaking by telephone to Western reporters at PLO headquarters in Tunis. He also claimed that he was not involved in the hijacking and that the four hijackers told him that they acted on their own. "When they were asked if they killed anyone," Abbas said "they replied, 'We are fighters for freedom, not killers, kidnappers, or hijackers.'" Given that Leon Klinghoffer's body was not found until the day after this interview, Abbas appeared to be comfortable with these denials.

Abbas went on to state that the hijackers surrendered to him because they sympathized with the PLF and trusted him. He also announced that he would attempt to have the four young men transferred from Italy to a Palestinian court. He averred that he was trying to do just that when the U.S. intercepted the EgyptAir plane.

In a revealing sidelight, Abbas's thirty-year old wife, Reem, attended the Tunis end of the half-hour interview. Abbas seemed to be attempting to polish his image as a humble family man seeking Palestinian freedom.

In interviews with the *Middle East News Agency* of Egypt and the Kuwaiti news service *Kuna* that same day, Abbas thanked Italy for permitting him to leave despite the U.S. request for his arrest. He also said that the four hijackers intended to get off *Achille Lauro* in Ashdod, Israel and conduct a suicide mission ashore. It was a "pure accident," Abbas claimed, that they aborted their scheme and hijacked the ship in order to avoid arrest in Israel.

Abbas gave a third interview on October 14, also via telephone to PLO offices in Tunis, in which he challenged the United States to present evidence linking him to the hijacking. He maintained that his radio contact with the hijackers was part of the negotiation aimed at arranging their surrender. He spun a Western reporter with more details of his family origins, and first and second wives. He said that he was unafraid of U.S. intentions to arrest him.

Just after his last interview, Abbas flew from Belgrade to Aden, a city in what was then called Southern Yemen (now simply Yemen). After a brief layover, he flew to Baghdad, Iraq.

The Reagan administration requested Yugoslavia hold and extradite Abbas, but Belgrade rejected the petition, saying it was legally groundless. The Yugoslavs whined about USS *Saratoga*'s participation in the capture of the hijackers. Apparently the United States promised Yugoslavia, in a routine formality, that the ship would not engage in combat operations either prior to or soon after its port visit to Dubrovnik.

"How could four idiots fail in their mission and still cause so much trouble?" said one senior State Department official as he surveyed the diplomatic damage that followed the intercept of the Egyptian plane. Italy, Egypt, and the United States were mighty peeved at each other.

"Frankly, I am very upset," Egyptian President Hosni Mubarak told reporters on October 14, three days after U.S. Navy aircraft intercepted EgyptAir Flight 2843. He also said he was "deeply wounded," "stabbed in the back," and that "we had not expected this attack from a friend." Mubarak called the U.S. action an "act of piracy."

Mubarak, who courageously ignored fellow Arab sentiment by strengthening ties with the United States and respecting Egypt's peace treaty with Israel, was furious at America for undercutting his political standing in the Middle East. One Egyptian observer remarked that "Reagan has humiliated Mubarak and in the Arab world, that is unheard of if you are supposed to be a friend."

The problem was not just one of personal ignominy; Mubarak also had troubles in the streets of Cairo. Immediately after the intercept, demonstrators shouted "Mubarak, assassination awaits you!" Perceiving that their president weakly allowed the U.S. action, the protesters warned that Mubarak might suffer the same assassination fate as his predecessor, Anwar Sadat. The demonstrators also burned U.S. flags and proclaimed "No America after today."

During the demonstrations, Mubarak awarded medals for valor to the crew of the EgyptAir jetliner. The pilots deserved commendation for their coolness, but some viewed the awards as an attempt by Mubarak to restore some of the country's lost honor.

Mubarak wanted an apology from Ronald Reagan, but he understood the difficulty of gaining such a concession. "You know every country has its national pride and its national dignity, so there are different means and ways to extend apologies," Mubarak told a reporter. "If I were in President Reagan's position, I would not go to the media and say 'I apologize.' It will never happen anywhere in the world like that."

Reagan saw it the same way. When the news media asked him if he intended to apologize, Reagan succinctly replied, "Never."

President Reagan did send a carefully worded letter to Mubarak in which he did not explicitly apologize, but attempted to explain U.S. reasons for the action. The Egyptian said he refused to open the letter for several days. Reinforcing Reagan's message, U.S. Ambassador Veliotes publicly stated in Cairo that the "U.S. regrets the need to intercept the Egyptian aircraft." Veliotes said later that the Egyptian news media picked up on the word "regret," which he said helped ease the situation.

The United States never intended to simply thumb its nose at Egypt, for the country was invaluable to the peace process in the Middle East.

The U.S. government recognized Egypt's pivotal role by granting the country $17.5 billion in economic and military assistance between 1974 and 1985, an amount second only to Israel in U.S. foreign aid. To further the healing process with Mubarak, Reagan sent Deputy Secretary of State John Whitehead to Egypt. Both sides described his meeting with Mubarak on October 21 as a positive step.

There was also a lingering problem in Egypt regarding Nick Veliotes calling the hijackers "sons-of-bitches." Local news media recorded his burst of profanity while he used a ship-to-shore radiotelephone on *Achille Lauro*. Described as a feisty, yet seasoned diplomat, he reportedly often spoke bluntly in what he thought were private conversations. Unaware that his comments were recorded, Veliotes inflamed Arab sensitivity.

"I was the target of a vicious media campaign in Cairo," Veliotes told me in 2002. "Suggesting that the Palestinians were sons of dogs was a terrible epithet, because dogs are not popular in the Islamic world. I had, in effect, sullied Arab womanhood."

Veliotes realized that his call had been taped when he visited Egyptian Foreign Minister Meguid during the turmoil following the hijackers' surrender. "He angrily handed me a bunch of wire service reports, all highlighting my remarks," Veliotes said. "I told him that the men were murderers and deserved harsh language, but Abdel Meguid asked, 'Why did you have to say it on the radio?'"

Two issues exacerbated the U.S.–Egypt rift, Veliotes explained when we talked. "The Egyptian ministry of defense viewed the U.S. intercept as a stain on the country's honor. The awards Mubarak gave the airliner crew masked part of the stain. Plus, many Egyptians regarded the event as a gross violation of Arab hospitality; Abbas and Badrakkan were Egyptian guests and the U.S. treated them rudely."

"The Egyptians also had a wholly different perspective on the fate of the hijackers, although both countries looked at the same facts," Veliotes said. "The Egyptians noted that the United States condoned third party negotiations with the hijackers of the TWA airliner the previous June, even accepting the terrorists' surrender without consequence after they murdered a U.S. sailor aboard the aircraft. Why, the Egyptians asked, did America not take the same approach this time?"

"We were bound and determined to do something to counteract terrorism," John Poindexter recalled. "This time we had the chance."

The *Associated Press* ran a story several months later reporting Veliotes's pending retirement from the Foreign Service and that it was involuntary. The U.S. government, according to an unnamed diplomat, was forcing him out to "placate the Egyptian government and to demonstrate the United States wants to smooth relations with Cairo." Further, the diplomat said that Veliotes had a shouting match with Secretary of State George Shultz, who wanted him to return to Washington for consultations.

"No truth to that story, whatsoever," Veliotes said years later. "Barry Schweid wrote the piece which simultaneously said that I was being forced out of Egypt by the Egyptians because I was too tough, and that Shultz was forcing me out because I was too soft!" Veliotes, who had previously been deputy chief of mission in Israel, ambassador to Jordan, and assistant secretary of state, said it was simply time to retire.

"I am not at all happy about what happened here today," U.S. Ambassador Max Rabb said in Rome late Saturday, October 12. An experienced diplomat, Rabb was relatively polite in his assessment. The White House, however, in an extraordinary statement at 1:30 A.M., bluntly condemned the Italian action. "The U.S. government finds it incomprehensible that Italian authorities permitted Abu Abbas to leave Italy despite a U.S. government request for his arrest and detention." Further, the statement read, the United States "is astonished at this breach of any reasonable standard of due process and is deeply disappointed."

As sharp as these words were, the rift between Italy and the U.S. was relatively short lived. Although Foreign Minister Giulio Andreotti said "the tone of certain prose with regard to us is unacceptable," both sides moved toward reconciliation. Perhaps each party realized it was not above criticism. The United States flouted international law and custom by intercepting the Egyptian aircraft; Italy ignored its 1983 extradition treaty with the United States by releasing Abbas.

To hasten the healing process, Reagan asked John Whitehead, en route to Cairo to tend to wounds there, to stop in Rome and deliver a personal letter to Prime Minister Craxi. The "Dear Bettino" letter, made public by the Italians, soft-pedaled the problem. "During the past week, we have had differences on the best way in which to respond to the hijacking of *Achille Lauro*. Despite these differences, which we have dealt with in a frank and friendly way. . . ." The United States eased its position from "astonished" to "frank and friendly" in one week.

The Italian government had a bigger problem than a temporarily irate America in the immediate aftermath of the *Achille Lauro* hijacking. Craxi's coalition government, split over how to handle the hijacking and Abu Abbas, collapsed on October 17, six days after the U.S. Navy deposited the hijackers in Italy.

Craxi headed a five-party coalition, the forty-fourth government in Italy since World War II. The frequency of government change in Italy, perhaps alarming in the United States, has long been an accepted part of Italian politics. Most were coalitions in which divisive forces were always at work. The *Achille Lauro* incident provided the Republican Party a chance to challenge Craxi's Socialist Party's approach to foreign relations.

Defense Minister Giovanni Spadolini and his two fellow Republican Party cabinet ministers opposed Craxi's pro-Arab foreign policy, instead generally supporting Israel and the United States. Spadolini also wanted Abbas turned over to the United States. He criticized Craxi for leaving him out of the decision to release Abbas; Spadolini was not in Rome when the cabinet met to consider what to do with Abbas.

When Spadolini withdrew his party from the government, Craxi did not have the votes in the Italian parliament to keep the majority, so he resigned. Regardless, Italian President Francesco Cossiga, the head of state in name only, asked Craxi to stay on as a caretaker, while the non-Communist parties worked to cast a new coalition.

The U.S. government, which had given the Italian politicians an issue to argue about, helped Craxi regain enough stature to reassemble his coalition. Craxi and Andreotti had been scheduled to meet with Reagan in New York the following week as the United States consulted with its allies about its pending summit meeting with the Soviet Union. Reagan told Craxi in his letter that he was "anxious to see you next week in New York," so the caretaker prime minister traveled as planned to America.

The Reagan letter and Craxi's visit to the United States gave him sufficient standing to ask Spadolini to withdraw his resignation. In return for accepting several Republican foreign policy goals regarding the Middle East and terrorism, Craxi reconstituted the government in its old form.

-◄- -►-

The hijacking was a setback to the PLO's attempt to both separate itself from terrorism and gain the world's acknowledgment that it was the legitimate representative of the Palestinian people. At first, Arafat and his representatives claimed to have defused the incident by negotiating the hijackers' surrender. But as evidence of Abu Abbas's role in the affair surfaced, his continued position on the PLO Executive Committee was reason enough for many to conclude that the PLO was still synonymous with terrorism. Israel always held this position, but even another member of the PLO Executive Committee admitted Abbas's involvement in the hijacking was detrimental to the organization: "Not even the Israelis could have achieved so much [damage] in so little time. Abbas has a lot to answer for." A senior U.S. government official (usually a cabinet level executive who is speaking off the record or on "background") echoed that assessment: "This time Arafat has shot himself in the foot with both barrels."

Reaction to the PLO's implicit role in the incident surfaced also at the United Nations. The UN General Assembly earlier had proposed inviting Arafat to speak at the UN's fortieth anniversary meeting in late October, but President Reagan threatened to cancel his appearance if the UN extended an invitation to Arafat. The UN yielded to U.S. pressure.

The U.S. government's hostility toward the PLO, however, was not limitless. U.S. Deputy Secretary of State John Whitehead also visited Tunisia during his fence-mending tour of the Mediterranean basin. During that visit, the Israeli bombing of PLO headquarters in Tunis and the subsequent *Achille Lauro* hijacking became examples of the complexity of the Middle East peace process.

Immediately after the attack, the White House termed the raid a "legitimate response" to the murder of three Israelis in Cyprus. Tunis complained about that characterization, so the United States recast its assessment and called the attack an "expression of self-defense" that could not be condoned. After Whitehead met with Tunisian President Habib Bourguiba, the envoy put yet another spin on the Israeli raid: "The bombing surprised and shocked Americans as much as it did Tunisians. We deplore it, as we deplore all acts of terrorism." Of course Israel didn't like that statement, and so on. . . .

Arafat sought a measure of damage control a month after the *Achille Lauro* incident when he issued on November 7 what has become known as the "Cairo Declaration":

The PLO reaffirms its declaration issued in 1974, which condemned all operations outside [Palestine], and all forms of terrorism. And it restates the adherence of all its groups and institutions to that declaration. Beginning today, the PLO will take all measures to deter violators.

Additionally, Arafat made a statement that might have been an acknowledgement of the impact of the *Achille Lauro* hijacking on the PLO. "Incidents have affirmed the PLO's conviction that terrorist acts committed outside [Israeli-occupied territories] have adverse effects on the Palestinian people's cause and disfigure their legal resistance for freedom." Of course Arafat also reiterated that Palestinian people have the right to "resist the Israeli occupation of its land by all available means."

In the United States, reaction to the intercept of the hijackers' plane was uniformly positive, save for a few diehards in the striped-pants set at the State Department who recoiled from upsetting relations with friends and allies. Congressional critics of Reagan's terrorist policy reversed their stand and hailed the chief. Calls to do *something* about terrorism were answered.

Pundits trumpeted the return of America's honor. They had been faulting the administration for its seemingly listless responses to the 1983 bombing of the Marine barracks in Beirut, the abduction and murder of Americans in Lebanon, and the murder of Robert Dean Stethem during the TWA airliner hijacking. The *Washington Post*'s Haynes Johnson captured the feeling in the country: "After what seemed so long a skein of national failure, humiliation, and weakness, the United States had demonstrated its capacity for success. It employed its power flawlessly and quickly, and it prevailed."

The Navy awarded medals to the units and individuals who identified, tracked, and intercepted the EgyptAir plane. Ralph Zia received a Legion of Merit, a distinguished award in the military. The Navy flew Zia and others to London for a public affairs show-and-tell, but Zia said it was cancelled at the last minute for "political" reasons. "I was told that the PLO was meeting with the Brits and our appearance on television might create a problem," said Zia. "We got back on an aircraft and returned to *Saratoga*."

Lance Morrow of *Time Magazine* responded to Yasser Arafat's accusation that the United States was guilty of "cowboy logic." "Arafat meant the word [cowboy] as an indictment. Americans might take it as a compliment. 'Damn straight we used cowboy logic, if that's what you want to call it.'" Morrow wrote that many Americans grew up enjoying old west morality plays between the good guys (cowboys) and the bad guys (cattle rustlers and varmints), the lore of Zane Grey and John Wayne. Although Morrow suggested that Europeans use cowboy as a term of derision and resent cavalier and boisterous American behavior, they "often harbor a sneaking admiration of the individualism and freedom that the idea of the cowboy implies."

Time also carried a lengthy piece in late October that examined the *Achille Lauro* incident. Reporter George Russell addressed several issues, recognized only through hindsight of course, that have extraordinary prescience of the aftermath of the terrorist attacks in America on September 11, 2001, sixteen years later. One might only exchange Osama bin Laden for Abbas and George W. Bush for Reagan in the story and *Time* could have run it again after the United States attacked Afghanistan following 9-11. Here are several of Russell's points from the *Time* article:

- But Washington had turned Abbas, the PLF leader who it believes helped plan the hijackers' mission, into the personification, at least for the moment, of a contest that CIA Director William Casey describes as a "war without borders."
- America's anti-terror policy, a State Department official predicted last week, "will now become more muscular."
- "How many young Palestinians are now burning to emulate those four yokels who captured the attention of the world and caused an earthquake in America's relations with Egypt and Italy?"
- Washington had already decided to take a strong stand against any objections by its allies to the terrorist-interception effort. Any subsequent repairs in relations, the White House had decided, would take place largely behind the scenes, and at a lower level of priority than the pursuit of the antiterror policy.
- "The world is getting very small for Abbas. His days as a free terrorist are numbered."

◄- -►

In Los Angeles, immediately after Alex Odeh's death on October 11, Irv Rubin, chairman of the Jewish Defense League, reacted to the incident with several public statements:

"Odeh appeared on television to whitewash the PLO murder of Klinghoffer."

"No Jew or American should shed one tear for the destruction of a PLO front in Santa Ana or anywhere else in the world."

"I have no tears for Mr. Odeh," Rubin said. "He got exactly what he deserved."

"I'm not crying over the death of Alex Odeh. My tear ducts are dry. My tears were used up crying for Leon Klinghoffer."

This kind of remarks was not foreign to members of the Jewish Defense League. New York Rabbi Meir Kahane started the organization in New York in the late 1960s. Bent on protecting Jews from another Holocaust, the group's motto is "Never Again." Initially, the League was connected to a series of attacks in the United States against interests of the Soviet Union, protesting that country's treatment of Jews. Attacks on Arabs, neo-Nazis, and others followed. FBI statistics show that between 1981 and 1985, there were eighteen terrorist attacks in the United States conducted by Jews, fifteen of them by members of the Jewish Defense League.

Rubin became chairman of the League in 1985. Born in Montreal in 1945, Rubin and his family moved to Los Angeles in 1961. He became a U.S. citizen in 1966, then served four years in the U.S. Air Force. During the early 1970s Rubin went to Israel, later serving in the Israeli civil defense force during the 1973 Arab-Israeli War. In the early 1980s, Rubin headed Jewish Defense League's west coast operations.

To most, Rubin was a brutish bully who offered a $500 reward to anyone who would kill or wound a member of the American Nazi Party. In 1980, Rubin was tried for soliciting such murders, but acquitted. He urged Jews to protect themselves with weapons, chanting "Keep Jews Alive with a .45" and "For every Jew, a .22."

The Jewish Defense League should not be confused with mainstream Jewish advocacy groups such as the B'nai B'rith and the Anti-Defamation League that it founded in 1913, as well as the American Jewish Committee. These groups are very aggressive in combating anti-Semitism, but eschew the violence that the Jewish Defense League has advocated. A representative of the Anti-Defamation League denounced the murder, as did the American Jewish Committee. (Also, please do no confuse the ADL—Anti-Defamation League—with the pro-Arab group—ADC—the American-Arab Anti-Discrimination Committee.)

The Santa Ana Police, FBI, U.S. Bureau of Alcohol, Tobacco, and Firearms, and the anti-terrorist division of the Los Angeles Police Department launched an investigation of the bombing. No person or group claimed responsibility for the incident. The FBI assumed jurisdiction over the crime within a few days and began an attempt to link the bombing to telephone threats made to Anti-Discrimination Committee offices prior to the incident.

Four weeks after Odeh's death, FBI spokesman Lane Bonner issued a statement that linked the incident to two other recent bombings on the East Coast: "We are attributing the bombings to the Jewish Defense League. There are similarities in all three bombings."

Rubin quickly reacted to the FBI's assertion that the League was behind Odeh's death. "I really resent the fact that they are implying that without any evidence whatsoever. We had nothing to do with the death of Alex Odeh." Rubin added a suggestion for the FBI: "They can take their possible link and shove it."

The rash of terrorist incidents in the mid-1980s, mostly attacks by Palestinian or Middle East groups on U.S. citizens, triggered a widespread, knee-jerk reaction against any Arab or Muslim, especially in the United States. This bigoted, gut-level response was an exact parallel to domestic reactions after the terrorist attacks in September 2001. The news media reported a number of incidents of arson at facilities associated with Arab-American causes, as well as threats to, and beatings of, Arab-Americans in 1985 and 1986. Many occurred during Middle East terrorist events, especially during or just after the hijacking of the TWA airliner and *Achille Lauro*.

In December 1985, FBI director William Webster warned that "Arab individuals or those supporting Arab points of view have come within the zone of danger, targeted by a group as of yet to be fully identified and brought to justice." Webster added two months later that there had been a resurgence in the actions of Jewish extremist groups against Arab-Americans and neo-Nazis.

"The same degree of vigor with which the terrorists who killed Mr. Klinghoffer were pursued should be used in the pursuit of the killers of

Alex Odeh." With this statement, the Rev. Jesse Jackson challenged the U.S. government and law enforcement agencies to find Odeh's killer. His comment was not the only one of that nature. The issue of a double standard for the treatment of the Klinghoffer and Odeh murders in the news media and the government started immediately after the *Achille Lauro* incident.

A week after Klinghoffer's death and four days after Odeh's, a *Washington Post* editorial was the first to hint at an imbalance of attention. "Leon Klinghoffer is now a familiar name; his death at the hand of terrorists precipitated a chain of events of international consequence. Mr. Klinghoffer, however, was but one of two Americans with some sort of Middle East connection killed savagely in recent days. The other was Alex Odeh." The *Post* urged the government to bring its full resources to bear to locate and prosecute the killer of Alex Odeh.

The *New Republic Magazine* was more pointed in a short article in its November 4 issue; it was titled TERROR DOUBLE STANDARD.

> Arab-Americans could be forgiven for feeling a bit paranoid about news coverage—that is, lack of coverage—of the bomb that exploded October 11 in the Santa Ana, California, office of the American-Arab Anti-Discrimination Committee. The bomb killed the committee's regional director, Alex Odeh, and injured seven others. This horrible story of terrorist murder within our borders didn't even make page one of either the *New York Times* or the *Washington Post*.

The editorial ended with a plea for equal justice:

"It ought to go without saying that the murder of Alex Odeh was as heinous as that of Leon Klinghoffer, and bringing Odeh's murderers to justice is just as urgent a task."

Washington Post columnist Philip Geyelin agreed with the magazine, writing, "Two equally heinous crimes—it ought to go without saying. And yet the *New Republic* saw a need to say it. The point is that, with some notable exceptions, nobody had."

Geyelin suggested the difference in attention to the murders had to do with the drama of the shipjacking. "The slaying of Klinghoffer also fits a familiar pattern: violence in far-off places directed at Americans caught up in the Arab-Israeli conflict. Odeh's murder, on the other hand, had the look of an isolated incident, an 'assassination' carried out by a lone crazy, inflamed by Odeh's sympathy with the Palestinian cause."

The *Post* reported on November 9 that "Arab Americans have sharply criticized the U.S. media and the White House for failing to give Odeh's death the type of attention paid the recent murder of Leon Klinghoffer." The *New York Times* carried the White House statement on the Odeh murder, "The Administration deeply deplores this tragic event," in a three-paragraph story on page 25. Barbara Shahin, Anti-Discrimination Committee deputy executive director in Washington, criticized U.S. newspapers for limiting their coverage of the Odeh killing to short pieces while committing multiple pages to the hijacking.

Norma Odeh, Alex's widow, added her feelings to the matter. Speaking before the U.S. Human Rights Commission, Mrs. Odeh told its members that after Alex's death, President Reagan, other politicians, and news media treated her with "blatant disregard." She said that Alex was a regular contributor to the Republican Party, even receiving a gold medal from President Reagan for his support.

"Reagan sees Mrs. Klinghoffer," Norma said to the news media. "It's as though her husband was something and mine wasn't. . . . No one had ever heard of Mr. Klinghoffer. A lot of people knew Alex."

The reactions throughout Europe, the Middle East, and in the United States to the hijacking and the apprehension of the four hijackers are clear evidence that terrorism is rife with power and politics. Only Americans saw their Navy's intercept of the hijacker's plane as a "good" act. The rest of the world saw it as something closer to an "evil" deed. Italy thought releasing Abbas was a good idea; America considered it a bad move. Egypt thought it was doing the right thing by sending the hijackers to Tunis; America viewed that as an act almost as evil as Klinghoffer's murder. Youssef Majed Molqi and Abu Abbas must have thought killing Klinghoffer was good for the Palestinian movement, but I join Lisa and Ilsa Klinghoffer in denouncing the act as evil.

There is no universal set of values in the world that prescribes what is good and what is evil. Individual societies make those determinations on their own. Regardless of its values, a government may still ignore them and act in its best interests. Politics usually prevail over values.

Prejudice is another powerful force in terrorism, as Alex Odeh's murder demonstrates. Prejudice shows up in the imbalance in the news media reporting of the two deaths—Odeh and Klinghoffer, as well as in the perceptions in the Odeh family about FBI foot-dragging. Terrorism provokes an upwelling of racial and religious biases that underlie U.S. society.

CHAPTER

4

"Terrorvision" and Trials (1986)

MARILYN Klinghoffer died of colon cancer February 9, 1986, just a few months after her husband's murder.

"She went downhill fast after she came home," said Lisa Klinghoffer. "On her drive down to Washington to testify before Congress, she was in such pain that she lay on the back seat the whole trip. She just gritted her teeth and marched ahead. She didn't talk about her illness lest it detract from her objective to memorialize my father."

Marilyn's death did not end the public tragedy of the Klinghoffer family. Lisa and Ilsa soon found that the reverberations of their loss would last for years.

Abu Abbas ushered in the new year, 1986, with another contact with the Western news media. Declining to say how or exactly when it contacted Abbas, the *Irish Times* in Dublin published an interview with him on January 9. Irish writer Faris Glubb, who wrote frequently on Middle East issues, quoted Abbas as saying that revolutionary forces would meet soon to discuss "U.S. terrorism" and create a war strategy against the United States.

Maintaining that the United States had declared war on the Palestinian people, Abbas said "this must be confronted by a declaration of war" by the Palestinians. While giving no specifics, Abbas said that the U.S. military could be the target of PLF operations.

Despite the fact that Abbas was the subject of an active arrest warrant, there was little discussion in the United States about the propriety of a Western reporter contacting a terrorist on the run. That silence changed dramatically, however, on May 5, when NBC TV aired an interview with Abbas.

"America is now conducting the war against us on behalf of Israel," Abbas said in the interview. "We therefore have to respond against America in America itself." He said that U.S. citizens might be targets.

Abbas admitted responsibility for the hijacking, a reversal of the position that he maintained for the previous seven months. Yet he continued to claim that the United States and Syria fabricated the murder evidence. "What is the use of killing an old man anyway?" he asked. "After all, he is old and would be soon dead anyway without killing. I do not believe our comrades on the boat carried out any killing."

In threatening America, Abbas described President Reagan as "enemy No. 1." Traveling in Tokyo at the time, Reagan, when asked about Abbas's threat, narrowed his eyes and, as if he were back in Hollywood, replied: "Let him try."

"You're not scared?" asked a reporter.

"No," Reagan said. "He's going to strike out."

Cinematic bluster aside, NBC's contact with a known terrorist created quite a stir. The main issue was NBC's potential complicity in terrorism by providing a venue for Abbas's rhetoric, but implicit in the event was a criticism of the CIA and FBI. If NBC News could find Abbas, why couldn't the U.S. government?

NBC broadcast the three and one half-minute segment with Abbas during *NBC Nightly News* on the evening of May 5, 1986, and repeated it the following day on the network's *Today Show*. Additionally, NBC included the interview in a one-hour special on the *Achille Lauro* hijacking on June 17.

Correspondent Henry Champ conducted the interview with Abbas at an undisclosed location. NBC News staff members spent two months looking for Abbas and negotiating the meeting. The only condition that Abbas requested was that NBC not reveal his location, a circumstance that NBC defended throughout the ensuing controversy.

Shortly after NBC aired the interview, U.S. government sources told the *New York Times* that they learned after the fact that Abbas was in Algeria when Champ met with him.

Reaction was immediate to the network's interview with a wanted terrorist.

"Terrorism thrives on this kind of publicity," said State Department spokesman Charles E. Redman. He also claimed that publicity, such as the NBC interview, "encourages the terrorist activities that we're all seeking to deter." State's head of counterterrorism, Robert B. Oakley, said the interview made NBC an accomplice to terrorism. "We think it's reprehensible, but nevertheless, they are free to do it."

"American television viewers might have been excused for flinging a shoe at their television screens last week," *Newsweek Magazine* wrote about the interview, one of many negative reactions to the NBC segment. Most of the critics faulted NBC for withholding Abbas's location, not for talking with him. "But it was clear when NBC put him on the air; he was a fugitive from justice," wrote the *Washington Post*'s Philip Geyelin. "The most newsworthy thing about him was where he was. . . . With his hiding place safely protected, Abbas was able to deliver to any impressionable follower of his own Palestine Liberation Front, or any other terrorist group, an incendiary call to arms." *Chicago Tribune* Editor James Squires seconded that thought: "They missed the news. We're in the news business and the news is 'Where is Abbas?'"

Nat Hentoff, also a *Post* columnist, likened the Abbas interview to a reporter talking to a common criminal on the run, a questionable decision for anyone in the news media. "The deal NBC struck with him seems to make sense only in terms of that network's current surge to overtake CBS News in the ratings," he wrote. "And that kind of mechanical thinking, when lives are in danger, does no honor to any news organization."

U.S. News and World Report's chairman and editor-in-chief Mortimer B. Zuckerman wrote that NBC News "got it badly wrong," claiming such coverage is merely "free political advertising" for terrorism. Zuckerman acknowledged that the common media reply to criticism is "the public has a right to know," but "this does not mean providing an unlimited platform for the terrorist to state his 'case,' as NBC did with Abu Abbas. The line can be drawn between responsible coverage and terrorist exploitation."

"The profession of journalism gives its practitioners frequent opportunities to take pride in the contributions of a free press. This is not one of them," wrote the *Chicago Tribune*'s Stephen Chapman. "By entering into a solemn covenant to shield a man who is credibly charged with a role in the murder of Leon Klinghoffer and who is forthright about his intention to murder other Americans, NBC News becomes a party to his contemplated crimes and degrades journalism."

Warren Hoge, foreign editor of the *New York Times*, said that his paper had been offered an Abbas interview shortly after the hijacking, but rejected the idea because of a similar requirement to keep his location secret. That didn't stop *Reuters* and the *Irish Times* from meeting with Abbas and running stories about the Palestinian about the same time as the NBC interview. Other news media representatives also approved of the segment.

"We would have run it," CNN's Ted Turner said. "There's no question that Abbas is a major news figure, for good or for ill." CNN had only been in business for five years at that point and likely would have run most anything. Charles Lewis, *Associated Press*'s Washington bureau chief, agreed, citing the mystery surrounding Abbas as reason enough for conducting the interview.

"NBC is neither a national intelligence service nor a law enforcement agency," said Lawrence Grossman, president of NBC News, vigorously defending his network's decisions. "We do not have the authority or ability to arrest fugitives. Our role is to report the news." Additionally, Grossman said that NBC sought the interview because "today, unlike the past, Americans are prime targets for terrorism. It is essential that we know who our enemies are and what we are up against." Grossman, in a bit of hyperbole, also claimed that Abbas was a "major international performer with major international contacts and major international clout. That's what makes him so dangerous and that's what makes him newsworthy."

Grossman also chided the U.S. government for failing where Henry Champ succeeded.

NBC News anchor Tom Brokaw said at the time that NBC "would do it in roughly the same manner" if they had it to do over. He said the interview's "news value" outweighed the negative aspects of the interview. NBC News Vice President Tim Russert saw some envy in the criticism from others in the news media. "Everybody was trying to get an interview with Abbas. That's the nature of the business."

"NBC gave Abbas the ideal forum," wrote Lisa Klinghoffer's husband Jerry Arbittier in a letter to the editor of the *New York Times* published May 18, 1986. "In the past," Arbittier, the president of the Leon and Marilyn Klinghoffer Memorial Fund, continued, "terrorists had to kill, hijack, or take hostages to get attention. Abbas used this unchallenged forum to threaten to kill Americans on their own shores." Arbittier criticized NBC's willingness to make a deal with Abbas and for "consorting with a known felon and helping further his cause."

"On behalf of our foundation and for all who would strike a blow against terrorism, we ask that this act, masquerading as a news event, be examined by the State and Justice departments to determine if there are any criminal implications relative to aiding and abetting a known and wanted international criminal."

At the U.S. Justice Department's request, NBC provided government lawyers with a transcript and tapes of the interview and turned over some of the interview's outtakes. The Justice Department took no action against either Abbas or NBC as a result of what it learned from the tapes.

A Gallup Poll found that seventy-two percent of those polled had heard nothing about the interview or the reaction it caused. Once pollsters explained the background, forty-five percent believed NBC was wrong in airing the interview and forty-four percent approved.

The same poll revealed that fifty-one percent of those polled said that the news media gave too much coverage to terrorist incidents, and fifty-six percent say terrorists were given too much opportunity to promote their causes. Sixty-eight percent blamed news media competition for the industry's disappointing coverage of terrorism.

It is extraordinary to think that a man who had been on the FBI's "Most Wanted List," named by the U.S. State Department as an international terrorist, the subject of a $250,000 reward, and a convicted criminal could gain access to the news media in the manner that Abu Abbas enjoyed since 1985. He gave at least three dozen interviews since the *Achille Lauro* hijacking. No other known terrorist came close to Abbas's record of public discourse. Abu Nidal, a notoriously dangerous terrorist and a man with whom the public sometimes has confused Abbas, appears to have given no interviews between 1984 and his death in 2002. Other terrorists claim credit for acts of violence, but usually through written communiqués or anonymous phone calls, and stick carefully to the shadows.

"The terror of terrorvision continues," wrote the *Los Angeles Times*'s Howard Rosenberg in the aftermath of Abu Abbas's interview on NBC News. "Besides murdering innocents and threatening world peace, international terrorists have put the news media in a terrible bind. How do they report on terrorism without advancing it? . . . Suffice to say, however, that terrorism is a story in need of a stage and the media are a stage in need of a story." Great Britain's prime minister Margaret Thatcher went a step further, calling news coverage of terrorism "oxygen" for the terrorists.

"Terrorvision," that marriage of convenience between political violence and the small screen, did not end in the 1980s. Just as Secretary of State George Schultz appealed to the news media to not further terrorist's publicity goals in 1986, President George W. Bush's national security advisor, Condoleezza Rice, asked the media not to assist Osama bin Laden's propaganda war after the 9-11 terrorist attacks in the United States. The news media lusted after video tapes of bin Laden, defending their interest just as NBC did sixteen years earlier.

This news-terrorism marriage forces the news media to choose carefully the words they use to describe politically inspired violence. "Terrorist" is a pejorative word, and reporters and editors seem to use it discreetly. Brigitte L. Nacos reported in her book *Mass-Mediated Terrorism* that the three leading American newsmagazines used the "T" word seventy-nine percent of the time when describing attacks on U.S. citizens during the 1980s. The magazines ascribed terrorism to incidents involving non-Americans in only fifty-one percent of the stories.

In 2001, according to the organization Fairness & Accuracy In Reporting (FAIR), the *Wall Street Journal* directed reporters to use the "T" word carefully, and *Reuters*'s policy prohibited the use of emotive terms such as "terrorist" and "freedom fighter" unless they were either in a direct quote or otherwise attributable to a third party. For news media entities such as *Reuters* that distribute news around the world, they see validity in the adage "one man's terrorist is another man's freedom fighter."

Nacos wrote that the news media describe those who murder abortion doctors as "criminals," but arsonists who burn newly constructed homes in previously rural areas are "eco-terrorists." The words "Arab," "Muslim," and "terrorist" seem to combine easily in the news, but Nacos found far fewer instances of reporting on "Jewish" or "Christian" terrorism. She cited the reporting on Brooklyn-born Jewish fundamentalist Dr. Baruch Goldstein, who killed twenty-nine Palestinians in 1994 in a West Bank mosque. According to Nacos, the news media referred to Goldstein as a "gunman" and "mass murderer," yet always termed Palestinian attacks on Israelis as terrorism.

This selective use of the "T" word has been relevant in the news media's reporting on Alex Odeh's death since 1985. The phrase "terrorist bombing" appeared in only a handful of the dozens of articles written about the incident.

John C. Bersia, a Pulitzer Prize-winning editorial writer for the Orlando Sun, tried in 2002 to make sense of the debate on the news media's coverage of terrorism.

> I would rather have news organizations covering terrorism excessively than for blinders of ignorance to slip over the public's eyes.
>
> Yes, to some extent the featuring of terrorists' exploits assists those miscreants by providing the attention some of them seek. But let's be serious and practical about this. If news organizations suddenly stopped or minimized their coverage of terrorism, would that and other forms of political violence simply scurry from sight?
>
> Hardly. Those problems dwell deep inside human society and have endured for ages.
>
> It's also worth mentioning that many of today's terrorists have little interest in taking responsibility for their acts or in explaining their motives and goals.
>
> On balance, news-media coverage of terrorism provides far more oxygen to the public than it does to terrorists.
>
> My advice would be for people to breathe deeply; press their news providers for as much coverage of terrorism and other international issues as they can manage; and perhaps attach less blame to the messenger.

Despite all of the flaps about the news media's apparent assistance to terrorists' publicity plans, the reporting has not led to more favorable public attitudes toward either terrorists or their causes. The U.S. research organization RAND found that despite intense news coverage of terrorism, public approval of terrorists was effectively zero. These findings fit with the 1986 Gallup poll taken just after NBC's Abbas interview. Gallup said that seventy-seven percent felt that terrorism would likely occur even if the news media reduced its coverage.

NBC's interview with Abu Abbas introduced a fourth factor—profits—to my argument that terrorism is about power, politics, and prejudice. Terrorism makes money for the news media. Grief sells. NBC consciously scheduled the highly criticized interview for one of the "sweeps" months in the U.S. television calendar. Reviewers measure audience reaction to network shows during those months, May being one of them, so that the networks can set advertising rates. Higher ratings during one of the sweeps months translate into more revenue.

Human tragedies bring the cable news networks to temporary prominence, up from the lower levels of television noise where they routinely lie, because they can stay with the story more easily than the networks. Newspapers, often a step behind television these days, focus on the human interest facets of a terrorist act—the victims families—in order to stay relevant to the story. It's almost as if tragedy is an industry, one that supports cameramen, far-flung correspondents, even the coffee and doughnut guy who serves the cluster of media people outside a victim's home.

Deaths from automobile accidents don't catch as many of the leering lenses of the grief industry. There is more tragedy, more pathos in terrorism. "Terrorvision" is an important part of terrorism.

Regardless of NBC TV's taunts, the CIA was indeed trying to catch Abu Abbas in 1986. Dewey Clarridge, a career CIA agent, went to Baghdad about the time of the NBC Abbas interview to persuade Iraq to facilitate the U.S. capture of the PLF leader. In his book, *A Spy for All Seasons*, Clarridge, who later became enmeshed in the Iran-Contra imbroglio, described his objective.

> I was in Iraq for the explicit purpose of returning Abu Abbas to the United States to stand trial for murder. I was not naïve enough to expect that Saddam Hussein would hand over Abbas directly to us. In the Arab tradition, that simply was not done. Instead I had formulated a plan to extract and capture Abbas in a way that would not implicate the Iraqi government, but would require its connivance, involving our forcing down an Iraqi plane headed for Yemen with Abu Abbas aboard. Yemen

was one of the few places left in the world where Abu Abbas would be welcome.

The U.S. government supplied Iraq with intelligence during that country's war with Iran in the 1980s. In return, Iraq agreed to stop its own terrorist acts, quit providing a haven for other terrorists, and give the United States helpful information on terrorists. An intermediary, who thought he was crazy, helped Clarridge arrange a meeting with the Iraqi government. Clarridge then flew to Baghdad to collect on the Iraqi part of the intelligence sharing agreement. He and another CIA agent made their pitch to the head of the Iraqi Directorate of General Intelligence, Dr. Fadil Barak.

> As I explained the purpose of our visit and sketched the outlines of the plan, Barak's cold eyes grew wider and wider. By the time I was finished, his demeanor clearly signaled that he, too, thought I was insane. In a bizarre way, Barak took it almost personally. He seemed insulted that we would dare ask such a thing. He began to sulk.

Although Clarridge also talked with the Iraqi foreign minister, Tariq Aziz, the Iraqi response to his proposal was wholly negative. On the way to the airport at the end of his short stay in Baghdad, Clarridge, angry with Iraq for not holding up its end of the bargain, confronted Barak. "Tell Abu Abbas I am coming after him, and when I find him, and I will, I will kill him."

Clarridge, fully aware that a Presidential order prohibited CIA assassinations, felt he had finally said something Barak understood. "I knew my remark was bluster born out of frustration, but did Barak? I doubt it, for it fit with his view of the world and I hope he conveyed it to Abu Abbas."

The next time a high-ranking CIA official went to Baghdad with Abu Abbas on his mind, the situation would be far different.

In February 1986, the FBI classified the bombing that killed Alex Odeh as a terrorist act, and began investigating whether the bomber violated Odeh's civil rights. Later that year, in July, the FBI released a report that said "elements" of the Jewish Defense League probably were responsible for the bomb blast that killed Odeh, as well as three other bombings. The bureau eased away from its earlier, unequivocal position by saying that final attribution to the Jewish Defense League or any other group "must await further investigation."

Irv Rubin again denied League involvement in Odeh's death. "What the FBI is doing is simple. Some character calls up a news agency or whatever and uses the phrase 'Never Again,' which is Jewish Defense League's slogan, and on that assumption they can go and slander a whole group. That's tragic."

On July 15, Jacqueline Salit, editor of *National Alliance*, a New York newspaper concentrating on Arab issues, announced that her newspaper had discovered that the FBI had closed its investigation of Alex Odeh because it had run out of leads. The newspaper acquired a Secret Service memo through the Freedom of Information Act that said the investigation had "met with negative results" and the case was closed in Los Angeles. The memo also stated the investigation "has failed to identify the perpetrators." [The role of the Secret Service in this matter was unknown.]

FBI spokesman Ray McElhaney responded immediately, saying the bureau was vigorously investigating the murder. "I assure you it is pending and ongoing."

"The Alex Odeh case is the highest priority investigation in our domestic terrorism program and it will continue to be until it is solved," FBI executive assistant director Oliver "Buck" Revell said at a House of Representatives Judiciary subcommittee meeting the next day. "We have suspects in this case and we are pursuing these suspects." Revell added that the FBI had insufficient evidence to bring charges. Lastly, Revell said that the bureau was working with Israeli police to identify possible support to American Jewish extremists by Israeli citizens.

"While our government apprehends terrorists halfway across the world, it seems helpless in the face of domestic terrorism directed against Arab-Americans," said Odeh's widow, Norma, in a written statement to the same subcommittee. Odeh's brother, Sami, repeated Norma's theme several months later: "Approaching a year . . . we don't have an arrest. At this point I can't honestly, truthfully say I am satisfied." Sami Odeh added that he had not yet lost faith in the FBI, but said, "time will tell whether my optimism is justified or not."

Sami, seven years younger than Alex, emigrated with his brother from the West Bank in 1975. He, too, became a U.S. citizen, in 1979,

and works as a real estate agent in Orange County, California. His
America-born wife, Lisa, echoed her sister-in-law's comment about
ethnic biases in the United States, "When I say my husband is a Palestinian, they react as if my husband is a terrorist."

Faris Bouhafa, national spokesman for the American-Arab Anti-
Discrimination Committee, added to increasing criticism of the FBI's
investigation. He said there is "growing skepticism within the Arab
community nationally as . . . to the extent to which the FBI has
devoted resources in its investigation."

Reportedly frustrated by the inability of the police and FBI to make
progress, the Anti-Discrimination Committee offered on October 11,
1986, a $100,000 reward for information leading to the arrest and con-
viction of those responsible for Odeh's death. The reward was good for
ninety days.

The Committee hosted a memorial dinner, also on October 11, to
honor Odeh. Many at the dinner expressed doubts that the killer would
ever be captured. Abdeen Jabara, national president of the Committee,
said that the killers might have left the country for Israel. Jabara said
that the Committee was concerned that Israel might not fully support
capture and extradition of suspects. "We are afraid the FBI's effectiveness in the case will be limited," Jabara added. The FBI has tried to
prove Jabara wrong in the years since, but his concerns were not completely unfounded.

Several organizations honored Alex Odeh in the year following his
death. In March 1986, the Orange County Human Relations Commission saluted Odeh and eighteen other men and women who had made
noteworthy contributions to human rights activities. The commission
singled out Odeh for his efforts to bring Arab and Jewish leaders
together to discuss their differences.

The following May, Cal State University-Fullerton erected a seven-
foot sculpture to "individuals who died while part of the university
residency." The University honored Odeh and two others at the sculpture's dedication.

On the first anniversary of his death, the Los Angeles Human Relations Commission honored Odeh for his efforts to advance "understanding about emerging ethnic groups" in Los Angeles County.

Alex Odeh was a poet with one book of poetry published, and a second in preparation when he died. One of the poems in the pending

book captured many of the feelings that encircled the events of his death.

> Lies are like still ashes.
> When the wind blows,
> The lies are dispersed like dust and disappear.
> At least we owe thanks
> To the one who tries to speak, write or paint
> An honest thought to the world.

After Marilyn Klinghoffer identified the four Palestinian hijackers in a Sicilian jail on October 11, 1985, the Italian justice system began in earnest its investigation of the incident.

As the Italian government transferred the four men to the Spoleto high security prison in central Italy on October 13, two sets of magistrates began gathering information. Luigi Carli and Francesco Meloni, public prosecutors in Genoa, claimed jurisdiction over the incident because *Achille Lauro* was based in Genoa and the hijackers boarded the ship there. Sicilian magistrates Dolcino Favi and Ettore Costanzo from Cantania also pursued the case, since they arrested the hijackers.

All four magistrates boarded *Achille Lauro* at sea on October 15, thirty-six hours before its belated return to Genoa. They questioned passengers and crewmembers about the hijacking and Klinghoffer's murder. Upon the ship's arrival, Magistrate Favi announced that he had "reconstructed the killing of the American in all its details." The magistrates also said that they issued arrest warrants for seven men: the four hijackers, a fifth who police arrested on a separate charge on September 28, and two others who were still at large. The prosecutors did not identify the seven. The hijackers had false passports and although they had given their names and personal information upon their arrest, the Italians had yet to corroborate the information.

A week later, on October 23, the Italian news media reported that one of the hijackers told prosecutors that Abu Abbas commanded the operation. The Genoese magistrates did not comment on the news report, but acknowledged they had transferred one of the four from Spoleto to a jail near Genoa. This story fit with another earlier in the week in which a senior PLO official also claimed Abbas directed the action. The unidentified official said that Abbas gave written orders to undertake a suicide attack as soon as they got off the ship in Ashdod. He went on to say PLO chairman Arafat was ignorant of the mission, but when he heard about the incident, angrily told Abbas to stop the operation.

A few days later the Sicilian magistrates acknowledged that one of the seven arrest warrants they had issued was for Abbas. This surprised Genoese magistrate Luigi Carli. "We are somewhat perplexed by this move since in our investigation, as things stand at present, nothing incriminating has emerged against Abbas."

The leaks and bureaucratic bickering ended October 30 when the Court of Cassation, Italy's highest criminal court, granted jurisdiction in the case to the Genoese magistrates. The court also upheld the Sicilian arrest warrant for Abbas.

A previously undisclosed issue arose during the court proceedings, one that substantiated U.S. claims that the Italian government manipulated the judicial system in order to justify its release of Abbas. On October 12 the Sicilian magistrate issued an arrest warrant for Abbas before he left for Yugoslavia. Yet Craxi asked judges from the Ministry of Justice to rule on evidence presented by the United States in its request to hold Abbas. The Ministry of Justice not only usurped the provincial magistrate's jurisdiction in reviewing extradition requests, but also ignored the Sicilian warrant. Italian politics won out over the Italian legal system.

With the Genoese investigation gathering momentum, Luigi Carli announced on November 11 that he had issued sixteen warrants, including one for Abbas. Although he mentioned no other names, Carli said all suspects were PLF members and all were directly involved in either planning or executing the hijacking. "There are no minor accomplices," he said. Carli said that he integrated the seven warrants from Sicily into the Genoese total of sixteen. The magistrate planned to try the five men in custody on November 20 on explosives and weapons charges. The Italian judiciary would hold a second investigation and trial for the hijacking crimes.

Two days later the Genoa magistrate office identified five individuals accused of owning and importing the arms and explosives used later in hijacking *Achille Lauro*. Four were the hijackers: Youssef Majed Molqi, twenty-three, born in Jordan; Ahmad Marrouf al-Assadi, twenty-three, of Damascus, Syria; Ibrahim Fatayer Abdelatif, twenty, of Beirut, Lebanon; and Bassam al-Ashker, nineteen, of Tripoli, Lebanon.

The fifth man, identified as Mohammed Issa Abbas, twenty-five and born in Damascus, was the cousin of Abu Abbas. The Italians arrested him before the hijacking on a false passport charge.

The magistrates said that testimony from the jailed men indicated a ten-month preparation period for the operation, including a survey of the ship and crew by Molqi and another Palestinian. Two hijackers used aliases of Antonio Alonco and Walter Zarlanga, both carrying Argentine passports. Another, with a Portuguese passport, called himself Diamontino Riberia; the fourth had a Norwegian passport with the name Stale Wan. Officials said that the men smuggled the guns and grenades into Italy via an automobile ferry from Tunis, carrying them on board ship in their luggage.

On November 18, 1985, a three-judge panel in Genoa convicted the five men of arms and explosives possession. Chief Judge Carlo Maria Napoli said that he accepted the prosecutor's recommendation that the sentence imposed on each defendant should vary with both the degree of involvement and the cooperation each extended to the prosecutors. The court sentenced Molqi to eight years in prison, and Abdelatif seven years, three months and a fine equivalent to $570. Assadi received four years and a $1,000 fine, Ashker six years and six months. The court sentenced Mohammed Issa Abbas to nine years and a $1,700 fine.

Magistrate Carli said he did not seek the maximum sentence of twelve years for the men, despite their "terrorist methods," because they espoused a cause "that cannot be considered devoid of valid motivation." Since Carli had been instrumental in gaining the defendant's cooperation during the investigation, one reporter asked him about his apparent support for the Palestinians. Carli answered, "I do not indulge in politics. I have no interest in it."

Regardless of Carli's claim to have ignored politics, he did not see the men as completely evil, ascribing their actions as quasi-political roles.

Abbas told investigators he carried a letter from his cousin, Abu Abbas, to the four hijackers, which he supposed contained instructions. When stopped by the Italian police, Abbas said that he swallowed the letter.

The defendants, held in cages during the eight-hour trial, formed a "V" signal with their fingers when the court rendered its judgment.

They also chanted together, "In our souls and in our blood, we defend Palestine."

The following day, Genoese magistrates issued the names of the remaining eleven Palestinians they want to bring to trial for the *Achille Lauro* hijacking.

- Mohammed Abbas, aka Abu Abbas.
- Ozzuddin Badrakkan, the PLF official detained with Abbas on board the EgyptAir jetliner.
- Abdul Rahim Khaled, an alleged PLF colonel who also boarded the ship, but disembarked in Alexandria before the hijacking.
- Ziad al-Omar, the suspected treasurer of the operation who Italy alleged oversaw activities in Tunis and Genoa before the cruise.
- Abu Kifah, PLF soldier.
- Mohammed al-Khadra, PLF soldier. Khadra and Kifah allegedly helped Issa Abbas transport the arms to Genoa.
- Mohammed Jarbura, a member of the hijack team who was reportedly too sick to board the ship.
- Abu Ali Kazem, one of Abu Abbas's bodyguards.
- Yussef Hisham Nasser, accused of aiding the hijackers in Italy.
- Yussef Ali Ismail, arrested near Rome, but not tried for arms possession.
- Mowffaq Said Gandura, a Palestinian acussed of supporting the hijackers.

Carli also announced Molqi confessed to killing Klinghoffer. Carli said that in his opinion, Abu Abbas masterminded the hijacking.

The following day, Italian officials said that they had just discovered that Bassam al-Ashker was only seventeen years old. The court later annulled his conviction and re-tried him as a juvenile.

An Italian appeals court reduced the sentences for arms possession for two of the hijackers and an accomplice on May 8, 1986, citing no reasons. The court reduced Issa Abbas's sentence from nine to seven years and Molqi's from eight to six years, six months. It reduced Abdel-atif's sentence to five years, nine months from seven years, three months.

The Italians set a trial date for those accused of hijacking *Achille*

Lauro and killing Leon Klinghoffer, as well as those who supported the operation, for June 18. In preparation for the trial, prosecutors released a 115-page document that detailed their case.

The report considered Abbas to have "created the action, chose the perpetrators, trained them for their particular task, and gave orders to the commandos." It said that while Italy viewed as inadequate American evidence of Abbas's leadership the previous year, the U.S. assertion later proved correct.

The report showed a bias toward the Palestinian cause remarkably similar to the political position held by many in the Craxi government. It said that the Palestinians, "having lost their own land, intend to carry out a struggle to reconquer their national territory and end the disastrous (and at times, inhuman) effects of the new diaspora." The report also praised Yasser Arafat for ending the hijacking, identifying PLO policies as distinct from those of Abbas. In testimony to the political correctness, at least in Italy, of the judgments, Antonio Badini, Craxi's national security advisor, expressed his approval, "I think it's rather objective, a good report, accurate."

Lastly the document described the murder of Leon Klinghoffer as "the extreme of ferociousness and inhumanity." Klinghoffer was the "victim of the violence which annihilated life simply because he was American, Jewish, and handicapped."

This was to be an absorbing criminal trial, a tense, three-week circus of violent threats, demonstrations, and recriminations. The news media was out in force and politicians on both sides of the Atlantic hovered expectantly, fearful the court might upset diplomatic apple carts with an inconvenient judgment. Also, Lisa and Ilsa Klinghoffer were waiting for justice.

The trial of fifteen men accused in the *Achille Lauro* hijacking started on June 18, 1986, in Genoa. Carabinieri officers escorted the chained men into an underground room, placing each in separate cages along the sides of the chamber. All others present passed through metal detectors upon entering the courtroom, their possessions examined by X-ray machines. Armed policemen, stationed six feet apart, formed a phalanx facing the gallery. Other guards patrolled the entrances and armed helicopters circled over the building. Hundreds of onlookers and news camera crews pressed against the barricades set up around the entire building.

Despite the security measures, four West Germans disrupted the proceedings as they commenced. They stood up in the public seating, shouting support for the defendants. "Comrades, we are here to express support for the Palestinian revolution," one of them said. As police hustled them out of the room, the demonstrators screamed, "Long live Palestine."

Events outside the crowded courtroom added to the already taut atmosphere. An anonymous PLF member called a news agency in Beirut, claiming the organization planned attacks on Italian interests, especially the judicial system, in retaliation for the trial. In Athens, a bomb exploded at an Italian trade office; a second, placed at the Italian Consulate, failed to detonate.

Abu Abbas was present in spirit. NBC TV re-broadcast its May interview with him on June 17, timed to coincide with the trial. Terrorism sells.

Presiding Judge Lino Monteverde started the trial by reading the charges. They varied among the defendants, ranging from murder, kidnapping, and hijacking to complicity. Only six defendants were in the courtroom—the three adult hijackers and three accomplices. The court would try nine others *in absentia*. Monteverde then announced he had summarily acquitted one of those in custody, Yussef Ismail, a Lebanese resident of Italy charged with running errands for the hijackers. The judge, however, added another person to the trial, Petros Floros. The court charged Floros, a Greek national, with assisting the hijackers. These changes left five defendants in custody and ten at large, to be tried in their absence. Bassam al-Ashker, a minor at the time of the hijacking, did not appear in court.

The chief prosecutor was Luigi Carli, the magistrate who investigated the incident. Gianfranco Pagano, a court-appointed attorney, represented the defendants. In accordance with an Italian law that permits victims of crime to participate in trials, attorney Oreste Terracini attended the trial, representing Lisa and Ilsa Klinghoffer. Lazzaro Bori acted as the attorney for the absent, but not distant, Abu Abbas. Six Genoese citizens and two judges constituted the jury.

The prosecution opened its case by announcing that all four of the hijackers had confessed to the hijacking prior to the trial. Molqi admitted that he killed Klinghoffer. Two, however, were not completely forthcoming—Molqi and his alleged assistant, Abdelatif. The location of the defendants' cages reflected the differences in their degree of cooperation. Those two were on one side of the courtroom, while Assadi, who prosecutors said renounced terrorism and cooperated the most fully, Issa Abbas, and Gandura sat in cages across the room.

On the second day of the trial, Thursday, June 19, Molqi startled the courtroom by recanting his confession that he shot Klinghoffer.

Judge Monteverde read the confession Molqi made on November 8, 1985, a month after the hijacking. In that statement, Molqi said that his group decided to kill a hostage because Syria refused its demands to enter port, negotiate the hostages release, and convince Israel to release Palestinian prisoners. In his confession, Molqi said, "I remember that it was 3:12 [P.M.]. (Everyone—Molqi, De Rosa, and Marilyn Klinghoffer—remembered slightly different times.) I went down where the hostages were and I forced a Portuguese waiter to bring the American to the stern of the ship. I shot him twice, once to the head and once to the chest."

When the judge finished reading Molqi's statement, he asked the Palestinian, "How do you defend yourself?"

"I have not killed," Molqi responded. "This is not true. This person was never on the ship. He was never seen by me or my comrades. It is a scheme created by the United States and Syria." Monteverde then read passages from the confession again, but Molqi denied each. Asked why he renounced his confession, Molqi said, "I don't know what I said. I was tired when these interrogations were done in the evenings, and I was given injections to help me sleep."

On the following day, Abdelatif also disavowed his pre-trial statement in which he claimed Molqi told him of killing Klinghoffer. Abdelatif had told prosecutors earlier that he and the two other hijackers had kept Molqi from killing Marilyn Klinghoffer, but he denied such a plan in court. "None of us killed," he said to the judge.

Gandura, accused of arranging logistic and financial support for the hijacking, testified of his innocence. He admitted being an officer in the PLO's secret police, merely passing through Italy. He said Arafat had sent him to Beirut to help locate and free foreign hostages held there.

Judge Monteverde then called upon Assadi to testify. He told the court that Molqi, covered with blood, admitted the murder just after firing the shots. Assadi said he saw Molqi order a steward to take Klinghoffer away in his wheelchair, but did not see Molqi shoot the American. Assadi went on to say the shooting upset him and he tearfully consoled Klinghoffer's wife later. "I embraced her and kissed her on the forehead and told her I had nothing to do with it."

Assadi confirmed all of his pre-trial confession and identified Abu Abbas as the person who planned, organized, armed, and financed the hijacking. Prosecutors, as part of their broader attempt to distinguish between the policies and actions of Abbas and Yasser Arafat, asked Assadi if the two Palestinian leaders were different. "The difference between them is like sky and Earth," he said.

As Assadi spoke, Molqi and Abdelatif angrily yelled in Arabic at their comrade from their cages, upset with Assadi's cooperation with the court. Perhaps thinking some of the invectives were aimed at him, prosecutor Carli hurriedly left the courtroom. Before abruptly adjourning the session, Judge Monteverde instructed the court reporter to ignore the defendants' menacing shouts.

But before the adjournment, Assadi also told the court of Abu Abbas's reaction to the hijacker's sympathy toward Marilyn while on the plane from Cairo to Sigonella. "He told me that I would be tried and shot for treating the hostages too kindly."

While the court was adjourned over the weekend of June 21 and 22, Petros Floros, the Greek accused of giving his passport to one of the hijackers, told a Greek newspaper someone had stolen the document. Floros, a truck driver from northern Greece, maintained he lost it on the Athens subway. "My passport was grabbed on the metro," he said. "How could I imagine it would be used by terrorists. I've never been in touch with Palestinians. I reported the loss of the passport to the police immediately."

The testimony from the ship's crewmembers about Klinghoffer's death dominated the trial session on Monday, June 23.

Steward Manuel De Souza, pointing at Molqi in his steel-barred cage, said the Palestinian ordered him to push Klinghoffer in his wheelchair to the stern where "no one would see him." Molqi then told De Suza to leave him alone with Klinghoffer.

"I heard shots ring out," said De Souza. "When I came back I saw a hole in Klinghoffer's chest. He was obviously dead. He [Molqi] told me to throw the American into the sea."

When the steward could not lift Klinghoffer's body over the life rail, Molqi summoned another crewmember to help, hairdresser Ferruccio Alberti. "I saw this man and body on the deck, and he gestured to throw it into the water," Alberti testified. "I was so afraid." When asked if he could identify the man in the courtroom, Alberti replied, "I never looked him in the face. I only saw blood on the deck."

De Souza said Molqi ordered both crewmembers to change clothes because they were covered with blood. Molqi also warned them later in the presence of the ship's captain to keep silent about the incident or he would kill them.

A British crewmember, Cheryl Herrington, testified Molqi joined a group of hostages after the shots, miming the firing of a gun and saying "Americano, boom, boom."

On the next day, the fifth of the trial, *Achille Lauro* Captain Gerardo De Rosa and Prime Minister Craxi's national security advisor, Antonio Badini testified. De Rosa said that Molqi and Ashker, the teenager, confronted him on the bridge. As Molqi raised one finger, Ashker said, "This is the first one we have eliminated," handing Klinghoffer's passport to the captain. "Molqi had bloodstains on his pants," De Rosa said. "I hoped it was just from a scratch." De Rosa said that Molqi and Ashker indicated Mildred Hodes would be the next victim.

Badini's testimony was important to the prosecutor's examination of the relationship between Abbas and Arafat. Badini had spoken with Abbas while the Palestinian remained on the Egyptian airline after the U.S.–Italian standoff at Sigonella. The official said that the "essential element" he gained from his conversation with Abbas was that Arafat sent Abu Abbas to Port Said to convince the hijackers to surrender. "We knew that Abbas had offered his good offices as sort of an intermediary," Badini said. This allegation conflicted with Assadi's earlier declaration that Abbas was in charge of the hijacking. That conflict would linger.

Prosecutor Carli read a statement the following day that Marilyn Klinghoffer made before she died four months before the trial. "About 3:15 or 3:30 [P.M.], I heard two shots," she wrote. "Right after, I heard a noise of something going into the water . . . a splash." Marilyn still clung to the idea that Leon was in the ship's infirmary at that point. In her statement, she also acknowledged that one of the hijackers tearfully kissed her later.

On Thursday, June 26, another bit of drama interrupted the flow of the trial. Judge Monteverde announced that defendant Gandura unsuccessfully tried to hang himself in his cell earlier that day. When he appeared in court, Gandura told Monteverde, "I would rather die than be humiliated."

Actually, as the court soon learned, Gandura's action was really a mock suicide attempt in protest of prison conditions. Four of the other defendants also complained about unhygienic conditions, frequent body searches, lack of medical care, and physical assaults by guards.

Molqi also protested, through his lawyer, about "so much fuss being made of one dead American while nobody speaks of thousands of dead Palestinians."

On Friday, Judge Monteverde unexpectedly suspended the trial because of a problem with the jury. Juror Silvio Ferrari, head of the Communist Party delegation on Genoa's provincial council, told the judge that one of the prosecutors had "invited" him to leave the jury. Responding to this unorthodox situation, the judge adjourned the trial until the following Tuesday.

Upon the resumption of the trial on July 1, Judge Monteverde opened the session by replacing juror Ferrari with an alternate because the local Communist Party had contacts with the PLF, the defendant's organization.

Then the judge, as part of the civil portion of the trial, entertained arguments from the attorneys for Lisa and Ilsa Klinghoffer, and the Lauro shipping line. Since the PLF was part of the PLO umbrella of organizations and dependent on Arafat for funds, the Klinghoffers's lawyer, Terracini, sought damages from the PLO for Leon's death. "The groups that belong to the PLO identified Klinghoffer as their enemy. Their enemy is the Jew, whoever he is, and whatever his nationality," Terracini said. "Klinghoffer was killed because he was Jewish. If he had not been Jewish, some other passenger would have been killed."

"No organization, even the noblest, has the right to kill in the name of freedom for its people," Terracini concluded.

The prosecutors summarized their case the next day, demanding life sentences for Abu Abbas, Molqi, Badrakkan, al-Omar, and three others. For the remaining eight defendants, they sought lesser prison terms.

During the next two days, July 3 and 4, defense attorneys presented their side of the case. Abbas's court-appointed lawyer, Lazzaro Bori, argued his absent client's innocence. "Abbas was not the mastermind. He was merely sent to Egypt by PLO leader Arafat to negotiate the surrender." The defense lawyers asked the court for lenience for the defendants, reasoning that their clients were not terrorists, but rather Palestinians fighting to regain their homeland. One compared the defendants to Carlo Pisacane, an Italian patriot who, during the hostilities surrounding the unification of Italy, seized a passenger ship in 1857.

On Saturday, July 5, Prosecutor Carli, in his final remarks, rebutted the defense's arguments and addressed the jury. "There were 385 [sic] pairs of eyes aboard the ship that saw the weapons and the bombs," Carli said. "You are not here to judge the struggle for the liberation of Palestine, the Palestine Liberation Organization, or the Palestine Liberation Front. You are concerned with the crude facts and the criminal actions." Carli also said that he was "astonished" at the comparisons of the hijackers to Pisacane.

On the day the judge sent the case to the jury, he allowed the defendants to make statements. Both Molqi and Abdelatif echoed their lawyer's line, saying they were not terrorists, just Palestinian fighters. Molqi said, "This case is not about terrorism, not even about a killing."

"Long live Arafat," Molqi and Abdelatif shouted as the jury left the room.

After seventy hours of deliberations, the jury rendered its verdicts and sentences on July 10. The jury found six defendants guilty of "kidnapping for terrorist ends that caused the killing of a person": Abbas, his top two deputies—Badrakkan and al-Omar—and the three hijackers. The three that got away received the harshest sentences, life imprisonment. Molqi received a thirty-year sentence, Abdelatif twenty-four years and two months, and Assadi, the most cooperative defendant, fifteen years, two months.

Judge Monteverde later told reporters the jury gave the three senior persons the maximum sentence because they planned the hijacking as "a selfish, political act" conceived to "weaken the Leadership of Yasser Arafat." They also judged Arafat to be unaware of plans for the hijacking.

Conversely, the jury accepted the suggestion the actual hijackers were "soldiers fighting for their ideals," not terrorists. Also, the court dropped the charge against all defendants that they were members of an "armed terrorist band." Judge Monteverde explained that the PLO did not meet the Italian legal definition of such a band because the PLO "has as its goal the restoration of a homeland to the Palestinian people."

Both the jury and Judge Monteverde cited what they called attenuating circumstances as reasons for giving the hijackers shorter prison sentences. Monteverde said the main circumstance was their childhood environment. "They have grown up in the tragic conditions that the Palestinian people live through," a reference to the refugee camps of Jordan, Syria, and Lebanon.

The court reiterated this theme three months later when it published the "motivation," a document required by Italian law that explains the justification for sentences. In Molqi's case, the court defended the decision to sentence him to only thirty years. The motivation not only cited Molqi's confession, despite his retraction, but also his background as a "Palestinian refugee passed from one military camp to another and ending up (at a young age) in a 'suicide unit.'"

The court cited insufficient evidence in acquitting Molqi of the specific charge of murdering Klinghoffer. No one saw him do it.

Mohammed Issa Abbas received a six-month sentence, although he was serving a seven-year term for arms possession. The jury sentenced Mowffaq Said Gandura to eight months, a better outcome than suicide by hanging.

The jury convicted *in absentia* three accomplices of lesser crimes—Mohammed al-Khadra, Yussef Hisham Nasser, and Abdul Rahim Khaled—with their sentences ranging from six and one half to seven and one half years. Khaled boarded the ship with the hijackers in Genoa, but disembarked in Alexandria with most of the passengers. The jury acquitted four others—Abu Kifa, Mohammed Jarbura, Abu Ali Kazem, and Petros Floros.

The court fined Abbas, Badrakkan, and al-Omar $20,000 each, payable to each of Klinghoffer's daughters. It also fined each of the three hijackers, ordering them to pay Lisa and Ilsa $20,000 apiece. The hijackers never paid the fines.

Lisa and Ilsa Klinghoffer were infuriated with the relatively mild sentences handed down to the hijackers. Appearing before a news conference later that day in New York, they blasted the Italian judicial system.

"They are all guilty of a horrible, heinous crime and they should all receive the maximum penalty," said Ilsa, who said she was sick to her stomach when she heard of the sentences. "An opportunity has been lost to deliver a clear message to terrorists everywhere that barbaric criminal acts in the guise of political activism will no longer be tolerated."

The Italian decision on Abbas outraged and frustrated Lisa. "I don't understand the Italian government," she said. "They let him go and now they give him a life sentence. If they want to send a message, let them find him and have him serve his life sentence."

"It's not over yet," said Lisa. She and her sister vowed to continue the fight, asking both their Italian lawyers and the U.S. government to seek extradition of those in custody.

Viola Meshkin, one of the hostages on board *Achille Lauro* said, "I think they deserve more because they've ruined so many families and interrupted so many lives." Frank Hodes, whose wife Mildred was to be the hijackers' next victim, said, "I'd prefer that they all be hanged, but the Italian system doesn't have capital punishment."

In Washington, State Department spokesman Bernard Kalb said, "the United States is pleased that persons responsible for the death of an American citizen and injury and damages to others have been convicted." Kalb also said, "We regret that the murder of Leon Klinghoffer was not treated more severely."

In Italy, Attilio Bastianini, deputy Liberal Party leader in the Senate said the sentences "leave Italian and international public opinion baffled. No matter how long I think about it, I really cannot understand what attenuating circumstances there can be for someone who in cold blood kills a defenseless and impaired person, chosen only for his religion and his nationality." *Voce Repubblicana*, the newspaper of the Italian Republican Party that faulted Craxi for releasing Abbas, also criticized the sentences. Other newspapers praised the outcome of the trial.

In late 1986, an Italian juvenile court convicted Bassam al-Ashker of hijacking-related crimes, sentencing him to sixteen years in prison.

During the two-day hijacking of *Achille Lauro*, someone removed $2.2 million in cash and jewels from the ship's safe. When Molqi ordered the ship's purser into the lounge during the initial takeover, the crewmember had no time to lock the open vault. The hijackers were the prime suspects until Genoese magistrate Luigi Carli began to investigate the theft.

A year later, Carli exonerated the hijackers, describing them as cruel, yet honest terrorists. They not only ignored the money and jewelry, Carli said, but also reimbursed the purser in dollars for the cigarettes they took from the bar during the incident. Carli also said that the four men paid for the damage they caused when firing their Kalashnikovs to scare the passengers and crew. Carli determined a crewmember must have been the thief and assigned investigators to interview staff members. The theft was never resolved.

Italy is a modern democracy. The country shares its culture and religion with many Americans. America fought Italy in World War II, but once the country's fascist dictator, Benito Mussolini was deposed, the people sided with the United States and Great Britain. They have been close allies and friends to the United States since then. Why is it that Italy sees terrorism differently than the United States? Had those hijackers been tried in New York, would the judge and jury have ignored their childhood?

Many of Italy's governments achieved rapprochement with the Palestinians and most of the Arab world through political discourse. Italy's judicial system reflects that political equilibrium. The United States has tried to accomplish similar goals, but our unwavering support for Israel has prohibited lasting relationships with all but a few moderate Arab states. That makes the United States a co-target of Arab and Palestinian extremists, who are bent on killing enough Israelis to drive that country out of Palestine. The fact that Americans, especially Jewish-Americans, are prime targets for Arab and Palestinian terrorists reflects our political situation. Yet Americans attempt to divorce terrorism from politics, casting the phenomenon as an issue of crime and punishment.

CHAPTER

5

"Swim for It?" (1987–1989)

TWO families. Two American families, both struggling with grief, anger, and frustration. Both the objects of hate, both victims of prejudice.

One was Jewish, mourning the murder of the father and the premature death of his wife. Despite their grieving, Lisa and Ilsa Klinghoffer showed grit and tenacity in their quest to have Abu Abbas arrested.

The other family was Catholic and Palestinian, also lamenting the murder of the father. The Odehs of California deplored the U.S. government's inability to find Alex's killer and were bitterly upset at their country's intolerance of Arab-Americans. They asked why would someone kill Alex Odeh simply because a Palestinian murdered a Jew halfway around the world?

Most Americans would have refused to accept Youssef Majed Molqi's claim that when he shot Leon Klinghoffer he was a freedom fighter attempting to regain his homeland from Israeli occupation. Most also would have agreed that Alex Odeh was entitled to his opinion. Yet many of us are bewildered at the American public's propensity to lash out at innocent people who share a religion or ethnicity with terrorists.

"When people ask me what I am, I say Palestinian," said Joyce Nassab, Alex Odeh's niece, in a 1988 statement that echoed a previous comment made by her aunt Lisa Odeh. "Then they point their finger at me and say 'Ah, a terrorist.'"

97

Just as Klinghoffer's death was not the only terrorist act in the 1980s, Odeh's murder was not the sole instance of bigotry. There were enough knee-jerk, anti-Arab reactions in America during the eighties and nineties to cause authorities to immediately suspect that the 1995 Oklahoma City bombing was the work of Arab terrorists.

FBI data showed a seventeen-fold increase in hate crimes against Muslims in six U.S. cities with large Arab populations after the 9-11 attacks. In Los Angeles County, anti-Arab incidents rose from twelve in 2000 to 188 in 2001. President Bush and others urged tolerance, but there are bigots among us.

"Occasionally I talk to the FBI," Sami Odeh said on the second anniversary if his brother Alex's murder. "I talked to them about a month ago. They constantly tell me they are working, they have the same number of people working as before, they haven't dropped it. But after two years, is it really a priority or is it not?"

"They ignored an act of terrorism in our own back yard and instead talked about terrorism around the world for their own political advantage," said former U.S. senator James Abourzek in October 1987, referring to the Reagan administration. The national chairman of the American-Arab Anti-Discrimination Committee blamed the stalled investigation on the administration's "attitude."

In the two years that had elapsed since a bomb killed Alex Odeh in his Anti-Discrimination Committee office, his family had few chances to savor good news about the investigation of the murder. During the previous April, Buck Revell, executive assistant director of the FBI, told the annual meeting of the Anti-Discrimination Committee that a federal grand jury in Los Angeles was investigating possible criminal activities aimed at Arab-Americans by Jewish extremist groups. Although Revell refused to link the grand jury activity to Odeh's murder, Anti-Discrimination Committee officials and Odeh's family viewed the announcement as a positive development.

"It's really good to hear that good news," said Norma Odeh, Alex's widow. "I really hope they do something and mean what they say. My kids and I will be very happy when this case is done."

"The Anti-Discrimination Committee is obviously very pleased to hear that . . . there appears to be a significant break in the Alex Odeh investigation," Committee spokesman Faris Bouhafa said. Bouhafa went on to suggest that if a grand jury was at work, the federal attorney's office must have some evidence.

In a related development in New York, Assistant U.S. Attorney Charles Rose said that the Odeh bombing could be related to two similar incidents in New York and New Jersey in August and September 1985. Although those incidents were directed at persons with alleged Nazi ties, Rose said, "There is a similarity in method and similarity in device. Suspects have been identified and the investigation continues."

More specific information about the Odeh investigation surfaced in November 1987 when a grand jury subpoenaed Hind Baki, Odeh's former assistant. Neither Baki, nor J. Stephen Czuleger, the assistant U.S. attorney assigned to the Odeh case, commented on the development. Czuleger did say, however, that the Justice Department attached a high priority to the Odeh case.

The development in the fall of 1987 that really got the Odeh family's attention was the revelation that Israel was hindering the FBI's investigation of the Odeh bombing. An internal FBI memo, obtained by New York's *Village Voice* newspaper and confirmed by unidentified government sources, said that Israeli responses to FBI requests for information on terrorist suspects living in that country "have been untimely, incomplete, and in certain cases, no response was rendered." In the memo, Assistant Director for Investigations Floyd Clarke wrote Buck Revell that a response to the leads "is crucial for the solution of the 25 terrorist incidents and other criminal activity perpetrated by the Jewish Defense League." Clarke also wrote that key suspects had fled to Israel and were living in the West Bank town of Kiryat Arba, which the memo described as a haven for right-wing Jewish extremist elements. Clarke did not reveal the names of the suspects.

Just as terrorism respects no borders, no country puts aside politics in the face of terrorism. Italy, Egypt, and the United States ignored diplomatic protocols in dealing with the *Achille Lauro* hijackers; Israel made similar, politically motivated decisions. The Israeli government was quick to urge both Italy and the United States to try Abu Abbas and the hijackers for the death of Leon Klinghoffer. That was the right thing to do, but, of course, it was also politically correct in Israel. It was not politically correct to provide swift and full cooperation with the United States during the investigation of Alex Odeh's murder in which suspects successfully sought shelter in Israel.

As 1987 drew to a close, the Odeh family and the Jewish Defense

League found themselves face to face in a church parking lot. On Christmas Eve, Sami Odeh joined a hundred other Palestine supporters in a candlelight protest of recent violence in the West Bank and Gaza Strip. They gathered outside Crystal Cathedral in Garden Grove, California for a brief demonstration to show their outrage with recent clashes between Israelis and Palestinians. "We are hoping to bring some awareness to our American friends," Sami said.

Nearby, Irv Rubin, chairman of the Jewish Defense League, stood with several members of his group. Rubin, who was particularly callous in his reaction to Alex Odeh's death, said that he came to the demonstration "because wherever they [the Palestinians] go, we've got to show up. There has to be a Jewish presence." Odeh and his friends did not respond to racial taunts from the Jewish Defense League members.

In the first real break in the Odeh investigation, the FBI announced in late June 1988 that they had arrested Rochelle Ida Manning. A federal magistrate ordered her held as a suspect in a 1980 mail bomb death of Patricia Wilkerson in Manhattan Beach, California. The justice also charged her husband, Robert Steven Manning, an American who emigrated to Israel in 1973. Federal officials also considered Robert Manning, a former Los Angeles resident and active member of the Jewish Defense League, a prime suspect in the Odeh bombing.

Born in Los Angeles in 1952, Robert Manning engaged in petty crimes as a youth, dropped out of high school, and spent a year in the U.S. Army. Discharged for not "adjusting" to Army life, Manning worked as a machinist, draftsman, and private investigator. He became a charter member of the Jewish Defense League's West Coast chapter in 1971. Convicted in 1972 for bombing the home of an Arab in Hollywood, Manning was sentenced to three years probation. During the investigation, police found a copy of *The Anarchist Cookbook*, a do-it-yourself bomb-making book.

Also in 1972, Manning threatened producer Ralph Riskin, who was working on the TV show "Bridget Loves Bernie," a sitcom about a Jewish husband and a Catholic wife. "If you don't take this show off the air right now, we'll come over and blow your ass off," Manning told Riskin on the phone.

After his probation ended, Manning moved to Israel. He and his wife Rochelle, also a dual Israeli-American citizen, traveled occasionally between the two countries. His trips to the United States reportedly coincided with three bombings in 1985, all thought by authorities to be the work of Jewish extremists. The same officials said that Manning was one of several suspects, all living in Israel, who could be connected to the Odeh bombing.

The FBI seized Rochelle Manning as she arrived at Los Angeles International Airport from Israel. They also confiscated a letter she was carrying from her husband to the American Civil Liberties Union, which complained of FBI harassment. Robert Manning's lawyer, Samuel Abady, said the letter referred to one sent Manning by FBI Agent Larry Wack. Abady claimed Wack threatened to put Manning on "Death Row" for Odeh's death. Attorney Abady also claimed that Rochelle's arrest was an FBI trick to lure her husband back to the United States.

At the time of his wife's arrest, Robert Manning was living in Kiryat Arba, the same West Bank town that Floyd Clarke wrote about in his memo to Buck Revell the previous year. Manning remained inside his home, refusing comment to reporters.

Assistant U.S. Attorney Nancy Wieban Stock, in charge of the 1980 Manhattan Beach bomb prosecution, said that Rochelle's fingerprints were on the letter accompanying the bomb, while her husband's were on the package. Stock said on July 13 that she was preparing an arrest warrant for Robert, the first in a series of steps required to extradite him to stand trial for the murder of Patricia Wilkerson in the Manhattan Beach office.

Manning's extradition became caught up in a renegotiation of the U.S.–Israeli extradition treaty. Internal Israeli political divisions also complicated the matter, as liberal and conservative factions argued over how best to protect Israeli citizens from foreign prosecution. "There's a sort of feeling here that you can't hand a Jew over to be tried by Gentiles," one Israeli official said. "It has to do with 2,000 years of Jewish history, of Jewish persecution at the hands of Gentiles."

A further dilemma involved the diplomatic status of the Israeli-occupied West Bank. The State Department felt that a U.S. request for extradition of Manning from the West Bank would be tantamount to a U.S. acknowledgment that the area was Israeli territory.

The exact nature of the 1980 Manhattan Beach bombing came to light in August 1988, two months after Rochelle Manning's apprehension. Federal agents arrested William Ross, a millionaire real estate broker in Los Angeles, charging him with conspiring to plant the bomb. Ross reportedly was enraged at William and Brenda Adams over a real estate deal. The Adams owned a computer services company and one of their employees, Patricia Wilkerson, was the victim of the bombing. She opened a package addressed to Brenda Adams, followed instructions inside by plugging a device into an electrical outlet, and died in the blast.

Federal officials reported that Ross and his brother, Arthur, were friends of the Mannings, as well as fellow members of the Jewish Defense League. U.S. attorney Stock said the bombing "was not committed at the request or with the knowledge of the Jewish Defense League," but rather was likely tied to a real estate dispute. Ross apparently recruited the Mannings to plant the bomb.

The Odeh family applauded Rochelle Manning's arrest and the revelations that the FBI suspected Robert Manning was involved in Alex's death. "I'd like it to be settled somehow," said Norma Nassab, Alex's sister. "I don't wish death on anyone. But I feel there has got to be some sort of trial and confirmation.

A federal court in Los Angeles tried Rochelle Manning and William Ross on charges of killing Patricia Wilkerson. In January 1989, the jury, after five days of deliberation, reported to the judge that they could not reach consensus on the guilt of either person. After the judge declared a mistrial, federal prosecutors sought and received a dismissal of all charges against Manning and Ross. Stock said the government would continue to seek the extradition of Robert Manning from Israel.

However hard Lisa and Ilsa Klinghoffer tried to put their father's death behind them, Abu Abbas hindered their healing. With a "catch me if you can" attitude and a smirk on his face, he continued to resurface periodically, especially when the news media were handy.

Abbas arrived in Algiers in April 1987 to attend a meeting of the PLO's parliament-in-exile, the Palestine National Council. Yasser Arafat used the meeting to reconcile with quarreling factions that split from the PLO after Arafat agreed in 1985 to coordinate PLO peace efforts with Jordan. He succeeded, but Arafat had to renounce his relationship with Egypt to gain rapprochement with hard-line groups supported by Syria.

Abbas, a member of the PLO Executive Committee, made news at the meeting because the committee talked of expelling him as a public relations measure. Alluding to the repercussions of the *Achille Lauro* hijacking, one PLO official said that Abbas didn't fit the PLO image that they wanted to project. "Abbas is out," said another Council member. "He is losing his seat on the Executive Committee because of what he did," a reference to the *Achille Lauro* hijacking. Yet another conceded that Abbas had become a political liability to the PLO.

Still other attendees resented the news media's interest in Abbas. PLO spokesman Ahmed Abdul-Rahman acknowledged that cameras seemed to follow Abbas, but dismissed the significance of Abbas's presence, "This issue is not so important to the PLO." Another PLO official challenged a reporter, "He is unimportant. Don't waste your time on him."

"We are protesting to the government of Algeria for allowing this notorious terrorist into the country," said U.S. State Department spokesman Charles Redman. The U.S. State Department didn't like Abbas's continuing role in the PLO leadership any more than some of the conference participants. Since both Italy and the United States had no extradition treaty with Algeria at the time, neither country could attempt an arrest. At the White House, no one said anything about mounting another cowboy operation.

Abbas reaffirmed his affinity for a microphone by tossing a few nuggets to an *Associated Press* reporter during the conference. "How many times do I have to apologize and clarify the *Achille Lauro* affair?" Abbas asked. He also said there was a "tactical error in the affair," presumably referring to the hijackers' deviation from the planned mission. "If I had not personally intervened quickly, a catastrophe would have occurred." He added that his PLF's policy is to only strike Israel, "never to undertake terrorist attacks or kill innocent people." Interestingly, Abbas referred to the hijacking as an "affair," while preferring to "strike" Israel.

"In all struggles, errors and blunders can happen, and they are not understood by the public," Abbas told a French radio reporter.

Despite the huffing and puffing about Abbas ruining the PLO's image, the Palestine National Council voted to keep him on the Executive Committee. Power politics are not unique to Western democracies. You rarely get what you see in the PLO.

Speaking of power politics, on September 15, 1987, the U.S. State Department ordered the Palestine Information Office in Washington to close within thirty days. The department cited the continued affiliation of terrorist groups with the PLO, which used the Information Office as a foreign mission of sorts, as the reason for the order. The government singled out Abu Abbas's membership on the PLO Executive Committee and his attendance at the Algiers meeting as examples.

The PLO described the order as hostile and an attempt to satisfy Jewish voters. James Zogby, director of the Arab-American Institute, called the move a cowardly election-year stunt. (The Institute is a mainstream lobbying organization headquartered in Washington.) Israel and American Jewish organizations praised the action. U.S. Senator Charles Grassley, a Republican from Iowa who earlier had sponsored legislation aimed at closing the office, supported the order. Grassley said the State Department consulted the American Israel Political Action Committee, a pro-Israeli lobbying group, before making a decision. In response, the American Civil Liberties Union lodged a flurry of protests that argued the order was an infringement of free speech rights enjoyed by Palestine-Americans working at the Information Office.

Palestinian youths started the first intifada ("shaking off") in Gaza in December 1987. The movement started spontaneously when thousands marched in protest of Israel killing four Palestinians. Rioting began in the next several days, with young protestors throwing rocks at Israeli forces. Violence escalated and continued until the 1993 Oslo peace meetings. To many, the 1987 intifada was an explosive response to Israel's twenty-year occupation of the West Bank and Gaza. (Israel captured the two areas during the 1967 Arab-Israeli War (the Six-Day War)—Gaza from Egypt and the West Bank from Jordan.)

Coincidentally, or perhaps in concert with the emerging intifada, Abu Abbas's PLF started a series of cross-border raids into Israel from Jordan and Lebanon. One coincided with the April 1988 visit to Israel by U.S. Secretary of State George Shultz, traveling to promote a U.S. proposal for limited Palestinian self-rule in the occupied territories. All were small operations that always resulted in one or more of the raiders dying. Because of the timing, Abbas may have been intent on embarrassing Arafat when Shultz was present. Also, considering the futility of the operations, Abbas may have been simply trying to justify his anti-Zionist standing among the members of the PLO Executive Committee.

Another event that drew more attention to Abbas than PLF attacks was a surprise announcement by the U.S. Justice Department. It withdrew the U.S. arrest warrant for him. The department took the action on November 9, 1987, but chose to keep it from the news media until the following January. Department spokesman Patrick Korten said on January 16, 1988, that Justice decided to announce the decision only after Italian Foreign Minister Giulio Andreotti publicly mentioned the withdrawal.

"We do periodic reviews of outstanding indictments to see what we have to support arrest warrants and we concluded at this point we do not have the evidence to win in an American court," Korten said. He said that the department also took into consideration Abbas's conviction in an Italian court.

The Klinghoffer daughters reacted to the news with their usual alacrity. They issued a statement that read: "This was forfeiting our right for our father's murderer to be held accountable in an American court of law. We see no purpose served by abandoning the warrant and we appeal to the President to have the Justice Department retract the decision." Lisa and Ilsa's statement also indicated they were disappointed with the government's failure to notify them directly of the cessation of the case.

"I'm dismayed," Lisa said. "I was really hoping that one day I would pick up the phone and hear that they had caught Abbas."

One of the men in Italian custody during the 1986 hijacking trial, Mowffaq Said Gandura, died after a fall from his fifth floor Rome apartment in July 1987.

During the trial, Gandura maintained he was a member of the PLO secret police, a claim the PLO denied. Although acquitted of hijacking charges, Gandura received an eight-month sentence for lying to investigators. He apparently became an informer for the Italian government at some point because a Rome hotel administrator said that the Italian interior ministry paid Gandura's hotel bills. That arrangement lasted from July 1986, until January 1987, when the hotel evicted Gandura.

According to his girlfriend, Stanislawa Honrik, Gandura traveled to Geneva on a false passport in 1987, withdrawing $100,000 from a numbered bank account. Upon returning to Rome, a Palestinian acquaintance stole Gandura's car, luggage, and the $100,000. The "friend" was found dead in Beirut two days later.

Responding to a Syrian request for his extradition on a fraud charge, Italian police arrested Gandura. He asked to return to his apartment to gather up several documents before being jailed. As Gandura and Italian police officers entered the apartment, he bolted for the bedroom and locked the door. By the time the police knocked down the door, Gandura was outside the window on a ledge. Despite police efforts to grab him, Gandura jumped to his death.

What information did Gandura sell to Italy? What was the source of the $100,000? What happened to the friend in Beirut? How does all this fit with the PLF and Abu Abbas? There are no answers to these questions.

"Maybe he was trying to swim for it."

Abu Abbas delivered that wisecrack, with a half smile on his face, to a stringer for the *New York Times* on November 13, 1988. The reference to Klinghoffer's body washing ashore in Syria was as clear as it was odious.

Abbas made the remark at the annual Palestine National Council meeting, again gaining more attention than perhaps he deserved. The real news at the meeting was the Council's discussion about renouncing terrorism and acknowledging Israel's right to exist. But the meeting, also in Algiers, gave him a platform and a chance to spin the news media.

"You have an accident on the way. Accidents happen," Abbas said, comparing the hijacking to an automobile accident during a trip. When a reporter asked if he regretted Klinghoffer's death, he first replied, "Who is Klinghoffer?" But later he said, "We are sorry when innocent people are victims of the situation, but we are not sorry for the operation because the operation was against Israel."

Attendees at the conference reacted like those the previous year to Abbas's continuing presence on the PLO Executive Committee. Mohammed Said, an American physician from Washington State attending by special invitation from Arafat, voiced his opinion. "I attacked him," he said. "*Achille Lauro* was a disgrace, and how can this man still be on the Executive Committee?"

In an interview with *Time Magazine* just before the Algiers meeting, Yasser Arafat responded to questions about Abbas and his position in the PLO.

Time: "Why do you defend particular terrorists, for example Abu Abbas Zaidan, who led the hijacking of the Italian ship on which the American tourist was killed?"

Arafat: "How? How?"

Time: "By keeping him on your payroll, so to speak, on your PLO Executive Committee."

Arafat: "Our payroll? He was elected. I can't prevent that. [Israeli Prime Minister Yitzhak] Shamir, who was wanted by Interpol, was later elected and is the prime minister. This is democracy. I did not elect Abu Abbas. It was the Palestine National Council that elected him. And a part of the reason is this, that it was a matter of indignity, national indignity; when Reagan breached the agreement with President Mubarak and they hijacked the plane and tried to put him in jail, that caused a reaction of sympathy for him."

A few days after the Algiers meeting, the PLO requested a U.S. visa for Arafat to address the United Nations General Assembly in New York. Secretary of State George Shultz, said to be offended by Abbas's "swim for it" remark, denied the request on November 26, 1988. Shultz referred also to the PLO's associations with terrorism, just as he had done the previous year.

In a *New York Times* piece on December 7, Walter Ruby acknowledged that he asked Abbas the question in Algiers that elicited his revolting response. The New York correspondent for the *Jerusalem Post*, Ruby wrote that Abbas's remarks after his casual celebration of Klinghoffer's murder generally went unreported. In Ruby's views, Abbas's follow-up statements disclosed a Palestinian resentment of America's double standard.

"Has Israel expressed regret about the millions [sic] of Palestinians who were shot at Sabra and Shatila?" Abbas asked Ruby. (Both were refugee camps at which pro-Israeli Lebanese Christian militia, in 1982, killed hundreds, perhaps thousands of Palestinian men, women, and children. Israel invaded Lebanon in 1982 to eliminate bases used by the PLO to launch attacks on Israel, aligning itself with the Lebanese militia during the operation.) "Did America express regret about the victims of Grenada? I wish the names of our victims and martyrs were as well known as the name of Klinghoffer. Can you name 10 Palestinians who died from Israeli gas, or 10 pregnant Palestinian women who were crushed and killed?"

Abbas's hyperbole notwithstanding, Ruby suggested in his article that the news media actually made Abbas's point by focusing on his Klinghoffer remark and omitting mention of his claims of Palestinian deaths. Ruby thought Abbas was trying to say that the death of one American is more newsworthy that the deaths of many Palestinians. But Ruby also offered an objective assessment of the impact of the news media's obsession with Abbas.

"By focusing so relentlessly on Abu Abbas's remark, we only strengthen those Palestinian groups that reject all compromise and are ready to fight to the death against Israel—even if it takes 100 years."

Lisa and Ilsa Klinghoffer didn't like Abbas's remark, either. These two women have been bulldogs when it comes to rebutting anything Abbas said to the press. So in a piece on the *New York Times* Op-Ed page on November 30, the sisters ensured that Abu Abbas did not go unchallenged.

> When the Palestine National Council was meeting in Algiers, the picture of our father's killer, Abu Abbas, in attendance in a front row seat, brought back all the bad memories. And then we read an interview with Abbas in which he snickered about our father's death. . . . To think that this man was running around free, being treated as a man of respectability, made the pain too much to bear.

The sisters applauded George Shultz's decision to keep Arafat out of the country. "Our reaction is, Right on Mr. Shultz! Stick to your principles! As Americans, we are best off when we do so, and, in the end, despite criticism from abroad, the world is best off when America takes the lead in fighting this evil."

Despite the Klinghoffers's endorsement, Shultz's hard line didn't last long. With Arafat barred from the United States, the United Nations convened a special session of the General Assembly in Geneva in December, inviting Arafat to address the body. There, on December 13, Arafat finally said the magic words, at least in the minds of the outgoing Reagan administration. The PLO formally accepted two United Nations Security Council resolutions, #242 and #338, which recognized Israel's right to exist in peace, and also renounced terrorism. Secretary of State Henry Kissinger had promised Israel in 1975 that the United States would not negotiate with the PLO until it accepted those two resolutions.

Willem Ruys in the 1950s. Its owners, the Dutch shipping company Rotterdam Lloyd, sold *Willem Ruys* to an Italian, Mr. Achille Lauro, in 1964. Lauro gave the ship his own name. *Peter Kohler*

Achille Lauro underway about the time of the hijacking. When Lauro Lines bought the ship, it reconfigured the funnels and some of the other exterior features, and painted the hull blue. *Peter Kohler*

Leon Klinghoffer in his wheelchair on board *Achille Lauro* shortly before the hijacking. *Lisa Klinghoffer*

Leon and Marilyn (far right) celebrated Marilyn's fifty-eighth birthday with friends on board *Achille Lauro* just two days before his murder. Three of the Klinghoffers's friends joined the party: Pearl Rosenthal, far left, Sylvia Sherman, behind Leon, and Charlotte Spiegel. *Lisa Klinghoffer*

Achille Lauro's captain, Gerardo de Rosa, left, greets American shipping expert Peter Kohler during a cruise a few months after the hijacking. During the hijacking incident, Kohler gave the U.S. news media insights on the ship's configuration and history. *Peter Kohler*

Jim Stark, a U.S. Navy captain assigned to the National Security Council staff at the White House, hatched the plan to intercept the *Achille Lauro* hijackers. Stark was later promoted to rear admiral, and when this photo was taken he was president of the Naval War College in Newport, RI. *Naval War College*

Vice Admiral John Poindexter approached his boss, Bud McFarlane, President Reagan's national security advisor, with the idea of capturing the hijackers. McFarlane then sold the plan to Reagan. All are shown in this 1984 photo in the White House Situation Room. McFarlane is second from left (his wife, Jondra, is behind him), Poindexter, chief of staff Jim Baker, Situation Room communications technician Bill Clark, and Reagan celebrated McFarlane's and Poindexter's birthdays. *White House Photo, courtesy of John Poindexter*

Bud McFarlane is shown here on October 10, 1985, presenting the plan to apprehend the hijackers to the President at the Sara Lee bakery in Chicago. With chief of staff Don Regan looking on, President Reagan, who was speaking at the bakery, authorized the plan in principle. Reagan later approved the start of the operation while returning to Washington aboard Air Force One. *Ronald Reagan Library*

Commander Ralph Zia, U.S. Navy, coordinated the Navy aircraft involved in finding the Egyptian airliner carrying the hijackers and forcing it to land in Italy. Zia managed this intricate aerial ballet from his station on a Hawkeye radar surveillance aircraft launched from the carrier USS *Saratoga*. *Ralph Zia*

"You can run, but you can't hide," proclaimed Ronald Reagan at a news conference in the White House on October 11, 1985. During a presidency plaqued by terrorism, Reagan was proud that the U.S. Navy had been able to take action against the *Achille Lauro* hijackers. *Ronald Reagan Library*

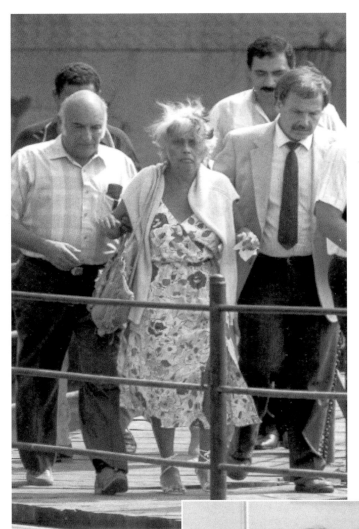

Marilyn Klinghoffer departed *Achille Lauro* on October 10, 1985, two days after her husband's murder, in Port Said, Egypt. Nothing could hide a widow's grief that day. *Barry Iverson/Time-Life Pictures/Getty Images*

Lisa (left) and Ilsa Klinghoffer, during the years after their father's death, pushed the Italian and U.S. governments to apprehend Abu Abbas, the leader of the hijackers. *Lisa Klinghoffer*

Nicholas Veliotes was the U.S. ambassador to Egypt in 1985. Appalled when he heard of Klinghoffer's murder, Veliotes created quite a stir in Cairo when he urged Egypt to "prosecute those sons-of-bitches." He was referring to the four hijackers who surrendered to Egyptian authorities. *Nicholas Veliotes*

Alex Odeh, the West Coast regional director of the American-Arab Anti-Discrimination Committee, was murdered on October 11, 1985. A Catholic Palestinian-American living in Orange County, CA, Odeh defended the Palestinian Liberation Organization and its leader, Yasser Arafat, in television appearances the previous evening. Odeh felt that Arafat had helped defuse the *Achille Lauro* incident. U.S. law enforcement authorities believe that the Jewish Defense League killed Odeh. *Sami Odeh*

Alex Odeh and his daughters, Helena, Susan, and Samia, shortly before his murder. He was almost universally loved by Christians, Jews, and Muslims in Southern California for his attempts at healing differences between peoples. Odeh was a victim of racial and ethnic stereotyping that rises from the U.S. population after terrorist attacks on Americans. *Sami Odeh*

Mohammed "Abu" Abbas, the man in charge of the *Achille Lauro* hijacking, appeared at a news conference in Gaza City in 1996. He and other terrorists were allowed to return for a Palestinian National Council meeting as part of a 1995 agreement between the Palestine Liberation Organization and Israel. *AP/Wide World Photos*

Abu Abbas and PLO chairman Yasser Arafat demonstrate their friendship at a 1987 Palestinian National Council meeting in Algiers. *AFP/Getty Images*

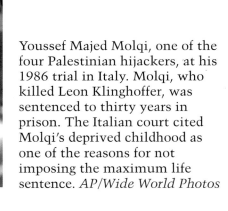

Youssef Majed Molqi, one of the four Palestinian hijackers, at his 1986 trial in Italy. Molqi, who killed Leon Klinghoffer, was sentenced to thirty years in prison. The Italian court cited Molqi's deprived childhood as one of the reasons for not imposing the maximum life sentence. *AP/Wide World Photos*

NBC TV aired the film *The Hijacking of the Achille Lauro* in 1989, which starred Karl Malden and Lee Grant. Marilyn Klinghoffer chose producer Tamara Asseyev, one of many filmmakers who vied for the rights to the story, to depict the violent death of Leon Klinghoffer. *Tamara Asseyev*

A joint Italian-U.S. production team created the second made-for-TV film about the *Achille Lauro* incident, *Voyage of Terror*, which starred Burt Lancaster and Eva Marie Saint. Producers rented *Achille Lauro* to serve as the primary set for the film and this scene shows the hijackers holding their hostages just below the ship's bridge. *Alberto Negrin*

In another scene from *Voyage of Terror*, Italian and U.S. military forces surround an Egyptian airliner carrying the hijackers at a NATO base in Sigonella, Italy. U.S. Navy aircraft forced the plane to land; in real life it was a Boeing 737, but the film producers used the McDonnell-Douglas DC-9 shown in this image. *Alberto Negrin*

The opera *The Death of Klinghoffer* premiered in Brussels on March 19, 1991. Composed by John Adams, the work was a minimalist tale of the hijacking, with a set that represented the various interior levels of the ship. *Martha Swope*

The city of Los Angeles dedicated this statue in honor of Alex Odeh in 1994. A plaque at the base reads, in part: "He taught the gentle wisdom of his land and sang the beauty of God's creation. To him Jews, Christians, Muslims, all were the children of Abraham." *Sami Odeh*

Irv Rubin, shown in this 1979 photo during a demonstration in Los Angeles, was the long-time head of the Jewish Defense League. He died in jail in 2002 while awaiting trial for conspiring to bomb an Islamic mosque and a U.S. congressman's district office. Rubin's secretly taped remarks during the conspiracy investigation indicate that the JDL killed Alex Odeh. *AP/Wide World Photos*

Achille Lauro burned and sank during a 1994 cruise from the Mediterranean to South Africa. The many fires, collisions, and deaths associated with the vessel prompted the news media to call it the "ship of death." *Rien/Corbis SygmaCorbis*

Shultz immediately responded to the PLO declaration, saying that the United States was "prepared for substantive dialogue with PLO representatives."

Shortly afterward, Arafat, who was back in Tunis, also pledged to do his best to stop Palestinian terrorism. One of his top aides, Khalid Hassan, addressed how the PLO was handling Abu Abbas under this new rubric in the peace process. Hassan said that Abbas was barred from Executive Committee meetings. "We can't kick him off because he was elected, but he does not participate," said Hassan. He also said that Abbas had no impact on PLO decision-making and equated the situation to one in Israel. According to Hassan, the Israeli parliament similarly isolated Jewish Defense League founder Meir Kahane, a radical who proposed expelling all Palestinians from Israel and the occupied territories.

All the rhetoric, as well-meaning as it seemed, did not stop Abu Abbas from planning more attacks on Israel.

The fact that the U.S. State Department negotiated the closing of the Palestine Information Office with a powerful Jewish lobbying group, the American Israel Political Action Committee, raises a sensitive issue. Jewish political advocacy groups have been deeply involved in the social, legal, and political manifestations of the *Achille Lauro* hijacking. In addition to providing clout to Lisa and Ilsa Klinghoffer's crusade to have Abu Abbas brought to justice, they have significant influence over the actions and votes of large numbers of U.S. politicians. That heft increases during the months leading up to a Presidential election.

Arab-Americans employ similar lobbying and special interest groups, providing support and encouragement to Alex Odeh's family. These groups also seek to influence politicians.

Each lobbying side, Jewish and Arab, struggles with the same complex issues and forces that have driven the Arab-Israeli conflict for years. Both sides think they were in the right during disputes such as PLO's retention of Abu Abbas on its Executive Committee and the resultant closing of the Information Center. Both sides were eager to seize both the moral and rational high ground during these situations. Both sides saw their respective positions as inarguable.

If terrorism is only about good versus evil, then everyone—

politicians, lobbyists, Jews, and Arabs—would have demanded Abbas's removal from the PLO Executive Committee. The fact that there was a difference of opinion is evidence that politics trump reason.

The complex debate between politicians about the Arab-Israeli conflict and the propensity of individuals and groups to regard the issue with diametrically opposed views seeps into many parts of American society, including the entertainment industry. Some believe that Hollywood reflects social mores of the day; others think it often sets its own agenda. In preparing to produce the first movie about the *Achille Lauro* hijacking, film producers either overlooked or minimized the major issues surrounding the status of Palestine in the late 1980s. Ignoring past Arab-Israeli wars, fighting over the West Bank, and the violence of the intifada, producers looked for more comfortable Hollywood themes. They cast the hijacking as a tragedy, a look at suffering caused by terrorism, much like the news media portrayed the event.

NBC TV aired a film about the *Achille Lauro* incident in 1989, *The Hijacking of the* Achille Lauro. Tamara Asseyev produced the film with the full support and assistance of the Klinghoffer family, and it starred Karl Malden and Lee Grant. Robert Collins wrote and directed the film.

Jostling for the movie rights began immediately after Marilyn Klinghoffer returned home in October 1985. Asseyev was among the first to contact the Klinghoffer family. "I phoned them and gave them my background," she said, then waited for a call back. Unbeknownst to any of the applicants, Marilyn Klinghoffer was dying, but struggling bravely to arrange a deal before she died.

"My mother wanted to tell my father's story," Lisa said. "She wanted to take advantage of every opportunity; she wanted his death to make a difference. Tamara just seemed the right person to tell that story." The family decided also that that television was the best medium for the project.

"She called me to come to New York and meet her daughters before we started," Asseyev said. "She sounded weak; explained it was the flu." Upon arrival, the family told Asseyev that Marilyn was in the hospital and could not meet with her. Marilyn Klinghoffer died that night, hopefully content that she had done her best to memorialize the death of her husband.

Asseyev, whose 1979 film *Norma Rae* was nominated for a best picture Oscar, set about to acquire story rights from other passengers in order to add multiple perspectives to the story. Those additional rights also give the dramatist greater flexibility. "If you don't have the rights, you cannot put words into someone's mouth," Asseyev said. Adding dialogue can enhance key dramatic scenes, a practice that came under scrutiny later. Asseyev also hired Lisa and Ilsa Klinghoffer as story consultants.

"Tamara approached me to write and direct the film, after NBC, her partner, recommended me," Bob Collins told me. "I was successful in making docu-dramas, especially biographies." (In a docu-drama, factual stories are embellished for dramatic effect.) "I had demonstrated that I could translate thorough research into a teleplay."

"I only take on stories that present life in a positive way," Asseyev said, setting the tone of the film. "This is the first time America dealt with terrorists in a very positive way. They intercepted the airplane, brought it down, took the terrorists to trial."

Armed with a good story, Asseyev and Collins began looking for a cast and a place to film.

"NBC suggested Karl Malden," Collins recalled. "He was honest and respected, and I thought he was a marvelous actor, one of the best that I have worked with." Further, Collins liked Malden because he wasn't Jewish. "I didn't want the film to be about Jews and Arabs. Besides, I knew Leon Klinghoffer. I knew how he lived, what he thought. He was just like my father—brought up tough in New York." To play Marilyn, Collins and Asseyev settled on Lee Grant, a veteran actress with an Emmy and Oscar to her credit.

"We needed a ship, film crews and extras; it was cheaper in another country," Collins said, explaining why he didn't film in the United States. Collins, however, encountered a problem that he had not considered—retaliation by Palestinian terrorists. "We heard that it would be too dangerous to shoot in Italy," Collins said. "Our contacts in Spain told us that the PLO threatened to target any production set established there; they would kill people!"

"Spain, Italy, Yugoslavia, Greece—they were all PLO centers," Asseyev explained later. "They would cause trouble, we were told. We couldn't take a cast and crew into that situation." In the face of these threats, Collins settled on Australia, making a deal with Sun Lines to use one of their ships.

"As soon as we got to Australia, Sun cancelled the deal, saying the threat to their ship was too great," Collins recalled. He also said that he was told the PLO had contacted government film commissions in Italy and Spain, threatening reprisals if they cooperated with the U.S. production. Collins found himself threatened by terrorists while trying to make a movie about terrorism.

Without a ship and only two weeks until the scheduled start of filming Collins got creative. "We found a coal ship that would be in port for a few days. Our production designer built a set on its deck for all of the outside scenes. It was close."

Lisa traveled to Australia to observe part of the filming and represent the family. The production team was sensitive to her feelings, holding back filming of emotional scenes until she left. Lisa was there, however, when the crew shot the happy scene where Leon and Marilyn said goodbye to their daughters at the start of the voyage.

To keep the right tension between cast members, Collins kept the actors playing the roles of terrorists away from the rest of the cast. "We didn't see the terrorists until the day they took over," said Grant. "It helped push us into the kind of situation they must have gone through. I know I was certainly frightened."

◄◄ ►►

NBC broadcast *The Hijacking of the* Achille Lauro on February 13, 1989.

"Terrorism as entertainment: NBC seems to be specializing in it," wrote Tom Shales, television critic for the *Washington Post*. NBC aired a film about the TWA airliner hijacking, *The Taking of Flight 847: The Uli Derickson Story*, the previous year, as well as its infamous interview with Abu Abbas in 1986.

Shales went on to write that the film told the story in a convincing and straightforward way. He felt that Malden and Grant added poignancy and impact to the story with their performances. "Even if they have been Hollywoodized, the Klinghoffers become more real here than they were as mere names in news reports, and the senselessness of what happened to them is made more immediate."

He was less pleased with the brutal prologue in which actors portrayed PLF guerrillas conducting the frightful 1979 raid on the Israeli town of Nahariya, which Shales felt was never connected to the rest of the film.

"That's where it began," countered Collins years later. "The hijackers demanded the release of the Nahariya terrorists. That incident set the whole meaning of the story for me."

In *USA Today*, Matt Roush also lauded Grant's and Malden's performances, but then wrote that the film "amounts to little more than an exercise in suffering. This hijacking seems an attempt to wring ratings from tragedy. That may work better than the movie, which adds nothing significant to our understanding of the unthinkable."

"That's what television does," answered Collins to the question of profiting from tragedy. "Look at CNN every day. The more tragic, the better the ratings."

The *New York Times*'s Walter Goodman grew weary quickly of the anticlimaxes, obligatory lines, and lame foreshadowing. "I don't know," says a friend of the Klinghoffers as she disembarks. "I somehow feel that I shouldn't leave you alone."

"As for the four young terrorists," Goodman wrote, "they all have good haircuts, do a lot of grimacing, and enjoy shooting their automatic weapons. The passengers were held for two days, but the viewers are on their own."

"Whether news or narrative, television is infinitely more comfortable showing the occurrence and impact of violence than examining its causes," Howard Rosenberg of the *Los Angeles Times* wrote, taking a more sophisticated approach in his review. "An event like the *Achille Lauro* tragedy is far easier to depict than a complex movement or cause like that of Palestinian nationalism. Movies like tonight's are made in part because the issues they depict—in this case an act of barbarism against unarmed civilian tourists—are an easy call, and the forces of good and evil are easy to identify."

"Collins obviously takes liberties, for there is no possible documentation for some of the private conversations depicted here," Rosenberg wrote, taking Collins to task on the private dialogue between characters. The critic believed that NBC's disclaimer on the fictionalization of characters for "dramatic purposes" was too vague.

"It was a play," responded Collins when we talked about the film's reception. "The dialogue was all mine. We based the conversations on real events. The characters represented real people. The story was a romantic tragedy about the sunset voyage of two old, sick people."

"What's more," Rosenberg continued, "[Collins] all but ignores the jurisdictional intrigues and political shell games and trickery underlying the ultimate capture of the hijackers and the escape of the man said to be their leader, the infamous Abu Abbas."

In writing the script, Collins said that he focused on the events on board *Achille Lauro*. He thought that the story was about a personal tragedy, a story about the unwitting involvement of an individual in political intrigue. He purposely stayed away from the greater international issues, concentrating on Leon and Marilyn Klinghoffer. "During my research, I became disgruntled with the behavior of everyone off the ship. I didn't want to deal with that."

Rosenberg completed his review with an essay about the Palestinian uprising in Israeli-occupied Gaza and West Bank in 1989.

"But the television industry rarely has the courage and vision to change course and make pioneering U-turns, so here is a prediction: Despite relatively steady newscast coverage, there will be no TV drama soon relating to the intifada, even though a good one could provide clarity and even though there are human stories and tragedies on both sides begging to be told."

Bob Collins told me that representatives from the American-Arab Anti-Discrimination Committee approached NBC to complain about potential biases against Palestinians in the movie. "NBC took a strong stand and did not ask me to change anything. I saw some truth in their allegations, however, so I added a scene in which one of the hijackers talked about the Palestinian cause."

Lisa and Ilsa Klinghoffer were pleased with the film. "I liked how it portrayed the relationship between my parents," Ilsa said.

CHAPTER

6

Mideast Machiavelli
(1990–1991)

ITTLE happened in the Odeh investigation during 1989, or in the first months of 1990. In May 1990, however, law enforcement officials said that they suspected three Jewish Defense League members had planted the bomb—Keith Fuchs, Andy Green, and Robert Manning. Federal officials provided evidence to grand juries in both Brooklyn and Los Angeles that linked the three men to several 1985 bombings. Manning was in Israel, Fuchs reportedly was living in a West Bank yeshiva, while Green ran a car rental business in Jerusalem. Finally, there was a reported similarity between the Odeh bomb to those detonated the same year in New York and New Jersey. A former FBI official said, "Characteristics that were similar in the three bombings indicate either the bomb-makers had the same teacher or the same group or person did it."

In light of these revelations, Robert J. Friedman wrote in the *Los Angeles Times* about Israel's alleged hindrance of the Odeh investigation, a matter initially described in the leaked Clarke-Revell memo in 1987.

Justice Department sources assert that Israel is still obstructing its investigation. While liberal Israeli politicians familiar with the case concede

115

as much, they hasten to add that this is not out of love for the Jewish Defense League trio, but because many Israelis view those who slay Arab-American supporters of the Palestine Liberation Organization or alleged Nazis as heroes. That makes Israel's compliance with an extradition request very difficult.

Israel advertises itself as a bulwark against terrorism in the Middle East. It has often chastised America for not combating Arab terrorism vigorously enough. But Israel's apparent lack of cooperation with the FBI in the Jewish Defense League investigation calls into question its sincerity in prosecuting the war against terrorism when the terrorism emanates from Israel itself.

Friedman's allegations of Jewish Defense League's complicity in the Odeh and other bombings drew immediate reaction from the League's Irv Rubin. "His crude attempt to blame the Jewish Defense League for the 1985 death of Alex Odeh is journalism at its worst," Rubin wrote of Friedman's allegations two weeks later. "His use of downright lies and innuendoes to indict the Jewish Defense League for the crime is nothing short of contemptible."

As he had in the past, Rubin denied any Jewish Defense League involvement in Alex Odeh's death, asking how government investigators had the chutzpah to blame the Jews for the killing. "Let's face it: The majority of terrorist attacks perpetrated in the world come from the adversaries of Jews. Instead of taking the authorities to task for possible anti-Semitism, as many a reputable journalist would have done, Friedman furthers a blatant assault on innocents."

Rubin, who once offered to arm Jews, tried to soften his image in 1989 and 1990. In August 1989, Rubin wrote to the *Los Angeles Times* editor to explain his heartless remarks about Odeh's death. He wrote that he reacted "emotionally" to Odeh's claim on television that Yasser Arafat was a man of peace. "Perhaps I should have chosen my words with more sensitivity, but . . . the reason I stated I had no tears for Alex Odeh was because I had already shed too many tears for the hundreds of victims of Arab terror."

In July 1990, Rubin told a reporter that his 1985 remark about Odeh was a turning point for the Jewish Defense League. He said that donations to the organization dropped immediately, and that national membership declined to a few thousand from the 11,000 the League claimed in 1972. "We lost a tremendous amount of support in the Jewish community," Rubin said. "People stereotyped us. They wanted to kill us."

Israel arrested Robert and Rochelle Manning in March 1991, three years after the country issued an arrest warrant for Mr. Manning. Diplomatic concerns in the United States over the status of the West Bank delayed the arrest. A U.S. Postal Inspector in Los Angeles—the Postal Service investigates mail bomb incidents—said the State Department removed that obstacle the previous March by withdrawing its objection to an Israeli arrest on the West Bank.

Israeli radio reported that the arrest was for the murder of Alex Odeh; Sami Odeh and Alex's family rejoiced when they heard the news. "I have been expecting that to happen for a long time. The Israeli government has been stalling."

And stall it did, because 1991 ended without any movement toward Israel's extradition of either Manning to the United States.

The second made-for-TV film about the hijacking aired in April and May of 1990. Its approach to the event was considerably distinct from the NBC movie the year before, proving that even in the entertainment industry there are two sides to every story. While NBC's version focused on the romantic tragedy, seen from the Klinghoffers's perspective, the second was a broader treatment that overlaid the political and nationalistic facets of the incident on the more personal Klinghoffer themes. *Voyage of Terror* starred Burt Lancaster and Eva Marie Saint. It was produced by RAI and Tribune Entertainment, written by Alberto Negrin and Sergio Donati, and directed by Alberto Negrin. The fact that the project was a joint Italian-American production almost guaranteed a different take on the story.

"There were so many political aspects to consider," Italian producer Fabrizio Castellani acknowledged. "For instance, the American partner cared about the emotional aspects of the event, and the Italian partner looked to the political aspects. It was a very delicate subject." This film gave Italians the chance to insert their view of the incident into the volatile mix of assertive U.S. terrorist polities, Middle East tensions, and the relationships between Jewish- and Arab-Americans. Negrin reflected part of the Italian perspective by anointing *Achille Lauro*'s captain, Gerardo de Rosa, the hero of the film, not Marilyn Klinghoffer or the American "cowboys."

Another distinct difference was the set used in this film. Castellani and American producer David Lawrence didn't search the world for a ship and locale for filming, they simply rented *Achille Lauro*. They hired Captain De Rosa to serve as the technical advisor, several of the original crewmembers to act as themselves, gathered the cast and 300 extras, then sailed. Paying the ship's owners $1 million, producers had free run of an otherwise empty ship for one week, then kept the cast and crew on board for another two and a half weeks after *Achille Lauro* resumed her regular cruises.

"We were never threatened," Negrin told me years later. "No one called, there was no pressure from the Palestinian movement."

Producers Castellani and Lawrence did not disregard safety issues altogether. "We kept the whole thing under wraps," Lawrence said later. "When Burt Lancaster and Eva Marie Saint came to Rome—they are big stars—we never released any information about their arrival. There were no interviews, and that held true until they were safe."

Lawrence also said that port officials hassled Egyptian and Israeli actors, a reflection of heightened security measures in the cruise ship industry. "We had an American actor who was Arabic by heritage who was awakened by the authorities in the middle of the night. We finally convinced them he was legitimate."

If the PLO did not pressure Negrin, others did, especially the Italian prime minister. "Craxi wanted me to make a film about him, about his role in the incident," Negrin told me, "complete with scenes of cabinet meetings, phone calls to President Reagan, and meetings with the American ambassador." After months of waiting for the Italian government's approval, Negrin managed to persuade Craxi to move the focus away from Italian politics.

The two-part, four-hour film aired on several dates throughout the United States in April and May 1990. Television critics did not praise it.

"*Voyage of Terror* comes off like an amateurish cross between 'America's Most Wanted' and the *Poseidon Adventure,* replete with songstress warbling a love song under the closing credits," wrote Tom Shales of the *Washington Post.* "In other words, it's a big hunk of junk and worth only the time it takes to hit the remote control channel changer." Shales also called the Reagan scenes the "most unintentionally funny impersonations of Ronald Reagan ever," and described the actor who plays De Rosa a "somnambulant stiff."

"This version of the story was filmed on the *Achille Lauro* itself, a supposedly authenticating detail," concluded Shales. "You have to wonder about the owners of a cruise line, though, who would lease their ship for such an enterprise. Wasn't once enough?"

"Perhaps not surprisingly, the Italians come off as the quietly reasonable heroes of the story," wrote John O'Connor of the *New York Times,* acknowledging the Italian influence on the production. "American officials tend to be characterized as cowboys. General Walter Davies [played by Robert Culp], who forces down the EgyptAir plane carrying the released terrorists, says things like, 'We're gonna take these bandits home with us.'"

The critics noticed that the film attempted to tell the hijacker's story, as well as that of the hostages. Shales was cynical of the melodramatic treatment of the issue and panned a scene in which one Palestinian hijacker wrote a letter to his girl back home, "Sometimes I dream of the day when I will be able to shake an Israeli's hand, look into his eyes and say, 'Let's stop fighting, let's find a solution.'"

From an international point, O'Connor wrote, there was a little something for everyone. He also noted that the film portrayed three of the four hijackers as dupes, with one realizing that they were "cards in a stacked deck in a dirty game played a long way from here."

"We are not saying the terrorists were good guys," co-producer Lawrence said just after the film aired. "We try to express their viewpoint. It's very difficult when you are juggling international situations."

George Paris, vice president of Tribune Entertainment, went on to say that the production team took great care to not portray the men as irresponsible terrorists. In his view, they were just "four young people—these were all kids in their teens and early twenties—who felt they were on a mission to help their countrymen. Those four kids looked at themselves not as terrorists but as patriots."

"I am a Jew!" Negrin said in 2003 when we talked about the film's alleged bias. "I told the truth. I wanted to show the hijackers as the puppets they were. I tried to be as honest as possible. I tried to do my job, not from an ideology point of view, but to tell the story as objectively as possible."

Negrin's treatment of how Italy allowed Abu Abbas to escape rankled the Italian government. Although the film aired throughout Europe and the United States, the state controlled television system in Italy banned it. "Listen Negrin," Craxi's personal secretary told the director, "this film will never be aired in Italy, never."

"Television's Palestinians never appear as enlightened, progressive humanists, or even as ordinary people. They never smile unless tossing a bomb," wrote Jack Shaheen, a frequent critic of the U.S. entertainment industry's portrayal of Arabs in films. He argues that a few men in New York and Hollywood have created a stereotype that is so pervasive, so ingrained in what the American public sees in theaters and on television, that the U.S. government shares and reinforces the bias.

In 1988, Shaheen noted that terrorist attacks in the United Kingdom by the Irish Republican Army or in Italy by the Red Brigades did not result in observers calling the UK and Italy terrorist nations. "Yet where are the voices contesting the myth that falsely brands more than four million Palestinians as corrupt and brutal?"

In both newspaper articles and his book *Reel Bad Arabs, How Hollywood Vilifies a People*, Shaheen documents that nearly one thousand movies and hundreds of television programs have shaped Arab Muslim stereotypes, bombarding their audiences with "rigid, repetitive and repulsive depictions that demonize and delegitimize the Arab." According to Shaheen, the treatment started with Rudolph Valentino in the early film *The Sheik* (1921), then continued in *The Road to Morocco*, with Bing Crosby and Bob Hope (1942), *Network* (1977), and *Jewel of the Nile* (1985). Television films reacted to the terrorism of the 1980s with *Hostage Flight*, *Terrorist on Trial*, and the *Achille Lauro* films. "My colleague, Alex Odeh, a Los Angeles poet, and Leon Klinghoffer were both killed by terrorists in October 1985," Shaheen wrote in 1990. "Viewers saw two TV movies based on Klinghoffer's death. Odeh was virtually forgotten."

"One event epitomized the imbalance between the attention given to Klinghoffer's tragic death and that accorded to Odeh," Shaheen told me in 2003. "I attended an event in Los Angeles that was a fund-raiser for the Odeh family, and I was approached by a producer from the CBS News show *60 Minutes*. I explained about Alex's murder, but he responded 'There's no story here,' and left. This rude, insensitive remark illustrates that according to this producer, the life of a Jewish-American is worth more than the life of an Arab-American."

Shaheen believes that the Arab stereotype continues to prowl movie screens because Arab-Americans don't have the organization or clout that other minorities—African, Asian, and Jewish Americans—have achieved. They have no effective lobby in Los Angeles, he contends. "There are no Arab-Americans imbedded in the industry—at the management, creative, directing, or producing levels," Shaheen said. "But just as importantly, both domestic and international politics associated with the Arab-Israeli conflict spill over into the entertainment world, creating misperceptions and dangerous stereotyping. Also, 'if it bleeds it leads' media coverage of Mid East problems influences public opinion, as well public policy."

"I was saddened by the portrayal of the Palestinians in the two *Achille Lauro* films," Shaheen concluded. "Only one person projected the deaths of Klinghoffer and Odeh equally—a political cartoonist at the *Los Angeles Times*. Soon after their deaths he showed the two men standing on a cloud in heaven. The cartoonist's point was that in heaven, they are equals."

The U.S. film industry makes movies to make money. Producers know that certain stereotyped bad guys will be readily accepted by movie-goers, thus assuring good box office receipts. Jack Shaheen is right in saying that producers would never cast a robed Arab or a Palestinian, even one without a machine gun, as a good guy, or even a character that has emotional depth. Filmmakers exploit the anti-Arab biases associated with terrorism to make money. Terrorism is not just about politics and power; it's also about prejudice and profits.

The helmsman turned the *Tiny Star* into the seas and cut its engines to dead slow ahead. Forward of the pilothouse, two men unlimbered a deck crane and began attaching lifting slings to one of five assault boats lashed to the deck of the small freighter. Just after 4:00 A.M., starlight and a sliver of a moon only partly illuminated the horizon set between the darkness of the sky and sea.

Three men conferred on the dimly lit bridge—Colonel Zuhayr, a Libyan military officer, Ozzuddin Badrakkan, and the ship's master—studying a chart showing the Israeli coastline 120 miles east of the ship's position. Cruising at 20 knots, Badrakkan estimated once all five boats were lifted off the ship into the water, the little flotilla could reach the beaches of Tel Aviv late that morning. The master signaled the deck crew to commence launching the boats.

Sixteen young Arab men must have talked and smoked on deck as *Tiny Star* pitched easily into each sea as it passed. Their feelings must have been mixed, as they contemplated what might be their last day on earth. Some must have been anxious, others even fearful. But all were committed to killing Israelis before their own death.

The men were also confident in their plan, one created by their commander, Abu Abbas, and his deputy Badrakkan, who they called Abu Oz. Their training in Libya for the past months would guide them through the darkness to the great glory of Palestinian freedom, Abu Oz assured them. Grabbing their Kalashnikovs, the men scrambled down a rope ladder to the boats bobbing alongside the ship.

The crew assigned to one of the boats started yelling at the others in the darkness. Their engine died and they could not re-start it. Abu Oz shouted from the ship, ordering his men to abandon the craft, even though it had been configured to carry extra fuel for all of the boats. The four remaining boats headed toward the gathering dawn.

Engine trouble on two more boats forced the team to abandon the craft before reaching Israel. Five of the men boarded one of the two remaining craft, and sped off toward their assigned landing point north of Tel Aviv. The second, overloaded with eleven men, steered toward Nizzanim, twenty miles south of Tel Aviv.

By midday, one of the boats slowed just off shore while one of the men scanned the shoreline with binoculars to find a recognizable landmark. Just then an Israeli helicopter appeared in the distance flying toward them. As the team argued about using the boat's 23 mm machine gun on the chopper, Israeli Navy gunboats approached at high speed. Their training deserted the PLF soldiers and the men decided not to resist. When ordered by the Israelis to jump into the sea, the humiliated men acceded. After Israeli sailors fished them from the water, the five sat wet, cold, and manacled on deck as the Israelis took them ashore.

Discarding the last remnants of the original plan, the crew of the last boat ran it through the surf and onto the shore of a crowed beach club. Running into the nearby dunes, they did not fire at the hundreds of beachgoers. The Israeli Army quickly engaged them in a sharp firefight. Four of the men died; seven capitulated and lived. No Israelis were killed or wounded.

Two years in the planning and funded with $3 million, Abu Abbas's grand plan to assault Israel from the sea fizzled and failed. Proving again, thankfully, that even terrorism is an acquired skill. Abbas's gang again couldn't shoot straight. In a previous sea-borne raid of similar scale in 1978, twelve guerrillas from Arafat's Fatah killed thirty-three Israelis and wounded eighty-two. What Abbas did successfully accomplish with this attack on May 30, 1990, as he had done in the past, was cause trouble for the United States, Israel, and the PLO.

The Palestine Liberation Front issued statements in both Lebanon and Iraq claiming responsibility for the raid. Since the PLF was still one of the PLO's constituent groups, focus in both Tel Aviv and Washington turned immediately to Yasser Arafat's renunciation of terrorism seventeen months earlier. Israeli Prime Minister Yitzhak Shamir asked the U.S. government to suspend its dialogue with the PLO.

"The U.S. is horrified at this terrorist attack," said State Department spokeswoman Margaret Tutwiler. At the White House, Press Secretary Marlin Fitzwater said that President George H. W. Bush was outraged at what appeared to be a cowardly attempt to target innocent people.

"We are not responsible as the PLO for this operation and we have no connection with it," Arafat declared. "I am talking about the institutions and the official forces which belong to the PLO." But Arafat also refused to condemn the raid, despite threats from President Bush and his administration to break off their talks with the PLO.

Central to the dispute was the mission of the PLF gunmen. Were they intent on killing civilian tourists?

Israeli officials firmly asserted the targets were civilians, citing documents and maps that showed hotel locations, which they found on board the two boats. Abbas told a Kuwaiti newspaper that the objective of the raid was "a resort for senior Israeli army officers. It was the storming of specific enemy positions . . . including the private camp for officers where they bathe," Abbas said. "Where are the civilian casualties? The actual fighting was with naval and air enemy forces." Arafat seized on this fine distinction between innocents and combatants in order to prove that no one associated with the PLO had engaged in "terrorism," but rather conducted a military operation. That contention lost air when two of the captured PLF soldiers began to talk.

"The goals of the operation were to kill civilians in the hotel area of Tel Aviv," Mohammed abu Shaash said in a videotaped interview released by Israeli officials. "We were supposed to shell it from the sea with Katyusha rockets and 23 mm and 14.5 mm shells and then land and kill anyone we came across. I was told to go to the Sheraton Hotel." Shaash also said that their superiors told the team not to identify who supplied the boats and arms. "We were told we must not admit this under any circumstances." A second commando, Ahmed Mohammed Yusef, said that his orders were to "cleanse the hotel and murder anyone we encountered."

As the United States pressured the PLO to condemn the raid and punish those responsible, the PLO leadership scrambled to find a way out of their pinch. The Executive Committee met in Baghdad to consider their situation, pointedly telling the news media that they had banned Abbas from the proceedings. The committee sent a representative to interview Abbas, who again claimed the mission was not against civilians. As proof, Abbas said the group did not shoot at the beachgoers when they landed. He also maintained that the raid was in reaction to an incident two days before in which a deranged Israeli citizen killed seven Palestinians. That assertion seemed silly since the Israelis had learned by then that the PLF teams had been training for months.

"The PLO is in a mess," one Arab diplomat said. "They don't know what to do, resume or not resume the dialogue. Punish or not punish Abbas. There are Arab voices saying they should accept the U.S. conditions and other Arab voices are saying no."

The PLO deliberations didn't assuage U.S. and Israeli concerns, and President Bush suspended his administration's dialogue with the PLO about peace in the Middle East on June 20, 1990. "We've given the PLO ample time to deal with this issue," Bush said at a news conference. "To date, the PLO has not provided a credible accounting." Bush acknowledged that the PLO, which separated itself from the attack, had factions within it that opposed negotiations with the United States and Israel. But Bush demanded Arafat categorically condemn the raid and discipline the PLF.

The Bush administration did not take this action simply because of its opposition to evil acts. Politics and the stalled Middle East peace process were the driving factors. Bush and his secretary of state James A. Baker III, wanted to get the recently installed conservative government of Israeli Prime Minister Yitzhak Shamir to engage in serious peace negotiations with the PLO. Weighing in on the matter was the American Israel Public Affairs Committee (AIPAC), just as it did in

1987 when the Reagan administration closed the Palestine Information Office in New York (also because of Abu Abbas). The Committee
was holding its annual meeting in Washington at the time and attendees made it clear that if Bush wanted American Jews and their allies
in Congress to help push Shamir to the negotiating table, he should
hold the PLO accountable.

Washington Post columnist Mary McGrory pointedly described the
influence AIPAC has on the U.S. government's decision-making process. "All are held in a circle of fear," she wrote at the time. "Bush didn't
dare let the terrorist raid go unpunished for fear of being held soft on
terrorism. He knew he would get no flak from the Hill: 47 senators
backed an amendment urging him to break off the talks. Members fear
AIPAC, fear alienating Jewish constituents. . . ."

Forced out of Jordan, Lebanon, and Syria during the previous twenty
years, Arafat had bases only in Tunis and Baghdad in the summer of
1990. Disciplining Abu Abbas, who enjoyed the full support of Saddam
Hussein, could jeopardize Iraqi support of the PLO. But the PLO problem with Abbas receded as fast as Kuwaiti defenses recoiled in the face
of invading Iraqi tanks on August 2, 1990. The Persian Gulf War had
started.

The PLF beach raid in 1990, along with the claims and counter-
claims about its objectives, and subsequent political repercussions,
offered an insight into the mind of Abu Abbas. Bright and clearly
manipulative by nature, Abbas was devious and cunning enough to
challenge Arafat for the right to be called the Palestinian Machiavelli.

The PLF guerrillas intended to kill Israeli civilians on the Tel Aviv
beaches, if one believes the confession of two of them, and Israeli analysis of the PLF documents they found on the boats. By claiming the
attack had been aimed at the Israeli military, regardless of the outcome, both Abbas and Arafat could plausibly deny the incident broke
the PLO's renunciation of terrorism. If the raiders had not fumbled and
bumbled their way ashore, but actually made it to the Sheraton Hotel
and killed tourists, Abbas would have said that it was an "accident," a
plan gone awry. Abbas's explanation sounded familiar.

Within hours after Molqi shot Klinghoffer, the PLF issued a statement claiming *Achille Lauro* was not the target of the four hijackers,
but rather Israeli military targets in Ashdod. Abbas echoed that line

every time he spoke to the news media, right up to September 1990. But he lied. He never intended for his *Achille Lauro* hijackers to go ashore in Israel.

In 1989, Italian legal scholar Antonio Cassese examined the Italian court's analysis of the true objective of the *Achille Lauro* hijacking. In order to consider whether the hijackers broke Italian terrorism laws during the 1986 Genoa trial, the court had to understand the men's objectives in the incident. Cassese wrote that the court firmly established that the PLF claim of conducting a terrorist attack in Ashdod was a "smokescreen," and the only objective Abu Abbas had in mind was the hijacking of *Achille Lauro*. The court cited five reasons for its conclusions.

First, the four hijackers offered contradictory stories about the planned attack at Ashdod. They even contradicted themselves.

Second, news media reports about the cabin attendant surprising the four men were false. The hijackers never tied and gagged the crewman as they previously claimed. The four stewards assigned to the men's cabin denied anything of the sort, and court interviews with other crewmembers corroborated the stewards' assertion. The hijacking was not a knee-jerk reaction to a premature discovery by the steward.

Third, neither Molqi nor Ashker, who stayed with the ship's captain constantly, told Captain De Rosa of any plan in Ashdod. The court concluded that Abbas created the Ashdod myth after Syria refused to cooperate with the hijackers.

Perfect timing was the fourth reason given by the court. The hijackers seized the ship after 651 passengers left the ship for a tour of the Egyptian pyramids. Only about 100 passengers remained on board ship, with most in the dining room and thus easily managed. The crew stayed out of the hijackers way, neutralized by the Palestinian's weapons and uncertainty about the hijacker's numbers. The court said the hijackers' coordinated movements and knowledge of the ship's layout were not consistent with an impromptu hijacking.

In the court's view, the most compelling reason for deciding that a hijacking was the true objective of the four Palestinians was the impossibility of an assault on Ashdod. During all previous port calls in Ashdod by *Achille Lauro*, Israeli security officials boarded the ship offshore, scrutinizing passports and matching them to the person. The hijackers' crude cover would not have lasted a New York minute under such examination. Further, Israelis always carefully searched all disembarking passengers. The Israeli security measures were so strict and so observable to the PLF during its planning of the operation that the court dismissed any claim that Ashdod was the target of the hijackers.

Abbas intended to hijack the ship, trading the hostages for PLF prisoners in Israel. He must have instructed Molqi to kill Jewish or American hostages to gain leverage. During the TWA airliner hijacking four months prior to the *Achille Lauro* incident, Israel, under discreet, behind-the-scenes pressure from the United States, almost released prisoners in a swap for the TWA hostages. Abbas may have been emboldened by that near miss about the potential for success during his hijacking. In May of 1985, Israel swapped 1,150 detainees for three Israeli soldiers captured by Arabs in Lebanon, another move that could have encouraged Abbas.

The Italian court's assessment of the PLF mission on board *Achille Lauro* is entirely consistent with the 1990 attack on the Tel Aviv beaches. In each instance Abbas kept the true goal of the operation from Yasser Arafat, thus giving Arafat the chance to claim that he did not authorize the attacks. In both cases, Abbas insisted that his men intended to assault Israeli military targets, not innocent civilians. This distinction is important to the Palestinian contention that a war of national liberation allows legitimate attacks on Israeli soil or the occupied territories. Arafat restated the PLO's right to attack Israel in his Cairo Declaration in November 1985 during the international ruckus following the *Achille Lauro* hijacking.

Both in 1985 and 1990, Abbas had a plan to justify each raid, regardless of the outcome. When his men hijacked *Achille Lauro*, Abbas called it an accident on the way to the liberation of Palestine. When Syria refused to negotiate with the hijackers, Abbas and Arafat took credit for ending the accident. If the PLF soldiers had gotten to the Sheraton Hotel and killed civilians in 1990, Abbas would have declared that the men panicked en route to their military objective. Since no civilians were hurt, he continued to maintain the target was the Israeli Army installation.

There is yet another facet to this complex situation—Abbas's relationship with Arafat. Regardless of Abbas's membership on the PLO Executive Committee, he timed PLF raids to provide maximum personal embarrassment to Arafat and disrupt PLO negotiations with Israel and the United States. Just as Abbas wanted it both ways during terrorist attacks, he wanted to keep up the armed struggle against Israel, while simultaneously offering public support to Arafat.

King Hussein of Jordan and Arafat signed the Amman Accord in February 1985, an agreement meant to provide a framework for joint Jordan-PLO peace negotiations with Israel. That agreement led to a rupture in the PLO ranks, as radical opponents to peace talks angrily denounced Arafat's movement away from violence. The October 1985 *Achille Lauro* hijacking ruined any prospects for a successful Jordanian-PLO strategy. Hussein angrily called Arafat to Amman after the hijacking, demanding explanations. The following February, Jordan announced the suspension of all diplomatic and political coordination with the PLO.

Abbas's highly visible presence at the 1987 Palestine National Council meeting in Algiers so irritated the United States, that the State Department closed the PLO office in Washington, further embarrassing Arafat. At the following year's Palestine National Council meeting, Abbas's "swim for it" remark prompted the United States to deny Arafat a visa to attend the UN General Assembly meeting in New York. The 1990 beach raid torpedoed the dialogue between the United States and the PLO. Abu Abbas was a smart guy, who used perfectly timed terrorist attacks to gain stature not only within the Palestinian movement, but also on the international political stage.

As you read this book, there will be many references to PLF operations against Israel, as well as attacks on that country by other Palestinian groups. Although not specifically addressed, there are an equal number of Israeli assaults on Palestinians. As of April 1989, just a year before the PLF raid on Tel Aviv, the death toll of the first intifada stood at 440 Palestinians and seventeen Israelis. During that month, Israeli Border Police indiscriminately killed five and wounded twelve Palestinians in the West Bank village of Nahalin after being assaulted by boys throwing rocks. Israeli officials acknowledged that the police used excessive force, lost control, and exercised bad judgment. The head of the Border Police, Commander Meshulam Amit, said that his forces "made mistakes" during the raid. My intention is not to highlight an isolated incident in an attempt to draw general conclusions about Israeli atrocities. Rather, the point is that both sides have killed large numbers of people during the Arab-Israeli conflict. Also, Commander Amit sounded just like Abu Abbas defending the *Achille Lauro* operation.

"We see this as the battle for Palestine," Abu Abbas said in September 1990 of Iraq's invasion of Kuwait and the resulting Persian Gulf crisis. Regarding the pending war between the U.S.–led coalition and Iraq, Abbas said, "Winning will get us closer to home. Losing it will put us further away." Asked if terrorism might be part of Iraq's planned strategy, Abbas responded, "We use many ways to reach our aim."

At his base of operations in Baghdad, Abbas found himself at the vortex of world affairs when Iraq invaded Kuwait. His position became even more central when Yasser Arafat decided to throw the PLO's support behind Saddam Hussein, a decision that later would yield severe consequences for the PLO.

"Strike with your long arms at all U.S. interests. Open fire at the enemies of our nation everywhere," Abbas said, ordering the PLF to attack American targets in support of Iraq. As the United States and others staged their forces in the theater in preparation for war with Iraq, Abbas told the news media that terrorist hit squads were in America and Europe, ready to attack targets if the coalition struck Iraq. Once coalition aircraft attacked Iraq in January 1990, Abbas used Baghdad Radio to call for all Arabs to "take up arms and strike and destroy the interest of the U.S, and its allies."

Abbas's bluster did not lead to any terrorism against America during the Gulf War, but the fact that Abbas and several other known terrorists—Abu Nidal and Ahmed Jibril—were in Iraq during the crisis, gave concern to many in Washington and London.

In his first lengthy session with the news media since the disastrous PLF raid on the Tel Aviv beaches, Abbas met clandestinely in early September 1990 with Tony Horwitz, a writer for the *Wall Street Journal*.

After taking him on a circuitous route through the back streets of Baghdad designed to shake any tails, armed guards patted down Horwitz and insisted that he test his tape recorder while pointing the microphone at his own neck.

"Broad-shouldered and six feet four inches tall, he has the strong but softening build of a retired lumberjack," Horwitz wrote, describing Abbas's imposing stature. "Ruggedly handsome, his thick black hair and mustache show no signs of gray at 41. His eyes don't give much away; in the dimly-lit office, they are so dark as to seem all pupil."

Abbas proudly showed off the effects of past battles with the Israelis—a scar on the forehead and bullet wounds in both thighs. Had he personally killed anyone? Responding with his now familiar smirk, Abbas said in fair English, "During the fight, you don't know what happens." He also tried to convince Horwitz that there was a distinction between "just killing" and war with Israel.

In response to the standard question about Leon Klinghoffer's death, Abbas turned prickly. "Klinghoffer, always I hear about this Klinghoffer," he said. "Nobody knows all the people who die in Palestine. But this Klinghoffer is like Jesus Christ."

He offered no regrets for the Tel Aviv beach attack, despite the consequences of the U.S. suspension of its dialogue with the PLO. Reflecting his intolerance of Arafat's shift from terrorism to diplomacy, Abbas lamented the PLO's progress in gaining a Palestinian homeland. "For two years we say yes, yes, yes to America, without results. Political ways have stopped now. Only we will fight." He said, however, that he would not spurn a potential negotiated settlement of the Arab-Israeli conflict.

Horwitz wrote that Abbas appealed to young, militant Palestinians who wanted action, rather than dialogue. PLF members apparently welcomed the paramilitary style of the organization, uniformly dressing in blue jeans, white shirts, and combat boots. One present during the interview, who claimed that all members must prove themselves in battle, said that he respected Abbas because of his focused and "rational" approach to fighting Israel.

This rational terrorist sat at a desk piled with papers, his reading glasses close by. Subordinates came and went in a manner similar to other Middle Eastern offices. Yet two things were distinctive. The staff carried guns, and the photos on Abbas's desk were not of his family. The pictures were of his PLF soldiers departing in their speedboats to kill Israelis out for a day at the beach.

Abbas granted interviews to *Le Figaro, Reuters,* and the Iraqi news agency INA that same month, but his remarks were mostly bellicose rhetoric aimed at the U.S. "aggression" in the Persian Gulf.

He was back in the news in November 1990 when Libya expelled 145 PLF members based in that country. While Libya offered no reason for the move, the action was thought at the time to have been the result of a PLO initiative to undercut Abbas in retaliation for the Tel Aviv raid. Abbas refuted that suggestion, saying "We rule out any possibility that the PLO leadership has asked for this, but some Palestinian circles who oppose our militant line might have done so."

During the period in which the Iraqi Army occupied Kuwait, hundreds of men from both the PLF and another small group under the PLO umbrella, the Arab Liberation Front, moved into Kuwait behind the military. They mounted an aggressive, and at times, murderous, campaign to convince Palestinians living there to support Iraq. Those Palestinians who resisted the demands for pro-Iraqi demonstrations were detained, even killed. The local leader of Fatah, Arafat's original organization and the major component of the PLO, was assassinated on January 18, 1991.

At the war's end, there was a severe backlash at Palestinians for the PLO's support of Iraq. Kuwait had long been a haven for Palestinians displaced from Israel and the West Bank. Hundreds of thousands of them worked and lived there profitably and peacefully. Yasser Arafat got his start there, owning a successful construction company. But as the Kuwaitis regained control of their country, they systematically detained thousands of suspected Iraqi collaborators. Dozens were reportedly tortured and two killed; many just disappeared. Kuwait expelled thousands of Palestinians, and the exodus was compared to the Israeli ejection of Palestinians in 1948.

Arab reaction to the PLO's support of Iraq yielded a staggering blow to the Palestinian movement. PLO officials said that the economic losses exceeded $12 billion. Political repercussions negated the gains Arafat accrued through years of moderation and diplomatic initiative.

In another move to isolate Abu Abbas, perhaps in concert with Libya's expulsion of the PLF, the Palestine National Council removed Abbas from its Executive Committee during its annual meeting in Algiers in September 1991. Abbas said at the start of the meeting that he would agree to leave if the United States respected Palestinian rights and did not, during any future negotiations, jeopardize those rights.

On March 5, 1991, Greek police arrested two men associated with the hijacking—Abdul Rahim Khaled and Petros Floros—after finding a bomb in Floros's house. Khaled had been convicted *in absentia* of complicity in 1986, while Floros was acquitted. In December 1991, Greece approved extradition of Khaled to Italy, but only after he finished prison terms in Greece for narcotics offenses and attempted escape.

Greece extradited Khaled to Italy in May 1996, where his previous sentence was increased to life imprisonment. Floros's fate is unknown.

The activities of Abu Abbas in 1990 were ample evidence that terrorism growing out of the Arab-Israeli conflict was then and remains a complex phenomenon. His expensive raid on the Tel Aviv beaches could have been a heinous and lethal attack on civilians had it not fizzled through inept execution. Perhaps knowing that his soldiers might fail, or even assuming they would, Abbas prepared two responses to the inevitable political reaction. He knew that if the raid succeeded, it would derail the ongoing dialogue between the United States and Yasser Arafat. If it failed, as it did, the resultant political imbroglio would have the same effect. Either way, his name is in the news. The attack on Israelis was merely a means to political ends.

Abbas gained even more leverage in the heated, triangular debate between Israel, the United States, and the PLO by talking to the ever-lustful news media afterward, maximizing the incident's publicity. Also, the interviews permitted him to shape his public persona—middle-aged father with a spreading paunch and reading glasses. He also stayed on message like any good politician—"Don't forget the terror wrought on Palestinians!"

CHAPTER

7

The Death of Klinghoffer (1991–1995)

I N 1991, five years after Italy's trial of the hijackers, their accomplices, and Abu Abbas, this was the status of the eleven persons that Italy charged with the hijacking.

Name	Sentence	Status
Hijackers		
Youssef Majed Molqi	30 years	In prison
Ibrahim Fatayer Abdelatif	24 years	In prison
Ahmed Marrouf al-Assadi	15 years	Free
Bassam al-Ashker	16 years	Free
Accomplices		
Mohammed Issa Abbas	7 years	Free
Mowffaq Said Gandura	8 months	Dead
Yussef Ali Ismail	Summarily acquitted at the trial's start	
Yussef Hisham Nasser	6 years	Free
Leaders		
Mohammed Abbas	Life	Free
Ozzuddin Badrakkan	Life	Free
Abdul Rahim Khaled	Life	In prison

Italy freed Issa Abbas and Nasser in December 1990 as part of a traditional Christmastime, early-release program. Issa Abbas served only
five years of his seven-year term. Nasser had the same sentence, but
served one year less since he was apprehended in 1986.

Italy paroled Ashker in June 1991 after he served six years of a
sixteen-year sentence. The Justice Ministry arranged for him to live
with a prison chaplain and work for the Italian Red Cross. Ashker
immediately escaped. Assadi, also released on parole in 1991, disappeared just as quickly. Molqi and Abdelatif remained in prison, but
that would change.

After the turmoil of the 1991 Gulf War and the subsequent damage
inflicted on the Palestinian cause by Arafat's support of Saddam Hussein, Abu Abbas stayed out of the news for a while. Since the Palestine
National Council replaced him on its Executive Committee in 1991
with his assistant, Ali Ishak, Abbas had fewer opportunities to make
news.

His diminished stature did not, however, keep Abbas from sending
his PLF soldiers into Israel on another seaborne raid. At 7:00 A.M. on
May 30, 1992, two men came ashore just south of the Israeli city of
Eilat after swimming three miles across the northernmost tip of the
Gulf of Aqaba from Jordan. They brought with them rifles, grenades,
and a small rocket launcher, using air tanks to keep the weapons
afloat. They killed Yosef Shirazi, a guard at a marine biology labora-
tory, then fired at people on the beach. As they attempted to set up
the rocket launcher, Israeli soldiers killed one and wounded the other.
Israeli authorities reported that two additional guerrillas drowned during the nighttime swim. The PLF claimed responsibility for the attack.

Later that summer, there were news media reports that Iraq had
arrested Abbas as he traveled from Baghdad to Amman to meet with
PLO officials. All proved to be false.

Abu Abbas was indeed in Baghdad in September 1992 and that fact
was the basis for a political tussle in Washington. A Democratic congressman, Henry B. Gonzalez of Texas, released documents that he said
proved that Secretary of State James Baker knew that Iraq was providing shelter to Abu Abbas when the Bush administration established its
pro-Iraqi policy in 1989. The Reagan administration had removed Iraq
in 1982 from the list of countries supporting terrorism in response to

Baghdad expelling Abu Nidal. President Bush extended that policy, according to Gonzalez, when he signed an order mandating closer ties to Iraq, stressing the importance of Persian Gulf oil to U.S. interests. "Our main goal was access to cheap oil," Gonzalez said in a speech in the U.S. House of Representatives. "Hussein wanted cash, credit and military technology. Oil made it possible."

This bit of international political maneuvering was in sharp contrast to the stand the Bush administration took in 1990 when it suspended its dialogue with the PLO. That decision arose after Abu Abbas's men raided the Tel Aviv beaches. In that case, the President used Abbas as a reason for a political action. In the situation regarding Iraqi oil, Bush ignored Abbas. Denouncing evil sometimes helps along the political process. In other times, it's best not to bring it up.

Perhaps sensing that he needed a publicity boost, or simply to disrupt ongoing Arab-Israeli peace talks, Abbas invited the ever-willing Western news media to meet with him in Baghdad in 1993.

"For two years, since the peace process began in Madrid, we have had the patience to stay calm and not take military actions," Abbas told Carol Morello writing for *Knight Ridder Newspapers* in late June 1993. "But our patience will finish. We gave everything to this peace process. We relinquished many principles. If the situation continues, we will have to be active militarily . . . to make the whole world remember we are here and we have our cause." Please note that many view Abbas's "military" operations as terrorism.

The 1990s peace process between Israel, its Arab neighbors, and the PLO started at an international conference in Madrid that the United States and the Soviet Union jointly sponsored in October 1991. The resultant face-to-face talks between Israel and Palestinians had bogged down when Abbas chose to give an interview in his Baghdad office. He was not the sole Palestinian critic of Yasser Arafat's dialogue with Israel, but he could speak out with relative impunity in the shadow of a protective Saddam Hussein.

Opportunist that he was, Abbas took advantage of the news media attention given to Iraq after the United States sent twenty-three cruise missiles into Baghdad a few days earlier in retaliation for a plot to assassinate former President Bush. He gave Morello his view of the U.S. military action.

"Up to now, there is no evidence [of a plot] to be sure. Even if it's true, I think there were many other recourses. Cruise missiles are a last recourse. If they describe us as terrorists, what can we call this act? This is just terrorism."

Abbas voiced his firm support for Saddam Hussein, clearly thankful for both his safe haven in Baghdad and Iraqi support for the Palestinian cause. He said that Hussein had not asked him to conduct terrorist attacks on Iraq's behalf.

Reporter Morello described the forty-four-year-old Abbas as alternately mellow and coy. In an office with lace curtains in the windows and a new Mercedes-Benz out front, he gave the kind of interview that every Western reporter seems to covet with terrorists. Abbas supplied good quotes, talked of past "military" missions, and threatened future violence in support of his fight for Palestinian freedom. He even polished up his cover story for the 1990 Tel Aviv beach raid. "We can kill thousands of civilians if we want, but we didn't do it that way. We told our fighters, if they reach the seaside, it is forbidden to shoot civilians. If you get to the end, shoot soldiers but not civilians."

In September 1993, nine weeks after Abbas's interview, Israel and the PLO announced that they recognized each other's right to exist. President Bill Clinton immediately restarted a U.S. dialogue with the PLO, which President Bush had suspended in 1990 after the PLF raid on Tel Aviv. Clinton also hosted Yasser Arafat and Israeli Prime Minister Yitzhak Rabin at a ceremony on the South Lawn of the White House. As the world watched on September 13, these previously mortal enemies hesitantly shook hands. These developments quickly led to an agreement between the PLO and Israel that allowed Yasser Arafat to form an interim Palestinian government for the Gaza Strip and designated areas of the West Bank. At a Tunis PLO meeting in October, the debate on ratifying the agreement heated up to the point of fisticuffs. Abu Abbas, although no longer a member of the Executive Committee, denounced the peace agreement and criticized Arafat's arbitrary leadership. The PLO eventually approved the peace plan.

Commemorating the tenth anniversary of Leon Klinghoffer's death, the Jewish advocacy group Anti-Defamation League sponsored an event at the National Press Club in Washington, DC, on October 27, 1995. Lisa and Ilsa Klinghoffer addressed the gathering, as did Samuel

R. "Sandy" Berger, President Clinton's deputy national security advisor.

"Our parents set out on a cruise to celebrate their wedding anniversary," said Ilsa. "Little did they know that tragedy would strike. A decade later, the pain is still great. No one knows when terrorists will strike. Terrorists put no value on human life."

"The story of Leon Klinghoffer reminds us why America must—and will—remain an aggressive leader in the global fight against terrorism," Berger said in an address about the threat of terrorism to Americans.

Just two days earlier, the *Achille Lauro* hijacking influenced an event in New York. In town for a celebration marking the fiftieth anniversary of the UN's founding, Yasser Arafat attended a concert for world leaders at the city's Lincoln Center. Part way through Beethoven's Ninth Symphony, aides to New York Mayor Rudy Giuliani forced Arafat to leave the auditorium. Unfazed by immediate criticism from the U.S. government, Giuliani called Arafat a murderer and terrorist the next day, citing the *Achille Lauro* incident as an example. Lisa, Ilsa, and Abraham H. Foxman, Anti-Defamation League national director, wrote to Giuliani, voicing their support.

"While we are strong supporters of the Middle East peace process, the memory of the victims of terror is always with us. While we support recent moves by the PLO toward reconciliation, we dare not forget those innocents who were the intended targets of that organization. Consequently, we believe that support for the peace process does not require embracing Arafat."

In response to a U.S. request for extradition, Israel finally arrested Robert and Rochelle Manning in 1991 for the mail-bomb murder of Patricia Wilkerson. The FBI long considered Robert Manning a prime suspect in Alex Odeh's murder. After a lengthy, two-year appeal by the Mannings, the Israeli Supreme Court rejected Robert Manning's request to remain in Israel and ordered his extradition to the United States in July 1993. The court reached no decision on Rochelle, who had been tried in 1989, but was released after a jury could not reach a verdict.

Israel permitted Manning's extradition solely for prosecution of Wilkerson's murder. Both U.S. and Israeli justice officials acknowledged that the U.S. extradition treaty with Israel prohibited U.S. prosecution for any crimes other than the one cited in the extradition request. As a result, Federal and California courts were barred from charging Manning with Odeh's killing.

"I am happy to hear that [Manning] will be here to face trial for a murder," said Sami Odeh. "And believe me, I can feel for the Wilkerson family and children. We all should have some measure of satisfaction when a criminal is convicted and put behind bars, no matter who the victim is." Odeh also said that investigators had told him the previous fall that the search for Alex's killer was at a standstill. "They are trying to follow all the leads and need to talk with some people in Israel and are not getting any cooperation with the Israeli government."

Manning delayed his departure from Israel a week by attempting to kill himself with an overdose of sleeping pills. On July 18, 1993, U.S. agents put him on a plane for America, with Manning, in chains, shouting to reporters, "I didn't do anything!"

Upon arrival in the United States, Manning pled not guilty in a Federal court in Los Angeles. His lawyer, Richard Sherman, gave his version of the Wilkerson killing, "What this is all about is they [the prosecutors] want to punish him for Odeh. But they can't make a case on Odeh, so they charged him with this."

"I don't want to get into this thing where we're being accused of using this [Wilkerson] case as a stalking horse for the Odeh case," responded Assistant U.S. Attorney Dean Dunlavey.

"This is a witch hunt," said Orthodox Rabbi Zvi Block, a long-time Manning friend and dean of Aish HaTorah College of Jewish Studies in North Hollywood, California. "Bob is not a violent person. He's the sweetest, gentlest guy. This man is loved. He's a pure mensch."

Manning, an Orthodox Jew, complained of the lack of kosher food in jail. Guards kept him separate from the general inmate population because of the bobby pins he used to attach his yarmulke to his head. Officials felt that other prisoners might take the pins and fashion them into weapons.

On October 14, 1993, Manning was convicted of complicity in the 1980 bomb death of Patricia Wilkerson. U.S. Attorney Terree Bowers said that Manning's conviction was very gratifying, especially in light of his extradition from Israel, an event that Terree termed as rare.

U.S. District Court Judge Dickran Tevrizian sentenced Manning to life in prison on February 7, 1994. Tevrizian cited the callous and hideous nature of the crime as the basis for imposing the maximum sentence, saying that the punishment was commensurate with Manning's utter disregard for the public.

"This whole thing is sickening to me," Manning said upon sentencing. "I wouldn't have anything to do with this sort of thing." Manning pressed unsuccessfully to serve his sentence in Israel.

A few weeks later police arrested William Ross, who along with Rochelle had been released after a 1989 mistrial. In March 1995, a Federal court convicted Ross of plotting the Wilkerson mail bombing.

Manning's wife Rochelle, who returned to Israel after her mistrial, died in an Israeli prison of an apparent heart attack on March 18, 1994. She had been awaiting extradition to the United States. She would not be the last person linked to Alex Odeh's death to die in prison.

At the same time Robert Manning was on trial in the fall of 1993, the Los Angeles City Council approved the creation of a statue in memory of Alex Odeh. Friends of Odeh, including radio and television personality Casey Kasem, raised $60,000 to pay for the sculpture.

Alex's wife Norma and brother Sami unveiled the statue on April 10, 1994, on the lawn outside the library at the Los Angeles Civic Center. Five hundred people listened as speakers recalled Odeh's contributions to the community.

"Alex Odeh . . . was an advocate for justice for his people," said Rabbi Arnold Rachlis of the University Synagogue in nearby Irvine, California. "He championed Palestinian rights, not because he wished to deny those of others, but because he wanted his peoples' voice to be heard."

The statue depicted Odeh in a Roman robe, holding a book and a dove of peace. A plaque at the base reads, in part: "He taught the gentle wisdom of his land and sang the beauty of God's creation. To him Jews, Christians, Muslims, all were the children of Abraham." The sculptor, Khalil Bendib, said that the statue "will remind us that an attack on any particular group is an attack on all groups."

"It's one thing to have a statue of Alex, it's another thing to have justice for Alex," said another speaker, Albert Mokhiber, president of the American-Arab Anti-Discrimination Committee. Mokhiber called for a renewed investigation into Odeh's murder.

The dedication of the statue drew immediate reaction from the Jew-

ish Defense League. Irv Rubin, whose remarks after Odeh's death—
"He got exactly what he deserved"—incensed all sensible people,
promised to bring a group of League protesters to the next City Council
meeting.

"We're going to make quite a dramatic protest because we feel in
our hearts that to paint Alex Odeh as a man of peace is not the truth,"
Rubin said. "This man was pro-PLO one hundred percent, and bottom
line, he was a PLO propagandist. The PLO has their hands covered
with Jewish blood." Sami Odeh quickly responded to Rubin's allegations.

"What Mr. Rubin thinks of my brother is not important to me. We
had over 500 people at the ceremony . . . including congressmen, a
mayor, a rabbi, priests, and other figures who knew Alex well, not just
heard about him. All testified in public to his being a man of peace and
to the good effort that Alex left behind."

The respective searches for justice by Sami Odeh and Irv Rubin par-
alleled the larger Arab-Israeli conflict. Their confrontation echoed the
standoff in the Middle East and the accompanying violence of the intifada during the early 1990s. As Palestinian and Israeli positions hard-
ened in those years, commentary on the conflict moved from the
newspapers and television into the arts. Opera was about to take on
the *Achille Lauro* hijacking.

> "Let the supplanter look
> Upon his work. Our faith
> Will take the stones [Israel] broke
> And break his teeth."

A chorus of Palestinians sang this refrain during the premier performance of the opera *The Death of Klinghoffer* at the Theatre Royale
de la Monnaie in Brussels on March 19, 1991. In the weeks following
the end of the Persian Gulf War, the world was sensitive to Middle East
politics, a situation that provided the arts and entertainment industry
with opportunities for creativity. Just as television broadcast the two
Achille Lauro films concurrent with Middle East violence, opera
inserted its relevance into the state of affairs. Reaction to the opera,
just as the response to the joint U.S.–Italian film in 1990, would reflect
the entire range of emotions surrounding the Arab-Israeli conflict.

To the uninitiated, a musical drama about the Arab-Israeli conflict and the murder of an elderly, paralyzed tourist was not your father's opera. No critic or knowing opera-lover was surprised, however, when John Adams and Alice Goodman set out to write an opera about death.

"Opera is a bloody business," wrote Katrine Ames in *Time Magazine* after the Brussels performance. "Composers have long found inspiration in violent history or mythology, filling their works with assassinations, suicides, beheadings, rape, and wholesale slaughter of war. When John Adams embarked on an opera based on the grisly [death of Leon Klinghoffer], he was following tradition."

Opera companies in both Europe and America occasionally have performed *The Death of Klinghoffer* from 1991 through the present. Many called it anti-Semitic, but others praised its avant-garde minimalism.

"Instead of a gory thriller a lesser crew might have put together, Adams and his colleagues . . . have concocted an operatic parable for modern times," wrote James Wierzbickie in a 1992 review. "Its moral, as suits today's confusion, is open-ended. There is no excusing terrorism, but often it happens that a sense of righteousness exists on both sides of a disputed fence."

In their first opera, Adams, Goodman, and Sellars created the landmark *Nixon in China*, a milestone in modernism that won a Grammy for a performance on PBS and an Emmy for a recording. The opera celebrates President Richard Nixon's triumphal 1972 trip to China and his meeting with Chinese leader Mao Tse-Tung. As he had with "Nixon," Sellars proposed another opera to Adams in 1988, with only the title in mind at the time—*The Death of Klinghoffer.*

"I knew as soon as I heard the title that this was the right thing for me," wrote Adams in 1991. "It struck me that figures like Mao or Nixon or a Palestinian terrorist had become, largely through their presentation to us in the media, figures of almost totemic meaning." Adams' grasp of the potential for an opera did not mean its creation would be easy, especially in light of what he described as two execrable television films.

The composer admitted that he was influenced less in creating *Klinghoffer* by the operatic traditions of Verdi and more by religious music such as the Bach *Passions.* The pillars of the production are seven choruses, full of sacred references, that, in Adams's words, "stand apart from the more mundane and often desperate actions of the people aboard the ship." They include the choruses of "Exiled Palestinians," the "Oceans, Night, Desert and Day," and the biblical tale of "Hangar and the Angel." The composer sought to frame the story with the choruses, and "remind us that this event, this hijacking and assassination, so seemingly lurid and 'newsworthy' in our minds, was in fact played out in the very womb of Western civilization."

Electing to tell the story through a few individuals, Adams limited the cast to Marilyn and Leon, three other passengers, Captain De Rosa and his first officer, and the four hijackers. Each character delivers his message alone, with little interaction with others, and their arias are interspersed between choruses. The captain laments his inability to prevent tragedy, Leon vents his anger at the hijackers, and Marilyn pours out her grief.

There is no gruesome scene of Klinghoffer's murder, no body thrown over the side. Singers and dancers allude to the event. "We don't show a sweet old man . . . in his Bermuda shorts," explained Sellars. "There is no boat. The entire opera is conducted on quite a higher plane."

Sellars dressed everyone in plain, non-committal clothes, eschewing costumes to reinforce the neutrality of the production and even out the audience's sympathy—hijackers and victims dressed the same. He also had actors portray multiple roles, reinforcing, in Adams's words, the "visual nonspecificity" of the cast. One actress played a Jewish-American housewife, then a teenaged hijacker; another was the first officer one minute, and "Rambo," a violent terrorist, the next.

George Tyspin designed a fifty-foot high set of tubular scaffolding, cables, and gangplanks that simulated the ship's interior and permitted the actors to be on several levels simultaneously. Sellars projected close-ups of singers on a large display hung on the steel latticework, a practice usually seen at rock concerts.

Interwoven into every scene were members of the Mark Morris Dance Group. Morris and Sellars had the dancers accompany the singers with allegorical movements tied to the libretto. The added dimension of dance, according to one opera critic, brought a "fusion of music and poetry; acting, singing and dancing; costume, design, and lighting."

The Brussels premier of the opera attracted critics from around the world, all eager to see how Adams would treat the *Achille Lauro* story.

European reviews were mixed, with the French-language press approving, but the English and German publications panning the production. A U.S. critic called the opera a powerful drama, with another praising it as a lyrical, poetic treatment, not an action drama. While classical music and opera critics wrote effusively about arias and choruses, costumes, and sets, other writers focused on the politics of the production.

"*Klinghoffer* is not an overt political manifesto," wrote Peter Catalano for the *Washington Post*. "Palestinian suffering under the Israelis is portrayed in *Klinghoffer* with sympathy one usually doesn't find in the U.S. press. Individual Palestinian hijackers are also depicted in a sensitive light." Adams gave Catalano his view of the Palestinian situation.

"These people really are oppressed, these people really are being killed. The terrible, terrible tragedy comes about as the result of people hating and misunderstanding each other and oppressing each other. I don't take sides, each side does it to each other. The Jews do it, the Palestinians do it, the Arabs do it, the Iraqis do it. It's not a question of us against them."

Sellars said that the opera is "pro-nobody." He said that the opera translated a contemporary event into the language of poetry, music, dance, and the visual arts. "Through this translation, we can begin to approach a reality which has nothing to do with cruise ships, tourists in Bermuda shorts, political correctness or racist cliches."

"I think we would have been very foolish if we had tried to change anyone's attitude," Goodman said, arguing that she, Adams, and Sellars had no political agenda. "We've tried to let the characters speak for themselves . . . and let the audience draw their own conclusions." And the characters do speak.

"We are soldiers fighting a war," sings the terrorist Molqi. "We are not criminals and we are not vandals but men of ideals."

"You just want to see people die," responds Klinghoffer. "You're crazy."

"You are always complaining of your suffering but wherever poor men are gathered they can find Jews getting fat," sings Rambo the terrorist. "America is one big Jew."

"On the 'politically correct' scale, we don't even register," said Sellars at the time. "People come expecting machine-gun fire and bodies being thrown overboard, and what they get is a bunch of art."

After Brussels, *The Death of Klinghoffer* played in Lyon and Vienna before opening in the United States at Brooklyn Academy of Music on September 5, 1991. The reaction to the opera in New York City took a sharper edge.

"A blazing bombshell has gone off to open New York's opera season," wrote Alan Rich in the *San Francisco Chronicle*. "*The Death of Klinghoffer* . . . opened its five-performance run last Thursday night . . . and the whole town's talking. They're not all talking ecstatically, of course. One way you can measure the brilliance and the importance of the event is by sizing up the number of early departures against the number who line up at the box office during the intermission for tickets to see the work again. At Sunday's performance . . . the count was about even."

Newsday's Tim Page was straightforward in his criticism, calling the opera "pompous, turgid, derivative, and hopelessly confused." Page faulted Goodman's libretto, which he believed portrayed the terrorists as "real men—Rousseau's noble savages made flesh—as opposed to the opera's nattering, ineffectual Jewish characters."

The opera's characterization of the Jewish passengers raised the ire of many and keyed Page's reference to "nattering" Jews. In the midst of the exiles chorus in the first act, Adams and company introduce the Rumor family, Jewish friends of the Klinghoffers. In their suburban New Jersey home just before the cruise, Mr. Rumor squabbles with his wife about her buying habits during their travels, while she rebukes him for spending too much time in the bathroom on trips. The scene looked like it had been lifted from a Neil Simon play. In later performances, the director replaced the Rumor family scene with the chorus of "The Exiled Jews."

"The opera has two arguments, which I take to be the work of Goodman," wrote Leon Wieseltier in the *New Republic*. "Both of them are morally obtuse. The first is that the conflict between two peoples, exiled and in love with the same land, may be represented by the conflict between Leon Klinghoffer and the terrorists who killed him. But it is not a conflict when a man with a submachine gun confronts a man in a wheelchair. It is a crime." Wieseltier objected to the lyric symbolism attached to the hijackers and the opera's focus on their romanticism, rather than their killing.

Others, however, found the opera too complex for simplistic condemnations. "There is nothing trendy about *The Death of Klinghoffer*, and you can dismiss its politics as naive only by dismissing those things in it you don't want to hear," wrote the *Boston Globe*'s Richard Dyer. Bill Zakariasen of the *New York Daily News* agreed. "Life and the world have never been that simple. It may be that no other opera has so definitely expressed the human condition of our time as *The Death of Klinghoffer*."

"I was told for months that I would not like it," Lisa Klinghoffer said of the opera. "I refused to listen to anyone. It's John Adams and I like all of his work. I gave Sellars, who I spoke with once, the benefit of the doubt right up until the opening."

"I couldn't believe it! Right off the bat the [Rumor family] scene mocked my parent's friends. I was mortified. They were seated right next to me."

The Klinghoffer families wanted to leave during the performance, but remained in hopes of seeing what they termed "something positive." "I liked the aria that my mother's character sang, and I liked the man who played my father," Ilsa said. "That was about it."

The Brooklyn Academy of Music approached the Klinghoffer sisters, inviting them to attend the openings as guests, even a party after the performance. Lisa and Ilsa declined, sensing that BAM simply wanted to use them to increase the buzz surrounding the U.S. premiere of the opera. "We bought our own tickets and stayed away from all the hype," Lisa said. Even opera companies know that grief sells.

Through a family spokeswoman, the sisters said that the opera exploited their father's murder and "appeared to be anti-Semitic." "While we understand artistic license, when it so clearly favors a point of view, it is biased. Moreover, the juxtaposition of the plight of the Palestinian people with the cold-blooded murder of an innocent, disabled American Jew is both historically naive and appalling."

After performances in New York, the opera was scheduled to open in Los Angeles, but *Klinghoffer* never played there or at Glyndebourne in the UK. Critics believed that these two co-commissioners didn't want the controversy surrounding the opera. It did play in San Francisco in November 1992. Reactions were mixed again.

James Wierzbicki of the *St. Lous Post-Dispatch* found the work to be balanced, philosophically speaking, especially in light of the removal of the Rumor family scene after the New York performances. "Only those who witnessed it can say if the domestic scene was or was not offensive. The San Francisco production, in any case, seemed perfectly even-handed."

"In terms of the shipboard action," Wierzbicki continued, "only the most biased of opera goers would disagree as to who the good guys and the bad guys are. At the same time, only the most callous could sit through the performance and not be reminded that more problems are far more complex than they appear."

Collectively, the making of the opera, its content, and the reaction to the production make my central point for me: Terrorism is not just about good versus evil.

An international arms dealer and narcotics smuggler sells weapons to a terrorist group so that it can hijack a cruise ship. Simultaneously, the arms merchant sells other weapons to a man who is illicitly supporting rebels intent on overthrowing a Communist government in Central America, a man who is also a staff assistant to the President of the United States. That presidential aide participates in the capture of the cruise ship hijackers. Meanwhile, the arms dealer does all of this while living in a luxurious, sea-side home on the Costa del Sol in Spain and hob-nobbing with the President of Argentina.

This may sound like a plot from a bad movie, but it's not. It's a true story about Monzer al-Kassar.

Kassar is a Syrian millionaire traveling on multiple passports who has been called the most successful private arms dealer in the world. Denmark convicted him of smuggling hashish in 1972, Great Britain banned him from entry in the 1980s for illegal weapons trafficking, and France once sentenced him *in absentia* for running a "criminal terrorist organization." *Time Magazine*, in a lengthy 1992 analysis of the bombing of Pan Am Flight 103 over Lockerbie, Scotland, alleged that Kassar helped the Popular Front for the Liberation of Palestine, General Command faction, plant the bomb on the airliner.

Ollie North's covert enterprise that led to the Iran-Contra scandal during the second Reagan administration sold weapons to Iran in return for help in releasing American hostages in Lebanon. Ollie overcharged the Iranians, using the extra money to buy arms for Contras fighting the Communist regime in Nicaragua. He bought some of the weapons, about $500,000 worth, from Kassar. During his testimony before a Congressional committee investigating North's program, John Poindexter rebutted criticism of North's deal with such an unsavory character as Kassar. "When you're buying arms on the world arms market . . . you often have to deal with people you might not want to go to dinner with."

There were several news media reports that Kassar provided his personal plane to carry Abu Abbas from Belgrade to Yemem to Baghdad after Italy released Abbas following the hijacking.

Spain arrested Kassar on arms charges in 1992. But it was not until 1994 that Spain's National Court accused him of piracy in connection with the *Achille Lauro* hijacking, as well as financing the operation. A member of the National Court, Judge Baltasar Garzon, who later gained notoriety by attempting to prosecute Chile's former dictator Augusto Pinochet, sought Kassar under Spain's universal prosecution law aimed at terrorists. While awaiting trial, the court freed Kassar on what was then a Spanish record $7.7 million bail.

For the December 1994 trial, Garzon convinced one of the imprisoned PLF hijackers, Ahmad Marrouf al Assadi, to testify of Kassar's involvement, but Assadi later recanted and refused to travel to Spain. Another accuser, Ismail Jalid, fell to his untimely death from a fifth-floor apartment; investigators said that Jalid was in an alcoholic coma at the time of his "fall." A third hostile witness, Syrian businessman Mustafa Nasimi, found himself in an uncomfortable position when armed men, thought to be Colombian drug dealers, abducted Nasimi's two teenaged sons during the trial. Kassar denied any involvement in the kidnapping.

The Spanish court acquitted Kassar in early 1995, citing insufficient evidence. Although Nasimi's sons were released after only two days as hostages, their father did not fare as well. An unknown assailant shot Nasimi in the head in the Syrian's Madrid home in 1998. Police suspected the murder was a settling of accounts dating back to Kassar's trial.

CHAPTER

8

The Ship of Death

URING the ten years following Youssef Majed Molqi's murder of Leon Klinghoffer, A*chille Lauro* was plagued by that death. Horribly, his was not the first death, nor the last on that ship. And the ship was not always the *Achille Lauro*. She began her life as a Dutch ocean liner.

With a crack of a champagne bottle on July 1, 1946, Mevrouw E. E. Ruys-Van Houten christened a new passenger ship *Willem Ruys*. The Dutch shipping line, Rotterdam Lloyd, commissioned the ship, naming it after two members of the family that owned the company. The first Willem Ruys founded the company, the second was a director of the firm during World War II.

The De Schelde shipyard in Vlissingen laid the keel of *Willem Ruys* on January 25, 1939, but before the ship could be launched, Germany invaded Holland, occupying Vlissingen in May 1940. The Nazis demanded that the shipyard continue construction of the ship, planning to seize the vessel upon completion. The Gestapo took many prominent Dutch citizens as hostages, including director Willem Ruys, in an attempt to dissuade the Dutch resistance from sabotaging German occupation activities. Undeterred, both the resistance and shipyard workers kept the pace of construction at a crawl. In response, the Gestapo shot Mr. Ruys and four others on August 15, 1942. He was the first of many who died because of this ship, this ship of death.

-<- ->>

The opening of the Suez Canal in 1869 dramatically altered the nature of maritime communications between Europe and Asia, with traditional colonial powers England, France, and the Netherlands relishing shorter transit times to their overseas possessions. Two Dutch shipping companies, Nederland and Rotterdam Lloyd, capitalized on the new route east. Both flourished by transporting passengers, mail, and cargo between the Netherlands and the Dutch East Indies. That success continued through the late 1930s.

In 1938, Nederland commissioned the construction of a new 20,000-ton ship, *Oranje*, to upgrade its quality of ocean liner service. Her maiden voyage on the East India route in 1939 was successful enough to prompt Rotterdam Lloyd to order a new ship to compete with *Oranje*. The shipyard referred to the new vessel as "Number 214," although Rotterdam Lloyd planned to name it *Ardjoeno* upon completion. The construction schedule called for launching in the spring of 1940 and the ship's first voyage to Batavia (now Djakarta) during the summer of 1941. World War II interrupted construction of the new ship and, if one believes the centuries of stories about jinxed and bad-luck ships, the violence of those years of war might have started a curse.

The Dutch attempted to protect the unfinished vessel by constructing masonry walls around the keel blocks, spreading sand over the deck plating, and sealing openings in the hull. While these measures largely protected the hull from Allied bombing during Germany's occupation, another threat emerged from the Nazis—they ordered the shipyard to resume construction in summer and fall of 1941. Should the Dutch continue to protect a ship that Germany intended to take?

The Dutch chose to work slowly and occasionally sabotage associated work to prohibit a launch. Despite the slowdown, workers installed four of eight diesel engines and her evaporators (machines that distill drinking water from the sea). As the German Army withdrew from Holland, it attempted to demolish the partially built ship, but the resistance defused the explosives at the last minute.

After Allied armies liberated Vlissingen, the ship's evaporators provided potable water to the city, and her generators, electricity. In recognition of this help and other contributions during the war, Queen Wilhelmina of the Netherlands granted the prefix "Royal" to Rotterdam Lloyd—Koninklije Rotterdamsche Lloyd.

Many ship enthusiasts and historians have cited the *Willem Ruys*'s unusual construction yet eventual completion as the basis for calling it a survivor, a ship fated to be favored, rather than a "hoodoo," or jinxed ship. The two competing reputations would continue through the ship's life.

At 21,118 tons, *Willem Ruys* was slightly larger than her competitor *Oranje*. She measured 631 feet long, with an eighty-two foot beam, and a cruising speed of 22 knots. She had 840 berths in First through Fourth Class, with a crew of 456 Europeans, Indonesians, and Chinese.

"Rotterdam Lloyd designed *Willem Ruys* specifically to be a Dutch East Indies mail ship," said Peter Kohler, a writer and keen student of passenger ships. "Her eight engines gave her the speed to cut the normal four week trip to Djakarta to three, plus her endurance permitted a non-stop trip." Kohler also said that the diesel engines were cheaper to operate than steam over these long voyages. The shape of her hull—wider at the waterline that at the main deck—allowed for generous machinery spaces, yet reduced her displacement. Since Suez Canal fees were based on displacement (weight), the operator could reduce toll expenses. Also, *Willem Ruys* accommodated Third and Fourth Class passengers, usually Indonesian nationals.

In recognition of the hot weather on most of the trip, the shipyard installed air conditioning in many of the First Class spaces. Designers provided several levels of covered decks so passengers could catch the breeze, yet stay out of the tropical sun.

Willem Ruys departed Rotterdam on December 2, 1947, on her maiden voyage to Batavia with 779 passengers. After transiting the Suez Canal on December 11 and stopping in Singapore on December 22, she arrived at Tandjong-Priok, Batavia's port, on Christmas Eve. *Willem Ruys* made the return trip January 3–23, 1948.

Competition between *Oranje* and *Willem Ruys* reached an uncomfortable level in 1953 when the two collided in the Red Sea. Maneuvering close aboard while passing at a combined speed of forty knots, *Oranje* lost part of her bow when she struck *Willem Ruys*, damaging several lifeboats on board her rival. Although both continued under their own power, a court of inquiry faulted the *Oranje* captain for trying to give his passengers too close a look at their counterparts on *Willem Ruys*. No one was injured.

In recognition of the demise of the Indonesian route, Nederland and Rotterdam joined forces to create a cooperative, round-the-world service using *Willem Ruys, Oranje,* and a third ship. During a 1958–59 refit, shipyard workers increased the number of berths on board *Willem Ruys,* upgraded furnishings, and added more air conditioning. Rotterdam Lloyd replaced the Javanese members of the crew with Europeans.

As air travel lured passengers from ocean liners and financial woes continued, Rotterdam Lloyd sold *Willem Ruys* in January 1964 to Flotta Lauro, a Naples shipping line. Lauro accepted the ship on January 5, 1965.

Achille Lauro, a former mayor of Naples, owned Lauro Lines. Lauro had considered building two new passenger ships, but instead bought both *Willem Ruys* and *Oranje.* He named the first after himself, the second, *Angelina Lauro,* in honor of his daughter. He sent *Achille Lauro* to a Palermo shipyard for overhaul and conversion, and *Angelina Lauro* to Genoa for similar work.

In the 1960s, Lauro owned fifty-nine ships, almost thirteen percent of the Italian merchant fleet. His father, Gioacchino Lauro, formed the family shipping business in 1927 and it prospered, with some downturns, until World War II. All but five of Lauro's ships, however, were lost during the war, but Achille Lauro rebuilt the line.

After buying both Dutch ships for $7 million, Lauro ordered upgrades totaling $22 million for both ships. Lauro wanted to compete in the deluxe category with other Italian ships such as the *Michaelangelo* and *Leonardo da Vinci.* He commissioned art and sculptures, installed extensive carpeting, air conditioning for all cabins, and verandas for the first class cabins.

While in dry dock in 1965, *Achille Lauro* suffered an explosion and fire, severely damaging the interior of the ship and extending the conversion by six months. Although shipboard fires are common during overhauls, the damage might have been more proof that the ship was jinxed. Change the name and change the flag, but the cursed fate remained.

Lauro also created berths for more passengers, mostly in tourist and immigrant classes. *Achille Lauro* gained enough accommodations to transport over 1,800 passengers, but only 152 in First Class. The shipyard extended the rake of her bow, thus streamlining her silhouette, added height to her two funnels, and increased her displacement to

23,629 tons. According to Peter Kohler, Lauro had the hull painted blue in recognition of Italy's national color.

From 1966 to 1972, *Achille Lauro* primarily carried European immigrants to Australia. During the 1967 Arab-Israeli War, she diverted from her normal Suez Canal route and steamed the long way to Down Under. Lauro Lines cancelled her scheduled cruises for July and August 1972, sending *Achille Lauro* into overhaul in May of that year. Fire struck the ship again in dry dock, resulting in five months of repair before her next sailing. Was this further evidence of poor safety precautions in Italian shipyards, or just a jinx?

Achille Lauro collided with *Yousset*, a Lebanese cattle carrier on April 28, 1975, in the Dardanelles, the narrow waterway between the Mediterranean and Black Seas. The small freighter sank with the loss of one life. *Achille Lauro* suffered minor damage.

In 1980, a South African travel company began annual winter charters of *Achille Lauro*. The cruise ship carried tourists from Southampton to Cape Town, and back. On one of those trips, in 1981, fire broke out in a bar and adjacent theater. One passenger jumped overboard in a panic and was lost at sea. Her husband, hearing the news, collapsed and died from a heart attack. Is this ship a lucky survivor, or a cursed devil of the seas?

Severe financial difficulties beset the Lauro Line in 1982, with creditors impounding nine of the company's twenty-two ships. Officials in Tenerife, Canary Islands, prohibited *Achille Lauro* from sailing, but the Italian government intervened eventually on behalf of the struggling shipping line. After months in Tenerife, *Achille Lauro* steamed empty back to Genoa where she was laid up for eighteen months beginning in January 1983. Negotiations between Lauro, its creditors, and the Italian government yielded a 1984 agreement in which Italy gained ownership of the cruise ship. Italy then leased *Achille Lauro* to Chandris Lines.

In late 1984, the "Great Blue Ship" began a series of eleven-day cruises in the Eastern Mediterranean, including the one Leon and Marilyn Klinghoffer booked for October 1985.

The *Achille Lauro* hijacking surprised the cruise industry. Not since 1961 had armed men seized control of a passenger ship, despite repeated aircraft hijackings through the 1970s and 80s, and the heightened security attendant to that violent trend. But the *Achille Lauro* incident prompted immediate attention to maritime security measures and legislation aimed at prosecuting terrorists, apparently successful steps since there have been no subsequent ship hijackings.

By 1985, the lesson of the Portuguese passenger liner *Santa Maria* had been lost on the cruise trade. In January 1961, Henrique Galvao and twenty-four men hijacked the ship after it departed La Guaria, Venezuela, reportedly to protest the governments of Spain and Portugal. The hijackers later surrendered without incident and the ship returned to Recife, Brazil.

Since the hijackers did not kill anyone, and CNN was not around to thrust a microphone in front of a former hostage, the *Santa Maria* incident had no effect on the maritime tourist environment. Klinghoffer's death, however, dramatically changed the scene.

According to travel industry spokesmen, the 1985 hijacking caused a "significant" number of passengers to cancel reservations for Middle East and Mediterranean cruises. Sea Goddess Cruise Line pulled out of the eastern Mediterranean, while Royal Viking cancelled seven of their ten cruises scheduled for 1986. Princess Cruises eliminated all of their spring and summer Mediterranean trips. For the rest of 1985, *Achille Lauro* changed her route, substituting Spanish, Portuguese, and Moroccan ports for those in Egypt and Israel. Further afield, Holland America decided to end its world cruises, citing fear of terrorism.

The 1985 *Achille Lauro* incident, coupled with the TWA airliner hijacking and fatal attacks at the Rome and Vienna airports that same year, altered tourism throughout Europe and the Middle East. Travel industry representatives said that almost half of U.S. travel agents reported clients cancelling trips or changing destinations after the 1985 terrorist incidents. Eight-hundred and fifty thousand Americans cancelled international trips after the TWA hijacking alone. Israel reported a 47 percent drop in tourism after the *Achille Lauro* event and subsequent airport assaults.

Immediately after the *Achille Lauro* incident, cruise lines began widespread use of metal detectors, bomb-sniffing dogs, and most ships banned the traditional pre-sailing, "bon voyage" parties on board ship. The industry began to develop terrorist profiles and reorder all of their security procedures.

In response to the *Achille Lauro* hijacking, the U.S. Congress passed legislation, the Omnibus Diplomatic and Anti-Terrorism Act of 1986, which provided, among other things, Federal jurisdiction over terrorism crimes committed against Americans overseas.

Prior to 1985, no regulatory agency set standards for maritime security the way the International Civil Aviation Organization did for airports. Subsequent to the *Achille Lauro* hijacking, the International Maritime Organization created uniform security guidelines for ships, although the provisions were voluntary.

By the spring of 1986, *Achille Lauro* returned to the eastern Mediterranean, but she ran aground off Alexandria, Egypt. On April 6, while an Egyptian pilot attempted to bring the ship into port, *Achille Lauro* grounded on a sand bar adjacent to the channel approaching Alexandria. None of the 940 passengers and crew was injured, and the crew, with the help of a rising tide, maneuvered the ship into deeper water within six hours. The *Associated Press* reported the incident, one that normally would have escaped notice, probably because anything that happened to *Achille Lauro* after 1985 became news.

Another incident brought the ship into the spotlight in July 1994. An Italian neo-fascist political party, the National Alliance, chartered *Achille Lauro* to take Alliance members, supporters, and Italian army veterans on a twelve-day tour of World War II battlefields along the North African littoral.

In an extraordinary confluence of ironies, a ship seized by Nazi Germany and a symbol of Middle Eastern anti-Semitism, carried passengers aligned with Italy's fascist past.

Gianfranco Fini, the head of the National Alliance, had been trying to separate his group from its roots in Mussolini's party, but the news media seized on the connection between two generations of Jewish opponents. Seeking a more positive spin, Fini threw a bouquet of flowers from *Achille Lauro*'s deck into the sea in Klinghoffer's memory, calling for a moment of silence.

Fire at sea is a mariner's worst fear. *Achille Lauro* had suffered more than most ships, but she met her stiffest challenge in the early hours of Wednesday, November 30, 1994.

The ship departed Genoa on November 19 for a twenty-one day cruise to Durban, South Africa, with intermediate ports of call in

Haifa, Israel; Port Said, Egypt; Mahe, Seychelles; and Port Louis, Mauritius. Five hundred seventy-nine passengers embarked, seeking the warmth of a Southern Hemisphere summer; 404 crewmembers served their every need.

Having passed the Horn of Africa earlier the previous evening, *Achille Lauro* steamed south through the Indian Ocean en route to her next stop in the Seychelles Islands. About 125 miles east of Somalia, she found a calm sea, light winds, and good prospects for a peaceful transit. At 1:30 A.M. many passengers were asleep in their cabins, but others still enjoyed the night's activities. Some danced in tuxedos and gowns as the evening's black-tie ball glided to its end. A few watched the late screening of the movie *Basic Instinct*. Then someone smelled smoke.

"We were alerted when the engines suddenly shut off," said British businessman Tony Webb. "Most people were at the social event, and the captain came on and said we all had to go up on deck because there was a fire."

Few remember hearing an alarm. As crewmembers banged on the doors of cabins, passengers, many clad only in dressing gowns or bedclothes, others in ball gowns, rushed for the open decks. Children screamed and family members clung to each other as smoke billowed up from the engine rooms where the fire started. South African cruise director Nadia Eckhard and her assistants tried to calm passengers and directed traffic on the decks. With passengers from South Africa, Germany, Great Britain, the Netherlands, Italy, and four other countries, language difficulties made matters worse. Below decks, crewmembers fought the blaze, but the fire consumed much of the machinery and pumps needed to control its spread.

"Then there was no water," said Peter Lategan of South Africa. "They were using buckets. The auxiliary pumps were dead. We had no power and no water to fight the fire so they used buckets." "It was so hopeless," said Esme Stratfold from South Africa. "The buckets were so small."

A bucket brigade is no way to fight fire at sea, but Captain Giuseppe Orsi tried, driving his crew through the rest of the night. They could not contain the fire, however, and *Achille Lauro* took on water. As the ship began to list to port (lean or tilt to the left side), he finally issued an SOS at 5:45 A.M. At 7:30 A.M., Orsi ordered the passengers and crew to abandon ship.

The passengers, huddled in knots on deck, more in search of comfort than warmth during the tropical morning, began to move toward their assigned lifeboats. Abandoning a listing ship is a tricky affair, especially when it's on fire. The crew could not lower boats on the starboard side because the ship leaned away from the water, so passengers pressed toward the other side.

"The business about women and children first does not apply in real life, I'm afraid," said Tony Webb's wife Lorraine. The Webbs pushed their way though from their assigned boat on the starboard side to one on the port side. The crew threw life rafts over the side and lowered lifeboats filled with passengers; one jammed on the way down, almost tipping its contents into the sea. "We had to climb up the side of the ship on ladders," said Kathleen Phillips, 67, one of those in the jammed lifeboat. "Then we climbed down a ladder to the life rafts. I don't know how we did it." Two elderly women fell off the rope ladders into the water, but passengers in life rafts plucked them from the sea.

One of the life rafts thrown from the ship hit British passenger Arthur Morris, 66, in the head as he sat in a lifeboat alongside the ship. "He was put in my life raft, but died three hours later," said Lategan. "We couldn't get a doctor. He died in his wife's lap." Another man, 68-year-old German Gerhard Szimke, died of a heart attack during the evacuation.

Several ships in the area responded to *Achille Lauro*'s distress call. The tanker *Hawaiian King* arrived first at 9:20 A.M., followed shortly by the bulk carrier *Bar Du*. Throughout the day passengers and crewmembers made their way in lifeboats and life rafts to the two ships, and up accommodation ladders to the relative safety of their decks. Everyone was accounted for, save a missing elderly man. As other ships closed to render assistance, over 900 persons spent the night on the open deck of the *Hawaiian King*.

U.S. Navy ships USS *Gettysburg* and USS *Halyburton* heard the SOS, but were 300 miles away. Changing course immediately, the ships made best speed to the burning *Achille Lauro*. During the night of November 30–December 1, the ships launched two helicopters that arrived on scene during the night, dropping medicines and supplies to the exhausted survivors. *Achille Lauro* continued to burn.

"The whole half of the ship is fully engulfed by flames," reported one of the Navy pilots. Nearby, Dinitrios Skapinkais, captain of another rescue vessel, tanker *Treasure Island*, reported his observations to an Italian news agency. "The *Achille Lauro* is listing by at least 40 degrees [almost half way over], and you can still see smoke and flames. The passenger decks on the stern are burning . . . I believe it will sink in the next 12 hours."

By the morning of Thursday, December 1, Captain Pete Smith, commanding officer of *Gettysburg*, organized the transfer of survivors from *Hawaiian King* and *Bar Du* to eight merchant vessels that had gathered to help, as well as the two Navy ships. During a ten-hour operation, small boats dispersed the survivors onto ships that agreed to take the passengers to the nearest ports. Five ships headed for Djibouti in the Gulf of Aden, while five steamed for Mombassa, Kenya. "Many had tears of relief" as they came aboard, said Captain Smith. Sailors gave them clothes to wear, food, and a hot shower.

Finally on their way to safety, many passengers spoke about their experiences. Some credited tour director Nadia Eckhard for saving their lives, others praised the crew. "The crew were absolutely marvelous," said British passenger Allison Panne. Yet another, German Hille Sieckmann, criticized Captain Orsi, "The captain did not keep his crew in line, he never showed his face, he never gave us a message." Later, after other passengers told of being shoved aside by crewmembers intent on getting into lifeboats, the Italian government initiated an inquiry into the crew's behavior.

Achille Lauro, meanwhile, burned on. On Friday, December 2, a salvage tug took the ship under tow, beginning a slow transit west in hopes of getting the hulk to port for either repairs or scrapping. A scant few hours later, an explosion near the bow shook the aged lady and, within minutes, she slipped below the waves of the Indian Ocean.

The events of her final day seemed to echo *Achille Lauro*'s early life as the Netherlands ship *Willem Ruys*. The tug belonged to a Dutch salvage company. An elderly woman, Evernentia Spiekermann, 74, died on board one of the merchant ships ferrying survivors to Mombassa. She was Dutch. One man was never accounted for during the evacuation of the ship and presumably died on board. He was Dutch. He was joined in a watery grave by the body of the passenger who died of a heart attack while abandoning ship—German Gerhard Szimke, who lived through the horrors of World War II.

Finally, the intense fires scorched the vivid blue paint of her hull, with the blackened steel resembling the original paint scheme of *Willem Ruys*.

Upon his return to Italy, Captain Orsi became the subject of several investigations, some of which were still ongoing in the summer of 2003. According to a Naples prosecutor, Federico Cafiero De Raho, a special commission found Orsi negligent regarding the fire, but exonerated him of charges related to the abandonment by the crew and passengers. De Raho told me that a safety inspection of the ship before it departed Genoa found the engine rooms to be dangerously dirty, with fuel and oil leaks creating potentially hazardous conditions. The Italian Coast Guard ordered Orsi to post crewmembers continuously in the normally unmanned engine rooms because of the conditions. The inquiry determined that Orsi did not comply and when the fire started, there were no crewmen present to either combat the fire or promptly sound an alarm.

The sinking of *Achille Lauro* put an end to the debate whether she was a survivor or a jinxed ship. The editorial board at the *Boston Globe* wrote the following about the ship of death:

"We say good riddance. Let there be no salvage of this ship of hell. Let the *Achille Lauro* put no more passengers in peril at sea."

CHAPTER

9

Terrorist Turned Politician (1996–1999)

MY face is not the face of a professional killer, is it?"

This rhetorical question, however disingenuous, was part of Abu Abbas's attempt to remake his image in the eyes of the Western news media during the second half of the 1990s. He entered the decade hurling polemics at the United States during the 1991 Persian Gulf War, but was trying to sell himself as a man of peace and just another Palestinian politician by 1996.

He came to this opportunity to claim that he was changing his spots through provisions of the 1993 Oslo peace accords between the PLO and Israel, and the subsequent 1995 Interim Agreement (Oslo II). Article XVI of the Interim Agreement read: "Palestinians from abroad whose entry into the West Bank and the Gaza Strip is approved pursuant to this Agreement, and to whom the provisions of this Article are applicable, will not be prosecuted for offenses committed prior to September 13, 1993."

Was this intelligent, Mideast Machiavelli, a man who simultaneously undercut and supported Yasser Arafat, telling the truth? Or was he simply expanding his web of lies, half-truths, and exaggerations?

Youssef Majed Molqi, the Palestinian who shot Leon Klinghoffer, walked away from his thirty-year prison sentence on February 28, 1996, after serving less than ten years. He disappeared while enjoying a twelve-day furlough from Rebbibia prison in Rome at a church-run shelter. He became the third of the four *Achille Lauro* hijackers to escape.

The prison granted Molqi four previous two-week passes before he disappeared. At the time of his escape, Rebbibia warden Maurizio Barbera considered Molqi a model prisoner. "I'm surprised," Barbera said. "He behaved very well here. He left and came back for years." This was a change for Molqi, who started a hunger strike on the first anniversary of the hijacking to protest prison conditions.

All fronts reacted quickly to Molqi's escape. U.S. ambassador to Rome Reginald Bartholomew called on Italian Prime Minister Lamberto Dini to voice his government's concern, an action reminiscent of the first Italian-American flap over the hijackers. President Bill Clinton's administration called for a widespread manhunt and State Department spokesman Nicholas Burns characterized Molqi's furlough as inexplicable. The Italian government, however, reacted initially with less enthusiasm.

"In Italy, after a certain prison term, people are allowed out on parole," said Foreign Minister Susanna Agnelli, defending the furlough program. Another government official shrugged, saying Molqi "is probably quite far from Italy by now." The attentive Klinghoffer daughters reacted, as well.

"The Italian government has to take responsibility," Lisa said. "The message given by your country is clear: If you are a terrorist and you want to kill Americans with impunity, Italy is the right place."

Several days after Molqi's disappearance, the Italian government began to take the matter more seriously, perhaps in response to the U.S. reaction. Dini, meeting with Italian intelligence officials, said, "We want to see clearly what happened." The Rome magistrate's office launched an investigation.

On March 13, Italy offered a reward of an unspecified amount—substantial, one Italian official said—while the United States declared the depth of its concern by offering $2 million for information leading to the apprehension of the missing Palestinian. The State Department also offered to protect any informants willing to come forward by resettling them and their families in America.

Pressures on the Italian government increased, also reminiscent of the 1985 brouhaha. The Jewish Anti-Defamation League voiced its criticism of Italy's "abysmal" record of penalizing the hijackers. The League and the Klinghoffers sent a joint letter to the Italian government.

The European Union criticized Italy for the incident, with some countries reportedly claiming Italy's approach to the terrorists undermined Union credibility as it attempted to take a stronger stand against terrorism. Prime Minister Dini acknowledged that the incident weakened his country's diplomatic stature. Dini, a caretaker prime minister caught between governments, as Bettino Craxi had been eleven years earlier, struggled to prepare for scheduled parliamentary elections in April.

"It is something . . . very civilized and advanced," Justice Minister Vincenzo Caianiello said, defending the furlough law. "In the United States, they look only at punishment and repression." An Italian legislator named Mario Gozzini pushed through reforms of the prison system in 1986, changes that rewarded good behavior with early release. Brief holidays out of prison were also part of the new regulations, which Gozzini claimed helped reduce prison violence.

To the relief of all, Italy recaptured Molqi on March 22, three weeks after he escaped. Spanish national police, in a joint operation with Italy, arrested Molqi in Estepona, a resort on the Costa del Sol. Traveling on a false Italian passport, which he reportedly bought on the black market, the unarmed Molqi surrendered peacefully. The Spaniards found Molqi through an intercepted phone call he made on March 16 from Seville to a woman in Prato, a town near Florence, Italy.

"For us," Italian police chief Fernando Masone said, "it was the end of a huge nightmare." Perhaps in response to U.S. sensitivities in the case, Dini called Ambassador Bartholomew directly with the news of the arrest. While Italy requested Spanish extradition of Molqi, the U.S. government began investigating how it might convince Spain to surrender Molqi to the U.S. justice system.

Ilsa Klinghoffer, traveling with her family in Italy after Molqi's escape, took advantage of her chance presence to urge the Italian government to redouble its efforts to not only extradite Molqi, but also pursue Abbas more aggressively. She met with several officials, later saying, "I was impressed by Italy's commitment and apparent close cooperation with the U.S. in fighting terrorism."

Spain did accede to Italy's request, transferring Molqi under tight security back to Rome on December 4, 1996. Italian Ministry of Justice officials said that Molqi must serve his complete sentence without parole at a maximum-security prison built to house Mafia criminals. According to his sentence, he will be released in 2016.

Defenders of the "Gozzini law," as Italians call the prison reform legislation, maintained that only one percent of prisoners remain at large after a furlough. Yet seventy-five percent of the *Achille Lauro* hijackers escaped. Did the Italian government, which valued good relations with the PLO and Middle Eastern Arab countries, give the hijackers opportunities to escape? Perhaps so, if you are to believe Youssef Majed Molqi. Upon his return to prison, Molqi told his lawyer, who later told the news media, that the Italian secret police helped him escape.

Yasser Arafat, Israeli Prime Minister Yitzhak Rabin, and Israeli Foreign Minister Shimon Peres shared the 1995 Nobel Peace prize for their efforts to seek peace between Israel and the PLO. Part of their historic agreement allowed a new Palestinian Authority to administer Gaza and parts of the West Bank. Progress toward the creation of an autonomous Palestinian state bogged down, however, in 1996 when Israel demanded that the PLO remove all references to the destruction of Israel from the PLO charter. In April, Arafat convened a meeting of the Palestine National Council in Gaza to consider the Israeli position.

Taking advantage of the Israeli promise to allow Palestinians to enter Gaza with immunity, dozens of self-professed freedom fighters, all previously on Israel's Most Wanted list, arrived to participate in the meeting. Leila Kalid, who hijacked El Al aircraft in the 1970s, was there. The fact that Mamdouh Nofel killed twenty-seven Israeli schoolchildren in 1974 did not keep him from attending. Abu Daoud, reportedly one of the organizers of the 1972 Munich Olympics massacre, appeared. Abu Abbas traveled from Baghdad for the meeting, joining others in posing for photographs and presumably swapping stories of past military operations.

"We were pals," Abbas told reporters. "We were like members of a football team."

There was a general feeling of reconciliation with Israel among the delegates. Some even talked of mistaken tactics for regaining their homeland. "We tried the way of blood, the way of Katyushas [rockets], the way of stone-throwing in the streets, and I think both sides now realize that was the wrong way," said Nofel. Abbas repeated his contention that the *Achille Lauro* hijacking was a mistake. Saleh Tamari, a council member from Bethlehem criticized Abbas, Nofel, and others, saying that their tactics caused the PLO to be "identified with groups like the Japanese Red Army and Carlos the Jackal."

The National Council voted overwhelmingly on April 24, 1996, to revoke clauses in the PLO charter that called for the annihilation of Israel.

While in Gaza and perhaps to reinforce his self-professed transformation from hijacker to peaceful politician, Abbas invited Associated Press reporter Ibrahim Barzak to a meeting on the eleventh floor apartment in a luxury Gaza City high-rise.

"The killing of the passenger was a mistake. . . . We are sorry," Abbas said. "We didn't plan at all to hijack the ship. The hijacking was a mistake, and there were no orders to kill civilians." Abbas had by now repeated his public version of the operation so many times that it must have seemed truthful to Barzak. What was missing from the interview, however, was Abbas's wise guy attitude that accompanied the "swim for it" remark in 1988.

Regarding peace with Israel, Abbas drew on phrases from the National Council deliberations that week. "We must open a new page in the relations" with Israel. "We choose the road of peace." His statements were in sharp contrast to his opposition to the 1993 PLO peace agreement with Israel.

Abu Abbas appeared to be dedicated to peace, not more violence. But his new attitude didn't sway the Klinghoffer sisters. Hearing reports that Abu Abbas was moving freely about the Gaza Strip, they quickly worked to have him arrested. New York Republican Alfonse D'Amato immediately introduced a resolution in the U.S. Senate calling for the U.S. Justice Department to seek Abbas's arrest and extradition. The Senate approved the resolution on April 30 by a vote of 99-0.

Some may view it a subtle distinction, but there were some serious killers at the Palestine National Council meeting, terrorists who had killed hundreds. But the U.S. Senate focused on one man whose organization had killed about two innocent persons between 1985 and 1996, Abu Abbas.

President Clinton met with Yasser Arafat on May 1 while the issue of Abu Abbas's status swirled about Washington, DC. During a brief session with the news media before the two men commenced their meeting, a reporter asked about Abbas's status.

REPORTER: Mr. President, 99 senators asked for you, and for Chairman Arafat, to authorize the extradition of Abu Abbas, the mastermind of the *Achille Lauro* hijacking. Will you ask the Justice Department to issue an extradition request? And Chairman Arafat, would you honor such a request if it came from the United States?

CHAIRMAN ARAFAT: We should not forget that Abu Abbas came and attended the Palestine National Council and voted to change the Covenant of the PLO and support the peace process.

President Clinton did not respond, as expected. He put a lot of his political capital on the line to broker a Middle East peace agreement. He had more to worry about than Abu Abbas. Pursuing Abbas did not fit into any of his political goals. The next President would have a different agenda.

Although the United States had no active arrest warrant for Abbas, a prerequisite to any extradition request, the Justice Department contacted the Palestinian Authority. That body quickly spurned the U.S. inquiry. "What is attributed to Abu Abbas could be said of all the Palestinian leadership—including Arafat," said Freih Abu Medein, the Authority's Justice Minister.

With the help of the Anti-Defamation League, the Klinghoffers asked the U.S. government to request Italy to apprehend him. Nothing came of that request. Italy had no reason to pursue the man at this point. It had its share of politically unpalatable dealings with Abbas eleven years earlier.

With apparent tacit approval from Israel, Abbas remained in Gaza for a while after the National Council vote. During that time, CNN reported that Abbas regularly consulted with Palestinian Authority officials, had lunch with politicians, and made himself seen about Gaza.

"If they want to make peace, they must allow me to come here," Abbas told CNN, referring to Israel. "If they don't allow me to come here, that means they don't want us to share peace . . . that means they speak to us: go and fight." Regarding his status, Abbas said, "It is true that a large percentage of the Western World hopes that I am imprisoned or dead. But all my people, the Palestinians and the Arabs, wish me a long life and freedom."

Abu Abbas returned to Baghdad in late spring of 1996, remaining out of public view for two years. During that period, the Israelis and the new Palestinian Authority established a relative degree of peace. The PA began organizing governmental services in Gaza and the West Bank and violence with remaining Israeli occupying forces decreased.

In April 1998, Abbas returned to Gaza. At a public rally to celebrate the anniversary of the founding of his PLF, 5,000 Palestinians cheered Abu Abbas. Politicians spoke to the crowd, praising Abu Abbas's contributions to the cause, and all those in attendance appeared to view the man as the epitome of armed Palestinian struggle for recognition.

Abbas entered Gaza through an Israeli checkpoint on the Egyptian border. Officials held him there for five hours while they consulted with the highest levels of the Israeli government.

Criticism of the government's decision within Israel was immediate, despite the provisions of the 1995 Interim Agreement and Abbas's 1996 attendance at the Palestine National Council meeting. David Bar-Illan, senior advisor to Prime Minister Benjamin Netanyahu, responded to critics by pointing to the 1996 precedent.

"I'm as puzzled by it as anybody," said Bar-Illan, referring to the strange twists in the peace process. "It's very difficult to rationalize. But we have to live by it. The political process sometimes overrides the theory on terrorism. It is quite difficult, admittedly."

Three Jewish activists quickly petitioned the Israeli High Court, requesting the arrest of Abbas and extradition to the United States. The Court referred the suit to lower panel for review. Israeli Ron Tarassian and two New Yorkers, Rabbi Avi Weiss, and state assemblyman Dov Hikind, pressed the legal action, arguing that Israeli law permits the arrest of anyone who harms a Jew in an anti-Semitic act. Tarassian called the Israeli decision to permit Abbas's entry despicable, and said that he was trying to form a private SWAT team to abduct Abbas.

"It is important that the government of Italy demonstrate that Mr. Abbas will not escape punishment for his outrageous act," the Anti-Defamation League and the Klinghoffer sisters wrote in a letter to Italy's ambassador to the United States. They asked Italy to "pursue all means available to bring this convicted terrorist to justice."

"My clients are deeply upset. . . . Any force of law that can bring him to justice should be carried out," said Jay Fischer, the Klinghoffer family lawyer.

The Jewish lobby showed its muscle again when the U.S. House of Representatives passed a non-binding resolution by a vote of 406 to 0, asking that Yasser Arafat seize and hand over Abbas and the PLF leadership to the United States for prosecution. Across town at the State Department, spokesman James Rubin gave his view of Abbas's status.

"Well, let me say that the United States strongly believes that Abu Abbas should be punished for the crimes committed on board the *Achille Lauro* in 1985. Abbas was tried in absentia in Italy in 1986, found guilty, and sentenced to life in prison. There are no charges pending against Abu Abbas in the United States. The statue of limitations has long since run out."

True to his form, Abbas took advantage of the controversy by speaking with the news media.

"Twenty years ago, I couldn't even pronounce the word Israel," he told Carol Morello, who interviewed Abbas for *USA Today* in May 1998. "They were the enemy. The Zionists. Now, peace is needed here."

Morello wrote that Abbas offered no remorse for his acts of terrorism, even joking about his past. In contrast, however, the reporter noted a tone of apology in his voice when Abbas spoke of Klinghoffer's death. "I didn't give a decision to kill that person. I didn't know he was handicapped. If I had been there, I would have seen he didn't get hurt. We were sorry this person was killed on the ship."

Abbas then entertained Julian Borger of Britain's *Guardian*. "Klinghoffer was not in our plans," Abbas said, staying with the "accident" line. "We didn't know him." Abbas said that one of the hijackers told him that the invalid American tried to organize a passenger revolt against the four Palestinians. "But I cannot defend what they did," Abbas said of the killing.

In his chat with Borger, Abbas explained the reasoning behind his unique hang glider attacks on Israel in 1979 and 1987.

"I was trying to work out how we could get into Israel from Lebanon across one very deep valley that was full of mines. One evening at that time, I was watching television and there was cigarette advertisement with people flying on hang gliders. That's how I thought of it."

Abbas said that he sent a PLF member to the UK to learn hang gliding, returning with a British instructor. The two then trained others to fly. Abbas kept the Brit in the dark about the purpose of the training. "He only found out later. I telephoned him to apologise." Again, Abbas claimed that his efforts, however fruitless and bloody, were worthwhile.

"Before, people in the rest of the world didn't know about Palestinians. Afterwards, they may have taken a negative position, but they knew about the problem."

Charles Sennott from the *Boston Globe* was next. Abbas told the reporter that he had remained free to that point by avoiding U.S. and Israeli security forces, moving frequently and wearing disguises.

"When America wants you, the whole world is part of the hunt," Abbas said. When asked, as always, about Klinghoffer, Abbas turned testy. "You Americans never forget, do you? You always want to ask about the man in the wheelchair."

"Look, we feel very sorry of all that happened on the ship," Abbas continued. "We know how hard and painful it is when someone is killed who is not related to the conflict. We have seen it happen to thousands . . . and the world never apologized to us. We hope one day the world hears our cries as loud as it heard Klinghoffer's."

Regarding peace with Israel, Abbas said that the chances for peace were diminishing at the time of the interview, June 1998. The diminution, according Abbas, meant that violence could again be an option. "If peace fails, all options are open."

"Abbas is spitting in America's face," said Morton A. Klein, president of the Zionist Organization of America. His group is the oldest, and one of the largest, pro-Israel organizations in the United States. "He masterminded the murder of an elderly, wheelchair-bound American, yet he is living comfortably in Arafat's territory and giving interviews in which he blames Klinghoffer for 'provoking' his own murder, attacks Jews and defends America's enemy, Iraq."

President Clinton traveled to the Middle East in December 1998, addressing the Palestine National Council on one of his stops. By that time, Abbas had returned to Baghdad. His spokesman said that the PLF leader would not be able to return to Gaza in time for the historic meeting. If nothing else, Abbas knew when to surface and when to lie low.

Israel's High Court ruled in October 1999, that Abu Abbas was immune from trial in Israel for the murder of Leon Klinghoffer. Even in Israel, the politics of peace were more important than bringing a killer of Jews to the bar of justice.

Federal and state investigators failed to uncover any new leads in the Odeh case during the mid-1990s. After a period of apparent inactivity, the Justice Department announced in August 1996 that the U.S. government was offering a million-dollar reward for information leading to the arrest of Odeh's killer.

A Justice Department spokesman said that such payments had been authorized by new Federal legislation signed by President Clinton the previous April. Cynics, however, suggested that the move was an election-year concession to the Arab-American community. Additionally, the Southern California Arab-American community continued to offer a separate $100,000 reward.

Unidentified vandals threw red paint on Odeh's statue in October 1996 and again the following February.

"For some group of people to try and dehumanize and smear our icons, such as Alex's statue, means a great deal: that they don't believe in the ideals of the United States and living in harmony," said Michael Sheadeh, a spokesman for the ADC. Rabbi Rachlis, who spoke at the statue's unveiling, said that if the vandalism "was political, [Odeh's relatives] and I have a common enemy."

"I just wish everyone would let him rest in peace," cried Odeh's widow Norma, holding her daughter Samya's hand in front of the statue.

When asked later about who might have defaced his brother's statue, Sami Odeh told me that only one person objected to the statue before the City Council, someone who was associated with the Jewish Defense League and Irv Rubin.

Shortly before her death, Marilyn Klinghoffer filed suit in the U.S. District Court, Southern District of New York, against the Port of Genoa, Italy, Crown Travel, Lauro Lines, Chandris Cruise Lines, and the PLO. The suit asked for $1.9 billion in damages. About the same time, two other *Achille Lauro* hostages, Sophia Chasser and Anna Schneider, both of Florida, each sued the two shipping lines and Crown for a total of $200 million. These suits started a chain of legal actions that would last for over a decade.

The Klinghoffer suit, carried on by the estates of Leon and Marilyn after her death, charged the shiplines and Genoa with negligence for not providing adequate security when the passengers boarded. It also claimed all defendants were liable for Leon's death and the terror inflicted upon him before he died. Crown Travel, doing business as Club ABC Tours, was charged with negligence and failure to bring to the Klinghoffer's attention the terms and conditions on the back of the cruise tickets. Those terms limited any liability for incidents to $10,000 and specified that any legal action must originate in Naples, Italy.

In May 1986, Chandris, which was marketing *Achille Lauro* cruises but not operating the ship, asked for dismissal of the two suits. Lauro Lines, which ran the ship, joined Chandris in denying any liability for the hijacking. Both also cited the passenger contract that limited liability and identified Naples as the proper court venue. Chandris also stated that the hijacking was a result of "unforeseeable, hostile, war-like acts" by others and claimed that third party defendants—the Port of Genoa, the Republic of Italy, and the PLO—should bear responsibility for the hijacking. The attorney for Crown/ABC, Rodney Gould, said at the time that the plaintiffs should sue a "culpable defendant," referring to the PLO, "not an innocent one."

As a follow-up to Gould's claim, Club ABC filed a lawsuit against the PLO, also in the U.S. District Court in Manhattan, holding the Palestinian entity responsible for the incident and subsequent business losses incurred by Club ABC as a result. The suit charged the PLO "conceived, conspired, organized, authorized and directed its agents . . . maliciously to seize by force" the ship and murder Leon Klinghoffer. Club ABC wanted the PLO to indemnify the travel agency for any damages it might incur through the lawsuits of Klinghoffer and others.

Former U.S. Attorney General Ramsey Clark, a liberal "movement lawyer" who defended many an unpopular client during his career outside the government, served as the PLO lawyer during these cases. In March 1987 the Jewish Federation Council of Greater Los Angeles cancelled Ramsey's scheduled appearance at the group's fund-raising dinner because of his defense of the PLO.

In response to Lauro Lines's claim that Naples was the proper forum for the Chasser lawsuit, U.S. District Court Judge Louis L. Stanton ruled that the wording on the back of the tickets was insufficient warning to the passengers. The forum selection clause, which essentially told passengers that they were waiving their right to sue outside Naples, was printed in letters only one-sixteenth of an inch high. Lauro Lines appealed that ruling all the way to the U.S. Supreme Court.

The Supreme Court sided against Lauro Lines on a technicality in May 1989. The court ruled that the issue of the proper forum could only be appealed after Judge Stanton conducted the trial. In other words, Lauro Lines' appeal was premature. The practical impact of the court's decision, however, was that the suit could continue in a U.S. court.

In a key development in June 1990, Judge Stanton combined multiple suits against the PLO. The consolidated action included the original Klinghoffer suit, Club ABC's third party complaint, and others. Despite Clark's assertion that Stanton did not have jurisdiction and the PLO was an unincorporated institution that could not be sued, the judge ruled that the combined action could proceed. He cited the PLO's New York activity as the basis for his decision. The PLO owned the building that housed its offices, had a telephone listing and bank account, and employed a permanent staff. Stanton also asserted that the PLO was not a member of the United Nations and could not benefit from diplomatic immunity. Jay Fischer, the Klinghoffer lawyer, praised Stanton's ruling, saying that it will "do much to relieve the agony of the Klinghoffer family and send a clear signal to the PLO and similar organizations that terrorist activity will not go unchallenged."

"Our lawyer called [and] said, 'I just wanted to let you girls know we won,'" Lisa said of Fischer's phone call after Stanton's decision. "That's all he said. We sat there with our mouths opened. You don't know how these things are going to turn out."

"It's beyond what most people would try," said Ilsa at the time. "People said to us, 'What? Sue the PLO? Are you crazy?'"

In 1993, Stanton ruled that the Klinghoffer estate could not sue Chandris Lines, but could press ahead with action against the PLO. The central issue in the PLO case, the subject of a series of appeals, reversals, and higher court rulings that occurred between 1990 and 1994, was the PLO's susceptibility to lawsuits in a U.S. court. A key ruling during this period was that the PLO did not meet the requirements of statehood needed to make it immune from lawsuits under federal laws in force then. Once all of the appeals were exhausted and

Stanton's jurisdiction was validated, the discovery process started, in which attorneys for all concerned shared information regarding the one, combined lawsuit against the PLO.

Complete discovery hinged on a March 1994 Stanton order to Yasser Arafat to give a deposition on his role in the hijacking. PLO officials agreed on several occasions in 1994 and 1995 to scheduling the time and place for the deposition, but backed out each time. Exasperated, Stanton ruled on November 12, 1995, that Arafat would be held liable for hijacking damages unless he complied by January 15, 1996.

"They've ignored all sorts of other deadlines," said Craig Harwood, a lawyer for Crown Travel, voicing his skepticism about Arafat's adherence to the ultimatum.

Rodney Gould, the lead lawyer for Crown, traveled with others to Gaza in December 1995 to take Arafat's deposition. Upon arrival, Gould told me later, he learned that the Palestinian was reportedly coping with a crisis in the West Bank and could not take time to meet with the U.S. lawyers. Gould said that they returned empty-handed, save for an educational tour of Gaza.

In a sharp turn of events, lawyers for both sides notified Judge Stanton on January 9, 1996, that they had reached a tentative settlement and were trying to negotiate the exact nature of a final agreement. In their letter to Stanton, the lawyers stated that one facet of the preliminary settlement was a PLO monetary contribution to the establishment of a peace institute aimed at preventing terrorism.

But it was not until August 1996, a few weeks before Judge Stanton was to have started the trial, that the two sides came to a final agreement and settled the suit. Attorneys for both sides described the settlement as "amicable," a word not previously used in discussing Leon Klinghoffer's death.

"The PLO's defense all along was that Yasser Arafat was a peace-loving president who had been done in by Abu Abbas, who was trying to embarrass Arafat," recalled Gould in 2003. "They claimed that Arafat should be praised for ending the hijacking and the renegade Abbas should be punished. But it would have been hard for the PLO to prevail with that argument in court because Abbas was on the PLO Executive Committee."

"I was not surprised by the settlement," Gould said. "Stanton was about to try the case and I don't think that the defense counsel felt they had a significant chance of winning. I think they felt that if they could unload the case, get rid of it, the PLO could carry on and succeed in the political arena." In Gould's opinion, the PLO valued the gradual recognition of the PLO by other nations at the time and the trial would have generated a heavy onslaught of miserable publicity. "The news media would have gone into a feeding frenzy and none of the attention it would have brought to the Palestinians would have been favorable."

Officially, there were two settlements, one with Club ABC and one with the Klinghoffers. The terms of each settlement were confidential, and the PLO admitted no wrongdoing, but it nevertheless agreed to pay an undisclosed amount of money to Club ABC and the Klinghoffer family. (Judge Stanton previously dismissed suits brought by other former hostages against Chandris Lines, and Lauro Lines settled all suits out of court.) The Palestine Observer Mission to the United Nations issued the following statement after the settlement:

> While the PLO was not responsible for the seizure of the *Achille Lauro*, or the tragic death of Leon Klinghoffer, and denied all liability, it believes that reconciliation is the more important consideration. The PLO recognizes the suffering of the Klinghoffer family and it is pleased to have achieved this amicable agreement, which is clearly in the best interests of peace, the Palestinian people and all concerned.

There were rumors that the settlement amounted to millions of dollars, but Lisa and Ilsa Klinghoffer told me in 2002 that only a small amount of money changed hands. They also said the "peace institute" never happened. "I thought that it was just a PR move by Ramsey Clark," Lisa said. Clark, however, said at the time that the potential agreement tentatively reached in January 1996 regarding the peace institute fell through because of new strains on the Arab-Israeli peace process at that point.

The early difficulties the Klinghoffer family experienced in finding a way to sue the PLO resulted in the U.S. Congress passing the Anti-Terrorist Act of 1991. The statute permits U.S. nationals to sue terrorists in the appropriate U.S. federal court for triple damages and attorney's fees. Using the law, the family of an American citizen, Yaron Ungar and his Israeli wife, Efrat, sued the Palestinian Authority for the couple's murder in Israel in 1996. Families of those killed in the 9-11 attacks on New York and Washington are pursuing claims via the same legal route.

"The Klinghoffer case was a legal landmark," attorney Gould said. "It had a significant impact on the jurisdictional issues surrounding civil retribution against terrorists."

Marilyn Klinghoffer, and later her daughters, were not thinking of setting legal precedents when they sued the PLO. They wanted punishment for the crime. Simple justice for a straightforward incident. Yet the PLO settled the suit for political reasons. Despite all of the rhetoric from Arafat about his abhorrence of terrorism, he implicitly conceded PLO complicity in Klinghoffer's death. A lawyer will disagree with me, but to a layman, that settlement was such a concession. He was willing to acknowledge PLO involvement in order achieve greater political gains, perhaps semi-admitting to be a bad guy because he knew that he had more important, political issues at stake. Besides, why not settle if the PLO's relations with the Klinghoffers were now "amicable"?

CHAPTER

10

Gotcha! (2000–2004)

THE Jewish Defense League must have killed Alex Odeh. Irv Rubin all but admitted it. His confession, however, didn't come from a session with the cops at the precinct house.

In 2000, the FBI's search for Alex Odeh's killer generally had ground to a halt. Although the investigation was still ongoing, FBI spokeswoman Laura Bosley said in Los Angeles that there were few leads and no firm suspects. A spokesman at FBI Headquarters in Washington declined to comment on the investigation.

"For years the FBI has told me that the case is still open and under investigation," Sami Odeh said at the time. "I find it very hard to believe that with all our resources, the killers haven't been brought to justice." Odeh also said that despite the FBI considering the case top priority, "If you ask probing, detailed questions, you'll get the standard answer: 'We cannot comment on open cases.'" When asked, Sami told me about his view of the FBI's efforts, "One has to conclude that either the FBI is incompetent, or they do not want to press charges for some reason, most likely political."

Lead agents in the investigation traveled to Israel in the summer of 2001, but declined to give Sami any details regarding their trip. The news media reported a slight increase in attention to Alex Odeh's case after the 9-11 attacks, with his name arising during discussions between law enforcement officials and the American-Arab Anti-Discrimination Committee. "We're frustrated," said Committee spokesman Hussein Ibish, "but there's not much we can do to shift the FBI into action."

Ibish said that the FBI told the Committee in 2002 that two suspects in the Odeh bombing still lived in Israel, but that diplomatic and political reasons prohibited their extradition. That remark fits with 1990 reports that two suspects, Keith Fuchs and Andy Green, were then living in the same West Bank village as Robert Manning before his extradition. The Committee spokesman said that the FBI claimed the uncertain status of the West Bank—is it occupied land or Israeli territory?—hindered the situation. This was the same issue raised during the 1991 Manning extradition, proving then to be an obstacle until the State Department withdrew any objection to Manning's extradition, regardless of his location on the West Bank. In 2002, State Department spokesman Duncan Maciness, probably unaware of the earlier precedent, said that the U.S.–Israeli extradition treaty did not extend to the West Bank.

Sami Odeh and the Anti-Discrimination Committee have not been able to convince either the U.S. Senate or House of Representatives to call for the arrest of Alex Odeh's killer. Despite the unique parallels between Odeh's death and that of Leon Klinghoffer—both were murdered for their race and religion—the Arab-American lobby in the United States. can't get Congress to move the way their Jewish counterparts can.

An unexpected development changed the dynamic of the stalemated investigation. Law enforcement officials arrested Jewish Defense League chairman Irv Rubin and an associate, Earl Krugel, on December 11, 2001, charging them with conspiracy to bomb a Muslim mosque and the office of a California congressman. U.S. Representative Darrell Issa (R-CA) was apparently targeted because of his Lebanese grandfather. (Issa later led the successful drive to recall California governor Gray Davis in 2003.) The two hired a third person, Danny Gillis, to plant the bomb. Gillis turned FBI informant, secretly taping conversations between Rubin and Krugel. Court records detailed Krugel's taped remarks, including his statement that Arabs "need a wakeup call."

Rubin's attorney, Peter Morris, said that the federal government's arraignment of Rubin and Krugel was an overreaction to the events of September 11 events. Rubin's wife, Shelley, called the arrest a "witch hunt against Jews to show that they're even-handed toward Muslims."

Rubin's long history of actions and statements previously had led to his estrangement from the mainstream Jewish community in the United States, so Rubin's arrest gathered no criticism from that quarter. David Lehrer, Western regional director of the Anti-Defamation League, said only "thugs and hooligans" belonged to the Jewish Defense League. And there weren't many thugs at that, according to Los Angeles County Supervisor Zev Yaroslavsky, who cast Rubin as a fringe of the fringe. "There are more teams in the American League then there are members of the Jewish Defense League."

In pre-trial hearings in October 2002, Rubin's lawyers asked presiding U.S. District Judge Ronald S. W. Lew to order prosecutors to turn over records of the FBI's investigation of Alex Odeh's death. The lawyers told the judge that the Odeh files would prove that the FBI was "out to get" Rubin because government officials could not prove Rubin was behind the 1985 bombing.

Before the judge could respond, Irv Rubin slit his throat with his safety razor then jumped head-first off the third level of the Los Angeles jail on Monday, November 5, 2002. He died nine days later.

Rubin had been awaiting trial that morning when, at 5:30 A.M., guards roused the prisoners for breakfast. All exited their cells onto a walkway that ran the length of each section of cells; Rubin's cell was on the third tier up from ground level. FBI spokesman Mathhew McLaughlin said that Rubin's death appeared to be self-inflicted. Reportedly, there was no one within fifteen feet of Rubin when he jumped. That did not stop rumors from starting about a revenge killing by Muslim inmates or neo-Nazis, groups that Rubin antagonized relentlessly.

"It's just counterintuitive and inconsistent with the man I knew," Rubin's lawyer Bryan Altman said about Rubin's alleged suicide. It is inconsistent with our discussions and his beliefs." Rubin was a devout Jew, and Altman said that Talmudic traditions prohibit suicide.

"I'm saying he was killed," contended Bill Maniaci, a retired police officer who became head of the Jewish Defense League after Rubin's death. Maniaci offered no justification for his assessment.

Rubin's estate filed a $5 million wrongful-death claim against the U.S. government in January 2003. Rubin's family lawyer, Peter Morris, charged the government with careless and negligent monitoring of Rubin, rather than claiming that Rubin was murdered.

Rubin's fellow defendent, Earl Krugel, pled guilty in February 2003 to conspiring to bomb the mosque and Representative Issa's office. Krugel implicated Rubin in the plot. Outside the courthouse during these proceedings, Rubin's widow Shelley and her teenage son, Ari, joined other League picketers to demonstrate on behalf of Rubin's innocence. "If you want to admit to committing a crime, so be it," Mrs. Rubin said in reference to Krugel's plea. "But you don't drag someone in with you who was totally innocent and is not here to defend himself."

The transcript of the secretly taped conversations between Rubin and Krugel was the basis of Rubin and Krugel's indictment and prosecutors revealed parts of that indictment at the two men's arraignment. Investigators said that Rubin wanted to "blow up an entire building," but lacked the technology. Further, the indictment read, "Rubin also said that the Jewish Defense League should not go after a human target because they still had not heard the end of the Alex Odeh incident."

To me, that statement means Irv Rubin was responsible for Alex Odeh's death. Rubin did not know that he was being taped when he made that statement. Given that, Rubin must have thought that he could speak frankly with his co-conspirators. Rubin's comments support long-held suspicions that the Jewish Defense League was behind Odeh's murder.

It's conceivable that Rubin may have been referring to the backlash felt by another group or person, and that lesson was useful to the League. The police and U.S. Attorney's office could consider this other conclusion, if the unreleased portions of tape-recorded conversation are sufficiently revealing.

How did the FBI view this development? Thom Mrozek, public affairs officer for the U.S. Attorney's Office in Los Angeles, refused my request to comment on the significance of Rubin's apparent confession. Laura Bosley, spokeswoman for the Los Angeles FBI office, also declined to discuss the development with me, citing the fact that the investigation of the Odeh murder was an open case. When asked about Rubin's taped remarks, Assistant U.S. Attorney Greg Jessner also refused to comment.

When asked about the significance of Rubin's taped statement, retired FBI Executive Assistant Director Buck Revell told me, "It's hard to say. That case drove us nuts when I was in the FBI, but we always believed that Jewish extremists were behind the bombing."

In June 2003 I passed along to Sami Odeh information about Rubin's secretly recorded statements; he was not aware of them. At my request, Sami asked the two investigators working on his brother's case about Rubin's statements, but Sami said later that the detectives declined to comment. Sami did say that the detectives were optimistic and hoped for positive developments in four to six months.

By the following month, unidentified sources familiar with the Odeh case reported that the Department of Justice had made a deal with Krugel—a lighter sentence in return to information about the Odeh incident. After Justice granted Krugel immunity from any self-incriminating statements, he began talking with the FBI. Yet by January, 2004, the FBI reportedly felt Krugel was holding back useful information, and was threatening that the government might renege on the offer of a lesser sentence.

No further information regarding the Odeh case was available by early Spring 2004. Nevertheless, the FBI continues to offer a $1 million reward for information leading to the arrest and conviction of Alex Odeh's killer.

Robert Manning, a member of the Jewish Defense League at the time of Alex Odeh's murder, remains imprisoned in a medium security Federal Correctional Complex in Victorville, California, convicted of the 1980 Manhattan Beach killing of Patricia Wilkerson. Law enforcement officials long considered Manning a suspect in Odeh's killing, but were prohibited by the U.S.–Israeli extradition treaty from prosecuting him for any crime other than Wilkerson's murder by mail bomb. Manning always denied any involvement in the Odeh bombing, a position that his former attorney, Richard Sherman of Los Angeles, confirmed for me in May 2003.

Manning did not respond to my request to interview him.

"Now even fundamentalists in Israel do not deny the right of the Palestinians to have a state," Abu Abbas told Suzanne Goldenberg of London's *Guardian* newspaper in April 2000. "It is handcuffed, but it is still a state," Abbas continued, referring to the nascent Palestinian government in Gaza and the West Bank. "Now we have to build bridges between their dreams and ours. If we can do that, it will be a blessing."

The Israeli Supreme Court rejected a petition the previous fall from Tel Aviv lawyer Nitsana Darshan-Leitner to have Abbas arrested. In the wake of that decision, Abbas traveled again to Gaza in the spring of 2000, arranging the interview with Ms. Goldenberg to keep his name in print. Abbas continued to maintain his terrorist-turned-politician role that he created in 1996, tossing off little platitudes like "we are fighters, but said yes to peace." Regarding his potential arrest while visiting Gaza, Abbas said, "Theoretically, any country in the world can arrest me. But everything is political. . . . Any harm that comes to us, harms the peace process and we will go back to what we did before."

Abbas told Goldenberg that he was proud of his career of terror, with the *Achille Lauro* hijacking an aberration, an "inglorious episode," to use Goldenberg's words. He repeated his story that the hijacking was an accident—"What happened did not go according to plan. It became famous because it failed. All we were trying to do was get a ship to go to Ashdod—the same as you would hijack a car." Abbas expressed no contrition for the hijacking during the interview, but rather said, "Always when you work, you make mistakes."

Speaking to Goldenberg, Darshan-Leitner said that even her clients—those whom she represented when she sued for Abbas's arrest—had "grown weary of fighting the by-products of peace. But the fact is he killed, he murdered, he acted criminally against the Jews and he should not be allowed here."

Goldenberg wrote that since Abbas was a close associate of Yasser Arafat and supported the peace process, the man was "to all intents unassailable. Nowadays," she continued, "the burly former guerilla admits that the greatest threat to his freedom comes from the extra kilos that he is carrying on his frame, and a related heart condition." Goldenberg never referred to Abbas as a terrorist in the article, only calling him a former guerrilla.

Later, in early September 2000, Abbas spoke with the *Chicago Tribune*'s Hugh Delios, reiterating his cover story of the hijacking, especially the falsehood of the cabin steward discovering the armed men. He also described to Delios his visit—authorized by the Israeli government—the previous spring to his family home near Haifa. Abbas told the journalist that he faked an Iraqi accent when talking to two Iraqi Jews, who invited the stranger to tea. "They told me that they don't dream about my land [Palestine], but about their own home in Iraq, and I saw my own picture in them," Abbas said. "My feelings were upside down." It was this revelation, Abbas told Delios, which made him realize that the Palestinians' problem was not "with the Israeli people, but only their leaders."

"I am proud of my past," Abbas said. "[But] we are with Arafat completely now. We need peace. We really do."

Peace did not have much of a chance at that point because the second intifada broke out a few days after Abbas's interview with Delios. On September 28, 2000, Israeli opposition leader Ariel Sharon, accompanied by hundreds of Israeli police, entered one of the holiest sites in Islam, Haram al-Sharif, to, in his words, "ascertain that freedom of worship and free access to the Temple Mount is granted to everyone: Christians, Muslims and Jews in particular." (The Temple Mount is co-located with Haram al-Sharif.) Violent Palestinian reaction ensued the following day, disrupting the stalled peace process between Israel and the Palestinian Authority, a peace that seemed tantalizingly close just weeks before.

As the Palestinian rioting gained momentum, Abu Abbas quickly discarded his talk of peace and reprised his role as agitator and terror-monger. Returning to Baghdad, he told Iraq's al-Rafideen magazine in October 2000 that his PLF would "start carrying out suicide operations" against Israel for the purpose of "liberating Palestine." In a telephone interview with the London-based Saudi newspaper Asharq al-Awsat, Abbas said, "As a result of the enemy's intransigence and the killing of our children, we have to respond to it in the manner it understands."

Iraq itself announced that it would start training Iraqi volunteers to fight with the Palestinians in the occupied territories of the West Bank and Gaza. Saddam Hussein also started a practice at the beginning of the second intifada that his government would continue until its demise—handing out substantial sums of money to the families of Palestinians killed or wounded by Israel. Iraq used both the PLF and another constituent member of the PLO, the Arab Liberation Front, to hand out the money—$10,000 for the dead, $1,000 to the injured. Those amounts grew later to $25,000 for families of suicide bombers.

Abbas remained in Baghdad, but in May 2001, he asked Arafat if he could return to Gaza. According to a PLF official, who spoke with Asharq al-Awsat, Arafat cautioned against Abbas's travel to Gaza because he was "targeted and his life may be at risk" were he to enter Gaza "in light of this situation," presumably the continuing fighting between

Israelis and Palestinians. No further details were available, but the warning might have reflected the potential for Israel's government to ignore the ruling of its supreme court and snatch Abu Abbas.

In the aftermath of the 9-11 attacks, the FBI dropped Abu Abbas from its "most-wanted terrorist list," apparently to make room for persons associated with the Al Qaeda terrorist network. Two Jewish advocacy groups, the Anti-Defamation League and the Conference of Presidents of Major Jewish Organizations, publicly criticized that decision. Malcolm Hoenlein, executive vice chairman of the latter, said, "I hope [Abbas] and others like him will be on future lists."

Lisa and Ilsa Klinghoffer wrote a letter to the editor of the *New York Times*, published a month after 9-11, drawing a parallel to their father's death and those of the 9-11 victims.

> We have read the letters and articles expressing outrage about the attack on America on Sept. 11. They brought back so many memories of when our father, Leon Klinghoffer, was murdered by Palestinian terrorists in 1985.
>
> After our father was murdered, there was much public outrage. But the outrage dissipated over time, and Abu Abbas, the mastermind of our father's murder, was allowed to resume his activities within the Palestine Liberation Organization. Such a loss of resolve only invites future acts of terrorism.
>
> If we are to defeat terrorism, out society must commit itself to taking an unwavering and sustained stand against terrorism. Our outrage today and in the future must remain as strong as it was on Sept. 11.

When the Boston Symphony Orchestra cancelled performances of the choruses from *The Death of Klinghoffer* after the 9-11 terrorist attacks, the reactions were as varied as the issues complex. Music and opera critics weighed in on both sides of the symphony's decision. "Ladies and gentlemen, the Boston Symphony Orchestra will now soothe you with its rendition of 'Kitten on the Keys,' performed on kazoos," wrote David Wiegand of the *San Francisco Chronicle*. "It hasn't quite come to that, but it just might, given the orchestra's ridiculous decision last week to cancel performances of 'Choruses' from *The Death of Klinghoffer*."

Anthony Tommasini, writing for the *New York Times*, thought it patronizing for the symphony's directors to presume what audiences might find offensive. "Of course art can provide solace and comfort. Yet art can increase and challenge us, make us squirm, make us think. The Boston Symphony missed an opportunity to present an acutely relevant work."

"Some have found *Klinghoffer* too soft on terrorists, too quick to caricature Jews," continued Tommasini. "What do three white Westerners know about ancient conflicts in the Middle East?" he asked, referring to Adams, Goodman, and Sellars. Tommasini also noted a prescient passage that critic Michael Steinberg wrote for a program booklet that accompanied a 1992 recording of *Klinghoffer*. Referring to the centuries-old conflicts that underlay the hijacking, Tommasini quoted Steinberg: "We can read about them in the Old Testament, and guaranteed, on whichever day you read these words, there will be some new installment in the morning paper."

"*The Death of Klinghoffer* trades in the tritest undergraduate fantasies," wrote respected musicologist Richard Taruskin of the University of California in the *New York Times*. "If the events of September 11 could not jar some artists and critics out of their habit of romantically idealizing criminals, then nothing will. But isn't it time for artists and critics to grow up with the rest of us, now that the unthinkable has occurred? If terrorism . . . is to be defeated, world public opinion has to be turned decisively against it. . . . This means no longer romanticizing terrorists as Robin Hoods and no longer idealizing their deeds as rough poetic justice."

"Censorship is always deplorable," Taruskin concluded, "but the exercise of forbearance can be noble. Not to be able to distinguish the noble from the deplorable is morally obtuse."

The Death of Klinghoffer was performed in Ferrara, Italy, and in London in January 2002 as scheduled.

The impact of the opera took on new dimensions in 2003 when BBC Channel Four released a film version of *Klinghoffer*. First shown in January at the Sundance Film Festival, the film was also exhibited at the San Francisco Film Festival on April 20–21, in New York at the Lincoln Center on May 13, then finally shown to its original target audience—the British television viewer—on May 24, 2003.

Critics maintain that filmed opera is a demanding medium, one apparently seldom staged with much success. In this instance, British director Penny Woolcock seemed the least likely person to succeed in such a difficult art form. With few directing credits and no operatic background, she undertook to bring Adams's score and Goodman's libretto to the small screen.

Her approach was unusual and, in the words of one critic, "broke all the rules she didn't know existed." She filmed scenes at sea on board a cruise ship off the coast of Egypt. The cast sang on camera, following music that Adams conducted and recorded earlier. Woolcock used handheld cameras to zoom in on singers' faces, bringing visuals to the audience not seen in opera houses. She interwove historical news footage into the film, as well as scenes staged to look like actual events. She did all of this while keeping the power of Adams's choruses and the arias of the major characters. And, in a major departure from the original opera's unseemly scene of a Jewish American family bickering about finances and bowel movements, Woolcock starts the film with Marilyn spitting in the faces of the hijackers in an Italian jail.

The result, according to *Los Angeles Times* critic Mark Swed, was "the first real masterpiece of cinematic opera." The *Guardian*'s Charlotte Higgins called the production "a piece of work that, at its best, combines the emotional kick of opera with the muscular power of film and the intimacy of television." Higgins went on to write that Woolcock "completely reimagined *The Death of Klinghoffer* in a way that stays true to the spirit of the piece, but that takes it in myriad directions unimaginable on stage."

The film drew criticism, however, about the politics of the hijacking, just as the stage version attracted strong reactions from both Jews and Arabs. "Is *Klinghoffer* anti-Semitic?" asked *New York Times* critic John Rockwell. He summarized the harsh treatment the opera received over the years from those who felt it over-dramatized the Palestinians' plight, but finally answered his own question. "In the end *Klinghoffer* is not anti-American or antibourgeois or anti-Semitic, but pro-human. It shows that murder is nothing more than that, vicious and unconscionable. To see the opera or the film otherwise, it seems to me, is to be swept up in the very tribal hatreds the opera so eloquently deplores."

The film attempts to find a basis for the Arab-Israeli conflict by retelling historical events that shaped the psyche of both peoples—the Holocaust and the 1948 expulsion of Palestinians from the newly created state of Israel. Woolcock's approach troubled *New York Times* writer Edward Rothstein: "The opera is based on the idea that the 'root cause' of Palestinian terrorism is Jewish sins; it accepts the terrorists' account of grievance and offers no alternative." Rothstein believed that Woolcock's "injustice theory," which blamed terrorism on a previous wrong, was unfounded.

"What I try to do in the music and what Woolcock has also done is to show that the Jews have a mythic past," opera composer Adams said, "but that the Palestinians also have a mythic past, and this drives a lot of people up the wall. . . . It doesn't condone terrorism. I think the film does great honor to (Klinghoffer) and his wife, but it also asks, 'Why are people willing to commit suicide bombings?'"

"It's not balanced—not at all," said Ken Jacobson, associate national director of the Anti-Defamation League. "Everything we've heard about the film suggests that it has the same message as the opera—that the Palestinians seem somehow like decent guys and good people, and Jews are cast in a negative light."

"I find it kind of astounding that anyone would interpret it like that," responded Penny Woolcock. "And I would have never have filmed it if I thought it was anti-Semitic. If the opera is about anything, it's that we have to forgive the unforgivable. Otherwise, we're lost as a species."

Abu Abbas's self-proclaimed conversion from terrorist to peaceful politician was irrevocably undermined in November 2001 when the Israeli Security Agency announced that it had uncovered a PLF-trained terrorist cell on the West Bank.

In a remarkable coincidence of events, the Agency reported that Bassam al-Ashker, one of the four *Achille Lauro* hijackers, was in charge of the cell's training, logistics, and planning. Only seventeen at the time of the hijacking, Ashker served but six years of a sixteen year sentence in Italy and disappeared immediately after his parole. By 2001, Ashker had risen to become Abbas's top deputy in the PLF.

The Israelis arrested three Palestinian members of the cell in the Ramalla and Jenin areas, one of whom confessed that the PLF trained the group at the Al-Quds military camp outside Baghdad. They practiced using automatic weapons and rocket-propelled grenades, and learned how to prepare bombs. By the time the Israelis reported the group's arrest, its members had abducted and murdered eighteen-year-old Israeli teenager Yuri Gushchin, bombed a checkpoint, injuring five, planted other bombs without injuries, and shot at vehicles. The Israeli

Internet Sites

http://www.adl.org
http://www.fbi.gov
http://imra.org.il
http://www.jdl.org
http://www.mfa.gov.il
http://www.palestine-un.org
http://www.pbs.org
http://www.radio.rai.it
http://www.zoa.org

Internet Articles

Anonymous. "SS Achille Lauro Chronicles," http://members.aol.com/_ht_a/
    drakare/achillelauro.html.
———. "Willem Ruys/Achille Lauro," http://www.allatsea.co.za/shipwrecks/
    achillelauro.htm.
Othfors, Daniel. "Willem Ruys/Achille Lauro." http://www.greatoceanliners
    .net/willemruys.html.

Unpublished Material

Research Papers

"The Achille Lauro Hijacking (A)," Case Program, C16-88-863.0, Kennedy
    School of Government, Harvard College, 1988.
"The Achille Lauro Hijacking (B)," Case Program, C16-88-864.0, Kennedy
    School of Government, Harvard College, 1988.

Interviews With Author

Collins, Bob, November 27, 2002
De Raho, Federico Cafiero, March 18, 2003
Gould, Rodney, March 16, 2003
Klinghoffer, Lisa and Ilsa, November 11, 2002
Klinghoffer, Lisa, May 2, 2003
Kohler, Peter, February 21, 2003
Negrin, Alberto, April 1, 2003
Odeh, Sami, October 21, 2002
Poindexter, John, November 28, 2002
Revell, Oliver, May 29, 2003
Shaheen, Jack, May 13, 2003
Stark, Jim, October 19, 2002

Security Agency also said the cell was planning mass killing attacks at Israel's Ben Gurion airport and targets in Tel Aviv and Jerusalem. The group allegedly smuggled some of their weapons into the West Bank in the car of a Palestinian Authority official, Abdul Razek Yehiye. The car bore Palestinian VIP license plates, allowing the car to go unsearched at border crossings.

Security proved too tight for the cell to detonate a bomb at the airport, so they prepared to attack Tel Aviv's seashore promenade, the Dolphinarium. One of the group, Muhammed Sha'ban 'Isa Qundus, traveled with Ashker to Baghdad to obtain Abbas's permission to undertake the operation, in which they would use a device to remotely trigger the bomb by cellular phone. Qundus told Israeli officials that Abbas instructed Ashker to get final authorization from him before planting the bomb.

Despite the cell's arrest, the PLF recruited three more West Bank Palestinians in June 2002, also sending them to Baghdad, where Iraqi intelligence officials trained them instead of the PLF. That training included the use of rocket-propelled grenades and Russian-made, shoulder-fired anti-aircraft missiles. During the training, both Abbas and Ashker visited with the men, with Ashker issuing detailed instructions for surveying targets and executing plans. Just as in 2001, the Israelis uncovered the terrorist cell, this time before its members could carry out any attacks.

In September 2002, the Israeli government released this information, as well as details of the relationships between Yasser Arafat, the Palestinian Authority, the PLF, and Abu Abbas. They gathered considerable materials on these matters when the Israeli army attacked and occupied part of Arafat's compound in Ramallah the previous spring. The Israeli Ministry of Foreign Affairs reported that documents seized during the attack revealed that the Palestinian Authority was then paying the PLF $12,000 a month to help underwrite its activities. The Iraqi government also gave money to the PLF, and Abbas donated funds gained from his real estate investments in Iraq. Other documents indicated that Arafat authorized the Palestinian Authority to pay PLF rents in buildings in the West Bank, $100 payments to each of fifty PLF members, and $100 each to PLF members wounded in the intifada.

The CBS News television program *60 Minutes* ran a segment on October 1, 2002, about the information that the Israelis found in Arafat's offices. Correspondent Lesley Stahl spoke of "smoking guns" and evidence of Iraqi support for terrorism, an issue that was on President George W. Bush's mind that fall as he started making his case for removing Saddam Hussein's regime in Baghdad.

As the Israeli Defense Force withdrew from Arafat's Ramallah compound and eased Palestinian travel restrictions in early October, Abbas sent a message of support to Arafat, praising the Palestinian's "steadfastness."

In November 2002 the U.S. government was campaigning throughout the world in an attempt to gather international support for the removal of Saddam Hussein from Iraq. President Bush most often cited the potential threat of Iraqi weapons of mass destruction as the reason for urging a "regime change" in Iraq, but he included among the lesser justifications Iraqi support to international terrorists. Bush and his advisors frequently referred to Abu Abbas and his PLF as examples of terrorists aided by Iraq. Those references, coupled with the revelations in the news media about PLF terrorist cells in the West Bank in 2001 and 2002, and Yasser Arafat's financial assistance to Abbas, put the publicity squeeze on Abu Abbas. He reacted just as he had previously, contacting the Western news media to spin his side of things.

Abbas granted an interview to reporter Rod Nordland of *Newsweek Magazine*, aggressively drawing a distinction between his activities and "real" terrorists like Osama bin Laden. "They say I am a terrorist. And Osama bin Laden is a terrorist. But terrorist is a very bad name to use." Abbas went on to say that he had renounced violence against civilians outside of Israel, but Al Qaeda wanted "universal war" and "war against everything." "*That* is terrorism," he said.

"There is a big difference between our ideas and aims and Al Qaeda's," Abbas told Nordland. "We Palestinians have lost our country, our homeland, our families, our land; we are fighting for our human rights. Osama bin Laden is not fighting for a national cause; he's not even fighting for the Arab nation. He wants an Islamic war." Nordland wrote that Abbas thought that Al Qaeda's 9-11 attacks on the United States hurt the Palestinian cause. As always, Abbas assiduously brought up personal issues as well during the interview to help cast himself as just a regular guy. He talked to Nordland about his five sons, one of whom he said was in a Canadian college.

Next was John Burns of the *New York Times*. The two-time Pulizter prize-winning reporter recognized Abbas in the lobby of Baghdad's Rashid Hotel in late October 2002. Burns was surprised that Abbas did not flee at the sight of a Western reporter. Burns later got Abbas's phone number from the Palestinian Authority's office in Baghdad and soon met with Abbas for two hours at PLF headquarters. The usual armed soldiers provided security, probably a measure more for show than in response to a potentially threatening reporter.

Abbas reiterated to Burns his goals—liberation of Palestinians and the recovery of their "occupied lands," differentiating that pursuit from bin Laden's broad war against Americans and Jews. Burns wrote that Abbas attempted to establish a moral argument that the 9-11 attackers were terrorists, but he and his group were not. The writer also hinted that Abbas might be preparing for the day when America might invade Iraq and could be attempting to "soften American anger against him." "I really haven't spent a moment thinking about this," Abbas said. "If the Americans want to attack, and destroy Saddam Hussein, they would be doing much, much more than the personal damage they will do to me."

When asked the inevitable question about Leon Klinghoffer, Abbas claimed the murder was not his fault and that innocent civilians are killed in war, referring to the atomic bombs the United States dropped on Japan as an example.

Abbas again mentioned his family, talking about his wife Reem and five sons: a fifteen-year-old living with him in Baghdad, two in Canada, one in Austria, and the fifth in Lebanon. As other reporters had in recent years, Burns contributed to the growing perception of Abbas as an aging terrorist, citing his weight, need for reading glasses, and a heart ailment. Abbas was 53 at the time.

In late December 2002, General Omart Suleiman, head of Egyptian intelligence, invited representatives from several Palestinian groups, including the PLF, to visit Cairo and discuss an Egyptian initiative for a Palestinian cease-fire with Israel. The Middle East news media reported that Abu Abbas arrived in Cairo January 6, 2003, for consultations with the Egyptian government. Abbas spoke with London's *al-Sharaq al-Awsat* newspaper by telephone from Cairo.

"My visit comes in response to the invitation from the brothers in the Arab Republic of Egypt and within the context of the consultations the Egyptian leadership is holding with all the Palestinian factions."

The fact that Abbas was in Cairo caught the attention of both the U.S. and Italian governments and rumors circulated that the United States had asked Egypt to extradite Abbas. That development later proved untrue, but a spokeswoman for the U.S. embassy in Cairo confirmed that the United States had indeed asked Egypt to confirm Abbas's presence there. Italy reportedly approached Cairo about Abbas's activities.

Rumors appeared to be sufficient cause for Abbas to abruptly depart Cairo for Baghdad on January 10. In interviews with both the London-based newspaper *Al-Hayat* and the *Associated Press*, Abbas confirmed that he had cut short his visit. He maintained that America's "reopening of old files compelled him to leave the country to avoid embarrassing his hosts."

As U.S. tanks rumbled toward Baghdad in late March 2003, Abu Abbas cast aside his bravado and fled toward Syria. Badgered publicly by the U.S. government to turn back terrorists and high-level Iraqi officials, Syria twice refused Abbas entry. He returned to his home on the south side of Baghdad. As Baghdad began to fall, Abbas tried again, moving to Mosul, then to the Syrian border, with Syria denying him sanctuary yet again.

On April 15, U.S. special operations forces, acting on a tip from an Iraqi, apprehended Abu Abbas at a house in Baghdad. The troops placed Abbas and a small group of his PLF members in a prison near the Baghdad airport.

While the Bush administration trumpeted Abbas's capture, quickly declaring that one of the war's goal had been satisfied—punishing Saddam Hussein for his ties to known terrorists—a debate erupted about what to do with the man.

Justice officials in Italy, which has an active warrant for Abbas, and the United States, which does not, immediately began discussions, with the Italians seemingly bent on deferring to the United States, perhaps to right old wrongs. "We are attempting to have him tried in Italy," said Italian Justice Minister Roberto Castelli, "but if the Americans have the possibility of detaining him and trying him on the strength of international law, we will have absolutely no objection."

Italy, which never pursued Abbas with any vigor after his conviction *in absentia* in a Genoese court, probably did not want the anti-Palestinian publicity that would assuredly arise out of Abbas's return to Italy. Abbas might have hoped for that outcome because the Italian legal system likely would not have held him for the entire life sentence that the court gave him in 1986.

The Israeli attorney, Nitsana Darshan-Leitner, who sued in Israel to have Abbas arrested in the late 1990s, urged the Israeli Attorney General to attempt to prosecute Abbas for the PLF's 2001 murder of Israeli teenager Yuri Gushchin. Gushchin was a victim of a West Bank terrorist cell that Abbas recruited while he was masquerading as a Palestinian politician.

The Lebanon office of the PLF demanded Abbas's immediate release, calling on everyone in sight—the United Nations, the Arab League, and the International Committee of the Red Cross—to help put an end to American aggression. Dr. Wasil Abu-Yusuf, a member of the PLF's Political Bureau in Al-Birah City in the West Bank, claimed that America asked Italy to extradite Abbas because America could not justify its arrest of Abbas. Abu-Yusuf also suggested that the PLO's payment to the Klinghoffer family, resulting from the lawsuit settlement in 1996, should be reason enough to let bygones be bygones.

The Palestinian Authority called for Abbas's release, citing the 1995 Interim Agreement and the 1993 Oslo Accords that grant immunity to persons committing crimes prior to 1993. The Authority also referenced the Israeli Supreme Court's 1999 ruling that Abbas did indeed enjoy that immunity.

Abbas's wife, Reem, chimed in, too. In an interview with the Arab news channel al-Jazeera, Reem declared that Abu Abbas was not a party to the war, and that the PLO–Israeli amnesty agreement should allow his release. She also said that she had spoken with her husband on the telephone from her home in Lebanon just before his arrest. Clearly, if he could not get to the press, this media-savvy Palestinian wanted his wife to get his message out.

In Washington, government officials quickly announced that the 1995 Interim Agreement, though co-signed by President Clinton, applied only to detention and prosecution by Israel or the PLO, not the United States. With that said, however, debate within the United States continued about what it should do with Abbas. "We're looking at the legal issues and possibilities and have nothing to say right now," announced Pentagon spokeswoman Victoria Clarke after Abbas's arrest.

Across the Potomac River, the U.S. Justice Department started investigating the legal grounds for prosecuting Abbas. Others examined the possibility of trying Abbas on the basis of forged passports, and documents and weapons in his possession at the time of his apprehension. The anti-terrorism legislation passed in the wake of incidents in the 1980s, as well as after the 9-11 attacks, may also provide cause for prosecution.

"They got him," a friend told Lisa during a PTA meeting at her son's school.

"They got Hussein?" Lisa asked. "Osama bin Laden?"

"No, they got Abbas."

"I was just dumbfounded," Lisa said. "I kind of froze for a second . . . I always wondered what my reaction would be, and how it would affect me. I thought, 'Thank God. Maybe we will get some justice.'"

Lisa told me a few days later that while she and her sister are overjoyed, they will not be content with Abbas returning to Italy. They feel that Italy will be soft on him and that he should be tried in the U.S. legal system. "We won't celebrate until he's locked up over here."

"When something like this touches your life, you are never the same," said Ilsa. "Our lives changed in such unbelievable ways from the moment when we heard 18 years ago. I know things that were important to me before were not. Petty things that used to bother me don't. Everything changes."

By the fall of 2003, Abbas's status had been simplified somewhat. News reports from Baghdad indicated that Italy was not seeking extradition, apparently deciding that political pressures outweighed legal matters. One report stated that the Justice Department "is not sure it can convict Mr. Abbas in the United States." As a result, the U.S. government continued to indefinitely detain Abbas at an undisclosed location. "He's in custody, sitting there, waiting for someone to decide what to do with him," declared an unidentified government official. "They'll probably decide just to let him sit there."

He didn't sit long because he died on March 8, 2004, apparently of natural causes, according to a U.S. Department of Defense spokesman. No U.S. government official would provide any details regarding Abbas's death, or additional information on the status of his interrogation or the U.S. Justice Department's intentions to prosecute him.

Abbas spoke of a heart ailment to the *Guardian*'s Suzanne Goldenberg in 2000, and to the *New York Times*'s John Burns in 2002. Perhaps the stress of the incarceration, which was so long in coming, led to his demise.

The Klinghoffer daughters wanted to see Abbas stand trial in the United States for their father's murder, but I think justice was done in some fashion. Abbas died an ignominious death, alone in a cramped cell in Iraq. He died prematurely at fifty-six, deprived of the chance to play with his grandchildren, enjoy this old age, and relish a peace between Israel and the Palestinians that the world hopes will come.

Lisa and Ilsa Klinghoffer reacted to Abbas's death with these thoughts:

> Our quest is over on a personal level in that all of the *Achille Lauro* hijackers are now accounted for in some way. On a larger, more global scale, our quest will never end until there is no more terrorism. Although we are just two private U.S. citizens, to many we symbolize the deadly realities of terrorism and the two of us are committed to fighting terrorism in whatever way possible, whether it's testifying in Congress, putting on educational seminars through the Klinghoffer Foundation or simply by raising the public's awareness.

With three other PLF soldiers, Samir al-Qantari killed Israeli Danny Haran and his four year-old daughter Einat in Nahariya, Israel, in 1979. Apprehended, convicted, and sentenced to 524 years in prison, Qantari was one of the jailed Palestinians that the *Achille Lauro* hijackers demanded Israel free. In May 2003 his mother still lived in Qantari's hometown, Aabey, a small village near Beirut, Lebanon. She showed a reporter a photo of her son, dressed in his Israeli prison uniform.

"Israel bombed and killed a lot of people," Siham al-Qantari said of a 1978 Israeli attack in south Lebanon. "He got affected by what he saw." Only seventeen, her son joined the PLF soon after the attack. "Samir is a hero. Palestine is Arab land. He was trying to liberate his land."

"He's a symbol of resistance," Bassam al-Qantari said of his brother. Bassam declared that Israel was his enemy and that he and others must fight for their land.

In 1995, Qantari called for an end to the violence from his prison cell. "We, the Palestinian nation must carry out some serious soul-searching," he said. "The decision taken by our organizations, principally in the early 1970s, allowing for the violence against civilians, was a terrible mistake—a boomerang. . . . The result was the creation of an environment among us that encouraged indiscriminate violence."

A few weeks after the Qantari family defended Samir, the only remaining member of the family he killed in Nahariya twenty-four years ago spoke out. Smadar Haran Kaiser, the young mother who suffocated her youngest child to keep her from Qantari, wrote an Op-Ed piece in the *Washington Post*. Remarried and still living in Israel, Kaiser wrote of her horrific experience. She also urged the United States before Abbas's death to attempt to bring Abbas to the States for prosecution.

> I am ready and willing to come to the United States to testify against Abu Abbas if he is tried for terrorism. The daughters of Leon Klinghoffer have said they are ready to do the same. Unlike Klinghoffer, Danny, Einat and Yael were not American citizens. But Klinghoffer was killed on an Italian ship in Abbas's attempt to free the killer of my family in Israel. We are all connected by the international web of terrorism woven by Abbas. Let the truth come out in a new and public trial. And let it be in the United States, the leader in the struggle against terrorism.

In November 2003 Qantari's fate was at the center of a proposed prisoner swap between Israel and the Lebanese guerrilla group Hezbollah. Israel refused to acquiesce to Hezbollah demands that Qantari be included in the exchange.

EPILOGUE

ABU Abbas was a terrorist in my mind. Lisa and Ilsa Klinghoffer considered him a terrorist. I am *not* saying that he was anything else. The most important point in the saga of the *Achille Lauro* hijacking, however, is that lots of other people viewed him as a freedom fighter. In my opinion, America can better deal with international terrorism, especially in deterring terrorist violence, by understanding that there is no universal judgment of Abu Abbas and others like him.

The best example of this diversity of opinions about Abbas and his men is found in the Italian trial. Faced with the facts of the hijacking, as well as the surrounding political realities, an Italian judge and jury considered Abu Abbas and his two top aides to have planned the hijacking as "a selfish, political act conceived to weaken the leadership of Yasser Arafat." Conversely, the jury found the four actual hijackers to be "soldiers fighting for their ideals," not terrorists.

John Adams and Alice Goodman explored characterizations in contrast to basic American conceptions of the hijackers in their opera *The Death of Klinghoffer*. Alberto Negrin also did in his film *Voyage of Terror*. Siham al-Qantari, the mother of PLF soldier Samir al-Qantari, who killed Danny Haran and his four year-old daughter Einat in Nahariya, Israel, in 1979, regards her son as a hero. Smadar Haran Kaiser, the young mother who lost her first husband and two children during that attack, deems Qantari as a criminal, a terrorist. How do these two people reconcile their disparate views? If they could, they may serve as an example for others. It seems to me that their only hope is through discourse rather than by more violence, criminal proceedings, or military actions by their respective countries or representatives. Israel and the United States have used these strategies in their attempt to deter terrorism, with uneven success.

If America does not understand why there are alternative views of Abu Abbas, the country will never develop the political approaches needed to counter the political foundations of terrorism emanating from the Arab-Israeli conflict. The unrivaled power of the U.S. armed forces makes a military solution seem feasible and attractive. That power might even yield some short-term benefits, but it could also lead to an arrogant, unilateral program devoid of any accompanying economic, cultural, and political initiatives.

If Americans call Abu Abbas a terrorist, they must also call the likes of Irv Rubin terrorists. The news media most often referred to Rubin as an extremist. America must rid itself of its double standards for terrorism. Deeply rooted racial and religious biases, and ugly stereotyping will, however, make that a challenge. These prejudices directly influence both America's understanding of terrorism and its policies for combating it. Slogans about the good guys versus the bad guys only strengthen these disruptive prejudices. America must get past the biases and the over-simplified morality play that those proclivities have created about terrorism before the country can hope to succeed in either deterring or living with terrorism.

In October 2002 President Bush addressed the nation, seeking public support for a congressional resolution that would endorse U.S. military action against Iraq. One of the reasons cited by the President for changing Iraq's regime was Saddam Hussein's association with known international terrorists, men who could attack America with chemical or biological weapons of mass destruction supplied by Iraq.

> Over the years, Iraq has provided safe haven to terrorists such as Abu Nidal, whose terror organization carried out more than 90 terrorist attacks in 20 countries that killed or injured nearly 900 people including 12 Americans. Iraq has also provided safe haven to Abu Abbas, who was responsible for seizing the *Achille Lauro* and killing an American passenger.

The Bush administration inflated the status of Abu Abbas to match that of Abu Nidal to raise political support for his invasion of Iraq. From 1984, the year Abu Abbas gained control of his faction of the PLF, to 2003, it appears that the PLF killed three people. In comparison, the Jewish Defense League has killed seven persons since 1968. Three or seven deaths at the hands of these two groups are three or seven too many, in my view, but whatever stature Abu Abbas gained since the *Achille Lauro* incident was through his skillful manipulation of an ever-hungry news media. Also, if Leon Klinghoffer had been an Italian, this terrorist, however bright and scheming he may have been, would have never been the lead story on CNN. But then, his men would have never killed an Italian.

The single issue that illustrates the complicated political nature of terrorism is a remark Abbas made to a reporter in 1990 about the long view he and others have about regaining the Palestinian homeland. "There is an Arabic saying that revenge takes forty years," Abbas said. "If not my son, then the son of my son will kill you. Some day, we will have missiles that can reach New York."

This last remark, a hollow piece of melodramatic bravado from a guy who sent hang gliders into Israel, caught the attention of a grievously ill-informed staff member at the U.S. House Republican Conference. (The Conference is made up of all of the Republican members of the U.S. House of Representatives.) A Conference point paper, issued in February 1999 urging the passage of legislation creating a U.S. missile defense system, absurdly cited this bit of rhetoric as a reason for a defensive shield.

The strength and lethality of Abu Abbas's Palestine Liberation Front did not emanate from its intercontinental missile program, but from Kalashnikovs in the hands of a few hundred young men. Except for the tragic death of Leon Klinghoffer and two Israelis, the PLF fighters don't even shoot straight. Abbas created this myth about the PLF by seducing the news media and spinning tales of derring-do. U.S. politicians, searching for a good-versus-evil reason for a weapons system that is a political hot potato, latched onto a bluff from a media-wise terrorist. Abbas used his remarks to gain attention. Republicans used that attention to make a political point. It's just circular politics spinning on the news media's carousel.

The news media, aided by filmmakers and powerful advocacy groups, inflated the significance of Abu Abbas. The media gained from his exaggerated status—interviews with major terrorists sell more newspapers than sessions with two-bit thugs. U.S. politicians can justify more politically motivated proposals and programs, even wars, if they can point to a seriously dangerous terrorist as a reason. Lisa and Ilsa Klinghoffer, who didn't need an inflated Abu Abbas to press their case, found that crusade easier every time Abbas spun a reporter to enhance his image.

Everyone seemingly profited from the *Achille Lauro* hijacking, save Leon Klinghoffer, Alex Odeh, and occasionally Yasser Arafat. Politicians, the Palestinian movement, the entertainment industry, reporters, cameramen, doughnut salesmen, and the whole industry of grief, opera-goers, missile defense companies, and bigots looking for revenge all used the incident and its aftermath to their advantage.

What is America to do about terrorism? Not a terrorism expert, I can't answer that question with authority. In my opinion, however, everyone can learn from the *Achille Lauro* story; and that the more a society is informed about a threat to its well-being, the better it can cope with that danger. The next most important lesson from the affair is that America cannot win its war on terrorism by simply casting its opponents as evildoers and sending in the stealth bombers.

Bruce Hoffman is an expert on terrorism. The head of the RAND Corporation's terrorism research unit, Hoffman offered the following observation in 1998: "Perhaps the most sobering realization that arises from addressing the phenomenon of terrorism is that the threat and the problems that fuel it can never be eradicated completely. Their complexity, diversity and often idiosyncratic characteristics mean that there is no magic bullet, no single solution to be found and applied."

Hoffman also wrote that the struggle against terrorism will largely depend on "continued, and continually strengthened, international cooperation." That makes sense, but America may never enjoy full collaboration with other countries if the American people and government ignore other societies' views of what America terms terrorism. Arrogant insistence that other countries sign up for this vastly oversimplified battle between good and evil will only isolate the United States and deny it critical cooperative assistance. Terrorism, at least that seen through the lessons of the *Achille Lauro*, is about power, politics, and prejudice. Solutions to terrorism lie in using power wisely and even-handedly, and finding political answers for political problems.

Lastly, the *Achille Lauro* story should remind America to rid itself of the racial and religious stereotypes that discredit any U.S. claim to the moral high ground in its war on terrorism. The suffering of Alex Odeh's family is reason enough both to acknowledge the existence of double standards for terrorism and move to eliminate them.

NOTES

ARABIC names are often spelled differently as they are transliterated into English. I used the spellings as they appeared in the source rather than adopt a common protocol. For example, the Palestinian jailed in Israel for an attack on an Israeli village in 1979 is called Samir al-Qantari in some sources, but Samir Kuntar in others.

Many of newspaper articles that I used as sources were undoubtedly generated originally by the Associated Press, then picked up by newspapers subscribing to the AP service. I accessed most of these newspaper stories through the Pro Quest database, which did not always identify the primary source of the information. Hence, I simply cited the newspaper in which the article appeared.

Prologue

Page

xii   *"the proximity of the events"*: "BSO Bows Out of *Klinghoffer*," *Boston Globe*, November 1, 2001.

xii   *"inappropriate to perform"*: Ibid.

xii   *"Adams and Goodman did not"*: "When Art and Sensitivity Clash," *Boston Globe*, November 16, 2001.

xiii   *"pompous, turgid"*: "Reaction Mixed to *Klinghoffer* in N.Y. Opera," *Los Angeles Times*, September 9, 1991.

xiii   *"Surely there is nothing"*: "Adamsweek: Klinghoffer Dies Again," *Wall Street Journal*, September 18, 1991.

xiii   *"only want comfort and familiarity"*: "BSO Bows Out of *Klinghoffer*," *Boston Globe*, November 1, 2001.

xiii   *"In this country"*: "The Witch Hunt: Why Is Composer John Adams Being Accused of Romanticizing Terrorism?" *The Guardian*, December 15, 2001.

xiii   *"The Death of Klinghoffer"*: "Boston Symphony Missed the Point on Art and Grieving," *San Francisco Chronicle*, November 7, 2001.

xiv   *"the unlawful use of force or violence"*: www.fbi.gov.

xv   *"You can run"*: Ronald Reagan news conference, The White House, October 11, 1985.

xvi   *"soldiers fighting for their ideals"*: "Italian Jury Gives Cruise-Ship Killer 30-year Sentence," *New York Times*, July, 11, 1986.

xvii *"They can run"*: "U.S. Captures *Achille Lauro* Mastermind," *Chicago Tribune*, April 16, 2003.

xviii *"For a case that has been a priority"*: Sami Odeh, interview with author, October 21, 2002.

Chapter 1

1   *"I started to run toward a door"*: "Hostages Tell of Death List," *New York Times*, October 13, 1985.

1   *"As soon as I got there"*: "Cruising on a Murderous Course," *Newsweek Magazine*, October 21, 1985.

2   *"We called them the"*: Lisa and Ilsa Klinghoffer, interview with the author, November 11, 2002.

2   *"a relaxing cruise with my friends"*: New York Times, October 13, 1985.

2   *"Her cancer was in remission"*: Lisa and Ilsa Klinghoffer interview.

3   *"It was like sailing on a lake"*: New York Times, October 13, 1985.

3   *"I noticed four people"*: Ibid.

3   *"We are Argentineans"*: Ibid.

4   *"Maybe that's how they got the guns aboard"*: Ibid.

4   *"I found two apples"*: "Passengers Tell of Terror Aboard," *Washington Post*, October 11, 1985.

5   *"That's when they started to threaten us"*: New York Times, October 13, 1985.

5   *"We had to sit very close"*: Ibid.

5   *"If some one wanted a cup"*: Ibid.

5   *"He followed me with his rifle"*: Ibid.

5   *"They kept saying 'Reagan no good'"*: Ibid.

8   *"The Brits gave us permission"*: John Poindexter, interview with author, November 28, 2002.

8   *"He also wanted me to help"*: Nicholas Veliotes, interview with author, December 10, 2002.

9   *"I attempted to push my husband"*: "Marilyn Klinghoffer's Story: Gun at Her Head," *New York Times*, October 29, 1985.

9   *"You go"*: New York Times, October 13, 1985.

10   *"We will start executing at 3:00 P.M. sharp"*: "The Achille Lauro Hijack-

ing (A)," Case Program, C16-88-863.0, Kennedy School of Government, Harvard College, 1988.

11   *"I have killed the American":* "Achille Lauro Hijacker Testifies Against Comrades," *New York Times,* June 21, 1986.

11   *"boom, boom":* "Why Italy Let Abu Abbas Go After Hijack," *San Francisco Chronicle,* June 25, 1986.

11   *"I was convinced they were going to kill":* "Skipper Denies Hush Over Klinghoffer," *Chicago Tribune,* June 25, 1986.

11   *"He was under immense pressure":* Peter Kohler, interview with author, February 21, 2003.

11   *"go back where you came from":* "Cruising on a Murderous Course," *Newsweek Magazine,* October 21, 1985.

11   *"I pleaded with the terrorists":* New York Times, October 29, 1985.

12   *"Who is speaking? Is this Majed":* Kennedy School (A).

14   *"The aim of the operation":* "Port in Israel Described as Target of Terrorists Who Seized Vessel," *New York Times,* October 11, 1985.

15   *"I can't believe this is happening to us":* "To Hostage Families, Waiting Back Home Is Also a Nightmare," *New York Times,* October 9, 1985.

16   *"We met at the Italian":* Veliotes interview.

16   *"Abdel Meguid, a formal":* Ibid.

16   *"The Italian agreed":* Ibid.

17   *"I am the captain":* New York Times, October 13, 1985.

17   *"When they left":* Ibid.

17   *"Fedayeen, fedayeen":* Ibid.

17   *"They had an assignment":* Ibid.

18   *"Several minutes later":* "Cheers, The Heartbreak At Apartment on 10th St.," *New York Times,* October 10, 1985.

18   *"It was such a shock":* Lisa and Ilsa Klinghoffer interview.

19   *"I and Bassam [al-Ashker] agreed":* "Terrorist Reverses Confession, Denies Killing Klinghoffer," *Houston Chronicle,* June 20, 1986.

19   *"I went to the bridge":* Veliotes interview.

19   *"Leon Klinghoffer was murdered":* "Ship-to-Shore Report," *Washington Post,* October 10, 1985.

Chapter 2

20   *"They have actually left Egypt":* "'Surprising' U.S. Action Angers Egypt," *Washington Post,* October 12, 1985.

20   *"They left Egypt":* "U.S. Jets Intercept Plane With Hijackers," *Washington Post,* October 11, 1985.

21   *"Klinghoffer and his wife were singled out":* "P.L.O. Aide Disputes Report of Killing," *New York Times,* October 11, 1985.

21   *"I tried to pass the"*: Veliotes interview.

21   *"Italy is a friend of ours"*: "P.L.O. Say Tunisians Refused Entry to Egyptian Plane Before It Left Cairo," *New York Times*, October 12, 1985.

22   *"a big lie fabricated by the intelligence service"*: "P.L.O. Aide," *New York Times*, October 11, 1985.

22   *"made no claims on the hijackers"*: "You Can Feel the Damage," *Time Magazine*, October 28, 1985.

22   *"all right"*: "Reagan Briefly Implies PLO Could Try Pirates," *Washington Post*, October 11, 1985.

23   *"If the captain had told us"*: "U.S. Jets," *Washington Post*, October 11, 1985.

23   *"If they were planing"*: Jim Stark, telephone interview with the author, October 19, 2002.

24   *"I didn't remember Yamamoto"*: Poindexter interview.

25   *"On behalf of the President"*: Ibid.

26   *"We got this thing off"*: Stark interview.

26   *"That's a terrible idea"*: William Crowe, *The Line of Fire* (New York, NY: Simon & Schuster, 1993), 122.

27   *"We knew we had a mission"*: Ralph Zia, interview with author, November 1, 2002. The other statements by Zia in this section are drawn from this interview.

27   *"I was ready to launch"*: Steve Weatherspoon, email to author, November 6, 2002. The other statements by Weatherspoon in this section are drawn from this interview.

30   *"I'm saying you are too close"*: Martin, David C., and Walcott, John, *Best Laid Plans* (New York: Harper & Row, 1988), 250.

31   *"I identified myself"*: Michael A. Ledeen, *Perilous Statecraft* (New York, NY: Charles Scribner's Sons, 1988), 178.

33   *"If it were up to me"*: "The Achille Lauro Hijacking (B)," Case Program, C16-88-864.0, Kennedy School of Government, Harvard College, 1988.

33   *"obtain useful elements"*: Ibid.

34   *"I am not worried"*: Tom Clancy, with Carl Stiner & Tony Koltz, *Shadow Warriors* (New York: GP Putnam's Sons, 2002), 285.

34   *"We could get the hijackers"*: Poindexter interview.

35   *"I think the media mistakenly"*: Jim Hattendorf at KABC-TV in Los Angeles played a tape of Odeh's statement for me over the telephone on October 23, 2002.

35   *"We Bag the Bums"*: *New York Daily News*, October 11, 1985.

35   *"the good guys finally won one"*: "Getting Even," *Newsweek Magazine*, October 21, 1985.

35   *"in a number of incidents"*: "Transcript of White House News Conference on the Hijacking," *New York Times*, October 12, 1985.

36   *"These young Americans"*: Ibid.

36   *"He rose from his chair"*: Poindexter interview.

36   *"We had the planes"*: "The Price of Success," *Time Magazine*, October 28, 1985.

36   *"hijacked the hijackers"*: "Kennedy School (B).

36   *"There is no difference"*: "Arafat Says Interception Showed 'Cowboy Logic,'" *New York Times*, October 13, 1985.

36   *"We did this"*: "Transcript," *New York Times*, October 12, 1985.

37   *"I heard the explosion"*: "Bomb Kills 1 in Santa Ana Office," *Los Angeles Times*, October 11, 1985.

37   *"Violence only begets"*: "Kahane Backers Rededicate Themselves to Cause," *Los Angeles Times*, November 7, 1990.

37   *"very committed to the idea"*: "F.B.I. Investigates Bombing of a U.S. Arab Group," *New York Times*, October 13, 1985.

37   *"condemned the hijacking"*: "Alex Odeh: Arab-American Victim of Hate," *Washington Post*, October 13, 1985.

38   *"If they want to kill me"*: "I Never Thought This Could Happen in America," *Los Angeles Times*, November 11, 1985.

38   *"He was a very quiet"*: "Alex Odeh," *Washington Post*, October 13, 1985.

39   *"We hope to resolve"*: Kennedy School (B).

39   *"he [Abbas] knew how to behave"*: Ibid.

41   *"did not, in the Justice Minister's opinion"*: Ibid.

41   *"I received a copy of the"*: Veliotes interview.

42   *"uncontrollable actions could result"*: "You Can Feel the Damage," *Time Magazine*, October 28, 1985.

43   *"I am familiar with your situation"*: Kennedy School (A).

45   *"Congress may be guilty"*: "Two Leaks, But by Whom?" *Newsweek Magazine*, July 27, 1987.

Chapter 3

46   *"I spit in their faces"*: "Hostages Tell of a 'Death List,'" *New York Times*, October 13, 1985.

46   *"I started knocking on cabin"*: Veliotes interview.

47   *"I was appalled"*: Ibid.

47   *"Get away"*: New York Times, October 13, 1985.

47   *"She told us not to"*: Lisa and Ilsa Klinghoffer interview.

48   *"It could have been my father"*: "Aged Victim, Portrayed as Helpless, Is Recalled as a Strong, Happy Man," *New York Times*, October 11, 1985.

48   *"I want to shoot him"*: Clancy, 293.

48   *"Thank God the President"*: "15 Passengers, on Return to U.S., Tell of Terror on the Cruise Liner," *New York Times*, October 13, 1985.

49   *"It was a bittersweet homecoming"*: Lisa and Ilsa Klinghoffer interview.

49   *"So many people called"*: *Ibid.*

49   *"a symbol of righteousness"*: "A Somber Homecoming for Leon Klinghoffer," *New York Times*, October 21, 1985.

50   *"an act of an unjust"*: "Klinghoffer Eulogized as Public and Private Hero," *New York Times*, October 22, 1985.

50   *"The world knows you"*: *Ibid.*

50   *"It was wonderful"*: Lisa and Ilsa Klinghoffer interview.

50   *"I'm so proud of you"*: "Reagan Meets Family of Slain U.S. Hostage," *New York Times*, October 26, 1985.

51   *"I believe that my"*: "Widow Urges World Fight on Terror," *New York Times*, October 31, 1985.

51   *"I have to do everything"* and *"We were afraid to go outside"*: Lisa and Ilsa Klinghoffer interview.

52   *"Some other people"*: "Klinghoffer Family Finds Pressures Hard to Escape," *New York Times*, October 31, 1985.

53   *"probably overplayed"*: "Evolution in Hijack Coverage," *Broadcasting*, November 11, 1985.

53   *"Pornography of grief"*: "Crisis Coverage and the Media," *Chicago Tribune*, June 28, 1985.

53   *"The terrorists seemed"*: "The Quick-Hit Crisis," *Washington Post*, October 12, 1985.

53   *"I have a problem"*: "America's Ordeal by Television," *Washington Post*, July 2, 1985.

53   *"the theater of the absurd"*: *Ibid.*

53   *"What the Shi'ite terrorists"*: "Shiite Spin Control," *The New Republic*, July 15, 1985.

54   *"There are millions of people"*: "P.L.O. Aide Bids U.S. Produce Evidence of Hijacking Link," *New York Times*, October 15, 1985.

55   *"a low-level thug"*: "A Terrorist Talks About Life, Warns of More Deaths," *Wall Street Journal*, September 10, 1990.

55   *"He was like a commander"*: "Wanted! Terrorist Abu Abbas Escapes with the Connivance of Italy and Yugoslavia, Setting Off Recriminations in the United States," *Newsweek Magazine*, October 28, 1985.

56   *"Danny helped our neighbor"*: "The World Should Know What He Did to My Family," *Washington Post*, May 18, 2003.

57   *"By the time we"*: *Ibid.*

58   *"fired warning shots"*: "In Yugoslavia, Freed P.L.O. Aide Says Fighters Fired Warning Shots," *New York Times*, October 13, 1985.

58   *"for a brief rest"*: *Ibid.*

58   *"If someone really died"*: "Palestinian Says Hijackers Told Him They Didn't Kill Anyone," *New York Times*, October 14, 1985.

59   *"pure accident"*: *Ibid.*

59   *"How could four idiots"*: "The Price of Success," *Time Magazine*, October 28, 1985.

59   *"Frankly, I am very upset"*: "Mubarak, Furious at U.S., Demands a Public Apology," *New York Times*, October 15, 1985.

60   *"Reagan has humiliated Mubarak"*: "A Chill in Egypt Ties," *New York Times*, October 13, 1985.

60   *"Mubarak, assassination awaits you"*: "Hosni Mubarak; The Angry Man of the Nile," *U.S. News & World Report*, October 28, 1985.

60   *"You know every country"*: *Time Magazine*, October 28, 1985.

60   *"Never"*: *Ibid.*

60   *"U.S. regrets the need to intercept"*: Veliotes interview.

61   *"I was the target"* and *"He angrily handed"*: *Ibid.*

61   *"The Egyptian ministry"* and *"The Egyptians also had"*: *Ibid.*

61   *"We were bound"*: Poindexter interview.

62   *"placate the Egyptian government"*: "Tough-Talking Ambassador to Egypt Quits Job After *Achille Lauro* Flap," *Houston Chronicle*, January 8, 1985.

62   *"No truth to that story"*: Veliotes interview.

62   *"I am not at all happy"*: Kennedy School (B).

62   *"the tone of certain prose"*: *Ibid.*

62   *"During the past week"*: "Reagan Sends Conciliatory Note to Italian Leader," *New York Times*, October 20, 1985.

63   *"anxious to see you"*: *Ibid.*

64   *"Not even the Israelis"*: *Time Magazine*, October 28, 1985.

64   *"This time Arafat"*: *Ibid.*

64   *"legitimate response," "expression of self-defense,"* and *"The bombing surprised"*: "Putting It Back Together," *Time Magazine*, November 11, 1985.

65   *"The PLO reaffirms its declaration"*: "Documents on Palestine," www.al-bab.com/arab/docs/pal/pal1.htm.

65   *"Incidents have affirmed"*: "Arafat Denounces Terrorism, Pledges to Punish Violators," *Washington Post*, November 8, 1985.

65   *"After what seemed so long"*: "The Reaction: Flash of Emotion, Surge of Pride, Sense of Relief," *Washington Post*, October 12, 1985.

65   *"I was told that the PLO"*: Zia interview.

66   *"Arafat meant the word"*: "Smile When You Say That," *Time Magazine*, October 28, 1985.

66   *"But Washington had turned Abbas"*: "The Price of Success," *Time*, October 28, 1985.

67   *"Odeh appeared on television"* and *"No Jew or American"*: "Bomb Kills Leader of U.S. Arab Group," *New York Times*, October 12, 1985.

67   *"I have no tears"*: "JDL Named in Probe," *Washington Post*, November 9, 1985.

67   *"I'm not crying"*: http://www.jdl.org/information/faq.shtml.

67   *"Keep Jews Alive"*: Jewish Militant to Plead Guilty to Bomb Plot," *The Guardian*, February 4, 2003.

68   *"We are attributing the bombing"*: "FBI Attributes Fatal Santa Ana Bombing to JDL," *Los Angeles Times*, November 9, 1985.

68   *"I really resent the fact"*: *Washington Post*, November 8, 1985.

68   *"Arab individuals"*: FBI Steps Up Efforts in Probe of Attacks on Arab-Americans," *Los Angeles Times*, December 12, 1985.

68   *"The same degree of vigor"*: "Jackson Critical of FBI Probe," *Houston Chronicle*, October 13, 1986.

69   *"Leon Klinghoffer is now"*: *Washington Post*, October 15, 1985.

69   *"Arab-Americans could be forgiven"*: "Terror Double Standard," *The New Republic*, November 4, 1985.

69   *"Two equally heinous crimes"*: "Victims of Terror," *Washington Post*, November 1, 1985.

70   *"Arab Americans have sharply"*: *Washington Post*, November 9, 1985.

70   *"The Administration deeply deplores"*: "F.B.I. Investigates Bombing of a U.S. Arab Group," *New York Times*, October 13, 1985.

70   *"blatant disregard"*: "U.S. Commission Told of Harassment, Discrimination," *Los Angeles Times*, February 12, 1986.

70   *"Reagan sees Mrs. Klinghoffer"*: "I Never Thought This Could Happen in America," *Los Angeles Times*, November 1985.

Chapter 4

72   *"She went downhill fast"*: Lisa and Ilsa Klinghoffer interview.

72   *"U.S. terrorism"*: "Terror Summit to Map U.S. War," *Chicago Tribune*, January 10, 1986.

73   *"America is now conducting"*: "Attacks Planned in U.S. Terrorist," *Chicago Tribune*, May 6, 1986.

73   *"Let him try"* and following quotations: "'Let Him Try' Reagan Says of Threat by Terrorist to Strike Against U.S.," *Houston Chronicle*, May 6, 1986.

74   *"Terrorism thrives on this"*: "Reagan Defiant After Threats," *Los Angeles Times*, May 7, 1986.

74   *"We think it's reprehensible"*: "NBC 'Complicity' Assailed," *Chicago Tribune*, May 7, 1986.

74   *"American television viewers"*: "Letting Terrorists Call the Shots?" *Newsweek Magazine*, May 19, 1986.

74   *"But it was clear"*: "NBC: How to Protect a Terrorist," *Washington Post*, May 19, 1986.

74   *"They missed the news"*: "Caught by the Camera," *Time Magazine*, May 19, 1986.

74   *"the deal NBC struck"*: "NBC's Abbas Interview: A Dishonorable Deal," *Washington Post*, May 17, 1986.

74   *"got it badly wrong"*: "Playing the Terrorist's Game," *U.S. News & World Report*, June 9, 1986.

75   *"The profession of journalism"*: "NBC's Covenant With a Terrorist," *Chicago Tribune*, May 11, 1986.

75   *"We would have run it"*: *Time Magazine*, May 19, 1986.

75   *"NBC is neither a national intelligence"*: "Why NBC Agreed Not to Tell Where Abu Abbas Was," *Washington Post*, May 31, 1986.

75   *"would do it in roughly"*: "The Crafty Art of Media Propaganda," *San Francisco Chronicle*, June 4, 1986.

75   *"Everybody was trying"*: "Arab's Interview Stirs News Debate," *New York Times*, May 7, 1986.

76   *"NBC gave Abbas the ideal forum"*: "NBC's Contribution to Terrorism's Cause," *New York Times*, May 18, 1986.

77   *"The terror of terrorvision continues"*: "Terrorism Crawls Under the Cover of Objectivity," *Los Angeles Times*, May 9, 1986.

77   *"terrorist,"* and *"freedom fighter"*: www.fair.org/media-beat/011001.html.

77   *"criminals," "eco-terrorists," "Christian," "gunman,"* and *"mass murderer"*: Brigitte L. Nacos, *Mass-Mediated Terrorism* (Lanham, Md.:, Rowman & Littlefield, 2002), 94–99.

78   *"I would rather have news"*: "Global Awareness: An Obligation to Inform and Listen," *Knight-Ridder/Tribune News Service*, September 17, 2002.

79   *"I was in Iraq for the explicit"* and following quotations: Duane R. Clarridge, with Digby Diehl, *A Spy For All Seasons* (New York, NY: Scribner, 1997), 15–20.

81   *"must await further investigation"*: " '85 Northridge Blast 1 of 4 Linked by FBI to 'Elements' of JDL," *Los Angeles Times*, July 6, 1986.

81   *"What the FBI is doing is simple"*: "Northridge Blast Cited FBI Links JDL 'Elements,' " *Los Angeles Times*, July 3, 1986.

81   *"met with negative results"*: "FBI Denies Having Suspended Investigation of Odeh Death," *Los Angeles Times*, July 16, 1986.

81   *"I assure you it is pending and ongoing"*: Ibid.

81   *"The Alex Odeh case"*: "FBI Attributes Fata; Bombing in Santa Ana to 'Extremists,' " *Los Angeles Times*, July 17, 1986.

81 *"While our government apprehends"*: Ibid.

81 *"Approaching a year"*: "A Year Later, a Bomber Is Still at Large," *Los Angeles Times*, October 10, 1986.

82 *"When I say my husband"*: "'I Never Thought This Could Happen in America,'" *Los Angeles Times*, November 11, 1985.

82 *"growing skepticism within the Arab"*: Los Angeles Times, October 10, 1986.

82 *"We are afraid the FBI's effectiveness"*: "500 Attend Dinner to Honor Slain Leader," *Los Angeles Times*, October 12, 1986.

82 *"individuals who died"*: "Fullerton Marker Honoring Dead of Cal State Dedicated," *Los Angeles Times*, May 5, 1986.

82 *"understanding about emerging"*: "Odeh's Message of Peace Lives On," *Los Angeles Times*, October 12, 1986.

83 *"Lies are like still ashes"*: "Alex Odeh: Arab-American Victim of Hate," *Washington Post*, October 13, 1985.

83 *"reconstructed the killing"*: "Italian Prosecutors Report Reconstructing the Killing," *New York Times*, October 17, 1985.

84 *"We are somewhat perplexed"*: "Sicilians Said to Issue Warrant for a Palestinian in Hijacking," *New York Times*, October 27, 1985.

84 *"There are no minor accomplices"*: "Italy Hints at Warrant for Abbas," *New York Times*, November 12, 1985.

85 *"terrorist methods"*: "Italy Convicts Palestinians in Arms Case," *New York Times*, November 19, 1985.

85 *"I do not indulge in politics"*: Ibid.

87 *"created the action,"* *"having lost their own land,"* and *"the extreme of ferociousness and inhumanity"*: "Italians Say Abbas Masterminded Ship Hijacking," *New York Times*, June 11, 1986.

87 *"I think it's rather objective"*: Ibid.

88 *"Comrades, we are here"*: "Achille Lauro Trial Opens," *Houston Chronicle*, June 19, 1986.

89 *"I remember that it was 3:12"*: "Terrorist Reverses Confession, Denies Killing Klinghoffer," *Houston Chronicle*, June 20, 1986.

89 *"How do you defend yourself?"* and *"I have not killed"*: Ibid.

89 *"I don't know what I said"*: Ibid.

89 *"None of us killed"*: "Outburst by 2 Defendants Stalls Ship Hijacking Trial," *Los Angeles Times*, June 20, 1986.

90 *"I embraced her"*: "Achille Lauro Suspect Accuses Terrorist's Leader of Killing Klinghoffer," *Los Angeles Times*, June 21, 1986.

90 *"The difference between"*: "Cruise Liner Hijacker Says Fellow Suspect Killed Klinghoffer," *Houston Chronicle*, June 21, 1986.

90 *"He told me that"*: "Los Angeles Times, June 21, 1986.

90 *"My passport was grabbed"*: "Greek Denies Giving Passport to an Achille Lauro Hijacker," *New York Times*, June 22, 1986.

90   *"no one would see him"*: Court Hears Man Who Dumped Klinghoffer's
      Body," *San Francisco Chronicle*, June 24, 1986.
91   *"I saw this man"*: "Waiter Points Out Klinghoffer Killer: al-Molqi,"
      Houston Chronicle, June 24, 1986.
91   *"Americano, boom, boom"*: Ibid.
91   *"This is the first one"*: "Skipper Denies Hush Over Klinghoffer," *Chi-
      cago Tribune*, June 25, 1986.
91   *"essential element"*: "Captain Implicates Accused in Slaying on *Achille
      Lauro*," *Houston Chronicle*, June 24, 1986.
91   *"About 3:15 or 3:30"*: "Statement of Mrs. Klinghoffer, Now Dead, Read
      in Court," *Los Angeles Times*, June 25, 1986.
92   *"I would rather die"*: "*Achille Lauro* Suspect Tries to Hang Himself,"
      Los Angeles Times, June 26, 1986.
92   *"so much fuss"*: Ibid.
92   *"The groups that belong"*: "Attorney Says Klinghoffer was PLO
      'Enemy,'" *San Francisco Chronicle*, July 2, 1986.
93   *"Abbas was not the mastermind"*: "Defense Hits Hijack Charge," *Chi-
      cago Tribune*, July 5, 1986.
93   *"There were 385 pairs of eyes"*: "Hijack Jury Asked to Ignore Cause,"
      Chicago Tribune, July 6, 1986.
93   *"This case is not about terrorism"*: "'Long Live Arafat!' Cruise Ship
      Defendant Says," *Chicago Tribune*, July 8, 1986.
93   *"kidnapping for terrorist ends"*: "Italian Jury Gives Cruise-Ship Killer
      30-Year Sentence," *New York Times*, July 11, 1986.
94   *"a selfish, political act"*: Ibid.
94   *"soldiers fighting for their ideals," "armed Terrorist band," and "has as
      its goal"*: "Italy Convicts 11 Men in *Achille Lauro* Hijacking," Los
      Angeles Times, July 11, 1986.
94   *"They have grown up"*: Ibid.
94   *"Palestinian refugee passed"*: "Italian Court Gives Reason for Sentence
      in *Achille Lauro* Case," *Los Angeles Times*, October 29, 1986.
95   *"They are all guilty," "I don't understand," and "It's not over yet"*:
      Klinghoffer's Family, Cruise Ship Passengers Decry Hijackers' Sen-
      tences," *Houston Chronicle*, July 11, 1986.
95   *"I think they deserve more"*: Ibid.
95   *"the United States is pleased"*: *New York Times*, July 11, 1986.
95   *"leave Italian and international public opinion"*: "Prosecution Appeals
      in *Achille Lauro* Case," *Houston Chronicle*, July 13, 1986.

Chapter 5

97   *"When people ask me"*: "Terrorist Stereotype Hurts Palestinians Who
      Try to Heal Wounds," *Chicago Tribune*, April 28, 1988.

98   *"Occasionally I talk to the FBI":* "Family of Slain Arab-American Still Waiting for Justice," *Los Angeles Times*, October 18, 1987.

98   *"They ignored an act":* Ibid.

98   *"It's really good to hear":* "Odeh Family Hails Grand Jury Probe of Anti-Arab Crimes," *Los Angeles Times*, April 4, 1987.

98   *"The Anti-Discrimination Committee":* Ibid.

99   *"There is a similarity":* Los Angeles Times, October 18, 1987.

99   *"have been untimely":* "Israel Unhelpful in JDL Terrorist probe, FBI Says," *Los Angeles Times*, November 19, 1987.

100   *"We are hoping to bring":* "Garden Grove Backers of Palestinians, Israel Protest at Church," *Los Angeles Times*, December 25, 1987.

100   *"because wherever they":* Ibid.

100   *"If you don't take this show":* "Bomb Suspect Called Dedicated Activist," *Los Angeles Times*, July 17, 1988.

101   *"Death Row":* "L.A.-Born JDL Man a Suspect in '85 Slaying of Alex Odeh," *Los Angeles Times*, June 25, 1988.

101   *"There's a sort of feeling":* "Bombing Trial Snarled in Treaty Issue," *Los Angeles Times*, July 30, 1988.

102   *"was not committed":* "Millionaire Broker Arrested as Suspect in Fatal Bombing," *Los Angeles Times*, August 13, 1988.

102   *"I'd like it to be settled":* "Alex Used to Say that Fighting Is for Animals," *Los Angeles Times*, October 11, 1988.

103   *"Abbas is out":* "PLO Drops Terrorist Abbas from Panel," *Los Angeles Times*, April 23, 1987.

103   *"This issue is not so important,"* and *"He is unimportant":* Ibid.

103   *"We are protesting":* "Palestinian Leaders Hail Rise in Attacks Against Israel," *San Francisco Chronicle*, April 22, 1987.

103   *"How many times":* "Abbas Limits Future Acts to Israel Targets," *Los Angeles Times*, April 24, 1987.

103   *"In all struggles":* "Ship Hijacker Fails to Fit PLO 'Image,'" *San Francisco Chronicle*, April 23, 1987.

105   *"We do periodic reviews":* "Justice Dept. Drops Warrant in *Achille Lauro* Hijacking," *Washington Post*, January 17, 1988.

105   *"This was forfeiting our right":* Ibid.

105   *"I'm dismayed":* "Killing Haunts Family," *USA Today*, January 19, 1988.

106   *"Maybe he was trying to swim for it":* "Hijacker Defends *Achille Lauro* Killing," *New York Times*, November 14, 1988.

106   *"You have an accident":* Ibid.

106   *"I attacked him":* "Diverse PLO Delegates Work Toward Consensus," *Washington Post*, November 15, 1988.

107   *"Why do you defend":* "Knowing the Enemy," *Time Magazine*, November 7, 1988.

107 *"Has Israel expressed":* "Abul Abbas Other Remarks," *New York Times,* December 7, 1988.

108 *"By focusing so relentlessly":* Ibid.

108 *"When the Palestine National Council":* "Yes, Mr. Shultz, Keep Arafat Out," *New York Times,* November 30, 1988.

109 *"prepared for substantive":* "U.S., in Shift, Agrees to 'Substantive Dialogue' with PLO," *Washington Post,* December 15, 1988.

109 *"We can't kick him off":* "Arafat Will Seek to Halt Terrorism but Cites Limits," *Houston Chronicle,* December 18, 1988.

110 *"I phoned them and gave":* "Meetings Between Widow, Producer Lead to Launching of 'Achille Lauro,'" *Houston Chronicle,* February 12, 1989.

110 *"My mother wanted":* Lisa and Ilsa Klinghoffer interview.

110 *"She called me to come":* "Tragic Story Told of Valiant Klinghoffers," *San Francisco Chronicle,* February 12, 1989.

111 *"If you don't have the rights":* Houston Chronicle, February 12, 1989.

111 *"Tamara approached me to write":* Bob Collins, interview with author, November 27, 2002. All of the statements by Collins in this section are drawn from this interview.

111 *"I only take on stories":* "News that Turns into TV Dramas," *USA Today,* February 13, 1989.

111 *"Spain, Italy, Yugoslavia":* Ibid.

112 *"We didn't see the terrorists":* Ibid.

112 *"Terrorism as entertainment":* "Reynolds, Wry and Spry in 'Stryker,'" *Washington Post,* February 13, 1989.

112 *"Even if they have been":* Ibid.

113 *"amounts to little more":* "'Achille Lauro' Suffering Aweigh," *USA Today,* February 13, 1989.

113 *"I don't know":* "*Achille Lauro* Tragedy," *New York Times,* February 13, 1989.

113 *"Whether news or narrative," "Collins obviously takes," "What's more,"* and *"But the television industry":* "'Achille Lauro' Centers on Personal Drama of Hijacking," *Los Angeles Times,* February 13, 1989.

114 *"I liked how it portrayed":* Lisa and Ilsa Klinghoffer interview.

Chapter 6

115 *"Characteristics that were similar":* "The California Murder Case that Israel Is Sweeping Under the Rug," *Los Angeles Times,* May 13, 1990.

115 *"Justice Department sources assert":* Ibid.

116 *"His crude attempt":* "Alex Odeh's Murder and the JDL," *Los Angeles Times,* May 26, 1990.

116 *"Perhaps I should have"*: "JDL Reply," *Los Angeles Times*, August 27, 1989.

116 *"We lost a tremendous amount"*: "JDL's New Patrol Leader of Militant Defense Group Wants to Change Its Approach, Image," *Los Angeles Times*, July 23, 1990.

117 *"I have been expecting"*: "Suspects in O.C. Bomb Slaying Held in Israel," *Los Angeles Times*, March 25, 1991.

117 *"There were so many political"*: "Reliving the *Achille Lauro* Tragedy," *Los Angeles Times*, April 29, 1990.

118 *"We were never threatened"*: Alberto Negrin, telephone interview with author, April 1, 2003. All other Negrin statements were drawn from that interview.

118 *"We kept the whole thing"*: *Los Angeles Times*, April 29, 1990.

118 *"We had an American actor"*: Ibid.

118 *"Voyage of Terror* comes off like"*: "Voyage of Terror," *Washington Post*, May 1, 1990.

118 *"most unintentionally funny impersonations"*: Ibid.

118 *"This version of the story"*: Ibid.

119 *"Perhaps not surprisingly"*: "New Film on *Achille Lauro* Hijacking," *New York Times*, May 2, 1990.

119 *"Sometimes I dream"*: *Washington Post*, May 1, 1990.

119 *"cards in a stacked deck"*: *New York Times*, May 2, 1990.

119 *"We are not saying"*: *Los Angeles Times*, April 29, 1990.

119 *"four young people"*: Ibid.

120 *"Television's Palestinians never"*: "Television Chose to Make the Palestinian America's Bogeyman," *Los Angeles Times*, January 10, 1988.

120 *"Yet where are the voices"*: Jack Shaheen, interview with author, May 13, 2003.

120 *"My colleague, Alex Odeh"*: "Our Cultural Demon—The 'Ugly Arab,'" *Washington Post*, August 19, 1990.

120 *"One event epitomized"*: Shaheen interview.

121 *"There are no Arab-Americans"*: Ibid.

121 *"I was saddened by"*: Ibid.

123 *"The U.S. is horrified"*: "Israelis Kill 4 in Thwarting Raid at Tel Aviv Beach," *Houston Chronicle*, May 31, 1990.

123 *"We are not responsible"*: "Arafat Denies P.L.O. Tie to Raid But his Mild Stand Troubles U.S.," *New York Times*, June 1, 1990.

123 *"a resort for senior Israeli army"*: "Raid Aimed at Israeli Officers, Abbas Says," *Los Angeles Times*, June 4, 1990.

123 *"The goals of the operation"*: "Guerrilla Says Raid Aimed to Kill Civilians," *Los Angeles Times*, June 6, 1990.

124 *"cleanse the hotel"*: "Alleged Raider Says Civilians in Tel Aviv Were His Targets," *Washington Post*, June 7, 1990.

124   *"The PLO is in a mess"*: "PLO Moderates Seeking Renewed Talks with
      U.S.," *Washington Post*, June 30, 1990.
124   *"We've given the PLO ample time"*: "Bush Suspends Talks with PLO,"
      Los Angeles Times, June 21, 1990.
125   *"All are held in a circle"*: "Making the Bad Guys Happy," *Washington
      Post*, June 24, 1990.
126   *"smokescreen"*: Antonio Cassese, *Terrorism, Politics and Law*
      (Princeton, NJ: Princeton University Press, 1989), 109.
128   *"made mistakes"*: "Mistakes Were Made, Israeli Says of Clash," *Chicago
      Tribune*, April 15, 1989.
129   *"We see this as the battle"*: "A Terrorist Talks About Life, Warns of More
      Deaths," *Wall Street Journal*, September 10, 1990.
129   *"Strike with your long arms"*: "Arafat's Iraq Debacle," *Wall Street Jour-
      nal*, August 24, 1990.
129   *"Broad-shouldered and six feet," "During the fight," "Klinghoffer,
      always I hear,"* and *"For two years we say"*: *Wall Street Journal*, Septem-
      ber 10, 1990.
130   *"We rule out any possibility"*: "Achille Lauro Terrorist Confirms Expul-
      sion of Group from Libya," *Boston Globe*, November 5, 1990.

Chapter 7

135   *"Our main goal was access"*: "Baker Knew of Terrorist, Iraq Ties,
      Records Show," *Los Angeles Times*, September 22, 1992.
135   *"For two years," "Up to now, there is,"* and *"We can kill thousands"*:
      "Terrorist Says His Patience Is Running Thin," *Knight Ridder/Tribune
      News Service*, July 1, 1993.
137   *"Our parents set out"*: "Urgent Need for Counterterroism Legislation
      Theme of 10th Anniversary Commemoration of Terrorist Murder of Leon
      Klinghoffer," Anti-Defamation League press release, October 27, 1995.
137   *"The story of Leon Klinghoffer"*: *Ibid.*
137   *"While we are strong supporters"*: "ADL Supports Giuliani's Position on
      Arafat," Anti-Defamation League press release, October 25, 1995.
138   *"I am happy to hear that"*: "Israel Will Turn Over 2 Suspects in 1980
      Bomb Death Extradition," *Los Angeles Times*, January 19, 1993.
138   *"They are trying to follow"*: *Ibid.*
138   *"I didn't do anything"*: "Suspect in '80 Bomb Death Extradited," *Los
      Angeles Times*, July 20, 1993.
138   *"What this is all about"*: *Ibid.*
138   *"I don't want to get into"*: *Ibid.*
138   *"This is a witch hunt"*: "Mail-Bombing Suspect a Man of Many Faces,"
      Los Angeles Times, August 5, 1993.

139 *"This whole thing"*: "Life Sentence for Man In Mail-Bomb Slaying," *San Francisco Chronicle*, February 8, 1994.

139 *"Alex Odeh . . . was an"*: "Statue a Tribute to Slain Activist," *Los Angeles Times*, April 11, 1994.

139 *"He taught the gentle wisdom"*: *Ibid.*

139 *"will remind us that"*: *Ibid.*

139 *"It's one thing to have"*: *Ibid.*

140 *"We're going to make"*: "JDL Protests Statue Honoring Slain Palestinian Activist," *Los Angeles Times*, April 13, 1994.

140 *"What Mr. Rubin thinks"*: *Ibid.*

140 *"Let the supplanter look"*: The opera's libretto can be viewed at http:// www.radio.rai.it/radio3/radio3_suite/archivio_2002/eventi/2002_02 _09_klinghoffer/libretto.htm.

141 *"Opera is a bloody business"*: "Opera As a Source of Healing," *Newsweek Magazine*, April 1, 1991.

141 *"Instead of a gory thriller"*: "Idealism as Opera, 'Klinghoffer' Is a Parable for Modern Times," *St. Louis Post–Dispatch*, December 6, 1992.

141 *"I knew as soon"*: "The Birth of *The Death of Klinghoffer*," *Harvard Magazine*, September–October, 1991.

142 *"stand apart from the more"*: *Ibid.*

142 *"remind us that this event"*: *Ibid.*

142 *"We don't show a sweet old man"*: "'Klinghoffer' Tries to Go Behind Headlines," *Christian Science Monitor*, September 5, 1991.

142 *"fusion of music and poetry"*: "In Its Finest Moments, 'Klinghoffer' Is Superb," *Boston Globe*, September 7, 1991.

143 *"Klinghoffer is not an overt"*: "Chorus of a Tragedy," *Washington Post*, March 21, 1991.

143 *"pro-nobody"*: "Opera Out of Terrorism," *Los Angeles Times*, September 1, 1991.

143 *"Through this translation"*: "'Klinghoffer' Librettist Revels in Power of Words," *Boston Globe*, September 1, 1991.

143 *"I think we would"*: "Sellars' 'Klinghoffer' Opera Premiers in Brussels," *Los Angeles Times*, March 21, 1991.

143 *"We are soldiers," "You just want,"* and *"You are always"*: *Ibid.*

143 *"On the 'politically correct'"*: "Adams: The Death of Klinghoffer," *Time Magazine*, April 1, 1991.

144 *"A blazing bombshell"*: "'Klinghoffer' Opera Causes Uproar," *San Francisco Chronicle*, September 12, 1991.

144 *"pompous, turgid"*: "Reaction Mixed to 'Klinghoffer' in N.Y.," *Los Angeles Times*, September 9, 1991.

144 *"The opera has two arguments"*: "The Death of Klinghoffer," *The New Republic*, September 30, 1991.

144 *"There is nothing trendy":* Boston Globe, September 7, 1991.

145 *"Life and the world":* Los Angeles Times, September 9, 1991.

145 *"I was told for months," "I liked the aria,"* and *"We bought our own":* Lisa and Ilsa Klinghoffer interview.

145 *"While we understand":* "Klinghoffer Daughters Protest Opera," New York Times, September 11, 1991.

145 *"Only those who":* St. Louis Post–Dispatch, December 6, 1992.

146 *"criminal terrorist organization":* www.pbs.org/frontlineworld/stories/sierraleone/alkassar.html.

146 *"When you're buying arms":* "Pan Am 103: Why Did They Die?" Time Magazine, April 27, 1992.

Chapter 8

150 *"Rotterdam Lloyd designed":* Peter Kohler, interview with author February 21, 2003.

155 *"We were alerted":* "Deadly Fire on Achille Lauro—Hundreds Flee," San Francisco Chronicle, December 1, 1994.

155 *"Then there was no water":* "Survivors of Cruise Fire Tell of Terror," Chicago Tribune, December 4, 1994.

156 *"The business about women":* "Crew on Blaze Liner 'Rushed for the Lifeboats,'" The Guardian, December 6, 1994.

156 *"We had to climb up the side":* Chicago Tribune, December 4, 1994.

156 *"He was put in my life raft":* "Survivors Tell Stories of Terror, Courage in Achille Lauro Fire," Houston Chronicle, December 4, 1994.

156 *"The whole half of the ship":* "Achille Lauro Burning," Houston Chronicle, December 1, 1994.

157 *"The* Achille Lauro *is listing":* "Liner Achille Lauro Blazes Uncontrollably," St. Louis Post–Dispatch, December 1, 1994.

157 *"Many had tears of relief":* "Achille Lauro Survivors Take Long Journey Home," New Orleans Times–Picayune, December 2, 1994.

157 *"The crew were absolutely":* "Survivors Laud Cruise Director," Houston Chronicle, December 5, 1994.

157 *"The captain did not keep":* "Achille Lauro Crew Criticized by Passengers," San Francisco Chronicle, December 6, 1994.

158 *"We say good riddance":* "Ship of Ghouls," Boston Globe, December 3, 1994.

Chapter 9

159 *"My face is not":* "Now Is the Time for Peace, Says Avowed Terrorist Abbas," USA Today, May 18, 1998.

159 *"Palestinians from abroad"*: http://www.israel.org/mfa/go.asp?M
     FAH00qa0.

160 *"I'm surprised"*: "Cruise Ship Hijacker Skips on Prison Pass," *Chicago
     Tribune*, March 3, 1996.

160 *"In Italy, after a certain"*: "U.S. Presses Italy to Recapture Terrorist Con-
     victed in Killing on *Achille Lauro*," *Washington Post*, March 6, 1996.

160 *"is probably quite far"*: "Rome Rejects U.S. Protests Over Hijacker, Law
     Cited in Escape of *Achille Lauro* Killer," *Washington Post*, March 8,
     1996.

160 *"The Italian government"*: "Killer's Flight in Italy May Spur Suit," *Bos-
     ton Globe*, March 10, 1996.

160 *"We want to see clearly"*: "Italy Probes How Hijacker Vanished," *Wash-
     ington Post*, March 12, 1996.

161 *"abysmal"*: "Italy, U.S. Offer Rewards in Search for Escaped Hijacker,"
     Washington Post, March 14, 1996.

161 *"It is something . . . very civilized"*: Ibid.

161 *"For us"*: "*Achille Lauro* Escapee Recaptured," *Chicago Tribune*, March
     23, 1996.

161 *"I was impressed by Italy's"*: "Daughter of *Achille Lauro* Victim in Italy
     Talks," *Reuters*, June 29, 1996.

162 *"We were pals"*: "Veteran Palestinian Fighters Reunite in Gaza for Major
     Vote," *Knight Ridder/Tribune News Services*, April 23, 1996.

163 *"We tried the way of blood"*: Ibid.

163 *"identified with groups"*: Ibid.

163 *"The killing of the passenger"*: "*Achille Lauro* Hijack Chief Talks of
     Peace," *Boston Globe*, April 23, 1996.

164 *"Mr. President, 99 senators"*: *Weekly Compilation of Presidential Docu-
     ments*, May 6, 1996.

164 *"What is attributed to Abu Abbas"*: "Request Denied," *USA Today*,
     May 2, 1996.

164 *"If they want to make peace"*: "Abu Abbas: From Terrorist to Peace
     Advocate," CNN, May 10, 1996.

165 *"I'm as puzzled by it"*: "*Achille Lauro* Plotter Recast as Proponent of
     Mideast Peace," *Boston Globe*, June 26, 1998.

165 *"It is important that"*: "ADL Urges Italy to Bring Convicted *Achille
     Lauro* Terrorist to Justices," Anti-Defamation League press release, May
     14, 1998.

165 *"My clients are deeply upset"*: *Boston Globe*, June 26, 1998.

166 *"Well, let me say that"*: "*Achille Lauro* Mastermind Says Klinghoffer
     'Provoked' Terrorists to Murder Him," The Zionist Organization of
     America news release, July 14, 1998.

166 *"Twenty years ago"*: *USA Today*, May 18, 1998.

166 *"Klinghoffer was not in our plans," "I was trying to work out,"* and *"Before, people in the rest"*: "Homecoming of a Hijacker," *The Guardian*, May 28, 1998.

167 *"When America wants you"*: *Boston Globe*, June 26, 1998.

167 *"Abbas is spitting"*: Zionist Organization of America news release, July 14, 1998.

168 *"For some group of people"*: "Red Paint Is Thrown on the Statue of Slain Activist," *Los Angeles Times*, February 7, 1997.

168 *"I just wish everyone"*: "Arab Americans Protest Statue Vandalism," *Los Angeles Times*, February 8, 1997.

169 *"unforeseeable, hostile"*: "Shiplines Deny Blame for *Achille Lauro*," *Travel Weekly*, May 15, 1986.

169 *"culpable defendant"*: Ibid.

169 *"conceived, conspired"*: "N.J. Agency with *Achille Lauro* Clients Files Suit Against PLO," *Travel Weekly*, November 6, 1986.

169 *"movement lawyer"*: "The Crusader," *Washington Post*, December 15, 2002.

170 *"do much to relieve"*: "The Very Long Arm of the Law," *The National Law Journal*, July 2, 1990.

170 *"Our lawyer called"*: "Klinghoffers Win Right to Sue PLO Over Their Father's Death," *Houston Chronicle*, July 8, 1990.

170 *"It's beyond what"*: Ibid.

171 *"They've ignored all sorts"*: "Hijack Suit Asks Arafat to Testify," *Chicago Tribune*, December 31, 1995.

171 *"amicable"*: "A Settlement with P.L.O. Over Terror On a Cruise," *New York Times*, August 12, 1997.

171 *"The PLO's defense," "They claimed that Arafat," "I was not surprised," "The Klinghoffer case"*: Rodney Gould, telephone interview with the author, March 16, 2003.

172 *"While the PLO was not"*: http://www.palestine-un.org/news/sep97_high.html.

172 *"I thought that it was just a PR"*: Lisa and Ilsa Klinghoffer interview.

Chapter 10

174 *"For years the FBI"*: "Pain of '85 Bombing Lingers," *Los Angeles Times*, October 6, 2002.

174 *"If you ask probing"* and *"One has to conclude"*: Sami Odeh, email to author on October 17, 2002.

175 *"We're frustrated"*: *Los Angeles Times*, October 6, 2002.

175 *"need a wakeup call"*: "JDL Chairman Accused in Plot to Bomb Mosque," *Houston Chronicle*, December 13, 2001.

175   *"witch hunt against Jews"*: "JDL Chairman Accused in Plot to Bomb Mosque," *Houston Chronicle*, December 13, 2001.

176   *"thugs and hooligans"*: "Jewish Activist Known for Tough Stance," *Los Angeles Times*, December 13, 2001.

176   *"There are more teams"*: "Jailed Jewish Militant Protector or Terrorist?" *Los Angeles Times*, January 22, 2002.

176   *"out to get"*: "Lawyers Seek to Sever Bombing Trial," *Los Angeles Times*, October 10, 2002.

176   *"It's just counterintuitive"*: "Jail Incident Is Not Fatal To Chairman of the JDL," *New York Times*, November 6, 2002.

176   *"I'm saying he was killed"*: "Jewish Defense League's Rubin Is Eulogized," *Los Angeles Times*, November 18, 2002.

177   *"If you want to admit to committing"*: "JDL Official Pleads Guilty in Bomb Plot," *Los Angeles Times*, February 5, 2003.

177   *"blow up an entire building"* and *"Rubin also said that"*: *Houston Chronicle*, December 13, 2002.

177   *"It's hard to say"*: Oliver "Buck" Revell, telephone interview with author, May 29, 2003.

178   *"Now even fundamentalists," "Theoretically, any country," "What happened did not," "grown weary of fighting,"* and *"the burly former guerilla"*: "Israel Lets In *Achille Lauro* Hijacker Turned Peacemaker," *The Guardian*, April 29, 2000.

179   *"They told me that they"* and *"I am proud of my past"*: "In Mideast, A Twist on Peace," *Chicago Tribune*, September 10, 2000.

180   *"ascertain that freedom"*: "The Temple Mount Must Be Open," *Wall Street Journal*, October 4, 2000.

180   *"start carrying out suicide"*: "Palestinian Group Plans Suicide Attacks Against Israel," *United Press International*, October 18, 2000.

180   *"As a result of the enemy's"*: "More Than 50 Palestinians Hurt in Clashes," *St. Louis Post–Dispatch*, October 29, 2000.

180   *"targeted and his life may be at risk"*: "Arafat 'Advised' PLF Secretary General Abbas to Postpone His Return to Gaza," *World News Connection*, May 3, 2001.

181   *"I hope [Abbas] and others"*: "Anyone Say Altalena?" *Jerusalem Post*, October 19, 2001.

181   *"We have read the letters"*: "Our Slain Father: The Outrage Lives," *New York Times*, October 12, 2001.

181   *"Ladies and gentlemen"*: "Boston Symphony Missed the Point on Art and Grieving," *San Francisco Chronicle*, November 7, 2001.

182   *"Of course art can provide solace," "Some have found Klinghoffer,"* and *"We can read about"*: "John Adams, Banned in Boston," *New York Times*, November 25, 2001.

182   *"The Death of Klinghoffer trades"* and *"Censorship is always deplor-able"*: "Music's Dangers and the Case for Control," *New York Times*, December 9, 2001.

183   *"broke all the rules"*: "Opera on TV Is a Disaster," *The Guardian*, May 1, 2003.

183   *"the first real masterpiece"*: "'Klinghoffer' Resonates Anew," *Los Angeles Times*, April 19, 2003.

183   *"a piece of work that"*: "Opera on TV Is a Disaster—Either a Laughable Hybrid or a Ghost of the Real Thing," *The Guardian*, May 1, 2003.

183   *"Is Klinghoffer anti-Semitic?"* and *"In the end Klinghoffer"*: "Is *Klinghoffer* anti-Semitic?" *New York Times*, May 4, 2003.

183   *"The opera is based on the idea"*: "Images of Evil's Flowering Disagree About Its Roots," *New York Times*, May 13, 2003.

184   *"What I try to do in the music"*: "Opera Film Caught Up in Mideast Conflict," *San Francisco Chronicle*, May 17, 2003.

184   *"It's not balanced—not at all"*: Ibid.

184   *"I find it kind of astounding"*: "Is Klinghoffer Anti-Semitic?" *New York Times*, May 4, 2003.

185   *"smoking guns"*: "60 Minutes," CBS Television News, September 29, 2002.

186   *"steadfastness"*: "'Achille Lauro' Hijacker Contacts Arafat," *Jerusalem Post*, October 1, 2002.

186   *"They say I am a terrorist"* and *"There is a big difference"*: "An Old Terrorist in Iraq," *Newsweek Magazine*, November 4, 2002.

187   *"soften American anger"* and *"I really haven't spent"*: "Ringleader of '85 *Achille Lauro* Hijacking Says Killing Wasn't His Fault," *New York Times*, November 8, 2002.

187   *"My visit comes in response"*: "PLO [sic] Secretary-General Abbas on Objectives of His Cairo Visit," *Asia Africa Intelligence Wire*, January 10, 2003.

188   *"reopening of old files"*: "Palestinian PLF Leader Cuts Short Cairo Visit After US Extradition Move," *Asia Africa Intelligence Wire*, January 11, 2003.

188   *"We are attempting to have him tried"*: "Italian Justice Minister Says 'No Objection' to Trial of Abu Abbas in USA," *Asia Africa Intelligence Wire*, April 20, 2003.

189   *"We're looking at the legal issues"*: "Tangled Legal Issues Complicate What to Do with Abbas," *St. Louis Post-Dispatch*, April 17, 2003.

190   *"They got him"*: "War with Iraq," *Los Angeles Times*, April 17, 2003.

190   *"We won't celebrate"*: Lisa Klinghoffer, telephone interview with author, May 2, 2003.

190   *"When something like this touches"*: *Los Angeles Times*, April 17, 2003.

190   *"is not sure it can convict"* and *"He's in custody"*: *New York Times*, November 3, 2003.

191   *"Our quest is over"*: Jerry Arbittier email, March 12, 2004.

191   *"Israel bombed and killed a lot of people"* and *"He's a symbol of resistance"*: "Lebanese Celebrate a Hero Killer Held 24 Years by Israel," *Chicago Tribune*, May 3, 2003.

191   *"We, the Palestinian nation"*: "Jailed Palestinian Calls for End to Violence," *San Francisco Chronicle*, May 26, 1995.

192   *"I am ready and willing"*: *Washington Post*, May 18, 2003.

Epilogue

193   *"a selfish, political act"* and *"soldiers fighting for their ideals"*: "Italian Jury Gives Cruise-Ship Killer 30-year Sentence," *New York Times*, July, 11, 1986.

194   *"Over the years"*: "Transcript," *New York Times*, October 8, 2002.

195   *"There is an Arabic saying"*: "A Terrorist Talks About Life," *Wall Street Journal*, September 10, 1990.

BIBLIOGRAPHY

Books

Aburish, Said K. *Arafat*. New York: Bloomsbury, 1998.

Buford, Kate. *Burt Lancaster: An American Life*. New York: Knopf, 2000.

Carey, Roane, ed. *The New Intifada*. London: Verso, 2001.

Cassese, Antonio. *Terrorism, Politics and Law*. Princeton: Princeton University Press, 1989.

Clancy, Tom, and Carl Stiner, with Tony Koltz. *Shadow Warriors*. New York: Putnam's Sons, 2002.

Clarridge, Duane R., with Digby Diehl. *A Spy For All Seasons*. New York: Scribner, 1997.

Crowe, William. *Line of Fire*. New York, Simon & Schuster, 1993.

Day, Beth. *Passage Perilous*. New York: GP Putnam's Sons, 1962.

Gormly, Captain Robert A., USN (Ret). *Combat Swimmer*. New York: Dutton, 1998.

Heyman, Philip B. *Terrorism and America*. Cambridge: The MIT Press, 2000.

Hoffman, Bruce. *Inside Terrorism*. New York: Columbia University Press, 1998.

Ledeen, Michael A. *Perilous Statecraft*. New York: Charles Scribner's Sons, 1988.

Lule, Jack. *Daily News, Eternal Stories*. New York: The Guilford Press, 2001.

Martin, David C., and John Walcott. *Best Laid Plans*. New York: Harper & Row, 1988.

Nacos, Brigitte L. *Mass-Mediated Terrorism*. Lanham, Md.: Rowman & Littlefield, 2002.

———. *Terrorism & the Media*. New York: Columbia University Press, 1994.

North, Oliver, with William Novak. *Under Fire*. New York: Harper Collins, 1991.

Olivero, Annamarie. *The State of Terror*. Albany: State University of New York Press, 1998.

Timberg, Robert. *The Nightingale's Song*. New York, Simon & Schuster, 1995.

Newspapers, Journals, and Internet Sites

Newspapers

Asia Africa Intelligence Wire, 2000–2003
Boston Globe, 1985–2003
Chicago Tribune, 1985–2003
Christian Science Monitor 1985–2003
Daily Variety, 2003
Houston Chronicle, 1985–2003
Jerusalem Post, 1985–2003
Knight Ridder/Tribune News Service, 1985–2003
Los Angeles Times, 1985–2003
New Orleans Times–Picayune, 1985–2003
New York Times, 1985–2004
Reuters, 1996
San Francisco Chronicle, 1985–2003
St. Louis Post–Dispatch 1985–2003
The Guardian, 1985–2003
United Press International, 2001–2003
USA Today, 1985–2003
Wall Street Journal, 1985–2003
Washington Post, 1985–2004
World News Connection, 2000–2003

Periodicals

Broadcasting, 1985
Good Housekeeping, 2003
Harvard Magazine, 1991
Newsweek Magazine, 1985–2003
Opera News, 2003
The National Law Journal, 1990
The New Republic, 1985–2003
Time Magazine, 1985–2003
Travel Weekly, 1985–2003
US News & World Report, 1985–2003

Anonymous. "Senator Achille Lauro," Shipping World, October 1966.
Kohler, Peter. "Back to Normal Aboard *Achille Lauro*," *Fairplay*, February 13, 1986.
———. "Voyage Report—*Achille Lauro*, 'The Great Blue Ship,'" Ships Monthly, June, 1986.
Von Kirvan-Pichette, Dr. Michael. "La Nave Blu—Willem Ruys," Steamboat Bill, Summer, 1987.

Veliotes, Nicholas, December 10, 2002
Weatherspoon, Steve, November 6, 2002
Zia, Ralph, November 1, 2002

Public Documents

Weekly Compilation of Presidential Documents, 1996

Audiovisual Material

Odeh, Alex. Appearance on KABC-TV in Los Angeles on October 23, 2002.

INDEX

Abbas, Mohammed "Abu," 54, 70: in Aden, 59; Al Qaeda, comparison to, 186; and Yasser Arafat, xvii, 57, 164, 179, 180, 185–87; Arafat, embarrassing of, 104, 125–28, 193; and Badini, 39, 91; in Baghdad, 165, 167, 180; background and life, 54–58; bin Laden, comparison to, 66, 186, 187; and Bush assassination attempt, 135–36; President Bush's references to, xvii, 186, 194; and CBS News *60 Minutes*, 185–86; capture (2003), xvii, 188–91; and CIA, 79–80; conviction and sentence, xvi, 93–94, 133; De Rosa contact with, 13; detainment in Iraq (2003–04), 188–90; in Egypt (2002–03), 187–88; EgyptAir intercept, 29–34; family, 187; family home, 179–80; FBI's Most wanted List, 76, 181; in Gaza (1996), xvi, 163; in Gaza (1998), 165; in Gaza (2000), 179; heart condition, 179; hijackers, contact with, 12, 15, 22, 59; hijacking, 8–9, 39; 58–59, 91, 103, 163, 166, 179; hijacking, coordination of, 13, 83–84, 87; hijacking, objectives, 125–28, 193; and Saddam Hussein, 135, 136, 186; intifada (2000), 180–81; and Iraq War (2003–04), 186, 188; Italy, custody in, 33–34, 38–43; Italy, release from, xv, 42–43, 62, 95; Italy, U.S. request for Abbas arrest (1996), 164; Iraqi support to, xvi, 194; Israel, attacks on,

xvii, 103, 104, 184–85; Israel, immunity from arrest (1999), 167–68, 178; Israel, U.S. request for Abbas arrest (1996), 163–64; and Klinghoffer, 130, 166, 167, 187; Klinghoffer death, apology for, 103, 106, 166; Libya, support to, xvi, 130–31; "man of peace," xvii, 159, 163, 164, 166, 179, 180; marriages, 55, 57; and missiles, 195; and NBC TV, xvi, 73–76; news media, use of, xvi–xviii, 55, 132, 195; and Olso Peace Accords, xvi; and PLF, xv, 55–58, 130; and PLO Executive Committee, 57, 102–3, 104, 106–7, 109–10, 124, 131; and Palestine National Council, 102, 106, 107, 162–63; Palestinian Authority, support from, 185; and Palestinian deaths, 107, 167; and Palestinian state, 178, 187; and peace process, 109, 135, 164, 179, 180; peace versus terrorism, xvii, 163, 164; trial, 83–96; and PFLP, 55; and PFLP (GC), 55; Reagan, threat to, 73; and Reem Abbas, 57, 187, 189; recruiting PLF members, xvii, 184–85; Tel Aviv beach raid (1990), 121–25, 130, 132, 136; trial, 83–96; war experiences, 130; weight, 179; and U.S., 72–73; U.S. arrest warrant, xvi, 84, 105; U.S. House resolution to arrest, 166; and U.S. invasion of Iraq, 187; U.S. Senate resolution to arrest, 163–64; West Bank, travel to, xvii; wounds, 130; in

223

THE

FRONTIER WORLD

OF

DOC HOLLIDAY

FARO DEALER
FROM DALLAS TO DEADWOOD

BY

PAT JAHNS

INDIAN HEAD BOOKS
NEW YORK

This edition published by Indian Head Books,
a division of Barnes & Noble, Inc.,
by arrangement with Hastings House, Publishers, Inc.

1993 Indian Head Books

ISBN 1-56619-159-9

Printed and bound in the United States of America

M 9 8 7 6 5 4 3 2 1

Contents

Acknowledgments

There were many people who went completely out of their way to help dig up Doc's past, and by their unselfishness and interest in his unhappy and romantic story they made the writing of this history possible. Some searched, some copied, some photostated, all were the researcher's dream of another self everywhere. My thanks go to Miss Lillian McKey of Valdosta, Georgia; Martin Wenger, Assistant Archivist, Department of State Archives, Denver, Colorado; J. R. Webb of Albany, Texas; Col. M. L. Crimmins of San Antonio, Texas; Mrs. Alys Freeze of the Western History Department, Denver Public Library; F. A. Hobble of Dodge City, Kansas; Ernest Dewey of Hutchinson, Kansas; F. B. Streeter, Librarian, Fort Hayes Kansas State College; Munroe d'Antignac, Griffin, Georgia. I also want to thank Miss Eleanor Sloan of the Arizona Pioneers' Historical Society, Tucson, Arizona, for her kindness and helpfulness while I was doing research there.

Others who were most helpful in running down references and passing them on were Henry G. Shearouse, Jr., Atlanta Public Library; R. A. Burns, Griffin and Spalding County Chamber of Commerce, Griffin, Georgia; Father Joseph E. Moylan, Vicar-General, Diocese of Savannah-Atlanta; L. P. Goodrich, Griffin, Georgia; Fred Mazulla, Denver, Colorado; Sister Mary Corona, St. Vincent's Hospital, Leadville, Colorado; Lynn I. Perrigo, New Mexico Highlands University, Las Vegas, New Mexico; Sister Superior Mary Bernardine, St. Vincent's Academy, Savannah, Georgia; Gardner Foley, Editor, *Journal of the Baltimore College of Dental Surgery*; Miss Marie Giles, Dallas, Texas; Llerena Friend, Barker Texas History Center, University of Texas, Austin; Mrs. Ida Lasater Huckaby of Jacksboro, Texas; Dean Krakel, Archivist, Library of the University of Wyoming, Laramie; Most Reverend Urban J. Vehr, Archbishop of Denver; Miss Corinne Palm, Albany, Texas.

My thanks also to Lillian Henderson, Director, Confederate Pension and Record Department, Atlanta, Georgia; William C. Wilkes, State of Texas Adjutant General's Department; Mrs. Dorothy Coleman, Reference Librarian, University of Kansas; Jim FitzGerald, Las Vegas, New Mexico; Mrs. Opie Vermillion, Big Stone Gap, Virginia; R. O. Ackerman, Phoenix, Arizona; Anna M. Berg, Public Library, Grand Junction, Colorado; C. W. McFadden, Chamber of Commerce, Glenwood Springs, Colorado; Agnes Wright Spring, Acting State Historian, Denver, Colorado; Roy V. Peel, Director, Bureau of the Census; Fred Shelley, Head Librarian, Maryland Historical Society; H. C. Byrd, President, University of Maryland; J. Ben Robinson, Dean, Baltimore College of Dental Surgery; Herbert J. Bain, American Dental Association; Mrs. Margaret Pratt, Dallas Public Library; Carl Coke Rister, University of Oklahoma; Mrs. Nellie Cox, Fort Concho Museum, Fort Concho, Texas; Margaret Baker, Librarian, Carnegie Public Library, Valdosta, Georgia; W. E. Cheatham II, New Mexico Highlands University; Thomas Z. Ortiz, New Mexico Highlands University; K. Jean Griswold, Wheatridge, Colorado; Chesmore Eastlake, M.D., Denver, Colorado; Mel Shepherd, Editor, *The Santa Fe Magazine*; I. W. Brock, Emory University; Ann Fisher, Decatur, Georgia; Mrs. John H. McGaughey, Albany, Texas; Frank C. Brophy, President, and H. W. Williams, Vice President, the Bank of Douglas, Phoenix and Douglas, Arizona; John Barr Thompkins, Bancroft Library, University of California at Berkeley; E. L. Turner, Editor, *Daily Times*, Valdosta, Georgia; John Crocker, Groton School; Herbert Gambrell, Dallas Historical Society; Harriet Dickson Reynolds, Librarian, Houston Public Library.

I also wish to thank Pete Barrett, outdoors editor of *True, the*

Man's Magazine, for permission to quote from *Lucian Cary on Guns.*

And my sincerest thanks to those very helpful people whose names, thanks to my stupid shyness, I never knew, who work at the Library of Congress in the newspaper reading room, the local history room, the rare book room, the folk-song section of the music department, the cartographic department and the copyright department. The same goes for those at the Department of Archives, in the census section, the Civil War section, the Army section, and—just to show there are no hard feelings—the Adjutant General's section, where I was mistaken for one of Senator McCarthy's investigators in a sad time of senatorial "probes." And my thanks also to those at the library of the Daughters of the American Revolution, for the use of their microfilmed 1880 census of Tombstone.

Last but not least, I wish to thank those old-time newspapermen whose writings make the best record of their day, the clearest picture of their way of life. When they had a story they told it front, back and center, so that you could understand what had actually happened and why. They have been run down as cowards who feared to anger the local killers by printing accounts of their misdeeds. I did not find them so. In fact, they seemed to delight in thinking up new insults with which to libel law-breakers of every sort. I hope here to have given the Old West newspapermen the means of clearing up the bad name tacked on them by elderly liars who had to explain why innumerable deeds of daring were not reported in the local papers.

Prelude

Doc Holliday's

World

Into the saloon where Charley White worked walked Doc Holliday, gun in hand. The first thing Charley knew, a bullet zinged past him. He ducked back, recognized his assailant and flashed behind the bar. Such commotions being no great shucks in Las Vegas, the patrons resignedly threw themselves flat on the floor. Charley having found a revolver behind the bar, placed there by an employer with his workers' welfare at heart, leaned over the marble top of the bar and returned Doc's fire. Doc stood his ground and shot back. Charley turned sideways, to make himself a smaller target, and fired at Doc in what approximates range-firing position for handguns. They stood there shooting at each other. Nobody hit anybody. Finally Charley got the bright idea that a moving target was the hardest to hit and backed into one of Doc's bullets.

He flopped on the floor, apparently dead.

But after Doc had gone, Charley surprised the patrons by resuming the perpendicular. The medical man called in diagnosed the wound as made by a bullet plowing along Charley's back just deep enough to graze the spinal column and stun him. Charley left town fast and, it was said, never ventured west of Boston, Mass., again.

Admirers swore Doc had just had a "bad" day. But the record shows he was an incredibly lousy shot. Which didn't mean that he wasn't still a dangerous man to tangle with and a killer. He had that sort of a reputation along the frontier and in the boisterous, murderous towns in whose tough joints he dealt faro. He was, in a way, a frontier paradox; he associated with the most redoubtable gunmen of the day, and though many of them met violent ends, Doc survived unscathed for a decade and a half, and finally died of the galloping consumption which had originally brought him to the west in hope of alleviation if not a cure.

In the story of Doc Holliday there is plenty of lead slinging, but don't be expecting corpses to fairly strew the landscape. Doc was not a homicidal maniac, as he has been pictured in the fantasy-West books which people the vast, barren spaces of the frontier with lively, mayhem-addicted ghosts. Yet he rather made up for his failure to live up to the role later invented for him, by the diversity of his real characteristics and accomplishments—being tubercular, an alcoholic, a professional gambler, a law officer, a murderer, a gentleman, a lover, a friend, a complex, intelligent person daily breaking down under the unremitting wallops of misfortune. And holding to his strange motto and fantastic loyalties though they killed him.

He and his companions are pretty poor specimens of humanity when seen through the eyes of their contemporaries and the local records, rather than in the astoundingly inventive memories of old men. The ones that fame has passed by were the heroes: Ed Masterson, mortally wounded, walking alone across Front Street in the dusk after shooting his drunken assailants; Johnny Slaughter lying dead in the road while the big maroon and gilt Concord stage he loved so well rocked driverless safely into Deadwood. It is time to tell the story of such men as these, too, and time to examine the actual deeds of the spurious heroes who built their fame with lies—and laughed at the city folks who believed them.

Good or bad in this plain telling, uncolored by reminiscences, with the fireworks demanded by a "good story" all outlawed, these are still unusual men. And they are unfailingly human; they, their friends, their enemies are people with hearts and hopes and needs that all men have. The thing that puts them apart from us is not their reputation but their place, their surroundings. Little cowtowns sprawled lonely on the plains, little mining camps choked by hills— small places where by contrast men felt as giants. Giants under that great sky which forever dominates the world that is West.

And why pick Doc Holliday to mirror their story? Because he went to nearly every boom camp of the old West—Dodge, Dallas, Fort Griffin, Denver, Leadville, Deadwood, Tombstone, all in their roistering heyday. Coughing, his hand poised to grab the gun tucked in his vest, already dying, he feared no man, he feared no thing. But he had not always coughed, had not always carried a gun. There had been another life, when a boy called John had lived in his father's house in Georgia, long years gone by. . . .

THE FRONTIER WORLD

OF

DOC HOLLIDAY

I

Boyhood in Griffin,

Georgia, during the

Civil War

No birth records were kept at the time he was born, but the First Sessional Record Book of the Griffin Presbyterian church at Griffin, Georgia, shows under *Infant Baptisms* that John Henry Holliday was baptised there on March 21, 1852, at a customary age of several months.

The two handsome blond Scots who were his parents were his world: Henry B. and Alice Jane McKey Holliday. And so close a part of their being that they seemed inseparable, were their white frame house on Tinsley Street near Second,[1] so carefully on the north or "right" side of the Macon and Atlanta railroad tracks, the numerous aunts, uncles and cousins coming on frequent visits, the six slaves his father owned,[2] the friends who amounted to most of the town, and all the close, belonging things of home.

John's mother was an admired personality in her small world: blonde, beautiful but unspoiled, gentle, kindly, a woman of education and refinement, a talented musician, a good wife and mother. He must have been very fond of her and very proud of her. She was born in South Carolina in 1829 and had moved to Georgia with her family as a child. She married Henry B. Holliday on January 8, 1849, according to the old McKey family Bible. On June 12, 1850, after an all-too-short period of happiness, her first child, Martha Eleanora, died at the age of six months and nine days. The baby's grave can yet be found in the old cemetery over near the Stonewall Confederate Cemetery in Griffin. On September 1 of the same year she left the Methodist Church, in which she had been raised, and joined the Presbyterians. She had ten brothers and sisters, so although John was her only surviving child her house was always full of young people, her husband being legal guardian of several of her younger brothers and sisters.[3]

Henry B. Holliday was high-strung and hot-tempered and intelligent. He was one of the unlucky men who see straight through to a logical answer to every question and then wear themselves out fighting everyone else to get there. He never learned that people hate being beaten over the head with anything, even the truth. He told the census takers that he had been born in South Carolina in 1820, and later moved to old Pike County, Georgia. He served as a second lieutenant in Captain Sargent's company of the First Georgia Volunteer Infantry Regiment in the Mexican War,[4] and was one of the first settlers of Griffin. When one considers that he owned some forty-six pieces of property in Griffin and several hundred acres in the county,[5] it is easy to conclude that he was, in common with so many men of his time, a land speculator, especially in view of his ownership of railroad property in other parts of the state.

Growing up is rarely easy under any circumstances, and going through the process in a model Victorian home which the father dominated as an iron-handed tyrant was a refined form of torture. Boys in those days were regarded as limbs of Satan and were early set upon to get their rough spots ironed out. Henry B. Holliday was too much the perfectionist to allow the opportunity to escape him of showing how a child that is raised right will be the right kind of adult.

4

John probably idolized his mother for being a refuge from the cruel-edged sarcasm and the constant "don't" that he came to associate with his father, but she was as much under her husband's thumb as John. Such an upbringing was doubly hard on John since he had a will of his own and just as hot a temper as his father. He probably clashed with his father from the start; but John could not escape this process that day in and day out sought to mold him into a pattern of manners and habits alien to his nature. He no doubt did his best to assimilate them into the native charm and cheerfulness he inherited from his mother. The code his father constantly preached was not concerned with social behavior alone—to get up when ladies entered the room and unfailingly say yes, sir; no, sir; yes, ma'am; no, ma'am; and generally to behave himself. It went deeper. Constantly nagged at to plan his actions ahead, to use his brains, to be a credit to his father, John was taught never to run crying to anyone, made to figure a way out of his childhood predicaments for himself.

Having other children in the house who were at least ten years older than John was no help, either. Always, people were expecting too much of him.

Griffin stands in the heart of one of the richest farming areas in the country, the tough red clay of that part of Georgia which lies between the coastal rice belt and the Piedmont. The early pioneers' wooden plows had not been able to handle so rugged a soil, and so settlement had jumped from the coast to the hills,[6] leaving this land to be settled in the 1830's and 1840's when somebody at last got the idea that Jethro Wood's cast-iron plow [7] and this tough clay were made for each other. Both the Holliday and McKey families had come from South Carolina and bought up this new land in the big boom when the hardwood forests and the little scratch-dabbly fields of the hunter-pioneer folks gave way to cotton fields that were the pride of the South.

Griffin was a miniature metropolis of this fertile black belt (so-

5

called from the large number of slaves used), about halfway between Macon and Atlanta on the little railroad of that name. It was a fast-growing town and a lively one for a kid to grow up in. John would have been on the run all day long keeping up with the building of the new courthouse, "manufactories" weaving cotton cloth, the nearby gin houses racketing away as the fearsome cotton gins separated the cotton fiber from the seeds and occasionally an operator from a hand or arm, the station busy with the coming and going and the loading and unloading of the cars and tending to the needs of the whimsical little wood-burning locomotives.[8] And of course one had to learn to ride as soon as one learned to walk, or mighty near, and was besides born with the right to carry a gun in search of possum and rabbit on any and every occasion. Like any kid John was right in the thick of the horse races and barbecues and picnics and church "jollifications" and parties and medicine-show parades and town celebrations—but most exciting of all was Court Week.

Not only John, but everybody in the county got excited over Court Week.

The South produced its own frontier customs when the hunter-pioneers moved west out of the old, settled areas in search of wild land. Traditions of a type of law were evolved that suited the necessities of the region. When later the ruined ex-Confederate trekked still further west in search of his fortunes, he took these traditions with him, and they proved just as well adapted to this remoter frontier. In the spring and fall the Circuit Court met at Griffin and everybody in the county came to town, some of them looking for trouble, and this type of law blazed forth outside the courtroom and was beyond it. The town had a wagon yard where the visitors could park their Conestogas and feed and water their animals and here, after the excitement and drama of the court scenes, the men would gather at night to swap stoneware jugs, lies, and fists. Sometimes the fights were just drunken brawls which anyone might attend. Sometimes a couple of the young bucks had to raise a ruckus or bust. And occasionally everybody would know that there were

6

two men in town looking for each other right peckish-like. First place to look was the wagon yard. There was no keeping kids away from the breeding ground of these fracases, short of chaining them to the bedpost; so John probably learned early the expediency of having the law on your side when you are planning to do someone in. It was easy enough to kill legally: taunt your enemy before witnesses into reaching for a weapon or even threatening you, and you had a free ticket to shoot him. Murder? It was an on-the-spot duel, which was to become the law of the frontier. Forget the preliminary niceties and there was the messy, unpleasant task of hanging you. John was an extremely intelligent, sensitive boy. He never forgot.

But, however many bodies had spouted gore on Saturday night and however hair-raising John's nightmares may have been as a result, come Sunday morning he went to Sunday school and church and got the terrors of hell poured into him. Instead of this invariably producing a stainless life, some of the little fiends actually managed to go astray. One has to marvel at the fortitude of men who went bad after being choked to the gills with the Old Testament, the Shorter Catechism and everlasting hellfire. Breaking the law of the land was nothing. But sinners knew they were going to hell. Hell was no figure of speech.

School began at about the time that John realized what was going on around him. Every morning, in company with his young aunts and uncles, he would be plunked down at a convenient table where his mother could keep an eye on them and they were set their little lessons. If they were attentive and managed to finish, they were permitted to play in the afternoon. If not, more lessons. If they were exceptionally good, they might have a story read to them, one of the nauseating moral tales of the times such as that patent jewel, "Little Paul; or, How to be Patient in Sickness and Pain," or possibly "Jasper; or, the Spoiled Child Recovered," compared to which "Willie and the Mortgage" seems almost bearable.[9] No wonder the impossible romances of Ned Buntline, waist-deep in blood and thunder and revenge and oaths and fainting heroines

7

and heroes who were forever manfully repressing a sob, were read to carefully hidden tatters.

On winter nights everyone would gather around the ornate cast-iron stove in the parlor. The camphine lamps would spread golden light over the heavy walnut and mahogany furniture, the oriental rugs, the elaborate double drapes, the floral wallpaper, the sentimental pictures and bric-a-brac, and the blond heads of the Holliday-McKey clan with their fine-boned Scotch faces. If no one was reading Scott or Dickens aloud, Mr. Holliday might be absorbed in the local weekly paper, pointedly called *The Independent South*; Mrs. Holliday would probably be sewing; one of the older girls might be playing the new rosewood melodeon; and the younger children would be playing with dolls, wooden blocks, soldiers and tin horses on wheels.[10] Occasionally everyone would join in a chorus of one of the popular songs.

Perhaps somewhere in the house hung a Currier and Ives print, "The United States Army Leaving the Gulf Squadron—9th March, 1847," drawn by J. M. Ladd. Always a reminder, always there to prompt one of the favorite pastimes of the day, telling stories of one's adventures.

John's father had been a twelve-month volunteer in the war with Mexico. Fannin's Avengers, his outfit had called themselves, for the murdered hero of Goliad,[11] and they had swept the dirty Greasers out of Vera Cruz and up over the hills past the Cerro Gordo to Jalapa under a lone star banner reading across the top "Young Hickory" and at the bottom "Dallas and Victory." [12] Forgotten were the log-barricaded trenches hastily dug for protection against the Mexican cannon; the scorching days and icy nights; the swift, perilous clash of hand-to-hand fighting in strange country; the steady diet of coffee, hard bread, salt pork and maggots; the terrible battle at the Cerro Gordo; the cold reception at Jalapa,[13] where Henry B. Holliday, second lieutenant, Company I, resigned on May 7, 1847, and with the rest of the twelve-month volunteers was shipped back to New Orleans, to be duly mustered out on May 29, 1847.[14] Also forgotten was the fact that of the 18,000 men

8

in the Georgia and Alabama regiments, only 12,000 came safely back.

John heard talk of war all the time, only the words now were mostly "secession, damned interfering Yankees, States' rights, crackpot abolitionist." He heard that the Yankees actually believed *Uncle Tom's Cabin* and you couldn't trust people who were that stupid. Words were setting fire to trouble. The South was a ferment of hotheads and the North was behaving like a smug elder brother accustomed to ruling the whole family.

But all was not grim under the greying skies; they had fun and romping good times. They danced lively dances, galloping down the room and sashaying back; hoopskirts flew up to reveal ruffled pantalettes and frock-coat tails fairly snapped in the breeze. They had energy and loved to show it off in the reel, the waltz, the cachucha, the polka, the redowa and all the other gay and lively dances of the day. If there wasn't room enough to dance, they expended this same energy on tableaux or pantomimes and would even compose impromptu take-offs on the popular blood-and-thunder novels, hilarious mockeries of stories which secretly thrilled their souls. They used cherry bounce for blood, gallons of it. They played games: Copenhagen, Fox and Goose, Consequences, Pencil, Change Partners, and asked riddles and sang songs by the hour.

Little boys of nine were allowed to play too, being useful as butts for jokes, messengers, and as corpses strewing the battle field when they could control their giggles. And John was allowed to help make the decorations for that new fashion, the Christmas tree, an idea lately brought over from Germany. There were cutwork paper baskets on it, artificial flowers, tiny presents fancily wrapped, and little tapers that burned under watchful eyes. There were fireworks for Christmas here in the South, and guns going off all day, and visitors and flocks of relatives and the most marvelous ham and wild turkey and oysters. It was the last Christmas for a long time. South Carolina had seceded from the union that year of 1860, on December 20.

9

Ten more states joined with South Carolina (Georgia on January 21, 1861), and for several months it looked very much as if there might be a peaceful separation. But this auspicious beginning—auspicious certainly from the Southern point of view—ended decisively with Bull Run. The South called it Manassas, "First" Manassas, as it turned out. News of the rout of McDowell's Union army by Beauregard's boys in grey was whooped from the Macon and Atlanta telegraph office in Griffin, and the bonfires roared skywards in the streets. The war was over. Washington would fall any minute now.

The rejoicing proved premature. The celebrations and the belief that the war was over disrupted Beauregard's army to such an extent—lots of his men simply went home—that it had to be reassembled before it could move into action once more. Which gave the Federals a breathing space to pull themselves together. Most important of all, General Winfield Scott, Mexican War hero, slapped a blockade around the southern coast that was tighter than the hide on a catfish; this blockade, jeeringly known as Scott's Anaconda,[15] nevertheless was eventually to assure the defeat of the Confederacy and the ruin of thousands of Southern families, the Hollidays among them.

To John's great delight, soldiering being all glory and no blood when one is nine, Georgia had immediately organized her volunteer infantry regiments again. The Twenty-Seventh formed at Camp Stephens near Griffin. Henry B. Holliday was appointed quartermaster with the rank of captain on September 2, 1861.[16] The remaining officers were elected by the men of the regiment from their own number, a device which, while producing some odd results, at least effectively prevented pusillanimous pups with money and pull from ever reaching a position where their own men would have to shoot them for the good of the outfit. On October 31, 1861, the Twenty-Seventh Georgia Volunteer Infantry regiment was ordered to Richmond.[17]

Flags waved. Crowds cheered. The band played. And the cars went chugging away in a pall of black woodsmoke.

John Holliday was almost ten years old and war was not quite what he had thought it would be.

Letters came, calming that terrible feeling of emptiness and panic. The Twenty-Seventh had been ordered to Manassas Junction where they were put to work, without arms, building a bridge across Occoquan Run, five miles south of Manassas. Here the Occoquan races through a deep, wooded ravine full of boulders, so the bridge was a complicated affair built on high, well-protected trestles. Captain Holliday settled down to a long battle with red tape and the mammoth Confederate record sheets of thick grey paper which were to hold up so poorly through the years.

At home the slowly increasing pinch of the blockade lived like misery in every house, sharpening the black shadow of sorrow and worry over the men and boys who were far from the women who ached to care for them. And John had been ordered to take care of his mother and not let her worry. If he could think of all sorts of comforting remarks about building a bridge instead of fighting, there was little he could do to make life easier for her physically. Odd how the little things in times of stress are hardest to bear: no pins, thread, paper, ink, soap, cloth, dyes, tea, coffee, shoes. Quinine and opium stores were turned over to the army and bandages were made from sheets and pillowcases. It was everybody's war, not just the soldiers'. And everyone suffered. If some poor footslogger waxed joyous over a captured Colt revolver,[18] his wife would gloat over a copy of Godey's *Ladies Book* brought down secretly by the Confederate mail route through Maryland, even if she could never have any of the fancy things in it.

To the relief of the folks at home Captain Holliday's regiment went into winter quarters at Camp Pickens near Manassas on December 15. Soon there was good news for them to read. To fill a vacancy in the regiment he had been elected major on Christmas day. His pay had gone up from one hundred forty Confederate dollars to one hundred fifty per month. Early in January he was granted "leave for less than one month." [19] And so the Hollidays had a second Christmas and were happy for a while.

The Twenty-Seventh, under Colonel Levi B. Smith, was ordered on March 9, 1862, to Clark's Mountain to become part of a new brigade composed of the Fourth North Carolina Troops, the Forty-Ninth Virginia Infantry and themselves. On April 9 they marched through half a foot of sleet and snow to the railroad to take the cars to Richmond.

John was old enough to read his father's letters: they were all-important now, because he knew his father was going where the fighting was. Apprehension filled the house like a damp mist.

McClellan had launched his Peninsula campaign and Lee, now in command of the Confederate forces, moved to block him off from Richmond. Newly-elected Major Holliday and the Twenty-Seventh managed to get down the James River as far as Grover's Landing. Fort Darling was holding back the Lincoln gunboats now that the gallant ironclad *Virginia* (known to the Yankees as the *Merrimac*) had been destroyed by her own crew by unfortunate necessity.[20] The Twenty-Seventh marched across the Peninsula to Yorktown, getting there just in time to dislodge some Federal snipers, and then joined the retreat to Richmond. The rains had turned the Peninsula into a morass. They suffered terribly from rain, cold, mud, fatigue and hunger.

Then the battles came. The big battles. The Twenty-Seventh fought at Williamsburg on May 5, in the battle of Seven Pines on May 31, Mechanicsville and Cold Harbor both on June 27, White Oak Swamp on June 30, and Malvern Hill on July 1, 1862. On July 6 the Twenty-Seventh was returned to Richmond. Its losses in killed and wounded were around a third of its 1,151 men. The majority of the survivors were sick from over-exposure and exhaustion.[21]

At the National Archives one can read Major Holliday's resignation, the original document with its old-fashioned long S's, and the harried handwriting of the surgeon's certificate accompanying it, stating that the major was no longer physically capable of carrying out his duties and that there were no prospects of his recovery under the necessary conditions of military service.

Major Holliday's resignation had seven indorsements by August 7 and finally on August 24 (the delay being due to the fact that it got lost) was approved. He went back to Griffin sick, discouraged, and with a thousand dollars (Confederate) in back pay.[22] And the Twenty-Seventh, SOL, went on to Antietam.

Having sacrificed his business to support the cause, Major Holliday returned home to find himself all but ruined. In June of 1861 the Confederate dollar had been worth a gold dollar; [23] and the tax digest for the Griffin district of Spalding County for that year shows that H. B. Holliday was worth $17,365. This was very good indeed for the times. Now it was all over. The Confederate dollar was dropping in value daily. Almost everything either had to go or was lost already. He was forty-two years old, sick and broke. And any fool could see by looking at a map that there were too many railroads leading into Atlanta for the Federals to fail to try to grab it. Once there, it would be logical to try to split the South by driving on to Savannah. And Griffin was between Atlanta and the sea.

He had managed to hold on to a few things. He refused to touch his wife's property in Griffin, but he had saved a property down in southern Georgia, near the Florida line, which he had bought when the Savannah and Gulf railroad went through there. It was near a raw little town newly built on the railroad, called Valdosta. As soon as he was well enough to travel, the Hollidays packed up their few remaining possessions, assorted small female McKeys (the boys were all in the Confederate army) and moved.

John had seen war snatch his father away strong and confident and fling him back sick and worried. Major Holliday's short temper was now hair-triggered and John, never exactly at ease around him, had to jump. In the tenseness of such an atmosphere John now saw the comfort and security of his home vanish and a journey undertaken to new and frightening surroundings. Here were the first small cracks in the wall of his integrity, although he held tight to his mother and was sure in her care and affection.

FOOTNOTES TO CHAPTER I

1. Because of the large quantities of property in Griffin that Henry B. Holliday owned, it is difficult to locate their home. However they did own this property and it agrees with the general location of the Holliday home according to the old-timers.
2. Tax Digest for Griffin district of Spalding County, 1861.
3. Minute Book A, pp. 62, 100, 132, of records of the Ordinary's office, Spalding County Courthouse, Griffin, Ga., and *The Independent South*, Griffin, Ga., July 7, 1859.
4. Mexican War records at the National Archives, Washington, D.C.
5. Tax Digest for Griffin district of Spalding County, Ga., 1861.
6. *Plain Folk of the Old South*, Frank Lawrence Ousley, Louisiana University Press, 1949. This book is not based on who said what, but on the actual records of the times. It is a refutation of the popular idea of the whole pre-war South and proves every word it says.
7. *Harper's New Monthly Magazine*, December, 1874, ascribes the cast-iron plow to a Scot, James Small, in 1785. It continues, however, that this plow did not come into general use until a Yankee, Jethro Wood, made a lighter, cheaper version with replaceable parts.
8. *Gazeteer of Georgia*, Adiel Sherwood. Griffin, Ga., 1860.
9. All by Jacob Abbott, advertised as the best in children's literature in *Harper's New Monthly Magazine*, December, 1857.
10. *Pioneer America, Its First Three Centuries*, Carl Dreppard. Doubleday and Co., Inc., Garden City, N.Y., 1949.
11. On March 27, 1847, during the Texan fight for independence, the remains of Colonel James W. Farming's army, which had surrendered to the Mexicans a few days before, and some other Americans also taken prisoner, were shot by Mexican soldiers near the little town of Goliad, Texas.
12. Now in the possessin of a descendant of Captain Sargent.
13. *The Twelve Months Volunteer*, George C. Furber, J.A. and V. P. James, Cincinnati, Ohio, 1848.
14. Mexican War records at the National Archives, Washington, D.C.
15. *A Short History of the Civil War*, Fletcher Pratt. Harrison Smith and Robert Haas, Inc., 1935.
16. From the individual records of Confederate soldiers at the National Archives, Washington, D.C.
17. *Heroes and Martyrs of Georgia In The Revolution of 1861*, Volume I, James M. Folsom, Macon, Ga. Burke, Boykin and Co., 1864. (From the Rare Book Room of the Library of Congress.)

18. The Confederate army largely used as its side arms captured Colt 1860 models issued to the Union army and available to the Rebels as they could capture them. That they were desirable as a shooting iron and as a bludgeon or other implement of mayhem is seen by the stacks of them in the Confederate museums, each one neatly labelled as to who captured it and where.

19. From Major Holliday's record as a Confederate soldier, now at the National Archives, Washington, D.C.

20. There are four excellent articles written by former participants on both sides about the ironclads in *The Century Magazine,* March, 1885.

21. *Heroes and Martyrs of Georgia,* op. cit.

22. Records at the National Archives, Washington, D.C.

23. *A New American History,* W. E. Woodward. The Literary Guild, New York, 1937.

2

Doc Grows Up

and

Falls in Love

Holliday Street in Valdosta was named for John's father.[1] He was one of the town's leading citizens later on, when there was town enough to matter. Right now Valdosta was ruined. There had been a little placed called Troupeville on the banks of the Withlacoochee River. When the Savannah, Albany and Gulf railroad came along and missed the village by four miles, it was quite a disappointment but instead of abandoning their little community the folks jacked it up piece by piece and moved it over to the railroad tracks. They also changed its name to that of Governor Troupe's plantation, Valdosta. They had just secured the buildings on their foundations and were getting the town started as a trading center when the men of the Confederate States of America were called upon to defend their country. In the period that followed Valdosta at first stood still and then commenced to fall into ruin, despite the heroic efforts of the women and children and old men.[2]

When the Hollidays first saw it Valdosta was a backwoods dump, to describe it pointedly. But after all, backwoods and frontier mean the same thing; they are just different ways of looking at a raw,

16

new settlement in a raw, new country. Dodge, Dallas, Tombstone, Deadwood were all backwoods when John first saw them. No place could have been a shock after Valdosta. Dust fogged everywhere from the dry, untended dirt streets; pine seedlings appeared determined to claim their own again; the sun-warped, unpainted boards were popping loose from the buildings and there were more old men loafing in Tom Griffin's general store of a Monday than there were people buying on a Saturday.

Scott's Anaconda had put its mark upon Valdosta. And upon the hearts of the people of the South. It was no wonder, then, that the Confederate raiders, the *Alabama,* the *Shenandoah* and the *Florida,* which preyed upon Yankee shipping on the high seas (the *Alabama* alone sank over six-million-dollars' worth) were so beloved by the home folks. John McIntosh Kell, executive officer of the *Alabama,* was a Spalding County man and known to the Hollidays. There were many prayers said for them and the other Confederate officers of these raiders, and for their British crews and the Scotch shipbuilders who built them.[3]

Everyone had to work themselves to death to keep the Confederate army in the field and themselves from starvation. They had an occasional "starvation" party at which no refreshments were served, but they made themselves cheerful over substitutes for tea and coffee, and in rooms dimly lit by stinking old Betsy lamps [4] no one could see the once-lovely hands roughened by homemade lye soap. There were things to do, more than enough.

Since the first church in Valdosta was a Presbyterian church, started mainly by a group of refugee families during these hard years, it would seem logical to suppose that the Hollidays were among its founders. They met in the courthouse, a square, unpainted, two-room structure, not even finished on the inside, located at the corner of Central Avenue and Ashley Street. Later on they had the first church building in Valdosta, neatly made out of a converted warehouse.[5]

John was too old now for home teaching. There were no public schools in Valdosta and nobody could afford private tutors, so the parents all got together and founded a private school which they called the Valdosta Institute. A teacher was hired and classes met in one room of the courthouse, which if not elegant at least boasted plenty of windows.[6] Tuition for the primary department was about fifteen dollars for a ten-month school year and in the upper school was twenty-six.[7] The teacher was necessarily a man of iron; he had to enforce discipline with clubs (euphemistically referred to as "sticks"), not because he was a sadist but because the theory of teaching stopped with such measures. The school day and the term were too long and the subjects were often too difficult for the ages of the pupils, and moreover were presented in as dry and pedantic a manner as possible, the idea doubtless being that one learned fortitude by suffering. The classes included Greek, Latin, French, astronomy, analytical geometry, trigonometry, calculus, chemistry, physics, logic, composition, economic geography, history, ethics, and of course reading and writing and 'rithmetic.[8] Fortunately Southern children have always been taught good manners at home, so few brawls resulted. The teacher would have been more astounded at a plain "yes" or "no"[9] than at getting a spitball in the eye, the latter being classed as a prank while the former was plain evidence of ill-breeding.

It sounds somewhat pathetic, Greek, ethics, calculus taught in one unfinished room by a man who but a moment before had been guiding grubby fingers that labored over spelling C-A-T. Actually, the enrollment was very small and the pupils received rather more individual attention than they wanted, particularly in the tougher subjects, because in these hard times many of the pupils had to drop out to work to help feed the family.[10]

Nobody could keep John in school that day of February 15, 1864, when his father's old regiment arrived on the cars from Savannah. Down they went to see them, hand in hand, the remembered heroes, their deeds not written on their faces, all honor, all courage, all self-denial masked by the unbreakable weariness of having to work too hard, be too lucky, to keep alive. And ask about so-and-so? Dead at Frederick, or Sharpsburg, or Chancellorsville! The best, always the most kindly thought of, gone! They came to Major Holliday's house to eat and sleep, some of them, and to stare at a blond, blue-eyed kid who was to them all little boys, every man's remembered son, in his youth and his laughter. And stories would come, not of the fighting but of episodes of their own childhood, and they could forget for a moment. And then they marched away to the battle of Ocean Pond (a large fresh-water lake about fifteen miles south of town) where the Federals were "utterly routed and defeated" and then back to Petersburg to defend Richmond against Grant.[11]

The countryside around Valdosta is very pleasant, especially to a boy getting to be twelve or thereabouts, and in those days had not been cleared to the extent it is now. There were vast stretches of the sunniest and brightest of forests, that of the Southern longleaf pine. It was a delight to smell the clean-scented air, to tramp the parklike glades, grass-grown instead of choked with underbrush, to feel in his pants pocket the businesslike bulge made by an ancient cork bobber wound with string and stuck firmly with a fish hook. Here and there would be a huge old oak or hickory, festooned with long streamers of grey Spanish moss, where a mockingbird sang his song of joy while plotting what evil thing to do next. The warm dust would billow about John's bare feet on the dusty trails as he wandered to a little clearing owned by a beekeeper or to a few acres of cane or corn newly scratched from the wilderness; the sky was a blue sample of the blaze of Glory, a squirrel would rush scolding away to hide and one would whistle "The Yellow Rose of Texas" or "Just Before the Battle, Mother," and everything was perfect and wonderful. And then there was the Withlacoochee, a considerable stream, the main tributary of the Suwannee, to play around, to fish in, and, if there were no 'gators in evidence, to swim in.

In the evening they would sit on the porch as the great moon of the Southland rose from way east over Okefenokee swamp, and they would talk of the news of the siege of Atlanta yelled down that morning from the train.[12] The night birds sang in the deep woods,

19

the busy fingers of John's mother and her little sisters kept their knitting needles clicking with no need to see what they were doing; they had knit so many pairs of army socks, so many Confederate grey mufflers, so hopefully. Someone began to sing and they all joined in, very softly, in the evening, by the moonlight. Soon it would be autumn, soon it would be the worst winter of the Confederacy, soon it would be the spring of defeat.

On the first of September Atlanta fell. John went back to school. It was canning and preserving time now that the crops were in. The winter vegetable garden had to be planted [13] and the eternal cotton picking still went on. But Atlanta was in the hands of the enemy, and the chill that had been spreading in the Confederacy since Gettysburg settled about its heart like the cold of the tomb. Their railroad link with the money and food of the West was gone; Richmond was isolated from half of its nation.

Atlanta was burned.

"You could see Atlanta burning from Griffin," the refugees said.[14]

The Federals now set off for Savannah with some misgivings at their own daring in abandoning their supply lines. (Hadn't Napoleon overreached himself doing something like this when he marched to Moscow?) The Union army had to depend entirely on the country to feed itself. One Judson Kilpatrick, in command of the cavalry, attended to that and a lot more.

John's blood boiled when he heard the stories of that infamous march to the sea.

The food hard-won by the women and children to feed them through the winter was lugged into the parlor by the marauders and stomped into the carpet—molasses, corn meal and Aubusson being a permanent combination, Union cavalry commander Kilpatrick's gay young blades had discovered. The family portraits were slashed, being of value only to their owners; the furniture was smashed, being unwieldy to carry off; the silver, the jewelry, the imported French underwear and everything else either portable or pawnable was taken. The livestock was driven away, the chickens were devoured on the spot and the houses were burned for barbecue pits.

Sherman's men stole everything, even the things that were nailed down, and burned what couldn't be carried away, leaving as a monument of their passing the standing chimneys of the burned houses. Even Sherman called them his "bummers" and when his chaplain protested against such destruction, he replied that orders had come from Washington that no Union soldiers were to be shot as vandals and that consequently he had no control over them.[15]

It was Christmastime.

The refugees came to Valdosta starved and in rags and some of them admitted that John's father was smart to have gotten out of that trap when he had.

It was a hard winter for the South, 1864–5. But Valdosta was spared the rare hard frost that in some years took the winter gardens. They had kale and collards for greens all winter and new turnips by January, and snap beans in a sheltered spot, and beets all winter long, and while they couldn't raise corn or tomatoes or peppers or squash the way they did in summer, still they had food to eat and could get warm in the sun and sometimes think of other things than war and destruction and death and hunger.

And then, in the spring, it was all over.

Defeat was worse than war.

John was thirteen and, as children think, getting to be somebody, if being somebody mattered in his downtrodden and despoiled world. He could not, in this environment, be an average small boy. There were Negro troops stationed in Valdosta and the courthouse had been taken over by the Carpetbaggers and their Scallawag friends. Because of the violent reprisals which had resulted from insults to these groups in other parts of the occupied states, the people of Valdosta went in daily fear lest some fool start something that the Yankees would finish for him.

Over and over again John's father pounded it in that logic could prevent trouble, that it was too expensive to live by one's emotions. Emotion had plunked him into the Confederate army and

21

ruined him. Logic had brought them all safely to Valdosta out of Sherman's way. John was to profit by his father's mistakes—lessons, however, which he learned rather too well.

The Negro troops went unrocked, the damyankee Carpetbaggers were called "Mister" and the traitor Scallawags, most hated of all, the Confederates who had turned Yankee-lovers, wore their tall silk hats in safety. And under the gun of Reconstruction, made to toe the line before Yankees who were master by force, the proud and impish kid might have figured that the code for him was that any means were all right so long as they insured survival. The thought lay cold in the back of his mind, with all the confusing and contradictory things that come with growing up.

Fortunately Valdosta was too poor and insignificant to be worthy of the harsher forms of oppression. The Negro troops stationed in the town were there to maintain a peace that was never violated and after a year were removed to return regularly only at election time. But Carpetbaggers took over not only the courthouse but all public offices and saw to it that every cent of tax money was paid in cash on the day due, or else they took over the property as lawful owners. What they did with the tax money was not accountable. Many a family lost now even the little that the war had left them, and the others were scraping along by the skin of their teeth.

It was at this time that the western part of the nation got a large migration of Southerners, and thus many of the habits and customs of the South became deeply ingrained in the accepted code of western behavior: the hospitality, the friendliness, the code of the duel.

School still went on. It was eternal. It even survived the Carpetbaggers taking over the courthouse. Mr. McWhir Varnadoe was in charge now, a man who loved learning for its own sake and who could make it attractive to others. If the children were stubborn about being charmed into knowledge, he wasted no time with psychology; it was just *boffo!* and no hard feelings. A most intelligent man. The Valdostans built him a one-room school with living quarters above it for himself and his family [16] and confidently sent him their children to be taught book-learning and what to expect of life. Unfortunately the starvation economics of the South allowed too few to attend school long enough for it to do them any good. There was not only a living to be gotten for every mouth, but still more to earn to pay the ever increasing taxes. That took every hand and long hours and old age before it was half due. And, never to be forgotten, the damyankees to blame it on.

So John would seem to be lucky. He got to finish school. There were those who envied him.

On September 16, 1866, John's mother died.[17]

The person that was young John Holliday died when his mother died. It was to be years before he realized it and that nothing could ever be done about it. He was completely stunned right after it happened, and when he began to realize his loss his crowd of relatives kept him purposely so busy that the dead-inside was hidden to fester and to break out as corruption when he needed strength the most. It was another blow at foundations which had had shocks aplenty; a rift that once made would deepen and widen under the smallest of blows until the house of morality collapsed and "Doc" Holliday escaped from the wreckage of "John" Holliday.

A year later John's father remarried. Her first name was Rachel, according to the 1870 census, and she was twenty-four when she became John's stepmother. Just the right age to be a young war widow, or one of the girls whose sweethearts had been killed in the war.

John's father was not a man to let sentiment stand in the way of practical considerations. He needed someone to keep his house, so he married one of the many women in black who had lost every hope of love in the war. There was a fine point in his father's behavior which John was never to grasp or never to heed. That was the need always to preserve his position of respectability in the community. Major Holliday knew that he could easily regain his fortunes if he became a Yankee sympathizer. It would have been very sensible of him to forget the old differences and join the winning team. But he didn't. No Holliday Street would have been

23

named for a Scallawag. No Scallawag became mayor of Valdosta, none signed the charter of the Valdosta chapter of the Royal Arch Masons No. 107, and John's father was mayor and charter-signer both,[18] and always a hard worker for the welfare and improvement of Valdosta and Lowndes County.

John's bitter resentment of his father's remarriage was swept away underground as the family again began to keep "something for John to do" always hatching in their minds. The fifteen-year-old orphan had aunts to cook fancy trifles for him, uncles to take him hunting in the buggy down to the Ocean Pond, pretty young girl cousins to dance and flirt with and plenty of boy cousins to get into mischief with. The clannishness of the Scotch family drew relatives from near and far—even relatives who were eyed slightly askance by firmly-raised Calvinists, such as Major Holliday's brother who had married a Catholic and had a daughter also of that persuasion. But whatever the religious doctrines of saints and sinners may be, here enters that daughter, the love of John's life.

Meet Mattie Holliday, the young, the lovely, the gentle, the kind, John's first cousin, a most devout Catholic.

John's Presbyterian relatives must have charitably wished everything good to this lovely blonde girl—save John's affections. As for her, fate could not have served her worse than to cause her to fall in love with him. Yet if he was good-looking, spirited and forever thrown into her company, how could she have escaped? Moreover, the marriage of cousins in this case was more to be desired than not. John's mother had left him her property in and around Griffin, and while the Yankees hadn't left much of it, still it was of a sizeable value for poor-but-respectable folk and a good thing to keep in the family.

The times, while hard in Valdosta, were not completely bleak. Beekeeping was increasingly important, and the planters were growing cotton, sugar cane and corn. The political situation in the state, as indeed throughout the South can be seen in this quote from an unnamed, undated Virginia newspaper in the *Atlanta Constitution*: "A man from Maine has our Post Office; a Vermont man represents us in Congress; a fellow from Pennsylvania is our Street Commissioner; our Revenue Commissioner is a Massachusetts man; a fellow from Philadelphia is jailer; the Chief of Police is a Pennsylvanian; two negroes represent us in the Legislature; and a man from Maine represents us in the Senate." [19]

Arthur McRae [20] comments on the number of guns being worn in the South in 1868, and the fact that they were used. John must have grown up in the company of guns; used them from his childhood. His flock of young uncles would have been forever going hunting and not without him, and rifle and pistol matches were sporting events of importance.

There were social functions, too. Valdosta had a new hotel, Stewart's, which had a ballroom for important events. Valdosta's branch of the Sons of Temperance was composed of sterling lads who had sworn to renounce drinking, smoking and swearing and were privileged to wear their fancy uniforms at celebrations of Lee's birthday, funerals of public figures, and in every little one-horse parade. For a young man not to belong was almost a disgrace. One can see the blue ribbon in John's buttonhole—and the twinkle in his eyes.

At eighteen John was about five feet ten, blond, blue-eyed, lively and always doing something. If his mother had been alive she would have worried because he wasn't stronger—and he would have said he wasn't fat, true, but he was tough, like the swamp sapling that you could pull and bend and twist and never break. He was still in school, ready this fall to start college or go to reading law, and having himself a wonderful time. That is, when his father, who put all his hopes in him and demanded an impossible perfection from him, would let him expand into his natural pleasantness and joke and pull pranks and not be serious. Mattie was part of everything he did, so lovely, so fine that he could never get the thrill of her out of his heart. He had so much: personality, love, property, social position, and a thoroughly good reputation. People liked him, this gay young John Holliday; he was a very pleasant kid to be around.[21]

FOOTNOTES TO CHAPTER 2

1. *History of Lowndes County, Georgia—1825-1941*, published by General James Jackson Chapter, DAR, Valdosta, Ga., 1941.
2. *History of Lowndes County*, op. cit.
3. Three articles on the *Alabama* by former participants on both sides, *Century Magazine*, April, 1886.
4. Camphine and other patent burning fluids being unobtainable, the old grease-burners of colonial days were resurrected. This was prior to the invention of the kerosene lamp.
5. *History of Lowndes County*, op. cit.
6. *History of Lowndes County*, op. cit.
7. *Plain Folk of the Old South*, op. cit.
8. Schoolbooks of the period in the author's possession.
9. In *The Americans At Home*, McRae comments at length on the vile manners of American children. However, when his travels brought him to the South he revised his earlier impression to state that only *Northern* children were mannerless and that Southern children had every evidence of good breeding. This was in 1868.
10. *Plain Folk of the Old South*, op. cit.
11. *Heroes and Martyrs of Georgia*, op. cit.
12. *History of Lowndes County*, op. cit. I wondered why they depended on the train crew instead of the railway telegraph for news, since the Yankees had not yet taken Savannah. However, there were many railroads that did not have telegraphs at this time, according to an article entitled "The American Railroad" in *Harper's New Monthly Magazine*, August, 1874.
13. *Reminiscences of Georgia*, Emily P. Burke, James T. Fitch, Ohio. (In the Rare Book Room of the Library of Congress.)
14. *Marching with Sherman*, Henry Hitchcock. Yale University Press, New Haven, 1927.
15. *Marching with Sherman*, op. cit.
16. *History of Lowndes County*, op. cit.
17. The McKey family bible.
18. *History of Lowndes County*, op. cit.
19. July 4, 1872.
20. *The Americans At Home*, op. cit.
21. On the eighth day of June, 1870, came Charles O. Force, Assistant Marshal of the Corporation of Valdosta, to enumerate the Holliday family in the census. He wrote as follows: "Holliday, Henry B.; age 51; male; white; occupation, General Agent; value of real estate, 1700; value of personal estate, 1000; born in South Carolina; father of foreign birth; male citizen over 21. Holliday,

Rachel; age 27; female; white; occupation, Keeping House; born in Georgia. Holliday, John; age, 18; male; white; occupation, Student; value of real estate, 3500; born in Georgia; attended school within the year. Troup, Lizie; age, 17; female; mulatto; born in Georgia."

3

Doc Acquires a

Title and T.B.

1870 was a good time for any father to get a hot-tempered son out of Georgia, no matter how he had been lectured on practical behavior. Rufus Butler had by means commonly known as illegal gotten himself elected governor and had packed the state legislature with Negroes hired to vote as they were told. It was a sad time for Georgians, taxed to the hilt, seeing the tax money, bond issues, everything, going into the pockets of the Carpetbaggers and Scallawags. Tough Negroes, protected by the Freedmen's Bureau, were completely out of hand. Retaliation was continually being talked by ex-Confederates and occasionally taking place.

John was old enough to be finishing school now, and there were fine dental colleges in Baltimore, far from the trouble and yet still a place where a Southern accent did not set one apart. The very idea of becoming a dentist in those days shows either excellent calculation or a happy preference in the matter of a profession. In the better families it was of course necessary to be a professional man, to have a degree of some sort. And no field offered more than dentistry for so small an investment. About sixteen months of technical training and one was entitled to be called "Doctor" and that made a stunning impression. The profession's respectability was new, but then, nobody can have everything.

Mattie and John parted with exhilarated hopes for their future days. A few months at school, a few more practising with another dentist, a year or so to build up his practise in his own office and they would have enough to be married. Ah, well; we might all hang ourselves if we could see the future.

The family took John to the station in the buggy and loaded him on the cars with much parting advice. Travel was considered as much a part of education as schooling; it was one of the things that were "done." Compared to the terrible roads of the day which plated you, your clothes and the buggy with an even coat of either mud or dust every time you went out, even in the largest cities, the railroads were heaven.

Tiny four-drive-wheel locomotives, often weighing no more than three or four tons, went scooting across the dead level countryside with majestic gushings of smoke, cinders, sparks, and even live coals, pulling three flimsy wooden cars at a steady twenty miles an hour if all went well. They died game on three-percent grades; they had to sand the rails or the drivers slipped trying to start any load at all; they jumped the track on the straight-a-way; and if not treated in return like very queens, they would eat out their boilers and retire to the roundhouse to sulk. The coaches were evidently planned either for a race of midgets or for people who behaved with studied decorum in public, there being a scant six or eight inches of leg room between the edge of your seat and the wooden back of the seat in front of you. It was sit up straight and die of fatigue or hang your feet out in the aisle. As a result the conductor picked his way through a forest of legs. The windows were all open in summer to let in air, engine smoke, cinders, wasps, sudden showers and other items which enlivened the journey as the cars rattled and rocked and swayed over the uneven roadbed. At least there were inside shutters which could be closed to keep the sun out—and then you couldn't see the scenery. At one end of the coach was the "convenience" and the drinking fountain, at the other the cast-iron stove which heated the cold and drafty wooden car in winter and invariably set it afire in a wreck.[1] And over all these human lives and all this magnificence ruled the engineer, a colossus of integrity and judgement, one hand on the "throttle-valve" and one free to wipe the tobacco juice out of his whiskers or make a fast grab for the Johnson-bar.[2]

One section of the Southern countryside is pretty much like another—it is rolling and green and sparkling with rivers, the degrees of each depending on where you happen to be. There are cotton areas and tobacco areas and naval stores areas, and just plain forests and fields. There are dead-asleep villages where nobody but a mule looks up as the rain puffs by, and bustling towns where the train stops for business and everyone seems to fall upon it with demands. And there at last was Richmond, storied Richmond to John, not just the capital of the Confederacy. His father had told of it as one vast hospital during the Seven Days' fighting, and the terrible heat when he had been so sick that he thought he would die. That week every building had been opened and the women and girls turned nurses and colored butlers had carried trays set with silver and loaded with food from the homes of Rich-monders to help feed the sick and wounded. Everything had been one vast bustle and hurry, the whole city an armed camp, until Jackson defeated Pope and the Confederacy had won another breathing spell.[3] Now the water front along the James was lined with the blank walls of burned warehouses, but further up the hills business had started up again. Everything was very quiet, though, as if remembering.

Eight hours more on the cars and John was in Washington, the mudhole capital, which was ignoring the unfinished stump of Washington's monument, listening to agitation from the prospering Western states for the removal of the capital to the center of the country, and completely taken over by low-class whites and armed gangs of Negroes.[4] Here he changed trains for the last time, gave up the last section of his yard-long ticket, and finally came to Baltimore. If Washington was temporarily at low ebb, Baltimore was

30

at high tide and flourishing, the great port of the Chesapeake, terminus of a railroad which carried the products of a huge and fertile farming area, a city of 300,000 persons.

So here is our young gentleman, alone in the big city. The Eastern cities at this time were in no position to criticise the raw new towns of the West.[5] The Boss Tweed scandal in New York had brought to the surface corrupt city governments all down the seaboard. Baltimore's slum areas were dreadful pigsty hovels of trash-pickers, prostitutes, thieves, beggars, alcoholics, derelicts, the depraved, the dying, the damned. The streets were every bit as unpaved and full of mudholes as Washington's. Open privies lined the alleys. The beautiful tall clipper ships crowding her wharves brought an active trade from other foul ports of the world, and some of the items not listed on the manifests were women, opium and cholera.

Which was the largest and best-known dental college of the time is apparently debatable. The Baltimore College of Dental Surgery was the first, but the Colton Dental Association at 81 West Lafayette Street advertized themselves as the discoverers of dental anesthesia. ("Gas" or nitrous oxide, was discovered by Horace Wells, a dentist of Hartford, Connecticut, in 1844, but it was quite a while before anyone paid any attention to his discovery. He died a suicide [6] and I have been unable to connect him with any institution in Baltimore, so it would appear that this advertizement of the Colton Dental Association was another of the many fraudulent medical claims of the times. At any rate, Colton made such a big splash [7] that it doubtless attracted a large number of students.)

Whatever school John attended, there wasn't too much to learning to be a dentist. "Open wider, please," came naturally. The Merry drill, which looked like an egg beater and was just about as practical for dental work, was being replaced by the foot-pedal-operated pneumatic drill which at last allowed the secure anchoring of fillings, crowns, and bridgework. Gold foil was the standard medium for fillings and saving teeth was a paying proposition, for

31

the dentist. However, having them pulled no longer struck the same terror to the heart. Nitrous oxide gas put you out for the unpleasant operation, which was performed by a dentist wearing a frock coat, an embroidered vest and vast quantities of whiskers, just like a doctor of medicine in his operating room, and cheap dentures were quickly made of a new hard rubber, Vulcanite. All in all, it was a good profession, satisfying to both the patient and the dentist. And moderately priced: extractions were fifty cents each, with gas, and complete sets of teeth could be had for as low as fifteen dollars.[8]

For amusement there were the innocent game of pool and cultural lecture series, and concerts and plays and church affairs and plenty of innocent entertainment. Indeed, one might have found them sufficient if it had not been for East Baltimore Street being there, so close and all, and so very lively and unpardonably wicked. But one had to go just to see the elephant and once there, have at least a glass of lager beer and watch the girls in pink tights and the calm-faced gamblers, and listen to the funny men in plaid suits and perhaps to a smooth-talking roper-in.[9] But whatever, John was no innocent when it came to cards or drinking. They were part of the education of a young Southern gentleman, even those who wore a bit of blue ribbon to keep peace in the family. He knew the right bower from the off-jack when those gentlemen winked in his hand, and the dandy spots of big casino, and the grandeur of the royal family and all they could do for him. He knew the feel of a crooked game from a straight one.

In those days playing cards were vastly different from the cards in use today. They were quite large, the corners were square instead of rounded, there were no figures and pips in the corners to tell you that you held the queen of hearts or the deuce of clubs without spreading the cards way apart, and none of the court cards were double-headed—you had to know how the feet of the jacks were different from those of the kings and what they looked like in the various suits, or you gave your hand away by reversing cards in it. It took a degree of concentration to know what you had in your hand, let alone how to play it. The backs were generally very simple and the whole effect was crude and garish.[10]

John probably could afford to spend very little money on East Baltimore Street, but the flaring gaslights, the whir of the wheel of fortune, the flashing legs of the can-can dancers, the high-pitched voices carolling "The Old Man's Drunk Again," and the tense silence of the faro table combined to make a tapestry of pleasant things, shallow and satisfying, where one could relax completely. In the honky-tonks and gambling hells it was not necessary to be anyone or have anything except money.

Baltimore was not a moral town, neither was it a clean town nor a healthy one. The *Baltimore Sun* printed a monthly vital-statistics column which practically amounted to a tuberculosis casualty list, fourteen dying of the white plague one month, twenty-one another, and no other cause of death showing more than five victims. And here was John Holliday who wasn't accustomed to the continual penetrating damp coldness, who had suffered the South's malnutrition for years, peering into the mouths of a tuberculosis-ridden population.

Who could wonder then that he felt tired almost all the time, that his appetite faded and he began to lose weight, that he had unexplained spells when he felt feverish and sick all over, and that he grew nervous and irritable. But he was certain to feel all right when he got back to Georgia, away from this fog and chill.

He went home with a dentist's degree and an early case of chronic pulmonary tuberculosis.

It was customary for the young graduate, even if he could now call himself "Doctor" to spend a while assisting an established dentist before going into business for himself. Young Dr. Holliday, after a triumphal visit home, went back to Griffin, by this time grown into a prosperous little burg. According to the memories of old-timers his office was in the old Merritt building on the southwest corner of West Solomon and State Streets, but whom he was working with no one can remember. His return to the South had not brought about the desired change in his health, so it wasn't long before he moved to Atlanta, the new capital of Georgia, which was bragging about its healthful climate. We may also note that it was the most prosperous town anywhere around.

Atlanta was still rebuilding, completely on its own hook,[11] from the destruction it had suffered at the hands of Sherman's invading army. Blocks of blackened ruins still were scattered through the town, but the main industries, the railroads, rolling mills and iron-works had been patched up enough to operate and were pouring all of their profits back into the business. And Atlanta wasn't slow. Some of its streets were actually macadamized, which was more than many a larger town (Atlanta had a population of 30,000) could boast, and the street railway system was expanding rapidly. However, it was still small-town enough so that when a new line was opened all rides on the horse cars were free that day and the town had a real celebration.

Atlanta is on the dividing line between the cotton and wheat growing areas of the state, right in the heart of the melon country. It was at this time on its way to being one of the South's big marketing and manufacturing centers, but the going was tough on occasion. Milledgeville had formerly been the capital. Now Kimball's Opera House in Atlanta had been taken over to house the Legislature and all the state's business offices, as well as the post office. Federal troops under Colonel Ruger were garrisoned at McPherson Barracks. DeGive's Opera House was the sole theater (double feature night: "Notre Dame; or, The Monk, The Hunchback and The Dancing Girl" together with "Irish Doctor; or The Jack of All Trades"), and Fair Week was the big event of the year with a Grand Trotting Race for a purse of eighteen hundred dollars. Also on the program were the names of five youths entered for a contest entitled "spitting at a mark" and it was noted regretfully that the slow mule race did not come off.

"The fact is, so intense are the business pursuits of most men here that they cannot find time to loaf on the corners, get drunk in the daytime, and indulge in other disreputable acts," says Dr. J. S. Wilson in *Atlanta As It Is*, published in 1871.

34

There was a lot for a young dentist to do in Atlanta besides extract neglected teeth. Pease and His Wife's saloon was a popular meeting place for anything from a White Hat (milk punch) to a modest glass of lager beer, and Thompson's restaurant was offering cooling ice cream soda water. The *Atlanta Constitution* occasionally named men up before the mayor's court (Mayor Hammond being referred to as "Old Ten Dollars and Costs") for conducting "faro or gaming tables" and they were lucky to get off with even a much larger fine than His Honor's nickname would indicate. There were a number of libraries in town, a flourishing lottery racket, and, "immediately in the city, accessible and pleasantly located, is a free mineral spring, which by analysis, proves highly beneficial to consumptives and dyspeptic sufferers, and an excellent spring it is." The same article [12] continues, "The climate of Atlanta cannot be excelled anywhere; it is healthy, pleasant and salubrious." On the following page two local deaths from sunstroke are listed.

Any number of Gentlemen of the Old School were still around. If one of them felt that another had injured his feelings, he would buy advertising space in the paper and under the heading, "A Card," would proceed to describe his enemy as a cad and a rascal and a person with whom no gentleman would associate. Instead of a suit for libel, the next day's paper often carried a news story about the resulting duel between the old boys, out near the cemetery. One of these, with shotguns at forty yards, was no laughing matter,[13] but more and more "A Card" was something to laugh at, and became a part of our language to mean that.

When such entertainments as "East Lynne; or, The Elopement" [14] (next week, "Ten Nights In A Bar Room") grew tiresome and it was a long time before the minstrel show was due, and when the Chicago Ale Depot was just another saloon and Chief Marshal General G. Tige Anderson, late of the Confederate States Army, had all the faro layouts under lock and key, and one's room was a stifling oven echoing back the remarkably persistent coughs, then there was always Humbug Row: "A kind of camping ground for lottery men, patent medicine venders [*sic*], and all kinds of small shows. Here flourish the prize package business; the educated hogs and uneducated men; corn doctors, root doctors, and all kinds of doctors except *regular* doctors. Here are the microscope men, the balloon men, the telescope men, the sham-jewelry men, and all kinds of men except hard-*working* men, who are seldom seen among the exhibitors." [15] Under huge flaring torches they stood, shouting you up to their booths with practised tongues; a year-around carnival, grimy and smelly and cheap and exciting. And good Officer Kicklighter to see you safe home after you'd been rolled for your wad.

Governor Smith's inaugural ball in 1872 was the social event of the year, since he was a Democrat. The *New Orleans Bee* congratulated Georgia on having "escaped from the bonds of the oppressor." [16] Atlanta boomed even more. A stove factory was built (models were called the Stonewall, the Ku Klux, etc.), and foundries and breweries and tobacco factories and warehouses, to say nothing of a flourishing "candy, soap, cracker and hoopskirt manufactory."

The *Atlanta Constitution* carried local news items taken from papers published all over the state and we note frequent quotes from the *South Georgia Times*, published in Valdosta, such juicy items as could be used to fill up space. "Valdosta has the largest Division of the Sons of Temperance in the State," on November 11, 1871; "Four brick stores are going up in Valdosta," on July 27, 1872; the birth of twin mule colts and a pig with six legs in John's home town were noted in October of 1872, and on November 24, 1872 the quote read, "James Robinson's Circus exhibited here on Thursday last. Mr. H. P. Morris, of Valdosta, and family, have moved to Texas. Valdosta has 1500 inhabitants."

Old records being what they are—sacred but scanty—no mention could be found of where Dr. John H. Holliday lived in Atlanta or the name of the dentist with whom he worked. Two old legal documents were unearthed which gave his legal residence as Fulton County, in which Atlanta is located. No doubt he roomed with some respectable family, possibly relatives, in the manner of young professional men of the times, the bachelor apartment of many uses being rather expensive. Dr. E. S. Billups, located upstairs over Chamberlin and Reynolds on Whitehall Street, was the only dentist advertising in the *Atlanta Constitution* at this time, although Hanleiter's *Atlantic City Directory* for 1870 and Wilson's *Atlanta As It Is* listed some ten dentists "of high repute in their profession," as well as Hapes Dental Depot, which specialized in making dentures.

Everything in John stubbornly refused to feel better. He was more tired than ever, thin to the point of emaciation, the spells of feeling sick all over came more frequently and he was generally feverish by nightfall. He began to wake up in the night drenched with perspiration from his scalp to the soles of his feet, and got up in the morning choking and coughing and spitting. Tuberculosis was so common then that surely he must have suspected something more was wrong with him than just being in a run-down condition. Boosters to the contrary, Atlanta winters were bleak and raw. While they had snow occasionally, the storms were usually sleet and freezing rain. The summers were hot and muggy, and the pesky mosquitoes, which were supposed to have blown over from Macon, were heatedly described as giving a man "conniptious duck fits, high strikes, Asiatic cholera and the itch." Mineral spring water was to no avail. Neither was Stafford's Olive Tar, warranted a specific for all forms of consumption, whether it is taken, applied or inhaled. The only fluid to contain magnetism. Price, fifty cents a bottle.[17]

Finally he must have had a small lung hemorrhage which scared him into going to a doctor.

There was nothing the doctor could do for him—except tell him. Six months to live if he stayed in Georgia, he was told. A year, two years at the very most if he moved to the high, dry plateau country of Texas. And then some cold and lonely night he would die strangling.

This was the end of young John Holliday.

Strangely enough, of all the towns explored through their old newspapers, battered Atlanta was the only one that had very few suicides. Everywhere else in the seventies and eighties people were "dousing their vital glim" and "jerking themselves over Jordan by their own bootstraps" and just plain "suiciding" right and left. John, undergoing a lengthy and painful death, had something indestructible deep inside. Whether it was courage or madness doesn't matter; it was there and drove him on as long as he was strong enough to take a step.

While there was no hope, there was at least an intelligent approach to this matter of dying. John wrote to his father and told him the news, asking for suggestions. Major Holliday came to Atlanta, bringing with him the deeds to the property which had been left to John by his mother, some letters of introduction to former Georgians now living in Dallas, and a legal guardianship paper. They agreed to sell one piece of property in Griffin to finance John's trip to Dallas. The remaining and most valuable one could be sold for John, whenever he needed the money, by his father if he were John's legal guardian. John's coming of age would not affect such a guardianship, which would have had to be legally dissolved and the guardian dismissed. This enabled John to get at money tied up in property even when he was far away. This first deed is dated November 12, 1872.[18]

FOOTNOTES TO CHAPTER 3

1. "The American Railroad," *Harper's New Monthly Magazine*, August, 1874.
2. *Santa Fé, the Railroad that Built an Empire*, James Marshall. Random House, New York, 1945. There being no brake lever it was necessary to put the engine in reverse to stop.
3. "A Virginia Girl In The First Year Of The War." *Century Magazine*, August, 1885.
4. "New Washington," *Harper's New Monthly Magazine*, February, 1875.
5. *The Wild Seventies*, Denis Tilden Lynch. D. Appleton-Century Co., Inc., New York, 1941.
6. "The First Century Of The Republic—Medical And Sanitary Progress," Austin Flint, M.D. *Harper's New Monthly Magazine*, June, 1876.
7. *Baltimore Sun*, December 11, 1869.
8. *Baltimore Sun*, October 4, 1869.
9. Admirers of the old days, hellers and bluenoses, will be interested to note that East Baltimore Street is still operating full tilt, the only difference being that the girls have discarded their pink tights and now operate in the raw.
10. *A History of Playing Cards and a Bibliography of Cards and Gaming*, Catherine Perry Hargraves. Houghton Mifflin Co., New York, 1930.
11. At the time of the great Chicago fire, October 9, 1871, editor I. W. Avery of the *Atlanta Constitution* got quite annoyed that Atlanta was asked to contribute money to help rebuild Chicago. No one had helped Atlanta to rebuild, he pointed out, and the town was still not restored to anything like what it had been.
12. *Atlanta Constitution*, July 14, 1871.
13. *Atlanta Constitution*, October 19, 1872.
14. Reserved seats, $1.00; general admission, $.75; family circle, $.50; boys and colored gallery, $.25. *Atlanta Constitution*, September 9, 1871.
15. *Atlanta As It Is*, John Stainback Wilson, M.D., New York. Little, Rennie and Co., Printers, 1871. (From the Rare Book Room of the Library of Congress.)
16. *Atlanta Constitution*, January 12, 1872.
17. *Atlanta Constitution*, October 27, 1871.
18. Spalding County Deed Book F, p. 1.

4

The Shooting

in Dallas

Mattie most likely knew she would never see him again, that he was going to his death alone. Aside from the difference in religion which may have stood between them heretofore, there could now be no question of their marrying. What had he to offer her? His only prospect was the grim reality that he would soon be coughing himself to death somewhere in the distant, raw frontier country. But Mattie's love remained unalterable. Perhaps everyone in the family was depressed when he left, although they also felt a sense of relief, as people do when they have pulled down the blinds on a dreary outlook—all except Mattie.

The *Atlanta Constitution* of July 15, 1871, quotes the itinerary of a person who traveled from Atlanta to Galveston; Dr. Holliday probably followed the same route a little over a year later. He would have been all night on Kimball's sleeping cars, the three rows of berths so close together that, as Robert Louis Stevenson commented,[1] going to bed was rather like undressing under a sofa, and would have arrived in Chattanooga the next morning. From here to Memphis it was 310 miles and the train took twenty-nine hours. These trains could now do sixty if the throttle-puller let them, but local laws and public opinion held them down to twenty or thirty miles an hour. The long delay in this case was possibly due to a washout or derailment on the line, but the usual cause for a hiatus in the schedule was the engineer's refusal to move without precise telegraphic orders signed by competent authority. There was a constant stream of gory train wrecks in these days, but the passengers would in a group fall on the engineer and berate him for not getting going. They would even hold indignation meetings and wire protests to the president of the railroad [2] . . . and then stand there looking silly as another train pooped toward them on the single track. When at last they chugged away themselves, with their anger only aggravated by the assurance that now they were traveling safely, they had to stop again and again for water, fuel and meals, the latter usually fifteen minutes at the Railway House where for a standard payment of fifty cents a standard meal of bacon, beans and coffee was slopped at them by ill-tempered waitresses. They paid, bolted the grub and ran—or ate the stale sandwiches, candy and fruit offered by the train's newsboy. Hours and hours and forever of this in the November cold, cramped, coughing and sick. . . .

But there was compensation waiting in Memphis, the steamer *Natchez*, that of the race with the *Robert E. Lee*, famous as the best and safest ship on the river. And there she was, like a four-layer bridal cake come alive and breathing,[3] the most gorgeous, delightful and hazardous form of transportation ever invented. The huge open decks all around gave her an air of fragility, the gilt and white salon running the length of the cabin deck gave her an undeniable look of opulence, and the compact but comfortable little cabins, opening off the salon, each had a life preserver under the bed and a notice on the door saying it could easily be removed and used as a raft.

The high-pressure boilers had a well-deserved reputation for exploding, and the cotton bales piled around the furnaces had a similar reputation for catching fire. The boilers were just iron plates riveted together into a cylinder; there was no inspection to see how much pressure they would carry; they had no insulation or protection of any sort and could be seen to "pant" alarmingly—and almost anything could be found as weight on the safety-valve beam. Each of the big side-wheels had an engine with a battery of about ten great long boilers, so the possibility of something goofing off somewhere was enormous.[4]

But the food was delicious, every comfort was provided for the passengers, and after a while the breathing stroke of the engines faded, as did the nervous expectation of a loud bang and subsequent catastrophe. In fact, since New Orleans was two and a half days and eight hundred miles away, things began to have a certain sameness most irksome to a person whose last desire was a little quiet in which to do some thinking. The barroom afforded certain "gentlemen's games" as well as the Brandy Smashes, Stone Fences and Earthquakes dispensed by the bartender, and Dr. Holliday probably joined in the enjoyment of all to pass the time. Here he saw the pure quill in professional gamblers, those who rode the river queens up and down the navigable waters of the Mississippi Valley, living off what they could earn by wit and skill from passengers with some visible means of support. A quiet and gentlemanly-looking lot, to be sure. Whatever his luck at their hands, the time passed and here was the *Natchez*, burning pitchpine and rosin to throw out a column of smoke that could be seen all over town to announce her arrival, steaming grandly alongside the levee in New Orleans.

From New Orleans he took a ninety-mile train ride across the peninsula to catch the Morgan Line iron steamer to Galveston. He paid eighteen dollars for this passage, the most he had paid for any transportation yet, because the Morgan Line had an absolute monopoly on traffic across the Gulf and consequently could charge anything it wished. In Galveston he took the train and rattled and bumped his way behind a little wood-burning coffee-pot engine of the Houston and Texas Central into Dallas, at last.

While Dr. Holliday collapses, ginned to the hilt, let us look at Dallas on the Trinity. The town originally had been built around a courthouse square in a grove of cottonwoods by a ford over the river, and then the H and TC had plunked itself down a mile away. The town immediately built Elm Street straight out to it, Dallasing station, connecting land, courthouse, town, *et al.* A street railway, the cars pulled by mules, provided public transportation for the spread-out town. Dallas was building up amazingly, prosperity was rampant, the Texas and Pacific Railroad was due soon, running from east to west, and Dallas saw itself the trading crossroads of central Texas. According to a circular entitled "Dallas and Dallas County," published in 1873 by a group of prominent citizens, the town had 6,000 inhabitants, one hundred stores and several manufactories.[5] Although Dallas was a great cotton market even then, it was also on the very edge of the wild West [6] and saw longhorns driven through its streets, buffalo hunters outfitting, Indian scouts passing through, and plenty of gamblers, saloon keepers, confidence operators and prostitutes setting up in business.

Soon after his arrival Dr. Holliday met Dr. John A. Seegar, a dentist and a former Georgian. The second deed sold by Henry B. Holliday for his son is dated March 25, 1873.[7] The Dallas City Directory for 1873 shows Seegar and Holliday listed under dentists and refers to J. H. Holliday as the partner of J. A. Seegar. Their office was on Elm Street between Market and Austin in one of the busiest parts of town. Dr. Seegar was about twenty years older than Dr. Holliday and a fine dentist, since he later advertised himself as a surgeon dentist and had an active practise in Dallas for many years. The two of them evidently practised dentistry in harmony, though allowances must have had to be made for the younger man's edgy nerves, his fits of depression and his gradually increasing number of hangovers.

Julian Bogel's "swell" saloon began to see a lot of Dr. Holliday. The days were slipping past, faster than he had ever imagined that time could go, with the inevitable end moving swiftly, if silently, toward him. If one could not bear it, one could forget it. Dr. Holliday was no saint, no soul of iron. He could not bear it.

Nobody knew what to do for consumption but everybody had a suggestion. Five mile walks twice a day, each followed by a cold bath, at least had the advantage of cutting short a painful existence. The patent medicines of the day stopped all the pain and left you feeling tip-top, but also a drug addict; this complicated matters dreadfully when it came to making out the death certificate. Many doctors prescribed whisky for relaxing the tension and gloom which are such unfavorable attitudes in consumptives, cheerfulness and a hopeful outlook being half the cure. Consequently the papers were flooded with whisky ads, recommending the purely medicinal value of their product. "Positively guaranteed to cure consumption," the distillers boasted. "We have thousands of testimonial letters in our files." [8] Whether large quantities of whisky will cure anything but sobriety is not for persons outside the medical profession to argue, surely. Something, we are not sure what, arrested (for a while unknown to him) the progress of Dr. Holliday's chronic pulmonary tuberculosis. At any rate, he became a heavy drinker.

All of the actions of "Doc" Holliday, starting here in Dallas and continuing to his death from what had in the last days become the miliary type of tuberculosis, show the behavior pattern of alcoholism. The disappointments and insecurity which he had known in his childhood were climaxed by the shock of finding himself to be dying; all this resulted in a personality maladjustment, a neurosis, in the inability to live with the real Dr. Holliday. When drunk as a skunk he was another person, a person he could bear to be. Sober, he was as mean as all hell, hating himself and everybody else.

It didn't come all at once. He was a respected businessman in Dallas for some time and only slowly slid into the half-world of the saloons and gambling halls, maintaining a footing in both camps almost until the last. The nights were so dreadful: the pain, the imagined horrors, the fear, the tossing and coughing, staring at the blackness of despair. He had to forget, and since the nights were the worst he began to spend them quietly drinking himself into amiability. There were the friendly girls in the cribs and the jolly girls in the honky tonks; there was the burlesque-show atmosphere of the variety show and the blood-and-thunder dramas at

Field's Opera House. There was in a quiet corner of every gambling house the mainstay of the business, the faro bank.

Faro is more than a gambling game. It is an involved form of investment, conducted with all the propriety of dealings in high finance. It demands a technical knowledge, a concentration so complete as to shut out everything else if one is to pursue it successfully. Here is a rectangular table with seats around three sides for the players and one behind it, against the wall always, for the dealer. The dealer slips a deck of cards into a dealing box, open on the top and at one side and fitted with a spring at the bottom to keep the cards forced up. The top card, which can be seen by everyone waiting for the game to start, is called "soda" and counts as nothing. When the game starts it is slipped aside and the card immediately under it is pulled out and laid alongside the box. Thus a card, which wins, shows in the box, and one, which loses, shows alongside the box. This is one turn of the twenty-four which make up a game. The last turn, in which three cards are shown (the cat-hop), pays double and the order of the three cards may be guessed in a special bet. The layout on which the betting is done is a strip of green felt on which are pasted the thirteen spades from a deck of cards. Some of the old decks showed a tiger on the ace, hence the nickname "bucking the tiger" for faro. To play you put your money on a card, by itself if you expected that card to come up in the box (win), or with a penny or a copper token on top of it if you expected the card to lose, hence the term "coppering a bet" for betting to lose. In order to keep track of what cards had been played a casekeeper was employed. He operated an abacus-like affair in which colored beads strung on rods were moved beside miniatures of the layout cards on each turn. You could tell how many queens, or deuces, or tens, for instance, had been played at any point in the game, but not of course whether they had won or lost. He sat directly across the table from the dealer, among the players, and his little flat folding box was visible to everyone. It was carefully consulted by the players before each turn. Keeping the case was known as "riding the hearse." A lookout, sitting on a swivel chair mounted on a box beside the dealer, was employed to help the dealer watch the complicated betting, since it was possible to bet on many cards simultaneously by a certain placing of the money on the layout. For instance, placing money on the outside right-hand corner of the eight meant that the money was on both the eight and the ten; on the inside left-hand corner of the king, that the bet was on the ace, king, queen. If the same card showed both in the box and alongside it, the house took half the bet. All bets paid one for one except the cat-hop. The odds were supposedly even; actually they were slightly in favor of the house and it was an excellent game for looking fair yet being easy for the house to cheat at by manipulating the deck, forcing certain cards and dealing seconds (this took a very expensive box), with the connivance of the casekeeper.[9]

Since Dr. Holiday spent so much time gambling, it might be well to take a look at the cards he used. They had by 1873 gotten indexed and the court cards were double-headed. They were known as "squeezers" or "indicators" from the way they could be held very close together. It was a great deal harder to read someone else's hand now when playing poker. Rounded corners, which did not bend easily to mark certain cards as the square corners did, came out about this same time also.[10] The cards were still a great deal larger than those in use today, but the back designs were becoming extremely fancy, with pictures of reigning monarchs in full regalia, locomotives, famous race horses, sportsmen, etc., and it was at this time that the familiar "Bicycle" back was put out by the United States Playing Card Company, probably the most famous back design ever made.

In other forms of finance things were beginning to get shaky. Another boost had been given Dallas's prosperity with the arrival of the Texas and Pacific Railroad, but the two railroads which served the town were destined to stop there for several years, proud to death and bragging as everyone was about them.

On September 18, 1873, the stock market crashed and there began one of the worst depressions the country has ever seen. Two large investment companies, Jay Cooke and George Opdyke, failed because of over-investment in railroad shares and precipitated a panic the results of which lasted well into the 1880's. It was the unemployment in the eastern manufacturing centers which did more than anything else to send people west. People were frantic for a means to make a living and they heard that in the west were rich mining areas where you could pick gold nuggets up off the ground [11] and great chunks of land which could be homesteaded for free. So the west in a decade became settled—the buffalo were killed off ruthlessly and the Indians were fought to a standstill; railroads were built on a shoestring and maintained themselves by bringing their future customers at half fare to buy the lands given to the railroads as a subsidy by the government. It was this year of business failure, 1873, that saw the back of the *wild* west begin to break, as determined people, tired of fighting apathy, moved to a place where there were real dangers to overcome and real rewards to win—wheat farms of hundreds of acres, cattle ranches of thousands of acres, mines whose richness made your eyes bug out to a fare-thee-well.

So what were desperately hard times in the east came to be a kind of semi-prosperity for the west, at least after some money got into circulation again. People were moving west in droves. The products they could grow sold cheap, it's true, but they had so much room to grow stuff that quantity made up for the low price. Dallas, like other western towns, continued to grow. There were plenty of teeth to work on, first fastening a rubber napkin around the patient's neck of course, but the scra-a-ape of sandpaper on a broken tooth got on the doctor's nerves as well as the patient's, it would seem, because the dentist's office saw Dr. Holliday but rarely now.

Mattie wrote bad news from home. They had begun to plant Sea Island cotton [12] around Valdosta and it had done so well that everyone changed to growing it. Then the boll weevil came and wiped

47

out the entire crop and half of South Georgia with it. Things looked very dim indeed for all the planters in the area, facing a depression and no money crop in sight.

Most of the time Dr. Holliday could forget Mattie, parents who were possibly going hungry, the prospects of his own approaching demise, anything. He could even crack a bitter joke about his sad lot between coughing spells and belting the bottle. He was not one to complain: he crowded his grouch toward life into compact, pungent verbal onslaughts on people and conditions that displeased him. Doubtless, God-fearing parents held up the dreadful youth's rapid moral decline as a picture of depravity to their own sterling lads, and they, once the lecture was over, doubtless headed breakneck for Dr. Holliday's favorite saloon to peek under the swinging doors and get a good look at this notorious character.

He was known as a gambling man and a steady drinker. His personality began to warp more and more; he became increasingly untrustworthy, untruthful, unpredictable and uncaring about his reputation—glossing over his behavior as if he thought himself invisible. His irritability when sober exploded into violent swearing outbursts when he was crossed by anyone. Daily his attitude toward responsibility faded. Sick mentally as well as physically, he was content to live his life at night in the saloons, the gambling hells, the honky-tonks and the disorderly houses in the southwestern part of town.

In such surroundings most men possessed a gun. Dr. Holliday's was probably the popular single-action Colt 1873 model, caliber .45. This was the famous Frontier Colt, and despite a hammer-fall that practically knocked the gun out of your hand, it was widely used and prized for being rugged, dependable and far-shooting. If you had a grip of iron you could even hit objects with it. Shooting, that is. In the longer barrel-lengths, of course, it did make a dandy bludgeon. But Dr. Holliday probably had his cut off short for hiding, which could help explain even better than the heavy hammer-fall some of his remarkable feats of shooting.

Sometimes he would help out his gambling friends by dealing

48

faro for them. (The professional gambler as a rule *dealt* faro and *played* poker.) His attention was so completely taken up with watching the betting, taking in the money and paying it out that, even with the aid of the lookout and the guy on the hearse, he had not a second to think of himself. If he made a mistake in favor of the house there was a loud angry scene, which gave the bank a bad name. If he made a mistake in favor of the players, the owner of the bank might clobber him one with a spittoon, just as a hint not to do it again. Dr. Holliday, not being one to take anything off of anybody, had built his house on a volcano. The house of counted days. . . .

At last the two years were up.

He was living on borrowed time—but behold the tragi-comic picture, the dying youth, the fair-haired boy pursued by a cruel fate. Only he doesn't die. The new days keep right on showing up; they are going to for years yet. But he doesn't know it. He doesn't know that he has been, as it were, reprieved. And at last his nerve breaks. It is New Year's Day, 1875.

"Dr. Holliday and Mr. Austin, a saloon-keeper, relieved the monotony of the noise of fire-crackers by taking a couple of shots at each other yesterday afternoon. The cheerful note of the peaceful six-shooter is heard once more among us. Both shooters were arrested." So the *Dallas Herald* of January 2, 1875, chronicles Dr. Holliday's sole shooting scrape in Dallas. The paper makes it out a piddling affair and doubtless its only result was that Dr. Holliday, his poor reputation now completely ruined, was requested by the law to make himself scarce. At any rate, he left town pronto, because in less than two weeks he was in jail again, this time in the little log hoosegow in Fort Griffin, Texas.

FOOTNOTES TO CHAPTER 4

1. *The Amateur Emigrant*, Robert Louis Stevenson. Charles Scribner's Sons, New York, 1925.
2. "The American Railroad," *Harper's New Monthly Magazine*, August, 1874.
3. The stroke of the connecting rods was about twenty to the minute, the average rate at which a person breathes. It could be felt all over the ship and gave these vessels an unusual amount of personality.
4. *Steamboats on the Western Rivers*, Louis C. Hunter. Harvard University Press, Cambridge, 1949.
5. This circular, a single sheet of paper like a handbill, is in the Rare Book Room of the Library of Congress. Dr. Seegar's name appears as one of the signers, but not that of Dr. Holliday.
6. *The Lusty Texans of Dallas*, John William Rogers. E. P. Dutton and Co., Inc., New York, 1951.
7. Spalding County, Georgia, Deed Book F, p. 95.
8. No federal or local laws at this time forced manufacturers to make their products live up to their claims. Cancer, tuberculosis, heart disease and syphilis cures were constantly advertized as unfailing remedies. Many of the cures contained habit-forming drugs or were only cheap whisky with something added to change the taste.
9. Faro has gone out of style now, but there are still some banks in operation in Nevada's gilt-plush gambling halls.
10. "Playing Cards," Frieda Clark. *Hobbies, The Magazine for Collectors*, April, 1952.
11. General George A. Custer, soon to get his at the Little Big Horn, but not soon enough, helped foster this story. He was leading an expedition through the Black Hills, the private property of the Sioux nation by United States treaty, and wrote glowingly of its wonders in his official reports. The newspapers naturally quoted him and even *Harper's* for October, 1874, stated: "The Black Hills region is in its floral beauty a new Florida and in its treasure a new El Dorado. As a grazing country it is not to be surpassed. Veins of lead and strong indications of silver have been found. Veins of gold-bearing quartz crop out on every hill-side. There are also unlimited supplies of timber."
12. *History of Lowndes County*, op. cit.

5

Trouble in

Fort Griffin, Texas

The friends he had, gamblers, saloonkeepers, bunco-steerers, prostitutes, familiarly called him Doc. He belonged to their world, particularly since his arrest. He was, in this January of 1875, twenty-three years old, of average height, very thin, very pale, with blond hair, blue eyes that sometimes seemed grey, and had an expression of constrained emotion—sometimes sorrow, sometimes petulance, sometimes rage. He spoke with a soft southern accent, dressed with extreme neatness and cleanness, and was, in this age of magnificent beards, clean-shaven except for a blond handlebar mustache. He appeared to be a gentleman and indeed, when stoked to the gills with the demon rum, his manner was pleasant and refined. Then he was feeling no pain, in every meaning of the phrase. When he was dead sober the tense nerves stretched through him so tautly that the most ordinary of experiences sandpapered him raw in a second and he fought back with virulently expressed hatred for everything and everybody. Just to keep matters straight, he managed to stay pleasantly soaked most of the time.

Being a small railroad town of average size for a farm and ranch trading center of the times, Dallas had its gossip and its social frame into which everyone fitted. Consequently, no one was surprised when Doc finally got into a shooting scrape; it had been expected for months. Now he was not wanted in Dallas: he was a trouble-maker and a souse. He'd been in one shooting scrape and no one knew when he'd succeed in killing someone. Neither did they see why it should happen in Dallas. Such things were bad for business.

To the north, clear up into Indian Territory, ranged the buffalo on their southern feeding grounds where the rolling hills were rich with grama grass. Alas, that in this bleak depression year their hides should make excellent machine belting and luxurious fur robes and be worth a dollar to a buck-fifty at the nearest trading center. That was enough, but there was even more, there was encouragement from the army, and sometimes free guns and ammo and even protection from the Indians, because the top brass were arguing that the Indians would be dependent upon the government for beef if the buffalo were gone and consequently could then be kept under supervision. Cattlemen looked at the grass. And the buffalo died.

Doc had seen the mile-long ox trains stacked high with buffalo hides come rolling into Dallas from Fort Griffin. He had heard that it was hell-on-the-border, that anything went. That the hunters and skinners threw away their money like water when they hit civilization again after weeks in the wilds.

Fort Griffin was the southern metropolis of the buffalo hunters. Acres of drying hides sent up a stench that marked the town like a beacon for miles and gave the local goings-on a peculiar flavor and gustiness. Conrad's Gen'l Merchandise did a land-office business in ammunition and supplies for the hunters, and a dozen saloons, most of them with a dance hall or honky-tonk attached, supplied anything else that might be desired. One of the last of the great cattle trails, known locally as the Dodge City trail, ran from Bandera, Texas, through Fort Griffin, to Doan's Crossing on the Red River, to Camp Supply on the north fork of the Canadian River in Indian Territory, to Dodge. Only Fort Griffin could call itself a town along the way, and many of the trail bosses outfitted there entirely or in part. All summer long the herders fogged in to

52

see a real live town and have a drink if nothing else. In keeping with the "wild" west character of the town, an army post was located within whooping distance. The unreconstructed Texans and the military delighted in disturbing one another and what with frolics and lynchings in the night and bugle tootings in the dawn, they succeeded admirably. The local Indians were a peaceable, friendly bunch of Tonkawas who, having forsworn scalps, proceeded to lift everything else in sight.

When Doc came rolling in on the stage he saw a bunch of unpretentious frame and adobe buildings and piles of buffalo hides scattered among the cottonwoods beside the Clear Fork of the Brazos river. A bluff rose immediately behind this little flat and on top of it was situated the army post for which the village was named. Only the year before Shackleford County had come into being and control had passed out of the hands of the army. A gang of toughs, gamblers, skin-game operators, prostitutes and drifters had immediately set up business in town and was flourishing mightily.

Doc found a prosperous-looking spot and went to work. No more the fancy plush chair with the adjustable head and foot rest, no more the finicky drilling, no more the hard labor of extraction. There remained the professional manner. He did his day's work at a round wooden table under a hanging kerosene lamp, sitting on an uncomfortable straight wooden chair that helped keep him alert, watching the cards, the faces, the hands; concentrating; coughing.

Men standing behind the players, watching, were expected not to crowd close, not to talk, and not to give the hands away; no interruptions to the game were permitted. Three card draw, jacks or better, was the usual type of poker played. A houseman dealt but did not play, taking a percentage of each pot for the house. If everything was perfectly square and aboveboard, the suckers as a rule still got taken, by their own stupidity. The professional player followed certain rules: "He must study the players more than the cards. He must never allow anyone to get on to his game, and must bluff lively every now and then to throw the other players off the scent. He must be the same, winning or losing—must never smile or growl, but lay low, keep still, and watch the game. Let him watch the draw closely and in a short time he will be able to know just what the player is drawing to—a pair, two pairs, threes, a straight or a flush. Then if he thinks he has the best hand after the draw, even if one or all of his opponents have bettered their hands, let him shove in his chips to the full extent of the limit at once, and not wait for them to play his hand." [1]

There would have been playing this winter other professional gamblers, hunters and skinners, soldiers from the fort, ranchers and herders from nearby, and perhaps the fabulous Lottie Deno. [2]

Away from the quiet of the poker tables and the faro bank, making a background of gayety and liveliness, was the honky-tonk where, upon a small stage, appeared such variety acts as could be lured into the wilderness, and where pretty girl hostesses circulated among the customers, urging them to buy drinks at the bar that ran down one side of the room. The variety acts were of the not-good-but-loud type: the constant pratfall, the clumsily-contrived local joke. A chubby blonde in tights prances out to wring her hands through "Lorena," "I'll Remember You, Love, in My Prayers" and "Silver Threads among the Gold." A dapper fellow of the comic persuasion follows, distributing his humor to all fields in turn; the army joke, the one about how the buffalo skinner stinks, one about the most popular man in town and one about Grant's administration, interspersed with dirty jokes of the less subtle sort. Somebody does a clog—expertly dodging the missiles thrown by boys who want to see girls. The blonde hastily reappears minus part of her costume and her former look of pain, but no one cares. The riot at least temporarily averted, a blueshirt yells, "Harrigan and Hart!" another, "The Mulligan Guard!" The professor at the piano rips into "The Regular Army O" and all is joy on the Clear Fork of the Brazos.

After the soldiers finished celebrating the last chorus of their favorite song, a hit from one of the many New York stage successes by Harrigan and Hart, the dump had indeed livened up. Ed

Harrigan's "Muldoon, The Solid Man" followed, a song which was known the world over and gave "the solid Muldoon" to the language of the times. This was as much a part of daily speech as the phrase "the missing Charley Ross," which referred to a kid who had apparently vanished the year before and got more publicity than the kidnaping of the Lindbergh baby in more recent times. Then the party began to get rough, "Sweet Evalina" being sung in its original off-color version, "Marriage Bells," the sporting house anthem, being delivered, the can-can danced with whoops resembling the battle cry of the Comanches, a drunk being dissuaded from reciting "Thanatopsis," and an impromptu bottle-throwing contest coming off.

In the dance hall next door a hunter and a soldier fell to blows over one of the female entertainers and proceeded to wreck the surroundings pretty thoroughly before being chucked out. Shots resounded from the gun of a drunken herder who knew of no other way to express his emotions. A peal of giggles rang through the night, there was a scurry of running feet, a lamp crashed. . . .

In order to keep on the good side of the godly it was necessary to make a noise like cleaning up in this sink-hole of iniquity every so often. Sheriff Jacobs, fortified by a state law which prohibited gambling,[3] and also by various local ordinances, would make a raid on the wicked and round up such small-time operators as he could to make a showing in court.

At this time the legitimate merchants were still making plenty of money with bacon, for instance, seventy-five cents a pound. But soon the herds would be killed off and the buffalo hunters would vanish, the Indians would be pacified and the forts abandoned, the easy money and the gamblers would be gone—and only the respectable ranchers and farmers would be left.

While Doc had apparently drawn to a pair of deuces and filled in the health game, his luck was lousy in other quarters. He must have arrived in Fort Griffin in time to coincide with one of these morality campaigns. And, since news of shootings travelled so fast in these dull times, the Fort Griffinites knew they had a potential killer on their hands and didn't want him any more than Dallas did, so they gave him a boot on his way. At any rate, he was indicted by the Grand Jury on January 12, 1875, for "gaming in a saloon," along with Hurricane Bill, Liz, Etta, Kate, *et al.*, charged with keeping a disorderly house,[4] and flung into Fort Griffin's tiny log jail. This is precisely the reception a person with a reputation as a gun-punk and a hard drinker could expect in any community, west, east, up or down, for a choice in locations. It was necessary to be wicked in a certain way, to have a flair. Sin was a business in which he did not have an "in." So, being himself and thoughtful instead of emotional about such matters, he put up bail, hopped the first stage out of town, and was never seen in that particular hell-on-the-border again.[5]

In January of 1875 there was more than enough adventure in a stage-coach ride west from Fort Griffin. Doc had evidently thought it out: it was necessary to go someplace where that disgraceful shooting episode in Dallas was unknown. Two grown men plugging away at each other and neither of them hit: that was funny in a gun-toting town. No wonder he was sneered at by law officers in one-horse burgs way out in the sticks. So he recollected all he'd heard of the boom towns of the west and picked Denver as the most promising for a gentleman of his talents and delicate state of health.

There was a long line of army posts arching around north central Texas as protection against the Comanches, Kiowas, Arapahoes and Cheyennes who were in the habit of raiding in this area. A stage and mail road ran north from Dallas to Fort Richardson[6] at Jacksboro, then west to Fort Belknap, Fort Griffin, Fort Phantom Hill, Fort Chadbourne and Fort Concho. These posts were mainly cavalry stations, each one lonelier and more dangerous as they progressed deeper into Indian country. This was the mildest part of the country which it was necessary to cross to get to El Paso.

In the long stretch west from Fort Concho, crossing the Pecos at Horsehead Crossing, there were no forts, only the bullet-scarred

56

adobe walls of the stage stations. Here the country was barren and hostile, a harsh land of sudden bleak hills and endless arid plains so unpleasant that one could well understand the ancient witticism to the effect that, if given one's choice, one would rent out Texas and live in hell. Fortunately the army, under General Ranald McKenzie, had chased a large party of Indians to their main camp in Palo Duro canyon and trounced them thoroughly the preceding September. By January they had just about pacified West Texas. But no one knew when a bunch of young bucks would break loose, raise hell and scalps all over the place and vanish into the Staked Plains. The monthly reports sent to the Assistant Adjutant General, Department of Texas, at San Antonio, are now on file at the National Archives. In February, 1875, Nicholas Nolan, Captain, 11th Cavalry, in command at Fort Concho, wrote: "The troops are employed to the extent of their ability in giving protection to exposed settlements and routes of travel and in guarding against incursions of hostile Indians and other marauders."

So Doc, coughing and miserable, would ride to the limit of his strength and then rest up at one of the villages that sprang up in the shelter of the forts, gambling with soldiers and ranchers until it was time to move on. Fort Concho, in Tom Green County, must have seen him sometime that spring. A *capais* was issued for his arrest to Tom Green County by the sheriff of Shackleford County (Fort Griffin) on June 30, 1875. Doc was probably long gone when it arrived, because this was the last of the case.[7]

Here is the land of the sky, of a blue so bright and immense as to be terrifying, pressing down a heat that knocks you flat and then rolls over you. And a trail wound across the brown and hateful land and six horses dragged a stagecoach across a foretaste of the wages of sin. The line of army posts dipped too far south here.[8] They were on their own, a mote of dust that swirled valiantly across the desert. The passengers sat grim-faced and coughing, most of them on the top where three seats were bolted to the roof behind the driver's seat. Swathed in dust as they were it was better than the cramped and stifling interior, and Doc had plenty of spitting room. They had a magnificent view of nothing. To see cattle was an experience, a herder a thrill, a lone Indian hair-raising, and the crossing of the Pecos unforgettable. At the stage stations the miserable meals and their extortion prices could hardly be choked down. The beds available had to be shared with other riders of the same sex and a host of critters of both sexes and astounding appetites. A hefty drink was all that kept Doc going. Cramped, exhausted, having to get off and walk to rest the horses on every incline, almost sorry to get back on to be jerked and jolted dizzy, they forced their minds blank and existed through the misery of crossing the plains by stage.

At last the monotony dissolved into interest. There was the Rio Grande after an eternity of dry washes; there were irrigation channels feeding orchards, vineyards and gardens; there were groves of ash and cottonwoods shading a little clump of adobe buildings; there was moisture in the air like a blessing on the travellers' burned faces. Here was El Paso—three saloon-gambling halls, a hotel, three stores, two stage stations, a tiny plaza, a little open-air market under a grove of trees and perhaps twenty-five American inhabitants and six times that many Mexicans.

East and west ran the old stage routes, Butterfield and the Overland; north and south ran the oldest road in America, the *Camino Real* from Mexico City to Santa Fe, settled by the Spanish in 1609. All of this valley of the Rio Grande was settled by the Spanish and it was a place of their language and customs. El Paso was a sleepy little hamlet, occasionally enlivened by a bunch of soldiers from nearby Fort Bliss or the arrival of a wagonload of silver from the mines of Chihuahua. The stages came and left, a ripple on the placid surface. After resting up at the Central Hotel and investigating the illegal side of the place Doc knew he had to move on.[9]

The old road ran north, the valley wide away to the barren hills shutting it in east and west, studded here and there with groves of cottonwoods and tiny Spanish-speaking hamlets with their irrigated gardens by the cool river, and then off into the *Jornado del Muerte*,[10] and back to the river again, far on to Albuquerque.

58

This was before the railroad came, this was old Albuquerque, a sleepy village of low adobe buildings, crowned on the plaza by the church of San Felipe de Neri. The trees had been cut down and the plaza glared in a haze of dust. The stores surrounding it all had roofs extending over the sidewalk to cut the glare and break the sight of such raw ugliness.

And still north they went, climbing, the mountains steeper and crowding closer. There was a coolness, a briskness in the air, fresh, invigorating, cutting away the fog of pain, a bitter reminder of days when one felt *well* and happy to be alive. The little villages were more scattered now, the vivid chilis hanging red on the tan adobe walls, a veil of woodsmoke blowing grey against the blue sky and the purple mountains. The cottonwoods showed their white branches lacy beside the cold and rushing river. At last, in a high country surrounded by higher country, they came to Santa Fe. Santa Fe then was crowded all close together and piled with trash and smelling of stronger items than the burning piñon one smells there now. It was yet the terminal of the Santa Fe trail and business was pretty brisk for a predominately Spanish town. One whole side of the plaza was occupied by the long, low palace of the governor, built back in Spanish times, with its white walls, cool *portal* (porch) and forthright charm. On the other three sides were two-story store buildings, each with its porch over the sidewalk. A narrow alleyway lined with a continuous row of one-story adobe rooms led to the unfinished Cathedral of St. Francis,[11] then being built of a local stone about the color of an old, dusty pumpkin and in a style which to this day looks awkward and alien among the comfortable and sturdy adobes. The town harbored a plenty of saloons and other localities for getting into trouble, but the railroads were coming, even if slowly, and soon the bullwhackers' day would be gone and the traders would find the railroads liked the flatlands and would give them a spurline and then pass them by.

So by the Southern Overland Stage Company Doc went east through a pass to sleepy Spanish Las Vegas, then north to Raton Pass. The country gradually was losing its green and wooded look, becoming more and more barren. The stage passed Fort Union, guarding the Santa Fe trail—paying toll at Raton to the legendary Uncle Dick Wootton, the last of the mountain men who had trapped furs in the high Rockies and made a roaring town of Taos—and went on to Fisher's Peak, thrust grandly up over the little adobes of Trinidad. Here Doc changed to the Barlow, Sanderson and Company [12] coach and went up more valleys and across more flats to the two Pueblos defying each other across the Arkansas River. It was the first "American" style town he had seen in a thousand miles of travelling. It even had a railroad. Years later he was to live in South Pueblo, but now he had to get on. After paying seven dollars for a ticket, he got on the Denver and Rio Grande, the plug-puller let 'er out, and off they chugged for Denver.

FOOTNOTES TO CHAPTER 5

1. From an undated article in the Cincinnati *Inquirer* on how to play draw poker, reprinted in the Denver *Tribune-Republican* of August 1, 1886.
2. A woman professional gambler who lived for a while in Fort Griffin, working at Shaughnassy's saloon, mostly, or the Bee Hive.
3. "An Act to Adopt and Establish a Penal Code for the State of Texas," which contained an anti-gambling law, was passed by the state legislature on August 26, 1856.
4. Volume I, Shackleford County District Court Docket, pages unnumbered.
5. See Chapter Seven.
6. The monthly records of old Fort Richardson, on file at the National Archives in Washington, were examined carefully in the hopes of authenticating one of Doc's wilder adventures. Mrs. Ida Lasater Huckaby, author of *Ninety Years in Jack County*, and a lifelong resident of Jacksboro (where Fort Richardson was located) had never heard of Holliday being there, and no mention of him is found in Thomas F. Horton's *A History of Jack County*. The monthly reports of the fort contain no mention of any of the men being in shooting scrapes and there were only sick in the hospital. The correspondence deals with forage problems, officers being absent from reveille, and complaints about lack of funds for repairs. The twelve companies, under Colonel W. H. Wood, 17th Cavalry, were employed as escorts for officers, the mail, to carry dispatches, and to go out with the Jack County sheriff to catch horse thieves.
7. Volume I, Shackleford County District Court Docket, pages unnumbered.
8. It is possible that Doc's stage line followed the military road, which would have dipped through the same kind of countryside down to Fort Davis and Fort Stockton.
9. After Fort Bliss was abandoned in 1877, the town became a nest of thieves and killers so lawless that the fort had to be re-established the following year.
10. The "Journey of Death," a ninety-mile waterless detour around deep arroyos cutting into the river. The scene of great suffering by the early Spanish settlers of the Rio Grande Valley, from both thirst and the Indians.
11. United States Signal Corps photo taken in the early 1880's.
12. *Routes of Travel in Colorado*, published by the *Rocky Mountain News*, Denver, 1874.

6

Denver in the 70's

No matter who set out from Pueblo with his ticket, Tom McKey arrived in Denver, not J. H. Holliday.[1] In that long, miserable stage ride he had thought it out. Despite all their disagreements he was proud of his father and the position he held in Valdosta; he thought so much of Mattie that he did not want her to be hurt by reports of his failings; he wanted to be sure those unfortunate affairs in Dallas and Fort Griffin were not associated with him. He knew the kind of life he wanted: quiet, busy, having a few good friends, making a buck or two, keeping out of trouble. But having seen what happened in Fort Griffin, he was taking no chances. He looked, as always, for insurance on his proposition. And since Tom had the same vowel sound as John, and he would naturally look up on hearing his mother's maiden name, he chose Tom McKey for his Denver go-by.

Having at last realized that he was not, after all, so close to the New Jerusalem that he could see the dome of the courthouse, as Bill Nye (an American humorist in three letters, to crossword puzzle fans) put it, McKey had straightened out a great deal. He didn't stop drinking—he couldn't—but he had been drinking so heavily for so long that alcohol no longer had much of an effect on him. When cold sober or lugging around not much more than a quart, he might be dangerous, but this rarely happened. That his personality was that of an alcoholic is shown, of course, by his taking an alias. Subconsciously he did not want to be this unhappy, frail, pain-wracked Holliday person. He was conscious of

62

wanting to change his luck. Perhaps, to himself, he was a new person with this new name; it was symbolic of his starting a new life. The pleasant kid would never come back, but he still had the capacity for making friends when he wanted to; he could concentrate on cards for hours; he put on a faultless show of being a gentleman—and he couldn't see that whisky had any ill effects on him *what-so-ever*; it just made him feel superior to other people.

His faro dealing experience standing him in good stead, he went to work for Charley Foster at Babbitt's House [2] at 357 Blake Street. At this time, for an eight-hour day (the average working day of the times was at least nine hours), as alternate dealer and lookout he would have made about seven dollars to start and worked up to ten. Casekeepers made five dollars for the same shift.[3] It was extremely exacting work, but with the one-hundred-proof ego he had developed nothing was difficult and he dealt the best faro game in town. That he was actually at least adequate is shown by his long continuing in the profession. In these hard times, with decent meals available for two bits and excellent hotel rooms renting for a dollar a day, this was a job worth keeping.

He spent hours and hours and hours practicing with the cards, learning a flashy shuffle, a cut that really broke up the deck—and if he couldn't also false cut, deal seconds or off the bottom and stack a deck right in front of everyone undetected, then he was the most unusual professional gambler that ever lived. No magician could do more with a deck of cards than Tom McKey. But these shady dealings were not resorted to in the better houses except in times of the direst necessity. In a town the size of Denver a good reputation was everything and for a house to get a name for running a brace game was death. However, it was generally agreed that it was only proper to protect your interests in case of an exceptional run of luck. If nothing else, an adeptness at cheating was assurance that you would recognize the gestures when you saw someone else using them—and also the patent machinery: the sleeve holdout, the ring that marked high cards with a dent, the mirror-surfaced coin that reflected the dealt cards, the deck known as a "reader" with its marked back, and all the gimmicks that defied luck. A well-operated faro bank, running on an investment of at least three thousand dollars, would bring in a net profit of about five thousand dollars a month. It was a business worth protecting in every way and hiring the best men for.

Tom McKey spent most of his time in the handsome saloon-gambling houses along Larimer and Blake Streets. When not dealing his shift at Babbitt's, he might be found in a quiet game of poker there or at the Little Casino, the Mint, or Ed Chase's place. The free lunch counter supplied him with a snack, and drinks were always on the house to players at the gambling tables. He might spend a few moments on the street talking to someone and getting a breath of air or looking in the gun shop windows along Larimer Street, but he rarely loafed. He had work to do. Rumor has credited him with phenomenal runs of luck, but we can only be sure that he did win fairly large sums on occasion, large enough to afford him the usual in gambler's jewelry; a diamond ring and a gold watch and chain.[4] His friends were all of this gambling world, the halfway world between respectability and the chain gang, paying for police protection, laying low, making money. That these friends were mostly Yankees was not allowed to make any difference to Tom McKey. It took an effort to forget the past, more than any Yankee could ever know, but he was able to put his hatred for them out of his mind as a coldly calculated matter of policy.

Despite brick buildings, a population of 18,000, an abundance of railroads, twelve churches, and the fact that Larimer Street was paved with wooden blocks for a short stretch, Denver managed to retain a truly western character. It was situated over an ugly bunch of hills at the confluence of Cherry Creek and the South Platte, where the Great American Desert's thousand mile gentle up-slope abruptly ends in the Rocky Mountains, with 14,000-foot Mt. Evans towering over the town. Whereas other towns might, like Dodge and Dallas, grow up by a ford across a river, or like Tombstone and Leadville, be in the heart of a mining area, there was a

64

psychological reason for Denver being where it was. People who had crossed the vast plains felt they had to pause for breath before tackling the mountains rearing up so overwhelmingly before them. They wanted to rest, dawdled to repair their gear, needed new supplies, had to wind up their fortitude and courage afresh, kind of hankered after some fun, and finally found themselves rooted in Denver. The gold fields of Black Hawk and Central City never missed them, and getting a constant inflow of people kept a bright edge on Denver.

It was not a gun-toting town, but neither was it a law-abiding one, being so noted for its number of petty theft arrests that the streetcar conductors went armed in the line of duty (there actually were some smalltime Jesse Jameses who robbed horse-cars instead of trains), and there were loud cheers when a housewife butcher-knifed a burglar the police had been unable to catch. The same things that had brought Tom McKey to Denver, its healthy climate and its reputation for being a boom town, had brought a large number of drifters, and consequently the city always had plenty of men repairing the gravelly dirt streets, so many days on the chain gang at hard labor being the penalty for vagrancy. The drunk and disorderly furnished the police news with most of its items. There also was one puny effort to tree the town which was promptly put down by eight policemen. And quantities of fisticuffings—rocks were thrown at Chinese dwellings, women were arrested for using foul language, and one deputy United States marshal tripped while chasing a chicken and poked a piece of scantling in his eye. The Denver *Rocky Mountain News* also faithfully reported the occasional murders, cuttings, brawls, out-of-town gun fights, and one spring day boldly chronicled "the first robbin' of the season."

Denver was not a one-horse cow town. It was the big time, the only real metropolis for five hundred miles in every direction. It was organized. The gamblers, saloonkeepers, bawdy-house madams and confidence-game operators, together with the investors whose money was in these illicit enterprises—and these latter included

65

many a respectable name—did business out in the open, under the protection of the city government. There were no scandals, no shootings, no stink. The *Rocky Mountain News* editor printed it all in his paper and nobody cared.

"Harry King and J. W. Raymond keepers of the gambling house which was 'pulled' by the police Friday night, were fined $25 by Sayer yesterday," the *Rocky Mountain News* reported on July 25, 1875, and a week later,[5] "Election times are coming on apace and the gambling houses have to be occasionally 'pulled' just for the political effect it has, you know. Several sporting men, charged with keeping gambling houses, were brought before Justice Sayer yesterday. The case against G. H. Pierce was dismissed, while the case of three others was taken under advisement. The tiger will commence to roar again in a few days, no doubt." And on August 4, "Justice Sayer yesterday dismissed the gambling cases which he had held under advisement since Saturday."

The following day Charles Ward (operator of The Mint) was charged with keeping a disorderly saloon, fined twenty-five dollars and lost his saloon license. He was fined an additional fifteen dollars for permitting women to assemble in his place for the purpose of attracting customers.

"Some of the city officials spend most of their time now on the streets, and are hand and glove with everybody, not excepting the most notorious bummers and saloon loafers," was the comment on the sixth.

And on the seventh, "Charley Ward, of the West Side 'Mint' was again put under arrest yesterday by Policeman Smith, for dispensing 'Mint juleps' and the like, after his license had been revoked."

"Justice Sayer yesterday dismissed the case against Charley Ward, of the 'Mint,' for selling liquor without a license. The city stands no show at all in a contest with a powerful institution like the 'Mint.' " This was the report on the twentieth of August, 1875.

A gambler or any denizen of his world was as safe in Denver at this time as if he had been in God's pocket. Tom McKey had protection and influence exerted on his behalf as "one of the boys," and was not only allowed but encouraged to continue in his chosen profession of card sharp.

His world was a fast-stepping place. It knew the latest insult ("Pull down your vest") and the correct retort ("Wipe off your chin"), the latest off-color and political jokes, the skeletons in the church crowd's closets, the sob story behind every sporting girl's fall from virtue, and the story behind the world that Mrs. Denver knew. Everyone had a certain fast-thinking, hair-trigger alertness that came from a daily life of having to be ahead of the game, watching and judging rapidly so many cards, hands, faces. What wonder that they thought of slower-thinking folks as chumps, inferiors to be robbed by an easy playing on their stupidity and covetousness?

Often a pair of professional gamblers would get together and work out a sure thing for them to operate in their spare time.

"You see, poker sharps generally go in pairs, and a pair of them can skin the best man out. And it does not make a bit of difference how many may be in the game, three, four, or even seven, the two playing in partnership will have everything to their advantage. This business is worked so skillfully that it is next to impossible to tumble to it during the game. Poker partners pretend to have no use for each other during the game, and generally speak in very uncomplimentary terms to one another. They do this to throw the other players off their guard. In the game they sit next to one another so they can see each other's hand. Suppose one of these sharps holds the age and his partner is the dealer for that hand; [6] well, the age finds a pair of aces in his hand, which he takes particular pains to show in some way or other to his partner; then if any of the other players have chipped in, the age raises the original ante to the full limit, whatever that may be, depending on his partner, the dealer, to help him out. Now the chances are that the dealer has either an ace or a pair or some lower card in his own hand, so if he has an ace he slips his hand quickly on the deck with the ace on top and if he has a pair in addition they come next. No one notices this move because he does it so quickly, and besides as he is not going to stay and play his own hand the other players don't think it worth while to watch him. They only watch the dealer as long as they think he is after the pot.

"Well, what is the result? The age has taken three cards and the other players are pretty well aware of the fact that he, the age, is drawing to a pair of aces. Now, if they helped their hands at all, they feel confident that they have got the age in a close box, so off they go, betting the full limit, only to find that the age is ready and raises them back to the extent of the limit. To be sure they have to call, only to find the age loaded for 'bar'." [7]

And when the dealer is on the left, he stacks the deck and his partner appears to cut but does not. "If you are a boss player avoid a limited game, and if you are a natural chump never go beyond a ten-cent limit under any circumstances." [8]

Professional gamblers know better than to believe that their luck *has* to change when the cards persistently run badly for them. After a few rotten hands they accept it as the occasional off night everybody is bound to have, and change their game. If continually dogged by bad luck McKey would stop gambling altogether and either just watch the others or go elsewhere for amusement, leaving the natural chump to sit there losing pot after pot, frantically telling himself the law of the maturity of chances. One does not suppose that the fancy ladies who hung out in saloons like The Mint allowed Tom McKey to be lonely or bored at such a time.

In the way of legitimate amusement there were the orderly German beer gardens where blonde lady musicians played um-pah-pah-um-pah-pah until midnight, burly waiters served beer and pretzels and ma and pa had a sedate waltz while the kids snoozed on benches. Guard Hall presented an occasional play by a travelling troupe with sufficient reputation to get people to part with their scarce money for tickets. The Turnverein Society presented free programs of tumbling, acrobatics and weight lifting at Turner Hall. Montgomery Queen's Elegant and Moral Circus (the female performers in gold-spangled Mother Hubbards?) came too, but the big eye-knocker-out was a visit by Dr. Mary Walker, *in men's clothes,* actually out walking upon the public street.[9] In the musical vein there was every kind of ditty from "I'se Gwine Back to Dixie" to "Over the Hill to the Poorhouse." In the literary line the *Rocky Mountain News* commented that Richards & Co. had received a shipment of new books, among them *Wild Oats Sown Abroad,* by T. B. Whitman; *Miss Angel,* by Miss Thackeray; *Sigma,* by Ouida and "others of equal worth." [10]

Tom McKey began to feel a little better. The high altitude had at first made him subject to knock-down, drag-out fits of exhaustion, but after a while he got used to it. Fortunately this first winter he spent in Denver was very mild, there being no snow until after Christmas. This gave the editor of the *Rocky Mountain News* opportunity to crow about the local "Italian climate," Italy being the tourist Mecca of the day, and later he inelegantly cemented the comparison by complaining that Denver bid fair to become a modern Pompeii, buried under tin cans, it was so dirty. Old-timers recalled a winter sixteen years before when the mercury congealed in the thermometers,[11] champagne, vinegar, and the cheaper brands of whisky froze solid and were handed around in chunks at the bar Uncle Dick Wootton was running at the time in the tiny village on Cherry Creek, and the air had been filled with a fine frost, like fog.[12] But Denver climate boosters were legion and consumptives were particularly urged to come there.

In the silence of his room Tom McKey would have a last drink, take off his shoes and glance at the paper. The scandals of Grant's administration, particularly the Whisky Ring, were getting a big play, as was every move of the reigning families of Europe, this being the era when Americans with secure investments and insecure family connections were feeling particularly inferior to "all that there European culture stuff." At home the little Sunday school kiddies were being asked to donate their pennies to help complete Washington Monument,[13] it was all too evident there were plenty of non-agency Indians left, Charley Ross was still missing, the Denver Ladies Relief organization served oysters, roast turkey, baked

69

beans and hot coffee at their fair, and Hale's Honey of Hoarhound and Tar positively cured consumption. So ran the even current of Tom McKey's days. At Christmas the editor of the *Rocky Mountain News* commented that Saturday had been a very quiet Christmas, family pleasures predominating, and that anyone could enjoy them despite hard times, dull business, and the scarcity of money. The first snow of the season fell on December 30.

In 1876 the news perked up all around. There was gold in the Black Hills and the Sioux were refusing to go back on the reservation. The Denver branch of the Young Men's Christian Association was opened in January,[14] so please do not feel that this McKey-Holliday fellow *had* to hang out in saloons. He probably never even noticed the event, being too busy talking over the big doings in Cheyenne, Wyoming Territory. Everybody was going to Cheyenne. That was the coming town. It was the jumping-off place for the newly-opened prospecting areas of the Black Hills.

The Denver Pacific Express arrived in Cheyenne at 12:15 P.M.,[15] and Cheyenne looked this winter almost as wild and woolly as it had in the Union Pacific construction days ten years before, when Hell on Wheels had been the town and the Big Tent crowd had run everything. They were laying rails four to the minute, the construction gangs had boasted. A thousand men with a hundred teams pulling scrapers were grading the bed; wagonloads of ties were coming from the west and trainloads of track from the east; the Cheyenne Indians were killing off surveying parties, construction gangs, crews of stalled trains and stragglers of all sorts; professional hunters were hired to supply the workers with meat and they killed off whole herds of buffalo and other large game; and west the tracks went. Ex-Confederate and ex-Union soldiers, Irish, Dutch (Germans, not Holland Dutch), Mexicans, British, farm boys, ne'er-do-wells, escaped convicts, runaway mamma's darlings, all sorts and conditions of men had fought that railroad across the land and raised hell in Cheyenne on Saturday night. The rough old days seemed reborn in this winter of 1876.

"A fresh invoice of Denver gamblers and sneaks arrived yester-

70

day," the rugged editor of the Cheyenne *Wyoming Weekly Leader* stated on February 12, 1876. "That dying town seems to be 'taking a puke' as it were, of this class of citizen."

Cheyenne might boast such bon-ton items as the Inter-Ocean Hotel, the famous Bella Union variety theater, real Brussels carpets, gold-framed mirrors, porcelain cuspidors and oyster saloons, but the town's normal 8,000 population was also inundated by a flood of rough characters. The way to the gold fields led through the heart of the Sioux' pet hunting ground. Driven here by the depression, many of these men would have bearded the devil himself and feared neither Indian nor white man—when they started out, that is. The sight of a scalped body soon proved mighty persuasive to caution. This winter Cheyenne was jammed with prospectors, teamsters, miners, sheepherders from the grounds up towards Laramie, railroad employees, bullwhackers, gamblers, tramps, adventurers, soldiers from nearby Fort Russell, outfitters, investors, and ordinary businessmen who had gone broke and were looking for anything in the way of work. The UP dumped them down and abandoned them to their fate. The editor of the *Wyoming Weekly Leader* begged someone to start a branch of the YMCA, and the Excelsior, the New Idea and Frenchy's Place were making a mint.

The road to the gold fields went to Fort Laramie, then to Custer City, the first boom camp of the Black Hills. It was 246 miles and cost twenty dollars travelling by the Cheyenne and Black Hills Stage Company line—and hardly worth it if you didn't survive the mad race through Red Canyon, the hangout of the Indians. The white men were intruders here on treaty land, the property of the Sioux, but they came in such force and had so much support from government officials (who naturally wanted their constituents to suffer as little as possible from the depression) that the soldiers were unable to keep them out after the autumn of 1875. A hundred men a day were leaving Cheyenne for the Black Hills.[16]

The road from Fort Laramie to Custer City was reported lined with deserted wagons and corpses. This the *Wyoming Weekly*

Leader hotly denied, saying, on May 13, 1876, that there were only three deserted wagons on the road and "there have not been twelve men wounded by the Indians in the last three weeks." It continues that the route is so safe because the road between Fort Laramie and Custer City is patrolled by Captain Egan's troops. On May 20 the editor blew up: "In almost every issue of the LEADER we are compelled to chronicle the murder of some of our citizens by the savages who infest our borders. Day after day the telegraph brings to us the particulars of horrible atrocities committed upon the people of Wyoming and Dakota by the fiendish and blood-seeking Indians, whom the Government, under so-called treaty stipulations, is feeding and supporting with the utmost generous liberality. The very Indians who partake daily of the bounty of this great nation at their agency are found among the hordes who waylay the traveller to the mines, surprise the miner in his camp, and who now threaten to kill or drive out of the northern country the hardy pioneers and industrious miners who have reclaimed the northern country from the possession of the barbarians."

And as if that wasn't enough—two Chinese companies (tongs) were at war in Cheyenne—Kung Chow versus Ning Yung.

There was no peace in the land.

And more trouble was brewing. A large band of agency Sioux had been allowed to go buffalo hunting up in the Big Horn country, off their reservation. Led by Sitting Bull, with Crazy Horse and Gall as lieutenants, they refused to return to the reservation. Generals Terry and Crook set out with their commands to force the return of the Sioux.

Tom McKey, busily dealing faro and raking in the chips, living in ease at Ford's place, listened to the stories and waited to see what would happen.

There was plenty to do in Cheyenne. The Bella Union went full blast all night, presenting tragic and comic skits, Graeco-Roman wrestling, clog dancers, the Americanized cancan, minstrel show routines, acrobats and vocalists. Popular songs of 1876 were "Grandfather's Clock," "I'll Take You Home Again, Kathleen"

72

(powerfully moving to a bunch of homesick boys), "Where Was Moses When The Lights Went Out?", and the hits from the new Harrigan and Hart show "Are You There, Moriarity?", "Sons of Temperance," "Brannigan's Band" and "No Irish Wanted Here." New saloons and gambling houses opened continually, the madams brought their girls up from Denver by the carload, and the knifings and steel-knucklings were varied by a chin-biting-off and the arrest of a streetwalker whose clothes all came off when a young policeman grabbed her arm [17] on the public street.

The editor of the Cheyenne paper apparently didn't think much of George Armstrong Custer. He pointed out that Custer was only brevetted to the rank of major-general, that he was actually a lieutenant-colonel. He commented on Custer's love of publicity disparagingly and pointed out that his post was only Fort Lincoln, Dakota Territory. This was in May. On July 8, 1876, it was "General Custer's Command Slaughtered Like Sheep" and there followed the story of the battle of the Little Big Horn. Immediately Custer was the martyred hero of the Indian troubles [18] and the sickeningly sentimental phrases piled on him would have cost death its sting. Cheyenne's citizens planned militia companies to fight the savages, and the scare grew worse instead of abating.

It is something to state that under such circumstances (Custer City having failed) 25,000 people went to Deadwood Gulch that spring and summer to make it the big boom camp of the Black Hills. And not everybody could gallop in with Captain Egan's men protecting the mail on the stage. Long lines of jerk-line freight trains snaked through the Indian country, fourteen miles a day, driven by dirty, verminous men, reeking of anquitum (which kept down the lice) and Sheepherder's Delight (which kept up their morale), artists with a Winchester as well as a whip, and chewing tobacco strong enough to poison permanently anybody not as completely zinc-lined as themselves. Flip a coin. Heads it's foolhardiness. Tails it's fortitude. What matters is that the wilderness was conquered.

Deadwood Gulch was a dead-end canyon in which were located

three camps, Elizabeth City, Crook City and Deadwood City, all bustling and tough, so tough that a revolver was known as a Black Hills bustle, from being so commonly worn. Deadwood, at the head of the gulch, was the most prominent of the camps. The road ended there, dead against the canyon wall, and civilization had apparently come full tilt, hit the canyon and rebounded, stunned. The town looked like "a lot of lemon boxes in a backyard gulley," [19] the street weaved about crazily, full of ruts and mires, the ugly buildings of logs and raw lumber had sprung up in the street, ten feet back, on the line, five feet back, all facing in its general direction, and haphazardly spaced. This street was jammed with mule and oxen teams, horses, burros, wagons and confusion. Everybody was in a hurry, and the steep canyon walls kept the breeze out so that a stifling pall of dust hung everywhere. Tents and wickiups held most of the newcomers, but a few hotels had been hastily contrived where the latest arrivals had the privilege of sleeping on the dining room floor for a dollar a night. Saloons, cribs, gambling houses and honky-tonks were jammed with customers "shooting off their mouths and guns" as the mood struck them. The most exciting event of the week was the arrival of the stage, handsome Johnny Slaughter driving in ripsnorting style, the horses at a full gallop, the harnesses jingling, everybody yelling and cheering. The mail had come.

To Deadwood flocked the professional gamblers, like vultures, to snatch their wages in gold dust from the homesick miners, carefully measured out by the pennyweight in the best scales, twenty dollars to the ounce. And the most famous names in the west were there: long-haired Wild Bill Hickok, down on his luck, having outlived his day, innocuously spending his time gambling and drinking; here, too, was Calamity Jane Canary with her sweeping raven locks, gaiters instead of boots, beaded and fringed buckskins and a wide-brimmed Spanish hat. "She is still in early womanhood, and her rough and dissipated career has not altogether swept away the lines where beauty lingers." [20]

Along the close-crowding hillside ran the flumes carrying water

74

for the mining operations at the edge of town, where placer mining was making rich those lucky enough to have, and strong enough to keep, the good claims. The gulch was safe from the Indians because the opening to it ran for a mile with its sides so close together that two teams could barely pass, which made it so easy to defend that the Indians never dared attack.

The average daily run of shootings, knifings and sudden mayhem was climaxed by the murder of Wild Bill Hickok in the Number 10 saloon. A man named Jack McCall walked in and shot him in the back in as contemptible and cowardly a manner as any polite society slaying. The stories that went around about this would make one think it had been Hickok's time to go. It is one of the classic legends of the west. He was wary, having heard many a threat and seen many a look of hatred in his day, and always sat with his back to the wall. On this occasion, meeting with some friends of his for their usual game of poker, he was the last one to arrive. The others began to tease him and nobody would get up so that he could sit with his back to the wall. Being good-natured with his friends, he at last gave up and sat down for the first time with his back to the room. And on this, slimy Jack McCall walked in and saw him there. He figured that the man who could kill Wild Bill Hickok would get a reputation as the west's boss gunman. In his pocket was a stolen pistol which, although he didn't know it, was defective and had only one chamber that would fire. And that one chamber was the one that happened to be under the hammer when it fell, discharging a bullet into the back of Hickok's head. He fell onto the table dead—both hands clutching his guns. Later his friends looked at the cards he had held: aces and eights with a queen kicker—the Deadman's Hand which gambling superstition said would never let its holder leave the game alive.

No mourner for Wild Bill personally, this kind of a shooting made a profound impression on Tom McKey as it did on many of the gambling fraternity who had killed their man and gained fame as gun artists. Seats against the wall were now at a premium. With McKey it became a phobia about being shot in the back under any circumstances.[21] He was not a coward; he was to prove that at the OK corral, as we shall see, but if offered his "druthers" would figure out a way to make his gun fights as sure a thing as possible, both from the standpoint of legality and of having the drop. Hickok hadn't had a chance. And Tom McKey was a fighter as his claymore-wielding ancestors had been: he wanted a chance to fight and defy the world that had made him weak and an outcast.

On August 17, 1876, the Cheyenne paper said that Wild Bill's death was not generally lamented. "If we could believe the half of what was written concerning his daring deeds, he must certainly have been one of the bravest and most unscrupulous characters of these lawless times. Contact with the man, however, dispelled all these illusions, and of late years Wild Bill seems to have been a very tame and worthless bummer and loafer." He was run out of Cheyenne under the vagrants' act, tough reputation notwithstanding. He loved to drink the tenderfoot's liquor and regale them with wild stories of his hair-raising encounters with "red fiends and white desperadoes. In such moments he was the very personification of happiness."

As the cold weather came on, Deadwood slowed down. The gamblers weren't doing as well as they had been, so they came back to Cheyenne. On September 3, 1876, the *Wyoming Weekly Leader* said that oysters were expected soon,[22] and also the season was fast approaching for being scalped by stovepipes. Leadville news read: "Two sporting men, Storms and Barnes, fired several shots at each other on the eighteenth. They only succeeded in wounding a bystander in the thigh." Later in the month the paper reported that vagrants were standing around on the street corners in Cheyenne and that everyone was complaining of the hard times. The Deadwood *Pioneer* for October 7 said: "The town is now quieter than ever before; nobody killed for over three weeks. This may be due to our recent city organization, or to the exodus of many of our shooters and cutters." This latter was due to the cold, Deadwood being due to be snowed in for the winter. On December 21 the Cheyenne paper stated that these were dreadfully hard

76

times for everyone but faro dealers. And the winter dragged on, mighty slow and everybody mighty poor.

By March, after the hanging of Jack McCall,[23] Wild Bill's murderer, everybody was primed for something silly to catch their imagination. They had a flutter with Fluke McGilder, a mythical character of western towns—unofficial mayor and chief taker-of-the-blame for practical jokes. Then the blue glass craze came along. It was nationwide. A doctor was claiming that wearing blue-lensed glasses and living in a house with blue window panes would cure all of one's earthly ills. It was the wonderful relief of sunglasses to a people whose eyes were constantly strained by the brilliant light of the clear-aired plains. Everybody was wearing blue glasses, big hotels installed blue glass windows in their lobbies, streetcar lines put blue windows in the horse-cars. The unbridled tongue of the editor of the Cheyenne paper went into his cheek. He wrote: "Swallow half a peck of nitrate of silver and it will die you permanently blue."

And here let us take a wallop at a long-standing Old West myth: that newspaper men were afraid to print the stories of killings because the killers might be offended and cut them down with a hail of lead. That is a lot of piffle. None of the old newspapers so carefully perused for the material in this book provides even a hint that newspapermen were afraid of killers, organized gamblers, or pressure from their influential friends. In fact, they seemed to delight in calling a spade a spade when their articles concerned the sporting world. Witness the following from the *Wyoming Weekly Leader* of March 15, 1877:

> "THEY DIDN'T KILL EACH OTHER,
> BUT THE PEOPLE WOULD HAVE BEEN BETTER
> SATISFIED IF THEY HAD.
> A SHOOTING AFFRAY BETWEEN TWO DRUNKEN GAMBLERS,
> NEITHER OF WHOM WAS A GOOD MARKSMAN."

"Seven pistol shots, four of which were irregularly fired, and three in lightninglike succession, startled the business portion of the city at 7 o'clock Friday night, and caused a general rush for the corner of Eddy and 16th Streets where a man was lying on the snowy sidewalk, bleeding from a brace of wounds.

"The Drunken Gambler's Duel.

"Shortly after 6 o'clock that evening two gamblers, C. H. Harrison and J. Levy, entered the new saloon of Shingle & Locke, and sat down at a table. They had been drinking freely and were just drunk enough to quarrel with ease. They soon became involved in a dispute about some big game in which Levy had taken a hand and got 'sinched,' and finally Harrison insinuated that he hated Irishmen. Levy grew angry,[24] and as Harrison added fuel to the flames by repeated abuse, he

"Drew a Revolver.

"Harrison said he had no pistol, but that if Levy would wait for him to get one he would do so and then give him (Levy) 'a turn.' Levy said that would be all right, and the men walked up 16th Street together. Reaching the Senate saloon, Harrison entered and soon reappeared with a revolver. He crossed Eddy street, started north toward Dyer's hotel, and when in front of 'Frenchy's' saloon, stopped and

"Fired at Levy

"who was standing directly opposite him. Levy returned the fire and six shots were exchanged, only one of which took effect, striking Harrison in the left breast and felling him, though not being at all serious. He raised up after being hit, and fired once at Levy, who then ran across the street,

"Shot the Prostrate Man

"in the hip and left him. This last wound is a serious one and may prove fatal. It took effect in the right hip, taking a circular course across the lower abdomen, and lodging close to the surface in the

78

left hip, lower down than the point of entrance. Dr. Joseph and another physician were summoned, the wounded man was conveyed to his room at Dyer's, and prompt attention given him. When Dr. Joseph reached him

"Life Seemed Extinct

"but prompt and proper use of restoratives soon opened up his eyes and loosened up his tongue and limbs. At midnight he was sleeping quietly in the arms of morphine, and owing to the great extravasation of blood and stubbornness in refusing to allow the extraction of the ball, his condition is considered very critical. Harrison has a wife and daughter here."

Further down in the same column it goes on: "All the evidence goes to show that Harrison fired the first shot, and that he was struck by Levy's first ball, which struck him in the breast and felled him. He raised up a little and fired his second and last shot, which failed to take effect. Levy, who fired five shots in all, then ran across the street and inflicted the second wound. The plea of self-defense might well be set up in Levy's behalf had he not done this, but we believe he should be made to suffer the severest penalty of the law for thus carrying into effect an evident intention to kill his man."

On March 22 the *Local Leaflets* column says, "Levy, the pistoliferous gambler, has secured bail and is at large. Harrison is reported as improving, his medical attendant stating that he will recover, though with the loss of a portion of one leg."

But on March 29 "C. H. Harrison, the gambler who was shot by J. Levy, on Eddy Street, in this city, just two weeks ago tonight, died at 5 o'clock Thursday morning, in his room at Dyer's hotel. His funeral took place from the hotel at 4 P.M., the hearse being followed to the cemetery by a procession numbering about 40 carriages, with probably 125 occupants, embracing a majority of the sporting fraternity, with their wives, and other females. Mrs. Harrison is, we believe, left in very destitute circumstances."

In this spring of 1877 Indians were still shooting stray clumps of people "so full of holes that even the coarsest food is of no use," [25] the depression was worse, lots of British investors were buying up cattle empires because prices were so low, and the yearly rush to Deadwood was on. The "boys in blue" were so fond of fighting Indians that they would come to town on pay day, get drunk, buy secondhand civilian clothes and a ticket west—then walk into the arms of their officers at the station. The guardhouse was better than winding up as a decoration on a Sioux scalp stick. Ed Chase, the boss gambler from Denver, was operating a place in Cheyenne and the town was twice as jammed as the year before —as many coming out disappointed as were going in hopeful. Mexican Mustang Liniment was being boosted as every man's private Black Hills doctor, and the Indians were dressing their hair with Frazer's axle grease. A shave was ten cents and a haircut two bits; this was very steep. Gold was down to eighteen dollars an ounce.

And then the stagecoach robberies started, one practically every week.

On March 25, 1877, about two and a half miles out of Deadwood, five masked men called to the north-bound stage to halt. As ordered, the driver threw up his hands, but he also let out a yell his horses knew meant for them to travel and stay not on the order of their going. They lit out for town on a dead run and the robbers fired a fusillade at the coach. The driver fell forward between the wheelers into the road, one passenger was wounded, and the horses finally pulled up of their own accord in front of the stage station in Deadwood. Everyone came running at the sight of the driverless stage, the wounded passenger was helped out, the story hastily pieced together, and a posse hurried to the scene of the crime. The stage was safe—but the driver's body was found in the road, riddled with bullets. It was evident from his looks, the telegraphed report to Cheyenne said, that he never knew what hit him. This was kind, for Cheyenne's marshal was his father. The dead man was twenty-seven years old, famous as the best and the

80

bravest of the Black Hills stage drivers. His name was Johnny Slaughter.[26]

A flood of gunmen was hired to bring out the spring clean-up from Deadwood, guarding a shipment of about $200,000 in bullion. Among them were Boone May, who later killed Persimmon Bill, reputed as the murderer of Johnny Slaughter; Scott Davis; Gale Hill; Wyatt Earp; and others.

On June 25, 1877, near Hat Creek ranch, the stage was robbed for the third time in as many weeks. Fortunately the treasure box (full of bullion) was rivetted to the floor of the coach and the robbers didn't have tools to get at the contents. Two days later the stage was robbed again. This time the robbers dynamited the treasure box and got $10,000 out of it, and $2,000 from the passengers. On July 4 the stage was held up again. In Deadwood, they say, Luke Voorhees, manager of the line, nailed Johnny Slaughter's bullet-ridden vest to the door of the stage station and began to enroll vigilantes from among the hold-up victims. The robberies continued.

The gambling fraternity was always passing along recommendations for places of business. It was in Cheyenne that Tom McKey ran into a bunch from Dodge and got first-hand information about the wildest and wooliest of cow towns. It was really tough. Those drovers were *looking for relaxation* at the end of a difficult and dangerous cattle drive and ready to raise hell in six directions. Tom McKey looked the Dodge City bunch over pretty carefully that spring of 1877, but he didn't go to Dodge at the opening of the trailherd season when the Kansans left the hard work of the gold fields to return to an easy fleecing of the weary herders. Always loyal to his friends, it took a good deal to jar him loose from them, and he had good friends in the Denver gang which was now operating in Cheyenne and Deadwood.

This summer McKey is supposed to have been riding the Union Pacific to and fro while working a confidence game on its passengers—that ancient whisker, the gold-brick racket. He would, it is said, scrape up an acquaintance with a likely-looking sucker, pass himself off as a mine owner, and with great reluctance (pressure of a family emergency or some such) sell the guy a gold brick cheap—for gold bricks—and then hastily depart. Some friends of his in the guise of Pinkertons would then arrive, inform the sucker that he was known to have contraband gold in his possession and remove the gilded lead brick for further use. This left the sucker with no evidence to prove his tale, except the absence of several hundred dollars from his wallet and the intent to do murder in his heart. McKey's gentlemanly appearance would have been a great asset in this business, since everyone who rode the trains in the west in those days was acutely aware of the danger from train robbers, drunken herders, ruffians and other such hard cases. No one suspected quiet, refined-looking, well-dressed persons with weak lungs who were obviously going west for their health. McKey would have gotten many a hearty laugh from an operation of this nature, since avarice is the characteristic which puts people in the power of confidence men and makes them rob themselves, as it were. Several things incline one to want to believe this tale: the appearance of the main crook; the fact that no physical violence is involved; the fact that the perpetrator of the racket was smart enough to quit while he was ahead, and not persist in his own avarice for so long that he was finally nabbed by the real Pinkertons, thereby making himself no better than his gullible victims.

That fall back in Denver things looked pretty much the same, except for the morbid rash of blue glass that had broken out everywhere. Colorado had been admitted to the Union the previous summer of 1876, calling itself the Centennial state, and was feeling spunky, but it takes money to kick up your heels and nobody had much. McKey probably didn't work as a faro dealer steadily; there were other ways of making money, although they did not provide a "visible" means of support, and besides, every now and then he was bound to overdo it with the benzine and get himself fired. The poker games went on day and night. Win a little, lose a little; he kept ahead of the game. The oyster so dear to hearts of the day afforded a modest feast, as did fresh strawberries imported from California at thirty-five cents a dish, and the drug stores had ice cream soda fountains where that popular American refresher could be consumed. Tom McKey sipped a soda—well, consumption gave him a delicate stomach, dyspepsia, they called it, and a steady diet of snake-bite remedy didn't help it any. And the heart of his days was being spent in the saloons and gambling houses, playing, dealing, or now that times were so dreadfully bad, just sitting around the stove talking with his friends.

Talking was the pet sport of the times, anyway. Amusements were few and feeble and hard to come by; consequently the value of gossip was somewhat idealized. Much has been made of the lack of interest taken in a person's past in the Old West—it wasn't healthy to indulge in who-shot-John queries, but notice how almost invariably all the lurid details immediately follow. Telling stories of one's own past and those of others who had gathered a certain reputation was the favorite pastime of the old days, and in order to be entertaining most of these stories had to be embroidered and embellished out of all reason. The reputation of every gunman of the Old West is based on just such fal-lals and fabrications and collapses under even the most casual investigation. The busy tongue of an idle moment built the wealth of hair-raising "Western" adventures, snowing under the modest tales of heroism and the occasional drunken gun fight. Later these fancy lies were cemented by the bragging of old fools who wished to appear heroes to a younger generation. They gave us an Old West that never was.

Some of the stories that have been told about Holliday are included here, ones for which any explanation at all could be found. One of the most persistent fabrications is that of his knifing a gambler named Bud Ryan and consequently being run out of Denver by the police in the late 70's. In the May, 1907, issue of *Human Life,* Bat Masterson, after describing Holliday's bloodthirsty career in Texas (saying he killed a soldier from Fort Richardson over a game of cards in a Jacksboro saloon [27]) had him, tuberculosis and all, ride horseback pell-mell across the most dangerous of the Indian country to Denver, keeping one hop ahead of a bunch of irate soldiers the whole 800 miles. To continue the fanciful line, Bat has him carry a concealed knife in Denver and most frightfully carve up the neck and face of that gentlemanly sport, Bud Ryan. Mr. Masterson, please note, was not a witness to the affray. He never actually saw Holliday kill anyone. Holliday was very inoffensive, it would seem, until he got out from under the eyes of his friends—whereupon he went hog-wild and killed people by the carload lot. At any rate, no witness can be found for the cutting of Bud Ryan, though one may read the gory details in any number of Old West books. The Denver papers carry no contemporary account of such an affair until June 22, 1887. And then what a comedown. There is a Ryan involved in a knifing at last and see what a good imagination did to the story. The *Denver Republican* for that date reported: " 'Kid' Ryan, a waiter bearing a hard reputation, was arrested last evening by Officer Bohanna. Ryan early in the evening was drinking in Moses' Home, a low saloon located at No. 487½ Larimer St. During the evening Jack Brogan entered the saloon and accidentally brushed against Ryan. This enraged him and hastily drawing a pocket-knife he made a lunge at Brogan. The knife struck him in the neck and inflicted a deep gash. The wound bled profusely but it is not a dangerous one. Had Ryan used a larger knife the chances are that Brogan's throat would have been cut. The police were loud in their denunciation of Moses' Home. They characterize it as a resort of the lowest type, where tramps, holdups and other evil characters resort." And so it turned out to be a couple of other fellows.[28]

Other lying contests took place on the subject of shooting and feats seen performed with guns. The favorite yarn was having seen Hickok split a bullet on a dime. Oh, come now! *Think.* Or try it yourself. Granting that by some miracle the dime is hit—what happens? The part of the dime that is struck buckles back and the bullet continues on its way.[29] The Winchester rifle, Greener's choke-bore shotgun, Colt, Remington, and Smith and Wesson revolvers and the little two-shot derringers were all a constant subject of discussion. People liked to give an importance to guns as the

84

daily difference between life and death. They also told about their pet place of carrying a gun and odd places they had heard of others concealing them. Guns were not openly carried in Denver now; this seems to have been one city ordinance that was enforced. But a person who "reached back" during a fight or argument had better be prepared for the consequences and not expect that anyone would think he was going for a handkerchief. The same thing went for reaching toward the breast of one's coat. Here was perhaps the favorite place for concealing a gun, under a frock or box coat, since there was less chance of the gun showing.

In a rare lonely moment Doc would write Mattie a note describing his quiet life, the hard times and how well he felt. She had written him about the continued loss of every cotton crop to the boll weevil and how nobody knew what to do. Now she wrote that his father was planting a grove of pecan trees [30] in the hope of at last finding a money crop that would grow there. That was his father as it was himself; they were men who refused to give up, who would fight while they lived. And they both inspired good women to pray for them every day of their lives.

The year of 1878 was the worst year of the depression. Over 14,000 businesses failed. New people were still coming to Denver,[31] but they seemed to be bringing trouble with them instead of increasing local business. While not as badly off as the eastern cities, Denver was dragging its tail.

As spring came on and the financial outlook failed to improve, Tom McKey went over the things he had heard in Cheyenne and Deadwood about Dodge and the trailherds from Texas. Soon it would be time for the first herds to arrive. It was foolish not to go where the money was, especially since the hard times were causing a breakup of his Denver associates. One by one they were going off —to Dodge, Pueblo, Leadville, Deadwood, wherever there was money and something going on. So he packed his second well-tailored black box-coated suit, his colored and white shirts, his stack of white collars and the rest of his neatly-kept clothes, some fancy pieces of gambling equipment, a couple of choice gold nuggets he kept as souvenirs, and an emergency bottle of *spiritus frumenti*. He tucked his shootin' iron into his bosom, his money with Scotch carefulness went in his belt. He had one last excellent meal at Charpiot's and departed.

One thing he left behind: Tom McKey.

He had found out how to get around the law and consequently no longer feared any bad publicity being attached to J. H. Holliday. He was the "gen-u-wine" copper-bottomed, gold-plated article, the *beau ideal* of professional gamblers: quiet, gentlemanly-appearing, as fast with his hands and mind as greased lightning, and all but impossible to fuddle with liquor, women, or smooth-sounding tales.

FOOTNOTES TO CHAPTER 6

1. A long article on Holliday appeared in the *Denver Republican* of December 25, 1887, a little over a month after his death. The author, while not claiming to have known Holliday, had picked up some material on him and his use of "Tom McKey" as an alias was included. Since this name fits in so well with a part of Holliday's past which the author of the article knew nothing about, it seems logical that he did use it. No J. H. Holliday figures in the Denver news or city directories and there are McKeys, McKees, McKays and Mackys all over town.

2. In a personal interview on May 22, 1882, with a reporter from the *Denver Republican* Holliday made this statement. He probably meant the saloon owned by John A. Babb at this address, according to the 1875 Denver City Directory.

3. *Rocky Mountain News,* July 2, 1876.

4. *Leadville Daily Herald,* August 26, 1884.

5. *Rocky Mountain News,* August 1, 1875.

6. In some gambling houses the deal passed in turn but a percentage was still taken out of each pot for the house.

7. *Denver Tribune-Republican,* August 1, 1886.

8. *Ibid.*

9. *Rocky Mountain News,* August 20, 1875.

10. *Rocky Mountain News,* August 11, 1875.

11. Mercury freezes at forty below zero.

12. *Rocky Mountain News,* December 6, 1875.

13. The one in Washington, D.C. It was abandoned for so long when half-finished that the difference in the weathering of the stone gives it a two-layer look to this day.

14. *Rocky Mountain News,* March 16, 1877.

15. *A Reliable and Correct Guide to the Black Hills, Powder River and Big Horn Gold Fields,* J. H. Triggs, Omaha, Nebr. Herald Steam Book & Job Printing House, 1876.

16. Their heavy stands of pine give them a dark appearance.

17. She said, "Well, that's the kind of sardine I am!" In the *Wyoming Weekly Leader* of May 31, 1877.

18. In *Our Wild Indians,* A. D. Worthington and Company, Hartford, Conn., 1883, Colonel Richard Irving Dodge says: "It is said that Custer's body was found unscalped and unmutilated. If so, my knowledge of Indians convinces me that he died by his own hand." Dodge, for whom Dodge City was named, spent thirty years as an officer on the frontier and made a careful study of Indians and their customs.

19. *Wyoming Weekly Leader*, June 28, 1877.

20. *Wyoming Weekly Leader*, June 21, 1877.

21. Note that later on in Denver and Leadville when he was arrested, the papers would always say that he immediately asked the police not to let him be shot in the back.

22. When the *Baltimore Sun* was first consulted for this book I thought the frequent mention of oysters was due to Baltimore being on the Chesapeake and consequently near the best oyster beds in the world. A "Ladies' and Gentlemen's Oyster, Tea, Coffee, Chocolate and Ice Cream Saloon" passed but as notice that "saloon" in those days was still being used in its original meaning and had to have an adjective before it—a "lager beer saloon" being a beer hall and an "ice cream saloon" being a malt shop. While this was true, in Atlanta the respect for oysters continued to be marked, according to the local newspaper. In the west it practically amounted to veneration. Oysters were *it* in the eating line in Holliday's time and cost accordingly. When he was in Tombstone, a five-course meal at the best place in town cost exactly the same as one lonely plate of oysters.

23. McCall at first claimed to be a man named Sutherlin and that he had killed Hickok in revenge for Hickok's cold-blooded killing of his younger brother. A coroner's jury refused to indict and he was released. However, he was unable to keep from bragging about what he had done and when enjoying a snootful once told the truth of the killing to several people. He was rearrested, tried and convicted with a rapidity which made up for the amazing leniency with which he had been treated formerly. He was hanged at Yankton, Dakota Territory, on March 1, 1877, and "died game."

24. In the punning spirit of the times, it is sometimes difficult to tell a son of Erin from a son of Aaron.

25. The quotes from Bill Nye are from *Bill Nye and Boomerang*, by Bill Nye Himself. W. B. Conkey Co., Chicago, 1894. This book is evidently composed of articles written by Nye while working on the Laramie, Wyoming *Boomerang* in the boom days of the Black Hills gold rush. You may read it in the Rare Book Room of the Library of Congress if you can refrain from laughing aloud and destroying the hushed sanctity of the spot.

26. *Wyoming Weekly Leader*, March 29, 1877.

27. See Chapter V, footnote 6.

28. The biographical article on Holliday which appeared in the Denver *Republican* for December 25, 1887, contains an account of his knifing Bud Ryan. This is far from a *contemporary* reporting of the affair which supposedly took place in the seventies. Many of the frays ascribed to Holliday in this article are repeated in Bat Masterson's article on him in *Human Life*, so it is likely that Masterson was one of the reporter's sources. The reporter does admit that some of the gambling element told him Doc never killed anyone. Doc was of course long since dead.

29. "Those Stunt Shooters," in *Lucian Cary On Guns.* Fawcett Publications, Greenwich, Conn. After making his experiment with this result, Mr. Cary continues: "Of course my experiment with a .22 long-rifle bullet doesn't prove what a .44 or .45 caliber revolver bullet with three times the energy would do to a dime. My guess is that the dimes on which Wild Bill Hickok used to split bullets at twenty paces were, like the men of those days, much harder and tougher than the kind we have now. The only other possibility that I can think of is that Wyatt Earp was a liar." (See *Wyatt Earp, Frontier Marshal,* by Stuart N. Lake. Houghton Mifflin Co., Boston, 1931, p. 43.)

30. *History of Lowndes County,* op. cit. Major Holliday introduced the growing of pecans in what is today an important pecan-growing area.

31. Denver's population in 1870 was 4,750. In 1880 it was 35,629.

7

Enter

Big Nose Kate

Here was the barren nothing-nothing land, flat, arid, treeless—and boldly defiant under the great domineering blueness. Standing there, looking straight ahead, you saw not hills nor trees nor anything of relief, but only the sky. Since to see earth you had to look down to the distance-blurred horizon, you knew yourself to be standing on the top of a great and round globe. After a long time of feeling small and shameful under this immensity, you grow to know yourself to be as good as the next guy, and better, and ready to spit in anybody's eye to prove it.

Across this terrible plain roared a little 4-4-0 diamond-stacker, the *C. K. Holliday* of the Santa Fe line, pulling a baggage car and two coaches painted a bright and bilious yellow, headed east out of Pueblo for Dodge on the Arkansas. Rattle, bang, bounce, lurch, they went scurrying over the uneven roadbed on the long downhill run of the slanting land. Doc cursed the lousy Banana Line for keeping him awake on a ride through West Monotony and the engineer pulled a cord to let a long, lonely whoo-ah-whoo-ah-whoo-*ooo* roll echoing over the plain, the loveliest sound that anything named industry ever gave the world. A little prickle ran down Doc's neck. He coughed a couple of times and at last managed to doze off.

Stiff and cramped, he woke up at the conductor's cry of "Dodge City!" to have himself a terrible coughing spell. When at last he got himself coughed out, he was weak from the effort it had taken and bitterly resentful of the pitying and curious looks the other passengers were giving him. The train was slowing down between huge heaps of white-bleached buffalo bones piled as high as the train windows; beyond them he got a confused glimpse of a couple of blocks of poor-looking frame buildings and then he was shaking aside the porter's efforts to help the sick man down from the cars —and standing on the platform he gazed in amazement at Dodge City as seen in the glory of Front Street.

There, under the cold glare of an early March sun, three short blocks of shacks brazenly stared across a mud-bogged street at the tracks. On either side of them a few more unkempt buildings tried to stretch the town's length out to six blocks. After the train had left he could see across the tracks the scattered buildings and livery stable corrals of the South Side, the respectable width of the Arkansas River with its iron bridge, and the wide and far away roll of the plains to nothing. All was bare and treeless and ugly.

A colored man carried his luggage straight across to the Dodge House at the corner of Front Street and Central, the best hotel in town. Remembering the posh Inter-Ocean in Cheyenne and the gilt and cut-glass splendor of the St. James in Denver, Doc smiled wryly. Likely the local yokels thought the Dodge House very swell,[1] but—oh, well, if there was money here he wouldn't complain about anything, certainly not about room 24 [2] with its plain walnut furniture, mild floral-patterned rug and heavy white china pitcher and bowl. It was clean and there was a fine view of some of the most unpretentious false-front buildings which had ever adorned the main drag of any town. He had a large, steadying drink, a bath, changed his clothes, settled his canister firmly in its shoulder holster and set out to see the elephant.

Coming out of the frame, two-story Dodge House with its adjoining billiard hall, he was facing the south and toward the little depot. Turning right on Front Street, he walked past a large vacant lot and then came to some small stores: Mueller and Straeter's boot shop; Andy Johnson's saloon where relics from the battle at Adobe Walls were kept; an institution which advertized itself thusly: "C. M. Hoover—wholesale dealer in wines, liquors, and cigars—manufacturers of soda water, sasparilla and cider—agent for Val Blatz's Milwaukee Bottled Beer—No. 39, Front St., D.C., Kansas." There were other small stores, restaurants and saloons, all pretty shabby, the dust-carrying Kansas winds scouring the house paints of the day to the bare boards in a matter of months. Most of them had a roof of some sort built out over the board sidewalk to make an every-man-for-himself arcade nearly three blocks long. After Doc crossed 1st Street the buildings began to look a little more prosperous: Koch and Kolly's Pioneer Barbershop; Beatty and Kelley's Dodge City restaurant; the Alhambra saloon with Kelley's opera house upstairs; Hungerford's meat market; George Dieter's Centennial Barbershop; York, Hadder and Draper's ranch outfitting store; F. C. Zimmerman's hardware and gunsmith store with its big wooden rifle pointing out over the street; the Lone Star saloon; Dr. McCarty's office and drug store; the Long Branch saloon; and, on the corner, "Wright and Beverley's Corner Brick Store." Across 2nd Street was Herman Fringer's City drugstore, then more small stores and saloons. The center of town was that one block between 1st and 2nd on Front Street. The corner of Front Street and 2nd was the main intersection, since 2nd went across the tracks into the South Side, past a number of saloons, dance halls, corrals and a large hall (formerly the Lady Gay honky-tonk) to the bridge across the river. Doc turned and walked north up 2nd; there was another scattering of stores and saloons, the Wright House, and a few houses beyond. The cross street, parallel with Front Street, was Tin Pot Alley (now Chestnut Street), lined with shacks and filled with rubbish.

Dodge's permanent population was about 1200, and it showed.

Doc, recognizing the fact that everybody in town was giving him the eye and wondering who the hell, was careful to go into the Long Branch, since it looked like the best saloon in town. It was a neat and well-kept place, with a handsome bar, attractive hanging lamps, a large plate-glass mirror and a few gambling tables, in an area about one hundred feet by thirty. It was about as handsome as saloons are likely to be. After a large soothing drink and a few pleasantries with the bartender, he went down the street to Beatty and Kelley's restaurant where six large tables were set to serve seventy-five people. It was a "meals at all hours" house, so he sat down to the usual breakfast of his day, which he was in the habit of eating at about three in the afternoon, picking at his choice of "beefsteak, mutton chops, veal cutlets, ham, eggs boiled, scrambled, poached and stiffened into omelet, with the heaped-up outworks of hot biscuits, hominy and fried potatoes." [3] The service was good, the cooking not as greasy as his indigestion had expected, and the surroundings bright and cheerful.[4] He began to feel considerably more confident.

Going back out into the street he looked curiously at the buildings down on the South Side, but they looked too dead to investigate. Going back up the street he stopped at the Long Branch again. The bartender smiled at him like an old friend, then nodded to a small, intelligent-looking man who immediately stepped up beside Doc at the bar.

"My name is Short," he said. "Luke Short. We have a small game just starting back here. Would you care to join us, Mr.— uh—?"

"Holliday, J. H. Holliday. From Denver," Doc said. They walked to the back of the room where a poker table was set under a skylight, with monte and keno table on either side. He smiled a little, knowing that the ice was broken, and that Luke Short had known him for what he was instantly, as he had recognized Short's profession.

The talk was all of the coming trail herds and how Dodge was being fixed up to entertain and manage the cowboys—

"The who?"

"Cowboys. The herders. That's a nickname they got here last season, and now that's all anybody around here calls them."

The Lady Gay of former years (Springer's opera house) was being reopened this year as the Comique, named for Harrigan and Hart's variety theater in New York; everything was getting an optimistic coat of paint; at the Alamo the new owners, Colley and Marion, were setting out their new shipment of the heaviest glass available for the saloon trade; new saloons and hotels were opening; the Long Branch four-piece orchestra was practicing under the leadership of Chalk Beeson; and soon drinks and cigars would be fifteen cents each or two for a quarter.

A small, pleasant-looking young man came in and looked around and was pointed out as City Marshal Ed Masterson. "He is not very large, but there are not many men who would be anxious to tackle him a second time. He makes a good officer." [5] Doc was told how last fall Masterson, then assistant marshal, had single-handedly broken up an incipient killing in the Lone Star dance hall, and then very nearly got himself killed for his lenient attitude toward the participants. They had their guns out, but instead of shooting first and asking questions second, as caution demanded, Ed had whaled one of them over the head with his equalizer. Instead of felling or even stunning the Texan, this treatment only infuriated him. He shot repeatedly at Masterson and one bullet struck him in the chest. Ed fell, his right hand paralyzed, but he grabbed up his revolver with his left hand and put his assailant out of the running with a bullet in his left leg and another in his left arm. Several other people were struck by promiscuously flying bullets, but there were no fatalities. Assistance arrived to find the badly-wounded marshal holding all the tough crowd in a corner at gun point.

"They don't come braver or decenter than Little Ed. But he gives the other guy too many breaks. One of these days some mean drunk will kill him—just you wait."

Doc brushed his mustache with a slender forefinger and looked at the mild-appearing young marshal. There was something about him that reminded Doc of the men of his father's regiment who had come to Valdosta during the war. Haunted, wary-eyed, too

94

game to give up, proud of a record that few were brave enough to win. And kindly and pleasant-speaking to everyone.

Coughing, Doc turned away, only to have another man pointed out to him, Marshal Masterson's younger brother, William, known as Bat, sheriff of Ford County at twenty-four. He was quite a dandy, sporting a hard hat, a big cigar and a fancy watch and chain. Doc took as instant a dislike to him as he had taken a liking to his brother. Perhaps he felt that Bat was a phony, perhaps he was jealous, perhaps he just didn't like his looks. Possibly it was the simple fact that Bat was two years younger than Doc, and Doc was acutely sensitive about his age. Later we will see him cut four years off his age in a public record. He never had a friend younger than himself. He wanted so much to stay the swift rush of time, knowing his reprieve from death to be but a whim, a fancy of fate, no matter how careful he was.

Nearly everyone else pointed out was connected with a saloon or a dance hall in some way: Mayor Kelley of the Alhambra, city council members D. D. Colley of the Alamo, Walter Straeter of the Old House, and Chalkley Beeson of the Long Branch. And everybody was excited about the coming trail-herd season.

"Two hundred thousand cattle on their way!"

Someone laughed over the rattle of balls in the keno goose and a pleasant tenor sang exultantly, "In gambling hells de-lay-ing, ten thou-sand cattle stray-ing, stray-ing."

Dodge had gotten its start as a soddy by a long-used ford across the Arkansas River, five miles west of Fort Dodge on the old Santa Fe trail. H. L. Sitler, a teamster who supplied wood at the fort, built it as a camp for buffalo hunters and freighters, and before long some tent saloons were put up nearby. In 1872 the Santa Fe construction gangs arrived and put up some more tents and portable houses and called it Buffalo City. Later that year the chief surveyor of the Santa Fe laid out a townsite and a town company was formed, headed by Colonel Richard I. Dodge, commandant at Fort Dodge, and the town was renamed Dodge City. This seems logical. It was a fairly rapid little hell on the range and became even rougher with the beginning of passenger service on the Santa Fe in September. Land hunters, buffalo hunters, gamblers, outlaws, fancy ladies and all the scum of the frontier poured into the hideous little town. The Indian danger was such that the buildings were all built close together along Front Street and the backyards were solidly barricaded with high board fences. From outside the town resembled a fort. The buffalo hunters gave the town its chief income and thousands of buffalo hides drying and stacked awaiting shipment proclaimed this fact wherever the winds blew for miles around. The Santa Fe was struggling along on a shoestring, smarting under the nickname of "the Jerkwater Line" given it by big and powerful railroads, but it was determined to have track built across the Colorado line by March, 1873. They had to, or lose their land grant. One mile a day, their little crew laid the track, often right on the ungraded plain, and headed west blindly for Colorado, 125 miles away. A government surveyor told them the state line was still four miles ahead after they had run out of track, ties and spikes. The work train went back along the line, the crew pulled up four miles of sidings and got the line laid five *yards* into Colorado before winter set in. The cold and an empty till together put a complete stop to further construction.

Then came the depression. To all intents and purposes, the Santa Fe stopped at Dodge for the next two years. Besides being depression years, 1874 and 1875 were also drought years in Kansas, and the Santa Fe kept itself and half of Kansas alive by hauling away buffalo bones at eight dollars a ton (it took eight complete skeletons to make a ton) to the eastern fertilizer markets. There was nothing west of Dodge worth running trains for. At last the Santa Fe got a little money scraped together and managed to get to Pueblo on March 7, 1876. Here they could get coal and timber for treeless Kansas, connect with other passenger services, and bring in supplies for rapidly industrializing Pueblo and the nearby mining areas. The Santa Fe had finally found a little prosperity and now boasted itself the Bonanza line in reply to its second nickname, the Banana line, which referred to the color of its early cars. Now it set about to try to people the Great American Desert, gambling that people could make a living there, not knowing yet that they held the key to the greatest wheat-growing area ever seen. Dodge prospered along with the Santa Fe.

In 1875 came the first of the big trail drives of cattle from Texas. The herds had formerly taken the old Chisholm trail to Abilene, but the local farmers' fear that their cattle would catch Texas tick fever from the longhorns and their disgust with the antics of the rampaging herders resulted in the Chisholm trail being barricaded. It wasn't too much of a loss, since farms had spread over much of the open range needed to feed the cattle and thereby ruined the trail anyway. Newton, sixty-five miles south, was the next terminus of the trail and for one season roared as loudly as Abilene had for five, then gave way to Ellsworth. In 1873 Wichita was the boom town of the trail herds, only to be supplanted by Hays City, and at last the Chisholm trail was abandoned. A deadline was set up, marked by barbed-wire fences and patrolled by armed farmers. East of it no one dared drive the Texas cattle. Fortunately, further west, there was the Jones and Plummer trail to Dodge City. A truce was made with the farmers to protect the open range along this trail and around Dodge. From 1875 to 1886 Dodge was the end of the trail, *the* cow town of the wild and woolly West. Having a firm basis as a buffalo hunters' hangout and a railroad construction town, Dodge was not one to be swept off its feet by the howling herders. Just to make sure they knew their place, it publicly dubbed them boys, cow boys, and made them like it.

The cowboys were neither innocent, fun-loving Rover boys nor blood-thirsty murderers. They were an assortment of people of all sizes, colors and dispositions, largely in the mood to have a good time to celebrate the end of the drive. They had been known to get out of hand. In order to prevent a too-frequent occurrence of this, the forces of law and order in Dodge were in the habit of considering themselves an important group. The preceding season had boasted Larry Deger as city marshal with Ed Masterson as his assistant, and Charles E. Bassett as sheriff.[6] That fall had seen Bat Masterson elected sheriff and his brother Ed appointed city marshal, with Charley Bassett as assistant.

In other towns where Doc had lived the police force had been in the pay of organized saloonkeepers, gamblers, pimps and confidence operators and everybody knew the law officers were hired to protect the crowd with the most money and influence. The smooth operation of the Denverites had been carried by them to Cheyenne and Leadville when those towns boomed. You had only to belong to the outfit and you had no worries. Doc had belonged. The criminal element and the professional toughs in Denver, Cheyenne and Leadville had known the cops in those towns were paid to protect the saloon crowd and consequently had left them more or less alone, making their dishonest money off of suckers and other hard laborers. But in Dodge the so-called criminal element was a bunch of bat-brained kids fresh off the Texas trail and looking for fun. They never once bothered their heads about protection and influence and fixes and knowing the right people. They were as criminal as a bunch of pranksters on Halloween and were a good deal more dangerous to the saloon crowd than any bunch of professional crooks. There were so many of them and they could think of so much mischief, that about all the police could do was keep up with those who were firing guns or threatening to do so. Otherwise it was every man for himself. It had to be.

Doc could not face the thought of being man-handled by some bully. He was too proud. Since the police were obviously unable to protect his rights as the Denver police had, he would have to think of some way to get along here. He could make friends with one of the law officers (he placed that in a conspicuous spot in his mind so he wouldn't forget to take advantage of any opportunity to get on the good side of one of them), but in the meantime. . . .

And so came the first herds in early April, Kansas cattle. While not the frisky Texans, these herders were not exactly high types, either, being gents whose dispositions had been considerably injured by the fractious habits of beef critters. They had an intense dislike for being crossed, and no marshal of a one-horse cow town was going to tell them what to do.

Ed Masterson had his hands full. Instead of shooting and arresting and forcing his will on these cowboys and ruining whatever fun they might find in Dodge, he was content to let them carry their guns as long as there wasn't any trouble. When they began to throw their weight around he batted them over the head with his Colt a little harder than he had been used to, and threw them in the cooler. The editor of the *Globe,* a political opponent of the Mastersons, complained loudly about this easy attitude of Ed's, but he kept right on doing what he thought was right, the gamest and best-liked town marshal any town ever had. He gave in to pressure enough to appoint Nat Haywood his assistant on April 6.

"On Tuesday evening, about 10 o'clock, Edward J. Masterson,
      And then on April 9———
Marshal of Dodge City, was murdered by Jack Wagner and Alf Walker, two cattle drivers from near Hays City. The two cowboys were under the influence of bad whisky and were carrying revolvers. Early in the evening Marshal Masterson disarmed Wagner; later Marshal Masterson and Deputy Marshal Nat Haywood tried the second time to disarm Wagner. While in the act Masterson was shot in the abdomen. Walker in the meantime snapped a pistol in the face of Officer Haywood. Masterson fired four shots, one of them striking Wagner in the bowels from the left side. Walker was struck 3 times, one shot in the lungs and his right arm horribly shattered from the other shots.

"The shooting occurred on the south side of the railroad track. Marshal Masterson coolly walked over to the business side of the street, a distance of about 200 yards, and upon reaching the sidewalk he fell exhausted. He was taken to his room where he died about 40 minutes afterward.

"Wagner and Walker were removed to Mr. Lane's room, where the former died about 7 o'clock Wednesday evening. Walker is lying dangerously wounded, with no hopes of his recovery.

"Some of the flying shots grazed the faces of one of our citizens and a cattle man. The shots were fired almost simultaneously and the wonder is expressed that more death and destruction did not ensue, as a large crowd surrounded the scene of the shooting.

"The officers were brave and cool though both were at a disadvantage, as neither desired to kill the whisky-crazed assailants.

"The death of Marshal Masterson caused great feeling in Dodge City. The business houses were draped in mourning and business on Wednesday generally suspended." [7]

Dodge indeed felt the marshal's death deeply; the whole town was stunned with shock and sorrow. "As we see the draped doors, the solemn faces, and the cold quiet air of remorse, we see depicted that steady determination to give no quarter to the ruthless invader of our lives, peace, and prosperity," the *Times* said in its black-bordered editorial. It was notice to the cowboys that in their grief for their dead marshal the citizens of Dodge would be doubly vengeful to wrongdoers. No one was to expect to find Dodge cowed by the death of Ed Masterson. They had loved the kid and he had died for them. They could not let him down.

Doc had liked Ed Masterson, "dead in the 26th year of his age," [8] very much. As he watched the solemn funeral cortege move through the silent, black-draped street on its way to the post cemetery at Fort Dodge,[9] he wondered who could be found to take the job he had held.

After the funeral, the biggest and most impressive that Dodge had ever seen, Nat Haywood resigned and Joe Mason and John Brown were hastily placed on the police force to serve until a marshal could be found. Shotguns were placed behind the counters and bars, the better citizens openly carried guns, and probably the only thing that saved Dodge was that the big herds and large numbers of cowboys had not yet arrived.

At last ex-sheriff Charles E. Bassett accepted the appointment as city marshal, with John Brown as assistant. Everybody breathed a lot easier. Bassett was a big, quiet, capable sort of guy, a good dresser as compared to the flashy Bat Masterson. He was one of the very few men of his day who was completely clean-shaven, not even having a mustache. Because of a certain formality in his manner and an inborn knowledge of how to get along with people, he was called "Senator." He was an excellent man for a law-enforcement job and held the position of city marshal in Dodge for the following two years. Senator Charley Bassett, frontier marshal.

The approach of the first of the big herds was kept track of, about 6,000 head being expected on May 9, and thousands more in the weeks following.

On May 8 Doc went down to the Long Branch for his customary afternoon game. Sitting at the poker table in the back was a man he recalled having seen in Deadwood, a tall, thin, raw-boned Illinois plow-jockey named Wyatt Earp, who had been bumming around the boom camps of the west very much as Doc had been doing. A gambler by profession, he had also been a policeman in Wichita in 1875 and had served in the same capacity in Dodge during the season of 1876.[10] He was quiet and even-tempered, but lacked the finer traits that marked well-bred people—constancy, loyalty, integrity—being always ready to jump to the side of the fence where prestige and profit were offered. He saw himself famous, another Wild Bill Hickok, if his cards were played right in this wild country. That was his predominating characteristic: he wanted to be famous as the law of the frontier. He was brave to the point of foolhardiness before an audience who could spread the word about his feats (and rescue him if he got in too deep). He was a fool in the hands of a good politician. He was dignified, fancied himself a lady-killer and had no sense of humor about his career or his hopes. He had headed for Dodge as soon as he heard of Ed Masterson's death, hoping to get his job. He was too late.

The Dodge City *Times* for May 18, 1878, lists Charles E. Bassett as town marshal; Wyatt Earp as assistant marshal; John Brown and Charles Trask as policemen. It also lists the herds that had arrived during the week from Texas, thousands of cattle and plenty of herders.

At last had come the Texas cowboy.

101

They arrived with their side arms, whiskers, dirt, rags, long hair, powerful thirsts and possibly with an inhibition or two after their difficult and dangerous trip from Texas. They wanted to get rid of everything but the guns and proceeded to do so. The two-bit haircut and shave and the fifty-cent bath at George Dieter's Centennial barbershop, the fancy duds at Wright and Beverley's, the first-class meal at Beatty and Kelley's merely put the final edge on their desire to get soaked—so blind and gone in liquor that the hardships and dangers and sorrows of the long drive might be erased completely. Forget the dearest friend of your heart, buried after the stampede. Forget the clouds of dust and the quicksands and the Indians demanding a toll of beef or scalps for passage-fare through the Nations. Forget the pitch-black nights when lightning blinked along the far skyline and the cattle stirred restlessly in the still, tense heat, and beside them you rode singing softly and praying that the heart-stilling shout of *Stampede!* would not be raised. Forget the rotten food, the aching back after twelve or fourteen hours in the saddle, the sweat-stinking clothes and the mean horse in your string that seemed bound to kill you.

They poured the drinks down at the "two-fer" rate and when they weren't just quite yet walking on their knees they would make for the dance halls and the painted cats, the faded flowers, the fallen angels, the plain old whores. Hats pushed back, spurs a-jingling, hard heels stomping, guns whacking their thighs at every bound, they sashayed into the dance with rebel yells and after each number led their lady up to the bar with shouts of "With every five drinks you get one snake free!"

And then some bastard that couldn't hold his likker like a gen-gennelmum would have to get mean and start a fight. "Shoot out the lights and call the wagon!" was accounted as a witticism in a town which had no patrol wagon. Well, the lights were shot out often enough, but the shooters were frequently dragged off to the jug in a semicomatose condition after having one of the officers' gun barrels applied briskly to the brow.

By and large Dodge got the second generation of trail herders.

These cowboys were young, eighteen, nineteen, twenty, the sons of Confederate veterans and themselves veterans of Reconstruction as it had been practised in Texas. They revered the Confederate battle flag (this is the so-called "Stars and Bars" which looks something like the British flag and is not the actual flag of the Confederacy, which was almost entirely white and could not be used in battle by gentlemen because the enemy kept thinking it was a flag of truce and would stop fighting) and they loved "Dixie," and Robert E. Lee, and were ready to fight at the word go, in case anybody thought they were licked or cowed or feared the Yankees. They referred to the cow-town marshals as pimps and added some unvarnished adjectives to the word. They carried their guns as long as they stayed sober enough to hang on to them.

After whisky and whores their next desire was to cut a figure as a gambling man—astute, sardonic, coolly raking in the chips while chewing on a big black see-gar. Doc's southern accent stood him in good stead with them when they were sober enough to know what was going on. You could trust a man whose voice didn't sound like clinkers grinding through the cookstove grates.

"Gambling ranges from a game of five-cent chuck-a-luck to a thousand dollar poker pot. Nothing is secret but with open doors upon the main street the ball rolls on uninterruptedly. More than occasionally some dark-eyed virago or some brazen-faced blond, with a modern [word illegible] will saunter in among the roughs of the gambling houses and saloons, entering with inexplicable zest into the disgusting sport, breathing the immoral atmosphere with a gusto which I defy modern writers to explain. Dance houses are ranged along at convenient distances and supplied abundantly with all the trappings and paraphernalia which go to complete institutions of that character. Here you see the greatest abandon. Men of every grade assemble to join in the dance. Nice men with white neckties, the cattle dealer with his good clothes, the sport with his well-turned fingers, smooth tongue and artistically twisted mustache, and last but not least, the cowboy, booted and spurred as he comes from the trail, his hard earnings in his pocket, all join the wild revel; and yet with all this mixture of strange human revel a remarkable degree of order is preserved." [11]

And so the ball rolled merrily on.

Somebody remembered something about a Holliday, yes, a dentist, shooting somebody someplace in Texas. Everybody could believe it. He looked the type. His eyes were so piercing, he never backed down before anybody, and besides, from the way he coughed you could tell he didn't have long to live and with nothing to lose, why, he'd likely shoot you to see if you'd land on your front or your back—for a small wager. And Doc, frail as he was, determined never to be a butt for a bully to torment, helped the legend along. It grew to such respectable proportions that men came to be afraid of him and consequently hated him. He was a figure to be reckoned with in Dodge, particularly if he was feeling extra good and the whisky made him happy instead of just comfortable. At such a time the cow town found itself with a permanent resident who was more of a liability than a dozen drunk Texans. After all, the cowboys had something to live for. It was considered suicide to try to tame Doc Holliday and a matter of policy to stay on his good side, little as he might be liked.

And now, in the best tradition of life, a paradox arises. There it is, in the Dodge City *Times* for June 8, 1878, a very neat, rather large advertisement: "DENTISTRY. J. H. Holliday, Dentist, very respectfully offers his professional services to the citizens of Dodge City and surrounding country for the summer. Office at room No. 24, Dodge House. Where satisfaction is not given money will be refunded."

At first this looks as if it might be one of Dodge's famous practical jokes. But N. B. Klaine, editor of the *Times,* printed Doc's ad seriously, apparently, because he proceeds to point out with great dignity that soon Dr. G. W. Milton will be in Dodge on one of his visits and that everyone should patronize him because he is such a good dentist *and* so respectable. Tell that to an aching tooth. But Klaine continued to give the travelling dentist free puffs all summer. A more polite yet unmistakable disapproval of Dr. Holliday could not have been made public. It probably gave Doc many a large laugh.

How the practise of dentistry went there is no way of knowing. Frequent references were found in memoirs to his practising dentistry during this period, always on cowboys, desperadoes and other rough characters. The stories invariably include some version or the other of his pulling the wrong tooth and in return getting all of his pulled by an irate cowboy, or else Doc getting some enemy under gas and pulling all of his teeth out. What probably would have upset him more would have been to be confronted while suffering from a hangover with a howling child in need of a molar extraction. Since we do not read of any children being flung out of second-story windows at the Dodge House, he must have been spared.

The festive cowboy continued to arrive and celebrate. The Grand and Glorious Fourth was gotten through without loss of life, it being one of the days on which firearms could legally be discharged within the city, but not a holiday dear to the hearts of Texans; Eddie Foy opened at the Comique; Marshal Bassett was getting a hundred dollars a month and his two helpers each seventy-five; one gambling sport was chaired by a pugilistic concubine and another spittooned; then on July 27, 1878, the *Times* reported:

"Yesterday morning about 3 o'clock this peaceful suburban city was thrown into unusual excitement, and the turmoil was all caused by a cantankerous cowboy who started the mischief by a too free use of his revolver.

"In Dodge City, after dark, the report of a revolver generally means business and is an indication that somebody is on the war path, therefore when the noise of this shooting and the yells of excited voices rang out on the midnight breeze, the sleeping community awoke from their slumbers, listened awhile to the click of the revolver, wondered who was shot this time and then went to sleep again. But in the morning many dreaded to hear the result of the war lest it should be a story of bloodshed and carnage, or of

105

death to some familiar friend. But in this instance there was an abundance of noise and smoke, with no very terrible results.

"It seems that 3 or 4 herders were paying their respects to the city and its institutions, and as is usually their custom, remained until about 3 o'clock in the morning, when they prepared to return to their camps. They buckled on their revolvers, which they were not allowed to wear around town, and mounted their horses, when all at once one of them conceived the idea that to finish the night's revelry and give the natives due warning of his departure, he must do some shooting, and forthwith he commenced to bang away, one of the bullets whizzing into a dance hall nearby, causing no little commotion among the participants in the 'dreamy waltz' and quadrille. Policemen Earp and Masterson made a raid on the shootist, who gave them 2 or 3 volleys, but fortunately without effect. The policemen returned the fire and followed the herders with intention of arresting them. The firing then became general, and some rooster who did not exactly understand the situation, perched himself in the window of the dance hall and indulged in a promiscuous shoot all by himself. The herders rode across the bridge followed by the officers. A few yards from the bridge one of the herders fell from his horse from weakness caused by a wound in the arm he had received in the fracas. The other herder made good his escape. The wounded man was properly cared for and his wound, which proved to be a bad one, was dressed by Dr. McCarty. His name is George Hoy, and he is a rather intelligent looking young man."

But on August 21 the kid died following amputation of his wounded arm by Assistant Surgeon Tremaine of Fort Dodge. "Hoy, who was already weak from a long sickness, never rallied or spoke after the operation. Just before he died he opened his eyes and seemed to recognize Mr. Day and one or two others, then with a smile on his lips he closed his eyes in death without a struggle. He was buried in the cemetery north of the city, a large number of his Texas friends following him to the grave." [12]

Years later Wyatt Earp claimed this firing off of guns was an attempt to collect a thousand dollar reward which had been offered for his own death, and bragged that he had shot the young herder.

Why anyone would want to take credit for shooting this kid in the back is beyond imagining, weird tales of prices being offered for the killing of any law officer and all such notwithstanding. There were no officers in Dodge with a gun-slinging record sufficient to warrant killing for a reputation; certainly not Charley Bassett, even though he was a former sheriff and now a town marshal, nor Wyatt Earp, assistant marshal and former policeman, nor young Jim Masterson just starting out as a policeman. And none of these men had cracked the skulls of any notable quantity of Texans before tossing them in the clink. There was nothing to warrant the offering of any blood money. The picture of the Dodge City police force in action was not that of a lone, fearless marshal patrolling the town and making all quail before his presence. It was more that the policemen were busy following their actual profession of gambling and were on call merely in case of an emergency.

Kansas summers are hot and dry. The dust fogged up relentlessly from Dodge's unpaved streets and drifted into every corner of every room in town. Doc coughed himself into exhaustion regularly. Thunderstorms brought changes in air pressure that made him feel as if his chest were collapsing under a great weight. He had periodic spells of malaise, chronic indigestion and generally ran a low temperature. He coughed constantly and after a morning when he had been unable to sleep for coughing he was probably the meanest man in Kansas. And all this was no worse than he hoped to feel, familiar as he was with the nature of his disease. He was doing everything he could to take care of himself. In 1877 there had been a big lead-silver strike at Leadville and many of the Denver crowd had urged him to go along with them to that newest boom camp. He had refused. Leadville's altitude is over 10,000 feet. All the tourist and prospector's guides of the day warned those who were tubercular or suffering from weak hearts not to go there under any circumstances as death from the slightest exertion would immediately ensue. For Doc had, after all, something to live for. He was bolstered by faith, the secure knowledge that somebody believed in him. And in vain, in sorrow. But it was there. It was the thing that kept him going.

Mattie had not seen him for five years. She still loved him, trusted him, believed in him. The cruelest and dearest vision of his lonely night was her face. He was barred from her society forever, an outcast, despised, something no decent woman would speak to. And yet he would not disgrace her further by giving up. The carefully kept Colt lay cold under his hand, unused. The long miles and the empty years . . . he would reach for the bottle beside his bed and drink until the sharp swords of his thoughts melted into soft and formless clouds.

The next day he would force the sick heart numb by concentrating on the cards, the opium of his days.

Sometimes when he wanted to kill a few minutes he would play keno, the forerunner of bingo. You have a sheet of paper on which are printed numbers from one to eighty. On it you mark your choice of ten numbers and hand it to the operator who marks a duplicate and puts your name and the amount of your bet on both sheets. You get one back and he keeps the other. When all the sheets have been marked for that game, ten numbered balls are pulled out of the "goose" and set up in a rack. If you have half the numbers you win double your bet (usually fifteen to twenty-five cents), six numbers pay 18 to 1, seven pay 180 to 1, eight pay 900 for 1, nine pay 1800 for 1, and all ten guessed right pay 3600 for 1. This is all right to take an occasional flutter on, but for regular gambling—Man! figure those odds! Chuck-a-luck is rather livelier. The three dice dance so merrily as their cage is spun and 180 to 1 is a good payoff for all three dice showing the same array of dots. It was a favorite game of the cowboys, any amount from a nickel up being accepted as a wager. Poker continued as the prime pastime and Doc was a darb at the green table. His eyes saw everything and could get a look in them that chilled off any desire to get funny. The ranks of the poker hands had long been fixed, but still there were occasions when a stand-off resulted from identical hands. It was the custom to deal a round of showdown to settle the tie. This is five cards face up, no draw, often the highest card deciding the winner. This was to grow into stud poker in a few years.

A great deal of the business done in Dodge was done in the saloons. The better ones along Front Street were attractively decorated, clean, and preserved strict order. Moreover, they were open twenty-four hours a day. A hot deal made at any time never had to wait for a light to see by or a pen to write with and so possibly cool off. After the hassle of arranging for payment and delivery and yelling for a kid to find Phillips, the Santa Fe agent, to see about the shipping, one could relax with a cooling glass of lager beer and munch a bite from the free lunch counter—limburger and Swiss cheese, pickled herring and caviar, liverwurst and rye bread and crackers being generally offered. It was comfortable, relaxing. And appreciated, not abused. Persons who have only been in cheap beer halls where the furnishings are strictly designed to resist wear and tear, or in chrome-plated and imitation-leopard-upholstered cocktail lounges featuring a pansy at the piano singing dingy songs, can but try to imagine the atmosphere of a real old-time, high-class saloon. It was the gentleman's club, American style, everybody being welcome who did not annoy the other customers. There were no tables to sit at, no bar stools: one drank one's drink standing up like a man. The paneled-front bar ran along one wall for about twenty feet. Almost invariably there was a large mirror behind it, set in a "back bar" carved and paneled to match the bar proper and made to hold an array of glasses, bottles and ornaments. A cupboard and ice chest usually stood across the open end. In more sedate areas like Denver, bar screens were placed in front of the swinging doors so that passers-by could not ogle the customers. However, in Dodge and other wide-open towns there not only were no bar screens but the swinging doors were wired open. A cordial welcome to all.

Finally, since Dodge was getting to be a respectable town, cowboys and all, anti-gambling and anti-bawdy-house laws were passed by the city council. All law officers were instructed to enforce these ordinances. Every gambling house proprietor and even Dutch Jake herself, queen of the local madams, was hauled into court, fined, and turned loose. Those low-class drifters and saloon bummers who could not pay their fine were run out of town. Dodge was as splendidly moral as towns too large to yell across. And it boasted such peerless knights of the prairie as Wyatt B. S. Earp, to walk about wearing a badge and be a part of the corrupt pattern of city government which has by and large been the country's average since the first trading center sprang up beside every ford of every river.

The trail-herd season went on in Dodge. Things were generally smooth but when trouble came it came in large lots. One week's issue of the *Times* [18] carried the following items: "A shooting affray occurred Wednesday evening. Some words passed between Al Manning, a barkeeper, and Jack Brown, an ex-policeman, the former firing at the latter and the ball striking Will Norton, a by-stander, the shot taking effect in the instep of the left foot. Manning was taken before Squire Cook and bound over in the sum of $500." "Another shooting took place about 12 o'clock Thursday night. Skunk Curley, a bullwhacker, shot a man named Grogan, a resident of Great Bend, Kan., the ball striking the right shoulder and passing across the backbone into the left shoulder making 4 holes and inflicting an ugly wound. The wounded man is doing well. His friends say he was an entire stranger to Curley, who was drunk, and that it was probable the shot was intended for someone else. Curley skipped the town and no arrest was made." "A disgraceful row occurred in the afternoon [Thursday], in which it is said the officers failed to appear. These occurrences are the subject of much comment on the conduct of the officers."

Consider the fact that the total number of arrests made in Dodge City in all of 1878 according to the court records was only sixty-four. That is an average of about twenty-one per peace officer, which is not very many for a town supposedly so full of sin and loaded guns and quick passions. Perhaps the *Times* had reason to

110

complain about the failure of the officers to do their duty. Ed Masterson had never failed to attend a brawl. . . .

And he was dead to prove it.

Down at the Comique the two warring factions in Dodge (that is, the saloon-gambling-policeman crowd versus their customers) met on an equal footing. By the time the festivities got rolling the heat of the day had worn off, the plains' little evening breeze had sprung up, the stars were out in thick, bright clusters, and the coyotes had started their nightly concert consisting of variations on the theme, "Yap! Grrrr!"

Now the ladies of the evening blossomed, the painted prostitute, the professional dancing partner, the kids out for a good time, the common sporting girl. Doc couldn't bear the sight of pretty little blonde girls with their faces painted and their legs showing. In fact he was so rude to them that he completely gave away his secret attachment to someone who in a way resembled them. One of the faded *nymphs du pavé,* as the *Times* has it, was named Katherine Elder. She was so little faded that you hardly noticed it, being quite young, and was a tall, big-boned, buxom brunette with a nose so determined and handsome that she was known to her cronies in the cribs as Big Nosed Kate. None of that crowd was noted for delicacy of manner, and being no exception herself, Kate didn't let it hurt her feelings. She took one look at Doc and his air of class, the anguish deep in his eyes, and let out a yell of delight. He couldn't fight her off and she drove him to distraction. Every place he went there she was with a hungry look and hands she couldn't keep off of him. His friend Wyatt Earp advised him to belt her one, that was the way he treated these floozies,[14] but Doc only coughed dejectedly. She'd likely cool him off with a right to the choppers if she got the idea she didn't have a chance.

There is a fine story about Doc and Kate, having to do with his killing a man over a game of cards in Fort Griffin and being incarcerated in a hotel room because the town had no jail. Since his victim was quite popular locally Doc was soon nominated by a group of irate miners for the job of becoming trimming on a tree.

Before they could find a rope, Kate set fire to the back of the hotel and when everyone rushed to fight the fire she stuck up Doc's guards and rescued him. They hid out in some willows by the river until evening, when a friend brought them horses and clothes.

Well, Doc was wanted in Fort Griffin and would hardly have gone back there just to tempt fate; the town had a very sturdy log jail in which Doc had roomed and boarded long enough to cure him of wanting a return engagement; there were no mines anywhere around, though to be perfectly fair, there could have been a convention of miners meeting in Fort Griffin at the time of Doc's alleged second visit; but a twelve-year-old female child brought up in that area could have tracked the fugitives to their lair in the willows if they had really been there and memorized her Sunday school lesson at the same time. To add to the confusion, I found hints and rumors and half-remembered stories which variously placed the affair in Caldwell, Kansas, Hunnewell, Kansas, and at last, as having happened to a couple of other people.

Kate had certain charms—a true and loving heart, a ready laugh, no brains to perturb her with weighty problems, a fine, healthy body, a marvelous vocabulary of cuss words, and a deep and abiding fondness for cheap whisky. Perhaps the most attractive thing about her to Doc was her very coarseness and vulgarity, a surface quality so different from the memory in his heart that no shameful emotions choked him when he saw her.

One night, they say, he felt so bad that nothing could do him any good. He had to go to bed before his customary dawn. It wasn't that his consumption was worse; it was the black depths of depression that made him feel as if he were losing his mind. The loneliness and despair crushed him. The knowledge of Mattie's prayers and trust could not stop the shaking; whisky only made him sick. It was a violent reaction to his way of life. He lay on his bed staring at hell from the empty blackness of space, it seemed; alone, alone, alone. . . .

Came a knock at the door.

Doc cursed the knocker fluently and coldly.

A succession of blows shook the door in its frame.

Doc went off into a violent coughing spell. His hands jerked so that he could hardly get the lamp lit. The banging on his door continued. Just as he got the chimney rattled back on the lamp and was catching his breath after damn near choking to death, the flimsy lock gave.

Kate bounded into the room, a big Colt gun in her hand, yelling that Doc was a lousy son of a bitch for treating her the way he did and she was going to fill him so full of holes he wouldn't float in brine. Wherewith she punctured the mattress in his immediate vicinity with a .45 caliber slug.

Doc arose in his wrath and a long white night shirt. Fortunately Kate was so blind drunk she couldn't exactly tell where he was but she kept on trying to locate him with a bullet. He clobbered her one aside the head with nearly three pounds of .45-caliber Colt hastily snatched up from beside his bed, and rather put his heart in it.

Kate came to feeling sober and sorry and very fragile—and lying on Doc's bed with a wet towel on her head. The door was braced with a chair and the hullabaloo in the hall was dying down as irate patrons of Deacon Cox's hostelry went back to bed somewhat disgruntled with Dr. Holliday and his friends. Kate snuggled down in bed and grinned at Doc. He stood by the lamp for a long minute looking down at her and then swiftly bent over and blew out the light. . . .

Doc and Kate were not seen again until late the following afternoon, by which time they looked fully as bushed as before, but a great deal happier about everything. In fact, they gave a rosy glow to the dust and shabbiness of Front Street as they walked along the warped board sidewalk. They moved into one of the shanties in Tin Pot Alley, a hotel du dive, as the phrase-coining *Times* put it, supposedly located between 2nd and 3rd. Fortunately one of Kate's redeeming characteristics was a passion for personal cleanliness and a love of neat surroundings, so their one room, with a lean-to kitchen attached and separate outhouse, was in the best

Dodge tradition, ratty outside and cosy inside, and that was all right with Doc.

This little love nest was a nine-day wonder. Doc had made plenty of money all summer and while he was usually cautious with his spending, now he proceeded to deck Kate out like a lady. She was probably scornful of the clothes he had made for her as being too refined; she would have liked red satin so she could lord it over the tarts in the red-light district by posing as a wealthy kept woman.

Women's clothes of the period were at their most ridiculously ornate, being so involved in their construction that one referred to building a dress, not just making it. In the language of the day it was a "tied-back dress," everything being hauled back to hang down from atop a bustle, leading one paper to refer to all women as walking around looking like a Newfoundland dog dragging a wet tail. The following describes a dress [15] that probably would have delighted Kate's soul, although from this distance it sounds like a nightmare: "A very showy suit is of Nile blue Rhadames satin, with the skirt trimmed with 11 rows of puffing, over which fall flounces of guipure embroidery in cream-colored silk on cream-colored tulle. Over the skirt are panel-shaped trimmings in wood color and Nile blue, covered with detached appliqué work forming flowers in jet, wood color and brownish steel beads. These panels are lightly joined on the sides by means of passementerie brandebourgs. On the upper part of the skirt is a satin scarf which forms a pannier, and there are inserted puffings coming from under the basquette of the waist, forming, as it were, one piece with the train. This kind of careless draping is one of the novelties of the season, and only a very expert dressmaker can handle it properly."

Naturally, to men of Doc's day, as to everyone today, this was just so much double-talk and making fun of these descriptions of women's clothes was a delight to writers. Witness the following from the *Times* for July 28, 1877, describing a ball at the Dodge House: "Our special reporter who was detailed to write up the costumes of the ladies, and who was in our usual liberal way furnished with an excessive amount of pocket money to make himself agreeable with, has somehow got the hat on the wrong foot and submits the following varied description of the Lords of Creation: Mr. J. F. L. appeared in a gorgeous suit of linsey woolsey, cut bias on the gourd with red cotton handkerchief attachment imported by Messers H. & D. from Lawrence. Mr. H. was modestly attired in a blue lambs wool undershirt, frilled. . . . Mr. I. G. J. was the envy of all; he wore his elegant blond mustache ala gin sling and was tastefully arrayed in arctic overshoes with collar buttons and studs. . . ." To keep in the spirit of the times, one wonders why no one showed up wearing train number 4.

But dressed or undressed, she was still Big Nosed Kate. After a while Doc's drink-numbed conscience came to life. He didn't love Kate and he despised himself for needing her so badly that he couldn't leave her. He took out on her all the repressed hatred he felt toward life for killing him so slowly and disgustingly, for making him a weakling whose manhood had to hide behind the cardboard demon of homicidal mania. He would never even have looked at her if she had had any of Mattie's characteristics, and yet he cursed her for being trash. He told her what he thought about the flashy gewgaws with which she cheapened her appearance, about her uneducated speech, her vulgar mannerisms, about her charming friends like Hop Fiend Nell and Highpockets and Big Em, and, worst of all, about her pretensions to gentility. Quite naturally Kate would get a little upset over such remarks and not having been brought up to repress her feelings, would let fly at Doc with anything handy. Their relationship was more inclined to be off than on. Doc would move back into the Dodge House until the storm was over, Kate would break up some more of the furniture and go on a prolonged bat, but before long they would be back together.

By mid-September most of the trail herds had been shipped out or, after resting up, had taken the trail on north to Ogallala. The

115

cowboys had gone back to their dreary and lonely jobs on the range. Dodge was beginning to get dull. And then word came that the Northern Cheyenne were on the warpath.

Indians!

These Indians had been among the victors at the Little Big Horn and the Powder River, but had at last made another treaty with the government. They had been sent down from their northern hills to the agency of the Southern Cheyenne in the Nations, promised food and tools and land so they could live as well as they had in the north before the buffalo were all killed off. Corrupt government officials made themselves plenty of money on the deal instead of fulfilling their obligations: only half or less of the promised beef was bought, the tools were sold to hardware wholesalers, every contract was let to the person paying the largest bribe. The pleas of the starving Indians were ignored. Everybody knew the only good Indian was a dead Indian. To add to the tension, the Southern Cheyenne were more closely allied with the Arapahoes than with their northern relatives, and they in turn had become half Sioux. The dissension in the Nations was noted with growing concern by everyone but the men running the agency.

Finally a band of the Northern Cheyenne left the agency and started home. Colonel Richard I. Dodge tells their story in *Our Wild Indians* as follows:

"Courageous and confident, easily beating off the attacks of the few cavalry companies that were available for its pursuit, this gallant band of but one hundred and twenty-five fighting men, encumbered by more than four times their number of women and children, moved through the Indian Territory and Southern Kansas as nonchalantly as though a victorious and overwhelming army. Moving by easy stages, their march was only a picnic from one luxuriant grass-plat to another; the pleasure of the jaunt just agreeably varied by slight encounters with troops, and mimic buffalo-hunts among the herds of fat cattle.

"On Poison Creek in Southern Kansas they encountered herds of real buffalo, a temptation so strong as to prove irresistible, and

116

here the march was suspended to enable them to kill and 'jerk' sufficient meat to carry them to the Missouri River.

"These pleasurable commissariat duties were rather suddenly brought to an end by the near approach of a larger force of troops than they had hitherto encountered. Constant victory had given them such confidence in their own powers and 'medicine' that, though knowing that the troops outnumbered them more than two to one, they determined to set a trap, and give their pursuers such a lesson as would effectually send them to the rear and insure an unmolested journey to their destination.

"This portion of the Plains is a formation of carboniferous sandstone covered by a thin layer of alluvial. The running streams meander through valleys cut entirely through the stone. The lateral slopes or depressions gradually deepen until the stone foundation is reached, and following this with more or less wear for some little distance, plunge precipitately into cañons whose bottoms are alluvial deposits, but whose sides are perpendicular walls of rock, from the tops of which the plain rises smoothly, gradually, and without the slightest cover for an approaching enemy. These are, by plainsmen, called 'box cañons,' and even though but ten to twenty feet in depth, they afford positions and opportunities for defence almost equal to those of the best artificial defensive works. A 'box cañon' of unusually excellent defensive facilities was selected by the astute Cheyennes. It was exceptionally rich in luxurious grasses suitable for the stock; it contained several springs of water; its windings formed natural bastions; and toward its upper end it was so deep and narrow as to afford perfect protection to the women and children. The edges and weak places were strengthened by low walls of loose stones, behind which, entirely covered and hidden, the little band crouched for its deadly spring.

"The Indians evidently anticipated that in the eagerness of pursuit the troops would rush blindly into this pitfall. But Col. Lewis [commandant at Fort Dodge] knew his enemy. Vigorous as was his pursuit, his advance was always covered by scouts.

"The principal valley from which the Indians had entered the

117

'box cañon,' had for a day or two been the grazing-ground of their stock, and was everywhere marked with numerous tracks. The scouts would probably have passed without notice the entrance to the 'box cañon,' and thus led Lewis, in spite of his caution, into an ambuscade from which he must have suffered severely, but for the constitutional impatience and excitability of the Indians. Though they knew that the troops for whom the trap was laid were but a short distance off, they were utterly unable to refrain from firing at the few advanced scouts. These shots, by disclosing their presence and position, deprived the trap of its only really dangerous feature.

"The scouts promptly returned to the command and informed Col. Lewis of the situation.

"Two companies of cavalry were dismounted, and advanced deployed as skirmishers, occupying one whole side of the 'box cañon.' A company of infantry occupied the other side. The lines closed in and the battle soon raged entirely to the disadvantage of the Indians. After scarcely an hour of this sharp work, the savages, finding themselves completely environed, were so convinced of their own defeat as to have made a flag of truce to open communications, when Col. Lewis, incautiously exposing himself, was struck down by a rifle-bullet and died in a few moments.

"This so demoralized the troops that they fell back, and night coming on, they retired from the field, and went into camp. The Indians were not slow to take advantage of this opportunity, and under the friendly cover of darkness, they escaped from the cañon and continued their flight towards the north. Before the battle had fairly joined, Lewis had sent a few of the very best marksmen among the scouts, to lie, *perdu,* among the rocks about the mouth of the cañon, with orders to kill as many as possible of the Indian ponies. This order had been so admirably executed, that, in spite of the utmost care on the part of the Indians, not less than seventy of their ponies had been destroyed. What remained were sufficient for a few days' march, but not for such a race as they now realized

118

they had to run; so, deviating from their most direct route, the Indians turned to the eastward and made a raid into the settlements to procure a remount.

"The horrors of that raid are a part of the history of Kansas."

That raid was on Decatur County, Kansas, September 28, 1878, the last Indian raid in Kansas.[16] Nineteen settlers were killed and the Cheyenne got away into Nebraska with a large supply of fresh mounts.

If you will look at a map of Kansas you will see that all this took place far, far from Dodge, in fact, something like a hundred miles away.

But the terrifying words "Indian raid!" had been spoken. Mass hysteria gripped the whole town and all the settlers out in the county. The vaguest rumors were built up into hair-raising facts, people coming in from the west reported seeing Indians only a few miles outside of town and the bodies of the scalped and slain were reported littering the plains. A herder named Warren was reported to have been killed at Henry Kollar's camp southwest of Dodge, and near Sun City two men, it appeared, had been killed and also a babe in its mother's arms. All the settlers headed for Dodge as fast as their teams could pull their wagons, the women and children screaming and the old man with his shotgun between his knees.

In Dodge the fire bell was constantly rung as an alarm, proprietors of gun and hardware stores handed out all their guns to arm the population, confused groups of people dashed madly about pursued by barking dogs, a Santa Fe train pulled in loaded with tramps, prospectors, hunters and travellers that it had picked up out in the wilds and carried free as a public service,[17] women were having hysterics and babies were crying, Kate made Doc promise to shoot her rather than let her fall into the hands of the red fiends, and all in all Dodge more closely resembled a European village of the Middle Ages afflicted with the dancing sickness than a town full of us doughty and fearless Americans.

About 2 P.M. flames were seen rising from the farmhouse of

119

Harrison Berry about four miles west of town.[18] Pale with dread the frantic population of Dodge instantly realized that the Indians had set fire to the house. Here was proof the red devils were *close*. The invariably helpful Santa Fe had an engine ready with steam up just in case of such an emergency. Onto it piled a crowd of heavily-armed citizens and off they roared to the scene of the conflagration. Finding no Indians about, they went to work on the fire. They were unable to save the house, but got out some of the furniture and managed to save the haystacks and the stock. The *Times* for September 21, 1878, praised P. L. Beatty, Chalk Beeson, Wyatt Earp and S. E. Isaacson for their part in fighting the fire.

Night came and some of the edge wore off the tension. The next day everybody was still unscalped and somewhat shamefaced. The Harrison Berry family remembered they had left home in such a hurry that no one had thought to extinguish the fire in the cookstove, the dead and scalped showed up alive and whole, there was strong evidence that a murder had been committed and blamed on the non-existent Indians, and the very word Indian was a bad taste in the mouths of the valiant citizens of Dodge for quite some time.

And then Dodge had a murder. Nobody could think or talk of anything else. Fannie Keenan, alias Dora Hand, had been murdered in her sleep, it was said, by one Jim Kennedy. Supposedly thinking that he had killed Mayor Kelley, against whom he had a grudge, Kennedy hopped a fast horse out of town. After him hurried Sheriff Masterson, City Marshal Bassett, Assistant Marshal Earp and Deputies Duffey and Tilghman, who, when they caught up with him had to shoot both him and his horse to get him to stop. They lugged him back to Dodge where Doc McCarty (first we hope, in those all-but-modern times, giving him ether,[19]) removed a lot of shattered bone from his elbow and got him doctored back to health sufficiently to stand trial. After all the furor caused by this, since Fannie Keenan was a faded flower of the better sort and her passing was somewhat resented in Dodge, the *Times* reported on October 26, 1878, "James Kennedy, charged with the murder of Fannie Keenan, had a preliminary examination Tuesday before Justice Cook. The evidence being insufficient the prisoner was acquitted." Whereupon everyone went about clucking their tongues and reminding each other that young Kennedy's father was one of the richest men in Texas.

FOOTNOTES TO CHAPTER 7

1. The Dodge City *Times* for July 7, 1877, has a gentleman from Atcheson, Kansas, describe the Dodge House as one of the best and most commodious hotels in the west.
2. Dodge City *Times*, June 8, 1878.
3. *Harper's New Monthly Magazine*, April, 1876.
4. Dodge City *Times*, May 24, 1879.
5. Dodge City *Times*, June 9, 1877.
6. Wyatt Earp is supposed to have been on the police force of Dodge City in the summer of 1877, but the *Times* does not list him as a law officer and as late as July 7, 1877, refers to him with, "We hope he will accept a position on the force," and even later, on July 21, 1877, he is referred to as "the ex-officer"—and the season was at its height at that time.
7. Dodge City *Times*, April 13, 1878. Bat Masterson claims to have fought this fight for his brother, but the only mention of him in the paper in connection with this affair is the statement that he had gone to visit his grieving parents.
8. We note that Ed Masterson's obituary states that he was born in "Henryville, Canada East."
9. Boot Hill, of fame for those who died with their boots on, was the local potter's field. After Prairie Grove Cemetery was opened in Dodge, Ed Masterson's body was reburied there.
10. We have heard marvelous tales of Mr. Earp's law-enforcement activities in Ellsworth. There is no record or newspaper mention of it. All we could find out about similar activities of his in Wichita was that he was a policeman there "in the years A.D. 1874, 1875 and part of 1876," according to a testimonial letter sent—by men who had been the mayor and members of the city council and the city marshal in Wichita during those years—to help Mr. Earp establish a moral character for himself at the time of his trial for the killings at the O.K. corral. The letter was printed in the Tombstone, Arizona, *Daily Nugget*, November 18, 1881.
11. Dodge City *Times*, September 1, 1877.
12. Dodge City *Times*, August 24, 1878.
13. September 21, 1878.
14. "Miss Frankie Bell, who wears the belt for superiority in point of muscular ability, heaped epithets upon the unoffending head of Mr. Earp to such an extent as to provoke a slap from the ex-officer, besides creating a disturbance of the quiet and dignity of the city, for which she received a night's lodging in the dog house

and a reception at police court next morning, the expense of which was about $20. Wyatt Earp was fined the lowest limit of the law, one dollar." From the *Times* of July 21, 1877.

15. *Rocky Mountain News*, April 30, 1882.
16. *Kansas, a Guide to the Sunflower State*, W.P.A., Viking Press, New York, 1939.
17. The Santa Fe trainmen had standing orders to pick up all strays along the tracks and carry them to the nearest town when there was Indian trouble, according to *Santa Fe, the Railroad That Built an Empire*.
18. This gives some idea of how really bare this area was.
19. Ether and chloroform were both in common usage at this time. *Harper's New Monthly Magazine*, June, 1876.

8

Doc Saves

Wyatt Earp's Life

In the winter Dodge settled down to being a small railroad town. The most important events of the day were "train times," the town's chief income was derived from the workers on the railroad, and the Santa Fe's big news was Dodge's big news. The Santa Fe's very humble beginning made Kansans feel closely allied with it, as if it were as "Kansas" as they were, never a stranger intruding and demanding. No scandals were ever attached to it such as had clouded the Union Pacific construction, and it prospered and grew with the land it served. Years and years later William Allen White was to say the Santa Fe was one of the nicest things that ever happened to Kansas.

And this winter the Santa Fe was expanding. Hoping someday to get clear to the Pacific Ocean, their surveyors had turned the route south before the wall of Rockies and laid out the line over Raton Pass, where their friend Uncle Dick Wootton sold them his right of way. A tunnel was started immediately, since the pass was nearly 8,000 feet high, and the little 4–4–0 engines could haul only thirty-six tons up its six-percent grades to the construction crews working on the New Mexico side. But the tunnel was long and hard to cut, so the Santa Fe bought a special engine from the Baldwin Locomotive Works, a consolidated type 2–8–0 job with cylinders twenty by twenty-six. It was the famous "Uncle Dick" which was to see repeated rebuildings and service until 1921. Up a 3.5 grade it could haul 258 tons and was the most powerful locomotive yet built. Everybody in Dodge turned out to see it when it came through, even the editor of the *Times,* to count its eight drive wheels, gaze awestruck at its *size,* and admire the fearless engineer who controlled all that power and made three dollars and twenty-five cents for a twelve-hour day.

But even four trains a day and pride in "Uncle Dick" couldn't keep Dodge from fairly itching with inactivity during the winter. Sometimes it looked like all there was to do was cuss the mud. Western Kansas gets an average of fifteen inches of rain a year. That is only five inches more than it takes to qualify as a desert, and yet all winter long the streets of Dodge were either sloppy sheets of goo or frozen into wave-like ruts. There were many mild days, but quite a few, too, when the wind reminded you that there was nothing to break its force between you and the North Pole, and a few bad storms. Doc and Kate stayed reconciled for remarkable spells now, not that they didn't get on each other's nerves when confined for any period of time, but Doc's motto was *Man cannot do what he wants to do in this world, but only that which will benefit him,* and the nights were cold. Moreover, money was not as plentiful as it had been in the summer and Deacon Cox charged two dollars a night for a room in his hostelry.

Among the high types wintering in Dodge the practical joke was regarded as God's gift to suffering humanity. Business was dull, there were no amusements, and then Fluke McGilder from Cheyenne showed up, remembered as Luke McGlue, but otherwise unchanged. Luke McGlue, Honorary Mayor and Chief Squirter of the Fire Company. It was he who slipped the raw egg in the coat-tail pocket of innumerable Prince Alberts. He who was unable to bear the sight of a saloon loafer snoozing by the warm stove unmolested. A piece of wet paper would be gently placed on the loafer's thigh, then a penny well-heated on the stove was slid onto it. The resulting steambath produced howls and kickings which broke up the boredom of all concerned most effectively. Good old Luke. A drunk passed out in public would awake to find himself a victim of the Keely cure for alcoholism. In this the unconscious souse is placed in a coffin in a dark room, with candles flickering dimly at head and foot, and left to come out of it. Confirmed drinkers have been known to stay cold sober for three days after an experience like this. On one occasion an inebriate awoke to find himself nailed up in a large china-ware crate and being exhibited at so much a look. That Luke: he deserved to be mayor.

The plight of Doc and his friends is described in the *Times*: [1] "The festive sportsman is as keenly sensitive to a stringency in the money market as the merchant or mechanic. Just at present his stock in trade is light. His bank roll which last summer he flashed on every available occasion, now scarce ever sees the light of day, and when it does its diminished proportions frighten his landlord, his washer-woman and even himself, stern and bold as he is. In the place of 20's and 50's he has ones and twos, and only occasionally does a 'five-caser' meet his piercing eye. He makes no reckless bets, nor does he indulge in games whereof he does not understand. It is absolutely necessary that when he bets, he bets on a sure thing, and his hand trembles even then as he lays his dollar on the board and risks its loss. Time is more plentiful with him than anything else. He sits around in the sun during the day, or near some friendly stove by night, he relates to his comrades the thrilling scenes and incidents of his past chequered career—tells of the days when he won and lost by the thousands and wore a diamond pin. At the recollection of those past flush times he says, 'd—m such country as this, the Black Hills for me.' But after a second thought he takes it all back and concludes to wait for the cattle trade."

When the weather broke, half the demimonde took off for Deadwood or Leadville and a little excitement—and so missed the Loving-Richardson gun fight. This was a real riot. Frank Loving, a quiet-type gambler, and Levi Richardson, a bucko-boy freighter, had been at odds for some time, P. L. Beatty testifying later that about a month before the fight Richardson had told him he and Loving were having trouble and "that he would shoot the guts out of the cock-eyed son of a bitch any way." [2]

Finally, on a Saturday night, April 6, 1879, Loving came into the Long Branch between 8 and 9 P.M. and met Richardson face to face. Loving went over and sat down on the hazard table.[3] Richardson sat down beside him and Loving immediately sprang up and facing the freighter said:

"If you have anything to say about me why don't you say it to my face like a gentleman, and not behind my back, you damned son of a bitch!"

"You won't fight, you damned—" Richardson began hotly.

"Try me and see!" Loving cried.

By this time both men were in such a rage that they were beyond reason. Richardson was standing in front of the table, Loving by the end of the bar. Richardson suddenly drew a gun and fired at Loving, who dodged around the stove set out in the middle of the narrow room and pulled his own gun, a .44 caliber Remington. It failed to fire with his first shot at Richardson and he hastily cocked it again, tearing around the stove with Richardson in hot pursuit shooting at him wildly. The room filled with smoke from the black powder used in manufacturing ammunition then. The other patrons were flinging themselves flat on the floor, into the ice chest, behind the bar, and one man even went through the transom.[4] Deputy Sheriff William Duffey there present tore through the smoke after the shooters who were still running around the stove and banging away at each other, and handsome City Marshal Bassett lit out on a dead run from Beatty and Kelley's a few doors away on Front Street. Finally Frank Loving, in one of those unpredictable little flurries of luck that come to all of us at some time, succeeded in hitting Levi Richardson with a bullet. Just at this time Deputy Sheriff Duffey grabbed Richardson and took his gun and City Marshal Bassett disarmed Loving. Out of eight or ten shots fired only one took effect, and that was the one which hit Richardson in the left breast and from the effects of which he died almost at once.[5]

The coroner's jury agreed that it was an open and shut case of self-defense and Frank Loving was turned loose. He was not even officially censured for carrying a concealed weapon.

By the time this fracas had been talked threadbare it was time for the cattle season to start. Dodge got itself all spruced up. City Marshal Charles E. Bassett, Assistant Marshal Wyatt B. S. Earp and Policeman James Masterson were to get one hundred dollars each this season, the city council decided. Doc Holliday oiled up a little marvel that had cost him a hundred dollars, a handsome silver-plated faro dealing box that would, when a tiny lever was pushed, eject two cards instead of one from the carefully stacked deck placed in it, and rehearsed with his confederate, who was to keep the case, the simple signals that told him what extra card to sneak in as played on the case. He also steamed open several brand-new decks of Hart's Linen Eagle cards, removed the faintest little whisker of an edge from some of the higher denominations therein and sealed them all back up with unfailing neatness. These items were then placed in readiness for an emergency.

The freighters were busy now that the trails were drying up and those distant from the railroad were putting in their spring orders. The soldiers, who had to hole up in the winter to get their mounts in condition for a possible summer campaign against the Indians, were again seen hitting the high spots in Dodge. The Santa Fe issued its annual spring order: stop the night trains beyond rifle shot out of Dodge and douse the big coal oil headlamp and the car lamps.[6] Drunken herders loved to shoot at the moving lights. Also, when a trail herd was spotted near the tracks, the conductor would go through the train warning everybody to be very quiet and above all not to shoot out of the windows (trains in those days invariably carried several pasengers who shot at everything that moved in the vast sameness of the plains). The engineer would get 'er rolling full speed, then when even with the herd would cut the throttle and *coast* past the nervous cattle. The cowboys, their hair practically on end for fear of a stampede, would be plainly heard singing gentle and soothing songs to calm the herd—and the passengers would then refuse to believe any of the shoot-'em-up stories of the tough trail towns. With their own ears they had heard those innocent young herders singing hymns as they worked.

The Comique opened early in May. Being down south of the tracks on Locust Street between 1st and 2nd, it had a new illuminated sign which was quite up-and-coming to attract customers. Actually this was hardly necessary since you could hear the festivities all over town. It also had a new drop curtain advertising the wares and services of prominent Dodge City businesses, and all who loved burnt cork, the clog dance and minstrelsy were invited to attend—with the admonition that strict order would be preserved. A typical "hall" of the day, the floor of the room was flat and the floor of the stage slanted steeply up back from the kerosene-burning footlights. The show started at 8 o'clock and ran until past midnight without a let-up. This season again had Foy and Thompson who had been so popular the year before, and on with them were Belle LaMont and Nola and Billie Forrest.[7] These performers had to work to keep the ball rolling for four hours, and all the time out-shine the gambling tables going full blast at the other end of the room and the long bar running down one side. Clog dances and skits and banjo-playing were offered, but fortunately one of the most dearly-loved entertainment features of the day, and one of the least exhausting, was the singing of songs—sentimental, lively, comic, and items with a real bounce to the rhythm.

The preceding year James O. Bland had written "Carry Me Back to Ol' Virginny" and it was still a great favorite, as was the Tony Pastor hit "Piper Heidseick," and also "Keep in de Middle ob de Road," "Reuben and Rachel" and "Grease with Cash." Harrigan and Hart were still going strong with their satires on the foibles of their fellows in the Mulligan Guards series, producing everything from "The Mulligan Guards' Picnic" to "Miss Mulligan's Piano-Fortay." In the year 1879 Emmett's "Cuckoo Song" was introduced, one of the famous vaudeville routines of the decade. And Bland followed up his sentimental hit of the year before with the rollicking, made-for-square-dancing "Oh, Dem Golden Slippers" which was to assume the place of a folk song in the cow country and be sung for generations. There were other songs more or less in this category, "In the Bright Mohawk Valley" being relocated as "The Red River Valley" and "My Bonnie Lies Over the Ocean" remarkably becoming the cowboy's hymn: "Last night as I lay on the prairie and looked at the stars in the sky, I wondered if ever a cowboy would come to that sweet by and by." And a song ideal for soothing cattle and mooning over in dance halls was the strangely touching and sweet little one: "When the curtains of night are pinned back by a star, and the beautiful moon sweeps the sky; when a soft summer breeze wafts the sleepy clouds by, I'll remember you, love, in my prayers." The cowboys themselves made up and sang songs: "Ten Thousand Cattle" with its unforgettable chorus; the saddle-rock rhythm of "I'm A-Ridin' Old Paint and A-Leadin' Old Dan"; the tragic ballad that starts, "As I walked out on the streets of Laredo"; the mournful loneliness of "All day on the prairie alone I ride, not even a hound-dog to trot at my side"; "The Cow Boy's Life" with its advice, "Now before you take up the cow boy's life make your insurance out to your wife and cut your throat with an old dull knife"; the happy strains of "Whoopee-ti-yi-yo, git along, little doggies"; and verse upon verse of "Old Chisolm Trail" with its cynical comments on life's vagaries: "Oh, it's cloudy in the west and it's lookin' like rain and of course my old slicker's in the wagon again," "I went to the boss for to draw my roll an' he had me figgered out ten bucks in the hole," "With my seat in the saddle and my head in the sky I'll quit punchin' cows in the sweet by an' by." [8]

Down in Smith County, Kansas, in 1873, Dr. Brewster Higley, a homesteader on Beaver Creek, and Dan Kelly, from near Harlan, wrote the words and music of America's most widely-known and dearly-loved folk song, "Home on the Range." [9] It was a great favorite in Dodge and thousands of cowboys and railroad men and travellers heard it there and carried it away with them to sing all over the land. Kansas can forever hold up its head in musical circles because of this, the song in America's heart.

But the Comique was not only a honky-tonk, it was also a dance hall. After midnight, when the clog dances and songs and minstrel skits were over, the Fairy Belles began looking for partners. This was not a taxi-dance arrangement with any girl being available if you bought tickets. You asked politely for a dance, treated your partner like a lady and upon the square-dance caller's shout of "Sashay to the bar and treat your partners," you trotted her up to the bar and plunked out fifty cents for a couple of drinks—yours cheap whisky and hers cold tea. This courtesy was all that was requested in payment, the girl getting a rake-off on each drink from the house. A series of boxes ran around the three sides of the room facing the stage, in case you wanted semiprivacy in which to recount your life history to some plump little redhead.

The games at the back of the hall were not conducted in such a noisy manner as to interfere with the rest of the fun, but the churchlike atmosphere of the faro bank was missing. Perhaps the favorite gambling arrangement was a giant wheel of fortune, the lucky numbers thoughtfully being decorated with Confederate battle flags and pictures of Lee and Jackson. The bird cage of the chuck-a-luck game added the friskly rattle of its dice to the floppity-whir of the big wheel, cries of "Keno!" and the rustle of cards at the Spanish monte table.

The Comique was easily the most popular summer institution in Dodge; the permanent saloons along Front Street were handsome and respectable, yes, but they danced the cancan every night at midnight at the Comique. It was lively; it was great fun. That the name "Lady Gay," one of the most original ever given any place of entertainment, was abandoned for the Comique is to be regretted, but Americanisms weren't good enough for us then, we had to be aping European styles which fit us about as well as we deserved. Kate got all the demimonde mad at her when she stopped calling it the Commy-kew, at Doc's suggestion. "That big horse putting on airs," was the general comment. But they all knew Doc pronounced it correctly. He was educated. You could tell that by just looking at him.

There was so much that you could tell by just looking at Doc. He was a killer: see those cold blue eyes, see how nervous he is when anybody gets close to him, see the way he always sits with his back to the wall. Why, I heard. . . . And you can tell he hasn't got long to live. Listen to that cough. Now you know I'm not a coward, but *there* is a man I wouldn't cross. And Holliday worked day and night to feed and foster this impression. Since he felt so sick most of the time it was easy to have the disposition a desperate killer was popularly supposed to have. Completely fearless, proud, and frail—and full of hatred for the stupid big toughs around him, he hardly had to tax his intelligence at all to figure out a way to be safe around them. But he had to not care that people hated him: that was the price for his physical safety. So long as Mattie did not fail him he could bear it. He would look at Kate sprawled out on the bed with a cigarette in one hand and a piece of imported French chocolate in the other, one heel on top of her upraised knee, idly flipping through the latest issue of *Frank Leslie's Illustrated Weekly*, looking every inch a whore— and completely happy. Then his hand would go automatically to the fancy cut-glass decanter full of whisky that stood beside him.

Probably the most important thing that happened to Doc during his stay in Dodge was getting acquainted with Wyatt Berry Stapp Earp. Many years later Earp was to make himself out the *beau ideal* of the mesquite to such an extent as to completely justify his middle initials of B. S. But right now, when Doc knew him, he was well on in his career as a failure and yet the very embodiment of the silent, manly personality; so no one realized he was anything but a great guy and as good an assistant marshal as Dodge was likely to find. One of the clumsiest yet most indefatigable politicians and string-pullers that ever lived, he radiated integrity and trustworthiness. Anybody could tell by looking at him that he was above any kind of shady dealing, that he was thoroughly honest, brave, and sincere in every undertaking. Two more completely misunderstood men never lived than Doc Holliday and Wyatt Earp. They probably never understood each other until one day in Pueblo, Colorado, in the late spring of 1882. And then they never spoke to each other again. But now they were just getting to know each other well, the professional gambler and the gambler-law-officer meeting daily in the saloons and gambling halls and honky-tonks of the lively little cattle-shipping center.

Doc is supposed to have saved Wyatt Earp's life. Even Wyatt's most bitter enemy among those who survived to write memoirs, Allie Earp, widow of his older brother, Virgil, mentions it. Allie was no admirer of Doc's, either, speaking of him with a hatred that only jealousy or scorned attention could produce. Or, perhaps, since she hated Wyatt so cordially, she would naturally extend this same emotion to a person responsible for his continuing among the living. At any rate, we are forced to question Wyatt Earp's grandiloquent version of the affair: faced by prominent cattlemen Tobe Driscoll and Ed Morrison and a couple of dozen blood-crazed Texans who had the drop on him, he is rescued dramatically by one lone little Doc Holliday dashing up with a gun in each hand. Drawing his own gun in safety now (still faced by fifty guns, none of which is fired) Wyatt proceeded to slam his gun barrel over Morrison's head, felling him. Still none of the yaller-bellied Texans has guts enough to shoot the gritty upholder of law and order. He then yelled to the others to drop their guns —and at last one Texan was insane enough to twitch his thumb back on the hammer. Doc, fast and deadly as a cobra with a gun, saw the Texan throw down, beat him to it, and plugged him in the shoulder. He and City Marshal Earp (this is Mr. Earp's version, remember) then herded the mob over to the jail where they all spent the night and next morning they were fined from one hundred to twenty-five dollars each.

There is no mention of such a superlative deed of daring in

either of the Dodge City papers, neither does the very carefully kept docket of Judge Marshall show Driscoll and Morrison's names nor any twenty-some arrested in one fell swoop. Assistant Marshal Earp was responsible for thirty-five arrests in all of 1878 and for twelve during 1879,[10] which makes small potatoes out of the second year and doesn't leave much in the way of work for 1878 if he only arrested eight people beside the Driscoll-Morrison crowd. Others, speaking of the affair, make it out that Earp tried to arrest three drunken Texans, one of whom pulled a gun on him, only to have Doc leap up from a nearby poker game and invite the Texan to reconsider. The clincher on a milder version would seem to be Earp's earlier account of the affair, which appeared in Hearst's San Francisco *Examiner* for Sunday, August 2, 1896. Over Mr. Earp's signature and apparently written by him we find: "It wasn't long after I returned to Dodge City that his [Doc Holliday's] quickness saved my life. He saw a man draw on me behind my back. 'Look out, Wyatt!' he shouted, but while the words were coming out of his mouth he had jerked his pistol out of his pocket and shot the other fellow before the latter could fire. On such incidents as that are built the friendships of the frontier."

Whatever happened, though, one thing tells us that Doc did something important for Wyatt Earp: every student of psychology learns early that doing a favor for a person disposes one to like them. The more important the deed, the greater the attachment. Saving a person's life, then, would tend to produce a mutual admiration society and such apparently was the relationship between Doc Holliday and Wyatt Earp. Doc wasn't able to play the desperado continually; around Wyatt he seems to have relaxed and been himself, cross but not criminal, unhappy but not self-pitying, and lonely, faithful and brave.

For the next two years Wyatt Earp's story is to be Doc Holliday's story. Neither one of them did the other any good, and indeed, their very friendship may have caused many deaths, even Doc's own. Here is where the tragedy blazes up—these two and

134

their characteristics met under an evil sign. And the shadow of the bloody left hand of the McKey coat of arms falls on Doc and everyone he knows.

Anyway, the time came when Doc and Wyatt were always seen together, inseparable friends.

This trail-herd season was quite mild. The grass was short around Dodge, so the herds were somewhat delayed, and many cattle were not shipped from Dodge at all, but driven on north to Ogallala and beyond. There were two big events in Dodge this summer, a strawberry and ice cream festival to benefit the Presbyterian minister, Rev. O. W. Wright, the biggest social event ever seen in Dodge, and the payment by the Santa Fe, after eleven years of operation, of its first dividend to its stockholders. It was a civilized summer—the brawls of previous years had lost out in popularity to dances, the twenty bodies on Boot Hill were dug up and replanted at Prairie Grove Cemetery, a school was built on the site of the old graveyard, and two no-liquor hotels were opened.

This summer Wyatt's brother, Virgil, and his young wife, Allie, left their farm and headed for Arizona by way of Dodge. Wyatt had never met Allie, so Virgil, after locating him in a saloon, brought him to the wagon to be introduced. Allie, fresh off the farm and neither very bright nor very sophisticated, had taken her shoes off in the wagon and when Virgil introduced Wyatt she stuck her dirty bare foot into his nice, white gambler's hand—just for a joke.[11] Wyatt was too dignified and formal to be anything but disgusted by such childish behavior. His feud with his sister-in-law seems to date from this first episode. Virgil and Allie headed on west and settled down in Prescott, Arizona, at least temporarily.

Dodge got calmer and more citified in behavior every day. Wyatt Earp wasn't the kind to hide his light under a bushel, and while everyone called him "Marshal," he knew it was a courtesy title, like "Colonel" when one is really a lieutenant-colonel, and that he was not the big dog he longed to be. Stories galloped into Dodge that the new Arizona silver camp, Tombstone, was the coming boom camp of the whole west. It seemed to have no law, so perhaps here he could get to be the fearless enforcer of order that he knew he could be if he just had the chance. He saw glittering visions of sheriff's stars and marshal's scrolls, law of the frontier, Wyatt Earp, and also the possibility of a good income. That fall he set off for Prescott.

Doc and Kate stayed in Dodge and settled down for a cosy winter.

By now Doc had built the demon-self a little too well. He was beginning to believe it himself. As his mind soaked up more and more alcohol it withdrew more and more from reality, warping itself into the world that Doc wanted to live in. And yet his personality was such that no one thought to call his bluff. When he said "Jump!" people jumped. He was so obviously the cold-blooded killer that no one dreamed it was only an act, a suit of armor worn to protect him from the insults of an unrefined community. With no one to remind him of this, he forgot that it wasn't true, apparently.

Not content to let well enough alone, he wasn't above throwing his weight around. He liked to make people back down, and every time he came out master in some cold-eyed bluff, he believed more in the "dream" killer. For amusement in the long winter he ran a bartender named Charley White out of town, with the promise of killing him if he ever saw him again.

Wyatt Earp wrote that someone had gone along with him to Prescott—a most interesting person whom we shall meet presently. Also his oldest brother, James, and the latter's wife, Bessie, and step-daughter Hattie, had converged on Virgil Earp's place in the hills west of Prescott,[12] and from there had come to Tombstone,[13] arriving about December 1, 1879. Doc was advised to lose no time in heading for Tombstone. The town wasn't organized, but when things settled down the Earps planned to be on top. Doc couldn't lose.

As spring came on Doc began to weigh his assets. Bat Masterson, a very good friend of Wyatt's, had been defeated for re-election as sheriff of Ford County and had gone to Tombstone. Luke Short was there, too. All the gambling, gun-throwing element in Dodge was going where the money was now that the trail-herd crowd was getting so tame. And besides, miners had the reputation of being gambling fools—a reputation he had often seen proved in Deadwood.

Doc had to wait for reinforcements in the way of money, but soon after the trail-herd season started, he made a large sum at the poker tables and was ready to start for Tombstone. His most important purchase in preparation for the new venture was in the artillery department. A new model of the 1873 Colt had come out, chambered for the same bullet the popular .44–40 Winchester rifle took. This particular ammunition was available everywhere, even in the far desert of Arizona, so naturally old Be Prepared had to have one of the new models. Since he habitually carried his gun either tucked inside his vest or in a shoulder holster, he had the barrel cut off. Kate had a tantrum that was heard halfway to Kansas City, threatening to kill herself at first, and then to kill Doc, so he at last agreed to take her with him. It was the first part of June, 1880, when they left Dodge.

No one was ever heard to wish them back. . . .

FOOTNOTES TO CHAPTER 8

1. February 23, 1878.
2. Ford County *Globe*, April 8, 1879.
3. Hazard is a complicated dice game, the parent of craps.
4. Dodge City *Times*, May 4, 1882.
5. This account is based on testimony given at the coroner's inquest and printed in the Ford County *Globe*, April 8, 1879. Cockeyed Frank Loving got his almost exactly three years later in Trinidad, Colorado, the *Rocky Mountain News* for April 18, 1882, reporting that he had been killed in a gun fight with one John Allen. It was a chase-all-over-town affair. Loving ran out of ammunition and by coincidence went into the very hardware store in which Allen was hiding from him. Allen, barricaded behind a counter, shot him easily.
6. *Santa Fe, The Railroad That Built an Empire.*
7. Possibly these girls only appeared at the Comique during the season of 1878.
8. I learned these and many other folk songs from my maternal grandmother who, for all that she was a true pioneer and lived many years in a sod house, looked the opposite of the commonly-held picture of a pioneer woman, being chubby, cheerful, and always singing. The popular songs of Doc's day were found in the music section of the Library of Congress.
9. *Kansas, A Guide to the Sunflower State.*
10. *Dodge City, Queen of Cowtowns*, Stanley Vestal, Harper and Brothers, New York, 1952.
11. "Tombstone Travesty, the Memoirs of Mrs. Virgil Earp," by Frank Waters. Manuscript at the Arizona Pioneers' Historical Society, Tucson, Arizona.
12. Prescott, Arizona, *Weekly Arizona Miner*, October 3, 1879, and Mrs. Virgil Earp's memoirs.
13. *Weekly Arizona Miner*, November 14, 1879.

9

Doc Wings

Charley White

In Dodge the trainmen slung a whole rack of Winchesters into the baggage car and prepared for anything. This was the day of Jesse James, and Billy the Kid was yet alive, so it was considered a good policy to be foresighted about trouble out in the lonely stretches of the Great American Desert. As they rattled along, Doc was surprised at the way the area was filling up with people. Eight small towns had sprung up between Dodge and Pueblo and the scraggly outlines of windmills could be seen here and there in the vastness over which only cloud shadows had chased the year before. Pueblo was becoming a prosperous industrial town and here Doc and Kate spent a day or two seeing the sights before they got on the fanciest train the Santa Fe ran, the *De Luxe Express* to Santa Fe. It had four cars: a combination coach with one end for ladies and the other for smokers; a sleeping car; a chair car paneled in hardwood and furnished with huge chairs upholstered in red plush; and a baggage-express-mail car—all pulled by the mighty Uncle Dick. Where once the little 4-4-0 engines had struggled over Raton Pass hauling a baggage car and a lone coach decorated with a sign asking the passengers not to get off to pick wild flowers while the train was in motion,[1] they now breezed through the dark tunnel in a smother of coal smoke and were in New Mexico before they could get the cinders wept out of their eyes.

And in New Mexico was Charley White. Doc smoothed down his mustache and grinned. They said he was working in a saloon in Old Town in Las Vegas.

Over Kate's protests they got off in East Las Vegas.

Doc had been in Old Town (West Las Vegas) before, on his way to Denver from Texas, and remembered it as a sleepy little adobe village nestled under great cottonwoods around a little plaza. On July 4, 1879, the Santa Fe had come, missing the town by just enough to allow New Town (officially East Las Vegas) to spring up along the tracks. A bunch of roughnecks had immediately taken over New Town, filling all the positions of local government and managing things to suit themselves. This was precisely the same thing that had happened in Dodge, but with greatly different results. The cowboys were just average kids at heart who were apt to get out of hand when likkered up. The tough element ran the town with no trouble. In Las Vegas the tough crowd had a tough bunch to handle—the sporting set that flocked wherever the railroad construction crews had their headquarters, members of Billy the Kid's loosely-knit gang of friends and sympathizers, and a fine collection of road agents, horse thieves and paranoids. They all wanted a share in the city government pot. The result was that law and outlawry became indistinguishable as they fought over the plum, and decent citizens were forced to become Vigilantes. Things quieted down somewhat after various prominent residents were used to decorate the windmill in Old Town plaza.

Doc and Kate took a hotel room and Doc set out to look the situation over and ask a few questions. Kate was told to stay in the room and not make any trouble. After a while he came back and told Kate that Charley White was working as a bartender in a saloon on a corner of the plaza [2] in Old Town. The two had a silent, strained dinner, then Doc ordered his worried mistress

140

back to the room and set off through the mountain-shadowed twilight for the plaza.

The air is wonderful in Las Vegas, the fresh-from-the-mountains, invigorating, golden air of New Mexico, and a quiet atmosphere of old-time charm still lingers in the old buildings that Doc walked by that evening. But Doc wasn't just walking along enjoying the quaintness of Old Town or watching the windows turn to glowing golden squares as the lamps were lit. He was planning a plan: how to kill Charley White and get away with it.

In the best Old West tradition one should begin to say to oneself, "Alas for Charley White, stalked by the most cold-blooded killer in the West." But. . . .

The onslaught by Doc on Charley, as we have already seen, turned out to be closer to farce than to tragedy, with Charley merely stunned by a bullet crease along his back. It left not even a scar to remind him, when he was safely back in law-abiding Boston, Massachusetts, of his Wild West days. But in all fairness to Doc's lousy marksmanship, it may be said that the revolvers of those days were far from dead-shot weapons and their kick-back was often more injurious than their bullets.

Doc, having killed Charley (as he fondly imagined), returned his weapon to its holster and, before Charley's resuscitation, sauntered out of the saloon and down the street.

And everything in Doc was singing. People he walked by on the street glanced uncomfortably away from his blazing eyes and the mad smile on his face. Kate had seen him worn out and shaking after pulling a bluff on someone in Dodge, but she had never seen him like this. She straightened up quickly from lighting a cigarette [3] in the up-draft of the lamp chimney and cried, "Doc, you're hit!"

He could never explain the wild joy that was all of him. The pure love of a gun fight had swept away everything recognizable. "Got him," he said laconically, and automatically reached for the bourbon bottle.

No record or newspaper mention could be found to authenticate this story. Why accept it then, and not those in Jacksboro and Denver? Setting aside Bat Masterson's story of Doc killing a man in Las Vegas, we come to Miguel Antonio Otero. Mr. Otero was the Las Vegas representative of Otero, Sellar and Co., one of the largest government contractors in the west, when Doc came to Las Vegas. He had grown up in the west and was yet young; later he was to become the governor of New Mexico and to occupy a position of the highest respect. In his *My Life on the Frontier* [4] he tells the story of Doc versus Charley White. It is the very plainness of the tale that makes us want to believe it. Two men face each other across a saloon and shoot and shoot and shoot and shoot and nobody gets hit until the very last and then not seriously. Mr. Otero says Doc must have been having an off day with his marksmanship. It never seems to occur to anyone to wonder why Doc has his gun out and cocked, and why even with the drop on his victim, can usually be counted on to miss entirely or merely graze the man. That's indoctrination for you. Later on we shall see this identical pattern of the Charley White gun fight pop up in every shooting Doc gets into. Mr. Otero didn't know that Doc Holliday was one of the lousiest shots that ever jerked a trigger. He told his story as it happened and apologized because it didn't fit the mythical Doc Holliday better. Also on the side of believing this story is that there are people in Las Vegas who remember hearing about it, in contrast to the Jacksboro shooting and the Fort Griffin rescue by Big Nosed Kate, which nobody in those towns ever heard of. But most important, it sounds like Doc and not like the blood-thirsty-sure-shot killer he posed as and which the blowhard boys who survived him continued to make him out to be for the greater glory of the Old West.

Ah, well. Here is Doc, gun in hand, and he has shot somebody at last after nearly eight years in the most desperate society available.

He and Kate gave Las Vegas a thorough going-over and finally decided to go on to Tombstone. In the three or four days they

142

spent in town Miguel Antonio Otero had several opportunities to talk to Doc and found him very pleasant and agreeable. Why not? Otero belonged to one of the oldest and most prominent families in New Mexico and Doc was a gentleman speaking to a gentleman.

At last Doc and Kate got on the train, headed for Tombstone— and destiny.

FOOTNOTES TO CHAPTER 9

1. *Santa Fe, The Railroad That Built an Empire.*
2. Miguel Antonio Otero says the saloon was where the First National Bank now stands and some present-day Las Vegas-ites say it was the saloon of the Plaza Hotel.
3. Cigarettes had been invented the decade preceding the Civil War. The first mention I found of them was in the Cheyenne *Wyoming Weekly Leader* for March 1, 1877: "Cigarettes are very unhealthy, but there are a great many men who still borrow them."
4. *Press of the Pioneers*, New York, 1935, in two volumes.

10

Tombstone, Arizona,

1880-1881

To get one thing off my chest first: Wyatt Earp was married all the time he was in Tombstone. Why he chose later to pose as the prime mover of a fictitious bachelor establishment I have no idea. In her memoirs Mrs. Virgil Earp speaks of Wyatt as arriving at their place in Prescott and later moving to Tombstone with his wife, Mattie. The 1880 census for Tombstone lists as living in the same house on Allen Street the following persons: Earp, Virgil W., age 36, married, occupation, farmer; Earp, Alley, age 22, wife, occupation, keeping house; Earp, Wyatt S., age 32, married, occupation, farmer; Earp, Mattie, age 22, wife, occupation, keeping house; Earp, James A., age 39, married, occupation, saloon keeper; Earp, Bessie, age 36, wife, occupation, keeping house; Earp, Hattie, age 16, daughter. And the Tombstone *Epitaph* of March 27, 1882, says: "Mrs. James Earp and Mrs. Wyatt Earp left today. . . ."

What Mattie Earp looked like, what her past had been, I have no idea. There was no record of Wyatt Earp getting or being married in Dodge. Perhaps someone came riding after him when he left for Tombstone, someone who tied her horse to the back of his wagon and said, "I don't care what happens, take me with you." Perhaps they were married in some now-vanished settlement. Perhaps they were never legally married at all. But they passed as man and wife in Tombstone. After Wyatt left Tombstone she went to his parents' home in California. What eventually happened to her I don't know. Absolutely unverified rumor has it that she killed herself in Wilcox, Arizona, soon afterward.

This summer of 1880 Doc was twenty-eight years old. He was still very thin, very pale. His blue eyes were fading to a cold, hard gray and white hairs were plentiful enough now to make his hair seem ash blond. His consumption was a habit; he couldn't remember what it was like to feel good. Alcoholism was continuing to deteriorate his personality and his hangovers were perfect marvels to behold: until he got that first drink in the morning he felt as if he were dying. His heart fluttered wildly, it didn't feel as if he had any lungs left to breathe with, he shook uncontrollably, his mouth felt as if it had been painted with moisture-proofing compound, he couldn't see and couldn't bear to hear. Recovered from this, he looked at the day ahead with a wholehearted and thoroughly understandable foulness of disposition. Only his friends were any good of all the people that lived. A growing impotency made him actively hate poor Kate. Mattie was, over two thousand miles away, his saint, his star. If he had married her he would most likely have beaten her, accused her of infidelity, and used her as a doormat for his emotional outbursts just as he did Kate. But Mattie was inaccessible, chaste, another dream in his world of dreams. All in all, he was the perfect alcoholic. Vanity was large in his make-up and he knocked four years off his age; [1] he could, when he wanted to, charm the birds off the trees. When he didn't want to bother, as in the case of small, blonde, silly Mrs. Virgil Earp, he got himself described as cold and disagreeable.

You had to know him very well indeed to recognize his virtues. His fortitude was perhaps foremost, and least appreciated by his associates. Since he never complained, no one realized how really badly off he was until they saw the quantities of liquor it took to get him back on his feet after some strenuous physical exertion. In a state of mind where nothing was ever sacred, he still never men-

146

tioned Mattie even to his closest friends. He might approach a gun fight from the basest of motives, with his gun in his hand, with no warning to his opponent, but when he was being shot at in return he stood his ground in the midst of the flying bullets and never once flinched or made any effort to get away. Apparently the thrill of a gun fight was the prime exhilaration of his life. If you had been accepted as his friend, you were his friend and that was that, no matter what you did or what you were accused of. It was the sure knowledge of this that made his friends trust him so unquestioningly in return. And although he drank around two quarts of 100-proof whisky every day, he managed to stay on the wide fringe of normal life: his person and his clothes were immaculate, his manner was quiet and refined, he worked hard at his profession.

For Doc and Kate to arrive in the Sonoran Desert in mid-June, even to stay at an altitude of 4,500 feet, was not to undergo a pleasant experience. The temperature has a habit of getting stuck at 120 degrees [2] and they sweltered until the tropical storms boiled up from Mexico. Kansas dust was to the Arizona dust as a gnat's pee to a cloudburst. The animal life was beyond amazement: tarantulas, centipedes, wolf spiders, trap-door spiders, scorpions, and bugs, bugs, bugs, the majority of which were said to be poisonous unless their sting was immediately swabbed with ammonia.[3] And Tombstone was having a ruckus of some sort all the time—shootings, stabbings, fights and near things occurring around the clock.

After a few days in Chris Bilicke's fashionable Cosmopolitan Hotel, Doc got Kate settled in a little dwelling of a type frequent in the southwest at the time and still surviving quaintly in Tucson and defiantly in Tombstone: a long, narrow edifice runs along the length of the sidewalk; it is divided into a row of single rooms with a door into the street and another into the alley behind. Built of adobe, with long windows down to the ground, these rooms are very cool. Kate's was in a row on the disreputable north side of Allen Street, at the corner of Sixth,[4] with the Soma winery on one side of the building and a funeral parlor on the other. The furnishings hardly strained Doc at all. A table was six dollars, two chairs about the same, a curtain was a dollar and a quarter, a lamp six dollars, a stove and fixings were a little over eight dollars, a basin and glass one dollar, a good wool mattress was six dollars, and a pillow one dollar.[5] Perhaps it wasn't very bon ton, but they weren't planning on doing any lavish entertaining.

Of course the first thing Doc did in Tombstone was to find Wyatt Earp. He and his wife were living in the next block west on Allen from where Kate settled, in a little dirt-floored adobe just about across the street from where the Bird Cage Theater was to be built a year later. Wyatt was working as a shotgun messenger for Wells, Fargo & Co. The Virgil Earps lived on the other side of a vacant lot from Wyatt, and Virg was working on the Tombstone police force as a special officer.[6] James Earp, oldest of the brothers, was working as a faro dealer. He and his wife and step-daughter had lived for a while with the Virgil Earps and then moved to the corner of First and Frémont. Morgan Earp, youngest of the four [7] and a year older than Doc, lived with Virgil and his wife, doing such odd jobs around as he could pick up.[8] In the journal kept by George Whitwell Parsons [9] he quotes a friend of his, one Milton Clapp, manager of Safford and Hudson's bank, as saying that there was only one woman in town that he would allow his wife to associate with, and that was Mrs. Clum, wife of the editor of the *Tombstone Epitaph*. Good old pioneer stock, the Earps, but. . . .

From Wyatt Doc got the low-down on what was going on around town. Tombstone, hardly a year old, was located in Pima County, of which Tucson was county seat. Charley Shibell, complete with mustache and imperial, a resident of Arizona since 1862 and a real frontiersman in the Apache country, was sheriff. The mayor of Tombstone was Alder Randall, whose chief activity appeared to be the aiding and abetting of town-lot claim jumping by his friends. One's only resource was to defend one's property at gun point, the town patent not having been allowed yet and all property being mining claims. The town marshal, Fred White, was both brave and honest, and apparently tried to keep out of this mess and confine his activities to arresting shooters and such, although from the way they flourished his efforts seemed futile. Ordinarily miners were more in the habit of getting into fracases of the slugging sort, but just about everyone went heeled this year because of the lot-jumping in town, mine-claim jumping, armed assaults and robberies which were so frequent at night, and poisonous snakes, gila monsters, hydrophobia skunks and horse thieves abounding. Consequently there was more shooting than the natural inclination of the citizenry warranted.

Just as Kate was getting settled in her adobe, the heat broke and the dust which was Tombstone's curse was swept away by nightly rains. The days were a delight, so fresh, so sparkling, the world become young and filled with joy, confident with hope, a-glitter with song. The air was the jewel amethyst washed clean of dust, worth travelling the world around to see. Only squat little adobe and frame houses and stores, here and there an adobe of two stories housing a hall or hotel, everything ugly and real and vivid, but softly glittering in this amethyst light—Tombstone had not (nor has, still, when the weather is right) its equal for beauty in the world. At night the thunderstorms fairly rolled down the streets. Torrents of water beat the plaster sealing the porous adobe walls. In the early morning Doc would come in, leaving the gleaming grey world to turn gold and pink under the dawn, and examine the adobe walls for cracks which would tell that the rain had worked under the eaves and down inside the mud walls to bring the house collapsing around their ears. And then he would put on a clean nightshirt and lie down to enjoy in peace and quiet the dawn lighting the town named Tombstone, the feel of air that was the carefree air of boyhood when the day was born eternally without care—if he had to beat Kate senseless to do it. He, who could not remember when he had felt good, was beginning to remember what feeling good was like. The magic of the air of Tombstone was drawing him out of himself, into an awareness of his surroundings, away from being sunk in the misery of a painful existence which was but the threshold to death.

Tombstone, with a population of 2,000 (which would triple in a year and a half), was lively in a way Dodge had never dreamed of being. Despite the lack of legal building sites, new structures of all types were being erected thick and fast. All day and night the tall iron-rimmed tires of the ore wagons rumbled through the dirt streets carrying Tombstone's prosperity to the stamp mills on the San Pedro, meanwhile grinding the street dirt to a fineness that could sift through anything. The saloons catered to the various shifts of miners day and night and faro was king in the gambling halls, with poker as prime minister. Loose women paraded on the north side of Allen Street and solicited business as they pleased, dragging the ruffled flounces of their gaudy "tied-back" dresses through the dust with an air of incomparably sensuous negligence. Cowboys from the cattle country in which Tombstone was located; teamsters and muleskinners busy freighting supplies from the end of steel to Tombstone, the copper-mining area further south and on down into Mexico and back; wealthy investors; tourists; job seekers; local businessmen; cattlemen; Mexicans; drifters; professional gamblers and gunmen—all walked the warped board sidewalks under wooden awnings which lined Allen Street. The sound most frequently heard was the *swoosh* made by swinging doors as they were batted open.

The Oriental, on the northeast corner of Fifth and Allen, was the most elaborate and best-patronized saloon in town. On the corner across Fifth was the Eagle Brewery saloon and free lunch.[10] Adjoining it on Allen was a cigar store and card room, then a barber and bath shop, Wells, Fargo & Co., Campbell and Hatch's saloon, the Alhambra saloon, a clothing store, the Occidental saloon, the Cosmopolitan Hotel (also housing the Maison Dorée restaurant, the best in town, and Fortlouis' cigar store), the Sultana cigar store and card room, and Hafford's saloon on the corner of Allen and Fourth.[11]

Doc spent most of his time in this area, particularly at Meagher and Melgren's Alhambra saloon. His foresight in getting involved in a recent gun fight, even if he had yet to kill his man, was plainly seen now. They didn't sit around talking about who looked like gun fighters in Tombstone—they knew them. Soon after Doc's arrival the murdered body of a Mexican was found in the city water supply, with gruesome evidence of a couple weeks' sojourn.[12] Before anyone had stopped tasting poor Pedro, the Perrine-Killeen-Leslie gun fight took place. It was June 22, 1880.

Buckskin Frank Leslie, a bartender at the Oriental, was reported to be a fast man on the draw and a good shot. Mr. Leslie's opinion of himself included being a lady-killer. On this particular night he had taken May Killeen, who also happened to be Mrs. Mike Killeen, to a ball at the Grand Hotel despite her husband's threats to kill him if he did. At midnight he walked May over to the Cosmopolitan Hotel across the street (where his room was) and sat down with her on the porch. He put his "big Colt six-shooter" [13] on the floor beside him, just in case. Suddenly Mike Killeen arrived. He arrived shooting. Leslie shot back. Somehow his friend, George Perrine, coming to warn him that Mike Killeen was looking for him, got mixed up in the fray. When the smoke cleared Killeen was found seriously wounded. He died within a week. It was never decided whether Perrine or Leslie had killed him, but anyway Buckskin Frank and the Widow Killeen were married on August 6, 1880.

This was so delightfully scandalous that the rest of the summer's slayings seem quite ordinary by comparison. George Parsons listed such doings locally as he thought important: the arrival of the telegraph on July 13, a "terrible scene by a leading prostitute on the st. tonight" on July 14, and on the 24th, "Another man killed night before last. Too much loose pistol practise. Bradshaw killed Waters because Waters resented with his fist being teased about a shirt." "A lot of us had a good time at the ice-cream place tonight," he wrote on the 26th, and on the 30th, "Still another man killed—Wilson—shot dead this A.M. by King, an anti-Chinese agitator who is at the head of a movement here to drive out the Chinese." On August 9 it was, "Night foreman of Contention [one of the largest mines] stabbed by a discharged hand who escaped. Nearly killed." And on August 29, "Another man killed last night—shot dead—a

Capt. Malgan. Things are getting to a pretty pass. The death roll since I came here, I mean violent deaths—shootings—and poisonings—foots up fearfully large. I have not recorded all. Something must be done. Lynch law is very effective at times—in a community like this." The *Epitaph* printed what amounted to a box score for Pima County: twenty-five homicides, fifteen arrests, one trial in a year.[14]

Two years in Dodge hadn't produced such an array of killings as a little over two months did in Tombstone.

And tough as Tombstone was, the area round it, soon to be Cochise County, was even tougher. Old Man Clanton led a free association of friends and fellow hard cases largely formed from young men of the cowboy type who had drifted into Arizona looking for excitement and easy money. His right and left bowers were Curly Bill Broscius, a Texas tough notorious for being too free with his trigger finger, and John Ringgold, known as Ringo, a well-educated souse noted for his fearlessness. Clanton's kids, Phil (or Phin), Ike and Billy, were in the thick of the trouble. They styled themselves cowboys and ranchers and expected to be treated as respectable businessmen when they came to Tombstone from their headquarters in nearby Charleston. And why not—none of their victims had guts enough to swear out warrants for their arrest. They made their living by smuggling goods in and out of Mexico, by stealing cattle, and by armed robbery and gambling.

The extent of their depredations in the rustling line can be seen from the following letter which appeared in the *Epitaph*: [15] "Editor Epitaph: I am not a growler or chronic grumbler, but I own stock, am a butcher and supply my immediate neighborhood beef, and to do so must keep cattle on hand, and do try to and could do so always if I had not to divide with unknown and irresponsible partners, viz: 'Cow Boys,' or some other cattle thieves. Since my advent into the territory and more particularly on the San Pedro River, I have lost 50 head of cattle by cattle thieves. I am not the only sufferer from these marauders and cattle thieves on the San Pedro, within the last six months. Aside from 50 head of good beef

152

cattle that I have been robbed of, Judge Blair has lost his entire herd. P. McMinnimen has lost all of his fine fat steers (oxen). Dunbar at Tres Alamos, has lost a number of head. Burton of Huachuca, lost almost his entire herd, and others—and in fact all engaged in the stock business—have lost heavily from cattle thieves. And not always do these thieves confine themselves to cattle; horses and mules are gobbled up by these robbers, as well as cattle. Is there no way to stop this wholesale stealing of stock in this vicinity or in the county? (signed) T. W. Ayles, Cattle Dealer."

But if you said a dirty word on the street in Tombstone you were promptly jugged.

The Earps were apparently unable to do much about local law-lessness of other than a petty nature, although Virg was a special officer under Marshal White, and Wyatt was now appointed civil deputy sheriff for the Tombstone area by Sheriff Shibell. The July 31, 1880, *Epitaph* had congratulated him on his appointment and added, "Morgan Earp succeeds his brother as shotgun messenger for Wells, Fargo & Co."

It was evident that these Earps could be useful; two of them legally carrying guns, a third entrusted with protecting Wells, Fargo & Co.'s bullion shipments, and Doc Holliday, the killer, making a fourth. A gang to be reckoned with. And there was someone in town who needed a gang to be reckoned with. The popular Oriental saloon was being high-pressured by Johnny Tyler, a professional gambler with none too ethical a reputation, into taking him into partnership in the gambling room. Tyler, with the aid of his friends, was keeping the Oriental in a constant uproar, starting fights, getting loud, scaring away peaceably dispositioned gamblers, rattling the faro dealers with a string of caustic comments, and generally behaving like a gangster of fifty years later making a bid for "protection" pay-offs. Lou Rickabaugh, chief of the owners of the gambling concession, refused to be forced into hiring Tyler if it meant losing everything—and the way Tyler was keeping the customers away, it looked as if that might very well happen.

Finally Rickabaugh came to Wyatt Earp and offered to sell him a one-fourth interest in the gambling concession at the Oriental if he would tame Tyler and keep order in the place. Knowing how profitable such a venture would be, Wyatt promptly took it up. After telling the good news to his brothers and Doc, Wyatt started out for the Oriental with his chest all puffed out with authority.

Remembering how once in Dodge he had had to rescue Wyatt from the results of a grandstand play, Doc tagged along. Sure enough, Wyatt dragged Tyler out the door of the Oriental by his ear and Doc had to pull his gun to discourage Tyler's friends from shooting Wyatt in the back as he did so.

Tyler went straight to his room, armed himself and headed back for the Oriental.

"You think you're so much with a gun. Start something with *me*!" he cried, batting in the door and spotting Doc standing at the bar. "Come on out in the street. I'll have it out with you."

Cautious customers flexed their knees preparatory to hitting the floor.

Doc set down his glass and smiled contentedly. A fight. That was just his meat. He walked up to Tyler and said, "Why go out in the street? What's wrong with where we stand? Ready?"

Tyler looked at Doc in amazement. He was close enough to spit on, and there was not the slightest sign of bluff about him. In fact, he looked like a crazy man, his eyes clouded with fire, his lips thinned into a smile, his thin white hand inching steadily toward the bosom of his coat.

"No, let's—" Tyler gestured awkwardly toward the door, his eyes unable to meet Doc's.

"You wanted a fight—go for your gun!" Doc cried. His smile deepened and he took a swift step toward Tyler. "Go for your gun!"

Tyler turned and tore out the door.

Doc walked over and peered out after him. "Tsk! Still running," he commented mildly.

Everyone in the room burst out laughing. They laughed big-talking Johnny Tyler right out of Tombstone. "Stopped running,

Johnny?" met him every place he went. He couldn't even get in a game. And finally, swearing to get even with Doc, Johnny Tyler left town. He might have been lacking in certain characteristics, but he was aces with a grudge, as Doc was to find out years later.

Wyatt and his wife moved to a neat little frame house at the corner of First and Frémont, next door to James and his family. It was across the street from the Mexican section, but a great improvement over the wrong side of Allen Street. Later Virg and Allie and Morg moved in catty-corner and all the Earps were together, as usual.[16] The women, when not running in and out of each others' houses, made curtains and got their gardens started. Virg kept on as a special officer, Morg quit his Wells, Fargo job and went to work dealing faro at the Oriental, and Wyatt divided his time between such duties as his deputy-sheriff, tax-collector position called for and the "club room" at his saloon. Doc continued to hang out at the Alhambra.

The shootings and hell raisings continued almost as regularly as the changes of shifts at the Contention, the Tough Nut, the Lucky Cuss, the Grand Central and the other mines on Tombstone's plateau and across the bare Tombstone hills south of town. Boot Hill, on the other side of town, overlooking the San Pedro Valley, was filling up.

Marshal White was generally unable to prevent the impromptu gun firings for which Tombstone was noted, but when a bunch of the wild cowboys undertook to hurrah the town on October 28, 1880, he did promptly set out to subdue them. While disarming their leader, Curly Bill Broscius of the Clanton gang, Marshal White was wounded by the accidental discharge of the cowboy's revolver. Wyatt Earp, who was happening by, ran to the assistance of the marshal and crowned Curly Bill with the twelve-inch barrel of his special Colt [17] and dragged him off to jail. Then he, Virg and Morg rounded up the other cowboys and tossed them in after their stunned leader.[18] When it was realized that Marshal White was going to die from the effects of this shooting and that a vigilance committee was being formed to hang Curly Bill by due process of a rope, the Earps went into action again. Wyatt and one George Collins loaded the prisoner into a buggy and departed rapidly for Tucson, guarded for several miles out of town by Virg, Morg, and others.[19] Before he died Marshal White exonerated Curly Bill of any intent to injure him, and the cowboys were released. Curly Bill seems to have stuck pretty close to Charleston after this when he was in the mood to shoot up a town.

Virgil Earp was appointed town marshal in Fred White's place, to serve until the city elections in January, 1881. But the Earps never had a monopoly on local law enforcement. Sheriff Shibell fired Wyatt as deputy sheriff and appointed loyal Democrat John H. Behan (pronounced Bee-un) in his place. Behan was a Yavapai man, a former member of the Territorial legislature who was well known around Prescott and had friends in the right places. He had a fine working knowledge of politics; "influence" and "fixes" were second nature to him. He was an excellent politician and would probably have made Tombstone an acceptable mayor, but he didn't have law-enforcement gumption, as the Earps didn't have election-eering gumption. On the surface friendly with the Earps, he must have disliked them in his heart, because he was a sensitive fellow—and they had the laugh on him.

They had been in Prescott for a few months themselves, and they weren't above asking Behan how his Chinese friends were. Nothing mean, you understand, just a josh. The Prescott paper recorded the reason: "Hon. John H. Behan had occasion to call at the Chinese laundry this P.M., when a controversy arose, leading to some half-dozen of the pig-tail race making an assault on him with clubs. He tried to defend himself with a revolver, which, un-fortunately, failed to work. He received several severe cuts about the head." [20] Now, the Chinese were rock-bottom low in the western scale of things, and for an officer to have a history of not being able to defend himself against any number of them was just downright pitiful. The very next week's issue of the Prescott paper recorded that Behan had left town. But he never succeeded in run-ning away from the story of the Celestials beating him up.

156

Doc had a place all his own in the scheme of things in Tombstone. He knew that Wyatt wanted to be appointed sheriff of the new county which was soon to be formed with Tombstone as the shire town. So he stayed in the background. He had a reputation as a killer (which he valued more than diamonds) and this could be bad for the Earps with certain people. He never threw his weight around as he had in Dodge and he curbed his delight in running men out of town after showing what he was capable of with Johnny Tyler. But he saw to it that everyone in Tombstone knew that if there was any trouble the Earps had a dangerous man with a gun backing them up.

He spent most of his time in the Alhambra, running his own faro bank, working hard, keeping his nose clean. But knowing that Wyatt Earp and Johnny Behan were both edgy with each other, Doc was unable to resist the temptation to bite a large chunk out of the new deputy sheriff. He got a big charge out of it—and made himself an enemy with really amazing qualities in the hating line.

Johnny Behan's self-esteem was largely propped up by his picture of himself as being irresistible to women. His personality, looks, virility made a net no woman could escape. And Doc knew Behan had this opinion of himself. Doc also rather thought the women noticed him and not Behan (later we'll see at least one perfectly respectable woman recognizing Doc when she saw him on the street, but not the town marshal, his deputy, nor the deputy U.S. marshal).

Doc describes what happened: [21]

"He [Behan] first ran against me when I was running a faro bank, when he started a quarrel in my house, and I stopped him and refused to let him play any more. We were enemies after that. In the quarrel I told him in the presence of a crowd that he was gambling with money which I had given his woman. This story got out and caused him trouble. He always hated me after that, and would spend money to have me killed."

Kate probably had a few thousand words to say on the matter, too.

With Morgan Earp being around the saloons all the time, naturally Doc saw a lot of him. They got to be very close friends, and from much better motives than Doc usually had for picking his friends. Morg was fun; he was good-natured, always laughing; so vividly alive, so full of personality that people didn't know what he looked like. They were only conscious of the force of his being. And somehow he and Doc just hit it off right together. Doc could almost forget to cough around him. They'd go to the Alhambra lunch room for a midnight supper together and probably before they'd finished Virg would come and then Wyatt. "The Earps and Holliday" people called them. Their friends Fred Dodge, a professional gambler and reputed undercover man for Wells, Fargo, and Marshall Williams, the local Wells, Fargo representative, would stop to talk about the arrival of the town patent. Kate might pop in and get herself chased right back out again. Publisher Clum of the *Epitaph* and his friends McCoy, Vickers, Burke, Parsons, and others could speak to them about the late trouble with Mayor Randall and Justice Clark Gray—and also thank them for their support at the rally which had finally impressed the mayor and his crowd with the fact that the citizens did not intend to put up with them any longer. They all laughed over how Randall had fled town.[22]

Virgil Earp was having only a little better luck than Fred White as town marshal. The shooting affrays continued unabated, and when the gents weren't shooting at each other, they had target matches. George Parsons, in pauses between examining the state of his soul, wrote down some of the local affairs: "A shooting scrape this afternoon. Benson Corral man shot Calhoun but didn't hurt him much. Lively times awhile," on November 13, 1880; and the next day, "Well, it's pretty definitely settled now that Garfield is president." On the 20th: "Shooting match this afternoon. Plaite of S.F. best shot." "Thanksgiving day and a very pleasant day . . . went to the race . . . a dance at the 'Grand' enjoyed by many single men and their wives." On December 7, 1880: "Some pleas- antries exchanged on the street tonight between 'Shot Gun Collins' and 'Scotty'—none of the bullets took effect." December 10, 1880: "Shooting now about every night. Very lively town. Strange no one is killed." December 22, 1880: "Shootists again on the rampage. 'Red Mike' shot last night and another man reported killed tonight. Heard shots. Things lively."

Lively, indeed. Tombstone's population was about 3,000 now and still increasing despite the numbers getting killed off. More stores were constantly being erected. The three blocks between Third and Sixth and Allen and Frémont were filled solidly with businesses. The areas facing these blocks all the way around were pretty well filled with rooming houses, small saloons and stores and most of the town's corrals and livery stables. Tough Nut was the next street south from Allen; across it the mines and prospect holes started.[23] Flanking Tombstone were now-vanished settlements: Richmond, Stinkem, Pick-em-up, clusters of shanties and tents whose occupants walked the mile or so to Tombstone and back at night, with loaded and cocked revolvers in their hands, even the pious George Parsons. Eight or nine miles further away, down grade, were Contention, Charleston and Fairbanks on the San Pedro, where the stamp mills for the recovery of silver from the ore were located. Charleston, Parsons says, was a pretty place, fifteen or twenty low adobes clustered under green and white cottonwoods by the river. And that was a river! The San Pedro has water in it. Most desert rivers are worth about as much as promises in hell, but the San Pedro is different. It makes a fair oasis in the Sonoran Desert. One could almost believe that Charleston held the gentle green trees and the comforting buildings of home. For a second Doc would see the two beautiful faces he had lost forever, one worn and sad, the other fresh and smiling—and then a lumbering ore wagon would erase them with a pall of dust.

FOOTNOTES TO CHAPTER 10

1. The Great Register for Pima County, Arizona, September 27, 1880 shows: "Number, 1483; name, Holliday, J. H.; age, 24; local residence, Precinct No. 17."
2. *The Private Journal of George Whitwell Parsons*, Arizona Statewide Archival and Records Project, Phoenix, Arizona, 1939. Entry dated June 15, 1880.
3. The sting of the little straw-colored scorpion has been known to be fatal to small children and the sick and debilitated.
4. "Business Section—Tombstone, A. T.—May, 1882," map by R. N. Mullins, Toledo, Ohio, 1950.
5. Parsons' *Journal*, November 16, 1880.
6. *Tombstone Epitaph*, October 9, 1880.
7. There was a still older half brother, and a younger brother named Warren, who will show up presently.
8. In the memoirs of Mrs. Virgil Earp, describing who lived where, she has Morgan married to one "Lou," but I could find no other reference to her, not even at the time of Morg's death.
9. Mr. Parsons' careful entries give us an on-the-spot picture of Tombstone unequaled by any other source. We may complain because he spends pages examining his conscience and justifying his failures, but after all, he was writing for himself and not for us. He went to Tombstone in early 1880, aged twenty-nine, a perfect example of the Victorian gentleman—willing to do hard labor, always ready to stand up for his principles, brave in an emergency, and cruelly hard on sinners.
10. For a while called the Crystal Palace and again called that today.
11. From the Mullins' map, the Parsons' *Journal*, and the two local newspapers.
12. Parsons' *Journal*, June 23, 1880.
13. Borrowed from George Perrine, according to his statement printed in the *Epitaph*, August 24, 1880.
14. *Tombstone Epitaph*, October 20, 1880.
15. *Tombstone Epitaph*, October 20, 1880.
16. Mullins' map, based largely on records of the Huachuca Water Company.
17. *The Great Rascal, the Life and Adventures of Ned Buntline*, by Jay Monaghan, Little, Brown & Co., Boston, 1952. Buntline was a dime novelist who went to Dodge to gather material for his thrillers. He took with him some special guns which he had had the Colt factory make to his order, single-action .45's with 12-

inch barrels and "Ned" fancily carved on the handle. One of these was given to Wyatt Earp in polite payment for material.

18. *Tombstone Epitaph*, October 28, 1880.
19. *Tombstone Epitaph*, October 29, 1880.
20. *Arizona Weekly Miner*, October 3, 1879.
21. Denver *Republican*, May 22, 1882.
22. Parsons' *Journal*, November 7, 1880.
23. Rupert Brooke would have loved Tombstone; you can't take two steps on the plateau south of town without falling into a hole in the ground.

I I

Tombstone, 1881,

Continued

Doc was arrested more times in 1881 than one can keep track of, and mostly for murder. This year saw the lawless decade started by the crash of 1873 coming to a close: Billy the Kid was killed on July 14; the fight at the O.K. corral, probably the most famous gun fight of the Old West, took place on October 26; Jesse James was killed early the following year. 1881 started out ordinarily enough in Tombstone, with a ball at the schoolhouse. On January 4 the town elections were held, with editor Clum of the *Epitaph* being elected mayor over lawyer Mark P. Schaffer by a landslide,[1] and Ben Sippy beating Virgil Earp for the town marshal post by forty votes.[2]

For a short period now none of the Earps had any authority in Tombstone. Marshal Sippy, no coward, was finding law and order as difficult to enforce as they had, if Mr. Parsons told the truth in writing up his journal. On January 10, 1881, he recorded the "capture" of the Alhambra saloon by Curly Bill's gang of cowboys, who then raced through the streets firing off pistols. Doc and the Earps doubtless just sat there looking like butter wouldn't melt in their mouths. Things like that didn't happen when *they* were law officers. But they were ready enough to perform in the law-enforcement line when their aid was requested.

In Tombstone today a street marker in front of the site of Vogan's bowling alley states that there Wyatt Earp single-handedly stood off a lynch mob of three hundred and rescued his prisoner Johnny-behind-the-Deuce.

This is based on Wyatt Earp's story of what happened. His name does not appear in either George Parsons' eyewitness account of the affair or the story carried by the *Epitaph*. And since it seems unfair to Marshal Ben Sippy to deprive him of his one moment of glory, let us examine these contemporary accounts.[3]

From the Parsons' *Journal*, January 14, 1881: "Got into the midst of a terrible excitement in the main street. A gambler called 'Johnny behind the Deuce' his favorite way at faro rode into town followed by mounted men who chased him from Charleston he having shot and killed Schnieder, engineer of the T.M.&M. Co. The officers sought to protect him and swore in deputies—themselves gambling men—(the deputies that is) to help. Many of the miners armed themselves and tried to get at the murderer. Several times, yes a number of times rushes were made and rifles levelled, causing Mr. Stanley and me to get behind the most available shelter. Terrible excitement, but the officers got through finally and out of town with their man, bound for Tucson."

From the *Tombstone Epitaph*, January 17, 1881: "Dismounting in front of Vogan's saloon [John 'Johnny-Behind-the-Deuce' O'Rourke] asked for protection, acknowledging that he had killed his man. In a few minutes Allen Street was jammed with an excited crowd, rapidly augmented by scores from all directions. By this time Marshal Sippy, realizing the situation at once, in the light of the repeated murders that have been committed and the ultimate liberty of the offenders, had secured a well-armed posse of over a score of men to prevent any attempt on the part of the crowd to lynch the prisoner, but feeling that no guard would be strong enough to resist a justly enraged public long, procured a light wagon in which the prisoner was placed, guarded by himself, Virgil Earp and Deputy Sheriff Behan, assisted by a strong posse well-armed. Moving down the street, closely followed by the throng, a halt was made and rifles levelled on the advancing citizens, several of whom were armed with rifles and shotguns. At this juncture, a well-known individual with more avoirdupois than brains, called to the officers to turn loose and fire in the crowd. But Marshal Sippy's sound judgement prevented any such outbreak as would have been the certain result, and cool as an iceberg he held the crowd in check. No one who was a witness of yesterday's proceedings can doubt that but for his presence blood would have flown freely. The posse following would not have been considered; but bowing to the majesty of the law, the crowd subsided and the wagon proceeded on its way to Benson with the prisoner, who by daylight this morning was lodged in the Tucson jail."

One could like Wyatt Earp so much more if he had been contented with his own modest feats and had not posed as the Sir Galahad of the cactus country. As it is, one can but cry, "Throw him a fish!"

On February 2, 1881, Cochise County, named for the great chief of the Chiricahua Apaches, was formed from Pima County, with Tombstone as county seat. Word came in on the telegraph that John H. Behan had been appointed sheriff of the new county.

Doc gives us an angle to the rivalry between Wyatt and Behan for this position. The *Rocky Mountain News* for May 17, 1882, carried the results of an interview with Holliday, then a prisoner in Denver's new jail, but not quoting him word for word: "Wyatt Earp, a saloonkeeper at Tombstone, was an applicant for the office of sheriff. J. H. Behan was also an applicant. Behan secured the appointment. He is said to have sometime before the appointment agreed that in case he secured the place he would appoint Earp Under-Sheriff. After getting the place Behan is said to have refused to do this. From that time a coolness grew up between the two men."

Wyatt was so upset that his fellow Republicans had to get on the telegraph to Prescott and do some string-pulling before he made a public spectacle of himself. One L. F. Blackburn was deputy U.S. marshal for the Tombstone area, but he was kept

164

busy working for the mining interests, handling the legal and bookkeeping angle of his job and not doing much law-enforcement work outside of occasional process-serving and such.[4] Arizona's United States marshal, Crawley P. Dake, seems to have been an understanding, underpaid and vastly overworked official. Being a good Republican he appointed Wyatt Earp as one of his deputies upon request and, hoping for the best, turned back to the account books where he forever struggled to make order out of his vast number of deputies' feeble attempts at financial reports.[5]

Wyatt was now a Federal man. Blackburn wasn't jealous of his position; he was too busy, being in with U.S. Commissioner Wells Spicer as a lawyer and mining broker, so Marshal Earp was free to be as important as he pleased. This mostly consisted of wearing his badge and looking busy whenever Johnny Behan was around. Actually he was spending most of his time with his brothers in the Oriental as usual.

John Behan appointed William Breakenridge, a hail-fellow-well-met who had seen nothing wrong with Chivington's Sand Creek massacres in which he took part, as his deputy, and Democrat Harry Woods, editor of the Tombstone *Nugget,* as undersheriff. Others were appointed deputies as time went on, but never any of the Earp crowd. At the time of Behan's appointment John Dunbar was made treasurer of the new county. These two were partners in running the Dexter livery stable. Dunbar, as a member of the Territorial legislature from Pima County, had been instrumental in pressuring the formation of Cochise County. As members in the best standing of a political machine which was running the Territory over the inept body of Governor Frémont, they were well fixed to make things go their way in and around Tombstone. For a while Tombstone and Cochise County seemed to get along well enough.

"Quite peacable times lately," Parsons wrote on February 25, 1881, "but today the monotony was broken by the shooting of Chas. Storms by Luke Short on cor of Oriental. Shots—the first two were so deliberate I didn't think anything much was out of the way, but at next shot I seized hat and ran out into the street just in time to see Storms die—shot through the heart. Both gamblers. L.S. running game at Oriental. Trouble brewing during night and morning and S was probable aggressor though very drunk. He was game to the last & after being shot through the heart by a desperate effort steadying revolver with both hands fired 4 shots in all I believe. Doc Goodfellow bro't bullet into my room and showed it to me. 45 caliber and slightly flattened. Also showed a bloody handkerchief, part of which was carried into wound by pistol. Short, very unconcerned after shooting—probably a case of kill or be killed. Forgot to say that the Faro games went right on as though nothing had happened after body was carried into Storms' room at the San Jose House."

This seems to have started things popping again in Tombstone. On March 1, 1881, Parsons noted, "Another man shot this a.m. and will probably die. One-Armed Kelly by McAlester. Oriental a regular slaughter house now. Much bad blood today. Pistols pulled. Games at Oriental closed by Joice."

Wyatt Earp's fighting interest in the Oriental seems to have pooped out with Johnny Tyler. Things were lively all over. Luke Short left town, the games at the Oriental opened up almost as soon as the saloon's proprietor closed them, and the ball went on in gala style. The weather was brisk and brilliant. On March 15, 1881, there was a light fall of snow. "A strange and pretty sight," Parsons wrote of snow in the desert. And that night an attempt was made to rob Kinnear's stage.

From the *Epitaph* of March 16, 1881: "At about 11 o'clock last night, Marshal Williams received a telegram from Benson stating that Kinnear & Company's coach, carrying Wells Fargo & Co.'s treasure, had been stopped near Contention and 'Budd' Philpot, the driver, killed and one passenger mortally wounded. Almost immediately afterwards A. C. Cowan, Wells Fargo & Co.'s agent at Contention City, rode into this city bringing a portion of the details of the affair. In a few minutes after his arrival, Williams, the Earp brothers, and several other brave, determined men were in the saddle, well-armed, en route to the scene of the murderous affray. From telegrams received from Benson at the *Epitaph* office, the following particulars of the affair were gathered:

"As the stage was going up a small incline about two hundred yards this side of Drew's Station and about a mile the other side of Contention City, a man stepped into the road from the east side and called out 'Hold.' At the same moment a number of men —believed to have been eight—made their appearance and a shot was fired from the same side of the road instantly followed by another. One of these shots struck 'Budd' Philpot, the driver, who fell heavily forward between the wheelers carrying the reins with him. The horses immediately sprang into a dead run. Meanwhile Bob Paul, Wells Fargo & Co.'s messenger, one of the bravest and coolest men who ever sat on a box-seat, was ready with his gun and answered back shot for shot before the frightened horses had whirled the coach out of range. It was fully a mile before the team could be brought to stand, where it was discovered that one of the shots had mortally wounded a passenger on the coach named Peter Roerig. As soon as the coach could be stopped, Paul secured the reins and drove rapidly to Benson, and immediately started back for the scene of the murder. At Benson a telegram was sent to the *Epitaph* office stating that Roerig could not possibly live. There were eight passengers on the coach and they all unite in praise of Mr. Paul's bravery and presence of mind.

"At Drew's Station the firing and rapid whirling by of the coach sent men to the scene of the tragedy, where they found poor 'Budd' lying dead in the road, and by the bright moonlight saw the murderers fleeing rapidly from the place. A messenger was at once dispatched to inform agent Cowan of the circumstances, and within 20 minutes after the news arrived Mr. Cowan had dispatched nearly thirty well-armed volunteers after the scoundrels. He then rode rapidly into Tombstone, when the party mentioned above started out to aid in the pursuit. This, with Mr. Paul's party, makes three bodies of determined men who are in hot chase and Mr. Cowan stated to an *Epitaph* reporter that it is almost impossible for the murderous gang to escape, as the pursuers are close at their heels and have the moonlight in their favor. Should the road agents be caught they will meet with the short shrift which they deserve."

An attempt on the mail-carrying coach was entirely within his Federal jurisdiction, Wyatt Earp felt. Never say die! He'd catch these robbers, win a glittering reputation and defeat Johnny Behan at the first sheriff's election (nearly two years off). Over the desert they went, a combined and serious posse: Bob Paul (soon to be elected sheriff of Pima County), the three Earps, Marshall Williams and Bat Masterson, joined off and on by Sheriff Behan, Deputy Breakenridge and Buckskin Frank Leslie. Morg captured a local tough, Luther King, hiding out at the ranch on the San Pedro owned by Len Redfield. King, rattled, confessed that he had held the horses while Bill Leonard, Harry Head and Jim Crane, disreputables whose chief livelihood hitherto had been herding cattle with most remarkably illegible brands, had tried to hold up the bullion-loaded stage. Sheriff Behan insisted that since murder had been done in an area under his jurisdiction and no mail actually stolen, Luther King was his prisoner and what was done with him was none of the Earps' business. He started back to Tombstone with his prisoner, accompanied also by Marshall Williams at the Earps' suggestion, to make sure King wasn't turned loose. They got back to Tombstone all right. Then the Tombstone *Nugget* for March 19, 1881, printed:

"Luther King, the man arrested at Redfield's ranch charged with being implicated in the Bud Philpot murder, escaped from the sheriff's office by quietly stepping out the back door while Harry Jones, Esq., was drawing up a bill of sale for a horse the prisoner was selling to John Dunbar. Under-Sheriff Harry Woods and Dunbar were present. He had been absent but a few seconds before he was missed. A confederate on the outside had a horse in readiness for him. It was a well-planned job by outsiders to get him away. He was an important witness against Holliday. He it was that gave the names of the three that were being followed at the

168

time he was arrested. Their names were Bill Leonard, Jim Crane and Harry Head."

This is one of the astounding news items of all time. The editor of the Democratic organ, the *Nugget,* was Under-Sheriff Harry Woods. He let a prisoner walk out of the jail and then writes in his paper that the escape was well-planned by outsiders. The wonder is not that there were so many lynchings in the west, but that the only lynching in Tombstone was performed by a bunch from Bisbee who refused to put up with Tombstone's leniency in the legal line. And why the reference to King being a witness against Holliday, of all people? Well, Holliday is the person referred to in the following article from the Tucson *Star* of March 24, 1881:

"It is believed that the three robbers are making for Sonora, via some point near Tucson. The fourth is at Tombstone and is well known and has been shadowed ever since his return. This party is suspected for the reason that on the afternoon of the attack, he engaged a horse at a Tombstone livery stable at about 4 o'clock, stating that he might be gone for 7 or 8 days and he might return that night, and picked the best animal in the stable. He left town about 4 o'clock armed with a Henry rifle and a six-shooter, he started toward Charleston, and about a mile below Tombstone cut across to Contention, and when next seen it was between 10 and 11 o'clock riding into the livery stable at Tombstone, his horse fagged out. He at once called for another horse, which he hitched in the streets for some hours, but did not leave. Statements attributed to him, if true, look very bad indeed and which, if proven, are most conclusive as to his guilt either as a principle actor or as an accessory before the fact."

The Earps came back to Tombstone empty-handed and completely bushed from their seventeen-day search through an area inhabited only by the robbers' friends, to find Doc Holliday accused of being in on the robbery and in fact, being the one whose shots had killed Philpot and Roerig. Everybody in town had seen his rages. His detractors explained that he had been drunk and that the other robbers, but innocent lads at heart, had been

169

unable to keep him from shooting Budd Philpot and the passenger. "A homicidal maniac," people said, and remembering how he had started for Johnny Tyler, anybody could believe it.

Worst of all was that he had been known to visit an old adobe hacienda on the Benson road where the stage robbers had camped out for a week prior to their attempt on the stage. At first Doc laughed at the picture of himself mixed up in the undignified hugger-mugger of an unsuccessful stage robbery.

"If I'd robbed Kinnear's stage I'd have shot a horse and got the bullion," he said, with a little dry cough. Even the tone of that cough gave his hearers the idea he thought them all a pack of fools for not having thought of that themselves. And of course he had gone to the old adobe. Bill Leonard, even though a "hard case," had been a friend of his for years and was, in consequence, still his friend. He denied having been at the adobe house the afternoon of the robbery.

"I heard there was a big game going on in Charleston, so I rode over there that afternoon," he explained. "Foresight is a virtue, they say, so I carried my .44 and a rifle in case some of my many admirers were unable to resist the desire to take a large chunk of my hair for a tender momento. When I got there I found the game closed. I headed right back and met Old Man Fuller starting out with the water wagon for Tombstone from the wells. I tied my horse behind the wagon and rode into Tombstone with Fuller. Got here about six o'clock. After dinner I got in a game at the Alhambra that lasted until dawn."

He had explained. It'd been damned nice of him, he thought, considering that he didn't have to explain his actions to a living soul. Now he expected people to leave him alone.

Nothing in the stereotyped pattern of Doc's behavior admits so violent a deviation from his usual behavior as engaging in a stage robbery. But something points to his knowing that the robbery was going to take place, if not all the details—and that is the very perfection of his alibi: it was too perfect to be normal behavior. Leonard knew Holliday and his code of loyalty. Possibly he told

170

or hinted broadly about the planned robbery to Doc, knowing that he would never tell anyone, not even his law-officer crony, Wyatt Earp. It is even possible that Leonard, Head and Crane planned to use Doc as a patsy all the while, since attention was called to his actions of that afternoon so promptly. But Holliday was crazy like a fox and when he saw Bob Paul up on the stage, thereby advertising to the world that there was treasure aboard (he didn't ride the stage unless Wells, Fargo had a valuable cargo being shipped out), he got himself an alibi, and fast.

It is quite possible that Doc was an accessory before the fact in the attempted robbery of Kinnear's stage and the deaths of Philpot and Roerig. Note that he did not ride his hired horse back to Tombstone, thereby saving himself time and money. He is presently to go chasing off all over southern Arizona in a posse, so his health must have been able to stand riding long distances. But he poked along with Old Man Fuller for a miserable couple of hours behind a pair of old plugs. And when they got to Tombstone Doc didn't disappear into Kate's adobe. He had dinner at a downtown restaurant, then bucked the tiger in the Alhambra all night long, and had witnesses to prove it.

But there were people in Tombstone who believed Doc was mixed up in the robbery and had guts enough to say so.

The Earps were understandably outraged. To half kill themselves chasing Leonard, Head and Crane through the heart of the rustlers' own stomping ground in the interests of justice and their own glory—and then to find their best friend accused of a crime they knew he could not have committed. And worse, to have their most important witness escape—and have that escape blamed on them. Sheriff Behan had certainly cured them of asking about his Chinese friends.

And Holliday was fast losing patience with those foolhardy enough to shoot their mouths off to him about being a stage robber protected by the Earps. When he was nervous or upset he drank more heavily than usual and as a result had very little control over himself. Having known something about the robbery only increased his righteous indignation that anyone should connect him with it.

What actually happened I was unable to discover, what with the old records being extremely fragmentary and the newspaper files to which I had access for this period being by no means complete. But Doc sure was in hot water. This is from the report of A. T. Wallace, Justice of the Peace, for March 1, 1881, to December 31, 1881: "April 13, 1881—Territory vs. J. H. Holliday. Threats against life. Discharged on payment of costs." The *Epitaph* for May 30, 1881, carried: "Doc Holliday has been indicted by the Grand Jury on account of participation in a shooting affray some time since. He was released on bonds." A list of sheriff's charges for June 2, 1881, had: "Territory vs. J. H. Holliday. (Court) To subpoenaing witnesses Wm. Porterfield, Frank Mitchell, J. B. Robinson, mileage to Turquoise & return, costs, $10.60."

The threats against life are plain enough. Doc got to the point where he faithfully promised to kill the next son of a bitch that said stage or robbery to him, and he meant *you.*

The memoirs of Billy Breakenridge, Sheriff Behan's deputy, tell of Holliday shooting Mike Joyce and his bartender in December of this year. None of the December records or the newspapers (fairly complete for December) vouch for this. Wyatt Earp later mentioned the Holliday-Joyce shooting [6] but didn't say when it occurred.

With apologies to all the keen and unimpaired old memories, let us put the shooting of Mr. Joyce and his unnamed bartender ahead a few months.

Despite owning a part interest in the gambling concession at the Oriental, Wyatt never got along with the saloon's proprietor, Mike Joyce. Joyce was a member of the county board of supervisors and friendly with John H. Behan and his partner, Dunbar. He didn't like the Earps and Holliday and he made no bones about it. Someone told Doc that Joyce was persisting in shooting off his mouth about Doc being a stage robber. It was too much. Doc felt

172

that he and his friends were being persecuted, no less, and by a lousy bastard that wasn't fit to live.

He began to brood over this, and to stoke the fire of anger with a fuel known as forty-rod.

Then he went down the street headed for the Oriental, gun in hand. He charged in the door, located Joyce and commenced shooting. When the smoke cleared it was discovered that Mike Joyce had stopped a bullet with his hand and a bartender had been shot in the foot. This was the only time Doc plugged any innocent bystanders, which is astounding luck when one considers the evidence of his marksmanship. Needless to say, a prosperous local businessman like Joyce wasn't going to put up with being shot by some gun punk.

But Doc evidently got away with this little matter despite being indicted by the Grand Jury, because he was free to be in trouble again all too soon.

Wyatt Earp was worried about the coming elections. If only he could catch Leonard, Head and Crane. . . . He took to thinking and pouring over this and counting up items pro and con on his fingers and completely over-taxed his courageous and unastute brain. He came up with a plot so involved, so dependent on the good will of people that even a moron wouldn't trust, that one has to marvel at him. "Oh, what a tangled web we weave when first we practice to deceive!" Surely only a fool could have gotten himself so fouled up.

Deputy U.S. Marshal Earp went to the cowboys and made a deal with Ike Clanton to lure Leonard, Head and Crane into a trap. Wyatt Earp was to get the credit for capturing them—Ike Clanton and his cowboy helpers were to get the thirty-six-hundred-dollar reward (in the strictest secrecy, of course, so no one would know they had sold out their friends).[7] If Doc had known about this he probably would have died the death. But Wyatt believed Doc completely innocent and didn't tell a soul about his dealings with Ike Clanton, who immediately set about locating his friends Leonard, Head and Crane so he could betray them for the reward.

Now Tombstone was floored by a stroke of bad luck, the first of a notable series of such. Nearly two blocks in the heart of the business section burned to the ground. The *Epitaph* for June 23, 1881, tells what happened:

"Messers. Alexander & Thompson, proprietors of the Arcade saloon on Allen Street, three doors above the Oriental saloon, on the corner of Allen and Fifth had a barrel of liquor that had been condemned by them for a long time which they intended to re-ship and as fate would have it they had a team ready to take it away at this time. They rolled it out in front of the bar and knocked out the bung for the purpose of measuring the quantity in the package. Mr. Alexander, in putting the gauge rod into the barrel accidentally let it slip from his fingers into the same. His bartender got a wire to fish it out and came to the front with a lighted cigar in his mouth, one report says, and another that he lighted a match for some purpose, when the escaping gas caught fire and communicated with the liquor which caused an instantaneous explosion, scattering the burning contents in all directions. There were two men in the saloon at the time besides Mr. Hazelton the bartender. Their names L. L. Sales and David Cotter. Mr. Sales says the concussion was terrific. The three escaped through the backdoor, exit through the front being effectually blocked by the flames. Almost by a miracle they escaped unhurt. In less than three minutes the flames had communicated with the adjoining buildings and spread with a velocity equalled only by a burning prairie in a gale. The heated condition of the woodwork assisted the devouring element in its rapid spread. This, as also the Vizina & Cook block on the corner, was an adobe building. It was ceiled with cloth which acted as tinder for communicating the flame.

"Seemingly, instantaneously with the bursting of the flames through the door into Allen Street the alarm spread and people rushed to the scene, but lack of facilities for extinguishing the fire gave it time to spread to adjoining buildings. Before anything could be done to check it the store of Meyers Brothers, Glover & Co., and the Occidental were all ablaze. The firemen were promptly on hand but they were almost as powerless as the citizens, with only this difference, they had a head which they implicitly obeyed. The first thing was to save books, money and valuables by those whose premises were on fire, which was only partially done. It is said a demand was made on Meyers Brothers and Tucker & Pridham for blankets wet and put over the adjoining buildings which was peremptorily refused and this resource for fighting the fire was thus summarily cut off. The moment the alarm was given Mr. M. B. Clapp, manager of Safford, Hudson & Co.'s bank rushed all money and valuable into the inner safe—the books being taken outside to a safe place—and proceeded to lock everything up. While locking the outer door the plastering began to fall around his head and he escaped, after having performed his last duty, by the back door, the front being inaccessible from the flames. Joyce, of the Oriental saloon, rushed to his safe, the outer door of which was unlocked and made an effort to unlock the inner door to get the cash box out, but the flames came sweeping through with such fury that he had to flee for his life, leaving over $1200 in greenbacks, no gold or silver—of his own money besides a large amount of deposits. He did not save a farthing's worth of anything.

"Thus far we have only touched upon the first incidents of the origin of the fire which all told did not occupy more than five minutes in transpiring, so rapid was the progress of the work of destruction. The firemen, assisted by the people, all of whom gave freely, fully and voluntarily of their energies in herculean efforts to check the flames. At once the demolishing of awnings, porches, et cetera began, as they were found to be the great elements for spreading the flames. The heat of the fire—added to that of the sun —the thermometer standing 100 degrees in the shade at 4 o'clock, made it almost impossible to get within reasonable distance of the points most available for checking the flames. All was hurry and confusion among those in the line of destruction. One of the first acts of self-abnegation was that of Wells Spicer, whose office was on Fifth Street. After saving his official and private papers he gave orders to demolish the building which was a frame—as were the majority in the burned district. The work immediately began but the fire came sweeping down upon them so rapidly but little more than tearing down the porch was accomplished before they had to abandon the work and go to another outpost. In spite of the herculean efforts the fire swept onward to Frémont Street on the north and crossed over Allen on the south burning in its eastward course across to Toughnut Street, reaching as far as Seventh where, owing to the number of vacant lots it was stopped. On the north side of Frémont Street the fire was prevented from spreading by the use of wet blankets and water constantly upon the fronts of the buildings. Schaffer & Lord ordered the broad porch around two sides of their store to be demolished at an early stage, and by playing a stream of water from the hose attached to the water pipes connected with the store the fire was kept at bay.

"By 6 p.m. the fury of the flames had spent itself and nothing remained but the charred and ghastly skeletons of the adobe buildings while here and there thirsty tongues of flame would break forth as if the greedy element, not satisfied with having consumed everything in its course, still craved for more."

Later newspaper articles praised the work of the firemen and volunteers, and also that done by Virgil Earp in organizing an armed vigilante group to protect the burned area where valuables of all sorts lay strewn in the streets as they had been flung from the doomed and burning buildings. Marshal Ben Sippy had either by accident or in total defeat picked this particular day to resign. The city council promptly picked Virgil Earp to fill out Sippy's unexpired term.[8] The only person injured in the fire was George Parsons, who got his face well smashed when a burning frame balcony which he was attempting to chop loose from an adobe building collapsed.

The work of rebuilding began immediately and was pushed with such vigor that the burned area was restored almost at once.

And then collapsed Wyatt Earp's secret finagling with Ike Clanton, newly orphaned by the death of Old Man Clanton at the hands of some irate Mexicans who resented his killing off their friends and relatives in such droves. The Tucson paper, the *Arizona Daily Star*, for June 23, 1881, carried the following:

"The killing of Bill Leonard and 'Harry the Kid' at Eureka, N. M., by the Haslett brothers . . . has been summarily avenged. It appears that a cowboy named Crane organized and led a band of congenial spirits in the work of vengeance. They followed the Haslett boys for some twenty-six miles from Eureka before they overtook them, and as soon as they came up with them the fight to the death commenced. The Haslett boys were game and made a brave fight, killing two and wounding three of the Crane party, but being overpowered were finally killed."

Now only one of the stage robbers is left, the Crane mentioned above. Law-officer Earp's dickering with thieves and murderers is becoming an embarrassment to both parties, neither he nor the cowboys wanting anyone to know about their futile and shady arrangement. And note this date, toward the last of June. There is plenty of time for suspicions and imaginings born of a guilty conscience to stir up trouble, trouble that culminates at the O.K. corral on a chill October afternoon.

The big news on July 2, 1881, was the shooting of newly-elected President Garfield. Not to be outdone, Tombstone came up with a shooting the following day, Parsons describing it: "Carleton shot Diss, probably mortally . . . all a bad crowd. Diss has bro't it all on himself. Mrs. Carleton the cause." It rained on the Fourth of July, and Doc and Kate had a knock-down, drag-out fight for variation on the usual theme of what to do on a rainy afternoon.

They had had fights aplenty, but this was the worst. This was the end of everything between them, Doc swore. He packed up and moved into the Cosmopolitan, leaving Kate to break up the furniture. But Kate realized that this time he meant it. The fire was out. He looked at her with cold dislike and not the blind rage that would dissolve into one of those cosy affairs of reconciliation to which she was so partial. Instead of breaking up the furniture as usual, she began to tell her woes to anyone who would listen, the while liberally soothing her bruised feelings with a stoneware bottle of gin. One very interested party heard her slobberings and decided to do something to even up old scores.

The *Daily Nugget* for July 6, 1881, carried: "Court Proceedings. United States vs. John H. Holliday. For attempt to rob U.S. Mail at the time of killing Budd Philpot; awaiting examination. Territory vs. John H. Holliday. On charge of murder of Budd Philpot. Continued to July 6, at 9 a.m. Bonds, $5,000." In another column: "Important Arrest. A warrant was sworn out yesterday before Judge Spicer for the arrest of Doc. Holliday, a well-known character here, charging him with complicity in the murder of Bud Philpot, and the attempted stage robbery near Contention some months ago, and he was arrested by Sheriff Behan. The warrant was issued upon the affidavit of Kate Elder, with whom Holliday has been living for some time past. Holliday was taken before Justice Spicer in the afternoon, who released him upon bail in the amount of $5,000, Wyatt Earp, J. Meagher, and J. H. Melgren [9] becoming sureties. The examination will take place before Judge Spicer at 9 o'clock this morning."

Doc was probably interspersing his cursing with "Hell hath no fury like a woman scorned," as a triumphant Sheriff Behan conducted him to jail. Out on bail he no doubt turned his attentions to Kate again. She explained that she didn't remember what she had done that night; she had just been drinking with Sheriff Behan and that was all she knew. Doc told her what he thought of her loyalty and devotion to his enemies, with the result that the next day's *Nugget* carried, under the court notes: "Miss Kate Elder sought 'surcease of sorrow' in the flowing bowl. She succeeded so well that when she woke up she found her name written on the Chief's register with two 'd's' [drunk and disorderly] appended to it. She paid her matriculation fee of $12.50, took her degrees and departed."

Kate departed straightway for Doc. Her head was splitting six ways from Sunday, but she knew who was to blame for all her troubles. When she got through telling Doc off, he swore out a

178

warrant for her arrest on the charge of threatening to kill him (it was less than two months since a similar charge had been placed against him) and Virg Earp hauled her up before Judge Felter. She was convicted but after due consideration of all points in the case was let go.[10] Kate was evidently a very attractive woman, hangover, rage, tears and all.

"Court Proceedings," in the *Nugget* for July 10, 1881, had: "The case of Territory vs. John A. Holliday was called for hearing yesterday morning at 10 o'clock, the District Attorney addressing the court, said that he had examined all the witnesses summoned for the prosecution and from their statements he was satisfied that there was not the slightest evidence to show the guilt of the defendant; and he therefore asked that the complaint in this case be withdrawn and that the case be dismissed. The Court thereupon dismissed the case and discharged the defendent, and thus ended what at once time was supposed to be an important trial."

After this neither Doc nor Kate wanted to make up. The breach was complete on both sides. After an Earp-Holliday-Elder conclave she agreed to leave town if Doc would give her a fairly large sum of money. This was blackmail, but rather than have the constant possibility of her again getting drunk with Sheriff Behan and swearing Doc's life away, the money was paid. She and Doc parted with a few choice cuss words each had been saving up for a special occasion, and their illicit affair ended on as ungenteel a note as it had begun.

Doc was feeling quiet. "In Justice Felter's Court a man named Julius Cecil erected a mansard structure of elaborate proportions on the cabeza of August Gutzeller, for which he paid a fine of $10." [11] Virg Earp kept busy arresting people, serving notices to abate nuisances, seeing that the hospital was kept clean and getting the chain gang out to clean up the alleys. The following day, please note, all members of the chain gang paid their fines! On July 22, 1881, the *Nugget* gave Lou Rickabaugh's faro games at the Oriental a large puff: "The three games run by Lou and his partner resemble a funeral procession from the time of opening to the close.

The player walks up to the table, in all cases presided over by a gentlemanly dealer, puts down his bet, be it a quarter or a $20 piece; the turn is made, and if he is lucky enough to win, no kicking or scowling is done. The game is dealt squarely on business principles. If a player is lucky, he can win everything in sight, money, checks, lay-out and case-keeper, and when 'cashing in' will be invited to 'take a smile' and call again. E'en though his original stake might have been a smooth quarter."

The rains were so bad this summer that some of the adobe buildings actually did collapse. Also, on August 5, Deputy Sheriff Breakenridge is the best shot at Spangenberg's shooting gallery, with twelve bull's-eyes straight running. Doc was above such show-off practices, of course. But Doc was doubtless in on this occasion noted by the *Nugget* for August 21, 1881: "A big poker game was running yesterday at the Alhambra saloon. It took just a double eagle to get in and about five big river bits to see the first raise." The same paper also had Chief of Police Virgil Earp arrest John P. Clum, mayor of Tombstone, editor of the evening paper, the *Epitaph,* and a deacon in the Presbyterian church, for fast riding in the city limits. He also arrested Em Eastman, an Allen Street cyprian, for using vulgar and obscene language. A couple of days later he and officers Flynn and Bronk raided an opium den and arrested five opium-smoking Chinese.

All appeared to be quiet in Tombstone.

And then on August 25, 1881, the *Weekly Star* of Tucson printed:

"One of the parties recently killed by Mexican regulars in New Mexico was the notorious Jim Crane, the last survivor of the stage robbers who murdered Philpot near Benson last spring. From a party who met Crane a few days before his death, the Tombstone *Nugget* learns the following additional particulars concerning the attempted stage robbery: 'To many it has always seemed a mystery that the parties concerned should have killed Philpot and spared Bob Paul, Wells, Fargo & Co.'s messenger. According to Crane, however, when the ambushed robbers fired at Philpot, they thought it was Paul, as the two had swapped places, Paul acting as driver and poor Bud as messenger.' "

Now all of the robbers were dead and the uneasy alliance between law and outlawry had completely broken down. People began to think other people were doing what they would do if they were in the other people's position. . . .

On September 10, 1881, the *Nugget* reported that the Bisbee stage had been stopped by road agents and two thousand five hundred dollars in coin taken from the Wells, Fargo box and an additional five hundred from the passengers. Marshals Williams, Morgan and Wyatt Earp, Fred Dodge and Deputy Sheriffs Breakenridge and Nagle immediately started for the scene of the robbery. Here were discovered the marks of a most distinctive pair of boot heels in the mud. They rode into Bisbee and arrested deputy sheriff Frank Stillwell, the heels freshly removed from his boots and replaced by a local shoemaker fitting the marks in the mud it was claimed. They also arrested Pete Spence, partner with Stillwell in a livery stable in Bisbee but living in Tombstone—right across the street from the Earps, as a matter of fact, in the Mexican section. There seemed to be little doubt that they were the robbers, and the *Epitaph* howled for Stillwell to be fired as a deputy sheriff. However, on September 16 the charges against Pete Spence were dropped and on October 6 those against Frank Stillwell were also dropped.

Stillwell and Spence expressed themselves as disliking the Earps more than somewhat and indeed hankering to "get" them. Ike Clanton, who by now was sure Wyatt Earp had told half Tombstone that he had tried to sell out his stage-robber friends of the earlier attempted robbery, added his threats to the others. Doc felt safe at last. Leonard, Head and Crane were dead so there was no one to prove that he had known even a vague hint about the planned robbery. He went off to Tucson to celebrate. The trouble boiled along without breaking the surface, but always just on the verge —and then all was disrupted.

The Apaches went on the warpath.

Geronimo, the old butcher, the wiliest murderer that ever laughed up a dirty sleeve at the Army, and several hundred of his Apache followers left the San Carlos Reservation and headed for old Mexico. They were pursued by Colonel Bernard's command of one company of infantry and one of cavalry, who despite all their precautions, were forced into doing battle once with the Apaches. After the carnage it was discovered that a blind Indian had been killed, a squaw and two children captured, and two colored soldiers wounded. The Army was held in so little esteem, this mild foray being rather outstanding for them, that the loyal citizens of Cochise County formed a group of irregulars to catch Geronimo and protect county property themselves. They had no sooner set out than it started to rain. It rained the hardest anyone had ever seen it rain in the desert, a regular cloudburst. All of the Earps, Sheriff Behan and his deputies, the Wells, Fargo crowd, Mayor Clum and all the brave and civic-minded citizens, including George Parsons, got soaked to the skin. They finally floundered onto the Army, the second day out, and huddled together for mutual protection. The Cochise County irregulars sent to Tombstone for supplies, the *Nugget* facetiously reporting that they were sent ninety-nine dollars' worth of drinkables and one dollar's worth of crackers—but then, all the telegraph lines were down and the papers had to fill up space some way. Constant reports of lost stock kept coming in, notably the loss of some twenty-seven horses by Frank McLowry from his ranch at Soldier's Holes, near where the Army was camped. Finally, with loud bugle-tootings to warn any stray savages that might be around to get out of the way, the Army doddered off toward the Mexican border and the Cochise County irregulars took off for home. Geronimo's men dropped a few long shots on them from a nearby hill, just as a mark of contempt, and melted away. Parsons was amazed that the Apaches had known where they were all along. He was also thoroughly cured of chasing Indians.

As soon as it was safe to take one's scalp travelling again, Frank Stillwell and Pete Spence were again arrested, this time by Deputy

U.S. Marshal Earp on a charge of robbing the mails, and were taken to Tucson by Virg. They were arraigned before the U.S. court commissioner, Judge Styles. After a preliminary hearing the charges against Spence were apparently dropped, and Frank Stillwell was released on bond.

Morg Earp went down to Tucson to join Doc for a couple of days' relaxation and both of them returned to Tombstone on the evening of Saturday, October 22, 1881. They got back to find Ike Clanton no longer able to keep his suspicions about Wyatt Earp talking about his betrayal of his friends to himself. He was yelling all over town that Wyatt was going around telling lies about him. Seeing that Ike had a crowd of cowboy friends with him, City Marshal Earp appointed Wyatt, Morgan and Doc as his deputies in case it came to a fight. It did—on Wednesday, October 26, 1881, at 2 o'clock in the afternoon.

FOOTNOTES TO CHAPTER I I

1. Parsons' *Journal*, January 4, 1881.
2. *Helldorado*.
3. Wyatt Earp's version is available at any bookstore. This *Epitaph* is only at the Bancroft Library, University of California at Berkeley.
4. *Tombstone Epitaph*, January 14, 1881. Mullins' map.
5. Reports of the United States Marshal for Arizona, Attorney General's Division, Department of Archives, Washington, D.C.
6. This is from an unnamed, undated newspaper clipping at the Arizona Pioneers' Historical Society in Tucson, in regard to the Lotta Crabtree estate trial. Wyatt Earp was under oath on the witness stand: "Earp denied that 'Doc' Holliday was a notorious character, 'outside of this other faction trying to make him notorious,' although, 'of course, he killed a man or two before he went there.' There was another little fuss [besides the fight at the O.K. corral] in which 'Doc' wounded a man named Joyce and the latter's partner, Earp recalled." There is no mention of Doc getting into this scrape in *Wyatt Earp, Frontier Marshal*, but then it apparently was not told to Stuart N. Lake under oath.
7. *Daily Nugget*, November 17, 1881.
8. This was a temporary appointment, Mayor Clum being out of town. He confirmed Virg for the post upon his return. Virg's bond for $5,000 as chief of police, with himself as principal and J. M. Vizina and C. R. Brown as sureties, is dated June 29, 1881.
9. The latter two are the proprietors of Doc's house, the Alhambra.
10. *Daily Nugget*, July 9, 1881.
11. *Daily Nugget*, July 16, 1881.

1 2

The Earp-
Clanton Feud

Parsons' Journal, October 27, 1881: "Much excitement in town and people apprehensive and scary. A bad time yesterday when Wyatt, Virgil and Morgan Earp with Doc Holliday had a street fight with the two McLowrys and Bill Clanton and Ike, all but the latter being killed and V. and M. Earp wounded. Desperate men and a desperate encounter. Bad blood has been brewing for some time and I am not surprized at the outbreak. It is only a wonder it has not happened before. A raid is feared upon the town by the Cowboys and measures have been taken to protect life and property. The 'Stranglers' were out in force & showed sand. My cowboy appearance & attire not in keeping with the excited mind. Loud talking or talking in groups was tho't out of place."

Daily Nugget, November 1, 1881: "Coroner H. M. Mathews: 'Yes, know the cause of the death of William Clanton from that examination of the bodies at the death-house, 9 or 10 o'clock at night, after looking them over casually right after fight; they died from the effects of pistol and gun-shot wounds; there were two wounds on the body; did not examine them thoroughly; there was one two inches from the left nipple, penetrating the lungs; the other was beneath the twelfth rib, above and beneath; 6 inches to the right of the navel; think neither of the wounds went through the body; not probing the wounds cannot say positively what direction they took; both went in front through the body; my opinion was that those wounds were the cause of death; examined the body of

Frank McLowry at the same time and day; found in the body of Frank McLowry one wound penetrating the cranium, beneath the right ear; another penetrating the abdomen one inch to the left of the navel. I should say the wound beneath the ear caused instant death—same as if shot through the heart—the wound through the head was at the base of the brain, just beneath the ear; no, sir, did not probe that wound; probed it a little; it passed horizontally through the brain; the wound in the abdomen was a straight, penetrating shot; I examined the body of Tom McLowry at the same time and place; found on his body twelve buckshot wounds—on the right side of the body, near together, under the arms, between the third and fifth ribs; my opinion was they were buckshot wounds; laid the palm of my hand over them, it would cover the whole of them, about four inches in space; the wound penetrated straight into the body.' "

Coroner's report to the Board of Supervisors of Cochise County listing inquests performed and personal property found on bodies, dated November 8, 1881: "From the body of Thos. McLowry I recovered in certificates of deposit in the Pima County Bank, checks and cash in all the sum of $2,923.45. From the body of Frank McLowry one Colts six shooting Pistol, with belt and cartridges. From the body of William Clanton, one Colts six shooter, with belt and cartridges, and one nickle watch and chain." (This old record, as well as the newspapers and so on quoted in this chapter, are the property of the Arizona Pioneers' Historical Society, Tucson, Arizona. *Ed.*)

Daily Nugget, October 30, 1881: "Last Tuesday evening, after the cold rain experienced here, the Chiricahua Mountains were white with snow. The fall must have been light as it was all gone Wednesday evening."

Tombstone Epitaph, October 28, 1881: "The funeral of the McLowry brothers and Clanton yesterday was numerically one of the largest ever witnessed in Tombstone. It took place at 3:30 from the undertaking rooms of Messers. Ritter and Eyan. The procession headed by the Tombstone brass band, moved down Allen

Street and thence to the cemetery. The sidewalks were densely packed for three or four blocks. The body of Clanton was in the first hearse and those of the two McLowry brothers in the second, side by side, and were interred in the same grave. It was a most impressive and saddening sight and such a one as it is to be hoped may never occur again in this community."

Daily Nugget, October 30, 1881: "We, the undersigned, a jury of inquest, summoned by the coroner of the county of Cochise to determine whose the body is submitted to our inspection; when, where and under what circumstances the person came to his death. After viewing the body and hearing such testimony as has been submitted to us, find that the person was Frank McLowry, twenty-nine years of age and a native of Mississippi, and that he came to his death in the town of Tombstone in said county, and on the 26th day of October, 1881, from the effects of pistol and gunshot wounds inflicted by Virgil Earp, Morgan Earp, Wyatt Earp and one Holliday, commonly called Doc Holliday.

"Thomas Moses, R. F. Hafford, D. Calisher, T. F. Hudson, M. Garrett, S. B. Comstock, J. W. Cowell, J. C. Davis, Harry Walker, C. D. Reppy, G. H. Haskell and W. S. Goodrich.

"The verdict rendered in the case of Wm. Clanton and Thomas McLowry was the same as the above, excepting as to their names and ages, which were inserted in the body of the document. After which the jury adjourned sine die."

Daily Nugget, October 30, 1881: "Yesterday warrants for the arrest of Wyatt, Virgil and Morgan Earp and J. H. (Doc) Holliday, were placed in the hands of the sheriff, but as Morgan and Virgil Earp were confined to their beds [they were wounded in the O.K. corral shooting], through wounds received in the late street fight, the warrants were not, in their cases served, and only Wyatt Earp and Holliday placed under arrest. When those parties were taken before Justice Spicer he denied bail as a matter of right, but upon showing of facts by affidavits, bail was granted and fixed in the sum of $10,000 each, being justified in the sum of $20,000 for each of the defendants." Bail was duly put up.

Daily Nugget, November 1, 1881: "Morgan and Virgil Earp were both resting very comfortably last evening, although the former suffered considerably during the day."

Daily Nugget, November 1, 1881: "Yesterday afternoon at 3 o'clock, the examination of Morgan Earp, et al., concerned in the late street fight, was commenced before Justice Wells Spicer, with quite an array of legal talent for both sides. For the prosecution are Messers. Goodrich & Goodrich, Smith, Earll, Campbell & Robinson, Smith & Colby, J. M. Murphy and District Attorney Price. For the defense are Howard & Street, T. J. Drum and Thomas Fitch. E. J. Risley, court reporter taking short hand report. . . . The testimony for the prosecution was opened by the examination of Coroner H. M. Mathews."

The Coroner testified, establishing the deaths of Billy Clanton and Tom and Frank McLowry were caused by bullet and shot-gun wounds.

Daily Nugget, October 30, 1881: "B. H. Fallehy, sworn and testified: I heard some stranger ask Ike Clanton what is the trouble; he said there would be no trouble; then Ike Clanton went over to Dolan's saloon; I then looked over and saw the Marshal standing at Hafford's doorway; then saw the Sheriff going over to where the Marshal and Sheriff were talking; the Sheriff says, 'What's the trouble'; the Marshal says, 'Those men have made their threats; I will not arrest them but will kill them on sight'; Virgil Earp said this; the Sheriff asked the Marshal in to take a drink; did not see them afterward, as I crossed over the street to the other side; when I got over there I saw one of the Earp brothers, the youngest one, talking with Doc Holliday; looked across the street; saw the Marshal again; some one came up to him and called him aside; when this gentleman got through talking with the Earps; saw three of the Earps and Doc Holliday go down the street together; they kept on the left side of the street on Fourth; I was on the right side; when I got to the corner of Frémont and Fourth I started to go across to the southwest corner of Frémont; when I got midway between in the street I saw the fir-

188

ing had commenced; I kept my eyes on the Earps and Holliday until the shooting commenced; I saw Doc Holliday in the middle of the street; the youngest of the Earps brothers was about three feet from the sidewalk; he was firing at a man behind a horse; Holliday also fired at the man behind the horse, and firing at a man who ran by him on the opposite side of the street; then I saw the man who had the horse let go, and was staggering all the time until he fell; he had his pistol still when he fell; I never saw the two elder Earps; I did not know where they were situated; I then went to the young man lying on the sidewalk and offered to pick him up; he never spoke except the movement of his lips; I picked up a revolver lying five feet from him; then I saw Doc Holliday running towards where the young man was lying, still having a revolver in his hand, making the remark, 'The s— of a b— has shot me and I mean to kill him'; could not say who fired the first shots."

Daily Nugget, November 5, 1881: "The prosecution introduced as a witness Mrs. M. King, who, being duly sworn, testified as follows: . . . I was present in Tombstone on the day the shooting occurred; . . . I was in the butcher shop on Frémont Street when the shooting occurred; I heard the firing; while I was in the butcher shop remember of seeing some armed parties pass the door; could not say they were all armed; saw Mr. Holliday with arms; he had a gun; I mean a gun as distinguished from a pistol; can't tell the difference between a shotgun and a rifle; don't know whether this was a shotgun or a rifle; I can identify the man in this room who had the gun. [Witness here identifies Mr. Holliday as the person.]

"He is the person I mentioned as Mr. Holliday; he had on an overcoat; the gun was on his left hand side, with his overcoat over the gun and his arm thrown over it; I knew it was a gun because his overcoat flew back and I saw it; there were three persons with him; I suppose they were; all four were right together, walking in the same direction, down Frémont Street from the post office towards Third Street; I only know what I have been told who these persons were; I do not know the Earp brothers only by sight, and as they have been pointed out to me; persons pointed out to me as the Earp brothers were with him; I could not positively point out in this room any of the Earp brothers; I can say there is one man here who looks like them; these four men were on the sidewalk walking leisurely along, as any gentleman would walk, not fast, or very slow; when they got to the awning where the butcher shop is, Mr. Holliday and the man on the outside were just a little in front of the middle two; they were walking nearly abreast of each other; Holliday was on the left hand side, next to the building; I heard remarks from the party as they passed; I heard the gentleman on the outside, as I stepped into the second folding door, as he looked around say to Mr. Holliday, 'Let them have it'; Mr. Holliday said, 'All right.' I suppose he said it to Mr. Holliday, for he answered him; no names were used; I heard no other conversation, at this exact time; I saw nothing of the fight."

Daily Nugget, November 6, 1881: "The prosecution re-opened the case by introducing West Fuller, who being sworn testified as follows: Reside at Tombstone; occupation gambler; was at Tombstone, Cochise County, October 26, 1881; I saw a difficulty between the Earp brothers and Holliday on one side and the Clantons and McLowrys on the other side, on that day; the difficulty occurred on Frémont Street, near the corner of Third Street; the parties were Doc Holliday, Wyatt Earp, Virgil Earp and Morgan Earp on one side, and Tom and Frank McLowry and Billy Clanton and Ike Clanton on the other side; I was right back of Fly's photograph gallery, in the alley-way; . . . I was going down Allen Street to where the Clanton boys were standing for the purpose of telling Billy Clanton to leave town; I mean the parties I saw was Billy Clanton, John Behan [the Sheriff] and Frank McLowry; could not see any other persons from where I was; well, I expected he was going to get into trouble, as I saw the Earp boys and Holliday armed.

"Q. Where were the Earps and Holliday when you saw them armed? A. On Fourth and Allen Streets.

"Virg had a shotgun; the others had six-shooters; I did not get close enough to say anything to Billy Clanton or any of that party before the shooting commenced; I saw the Earps coming down; saw them just as they got there; heard some one say, 'throw up your hands'; some of the Earps said it; Billy Clanton throwed up his hands and said, 'Don't shoot me, I don't want any fight." At the same time the shooting commenced; I did not see Tom Mc-Lowry at the time; I did not see Ike Clanton at the time of the first shooting; I did not see Frank McLowry. The Earp party fired the first shots; two shots; almost together; I would not be positive whether they were gun or pistol shots; after these shots the firing commenced very rapidly; both parties were firing then; after the first two shots Billy Clanton staggered and fell up against the side of the house; there were five or six shots fired by the Earp party before Billy Clanton or Frank McLowry fired and they, Billy and Frank, were the only ones of the Clanton party that I saw fire a shot at all; at the time of the first two shots by the Earp party the hands of Billy Clanton were up. (By demonstration, witness shows hands up even with the head.) Frank McLowry, just at the time the shooting commenced, was standing by holding his horse; I don't think he was doing anything; I saw his hands and nothing was in them; if he had had a weapon in his hands, I would have seen it; I think the first two shots were both aimed at Billy Clanton; I saw he was hit; he threw his hands down on his belly, and partly turned around. I did not see, at that time, the effect of any shots on any one else; Frank McLowry drew a weapon and fired some shots during the fight; Frank McLowry was in Frémont Street when he drew his weapon; I think he was a little past the middle of the street when he pulled his pistol. . . .

"Q. Did you examine Tom McLowry after he was brought in the house? A. I did.

"Q. Did he have any arms on at that time? A. He did not.

191

"Q. Did he have a cartridge or other belt on? A. I did not see any.

"Q. State whether or not, during the shooting, you at any time saw Ike Clanton with any arms? A. I did not.

"Q. In what house was Tom McLowry brought? A. In the house on the corner of Third and Frémont; it was the second house below Fly's gallery, on the same side of the street.

"Q. What are your feelings toward the defendant, Holliday? A. We have always been friendly.

"Q. Are you so now? A. Yes, sir.

"Q. Did you not, on the 5th day of November, 1881, about 5 o'clock in the afternoon, in front of the Oriental saloon, in Tombstone, say to, or in the presence of Wyatt Earp, that you knew nothing in your testimony that would hurt the Earps but that you intended to cinch Holliday, or words to that effect? A. I told Wyatt Earp I thought Holliday was the cause of the fight. I don't think I used the words that I would cinch Holliday. I will not be positive."

Daily Nugget, November 6, 1881: "Motion was made by the attorney for the prosecution that the defendants be remanded to the custody of the Sheriff without bail. The point taken was that the proof was conclusive of murder. . . . The prisoners were remanded to the custody of the Sheriff until further order of the court."

Daily Nugget, November 6, 1881: "Andy Mehan, sworn: Am in the saloon business.

"Q. Did you know Thomas McLowry in his life time? A. Yes, sir.

"Q. Whose pistol is that which you brought into court? A. It was left with me by Thomas McLowry.

"Q. When did he leave it with you? A. On the 26th of October, 1881.

"Q. About what time in the day did he leave it with you? A. Between 1 and 2 o'clock.

"Q. Where has it been since the time he left it with you until you brought it into court? A. In my safe in the saloon."

Daily Nugget, November 10, 1881: "Ike Clanton being sworn, says: My name is Joseph I. Clanton; reside four miles above Charleston, on the river; my occupation is that of a cattle and stock dealer. . . . Myself and the McLowry brothers and Wm. Clanton and a young fellow named Willie Claibourne were standing in a vacant lot on Frémont Street, between Fly's building and the one next west of Fly's, talking; Sheriff Behan came down and said he would have to arrest us. He said he would have to arrest us and disarm us; I asked Behan what for? He told me to preserve the peace; I told him I had no arms; then William Clanton told him he was just leaving town; the Sheriff then said if you are leaving town all right; he then told Tom and Frank McLowry he would have to take their arms; Tom McLowry told him that he had none; Frank said he was going out of town and did not want to give his arms up, while the party that hit his brother was still armed; the Sheriff told him that he should do it; and to take his arms up to the Sheriff's office and take them off; then he (Frank) said he had business in town that he would like to attend to, and would not lay off his arms and attend to the business, but that he would leave town if the Earps were not disarmed; the Sheriff put his arms around me to see if I was armed; Tom McLowry said to him, I am not armed, and opened his coat this way (showing each hand on lapel and coat thrown wide open); the Sheriff then looked up Frémont Street and ordered us to stay there until he came back . . . just as Behan started up the Earps and Holliday appeared on the sidewalk . . . he held up his hands to them and told them to stop, that he had our party in charge.

"Q. State what they did when Behan told them to stop? A. They passed right on by him; did not stop but came on to where we were.

"Q. How far was it from where you were standing to where Behan met the Earps and Holliday? A. I would judge it to be about twenty paces.

"Q. You say they came on down to where you were, what did they do when they got there? A. They pulled their pistols as they got there and said: 'You s—s of b—s, you have been looking for a fight, and now you can have it'; Wyatt and Virgil said it, and at the same time ordered us to throw up our hands; we threw up our hands, and they at the same time commenced shooting.

"Q. Who commenced shooting? A. The first two shots were fired by Holliday and Morg Earp.

"Q. Who fired the next? A. Wyatt Earp and Virg Earp, in quick succession; just after Morg and Holliday shot, Virg fired, before Wyatt did.

"Q. How close together were the first two shots? A. They were fired so close together that I could not tell which fired first. . . .

"Q. At the time the Earp party came up to where you and the McLowrys and Billy Clanton were standing, what if anything, did Wyatt Earp do? A. He shoved his pistol against my belly, and said, 'throw up your hands'; and said, 'you s— of a b— you can have a fight.' I turned on my heel and took Wyatt Earp a hold of his hand and pistol with my left hand and grabbed him around the shoulder with my right hand and held him for a few seconds; while I was holding him he shot and I pushed him around the photograph gallery and jumped into the photograph gallery door; went right through the hall and out the back way, and went off across Allen Street and into the dance hall; as I was leaving and as I jumped into the door of the photograph gallery I heard one or two bullets pass right by my head; as I passed through an opening on my way from the gallery I heard another bullet pass me.

"Q. State if there was any previous difficulty between you and the defendants or either of them, if so, when and where? A. Yes, sir, there was a difficulty between Holliday and Morg Earp and me the night before the shooting, at a lunch stand in this town, close to the Eagle Brewery saloon, on the north side of Allen Street; as near as I can remember it was about 1 o'clock in the morning; I went in there to get a lunch; while I was sitting down at the table Doc Holliday came in and commenced cursing me and said I had been using his name; that I was a s— of a b— of a cowboy, and to get my gun out and get to work; I told him I had no gun; he said I was a d—n liar and had threatened the Earps; I told him I had not, and to bring whoever said so and I would convince him that I had not; he told me again to pull out my gun and if there is any grit in me to go fighting; all the time he was talking he had his hand on his pistol in his bosom; I mean he had his hand in his bosom, and I believed on a pistol; I looked behind me and I saw Morg Earp with his feet over the lunch counter; he also had his hand in his bosom, looking at me; I then got up and went out on the sidewalk; Doc Holliday said as I walked out, 'You s—n of a b—h, you ain't heeled; go heel yourself'; just at that time Morg Earp stepped up and said, 'Yes, you s—n of a b—h, you can have all the fight you want now'; I thanked him and told him I did not want any of it; I am not heeled. Virgil Earp stood then about fifteen feet from me down the sidewalk. Just about this time, Wyatt Earp came out of the door; while we were still standing there. . . .

Daily Nugget, November 11, 1881: "Examination of Ike Clanton continued: Just about this time Wyatt Earp came up; Wyatt did not say anything; Morgan Earp told me if I was not heeled when I came back to be heeled; I walked off and asked Morgan Earp not to shoot me in the back; I did not see Morg Earp or Doc Holliday that night to speak to them; well, that night I came back in half an hour to the saloon on the west, the Alhambra, I think; I sat down to play poker in the morning in that saloon; I think the name of it was the Alhambra; Tom Corrigan was tending bar there; those two saloons I have got the names mixed; the first row between me and Holliday was in the Alhambra, we were playing poker in the Occidental, Virg Earp, Tom Mc-Lowry, myself, John Behan and another gentleman, I don't remember his name; in the row with Holliday and Morg Earp on the sidewalk Virg Earp told them to let me alone while Jim Flynn was there, then again as I walked away; Jim Flynn is a policeman; there was no Jim other than Jim Flynn there at the time; when the poker game broke up in the morning I saw Virg Earp take his pistol out of his lap and stick it in his pants, I got up and followed him outdoors on the sidewalk; he was going down Allen Street in front of the Cosmopolitan hotel; I walked up to him and said from his actions the night before in regard to the policeman and what he said the night before, and playing poker with his six-shooter in his lap, I said I thought he stood in with those people who tried to murder me the night before; I told him if that was so I was in town; he said he was going to bed; I went and cashed my chips into the poker game.

"Had no more talk with him that morning; well, think it was about half-past 12 o'clock on Fourth Street, between Frémont Street and Allen Street, Virg and Morg Earp came up behind me; do not know where they came from, Virg Earp struck me on the side of the head with a six-shooter from behind and knocked me up against the wall; Morg Earp cocked his pistol and stuck it at me, towards me; Virg Earp took my arms, my pistol and Win-chester; I did not know or see that they were about there; did not know who struck me until I fell against the house; then they pulled me along and said: 'You damned s—n of a b—h, we'll take you up to Judge Wallace's office'; when I got there Wyatt Earp came in and cursed me, and said I could have all the fight I wanted; did not see Doc Holliday there; Wyatt Earp called me a thief and a son of a b—h, and said I could have all the fight I wanted, and said he could out-shoot me, or whip me, am not cer-tain which he said; Virg Earp came up and said, 'Yes, we will give it to you pretty plenty now'; Morg Earp told me he would pay my fine if I would fight him; I told him I would fight him; Wyatt Earp offered me my gun—rifle—by pointing it muzzle fore-most, and told me to take it; as he presented me the gun I saw Virg Earp put his hand in his bosom (this way), [showing] Mor-gan Earp stood over me, on a bench behind me; Wyatt Earp stood to my right and in front of me; then I told them I did not want any of it that way, Wyatt Earp asked me when I wanted to fight, and where and how.

"As well as I can remember, I said 'I will fight you anywhere

196

or any way'; this is all I remember of what occurred there; this all transpired while I was in Judge Wallace's court; I am inclined to think that Judge Wallace was not in court at the time; I was waiting there in court some time before the fine was imposed on me; there were a good many people at the door when this occurred; I was fined, paid my fine, and was released; this, I think, was about 10 o'clock; all this occurred on the day of the killing, about, as near as I can judge, about one hour and a-half before the shooting.

"Q. At the time you were released, who had your arms? A. Virg [word illegible] at least, he had taken them in charge when I was arrested, and had not given them to me.

"Q. When and where did you get your arms? A. I got them I think a couple of days after that from Billy Soule, the jailer."

Daily Nugget, November 13, 1881: "Continuation of testimony of Isaac Clanton. . . .

"Q. You were asked in your cross-examination if Billy Leonard, Jim Crane and Harry Head were supposed to be connected with the attempt to rob the stage at the killing of Budd Philpot, and to which you answered: 'I don't know anything about it but what Virgil Earp, Wyatt Earp, Morgan Earp and Doc Holliday and others told me.' Please state what Doc Holliday told you, upon that subject, and when you have answered as to him, state what Morgan Earp told you, then state what Virgil Earp told you, and then what Wyatt Earp told you?

"A. Doc Holliday told me, to the best of my recollection, this: I came up town a few days after Budd Philpot was killed; Doc Holliday asked me if I had seen William Leonard and his party; I told him I had; I had seen them the day before and they had told me to tell Doc Holliday that they were going to the San José Mountains. He then asked me if I had had a talk with them. I told him only for a moment. He told me then he would see me later in the evening. This was in front of the Cosmopolitan Hotel; later in the evening I met him at Jim Vogan's place and after talking with him a while he asked me if Leonard told me how he came to kill

Budd Philpot. I told him Leonard had told me nothing about it. He [Doc Holliday] then told me that Bob Paul, the messenger, had the lines and Budd Philpot had the shotgun, and Philpot made a fight and got left. About that time someone came along and the conversation ended.

"I told Doc Holliday not to take me into his confidence, that I did not wish to know any more about it. Doc Holliday told me he was there at the killing of Budd Philpot. He told me that he shot Philpot through the heart. He told me this at the same time and in connection with the sentence that, 'Philpot made a fight and got left.' He said he saw 'Budd Philpot, the d—n s— b— tumble off the cart.' That is the last conversation I ever had with Holliday in connection with that affair. He has often told me to tell Leonard, Head and Crane, if I saw them, that he was all right.

"Sometime in June, about the 1st, I came into Tombstone and I met Wyatt Earp in the Eagle Brewery saloon; he asked me to take a drink with him; while our drinks were being mixed he told me he wanted a long private talk with me; after our drinks we stepped out in the middle of the street; he told me then he could put me on a scheme to make $6,000; I asked him what it was; he told me he would not tell me unless I would promise either to do it or promise never to mention our conversation to anyone; he told me it was a legitimate transaction. And then the conversation as detailed in my cross-examination ensued.[1]

"The next morning after this conversation with Wyatt Earp I met Morg Earp in the Alhambra saloon, and he asked me what conclusion I had come to in regard to my conversation with Wyatt; I told him I would let him know before I left town; he approached me again in the same place four or five days after this; we had considerable talk about it then at that time, but I only remember that he told me that ten or twelve days before Budd Philpot was killed that he had 'piped off' $1,400 to Doc Holliday and Bill Leonard, and that Wyatt Earp had 'given away' a number of thousand dollars (I think he said $29,000) the day Budd Philpot was killed—which sum was going off on the train that

198

night; we talked a while longer, but I don't remember what was said, only I told him I was not going to have anything to do with it; I meant I would have nothing to do with killing Crane, Leonard and Head; Virg Earp told me to tell Billy Leonard at one time not to think he was trying to catch him when they were running him, and he told me to tell Billy he had thrown Paul and the posse that was after him off his track at the time they left Helm's ranch, at the foot of the Dragoon Mountains, and that he had taken them on to a trail that went down into New Mexico, and that he had done all he could for him, and he wanted Billy Leonard to get Head and Crane out of the country, for he was afraid one of them might be captured and get all his friends into trouble; he, Virg Earp, said in that conversation, that they had quit a trail of three horses and followed a trail of fifteen horses; he said I [should] send them this word to assure them that I have not gone back on them; he stated he knew the trail of Crane, Leonard and Head went south towards the San José Mountains, and the Sheriff and posse followed the other trail into New Mexico.

"Q. Why have you not told what Doc Holliday, Wyatt Earp, Virgil Earp and Morgan Earp said about the attempted stage robbery and the killing of Philpot before you told it in this examination?

"A. Before he told me I made him sacred, solemn promises that I would never tell it, and I never would if I had not been put on the stand, and another reason was that I found out by Wyatt Earp's conversation that he was offering money to kill his confederates in this attempted stage robbery, through fear that Bill Leonard, Crane and Head would be captured and tell on them, and I knew that after Crane, Leonard and Head was killed that some of them would murder me for what they had told me."

Daily Nugget, November 11, 1881: "J. H. Batcher sworn, says: My name is J. H. Batcher; residence, Tombstone, Cochise County, Arizona; am bookkeeper for P. W. Smith; was at Tombstone on the 26th day of October, 1881; on that day I saw a difficulty below Judge Wallace's office, on Fourth Street; saw Wyatt

Earp strike Tom McLowry with his pistol; first saw Wyatt Earp at Judge Wallace's office; as he left the office I started to the corner store, following behind him, perhaps fifteen feet behind; at this time Tom McLowry was coming down Fourth Street toward Wallace's office; Wyatt Earp stopped him and addressed him; he said something to him, and at that time I thought it was time to get out of the way, and I left; heard Tom McLowry speak rather loud and said he had always been a friend of his (Earp's); that he had never done a thing against him; Tom McLowry addressed him and after saying something said, 'If you want to fight I am with you'; then Wyatt Earp pulled his gun and asked him if he was heeled? Tom said something, I don't know what; then Wyatt struck him, first with the palm of his hand and then hit him with his right hand with his pistol on the side of his head to once; Tom McLowry fell down and Wyatt Earp walked away, and Tom McLowry got up and left."

Daily Nugget, November 12, 1881: "The inmates of the County Jail are complaining of the cold. Arrangements have been made for properly heating it on and after today."

Daily Nugget, November 18, 1881: "Robert S. Hatch, for the Defense, sworn: My name is Robert S. Hatch, reside at Tombstone, Cochise County, Arizona, occupation, saloon keeper.

"Q. Were you in Tombstone on the 26th of October last? A. Yes, sir.

"Q. Did you see anything of a difficulty on that day between Virgil Earp, Morgan Earp, Wyatt Earp and J. H. Holliday on the one side, and Isaac Clanton, William Clanton, Frank McLowry and Thomas McLowry on the other side? A. I did between a part of those parties.

"Q. State how you came to see the difficulty, under what circumstances, and what occurred between the parties, when and where it occurred. State all the matters you know in relation thereto. A. I was walking down Frémont Street in company with William Soule, jailer and deputy sheriff, here on the 26th day of October last, about 2 o'clock in the afternoon; I noticed the three Earp brothers and Doc Holliday in front of me going down the street; as I got down near the Recorder's office I saw Mr. Behan come out from near Fly's building—the photograph gallery—he advanced up the street a short distance, and met the Earps and Holliday; he made some remark to them, which I think was, 'I am sheriff of this county; and I want this thing stopped,' or words to that effect; they (the Earp party) walked right on, I mean the Earp party; saw at that time two men that had been pointed out to me as the Mc-Lowry brothers, and Billy Clanton, standing in the vacant lot below Fly's building; as the Earp party got within about eight or ten feet of them I heard some one, who I though was Virgil Earp, say: 'We came down here to disarm and arrest you,' or words to that effect; a few seconds after this was said the shooting commenced.

"I turned to Billy Soule and said to him, this is none of our fight, we had better get away from here; as I turned to go I saw Billy Clanton standing near the corner of the building below Fly's house, with a pistol in his hands in the act of shooting; probably there had been three or four shots fired at that time; I immediately ran up the street and went into Bauer's butcher shop— the market—probably went as far as the butcher block, near the back end of the shop, turned and went back to the door on the west side of the building; saw Doc Holliday and a man that had been pointed out to me as Frank McLowry near the middle of Frémont Street, ten or 11 feet apart, or somewhere like that; Frank McLowry made some remark like this: 'I have got you this time'; Holliday made some remark: 'You are a good one if you have,' or words to that effect; McLowry seemed to be retreating across the street, to the opposite side of the street; when he got near the adobe building on the opposite side of the street, he stopped and stood with his pistol across his arm, the pistol in his right hand and resting on his left arm and in the act of shooting; about that time I saw Doc Holliday and Morgan Earp shooting in the direction of McLowry, or at him; Frank McLowry fell to the ground at that time as if he had been shot; the shooting seemed

201

to be over at that time; I immediately went out of the butcher shop towards Fly's building; before I saw Frank McLowry fall and before he got across the street, I saw Morgan Earp fall in the middle of the street and I think he made some such remark as, 'I am hit,' or shot, or something of the kind; he, Morgan Earp, immediately got up and commenced to shoot, or was in the act of shooting towards Frank McLowry.

"I saw this man Fly come out of his, Fly's house, with a Henry rifle in his hand. He made the remark, pointing to Billy Clanton below, who had a pistol in his right hand, 'somebody take that pistol away from that man,' referring to Billy Clanton. Billy Clanton seemed to be in the act of trying to cock it, but did not seem to have the strength to do so. I said to Mr. Fly, 'Go take it yourself, if you want to.' Fly walked towards Billy Clanton and I was right with him. Fly reached down and took hold of the pistol and pulled it out of his hand. As he did so, Billy Clanton said, 'give me some more cartridges.' "

Daily Nugget, November 17, 1881: "Testimony for the defense—Statement by Wyatt Earp . . . witness took the stand and commenced his statement by reading a carefully prepared manuscript. . . . My name is Wyatt S. Earp; 32 years old the 19th of last March; born at Monmouth, Warren County, Ill., reside in Tombstone, Cochise County, Arizona, and have resided here since December 1st, 1879, and am at present a saloon-keeper; also, have been Deputy Sheriff and detective.

"The difficulty which resulted in the death of Wm. Clanton and Frank and Tom McLowry, originated last spring.

. . . .

"Shortly after the time Bud Philpot was killed by the men who tried to rob the Benson stage, as a detective I tried to trace the matter up, and I was satisfied that three men named Billy Leonard, Harry Head and James Crane were in that robbery. I knew that Leonard, Head and Crane were friends and associates of the Clantons and McLowrys, and often stopped at their ranch; it was generally understood among officers and those who have information about criminals, that Ike Clanton was a sort of chief amongst the cowboys; that the Clantons and McLowrys were cattle thieves and generally in the secrets of the stage robbers, and that the Clanton and McLowry ranches were meeting places and place of shelter for the gang.

"I had an ambition to be Sheriff of this county at the next election, and I thought it would be of great help to me with the people and business men if I could capture the men who killed Philpot; there were rewards of about $1200 each for the capture of the robbers; altogether there was about $3600 for the capture.

"I thought this might tempt Ike Clanton and Frank McLowry to give away Leonard, Head and Crane, so I went to Ike Clanton, Frank McLowry and Joe Hill when they came in town; I had an interview with them in the back yard of the Oriental Saloon; I told them what I wanted; I told them I wanted the glory of capturing Leonard, Head and Crane, and if I could do so it would help me make the race for Sheriff at the next election; I told them if they would put me on the track of Leonard, Head and Crane and tell me where those men were hid, I would give them all the reward and would never let anyone know where I got my information; Ike Clanton said he would like to see them captured; he said that Leonard claimed a ranch that he claimed, and that if he could get him out of the way that he would have no opposition in regard to the ranch.

"Clanton said Leonard, Head and Crane would make a fight, that they never would be taken alive; that I must first find out if the reward would be paid for the capture dead or alive. I then went to Marshall Williams, the agent of Wells, Fargo in this town, and at my request he telegraphed to the Agent or Superintendent of Wells, Fargo at San Francisco to find out if the reward would be paid for the robbers dead or alive. He received in June, 1881, a telegram which he showed me promising that the reward would be paid dead or alive.

"The next day I met Ike Clanton and Joe Hill on Allen Street in front of the little cigar store next to the Alhambra; I told them the dispatch had come; I went to Marshall Williams and told him I wanted to see that dispatch for a few minutes. He went to looking for it and could not find it just then; he went over to the telegraph office and got a copy and came and gave it to me. I went and showed it to Ike Clanton and Joe Hill and returned it to Marshall Williams, and afterwards told Frank McLowry of its contents. It was then agreed between us that they should have all the $3,600 reward, outside of necessary expenses for horse hire in going after them, and that Joe Hill should go where Leonard, Head and Crane were hid over near Eureka, in New Mexico, and lure them in near Frank and Tom McLowry's ranch, near Soldier Holes, 30 miles from here, and I would be on hand with a posse and capture them.

"I asked Joe Hill, Ike Clanton and Frank McLowry what tale they would make to them to get them over here. They said they had agreed upon a plan to tell them that there would be a paymaster going from Tombstone to Bisbee shortly to pay off the miners, and that they wanted them to come in and take them; Ike Clanton then sent Joe Hill to bring them in; before starting Joe Hill took off his watch and chain and between two and three hundred dollars in money, and gave it to Virgil Earp to keep for him until he got back; he was gone about ten days, and returned with the word that he had got there one day too late, that Leonard and Harry Head had been killed the day before he got there by horse thieves; I learned afterwards that the horse thieves had been killed subsequently by members of the Clanton and McLowry gang; after that Ike Clanton and Frank McLowry claimed that I had given them away to Marshall Williams and Doc Holliday, and we began to hear of their threats against us.

"I am a friend of Doc Holliday, because when I was City Marshal of Dodge City, Kansas, he came to my rescue and saved my life when I was surrounded by desperadoes.

"About a month or more ago Morgan Earp and myself assisted to arrest Stilwell and Spencer on the charge of robbing the Bisbee stage; the McLowrys and Clantons have always been friends of Stilwell and Spencer, and they laid the whole blame of their arrest

204

on us, though, the fact is we only went as a Sheriff's posse; after we got in town with Spencer and Stilwell, Ike Clanton and Frank McLowry came in; Frank McLowry took Morgan Earp into the street in front of the Alhambra, when John Ringgold, Ike Clanton and the two Hicks boys were also standing by, when Frank Mc-Lowry commenced to abuse Morgan Earp for going after Spencer and Stilwell; Frank McLowry said he would never speak to Spencer again for being arrested by us; he said to Morgan: 'If you ever come after me you will never take me;' Morgan replied if he ever had occasion to go after him he would arrest him; Frank McLowry then said to Morgan: 'I have threatened you boys' lives, and a few days ago had taken it back, but since this arrest it now 'goes.' Morgan made no reply and walked off.

"Before this and after this Marshall Williams, Farmer Daly, Ed Byrnes, Old Man Winter, Charley Smith and three or four others had told us at different times of threats to kill us made by Ike Clanton, Frank McLowry, Tom McLowry, Joe Hill and John Ringgold; I knew all those men were desperate and dangerous men; that they were connected with outlaws, cattle thieves, robbers and murderers; I knew of the McLowrys stealing six government mules and also cattle, and when the owner went after them—finding his stock on the McLowry boys' ranch—that he was driven off, and told that if he ever said anything about it they would kill him, and he has kept his mouth shut until several days ago for fear of being killed. I heard of Ringgold shooting a man down in cold blood near Camp Thomas; I was satisfied that Frank and Tom McLowry had killed and robbed Mexicans in Skeleton Canyon three or four months ago, and I naturally kept my eyes open, for I did not intend that any of the gang should get the drop on me if I could help it.

"Ike Clanton met me at Vogan's old saloon five or six months ago [2] and told me that I had told Holliday about this transaction concerning the 'giving away' Head, Leonard and Crane; I told him I had never told Holliday anything; I told him that when Holliday came up from Tucson I would prove it; Ike Clanton told him that

205

Holliday had told him so; when Holliday came back I asked him and he said no; I told him that Ike Clanton had said so; on the 25th of October—the night—Holliday met Ike Clanton in the Alhambra lunch room and asked him about it; Clanton denied it; they quarrelled for three or four minutes; Holliday told Clanton he was a damned liar if he said so; I was sitting eating lunch at the lunch counter, Morgan Earp was standing at the Alhambra bar talking to the bartender, I called him over to where I was sitting, knowing that he was an officer, and told him that Holliday and Clanton were quarrelling in the lunch room, and for him to go in and stop it; he climbed over the lunch counter from the Alhambra bar, went into the room, took Holliday by the arm and led him into the street; Ike Clanton in a few moments followed them out; I got through eating and walked out; as I opened the door I could hear that they were still quarrelling outside; Virgil Earp came up, I think out of the Occidental, and told them (Holliday and Clanton) that if they did not stop their quarrelling he would have to arrest them.

"They all separated at that time, Morgan Earp going down the street, home; Virgil Earp going in the Occidental saloon, Holliday up the street to the Oriental saloon, and Ike Clanton across the street to the Grand Hotel. I walked into the Eagle brewery where I had a faro game which I had not closed. I stayed in there a few moments and then walked out on the street and there met Ike Clanton. He asked me if I would take a walk with him, he wanted to have a talk with me. I told him I would 'if he did not go too far, that I was waiting for my game in the brewery to close, as I had to take care of the money. We walked about half way down the side of the brewery building on Fifth Street and stopped. He told me that when Holliday approached him in the lunch room, that he was not fixed just right. He said that in the morning he would have man for man, and that this fighting talk had been going on for a long time, and he guessed it was about time to fetch it to a close. I told him I would fight no one if I could get away from it, because there was no money in it. He walked off and left me saying, 'I will be ready for all of you in the morning.' I walked over

206

to the Oriental, he come in, followed me in rather, and took a drink, having his six-shooter on and playing fight and saying, 'you must not think I won't be after you all in the morning.' He said he would like to make a fight with Holliday now. I told him Holliday did not want to fight, but only to satisfy him that this talk had not been made. About that time the man who was dealing my game closed it, and brought the money to me. I locked it up in the safe and started home. I met Holliday on the street between the Oriental and Alhambra. Myself and Holliday walked down Allen Street, he going to his room, and I, to my house to bed.

"I got up next day, October 26th, about noon. Before I got up Ned Boyle came to me and told me that he had met Ike Clanton on Allen Street, near the telegraph office, and that Ike was on it; that he said that as soon as those d—d Earps make their appearance on the street today the ball will open; that Ike said, 'We are here to make a fight and we are looking for the s—s of b—s.' I lay in bed some little time after that; got up and went down to the Oriental saloon. Harry Jones came to me after I got up and said, 'What does all this mean?' I asked him what he meant. He says, 'Ike Clanton is hunting you Earp boys with a Winchester rifle and a six-shooter.' I said, 'I will go down and find him and see what he wants.' I went out, and at the corner of Fifth and Allen, I met Virgil Earp, the marshal. He told me how he had heard that Ike Clanton was hunting us. I went down Allen Street, and Virgil went down Fifth and then Frémont Street. Virgil found Ike Clanton on Fourth, near Frémont, in an alley way. He walked up to him and said, 'I heard you were hunting for some of us.' I was coming down Fourth Street at this time. Clanton then threw his Winchester around toward Virgil; Virgil grabbed it and hit Clanton with his six-shooter and knocked him down. Clanton had his rifle and his six-shooter in his pants. By that time I came up. Virgil and Morgan Earp took the rifle and six-shooter away and took them to the Grand Hotel after examination and took Ike Clanton before Justice Wallace. Before the examination Morgan Earp had Ike Clanton in charge as Virgil Earp was out.

"A short time after I went to Wallace's court and sat down on a bench. Ike Clanton looked over to me and said, 'I will get even with all of you for this. If I had a six-shooter now I would make a fight with all of you.' Morgan Earp then said to him, 'If you want to make a fight right bad I'll give you this,' at the same time offering Ike Clanton his own (Ike's) six-shooter. Ike Clanton started up to take it, and Campbell, the Deputy Sheriff, pushed him back in his seat, saying he would not allow any fuss. I never had Ike Clanton's arms at any time, as he has stated. . . .

"I was tired of being threatened by Ike Clanton and his gang; I believed from what they had said to me and others and from their movements that they intended to assassinate me the first chance they had, and I thought that if I had to fight for my life with them I had better make them face me in an open fight, so I said to Ike Clanton, who was then sitting about eight feet away from me, you d—n dirty cow thief, you have been threatening our lives, and I know it, I think I would be justified in shooting you down in any place I would meet you, but if you are anxious to make a fight I will go anywhere on earth to make a fight with you, even over to the San Simon, among your own crowd; he replied, all right, I will see you after I get through here, I only want four feet of ground to fight;

"I walked out, and just then, outside of the court-room and near the Justice's office, I met Tom McLowry; he came up to me and said to me, 'if you want to make a fight I will make a fight with you anywhere'; I supposed at the time that he had heard what had just transpired between Ike Clanton and myself; I knew of his having threatened me, and I felt just as I did about Ike Clanton, that if the fight had to come I had better have it come when I had an even show to defend myself, so I said to him, 'all right, make a fight right here,' and at the same time slapped him on the face with my left hand and drew my pistol with my right; he had a pistol in plain sight, on his right hip, in his pants, but made no move to draw it; I said to him, jerk your gun and use it; he made no reply; I hit him on the head with my six-shooter and walked away down to Hafford's corner, went into Hafford's and got a cigar and came out and stood by the door. Pretty soon after I saw Tom and Frank McLowry and William Clanton. They passed me and went down 4th Street to the gunsmith shop; I followed down to see what they were going to do; when I got there Frank McLowry's horse was standing on the sidewalk with his head in the door of the gunsmith shop; I took the horse by the bit, as I was deputy city marshal, and commenced to back him off the sidewalk; Tom and Frank McLowry and Billy Clanton came to the door; Billy laid his hand on his six-shooter, Frank McLowry took hold of the horse's bridle. I said 'you will have to get this horse off the sidewalk.' Frank McLowry backed him off on the street. Ike Clanton came up about that time and they all walked into the gunsmith shop. I saw them in the shop changing cartridges into their belts. They came out of the shop and walked along 4th Street to the corner of Allen; I followed them to the corner of 4th and Allen Streets, and then they went down Allen and over to Dunbar's corral.

"Virg Earp was then City Marshal; Morgan Earp was a special policeman for six weeks or two months, wore a badge and drew pay; I had been sworn in Virgil's place to act for him while he was gone to Tucson to Spencer and Stilwell's trial; Virgil had been back for a few days but I was still acting; I knew it was Virgil's duty to disarm those men; expected he would have trouble in doing so and I followed up to give assistance if necessary, especially as they had been threatening us as I have already stated.

"About ten minutes afterwards, and while Virgil, Morgan, Doc Holliday and myself were standing on the corner of Allen and 4th Streets, several persons said there is going to be trouble with those fellows, and one man named Coleman said to Virgil they mean trouble. They have just gone from Dunbar's Corral to the O.K. Corral all armed. I think you had better go and disarm them.

"Virgil turned around to Holliday, Morgan Earp and myself, and told us to come and assist him in disarming them. Morgan Earp said to me, they have horses, had we not better get some horses ourselves so that if they make a running fight we can catch them,

I said no. If they try to make a running fight we can kill their horses and then capture them.

"We four then started through Fourth to Frémont Streets. When we turned the corner of Fourth and Frémont, we could see them standing near or about the vacant space between Fly's Photograph Gallery and the next building west. I first saw Frank McLowry, Tom McLowry, Billy Clanton and Sheriff Behan standing there. We went down the left hand side of Frémont Street, when I got within about 150 feet of them. I saw Ike Clanton, Billy Claiborne and another party. We had walked a few steps from there when I saw Behan leave the party and come toward us. Every few steps he would look back as if he apprehended danger. I heard Behan say to Virgil, 'Earp, for God's sake don't go down there for you will get murdered.' Virgil replied, 'I am going to disarm them'; he being in the lead. When I and Morgan came up to Behan, he said, 'I have disarmed them.' When he said this, I took my pistol which I had in my hand under my coat, and put it into my overcoat pocket. Behan then passed up the street, and we walked on down. We came upon them close, Frank McLowry, Tom McLowry and Billy Clanton standing all in a row against the east side of the building on the opposite side of the vacant place west of Fly's photograph gallery. Ike Clanton and a man I did not know was standing in the vacant space, about half way between the photograph gallery and the next building west. I saw that Billy Clanton, Frank and Tom McLowry had their hands by their sides; Frank McLowry's and Billy Clanton's six-shooters were in plain sight. Virgil said, 'Throw up your hands: I have come to disarm you.'

"Billy Clanton and Tom McLowry [3] commenced to draw their pistols; at the same time Tom McLowry threw his hand to his right hip, throwing his coat open like that (showing), and jumped behind a horse. I had my pistol in my overcoat pocket, where I put it when Behan told us he had disarmed the other parties. When I saw Billy Clanton and Frank McLowry draw their pistols, I drew my pistol. Billy Clanton leveled his pistol on me, but I did not aim

210

at him. I knew that Frank McLowry had the reputation of being a good shot and a dangerous man and I aimed at Frank McLowry. The first two shots which were fired were fired by Billy Clanton and myself, he shooting at me and I at Frank McLowry. I do not know which shot was fired first. We fired almost together. The fight then became general.

'After about four shots were fired, Ike Clanton ran up and grabbed my left arm. I could see no weapon in his hand, and I thought at the time he had none, and so I said to him, 'The fight has now commenced; go to fighting, or get away.' At the same time I pushed him off with my left hand. He started and ran down the side of the building and disappeared between the lodging house and photograph gallery; my first shot struck Frank McLowry in the belly; he staggered off on the sidewalk, but first fired one shot at me; when we told them to throw up their hands Claiborne held up his left hand and then broke and ran, and I never seen him afterwards until late in the afternoon; I never drew my pistol or made a motion to shoot until after Billy Clanton and Frank McLowry drew their pistols; if Tom McLowry was unarmed I did not know it; believe he was armed and fired two shots at our party before Holliday, who had the shotgun, fired at and killed him; if he was unarmed there was nothing in the circumstances, or in what had been communicated to me, or in his acts or threats that would have led me even to suspect his being unarmed; I never fired at Ike Clanton, even after the shooting commenced, because I thought he was unarmed; I believed then, and believe now, from the facts I have stated and from the threats I have related, and other threats communicated to me by different persons, as having been made by Tom McLowry, Frank McLowry and Ike Clanton, that these men last named had formed a conspiracy to murder my brothers, Morgan and Virgil, Doc Holliday and myself; I believe I would have been legally and morally justifiable in shooting any of them on sight, but I did not do so, nor attempt to do so; I sought no advantage when I went, as Deputy Marshal, to help to disarm them and arrest them; I went as a part of my duty and under the

211

directions of my brothers, the marshals; I did not intend to fight unless it became necessary in self-defense or in the rightful performance of official duty; when Billy Clanton and Frank McLowry drew their pistols; I knew it was a fight for life and I drew and fired in defense of my own life and the lives of my brothers and Doc Holliday."

Daily Nugget, December 1, 1881: [6] "Opinion of Justice of the Peace Wells Spicer. . . . Defendants, Wyatt Earp and John H. Holliday, two of the defendants named in the above entitled action, were arrested upon a warrant issued by me on the 29th day of October on a charge of murder. The complaint filed upon which the warrant was issued, accuses said defendants of the murder of Wm. Clanton, Frank McLowry and Thos. McLowry on the 26th day of last month, at Tombstone, in this county.

"In view of these controversies between Wyatt Earp and Isaac Clanton and Thomas McLowry, and in further view of the quarrel the night before between Isaac Clanton and J. H. Holliday, I am of the opinion that the defendant, Virgil Earp, as chief of police, by subsequently calling upon Wyatt Earp and J. H. Holliday to assist him in arresting and disarming the Clantons and McLowrys, committed an injudicious and censurable act, and although in this he acted incautiously and without proper circumspection, yet when we consider the condition of affairs incident to a frontier country; the lawlessness and disregard for human life; the existence of a law-defying element in our midst; the fear and feeling of insecurity that has existed; the supposed prevalence of bad, desperate and reckless men who have been a terror to the country, and kept away capital and enterprise, and considering the many threats that have been made against the Earps, I can attach no criminality to his unwise act. In fact, as the result plainly proves, he needed the assistance and support of staunch and true friends, upon whose courage, coolness and fidelity he could depend in case of an emergency.

"Virgil Earp was informed by one A. F. Sills, engineer of the Atchison, Topeka and Santa Fe Railroad,[4] then absent from duty on a lay-off furlough, and who had arrived in town only the day before and was totally unacquainted with any person in town or the state of affairs existing here, that he (Sills) had overheard armed parties, just then passing through the OK corral, say, in effect, that they would make sure to kill Earp, the marshal, and would kill all the Earps. At the same time several citizens and a committee of citizens came to Virgil Earp, the Chief of Police, and insisted that he should perform his duty as such officer, and arrest and disarms these cowboys, as they termed the Clantons and McLowrys.

"Was it for Virgil Earp, as Chief of Police, to abandon his clear duty as an officer because his performance was likely to be fraught with danger? Or was it not his duty that, as such officer, he owed to the peaceable and law-abiding citizens of the city, who looked to him to preserve peace and order and their protection and security, to at once call to his aid sufficient assistance and proceed to arrest and disarm these men? There can be but one answer to these questions, and that answer is such as will divert the subsequent approach of the defendants toward the deceased of all presumption of malice or illegality. When, therefore, the defendants, regularly or specially appointed officers, marched down Frémont Street to the scene of the subsequent homicide, they were going where it was their right and duty to go; they were doing what it was their right and duty to do; and they were armed, as it was their right and duty to be armed, when approaching men whom they believed to be armed and contemplating resistance.

"There is a dispute as to whether Thos. McLowry was armed at all, except with a Winchester rifle that was on the horse beside him. I will not consider this question, because it is not of controlling importance. Certain it is, that the Clanton's and McLowry's had among them at least two six-shooters in their hands and two Winchester rifles on their horses, therefore, if Thos. McLowry was one of a party who were thus armed and were making felonious resistance to an arrest, and in the melee that followed was shot, the fact of his being unarmed, if it be a fact, could not of itself criminate the defendants, if they were not otherwise criminal. It is beyond doubt that William Clanton and Frank McLowry were armed, and made such quick and effective use of their arms as to seriously wound Morgan Earp and Virgil Earp.

"The testimony of Isaac Clanton that this tragedy was the result of a scheme on the part of the Earps to assassinate him, and thereby bury in oblivion the confessions the Earps had made to him about piping away the shipment of coin by Wells, Fargo & Co., falls short of being a sound theory, because of the great fact most prominent in the matter, to-wit: that Isaac Clanton was not injured at all, and could have been killed first and easiest. If he was the object of the attack he would have been first to fall, but as it was, he was known, or believed to be unarmed, and was suffered, and so Wyatt Earp testifies, told to go away, and was not harmed.

"Sheriff Behan further testifies that a few minutes before the Earps came to them that he as Sheriff had demanded of the Clantons and McLowrys that they give up their arms and that they 'demurred,' as he said, and did not do it, and that Frank McLowry refused and gave as a reason that he was not ready to leave the town just then, and would not give up his arms unless the Earps were disarmed, that is, that the Chief of Police and his assistants should be disarmed. In view of the past history of the country and the generally believed existence at this time of desperate, reckless and lawless men in our midst, banded together for mutual support, and living by felonious and predatory pursuits, regarding neither life nor property in their career, and at this time for men to parade the streets armed with repeating rifles and six-shooters, and demand that the Chief of Police of the city and his assistants should be disarmed is a proposition both monstrous and startling. This was said by one of the deceased only a few minutes before the arrival of the Earps.

214

"Another fact that rises up pre-eminent in the consideration of this sad affair is the leading fact that the deceased from the very first inception of the encounter were standing their ground and fighting back, giving and taking death with unflinching bravery. It does not appear to have been a wanton slaughter of unresisting and unarmed innocents, who were yielding graceful submission to the officers of the law, or surrendering to or fleeing from their assailants, but armed and defiant men, accepting the wager of battle and succumbing only in death.

"I have the less reluctance in announcing this conclusion, because the Grand Jury of this county is now in session, and it is quite within the power of that body, if dissatisfied with my decision, to call witnesses before them, or use the depositions taken before me, and which I shall return to the District Court, as by law required, and to thereupon disregard my findings and find an indictment against the defendants if they think the evidence sufficient to warrant a conviction.[5]

"I conclude the performance of the duty imposed upon me by saying in the language of the statute: 'There being no sufficient cause to believe the within named Wyatt S. Earp and John H. Holliday guilty of the offense mentioned within, I order them to be released.' " [6]

FOOTNOTES TO CHATPER 12

1. I was unable to locate the testimony of Ike Clanton regarding this. However the general idea appears in the following part of his testimony.
2. I believe he meant *weeks* ago, since, reading on, we discover that he refers to this being when Holliday was in Tucson—which had been five or six weeks previously. The word is "weeks" in the précis of this testimony which appeared in the *Tombstone Epitaph,* November 17, 1881.
3. This is probably a transcriber's error for *Frank* McLowry. It appears, "They—Billy Clanton and Frank McLowry—commenced to draw their pistols," in the *Epitaph.*
4. Constructing a route near Tombstone at this time.
5. It is very interesting to note the names of some of these Grand Jurors. From the *Daily Nugget,* November 22, 1881; these are: "L. W. Blinn, Foreman; C. W. Harwood, E. A. Harley, D. R. M. Thompson, Max Marks, T. F. Hudson, A. Barnett, W. A. Harwood, Dane Calisher, J. D. Kinnear, R. Cohen, O. F. Thornton, S. B. Comstock, T. R. Sorin, Marshal Williams, F. A. Rustig, and A. W. Buford. . . . Objection was raised by Judge Campbell to the swearing of certain grand jurors to act as such, because in the cases of Wyatt, Morgan and Virgil Earp and Doc Holliday, they were strong advocates of their actions in cases wherein they would come before the jury. Motion overruled."
6. Justice Spicer's opinion is printed in its entirety in *Tombstone's Epitaph,* Douglas D. Martin, University of New Mexico Press, Albuquerque, 1951. On page 202 Dr. Martin interrupts to correct Spicer, saying that Ike Clanton, not Sheriff Behan, testified regarding Frank McLowry's request that the Earps be disarmed. This statement also appeared in Sheriff Behan's testimony at the coroner's inquest. *Daily Nugget,* October 29, 1881.

   Also, please note, only the *Nugget* had a shorthand reporter covering the events of the trial.

13

The Feud Continued,

Final

Bloody Windup

Doc and Wyatt were released on Wednesday, November 30, 1881. Doc didn't get himself arrested again until Friday.[1] He was hauled in on a charge of firing off a pistol and acquitted.

The tension in Tombstone was really remarkable, every gun going off being listened to fearfully lest it be followed by a barrage. And now that Virg's deputy, James Flynn, was chief of police, there was plenty of shooting. U.S. Marshal Crawley P. Dake was catching hell from the attorney general's office in Washington because he and his men were unable to preserve order in Arizona. He sent the following telegram to the Attorney General: "Hon. S. F. Phillips, Actg. Atty. Gen., Washnt., D.C. Yours at the insistance of President received my deputies at Tombstone have struck one effectual blow to that element killing three out of five they had threatened the lives of my deputies on sight no braver men in Arizona than I have employed with a strong posse I have confidence will drive them from the border a special allowance for this particular purpose should be made and the paying of actual expenses of posse authorized wrote you December third on this subject I have acting Governor Josephs cordial support C. P. Dake US Marshal." [2]

It was at this time apparently that Virgil Earp was also made a deputy United States marshal.[3]

After the grand jury failed to indict Doc and the three Earps, they and Justice Wells Spicer, Mayor Clum and several members of the vigilance committee received threats against their lives in anonymous letters. Of those threatened, only Judge Moses left town. The others publicly took it as a practical joke and then on December 14, 1881, an attempt was made on the life of Mayor Clum, who was in the constant habit of making blistering criticisms of the cowboys. While riding the night stage (which was known to carry neither mail nor bullion) to Tucson to visit his brother, the stage was fired upon about four miles outside of Tombstone. Cries of, "Get the old bald-headed son of a bitch," were heard, and about fifteen bullets plunked into the stage loaded with people. One of the horses was hit and died after the string had bolted in a dead run for half a mile. Mayor Clum got off to help cut out the dead horse and somehow in the darkness the stage went on without him. A posse was sent out to search for him, it being believed that in the confusion he had been shot, but he was found safe at Benson, having borrowed a horse at the Grand Central mill and coolly ridden on.

The O.K. corral affair and the resultant hearing had gotten a great deal of publicity throughout the country. It was the Wild West as city dwellers fondly believed the real, daily, average life in the western part of the country to be. The Earps and Doc were six-shooter heroes. The San Francisco *Report* for November 2 summed up the whole country's feelings toward the state of affairs in Cochise County and the action of Virg Earp and his assistants: "We learn from the intelligent Associated Press agent at Tombstone, that 'the friends of the deceased are determined to prosecute the case to the bitter end in the courts.' We hope they will find the end bitter enough to suit the law-abiding citizens of

Tombstone. How would it do for the marshal to take that quick-shooting little posse of his and see whether these friends are carrying any concealed weapons around with them? The lives of Earps, Marshall Williams, Wells-Fargo's agent, and others have been threatened by the friends of the dead men. We hope the ruffians will try, at some opportune time, to carry out their threats and will get the same dose their pals got."

They say that Doc and Wyatt went into the Oriental, soon after their release and after Wyatt had sold his interest in the gambling room there, and walked up to the bar for a drink. Mike Joyce, understandably still resenting being shot by Doc and wanting to show him he wasn't afraid of him, said, "Look who they let run around loose. Guess there'll be another stage robbed any day now."

Wyatt leaned across the bar and slapped Joyce as hard as he could with his open hand. Doc drew his gun but didn't fire. The two of them looked around and then, remembering the pistol Joyce kept behind the bar, carefully backed out the door. Joyce stood there shaking with rage. Doc could shoot him and go un-punished—murder unarmed young cowboys and go unpunished! It wasn't right. And he intended to do something about it. Despite all the good advice of his friends, he grabbed up the bar pistol and started down the street to give Doc a dose of his own medicine.

He located Doc in the Alhambra, not knowing that certain of his friends had sent hot-foot for the sheriff to keep Joyce from getting himself in trouble.

Gun in hand, Joyce lunged toward Doc. "You cheap tinhorn, I'm going to see you get a dose of your own . . ."

"Drop that gun!" Sheriff Behan cried, grabbing Joyce from be-hind. They stood there wrestling for a moment, Joyce puffing with rage and Behan from running, while Doc smiled at them with calm superiority from behind a highball glass full of whisky. At last Behan got his friend disarmed and hauled him off down the street to Wallace's court where he was fined fifteen dollars and costs for disturbing the peace.[4] Joyce hated Behan as much as he hated Holliday after that, and would allow no one to tell him that the sheriff had probably saved his life.

Christmas Day there were imported oysters and champagne at the Maison Dorée, followed by an all-night brawl at the Eagle Brewery saloon.

The *Epitaph* for December 26, 1881, mentioned that Hutchinson's variety troupe was to dedicate the new Bird Cage Theater with "an entirely new and original series of plays, songs, dances, etc." It cost fifty cents to get in, and of course there was a bar in addition. The new songs were largely sentimental: "In the Evening by the Moonlight," "Forsaken," "Wait Til the Clouds Roll By, Jennie" and "When the Robins Nest Again." But in these joints were also sung songs of a robust and ribald nature; probably the most justly acclaimed was, "Son of a Gamboleer," newly come into popularity in this decade. It was sung to a tune not easily forgotten, still among us as "I'm a Rambling Wreck from Georgia Tech," and with words fit to be sung by the toughest old pro in town.

George Parsons was now sleeping at Doc Goodfellow's office, so the dressings on his nose (which had been operated on after his injury in the big fire) could be attended to. This office was upstairs over the Eagle Brewery saloon and across Fifth from the Oriental, now alternately owned and not owned by Mike Joyce and patronized and boycotted by the Earps and Holliday. It was a ringside seat at all the local disturbances. On December 28, 1881, Parsons wrote in his journal:

"Tonight about 11:30 Doc had just left and I tho't couldn't have crossed the street—when four shots were fired in quick succession from very heavily charged guns, making a terrible noise and I tho't were fired under my window under which I quickly dropped, keeping the dobe wall between me and the outside till the fusilade was over. I immediately tho't Doc had been shot and fired in return, remembering a late episode and knowing how pronounced he was on the Earp-Cow-boy question. He had crossed though and passed Virgil Earp who crossed to West side of 5th and was fired upon when in range of my window by men 2 or 3

220

concealed in the timbers of the new 2 story adobe going up for the Huachuca Water Co. He did not fall, but recrossed to the Oriental and was taken from there to the Cosmopolitan being hit with buckshot and badly wounded in left arm with flesh wound above left thigh. Cries of 'There they go,' 'Head them off' were heard but the cowardly apathetic guardians of the peace were not inclined to risk themselves and the other brave men more or less armed did nothing. Doc had a close shave. Van and I went to hospital for Doc and got various things. Hotel well guarded, so much so that I had hard trouble to get to Earp's room. He was easy. Told him I was sorry for him. 'It's hell, isn't it!' said he. His wife was troubled. 'Never mind. I've got one arm left to hug you with,' he said."

Two assassinations had been attempted—and Doc's name was on the list of those threatened. He must have gotten a slightly self-conscious feeling between his shoulder blades, thinking about the people who wanted to plant a bullet there. But he was deep in the habit of caution and no one noticed any difference in his behavior.

Mattie had of course read the story of the fracas at the O.K. corral in the papers and Doc had written her the complete law-officer's version. Now he had to reassure her of his safety. He just might have felt better if he could have believed what he was writing. But there was no question of the cowboys running them out of town: they set up fort in the Cosmopolitan Hotel and believed themselves invincible. At least none of them had been killed.

The Earps had switched their headquarters to Campbell and Hatch's Bank Exchange saloon (noted for the excellence of its billiard hall), located between the Alhambra and Wells, Fargo on Allen Street. The pool room was kept in top condition, having been completely renovated during the Earps' trial. The *Nugget* for November 3, 1881, described the saloon with: "It is the pleasantest place in town for billiard players, and a quiet game of cards, not taking into consideration the fine liquors and cigars to be had."

A Grand New Year's Ball was held at Schieffelin Hall [5] under

221

the auspices of Rescue Hook and Ladder Co., No. 1, and names of both factions appeared cheerfully on the lists of committee members. Everyone hoped the New Year would be one of peace and prosperity—except certain ones who nursed in their hearts the picture of three young men dead in the dust of Frémont Street and two others yanked off to jail for a little harmless stagecoach robbery.

The city elections produced respected John Carr as mayor and Dave Neagle, candidate of the "ten-percent county ring," [6] as town marshal. The local tension continued. The *Epitaph* printed on January 7, 1882: "Notice. In order that there may be no misunderstanding in the matter of permits to carry fire-arms granted by me for an indefinite period, notice is hereby given that all such permits expire January 1, 1882, and the same are hereby declared of no effect and void after that date. John P. Clum, Mayor. December 10, 1881."

On January 17, 1882, Parsons wrote in his journal: "Snow yesterday. Light fall. Much blood in the air this afternoon. Ringo and Doc Holliday came nearly having it with pistols and Ben Maynard and Rickabaugh later tried to kick each others' lungs out. Bad time expected with the cowboy leader and D.H. I passed them both not knowing bad blood was up. One with hand in breast pocket and other probably ready. Earps just beyond. Crowded street and looked like another battle. Police vigilant for once and both disarmed." The *Epitaph* for January 18, 1882, told the end: "Police court: J. H. Holliday, Wyatt Earp, Ringo, arrested for carrying concealed weapons; Earp discharged, Holliday and Ringo fined $30 each."

There are many versions of this in the old-timers' recollections, one side having it that Doc was all ready to perforate Ringo when he was arrested, the other claiming that Ringo invited Doc to duel on the spot and Doc declined. Actually, it appears that the police grabbed them before either had gotten beyond the brag and bluster stage. Surely Doc and Ringo were the most closely matched opponents the two factions could have picked: both educated;

222

both alcoholics; both loyal to their friends, both totally fearless. Anything other than their killing each other on the spot is unthinkable, but like the fight between Richard I and Saladin, it never happened—luckily for the nerves of the loyal Tombstoners.

Ah, well! Drinks are still twelve and a half cents.

There having been more stage robberies, on the 24th of January, 1882, the *Epitaph* printed: "To the citizens of Tombstone: I am informed by His Honor, William H. Stilwell, Judge of the Judicial Court, First Judicial District, Cochise county, that Wyatt S. Earp who left this city yesterday with a posse, was entrusted with warrants for the arrest of diverse persons charged with criminal offenses. I request the public within this city to abstain from any interference with said warrants. Dated January 24, 1882. John Carr, Mayor."

Well, they galloped all over southeastern Arizona and didn't accomplish anything. Fortunately for Doc's consumption, he knew how to ride and could save himself a great deal on these *pasears*, although it sometimes took half a bottle of whisky to get him on his feet the following morning. A joker in Charleston sent the following telegram to Sheriff Behan, which the *Nugget* and *Epitaph* both printed in all seriousness: "Charleston, A.T., January 25—To J. H. Behan, Sheriff of Cochise County. Dear Sir:— Doc Holliday, the Earps, and about 40 or 50 more of the filth of Tombstone, are here, armed with Winchester rifles and revolvers, and patrolling our streets, as we believe, for no good purpose. Last night and today they have been stopping good, peaceable citizens on all the roads leading to our town, nearly paralysing the business of our place. We know of no authority under which they are acting. Some of them, we believe, are thieves, robbers, and murderers. Please come here and take them where they belong. Charleston."

U.S. Marshal Dake came and made some more deputy U.S. marshals, Doc and Morg among them, for temporary duty with Wyatt. Others were the youngest of the five Earp boys, Warren, Sherman McMasters, Turkey Creek Jack Johnson and Texas Jack

Vermillion (so-called because he was from Big Stone Gap, Virginia). While this posse was tearing hither and yon over the landscape, many of the men named in the warrants given Wyatt came into Tombstone and gave themselves up.[7]

And while the Earps' posse was wasting its energy and the taxpayers' money, something happened back in Tombstone that no one thought much of except Campbell and Hatch and their steady pool-playing customers. However, in light of something soon to happen in Tombstone, we get a faint chill reading that they have just had the pool tables recovered.

To show how Tombstone continued in the public eye all over the country, and how little the goings-on in the west were understood by easterners of their own time, get this quotation from a New York paper in the Tucson *Daily Star* of January 27, 1882:

" 'Tombstone, Arizona, is well named. Few people there die in their beds. Between the cowboys and other desperadoes the uncertainty of life is constantly exemplified. A man with good luck and extraordinary vitality may manage to keep out of the tomb long enough to become a citizen, but such instances are rare. Not long since Deputy United States Marshal Earp was found with nineteen bullets in his body and he is alive yet. He seems to be the right sort of man for the place.'—N.Y. Exchange.

"Pshaw!" the editor of the *Star* commented. "This is not half, nor a twentieth part. The marshal had fifty-seven bullets extracted and it is believed there is about a peck yet in his body. Only a short time ago a cowboy had a Henry rifle rammed down his throat and then broken off; he spit the gunbarrel out with the loss of only a tooth. It is stated as a fact that more than four-fifths of the inhabitants of the district carry one or more bullets in their bodies. One instance is of record where birth was given to an infant who came forth armed with two bowie knives, and a columbiad strapped to its back. Everybody goes armed, men, women, and children. Every house has portholes from which the cowboys are shot down. It is a great place for suicides; if a fellow wants to die with his boots on he just steps out on the street and yells out, 'You're another,' and immediately he is plumped through from all sides with a shower of bullets. Sports play at cards with a knife in their left hand and a six-shooter in their right. It is no uncommon occurrence to see twenty men dumped out of a club room in the morning and pitched down some mining shaft where the ore has petered out. This is but a faint picture of the situation. Our New York exchange had better try and get the facts."

The loyal Tombstoners laughed heartily at the Tucson paper's satire on conditions in Cochise County—and checked their guns to see if they were loaded.

The storm had only lulled.

Ike Clanton now made a legal effort to get revenge for the killing of his brother and the McLowrys, egged on by Frank Stilwell, Pete Spence, Ringo and other peerless fellows of the cowboy persuasion.

"Wyatt Earp, Morgan Earp, and Doc Holliday were arrested yesterday on a warrant sworn out at Contention before Justice Smith, at the instance of Joseph Isaac Clanton. The charge upon which they were arrested, we are informed, was but a renewal of the one under which they were arrested last fall for the shooting affray in Frémont St. They were taken before Court Commissioner Drum last night to effect their release on a writ of habeas corpus, and the matter taken under further advisement until this morning. If it is a fact that this warrant has been allowed to issue without new evidence to warrant it, the code of rights that protects all alike has been violently infringed. Cleared by a lengthy examination before a magistrate and then by a grand jury, it is only in the province of another grand jury to take up the case, unless new evidence is brought forward before the issuance of a warrant. These are cold facts and not contingent turkey," said the *Epitaph* on February 11, 1882.

On February 15, 1882, George Parsons wrote: "Yesterday Earps were taken to Contention to be tried for killing of Clanton. Quite a posse went out. Many of Earp's friends accompanied, armed to the teeth. They came back later in the day, the good people below

225

beseeching them to leave and try case here. A bad time is expected again in town at any time. Earps on one side of the street with their friends and Ike Clanton and Ringo with theirs on the other side—watching each other. Blood will surely come. Hope no innocents will be killed."

Doc and Wyatt and Morg had only spent some four days in the rat-trap, dirt-floored county jail this time, finally getting out on a writ issued by Judge Lucas upon proof that no new evidence was forthcoming. Virg was still confined to his bed from the injuries received in his attempted assassination. Ike Clanton's legal effort came to nothing . . . and the Earps jeered at him for a fool. Wyatt and his posse again went out on "scouts" through the county, just to show the cowboys somebody was keeping an eye on them. It looked like scorn versus resentment. It looked like trouble.

"Mr. Virgil Earp was out upon the streets this morning for the first time since he was hurt," said the *Epitaph* on Wednesday, March 15, 1882.

But the Earps had made the mistake of underestimating their enemy. When you are dead, it doesn't matter that you were shot in the back by a coward. He got you, boy, and you were a fool for letting him do it.

"At 10:50 Saturday night, while engaged in playing a game of Billiards in Campbell & Hatch's billiard parlor, on Allen Street between Fourth and Fifth, Morgan Earp was shot through the body by an unknown assassin. At the time the shot was fired he was playing a game of billiards with Bob Hatch, one of the proprietors of the house, and was standing with his back to the glass door at the rear of the room that opens out upon the alley that leads straight through the block along the west side of A. D. Otis & Co.'s store to Frémont Street. This door is the ordinary glass door, with four panes in the top instead of panels. The two lower panes are painted, the upper ones being clear. Anyone standing on the outside can look over the painted glass and see anything going on in the room just as well as though standing in the open door. At the time the shot was fired deceased must have been standing within ten feet of the door and the assassin, standing near enough to see his position, took aim for about the middle of his person, shooting through the upper portion of the whitened glass. The bullet entered the right side of the abdomen passing through the spinal column, completely shattering it, emerging on the left side, passing the length of the room and lodging in the thigh of Geo. A. B. Berry, who was standing by the stove, inflicting a painful flesh wound. Instantly after the first shot a second was fired through the top of the upper glass which passed across the room and lodged in the wall near the ceiling over the head of Wyatt Earp, who was sitting a spectator of the game. Morgan fell instantly upon the first fire and only lived about one hour. His brother, Wyatt, Tipton and McMasters rushed to the side of the wounded man and tenderly picked him up and moved him some ten feet away, near the card room, where Drs. Mathew, Goodfellow and Millar, who were called, pronounced the wound mortal. He was then moved into the card room and placed on the lounge where in a few brief moments he breathed his last surrounded by his brothers, Wyatt, Virgil, James and Warren, with the wives of Virgil and James and a few intimate friends. Notwithstanding the intensity of his mortal agony, not a word of complaint escaped his lips, and all that were heard, except those whispered into the ear of his brother and known only to him, were, 'Don't, I can't stand it. This is the last game of pool I'll ever play.' The first part of the sentence being wrung from him by an effort to place him on his feet," said the *Epitaph* for March 20, 1882.

"It was and is quite evident who committed the deed," Parsons wrote the day after Morg's death. "The man was Stilwell in all probability."

Now, Wyatt, see what your ambition and your pride have done. Morg is dead. Morg. You stomped all over the feelings of others; now you know how they felt. Now you are going to react in the same way they did, and make your own revenge in this lawless country. You saw the men who shot Virg go unpunished. You know the murderers of Morg will escape the law, too. So you are going after them as marshal, jury, judge and executioner—and by this revenge become as mean and cowardly as your enemies, and as human.

The Earps' grief for Morg was shared very deeply by Doc. The insulation of alcohol failed him, and he swore to kill every man who had had anything to do with the death of Morg. His faltering ego told him he was as much to blame for Morg's death as the man who pulled the trigger, because he had been loyal to Bill Leonard. Well, he could not undo the net of his behavior. But he could fling that net over others. He pulled his gun, there in the saloon where the Earp women's weeping was the only sound over Morgan's body, and checked the loading and rocked the hammer thoughtfully.

He looked up and met Wyatt's eyes.

Morg was killed on Saturday the 18th of March, 1882. While his body was being embalmed, the rest of the family decided what to do. Virg, being still weak and crippled from the earlier attempt on his life, could do nothing constructive in Tombstone. Aided by the others, his wife got their stuff packed and by Monday they were ready to leave. The Earps' parents had moved to California, and it was decided Virg and Allie would go there and take Morg's body with them to be buried far from Tombstone. They left Tombstone Monday at 12:30, going to Contention, where the Southern Pacific now reached, and got on the train for California, accompanied for a part of their journey by Wyatt, Warren, Doc, Sherman McMasters and Turkey Creek Jack Johnson.

Everyone knew that Frank Stilwell, Pete Spence, a Dutchman and a couple of Mexicans or Indians or breeds or some such had murdered Morg. Spence's wife had heard some of their talk on the matter and seen some suspicious actions.

On the morning of Tuesday, March 21, 1882, the body of Frank Stilwell was found riddled with bullets beside the Southern Pacific tracks in Tucson. He had still been out on bail pending trial for robbing the Bisbee stage. "One load of seven buckshot

228

had entered the left breast and ranging downward, had passed out the back. A bullet, evidently that of a pistol or rifle, had passed through the fleshy part of the left arm and entered the body just below the armpit, and passing directly through, came out in line of entrance under the right arm into which it lodged. Another load of 11 buckshot had shattered the left leg above the knee and one bullet had gone through and into the calf of the left leg, while still another bullet, evidently a downward shot, entered the right leg above the knee, passed through, and into the calf of the left leg." His face was contorted with pain or fear, and the palm of his left hand was found to be burned and blackened by powder.[8]

Parsons commented on March 20, 1882: "A quick vengeance and a bad character sent to Hell where he will be the chief attraction until a few more join him." (The date makes it appear as if Parsons knew Stilwell was dead and who did it before the body was found, but this is due to his habit of going back and writing up several days at a time.)

The testimony given at the coroner's inquest [9] will have to tell as best it can what happened—the number of bullets in Frank Stilwell's body making Wyatt Earp's version in *Wyatt Earp, Frontier Marshal* a somewhat foggy recollection, as did also the presence of men Wyatt said were not there, and Morgan's body, which Wyatt thought had been shipped west the day before.

"David Gibson was at the depot with checks for passengers baggage. Met the train newsboy who said, 'I guess there will be hell here tonight,' and when asked why said that 'the Earps and Holliday were aboard and were going to stop here as they had told him that the man who killed Morgan Earp was in Tucson.' At this moment Doc Holliday, Wyatt Earp and another Earp and a short man walked from Porter's hotel toward the depot and appeared to be looking for someone. Holliday had an ulster over his shoulder and a gun under it. The two Earps had short Wells, Fargo's shotguns, believed the short man had no gun so paid but little attention to him as he was a stranger. As they reached the end of the sleeper one of them stepped on the platform and passed to the opposite side and then looked up and down the train, returning all four of them walked toward the rear end of the sleeper when they faced about and walked about towards the engine at the head of the train. The newsboy pointed out the wounded Earp who was sitting in the car with two ladies in front of him. The conductor's bell then rang and two shots were fired towards the head of the train, instantly followed by about five more, could plainly see the flashes of the guns, but could not see the Earps or the other man who he was informed by the newsboy was McMasters."

"Isaac Clanton—was acquainted with the deceased whose name was Frank C. Stilwell and who was a native of Texas, aged about 27 years. Had told him I was expecting a Mr. McDowell from Charleston who had been summoned as a witness before the court in session here. Deceased had asked him to go with him to the depot. Went as far as Morgan's livery stable and then returned to town, the deceased returning on to the depot. Afterwards went to the depot when the train from the East was coming in and was on the hotel porch when rejoined by Stilwell, who called him to the rear of the hotel and told him that the Earps and Holliday were aboard the train. After talking for a few minutes Doc Holliday, McMasters, Johnson, Wyatt and Warren Earp came out of the hotel and walked towards the train. I then started towards my room, and deceased walked down the track between the cars and the hotel. When below Morgan's livery stable, stopped for a while, thinking that deceased would come up. In a few minutes heard the shots; returned to the stable and inquired about the shooting but did not know that Stilwell had been killed until this morning."

"A. McCann was at the depot when the train came in, saw four men with guns, also saw Virgil Earp and wife get into the car, also the three men who were with them, but they immediately came out and walked toward the head of the train; in a few minutes heard six or eight or maybe ten shots, which were fired about as the train started, also heard some cheering. The tallest man was one of the Earps, two of the men were short, one was very short. Doc Holliday had a gun, saw him walk toward the new part of the hotel."

"James Miller: Fireman on west bound train on the evening of the 20th, saw a man running down the track on the east side of the engine and across the track in front of it. Eight or ten minutes afterwards saw four armed men pass on the west side of the engine and down to the left of the coaches standing on the side track. In about five minutes afterwards heard five or six shots in rapid succession. Saw but one man while they were shooting, but saw four men standing there when the train pulled out. Watched to see if they boarded the train. When they first passed down they all had guns; but when the train ran by a few minutes later the four men were standing where the firing had been done and had guns in their hands. Saw one man fire a gun. He was a middle-sized man. The shooting was done by the same party who passed the engine. The man who ran down the east side and crossed the track had no gun. Heard someone say before this took place that there would be murder done here."

"R. E. Mellis: Was engineer on the outgoing train, and while on the lookout for tramps, saw a man cross in front of the engine, and shortly afterwards four armed men walked down on the west side of the train to where the man was. Heard them fire. There must have been a dozen shots. This was in the neighborhood of the crossing. Pulled out fast so they could not get on the train. They did not speak while passing. Did not see any gun in the hands of the man who ran across the track in front of the engine. Did not recognize him. Heard the firing and saw the flashes of the guns. Saw four men standing where the shooting had been done."

"The case was submitted to the jury who after consultation returned a verdict that the deceased was named Frank C. Stilwell aged 27 years, a native of Texas and that he came to his death at Tucson, Pima County, A.T., on the 20th of March, 1882, 7:15 p.m. by gun-shot wounds inflicted by guns in the hands of Wyatt Earp, Warren Earp, Sherman McMasters, J. H. Holliday and Johnson whose first name is unknown, the persons by whose act the death of Frank C. Stilwell was occasioned."

Doc and Wyatt and the others rode an east-bound freight back to Contention, got their horses and rode into Tombstone Tuesday morning. They went straight to the Cosmopolitan and began to pack. Thanks to the telegraph everybody in town knew they had killed Frank Stilwell the night before in Tucson. The *Epitaph* tells how they left town: [10] "Sheriff Behan was standing in the office of the Cosmopolitan hotel when Wyatt Earp and the others comprising the party came into the office from the rear entrance, each one having a rifle in his hands, in the ordinary manner of carrying a gun, and passed through the room to the street. As Wyatt advanced to the front and approached Sheriff Behan, the sheriff said to him, 'Wyatt, I want to see you.' Wyatt replied, 'You can't see me; you have seen me once too often,' or words to that effect. He passed out into the street and turned around and said, 'I will see Paul,' [the sheriff of Pima County] and then the party passed on down the street. These gentlemen say that no word was spoken by the sheriff that implied a demand for an arrest, and that no weapons were drawn upon or pointed at the sheriff. Furthermore, one of these gentlemen [who are telling the story to the editor of the paper] says that he considers that the sheriff did well in not attempting to make the arrest last night, under the circumstances; that he expects the Earp party will surrender themselves to Sheriff Paul of Pima County, when he arrives."

But they didn't see Paul. They went off looking for the other men believed to be involved in Morg's murder. Pete Spence gave himself up to the sheriff promptly and was jailed armed, in case the Earps tried to force the jail to get at him.[11] Deputy Sheriff Hereford arrested the Dutchman, Frederick Bode, and Deputy Sheriff Bell brought in Indian Charley, suspected of being implicated in Morg's death.[12] The other Mexican, Indian or whatever didn't do so well: "This afternoon Theodore D. Judah came in from Pete Spence's wood camp, in the South pass of the Dragoons, and gave an *Epitaph* reporter the following information: Yesterday morning, about 11 o'clock, Wyatt and Warren Earp, Doc Holliday, McMasters, Texas Jack and Johnson came into the

232

camp and inquired for Pete Spence and Indian Charley; also as to the number of men there, and their whereabouts. Judah informed them that Spence was in Tombstone, and that a Mexican named Florentino was looking for some stock which had strayed away. Judah indicated the direction taken by the Mexican, and the party immediately left as directed, passing over a hill which hid them from view. A few minutes later ten or twelve shots were heard. Florentino not returning, this morning Judah proceeded in search of him, and found the body not far from the camp, riddled with bullets. Judah immediately came to town with the news. He states that had the sheriff's posse come a mile further, they would have had all the information they wanted." [13]

The coroner's inquest into the death of Morgan Earp produced the following statement by Pete Spence's Mexican wife, Marietta; [14] "On Sunday morning Spence told me to get breakfast about 6 o'clock, which I did—after we had a quarrel, during which he struck me and my mother, and during which he threatened to shoot me, when my mother told him he would have to shoot her too. His expression was, that if I said a word about something I knew about he would kill me; that he was going to Sonora and would leave my dead body behind him. Spence didn't tell me so, but I know he killed Morgan Earp; I think he did it, because he arrived at the house all of a tremble, and both the others who came with him. Spence's teeth were chattering when he came in. I asked if he wanted something to eat and he said he did not. Myself and mother heard the shots, and it was a little after when Stilwell and the Indian, Charley, came in, and from one half to three-quarters of an hour after Spence and the other two men came. . . . I judged they had been doing wrong from the condition, white and trembling, in which they arrived. . . . Four days ago, while mother and myself were standing at Spence's house, talking with Spence and the Indian, Morgan Earp passed by, when Spence nudged the Indian and said, 'That's him; that's him.' The Indian then started down the street so as to get ahead of him and get a good look at him."

Wyatt, Doc & Co. still did not surrender to authority, despite all the men indicted by the coroner's jury being either dead or in jail charged with Morg's murder. They were wanted for murder themselves now. "Sheriff Behan left with a posse of some fifteen or sixteen men, among whom were John Ringo, Fin Clanton and several others of the cowboy element, together with some of the permanent residents of Tombstone," the *Epitaph* said,[15] describing the local efforts to find the Earp party. Parsons wrote on March 23, 1882: "More killing by the Earp party [Florentino]. Hope they'll keep it up. Paul is here—but will not take a hand. He is a true—brave man and will not join the murderous posse here. If the truth were known he'd be glad to see the Earp party get away from all these murderous outfits."

The *Epitaph* for the 24th had: "Mrs. James Earp and Mrs. Wyatt Earp left today for Colton, California, the residence of their husbands' parents. These ladies have the sympathy of all who know them, and for that matter, the entire community. Their trials for the last six months have been of the most severe nature."

On March 25, 1882, Parsons wrote: "Rumors of a battle and 4 of Earp party killed recd. this a.m. Discredited. I got strictly private news though later that 'Curly Bill' has been killed at last—by the Earp party and none of the latter hurt. Sheriff Behan has turned all of the Cow-boys loose against the Earps and with this lawless element is trying to do his worst. I am heartily glad at this repulse and hope the killing is not stopped with the cut throat named. Feeling here is growing against the Ring, Sheriff, etc., and it would not surprize me to hear of a necktie party some fine morning."

Monday's *Epitaph,* March 27, 1882, had in it the verdict of the coroner's jury which had met to determine the cause of the death of "Florentino, a native of Mexico," who had taken off violently near Pete Spence's wood camp. It named Wyatt Earp, Doc Holliday, Warren Earp, Sherman McMasters, Texas Jack and one Johnson as being his killers. Now they were wanted in both Pima and Cochise Counties. Sheriff Behan took out after them with another posse of cowboys and after being refused cooperation by indignant ranchers who had lost cattle to rustlers, came back empty-handed. A Tucson item in this same Monday's *Epitaph* said: "Sheriff Paul has returned from Tombstone. He says he did not go in pursuit of the Earps because the posse selected by Sheriff Behan, of Tombstone, were mostly hostile to the Earps and that a meeting meant bloodshed without any possibility of arrest. Sheriff Paul says the Earps will come to Tucson and surrender to the authorities."

They did not go to Tucson. They did not surrender to anyone. The better class of Tombstone resident, as shown by the attitude of the editor of the *Epitaph* and George Parsons, apparently approved of the murders of Frank Stilwell and Florentino. They understood all too well the precarious state of justice in which they lived. The cowboy element, of course, was outraged. Young Billy Clanton, Frank McLowry, unarmed Tom McLowry, Frank Stilwell, the Mexican Florentino—all murdered by the Earps and the deeds applauded, not punished. The citizens of Tucson, despite the attitude of Bob Paul, were very upset over the Earps coming to their town to commit a cold-blooded murder. That kind of thing might do for Tombstone, but the Ancient Pueblo had its law and order and no Earp was going to run rough-shod over it. Sheriff Behan offered a reward for the capture of the Earps.

And in the meantime Wyatt, Doc & Co. quietly faded out of the desert landscape and into the irrigated green valley of the Rio Grande at Albuquerque. Here they scattered. Dan Tipton, who had joined the Earps after the killings, parted from them, fell among evil companions and got himself killed. McMasters and Johnson went off to the Panhandle of Texas where they did not long survive either. Texas Jack Vermillion went back to Big Stone Gap, Virginia, bought a farm, married, raised a family, and was a Methodist Sunday school superintendent, member of the school board and pillar of respectability until his death in 1910. Doc and the two Earps went to Colorado.

Back in Tombstone, trial was being held for the surviving murderers of Morgan Earp. Its result was precisely what everyone expected. "The case of the Territory vs. Pete Spence, charged with the murder of Morgan Earp, was completed in the police court this afternoon. The prosecution asked for Mrs. Spence as a witness this morning, but the defendant objected, whereupon the prosecution refused to proceed further with the case, and the court accordingly ordered the discharge of the prisoner. The same testimony was brought against Frank Bodie, who was charged with the same offense, and the court also ordered his dismissal." [16]

FOOTNOTES TO CHAPTER 13

1. *Daily Nugget*, December 3, 1881.
2. Records of the office of the Attorney General, National Archives, Washington, D.C.
3. "U.S. Deputy Marshal Virgil W. Earp," reads the *Epitaph* for December 29, 1881.
4. *Tombstone Epitaph*, December 18, 1881. *Helldorado*.
5. Named for Ed Schieffelin, who braved the Apaches to discover the silver deposits around Tombstone and named the camp and such mines as the Lucky Cuss, the Tough Nut and the Contention.
6. *Tombstone Epitaph*, December 26, 1881: "The *Epitaph* is opposed to the election of Dave Nagle to the position of city marshal of Tombstone, for the reason that he is identified with the ten-per-cent county ring."
7. Parsons' *Journal*, January 30, 1882.
8. *Arizona Daily Citizen*, March 21, 1882.
9. *Arizona Daily Citizen*, March 27, 1882. The testimony at this hearing is generally incoherent.
10. *Tombstone Epitaph*, March 22, 1882.
11. *Tombstone Epitaph*, March 25, 1882.
12. *Tombstone Epitaph*, March 23, 1882.
13. *do.*
14. *do.*
15. *do.*
16. *Tombstone Epitaph*, April 3, 1882.

14

Doc Has Trouble

in Denver

Pueblo, now grown to a city of about 30,000 in this year of 1882, was booming as an industrial town. The Colorado Coal and Iron Company had blown in the Minnequa blast furnace the year before, the Mather and Geist smelter was finished and work had started on the Eilers smelter. Being in a strategic spot on the railroads, Pueblo saw coal brought from Trinidad to smelt the ores from Leadville in her works. Lonely on the plains, the mountains far to the south and west, the smoking towers of Pueblo even then could be seen for miles. It was here in the gambling district south of the river, around the Santa Fe station, that Doc and Wyatt and Warren came to rest up, take stock of their condition and plan what to do.

Doc was all ready to go to work in some prosperous spot. Pueblo was full of old friends of his from his Denver days and any number of good set-ups were available. But Wyatt and Warren could feel the law breathing down their necks. To Doc's amazement they began to plan for a place in which to lay low until the furor over the murders blew over.

And at last they quarreled. Perhaps Doc accidentally let go some hint that he had known Kinnear's stage was going to be robbed by Bill Leonard and his friends. Perhaps Wyatt now wished he had not taken the law into his own hands after Morg's

238

death and so blamed Doc for sweeping him into two cold-blooded slayings. Perhaps Doc saw Wyatt as a swell-head and a blow-hard, since he was still so puffed up about having been city marshal of Dodge.[1] Perhaps Doc saw Wyatt more than himself responsible for Morg's death, since Wyatt had tried so hard for the public renown of catching Leonard, Head and Crane. Perhaps Wyatt saw his friendship with Doc would end up more of a liability than an asset.

Whatever the reason, they parted. Wyatt and Warren sneaked off to the remote Gunnison country which was later to be a fisherman's paradise, but was then isolated rangeland and almost unpopulated. Doc walked the streets of Pueblo unmolested. He and Wyatt never saw each other again. Wyatt went into saloonkeeping, following the gold and silver strikes, and finally wound up as a Southern California real-estate man. He spread far and wide the story of his dauntless deeds, enlarging on them and making up new versions in his spare time. Since he lived to be eighty (he died in Los Angeles in 1929 [2]) the stories really got quite a Muenchausen working over. And since we are ready to admire and give him credit for the good things he actually did, we wish he could have controlled his imagination a little more—but then all our idols turn out to have clay feet, often clear up to the neck, so it would be more to the point to complain about the high price of whisky. As for the rest of the Earps—Warren hadn't learned that the Earps would always have bad luck as law officers and he was killed while working as a special officer for a cattleman's association. Virg, who actually was the frontier marshal, became a prospector and died of pneumonia during the Goldfield's (Arizona) rush. James Earp seems to have avoided the strife and lawlessness of his brothers and is reported to have settled in California and lived to a ripe old age.[3] Newton Earp appears to have followed James' example.

Of the surviving Clantons, Finn died near Safford, Arizona, in 1882. Ike was killed in Bonita, Arizona, by a deputy marshal, in 1887.[4]

And Doc flourished in Pueblo like the green crab grass. The fight at the O.K. corral had recalled Tom McKey to his old friends and the late trouble with Frank Stilwell and that Florentino had cemented his fame. He had a rush of popularity with the South Pueblo sporting set, and relieved of his worries as a partisan of the Earps, began to relax and enjoy himself.

On May 14, 1882, he and two professional gambler friends went up to Denver for the races at the Fair Grounds on the 16th. Doc was certainly pleased with the change in Denver—the town was a fine example of the prosperity the whole country was at last enjoying. Big brick buildings were doubling the former size of the business section, new stone sidewalks had been laid, the horsecar lines had been extended and electric street lights installed, the grand Windsor Hotel was newly opened, and Charpiot's, Cella's, Cammelleri's and the Bon Ton were famous restaurants. There were 563 telephones in town—you rang for Central, picked up the receiver and said politely, "Hello, Central. Please connect 27 (your number) with 125 (the butcher shop)." The tourist business was a big thing with Denver, and the town was flooded with sightseers of every type from the old farm couple who had arrived on a pass provided by their railroad-employee son to European nobility travelling with an entourage of servants.

Oh, it was good to be in a big city again.

Doc got to Denver on Sunday. Monday night he was arrested.

"At about 8:30 o'clock last night persons passing along the sidewalk on Fifteenth Street, in the immediate vicinity of the Sheriff's building, might have seen a thin, spare man, with a blond mustache and a piercing eye, which glanced covertly and suspiciously from under the brim of a black slouch hat, passing quietly along the street. The stranger glanced restlessly from side to side without turning his head, as if he feared the approach of some unknown enemy. Had it not been for this, which would have created the suspicion in the mind of an acute observer that he had committed some great crime, ordinary suspicion of evil would have

240

been averted by the man's meek appearance and quiet demeanor. The stranger's hair was slightly streaked with gray, his clothes were custom made and such as are worn in civilized communities, and altogether there was nothing to denote that he was the desperate, blood-thirsty and notorious murderer, stage-robber and villain which he was soon afterward represented to be. The street at the point indicated is brilliantly lighted with electric lights at both ends of the block and all that passed could be as readily seen as in broad day light. But few people were passing at the time and the streets were momentarily deserted, when suddenly a man stepped from the deep shadow which is thrown by the electric light, and is seen in every place where its rays cannot penetrate, and accosted the first stranger. He accosted him in the most summary manner. His manner of salutation was to drop two six-shooters full into the face of the spare, quiet pedestrian and halt him with the words— more suited to the highway than to the smooth pavements and surroundings of a brilliantly lighted street—

" 'Throw up your hands!'

"A muttered imprecation and the words heard only indistinctly, 'Doc Holliday, I have you now,' were all that gave indication of the first stranger's crime or the need for this summary arrest. As the man with the pistols spoke his throat seemed to expand, his veins swelled, his chest heaved and it was evident he was straining every nerve to hold himself in check and keep from killing his victim.

"The two men, accompanied by Deputies Linton and Barney Cutler, hurried into the Sheriff's office, where another exciting scene occurred. It was almost impossible to tell what the prisoner was charged with, and the reticence of the Sheriff, together with the prisoner's own cool and rather intrepid actions, only added to the interest of the affair.

"It was afterwards learned, however, that the prisoner's name was John H., alias Doc, Holliday, a man very much hated in Arizona by the cowboys, and who was recently compelled to leave there through fear of being assassinated, as two of his friends and brother officers have been. The man who arrested him on the street gave his name as Perry Mallan and claimed to be a Deputy Sheriff from Los Angeles, California. To the officers here he gave Doc Holliday the record which the cowboys gave him in the South, charging him with every conceivable crime and exhibiting telegrams ordering Holliday's arrest as an accessory in the murder of Frank Stilwell in Tucson, the murder of a railroad conductor on the Southern Pacific road, the murder of a ranchman named Clanton near Tombstone, and attempted murder of his brother, the murder of Curly Bill, the noted cowboy, and half a dozen other crimes. Just what part Holliday had in these affairs is not known. He is represented by one side as a desperado and on the other side a well-known officer told a reporter last night that Holliday had been a United States Marshal in the employ of the government for years and stood well wherever he was known. The record of Holliday, as given by his enemies, however, has attained wide celebrity and this was what Mallan claimed for him last night.

"Although charged with these various crimes, the one for which Holliday was followed so closely occurred over seven years ago. The manner of his arrest reads more like the story of a mining camp than a tale of Denver in her metropolitan splendor and all the circumstances are tinged with the romance of a past and bygone day.

"Following close upon the capture a *Tribune* reporter was in the Sheriff's office, where a curious scene was witnessed.

"Behind the railing and partially screened by the desk stood a man demanding to know why he had been arrested. Deputy Linton was telephoning frantically for a hack. Just on the other side of the desk, from Holliday, stood a young, thick set man, with a short-cropped reddish mustache, his foot resting on the seat of a chair. A second glance showed that he held a revolver partially concealed behind his back.

" 'Oh you can drop that,' said the other man, who proved to be Holliday. 'Nobody is going to try to get away from you. I have no weapons.'

"Hot words passed between the two. Mallan, who held the weapon, was excited, but Holliday was cool, though with that coolness which knows that it is its only salvation, for he evidently feared that Mallan might kill him at any moment. A crowd of rough looking men, strangers to Holliday and most of those present, filed into the room. To the reporter, who did not know the circumstances of the case, it looked as if a murder or lynching was imminent.

" 'No, you won't get away from me again,' exclaimed Mallan, still holding his pistol in his hand. 'You killed my partner, you blood-thirsty coward, and I would have taken you in Pueblo if the men I had with me had stood by me.'

" 'I did not come here to be abused,' said Holliday, looking toward the Sheriff for protection.

"Just then a crowd of rough, ill-favored fellows filed into the Sheriff's office. To them Holliday appealed, saying he wanted to make a statement.

" 'This is not a court or jury,' said Deputy Linton.

" 'But I want to set myself right,' said the prisoner.

" 'Is it customary in this country to deny a citizen the right of speech? Is it right? Is it justice?'

"No answer.

"It was evident that the whole spirit of the Sheriff was with Mallan, and as he still grasped his revolver he held the winning hand.

"The little group which Holliday addressed appeared, several of them at least, to be strangers in Denver. One or two were citizens who happened in through curiosity, but there were several suspicious characters in the group.

" 'I can show who that man is'—said Holliday, vehemently, like a man at bay, but a threatening movement from the man with a pistol checked his speech for a moment. 'I can prove that he is not the Sheriff, and, in fact, no officer of Cochise County,' he continued boldly. 'I can show you his reason for bringing me here; I can show—' but Mallan and the Deputy Sheriff both cut short his speech. He desired to make a statement but they said it was no place for it.

"Mallan (if that be his name) stormed and threatened and fingered his pistol until he finally returned it to his pocket.

"He talked about 'his partner' killed by the blood-thirsty Holliday, and said he would show him no quarter even as he (Holliday) had shown his victims no quarter.

"The prisoner was taken to a hack and hurried to the county jail. Before going Holliday mentioned the names of several men he knew in the city, and. among others said that his friend Bob Masterson, Marshal of Trinidad, Colorado, had come up with him.

" 'Can I come with you—I am a reporter,' said *The Tribune* man collaring the hack at the foot of the stairs.

" 'Come on; you are just the man I want to see,' exclaimed Holliday eagerly.

"At the jail, however, Holliday had evidently repented of the statement he was so anxious to make. He made no further charges against the man Mallan, only saying that he first wanted to see his friend Masterson and then an attorney.

"Up to this time the names of neither prisoner nor debtor had been mentioned. The prisoner gave the name of John H. Holliday. He refused to say who Mallan was, only reiterating that he was no officer of Cochise County, Arizona. He said that Mallan came to him in Tom Kemp's variety theater, Pueblo, a few days ago and claimed to be his friend, telling him that the Stilwells were on his track to kill him and that he wanted to warn him.

"This is probably the fact and was the circumstance referred to with so much unction by Mallan when he said he would have arrested Holliday before had his friends stood by him, etc.

"As Holliday was hurriedly pushed into a cell the reporter heard Mallan address him as 'Doc' and then for the first time came the remembrance of who Doc Holliday was. The reporter had heard of Holliday only from the cowboy standpoint and had supposed he was a very hard and desperate man. He did not look so, but such was the record he had been given. While riding back in the hack the subject was more fully discussed and then it was first learned that Mallan had given the estimation of Holliday already described. This was what had confirmed the Sheriffs in the belief that they had such an important prisoner. Mallan further said that Holliday had killed his partner, Harry White, seven years ago and that he was following him at his own expense for revenge. Holliday's history was further given as a partner of the notorious 'Off Wheeler' and 'Six-shooter Smith,' the latter of whom was killed about six weeks ago.

"Coming down town the reporter met Mr. Bob Masterson, Marshal of Trinidad, Colorado, and known as the 'man who smiles.' The New York *Sun* once wrote him up for this characteristic. He is said to have killed twenty-one men in the discharge of his duty each time so politely and with such a pleasant smile on his face that it was almost a pleasure to die at his hands. Bob is a gentleman, every inch of him, and no man stands higher where he is known. He was the man whom Holliday had called for on leaving the jail.

"Being asked about the arrest, Masterson, who was even then with Mr. Frank Naylor on his way to get a writ of habeas corpus for Holliday, gave an entirely different account of the affair. He had just heard of the arrest. To tell the story would require a review of the cowboy troubles in Arizona. Masterson said that Holliday was a responsible man, a Deputy United States Marshal, and for a time Deputy Marshal of Tombstone, and that the cowboys only wanted to assassinate him as they had Virg and Morgan Earp. It was feared that he would be taken from the jail last night and murdered. This accounted, then, for Holliday's strictures against Mallan(?) which he did not dare to express. If, as was suspected, Mallan was a cowboy playing the detective, Holliday feared to say so for fear of being shot down in the Sheriff's office. The case is a peculiar and sensational one throughout. Holliday, in company with the City Marshal, Virg Earp, and his brothers, Wyatt and Morgan Earp, was in the fight in Tombstone last fall, in which Bill Clanton and Frank and Tom McLowry were killed. It was feared last night that Mallan was no other than Sim Clanton, a brother of the dead man, and that the arrest of Holliday was only a scheme to get him in their power and murder him. All the other men alleged to have been killed by Holliday are said to be notorious desperadoes.

"At 3:30 o'clock this morning a writ of habeas corpus signed by Judge Elliott was served upon Sheriff Spangler, ordering him to hold the prisoner until he could be brought before the Court this morning."

And so the Denver *Tribune* on May 16, 1882, starts off a newspaper feud that split Denver wide open. The *Rocky Mountain News* had come out violently anti-Holliday, praising Mallan extravagantly for capturing a criminal charged with everything but infanticide. The Denver *Republican* sided with the *Tribune* in championing Holliday, as did the Pueblo *Chieftain*. The importance with which the affair was regarded is shown by the above article occupying the two right-hand columns on the front page. And here we see Doc's position in society being decided in the Denver press: killer or frontier-type gambler-law officer.

The Pueblo *Chieftain* for May 17, 1882, adopted a proprietary air toward Doc, as a Pueblo man who got done dirt in Denver. Speaking of his activities locally it said: "He made no effort to conceal his identity, and when questioned as to his doings in Arizona, said he had nothing to fear from that quarter, as he had received full pardon from the governor for his bloody work, in consideration of the effective services he had rendered the authorities. In conversation here he said he had never killed anyone, except in protecting himself, and that all he asked was to be let alone; he had left Arizona for the single purpose of being at peace with everyone around him, and he hoped his enemies would allow him that privilege.

"A day or two after Holliday came here another man named Perry Mallen arrived upon the scene. . . . Mallen was recognized as being formerly from Akron, Ohio, where he now has relations: he met several Akron gentlemen here, ingratiated himself into their

246

favor, and succeeded in securing considerable money from them, which he failed to return, and he may be arrested by them for obtaining money under false pretenses. To his acquaintances from Ohio he simply said he was travelling around the country on business, but to strangers with whom he should certainly not have been so confidential, he asserted that he was a government detective, a United States deputy marshal, etc., etc. Those who know him here say he holds no official position whatever, which goes far to strengthen the belief that he is simply after the blood-money which may be given to him by the cowboys of Arizona for the capture of Holliday. He is a small man, with reddish face and beard, with small, ferretty eyes, and not an inviting cast of features. He is much the inferior of Holliday in every particular, in appearance at least. His home is in Ogden, Utah.

" 'Doc' Holliday is a man of light weight, rather tall, smoothly shaven, and is always well-dressed. Streaks of grey can be seen in his hair, which grows from a head a phrenologist would delight in examining. His eyes are blue, large, sharp and piercing. He is not over thirty years of age and straight as an arrow. He gained his title of 'Doc' in a legitimate manner, as he once practised medicine, in Los Angeles, California, notably. He is well educated and his conversation shows him to be a man of considerable culture. That he has killed a number of men in the southern territories, and that he is regarded as a hard, dangerous man there is no disputing, but his friends claim that extenuating circumstances existed in every case of murder with which he was charged.

"If he had been taken by the proper officials, his arrest might be hailed with delight by a great many who now look upon it as an outrage, because they believe Mallen is an impostor, and that he made the arrest simply to get a little blood-money and turn his prisoner over to the 'tender mercies' of his enemies. The interference of the marshal of Trinidad in Holliday's favor, and his assertation that the man is not the fiend that he is represented, would certainly indicate that he is being persecuted and that the captor is no better, if as good, as his prisoner."

On the 19th the *Tribune* reported that a warrant had been issued in Pueblo for Holliday's arrest on a charge of having robbed a man there of a hundred and fifty dollars in a confidence game. Marshal Jennison of South Pueblo tried to serve the warrant on Holliday while the latter was being brought into court in Denver, but was sent "through the door in the most approved one-two-three-bounce-'em style" by Sheriff Spangler. The courtroom was crowded with gamblers, bunco men and confidence operators, but the scene with the Pueblo marshal "had worked up the Saxon blood of the Sheriff" and he ordered everyone out. Holliday was returned to jail promptly.

"It is evident that if anything like a fair opportunity was presented, a break would be made by Holliday's friends to rescue him from the Sheriff," the *Tribune* continued severely, reversing its former attitude toward Holliday. "The latter has good reason to fight all efforts to release Holliday. He has received stacks of telegrams from the California and Arizona officers to hold Holliday at all hazards, and by fair means or foul. This he now intends to do. An officer is now expected to arrive within a couple of days with the necessary requisition, and then Holliday will doubtless be taken to the scene of his alleged crimes for trial."

Sheriff Spangler had telegraphed to Johnny Behan and Sheriff Bob Paul of Pima County that he had Doc Holliday *and the Earps* [5] in jail in Denver and was awaiting a requisition for them. To Behan's fury, since he had offered rewards and made what he advertized to be strenuous efforts to catch Wyatt, Doc & Co., Bob Paul was selected by Governor Tritle of Arizona to bring the murderous marshal and his posse [6] back to justice. Sheriff Byres, of Gunnison, wiring to ask if he should arrest the Earps (who were actually in his county), was dismissed by Behan as a fraud.[7] Why Spangler said he had the Earps in jail in Denver is a puzzle, until one recognizes the hand of crackpot Perry Mallan, who probably added the Earps to his telegram to give it importance and signed Spangler's name to give it authority.

Bob Paul had to go to Prescott, get the requisition from the governor and go all the way to Denver. This took quite a while, and in the meantime Doc was doing everything he and his friends could think of to get out of the really serious trouble which a glory-hunter had at last managed to get him into. The fake robbery charge in Pueblo, later made by one of his friends to produce the legal twist that Holliday was wanted in Colorado and hence should not be allowed to get out of the state, was still to be brought up. First Doc set out to impress everyone with the fact that the attempt to extradite him to Arizona was only an attempt by the cowboys to get him in their power and murder him.

On the Sunday following his arrest, the Denver *Republican* sent a reporter to the county jail to interview Holliday. This interview,[8] quoting Doc's own words, describing his actions and appearance, is the best picture of the man himself that could have been found. The facts take quite a shellacking, but then Doc was fighting for his life—desperately acting a part before the reading public of Denver: the martyred law-man who would kill himself rather than be lynched by an outlaw gang.

"Holliday has a big reputation as a fighter, and has probably put more 'rustlers' and cowboys under the sod than any one man in the West. He has been the terror of the lawless element in Arizona, and with the Earps was the only man brave enough to face the bloodthirsty crowd, which has made the name of Arizona a stench in the nostrils of decent men. The visitor was very much surprised at Holliday's appearance, which is as different as could be from the generally conceived idea of a killer. Holliday is a slender man, not more than five feet six inches tall and would weigh perhaps 150 pounds. His face is thin and his hair sprinkled heavily with gray. His features are well formed and there is nothing remarkable in them save a well-defined look of determination from his eyes, which the veriest amateur in physiognomy could hardly mistake. His hands are small and soft like a woman's, but the work they have done is anything but womanly. The slender forefinger which has dealt the cards has dealt death to many a rustler with equal skill and quickness, and the slender wrist has proved its muscles of steel in many a deadly encounter, when a quick motion of a six-shooter meant everything. Holliday was dressed neatly in black, with a colored linen shirt. The first thing noticable about him in opening the conversation was his soft voice and modest manners. He explained the case as follows:

" 'The men known as cowboys are not really cowboys. In the early days the real cowboys, who were wild and reckless, gained a great deal of notoriety. After they passed out their places were taken by a gang of murderers, stage robbers and thieves, who were refugees from justice from the Eastern States. The proper name for them is Rustlers. They ran the country down there and so terrorized the country that no man dared say anything against them. Trouble first arose with them by the killing of Marshal White by Curly Bill. Marshal White fell into my arms when he was shot and I arrested Curly Bill. The trouble then is familiar to all.'

" 'Do you apprehend trouble when you are taken back?' asked the visitor.

"Holliday paused for a minute and gazed earnestly out of the window of Jailor Lambert's room into the rain outside and then said slowly, 'If I am taken back to Arizona, that is the last of Holliday.' After a pause he explained this by saying, 'We hunted the Rustlers, and they all hate us. John Behan, Sheriff of Cochise County, is one of the gang, and a deadly enemy of mine, who would give any money to have me killed. It is almost certain that he instigated the assassination of Morgan Earp. Should he get me in his power my life would not be worth much.'

" 'But Sheriff Paul, of Tucson, will take you to that place, will he not?'

" 'Yes, and there lies my only chance for safety. I would never go to Tombstone. I'd make an attempt to escape right outside this jail and get killed by a decent man. I would rather do that than be hung by those robbers there.'

" 'Cannot Paul protect you?'

" 'I'm afraid not. He is a good man, but I am afraid he cannot protect me. The jail is a little tumble-down affair, which a few men

250

can push over, and a few cans of oil thrown upon it would cause it to burn up in a flash, and either burn a prisoner to death or drive him out to be shot down. That will be my fate.'

" 'Haven't you friends there who would rally to your assistance?'

" 'Yes, the respectable element will stand by me, but they are all intimidated and unorganized. They will never do anything until some respectable citizen is shot down, when the people will rise and clean them out, as they did at Fort Griffin, where twenty-four men were hung on one tree when I was there. The Tombstone Rustlers are part of the Fort Griffin gang.'

" 'You are charged with killing Frank Stilwell. What do you know about that affair?'

" 'I know that Stilwell was a stage robber, and one of Morgan Earp's assassins, and that he was killed near Tucson, but I do not know that I am in any way responsible for his death. I know that he robbed a stage, from the fact that he gave the money to a friend of mine to keep, and I know that he helped in the assassination of Morgan Earp, as he was seen running from the scene by several responsible citizens. Pete Spence was with him, and I am morally certain that Sheriff Behan investigated [instigated?] the assassination. He did it for two reasons. One was that he was the officer elected by the Rustlers and the other was that he was afraid of and hated Morgan Earp, who had quarrelled with and insulted him several times. He feared Earp and had every inducement to kill him. A word further about this man Behan. I have known him a long time. He first ran against me when I was running a faro bank, when he started a quarrel in my house, and I stopped him and refused to let him play any more. We were enemies after that. In the quarrel I told him in the presence of a crowd that he was gambling with money which I had given his woman. This story got out and caused him trouble. He always hated me after that, and would spend money to have me killed. He has always stood in with the Rustlers and taken his share of their plunder, and in consequence he is in their power, and must do as they say. This is shown by the fact that he has five Rustlers under him as deputies. One of these men is John Ringo, who jumped on the stage of the variety theater in Tombstone one night about three weeks ago, and took all the jewels from the proprietor's wife in full view of the audience. These are the men who want me and that is the kind of country I am going back to for my health.'

" 'It's a nice, sociable country, I must admit,' responded the visitor, who ran over mentally all the terrible outrages which had been committed of late by the noted Rustlers, including a train robbery or two and several stage robberies. Holliday, in response to a question, then turned his attention to Mallan, the officer who followed him and caused his arrest here.

" 'The first time I met him,' said Holliday, 'was in Pueblo just before I came to Denver. He approached me in a variety theater and introducing himself said he wanted to do me a favor in return for saving his life in Santa Fe once. I told him I would be very thankful for any favor he wanted to show me, but he must be mistaken about my saving his life in Santa Fe, as I had never been there. He did not reply to this, but told me that he had just come up on the train with Josh Stilwell, a brother of Frank Stilwell, whom I was supposed to have killed, and that he had threatened to shoot me on sight. I thanked him for his information, and he replied, "If you give me away I will kill you." I told him I wasn't travelling around the country giving people away, and he left me. I met him in a saloon a few days afterwards, and asked the barkeeper who he was. He told me that Mallan represented that he was a ranchman, who had sold out in the lower country, and was looking for a location, upon the strength of which he borrowed $8 at one time, and $2 at another. I met the barkeeper several times afterwards, and he told me that the money had never been paid. I then considered that there was no truth in his story which he had told to me.

" 'The next time I saw him was in Denver, when he dropped his guns on me and caused my arrest. Paul does not know him, and I believe he is a crank. He acted like one at Pueblo, when he took down his clothes and showed a mark which he said was a bullet wound, but which was the mark of disease. I laughed in his face, the thing being so funny that I couldn't help it.

" 'On thing which Mallan tells gives him away bad. He said in your paper that he was standing alongside Curly Bill when the latter was killed. The facts are these: We were out one day after a party of outlaws, and about 3 o'clock on a warm day after a long and dry ride from the San Pedro river, we approached a spring which was situated in a hollow. As we did so eight Rustlers rose up from behind the bank and poured from thirty-five to forty shots into us. Our escape was miraculous. The shots cut our clothes and saddles and killed one horse, but did not hit us. I think we would have been all killed if God Almighty wasn't on our side. Wyatt Earp turned loose with a shot-gun and killed Curly Bill. The eight men in the gang which attacked us were all outlaws, for each of whom a big reward has been offered. They were such men as Curly Bill, Pete Spencer and Pony Deal, all of them wanted by the authorities and Wells, Fargo & Co. Pony Deal, I am told, was killed a few days ago on the railroad by soldiers. If Mallan was alongside of Curly Bill when he was killed, he was with one of the worst gangs of murderers and robbers in the country.'

" 'Where are the Earps?'

" 'In Colorado, over in the Gunnison, I believe.'

" 'Didn't you have a quarrel with them in Pueblo a few weeks ago?'

" 'We had a little misunderstanding, but it didn't amount to much.'

" 'Would they help you now?'

" 'Yes, all they could; but they are wanted themselves, and of course couldn't go back with me without putting themselves in danger, without doing me any good.'

"Holliday in conclusion said that Mallan's claim that he, Holliday, had killed his partner in Utah, was false, as at the very time Mallan claims the killing was done, the speaker was here in Denver dealing for Charley Foster, in Babbitt's house, where Ed Chase is now located. Holliday further says he was never in Utah. After leaving Denver he went to Dodge City, Kansas, where he stayed some time, going to Arizona from there. In going back he said he would be safe until he reached a point below Albuquerque and that it would not be healthy for Mallan to go on the same train. . . .

"Today in the District Court of Arapahoe County the writ of habeas corpus will come up. The requisition will arrive today. As it is pretty well assured that Holliday will be killed if taken back, the case will be thoroughly investigated before a requisition will be allowed."

Bob Paul had arrived armed with warrants, only to find that Wyatt and Warren were several hundred miles away and Doc was the sole Arizonan in the Denver jail. The requisition was delayed to exasperation. That Doc and the Earps escaped being taken back to Arizona in leg-irons is due to the red tape which fouled up the entire proceeding as much as to Perry Mallan's odd behavior.

An interview with Bob Paul, who "is of large physique, weighing probably two hundred pounds, [and] has a frank, open countenance," [9] show that he was somewhat on the fence as to the position of Doc and his friends. Asked if Doc was a member of the Earp gang, Paul said, "He was, and in fact was one of the leaders. The so-called Earp gang, or faction, if you please, was composed entirely of gamblers who preyed upon the cowboys, and at the same time in order to keep up a show of having a legitimate calling, was organized into a sort of vigilance committee, and some of them, including Holliday, had United States marshal's commissions."

" 'Was Holliday regarded as a desperate character?'

" 'Not by any means. He was always decently peaceable, though his powers when engaged in following his ostensible calling, furthering the ends of justice, made him a terror to the criminal classes of Arizona.' " [10]

On May 23, 1882, the Pueblo *Chieftain* said: "Mallen, the man who arrested 'Doc' Holliday in Denver recently, has at last admitted that his story of a seven-years hunt for his man was a fabrication. The indications are at present that Holliday will be

254

acquitted in Denver and that he will not be taken back to Arizona."

But the very next day the *Rocky Mountain News* carried: "Sheriff Paul received a telegram yesterday from the Secretary of Arizona Territory stating that the requisition had been forwarded from Tucson last Friday, hence it is expected momentarily. The case has begun to look very dark for Holliday, and it is nearly settled that he will have to go back to Tucson with Sheriff Paul who guarantees him protection against violence. It is not strange, however, that he should object to going back for trial as he left there to avoid this inconvenience."

Perry Mallan turned up again in the *Rocky Mountain News* on May 25, 1882, stating that Johnny Behan had offered a $500 reward for Doc and that the Cochise County commissioners had offered $1000 for him. The more he attempted to justify his actions, the more it looked as if these rewards alone were responsible for Doc being in jail.

The requisition finally arrived and was formally presented to Governor Pitkin on Friday, May 26, 1882. It had been put to the governor pretty strongly that Holliday stood no chance of anything even resembling justice if he was returned to Arizona and on the following Monday he was released into the custody of the Pueblo marshal.

The Pueblo *Chieftain* for June 1, 1882, carried: " 'Doc' Holliday is in the city, and his troubles, for the present, are apparently over with. Yesterday morning he appeared before Justice McBride upon a charge of having swindled a man out of one hundred dollars—a complaint entered against him just after he went to Denver. He waived examination and was bound over to appear before the District Court, providing a true bill was found against him. He was placed under bonds of $300, which he furnished, thus securing his liberty. He will remain in this city until his case is finally disposed of. He has no fears of the outcome. . . . The Cincinnati *Enquirer*, of Sunday, contained over a column of twaddle devoted to this case. A biographical sketch of the principal was included, in which it was made to appear that he has in his time

255

killed over fifty men, and that Jesse James is a saint compared to him. The article in question has caused much amusement among Holliday's friends."

Mr. Perry Mallan vanished from Denver under somewhat of a cloud and in possession of $161 and a valuable revolver which didn't belong to him. He was arrested in Pittsburg and held for requisition from there by the Colorado authorities [11] but I was unable to discover the final disposition of his case.

Doc settled down to a quiet and routine existence as a gambler in South Pueblo. The romance of his story made him a well-known local character, a tame killer to brag about, just as Trinidad had Bat Masterson to boast about to visiting easterners. He went to court again on July 18, 1882, charged with larceny but got his case continued.[12] It was continued on into infinity, although he was careful to keep himself under indictment so that the Arizona authorities couldn't grab him.

Pueblo, he felt, was a lucky town for Holliday.

FOOTNOTES TO CHAPTER 14

1. See Wyatt Earp's testimony after fight at the O.K. corral.
2. *Arizona, the Last Frontier*, Joseph Miller. Hastings House, New York, 1956.
3. *do.*
4. *do.*
5. From an undated *Tombstone Epitaph* quoted in the Denver *Republican*, May 22, 1882.
6. The *Tombstone Epitaph* had recently been sold by ex-mayor and Earp-partisan Clum. The new owners stated their attitude toward the Wyatt, Doc & Co. brand of justice: "Since the Earps . . . left the country, perfect peace has reigned in this section. The *Epitaph* only maintains that there is no difference between a murderous cowboy and a murderous United States Marshal."
7. Quoted in the Denver *Republican* for May 22, 1882, another undated *Tombstone Epitaph* states: "We have half an idea that S. Byres, of Gunnison, is a fraud and a delusion, from the fact that he telegraphed yesterday to Chief of Police Neagle, making inquiries as to the character of the Earps. Gunnison is 275 miles from Denver, and the Earps, according to a telegram received late yesterday, are still in jail in Denver."
8. Denver *Republican*, May 22, 1882.
9. *Rocky Mountain News*, May 22, 1882.
10. *do.*
11. Pueblo *Chieftain*, June 6, 1882.
12. Pueblo *Chieftain*, July 19, 1882.

15

Doc's Last Gunfight

"I have decided to enter a convent, the Sisters of Mercy, in Savannah," Mattie would have written early in that winter of 1883.

Doc stared at the page, too stunned at first to comprehend what the words meant to him. Mattie went on to explain how she was overcome by a great need to belong, to serve, to do some good in the world. "This is a working order. I shall be a teacher or work in a hospital or do something like that. You mustn't think of me as being lost to life. I have *found* life. This is, to me, the perfect way to a rich and complete life. I am so happy, John, so very, very happy. I shall pray for you every day of my life. Needless to say, Papa is dismayed. . . ."

Perhaps in that moment Doc saw Tom McLowry's face. Knew the dreadful headache that fogged Tom's thinking after Wyatt Earp had beaten him over the head with his gunbarrel in that apprehensive Tombstone street. Saw Tom's hands grabbing the front of his vest to throw it open so everyone could see he was unarmed—only Doc had thought he was going for his gun. Tom had died and many men had died, and Mattie would never blame anyone. Only. . . .

Standing in his lonely hotel room, looking down on the twilight-grey street where suppertime had cleared most of the passers-by away, he coughed and coughed. Mattie had turned her back on him—and he knew at last the complete abandonment he had never let himself believe would ever happen to him. He knew Mattie had not meant to hurt him. Her prayers, she thought, would be shield enough. "I am so happy," she had written. *I am so happy.* And at

258

last he understood how it had been for her, all these long years. Her friends had had husbands and babies and homes, making a priceless contribution to their world. She had had nothing. Nothing but love for a man who had at last turned out to be a killer. And she was too good not to want to make sacrifices for others—to marry a man half dead, bear his children, and after his death slave to raise the children herself. She would have been inexpressibly happy, Doc realized. All of the emptiness of his life swept over him. He had very nearly ruined Mattie's life in the ruin of his own. He stood there wondering if he had unconsciously wanted to make her as unhappy as he was. Well, it was all over. She would be happy, he knew, working as a nun. And for himself . . .

Everything was over.

Doc turned away and lit the lamp. The chimney rattled faintly but with determination against the bracket in which it was set as Doc tilted it to get the match at the wick. He replaced the chimney, turned the flame up, and stared at his white hand. It trembled very slightly, but continuously. His eyes were cold green-grey in the yellow lamp light. He was completely alone in the world—Mattie had forsaken him. And he could not blame her. Now he saw plainly that his constant drinking was bringing about a slow deterioration of his physical control. A horrible picture of himself as a drunken, dirty old bum stood in the center of his vision. He knew the shameless self-pity which brought that on, and fought the vision away. He looked down at his finely tailored suit, spotless, pressed, neat.

And all alone. The dreadful black pit was right at his heels—the pit into which stumble the men who know that no one cares for them, not anyone, anywhere. He walked quickly over to the table by his bed and poured himself a large drink of the best Kentucky bourbon. He saw that his hand shook holding the glass even as he lifted it. He smiled wryly, knowing the net of behavior in which he was caught and how hard he worked to pull it closer around him, then swallowed the mellow fire in the glass.

Suddenly the tremor in his hand lessened with the tightening of his fingers around the glass. He was lonely, yes, but he was also free. He no longer had anyone to consider but himself—he could do anything his slightly warped code of morals permitted, go any place his health . . .

The coldness in his eyes deepened, the wry smile changed. He rang for a boy and hauled his little trunk out of the closet and wiped it off. When the boy came Doc gave him a double eagle and told him to go over to the Denver and Rio Grande station and get him a ticket on the early train to Leadville.

"Hey, Doc. You ain't going to Leadville," the kid said, "coughing like you do?"

"Get!" Doc said. He placed a pile of crisply fresh cotton shirts in the trunk, then picked his .44 up from under a scarf in the drawer. The kid still stood in the doorway, staring in fascination as Doc, a real, sure-nuff killer, spun the cylinder of the very gun he'd killed all them fellers with. Doc reached down swiftly with his left hand and came up with a well-polished boot. The bellboy exploded into the hall and hit the stairs running.

Doc sat down suddenly. His gun fell on the floor unnoticed. This was the point where his life reached its climax. From here on everything is downhill. He sat there trying to justify his decision to go to Leadville to himself—trying to make it out anything but what he feared was true, that he no longer cared what happened to him. Mattie had failed him. Mattie. He knew that the spark, the something undefinable that gave zest to his existence was gone. And that his life was over, then, when Mattie entered the convent of the Sisters of Mercy.

But habit was so deep that he picked up the gun, polished it carefully, and put it away. Then he gave the bourbon bottle an emptying. Ah, well, he had been looking at the gloomy side, making things out as bad as they could be. There were good and logical reasons for going to Leadville.

He opened another bottle and lowered the spirit level.

There were more good reasons than not for going to Leadville.

He finished his packing with his usual neatness, tipped the bellboy a magnificent dime for getting his ticket, had one last good-sized snort, put on his black slouch hat and went out to celebrate his last night in Pueblo. And as he turned down the lamp wick on his way out, he looked at the fine tremor in his hands and it did not bother him in the slightest.

Doc had succeeded in covering up his real reason for going to Leadville to himself, but all his friends thought he was crazy. Leadville is 10,200 feet above sea level, with a climate described as "ten months winter and two months mighty late in the fall." They said it never rained in Leadville, it only snowed, the year around. The tourist guides advised all persons going there to bring a heavy ulster overcoat and be prepared to have colds, catarrh, bronchitis, pneumonia and other respiratory complaints continually, and stated emphatically, "Persons troubled with weak lungs or heart disease should also give the new camp a wide berth. The rare atmosphere accelerates the action of both these organs, and unless they are in perfect condition, serious results may follow." [1]

But Leadville was wide open. Half of the town's population of 10,000 were miners [2] and from having been in Tombstone and Deadwood Doc knew how they loved to gamble. Some of the most famous saloons in the West were there, and many of Doc's friends. He would fit in there, he would get along fine. And he wasn't going to worry about his health, not when he was strong enough to ride all over half of Arizona.

The Denver and Rio Grande had had a real battle, guns and all, with the Santa Fe for the right of way to Leadville and the west through the Royal Gorge of the Arkansas, and it had won itself a scenic route rarely matched in the world. The train seems to charge straight at a towering wall of mountains, and then sweeps like magic into the narrow passage that is the Royal Gorge where sheer walls of rock leap up over a thousand feet. The height of the gorge is accentuated by the surging closeness of its mighty walls, which confine at their base only the rawly blasted-out bed of the railroad and the white, racing water of the Arkansas. And then the road climbs and levels off in the park-like valley of the Upper Arkansas, and climbs again, always higher and higher, always far below the vast snow-covered mountains, and at last the train pants gamely into Leadville, on the western slope of the Mosquito Range. Across the flat valley of the Arkansas, to the west, loom Mt. Elbert and Mt. Massive, the second and third highest mountains in the country. Behind the town, the Carbonate, Fryer and Iron Hills are scarred by yellow and grey dumps. The big strikes were over and Leadville had settled down from the riotous days of its youth (the town was about four years old), but the mines were still producing, the smelters still fouling the cold, piercing mountain air, and there was money and adventure to be found there that winter of 1883.

It was Haw Tabor's town, as the Little Pittsburg and the Matchless, two of the richest mines on the slope, were his. The Tabor Grand Opera House was presenting the best talent, and plans were being made for the Tabor Grand Hotel. He was also kind enough to provide Leadville with the most delightful gossip, as he made it plain that skinny, prim Mrs. Tabor was no longer good enough for him and that he was lusting after plump little Mrs. "Baby" Doe, a divorced woman, no less.

That it was an ugly town didn't matter to Doc. It had two paved (slag) streets, which was more than Denver could boast, and some of the most famous saloons in the West: the Texas House with its chandeliers where every gas shade was a different tint of opalescent hand-blown glass; the walls were covered with rose brocade and decorated with expensive mirrors and paintings and the long mahogany bar had a white marble top. Nearby was Pop Wyman's, which had a huge Bible just inside the door, chained to a lectern, and where no drunks were served at the bar and no married man was allowed to gamble, and where the clock had the pious admonition, "Don't swear," painted across its face. There was also the oddly-named St. Ann's Rest saloon and dozens of other clean and average places. There was the fine Leadville Trotting and Running Association which held weekly races in the summer at Malta, four miles west of town, and the painted ladies on Stillborn Alley, two Turnverein societies for moral uplift, and a

262

mine which had been named the Ragged Ass, for some aged burro, no doubt.

Doc checked into the Clarendon Hotel, next door to Tabor's Opera House and the swankest hotel in town. He couldn't appreciate its splendor; he was too sick. Any unusual exertion caused him to pass out cold. His sole prop, the contents of the bourbon bottle, produced intoxication so acute that he was reduced to walking on his hands and knees and dragging his chin. But no one turned aside from him with disgust and scorn. He was picked up, brushed off, set down in a chair and informed that he was new in Leadville. "It's the elevation. You'll be used to it in a day or two."

The next day, to his surprise, he felt well enough to try to make a trip around the downtown area, just to get his bearings. Harrison Avenue appeared to be the main cow path. The whole downtown area was cut up by oddly-interposed streets which cut some regular city blocks into slivers or uneven-sided rectangles and dead-ended at adjoining blocks. The business section wasn't so big, but it certainly was thick with saloons.[3] Everything had a worn and dingy appearance, the result of the air pollution caused by fumes and smoke from the eight smelters and reduction works, four foundries and a gas works.[4] Almost immediately Doc had run into familiar faces. They showed him the joints and the high spots and introduced him around. "Doc Holliday," was introduction enough; he was known to everyone in his day, not just the sporting world.

"Doc!" cried a familiar voice, important with the weight of bad news, and Doc turned to see a man he remembered from Tombstone, although he. couldn't recall his name. The ex-Tombstoner went on, while shaking Doc's hand and assuring him of his friendship, "Johnny Tyler is here."

"That son of a bitch!" Doc howled. "Of all the . . ."

"He's dealing at the Casino. He's right bitter about the way you treated him in Tombstone, Doc."

Doc coughed and cursed off and on for quite a spell. Johnny Tyler! There wasn't any peace and quiet anywhere.

"Well, I don't run from anyone," he said at last. "So I guess Tyler and I'll mix it up again one of these days."

This was precisely what everyone had known he'd say.

He moved into rooms upstairs over a building at 106 East Second,[5] right downtown and in the thick of everything. He went to work at the Monarch saloon at 320 Harrison Avenue, dealing faro for Cy Allen, the proprietor. He began to have constant colds, sore throats and severe respiratory complaints. Mattie wrote that she was completely contented as a postulant, proudly recounting her chores and the things expected of her. Doc ran into Johnny Tyler, making sure plenty of people were about when he did, so as to show his old enemy up as a bluff and a bully who was afraid of him. Hatred for Doc became one of the important things in Tyler's life as a result, and he went around behind Doc's back constantly stirring up feeling against him.

1883 dragged on, and closer crept the dread day when Mattie would enter the convent as a novice. Doc was putting a strain on himself, concentrating on dealing faro, coughing himself into exhaustion, worrying constantly about what Mattie was doing, and fighting the hostility Johnny Tyler was stirring up against him. In the spring, when mud was Leadville's only sign of the change in seasons, Mattie wrote that she knew she wanted to be a nun all the rest of her life. With great difficulty Doc turned his attention to his surroundings. He had gotten used to the elevation as far as liquor was concerned, and having more and more things to forget, he drank harder and harder and grew to be harder and harder.

He was living far beyond the strength of his physical and nervous systems; without alcohol to bolster him he would have collapsed. And the whisky was merely a house built on sand: the tremor of his hands was spreading all over him, he began to find he could not think as clearly and as easily as before, and that he had difficulty in concentrating. He fought this by drinking even more heavily, longing for the sharp edges of life to be soft and blurred for him always.

With summer, driving was the most indulged-in sport and the

week-end races on the half-mile track at Malta were always crowded with spectators. Doc was glad to get out of town on these little excursions and found himself feeling much better. His trouble with Johnny Tyler continued but was always kept from coming to a head by one thing or another. Winter closed in again all too soon, and the improvement in Doc's health brought about by the warmer weather rapidly vanished.

Back in Georgia late September was but a prolongation of summer. On October 1, 1883, Sister Mary Melanie Holliday entered the Sisters of Mercy at St. Vincent's Academy in Savannah.[6] It was a Monday, the beginning of a week, of a life, of cheerful and contented work and prayer for others.

"Sister Mary Melanie," Doc said. The name was strange on his tongue and Mattie was a stranger. When he saw some of the Sisters of Charity who operated St. Vincent's hospital in Leadville, he would stare at them out of the corners of his eyes, wondering if Sister Mary Melanie dressed the way they did and looked as busy and at peace with everything and everybody. And then turn away to his loneliness. He had known that he would lose her now, finally and irrevocably, for all that she had yet to take her final vows, but still, when it happened, it was a deeper shock than he knew. Beautiful Mattie in her white dress and veil, to be bound forever in the service of her faith. He came down with some kind of major respiratory infection, the doctor called it pneumonia and let it go at that, which laid him up for several weeks. It was a wonder that it didn't kill him, but the toughness and stamina which had defied the onslaughts of both whisky and tuberculosis were still holding together in some fashion and he pulled through.

He was very weak, however, as anybody could see, and was living close to the thin edge of collapse. The constant, racking cough kept him so tired that he could never get the rest he needed to throw off the persistent infection. It took every nerve he could strain to get through his eight-hour shift at the faro bank in the Monarch saloon. He managed to forget Mattie's defection for hours at a time, only to find the hurt waiting for him when the last turn had been called. Johnny Tyler and the crowd of enemies he had made for Doc faded from Doc's mind. He had too many other worries, the worst of which was keeping his job, since his concentration and memory continued to get poorer and poorer and he continued to be so weak and tired.

How long he might have gotten by there is no telling.

But now Johnny Tyler struck directly at him.

There had been a couple of complaints about Doc being so short-tempered, but Cy Allen had kept him on for his publicity value. Now Tyler and his crowd set about to change Cy Allen's sentiments toward Holliday—the cold-blooded killer that people were afraid of, the drunkard no one could trust, the worst faro dealer in Leadville. One of Tyler's crowd set out to pick a fight with Doc, to show how easily it was done, and got somewhat more than he had bargained for. Doc was fired as a result.

He flew into one of his shaking rages, accused Tyler of being behind his being fired, and promised to get him for it, and Cy Allen, too. Some of his friends dragged him away before it came to a shooting. His friends on the police force, of whom he continued to have quite a few, cautioned him to be careful.

Tyler was smart. He never threatened Doc. He was careful never to let Doc taunt him into any injudicious words or actions. And he continued to stir up feeling against him at every opportunity. One of Tyler's friends was a bartender named Billy Allen, no relation to Cy Allen of the Monarch. With Doc's reputation as a killer, Billy was careful never to let himself be known as an enemy, but he hated Doc and, like Tyler, wanted to see him get his.

Doc's health broke down again. The shock of losing his job, and worse, knowing that his poor showing as a faro dealer had come to everyone's attention, brought on another attack of pneumonia. He was a long time getting over this, and before he was well enough to sit in a game his money ran out. Mannie Hyman, who ran Hyman's saloon at 316 Harrison Avenue, let him stay in a room upstairs over the saloon until he could get on his feet.[7] Hyman was rather a rough angel of mercy hidden in the guise of a saloon-

266

keeper: the room was there; Doc could use it; don't expect no service. In a little while Doc stopped coughing himself into exhaustion and managed to win enough at poker to pay Hyman for the use of his room and then moved to 219 West Third.[8]

And now his luck ran out. Tired and sick, too game or too stubborn to leave Leadville, he needed money desperately. And Luck, crying, "Them that has, gets!" flew out the window. In the early spring he was ill again and crept around like a sick rat, broke half the time, still pursued by Johnny Tyler's hatred and lies. But even half dead he was too much for Tyler to face and have it out. Tyler could never again stand up to Holliday, and never forgave him for having proved it.

Summer came at last, and that, or Sister Mary Melanie's prayers, or Doc's own inherent toughness, or something, got him on his feet physically, even if his luck continued so bad that he had to pawn his jewelry. Needless to say, he did not also pawn his gun. Rather than do that, he borrowed small sums from his friends and acquaintances, something the gambler comes to, sooner or later.

After getting over his rage with Cy Allen for firing him, Doc had not boycotted the Monarch saloon, although he spent most of his time in Hyman's or at the Board of Trade down the street. And he had a speaking acquaintance with Billy Allen who had recently gone to work as a bartender at the Monarch. In line with his usual run of luck of late, Doc inadvertently handed himself over to Johnny Tyler's crowd. He borrowed five dollars from Billy Allen and was unable to pay it back. Nobody was going gunning for Doc for any reason short of madness, but there were other ways of hurting him, of proving him as much a coward as he had proved Johnny Tyler to be in Tombstone. He would find out what it was like to be laughed out of town, Tyler swore.

Billy Allen was determined to show Doc up. He promised to lick the stuffing out of him if he didn't fork over that five.

Doc knew that no man would ever shame him before a crowd.

The *Leadville Daily Herald* for August 20, 1884, tells what happened as a result: "Yesterday's Shooting. Billy Allen, a Bartender at the Monarch Saloon, Shot by Doc Holliday," read the headlines. Nobody who knew Holliday could be surprised that it had happened—or at how it happened. "It seems that some weeks or months ago Doc Holliday borrowed five dollars from Billy Allen the bartender at the Monarch saloon," the *Herald* explained. "From all accounts Allen had asked him for the money several times, but as Holliday was out of employment, he could not pay it. Yesterday, Allen learned that Holliday was in Hyman's saloon, and started in to see him. Some of the former's friends so they say, advised Allen not to go, but he insisted on going, saying he would not have any trouble, and just as he entered Hyman's place, Holliday who was standing behind the cigar case saw him and drew his gun, a cut off single action colts 44, and fired, the first shot missed Allen and went through the glass at the top of the folding doors and lodged in the upper part of the door frame. When the first shot was fired, Allen turned to get out, but stumbled and fell, and just as he fell, Holliday reached over the cigar case and fired the second time, the ball entering Allen's right arm from the rear about half way between the shoulder and elbow and passing out in the front. The bone was not injured, the ball passing through the muscular or fleshy part of the arm. Henry Kelleman, who was standing behind the bar at the time, caught Holliday after the second shot was fired and prevented him from firing the third shot, if he had been so disposed. Allen got up and got out of the store and fell against the side of the house in a fainting condition. He was put into a hack and driven to his room on East Fifth Street. Drs. Maclean and D'Avignon were sent for and dressed his wound. An incision was made into the arm and the clotted blood removed, and the wound made by cutting, sewed up.

"To return to Doc Holliday. After the firing of the second shot, Captain Bradbury, who was standing on the sidewalk, rushed in and disarmed Holliday, took him in custody and escorted him to the county jail, where he was locked up. As he walked off he made the request to be protected, that is, not to let anyone shoot him in the back.

"There are two sides to the story connected with the affair. A number of those who were Allen's friends were talked with, and the following is their account of the affair. They stated that Allen had no intention of any difficulty; but that he was only going in to see Holliday. As he started Cy Allen said to him, 'Billy, you would better not go; he will kill you.' But Allen did not heed the warning, saying he would have no difficulty. He did not get killed, but the bullet hole in his arm shows that Cy Allen understood the disposition of Holliday better than Billy did. Allen's friends contend that he had no ill feeling toward Holliday, and apprehended no danger, and intended to have no difficulty.

"On the other hand, those who are rather inclined to the side of Holliday say that there is a gang in town who have been wanting to kill Holliday for the sake of getting a reputation. One of them stated that Allen had told Holliday that he would give him until noon yesterday to pay back the five dollars, and that in case he did not pay it he (Allen) would take Holliday's gun away from him, if he had one, and then thump him. Holliday's friends contend that when he saw Allen coming into Hyman's he thought he was coming to fulfill the threat he had made, and being physically greatly the inferior of Allen he turned loose with his gun with the result already known. . . .

"Doc Holliday has been in Leadville for about two years. He came here from Arizona, where he had the name of being a dangerous man and utterly reckless of human life if any provocation to kill was offered. During his stay in Leadville however, he has been very quiet and has never got into any trouble until yesterday. It has been reported that a grudge existed between him and certain other gamblers that had its origin in Arizona, and that a 'killing' has been imminent for some weeks. Some of those connected with the Monarch saloon say that Holliday has been sore at the house for some little time, because he was discharged from his position as a faro dealer at one of the tables in the house, and that he has made threats as to what he would do. . . .

"He is said to be a southern man by birth and well cultured, and a dentist by profession, but he has not followed the business for a long time. It is said by a number of the sporting men that the trouble is not over yet, and that it is likely a killing will grow out of the affair before it is ended.

"At a late hour Holliday had not got bail, though he probably will today."

A week later the *Herald* reported: [9] "Doc Holliday's examination on the charge of assault with intent to kill Billy Allen on last Tuesday came off yesterday in the District court room before Judge Old. The room was crowded with spectators, anxious to learn the result. . . .

"Captain Bradbury was the first witness who testified for the prosecution: 'I am acquainted with Allen and Holliday; on the day of the shooting I saw Allen in front of Hyman's and asked him what was the trouble between him and Holliday; he replied, "Doc owes me five dollars and won't pay me;" I then said to him, "I heard he had a gun for you, and you had better not go into Hyman's, as he may be there;" he said he "wanted to speak to Doc," and went in; I could see Holliday as he raised the gun and fired; Allen fell and Holliday reached over the case and fired again; I don't think the first shot took effect; Allen, so far as I could see, made no motion to shoot; I went in and said, "Doc, I want your gun;" and I disarmed him and took him to jail. . . . Holliday said, "I want you to protect me." '

"Henry Killerman, the bartender at Hyman's testified to being behind the bar at the time of the shooting; that Holliday came in and said he had heard Allen was going to do him up, and that he did not intend to be murdered. . . . 'Allen was not employed in the house and had no business there; I heard Holliday say it was pretty hard for him to be disarmed when Allen was carrying a gun for him.'

"Pat Sweeny was the first witness for the defense. . . . 'Allen then said he would give Holliday until Tuesday noon to pay him, and if he did not he would knock him down and kick his d—d brains out.'

270

"Officer Robinson sworn: 'I told Doc Holliday the night before the shooting that "I have been told you carry a pistol, you have always been my friend, and I don't want to search you; if you have one go and put it away" . . . the man that told me was Bill Allen.'

"James Ryan testified: '. . . Bill Allen told me a man in town has not treated me right; he borrowed five dollars from me and if he don't pay me by Tuesday, I will whip him. . . . Allen is a stout, active man; Holliday is a small man and delicate besides.'

"Doc Holliday testified: 'I borrowed five dollars from Allen, and said I will pay it in five or six days or a week. There is a young man owing me and when he pays it, I will pay you. He did not pay me. He told me he had lost the money and could not pay. I said I am sorry, as I promised to pay Allen. I told Allen this but that I would pay it as soon as I got it. I walked into the Monarch before this trouble, and was coming out, when Allen came out, with an apron on, with his hand under his apron. He said, "Holliday, I'll give you till Tuesday to pay this money and if you don't pay it, I'll lick you, you son-of-a-b—." I said my jewelery is in soak and as soon as I get the money, I'll give it to you. I then went out and began to think of something that happened last winter.' (Prosecution objected.) 'I went to bed at 5 o'clock Tuesday morning, and got up about 3 o'clock and went to Hyman's; I started down street and was talking to Hyman when Sweeney came up and said, I want to see you; this man Allen wants to see you; he has a gun; I think it is a six shooter; I said to Sweeney, I want you to see the marshal, and don't think it is right that one should be disarmed and another allowed to carry a gun; I don't want to be murdered; I went over to Hyman's and Lomeister said he would see Faucett [the city marshal] or Bradbury; I saw Hyman and told him that I wanted him to see an officer, as I would not carry a gun, for I had no money to pay a fine, and I did not want to be murdered; afterward I was in at Hyman's; I saw Allen come in with his hand in his pocket, and I thought my life was as good to me as his was to him; I fired the shot, and he fell on the floor, and fired the second shot; I knew that I would be a child in his hands if he got hold of me; I weigh 122 pounds; I think Allen weighs 170 pounds; I have had the pneumonia three or four times; I don't think I was able to protect myself against him.'

"Cross-examined: 'I got up about three o'clock; I think the shooting was between 4 and 5 o'clock but am not certain as to the time; I knew Allen was then looking for me; I was in Hyman's waiting for Marshal Faucett to come and protect me; I expected Allen to come there or anywhere else; I expected to protect myself; I had been told he had a gun and was looking for me; when he came in his right hand was in his pocket; he was about three feet inside of the door when I shot; when I shot the first time he turned and fell; I did not see where his hands were when I fired the second time; I supposed he was going to get there if he could, for I thought he had come there to kill me.'

"Judge Old bound the defendant over in $8,000 bail."

With their usual perversity and lack of logic both luck and public opinion swung to Doc's side. Doc shot one of Johnny Tyler's crowd and everyone decided Tyler had gone too far. The eight thousand in bail was produced and Doc went back to the poker tables, where despite his impaired judgment and lack of concentration the know-how gained by a decade of practice kept him ahead of the game. He got his jewelry out of hock, had some new clothes made, and realized that he was a public figure in Leadville.

Leadville took sides in the matter. Doc's faction did everything they could think of to patch up the quarrel and keep Billy Allen from pressing his suit against Doc. Judge Goldthwaite's session of the criminal court of Lake County met the first Monday in September. Doc's case was not tried. The court met again the first Monday in December. Doc's legal counsel got his case continued again. Allen still refused to compromise. Doc had tried to kill him and he had the scars to prove it. Johnny Tyler's crowd felt that surely they would see Doc sent to the rock pile at Canon City for attempted murder.

272

Doc knew that Tyler had fostered Billy Allen's trouble, taken up his cause, and was keeping the trouble between them worked up. He determined to use this to his advantage when the case at last came up for trial.

The March session of the criminal court scheduled his case. It was started on March 27, 1885.

Back in Arizona the Tucson paper [10] printed: "Doc Holliday. The whereabouts and occupation of this notorious individual, so well known in Arizona, has for some time been lost sight of, and the following Leadville special to the Denver *Tribune-Republican*, dated March 27, may be of interest to his acquaintances:

'The trial of Doc Holliday, the man with a bloody record, in the charge of shooting Billy Allen, on August last, with intent to murder, began in the Criminal Court before Judge Goldthwaite this morning. A jury was impanelled and the evidence commenced, but the wrangling among the lawyers delayed it materially. The difficulty grew out of an old dispute in Tombstone, Arizona, in which Holliday was the ringleader on one side and John Tyler, who is now dealing for a faro bank here, was on the other.

Holliday and Tyler both left Tombstone after the latter had refused to fight a duel with the former at ten paces, and met in Leadville. Tyler was a Pacific and Holliday an easterner. There was an inextinguishable rivalry and animosity existing between the factions. The old imbroglio was rankling in their breasts here and Tyler and his friends did everything to prejudice the public against Holliday. Billy Allen was among those who sympathized with the Tyler crowd and Holliday put him down as an enemy.

Some financial difficulty arose between Allen and Holliday, the matter assuming the shape of a quarrel. Allen is alleged by Holliday's friends to have said that he would 'do him up,' while Allen asserts that he said he would whip him. At any rate, on the day of the tragedy a number of Holliday's friends went to his room and represented that Allen was seeking him with a revolver.

About noon he went across the street to Hyman's, and said laconically to the proprietor, 'The time's up.' He then returned to his room where he remained until 5 o'clock. He then sent his revolver by a friend to Hyman's, where it was placed behind one end of the bar. Holliday soon came over and took his stand within reach of the weapon, and near the cigar lighter.

Allen, having overlooked the action behind the bar, put on his coat and assured Mr. Allen, who remonstrated with him, that there would be no trouble, he went to Hyman's and had scarcely crossed the threshold when Holliday levelled his revolver and fired, the bullet striking below muscle of the right arm and emerging near the shoulder. Holliday sprang behind the bar again, and fired the second time, the bullet blazing Allen's head. He was then overpowered and disarmed, while Allen was removed to his apartments, recovering shortly afterwards.

Every effort was made to compromise the matter before it reached the courts, but Allen stood firm for the prosecution. The testimony will be resumed in the morning.' "

And nothing came of it. The very next day Doc was acquitted.[11] It was small comfort Johnny Tyler got from the fact that Doc was requested by the law to shake his freight out of Leadville, his friends on the force personally escorting him to catch the evening train to Denver via Colorado Springs. Doc himself was very glad to get out of the whole mess, but he sent word by one of the law-and-order crowd to Johnny Tyler that he would be back. He looked long at a wave of smelter smoke drifting like a black nun's robe across the clear outline of the mountains. Then, coughing, he got on the train.

274

FOOTNOTES TO CHAPTER 15

1. *Tourist's Guide to Leadville and the Carbonate Fields*, Lewis Cass Carpenter. The Denver *Daily Tribune* Publishing House, Denver, 1879.
2. *Crofutt's Grip-Sack Guide of Colorado*, George A. Crofutt. Overland Publishing Co., Omaha, Nebraska, 1885.
3. Twice as many saloons as grocery stores, according to Ballenger & Richard's *Leadville City Directory*, 1883.
4. *Crofutt's Grip-Sack Guide of Colorado.*
5. *Leadville City Directory*, 1883.
6. From the records of St. Vincent's Academy, Savannah, Georgia.
7. *Leadville City Directory*, 1884.
8. *do.*
9. *Leadville Daily Herald*, August 26, 1884.
10. *Arizona Weekly Citizen*, April 4, 1885.
11. *Denver Tribune-Republican*, March 28, 1885, and March 29, 1885.

16

Doc Bows Out

Under Catholic and

Presbyterian Auspices

In Denver Doc checked into the Metropolitan Hotel [1] at 1325 16th Street, right across from the big Academy of Music theater. It charged a dollar and a quarter a night, as compared to the Grand Central which charged fifty cents a night and was next door to the railroad yards, and the Windsor which charged four dollars a night and had diamond-dust mirrors.[2] Denver's population was 54,000. A five-room house rented for thirty-five dollars a month, the best eggs were twenty cents a dozen, city laborers were getting a dollar and a quarter to two dollars a day, foundry workers got three dollars. These were for ten- to twelve-hour shifts. Faro dealers wages had been cut to five dollars for eight hours. The big news was the charge made by Theodore Tilton that world-renowned Reverend Henry Ward Beecher had committed adultery with Mrs. Tilton. Labor strikes characterized by violence and bomb-throwing were chronicled almost daily in the newspapers. But the country was bragging of its prosperity. Denver had a brand-new Tabor Grand Opera House, big smelters, foundries, breweries

276

and railroad yards. The local rage was roller skating, and the streets were still not paved.

Ed Chase's Palace Theater was the most popular gambling place in town. It was located at the site of Babb's saloon, where Doc had worked ten years before when he first came to Denver. It was on the second floor, and except for the splendor of its decorations, very like the Comique in Dodge City.

Sporting events were big items in the gambling field. Horse racing was always popular, but it was temporarily overshadowed by a craze for bicycle racing of a style perhaps describable as public suicide. The bike we ride today was sneered at as a "safety" bicycle—these riders whizzed around on top of one towering fifty-four-inch wheel, so that a fall, which was too easy, generally drew blood, broken bones and public approbation. Baseball had newly come into its own this summer of 1885. The teams, in Damon Runyon style, were known by the name of their town— the New Yorks, the St. Louis's, the Denvers. On August 3, 1885, three thousand people turned out to see the Denvers beat the Hastings, nine to five, sitting or standing on the grass around the diamond in the absence of a stand. Two Hastings at bat were hit by pitched balls, but instead of taking a base could only curse the Denvers' pitcher. There were no contracts, and often a top-notch team would have its best players lured away in the midst of a series by better wages. On August 15, 1885, the Denvers were defeated eight to seven by the Leavenworths, in twelve innings. Of the Denvers' pitcher the Denver *Tribune-Republican* said: "[Martin] was only batted for 8 hits, with a total of 10 bases. He struck out 9 men, assisted 9 times and made 5 errors." In another game the Denvers' catcher, playing without a mask, was hit in the head by a foul tip. The game was delayed for ten minutes while he lay unconscious on the greensward, and continued when he was able to play! The gambling crowd ran the betting just as they did for the horse races, pools for the baseball games being sold daily at the Jockey Club saloon.[3] Ed Chase's Palace Theater was the scene of weekly wrestling matches, one fall to a finish,[4] often lasting two or three hours. The contestants were invariably Greek George and Antoni Pierre, with the former always winning. This was the heyday of John L. Sullivan and boxing of the slaughterhouse style, a round lasting until a knockdown and often going twenty or thirty rounds, or until it was stopped by the police. Mr. Sullivan usually appeared in cream-colored tights with a green sash.

Doc got along fine in Denver, but his friends were all struck by the change in him: the marked way in which a fine tremor shook him continually, the way his chest had sunk, giving him a very stooped appearance, the way in which the white hairs predominated over the blond ones, the way his accurate judgement had slipped. No one criticized him for his drinking: it was obvious that he was in constant pain. He was congenial with his friends and there were a lot of men who wanted to meet him. "I gambled with Doc Holliday." That was something to tell your grandchildren. A real killer and looked and talked like a perfect gentleman.

Doc wrote to Sister Mary Melanie far oftener than he had written Mattie. She wrote that she was praying for his conversion. The two women that he had loved, his mother and Mattie, stood at the two extremes of Christianity and he was lost in the middle. He kept on, lost though he might be, loyal, uncomplaining, brave. And it was hard, now. The alcohol which padded his nerves against the cruelties of existence was at the same time breaking them down. His follow-through to the point of an argument was likely to get side-tracked, his initiative was fading, his memory was very bad, he found himself with a glib excuse for every discreditable thing he did, and he was becoming increasingly impulsive and unpredictable. His actions, as his appearance, were those of an old man. He was thirty-four this winter of 1886.

As spring came on, the Denver *Tribune-Republican* began a crusade to force the gambling element out of town. There were anti-gambling-house and anti-bawdy-house laws, the paper pointed out. Why weren't they enforced? It made such a stink that all the

278

gambling-house proprietors and prostitutes were rounded up and fined—and turned loose to go back to their business. One gambler protested, saying he had paid two hundred dollars to the city government for the privilege of conducting a gambling hall with the understanding that he would also be protected, so it was unjust that he be fined, too. The judge commented mildly that such was contrary to the laws of the state. There was no investigation of the "fix." [5]

The arrests continued into summer, providing the paper with its largest quantity of local news, until July 6, 1886.

That night the Academy of Music burned down.

Doc hurried down the street, staring at the flaring red reflected all over the front of his hotel, and got there just as the windows started falling in from the terrific heat. The dozen or so firemen with their few pieces of equipment, even though they included the magnificent new Amoskeag steamers which could pump a sizeable stream of water, could do nothing with the flames. The theater, Kinneavy's saloon, the St. Cloud restaurant, two stores and the Western Union office were destroyed. Doc's hotel, the Board of Trade saloon, a warehouse, the German National Bank and Charpiot's restaurant and hotel were scorched and lost their windows from the heat.

At last the police let Doc into the Metropolitan. It was filled with smoke, but none of his things had been damaged. He coughed a good deal from the smoke, but counted himself lucky not to have lost anything. Indeed, his luck had swung up with the shooting of Billy Allen, and kept him pretty well off. Doc was careful to have some friends on the police force everywhere he went, usually men who had been through the wild seventies in the west as he had been, and with whom he could swap lies about his death-defying deeds as deputy marshal of Tombstone and deputy United States marshal for southern Arizona. These men now suggested to him that there were a bunch of young efficiency-cranks on the force, some of whom had noticed him at the fire. Doc's name was on the city list of undesirables and it seemed likely that he was due to get run in on a vagrancy charge. Denver now had a law that said all persons who had no visible means of support could be arrested as vagrants.

Doc left Denver, but in Pueblo he ran into an old friend named McCoy and they got to talking about the coming racing meet in Denver. Doc had not gotten any official notice to leave town, and the more he thought about it the more reasons he could find for going back.

The Denver *Tribune-Republican* for August 4, 1886: "The notorious Doc Holliday was arrested last evening by the police for vagrancy. J. S. Blythe and K. McCoy were arrested at the same time and on a similar charge. They were locked up in jail and opposite their names on the prison slate were marked the words, 'safe keeping.' When asked why such a charge was preferred, the reporter was informed that if a charge of vagrancy was preferred the prisoners must necessarily be arraigned in the Police Court in the morning where the sentence, in all probability, would be a slight fine only.

"The intention is to keep them in jail until this morning and then arraign them in one of the Justice Courts on a charge of vagrancy. This will insure them, so the police say, of going to jail for a long period of time."

There followed a recital of Doc's career as a criminal, winding up, "He then came to Denver and since that time has been living here—that is, when the police did not drive him out of town. His only means of living was gambling in its worst form and confidence work. Three weeks ago he left town on a penalty of being arrested, but returned a few days ago, the police say, in company with a score of other confidence men, thieves and sure-thing workers. Last evening Holliday, McCoy and Blythe were standing on Sixteenth st., when Officer Norkott called up the patrol wagon and they were gathered in."

The next day's paper explained what all the fuss was about, if you knew that Jewell Park was the local race track. "The cases against 'Doc' Holliday and Messers McCoy and Smythe, the al-

280

leged gamblers and bunko men, came up in the Police Court yesterday. The charge entered was vagrancy. None of the parties had attorneys. The cases of the first two men were continued. In Smythe's case, testimony was given to the effect that he was employed by Messers Bush and Hudson of Jewell Park as a watchman. For this he received $10 per week for 3 nights' work."

Doc got his case continued clear out of sight and proceeded to forget about it. The paper made no mention of it, but there must have been people around who could put two and two together. There was a racing meet due soon and a notorious gambler and confidence man was seen talking to one of the night watchmen at the track. This time Doc was officially requested to depart and stay departed. He went down to Pueblo, but things were too easy for him there. He had come to the point where the only interest in his life was doing things he wasn't supposed to do and getting away with it.

He was so restless that he didn't know what to do with himself. Everything in his life was shabby and pointless. He felt with dismay that he had outlived his day and the way of life he could get along in. Tuberculosis, gun fights, the eternal drenching in alcohol, the painful altitude of Leadville, losing Mattie, he had survived them all. And for what? To come to emptiness and defeat. He knew that his mind was clouded permanently now from over-drinking; he could only sense things clumsily, fumble dimly and uncaringly for answers to questions that he couldn't put into words. His stay in Leadville had set off the progress of his tuberculosis, largely arrested before, and his dreadful coughing, his painfully collapsed chest and consequently stooped posture, his constant indigestion, all combined to make his life a torment.

He went to Denver again, unmolested by the cops now that the papers were not putting the heat on, and took care of a few little business matters of his usual shady sort. But all the time he was looking for something. What it was he didn't know, but it was, he felt, the thing that was making him so restless.

At last he went back to Leadville.

Hyman's was now owned by Schultze and Dale, there was a fine new YMCA, Johnny Tyler ignored him even behind his back; the chubby dames [6] in the variety theaters on Second street were singing "My Darling Clementine," "Aloha Oe," "Stars of the Summer Night," and "Leaf By Leaf the Roses Fall," and here, with that kindness that he so little appreciated, luck was all his. He made a pile gambling that was the equal of anything he had ever done in his prime. It gave him a lift, made him feel that it was not too late, that something fine could yet be done.

It was May of 1887.

He had heard much of Colorado's newest health resort, Glenwood Springs. The hot springs were being boasted as a sure cure for consumption, the vapors being heavily charged with healing chemicals. So Doc had his trunk taken down to Carson's stage and express line, at 106 West 4th,[7] paid twelve dollars for his ticket and got on top of the big four-horse Concord for his last ride.

Glenwood Springs is set in a little valley of the Colorado River, shut in by snow-capped mountains. From Yampa hot spring flow daily six million gallons of water at an average temperature of 140°F, and there are hot-vapor caves and baths besides.

Doc checked into the Glenwood Hotel and began to take the cure. When not breathing the hot, steamy air he hung out in the sheriff's office talking over old times or did his serious drinking in one of the four local saloons. The town had some 400 permanent residents, but as summer came on the population increased enormously. Everyone seemed benefited by the hot mineral waters.

Everyone but Doc.

His chronic pulmonary tuberculosis suddenly developed into miliary tuberculosis, in which the germ attacks not only the lungs but every part of the body, and with vicious force and speed. Doc felt worse and worse, and one day he noticed an ulcer on his chest.[8] He promptly went to a doctor, suspecting syphilis no doubt, and after an examination was informed that it was a tubercular lesion. Another one was starting. The doctor told him that

282

he had developed galloping consumption and could expect to live but a few months.

Doc was thirty-five years old this summer of 1887.

He went back to his hotel room and found it marvelously peopled. The loneliness would never come back. The shadows were more real, more filled with unfailing companionship than the crowded saloon he had stopped at on his way from the doctor's office. He heard so faint and clear his mother's voice singing, Morg's laugh, the leathery rustle of gun belts on Frank and Tom McLowry, Billy Clanton, Frank Stilwell, Florentino. And he was not afraid. He wrote Sister Mary Melanie a letter to thank her for her prayers. But he was still Doc and coldly practical, and still an alcoholic to whom truth was something a lie was dressed up to look like in order to get you something you wanted. So he went right smack out and told the Catholic priest, Father Downey, that he had been baptised a Catholic, and told the Presbyterian minister, Reverend Rudolph, that he had been raised a Presbyterian.

By the first week in September Doc was so weak that he could no longer get around. His remarkable behavior with the sky pilots paid off in their unflagging attention to him, each determined to save the sinner's soul for their own particular heaven—as Doc had intended they should. His sufferings were so great, and his courage so marked, however, that others were attracted to his bedside and he would never have lacked for kindness nor care even without the clergy. He was rotting away before everyone's eyes, and yet he clung to the life which had been so grave a trial for him, and whose temptations had so often found in him a ready subject, without complaining, without blaming anyone else for his troubles.

He died at ten o'clock in the morning on November 8, 1887.

The obituary which appeared in the Glenwood Springs paper the following day [9] is typical of Victorian maudlinism on the subject of death, but it shows us what Doc told the people in Glenwood Springs about himself, and what they thought about him.

"Death of J. A. Holliday; died in Glenwood Springs, Colorado, Tuesday, November 8, 1887, about ten o'clock a.m. of consumption, J. A. Holliday," read the two-column headline. "J. A. Holliday, or 'Doc' Holliday as he was better known came to Glenwood Springs from Leadville last May, and by his quiet and gentlemanly demeanor during his short stay and the fortitude and patience he displayed in his last two months of life, made many friends. Although a young man he had been in the west for twenty-five years, and from a life of exposure and hardship had contracted the consumption, from which he had been a constant sufferer for many years. Since he took up his residence at the Springs the evil effects of the sulphur vapors arising from the hot springs on his weak lungs could readily be detected, and for the last few months it was seen that dissolution was only the question of a little time, hence his death was not entirely unexpected. From the effects of the disease, from which he had suffered probably half his life, Holliday, at the time of his death, looked like a man well advanced in years, for his hair was silvered and his form emaciated and bent, but he was only thirty-six years old.

"Holliday was born in Georgia, where relatives of his still reside. Twenty-five years ago, when but eleven years of age, he started for the west, and since that time he has probably been in every state and territory west of the Mississippi River. He served as Sheriff in one of the counties of Arizona during the troublous times in that section, and served in other official capacities in different parts of the west. Of him it can be said that he represented law and order at all times and places. Either from a roving disposition or while seeking a climate congenial to his disease, 'Doc' kept moving from place to place, and finally in the early days of Leadville came to Colorado. After remaining there for several years he came to this section last spring. For the last two months his death was expected at any time; during the past fifty-seven days he had only been out of his bed twice; the past two weeks he was delirious, and for twenty-four hours preceding his death he did not speak.

"He was baptised in the Catholic church,[10] but Father Ed.

Downey being absent, Rev. W. S. Rudolph delivered the funeral address, and the remains were consigned to their final resting place in the Linwood cemetery, at 4 o'clock on the afternoon of November 8th, in the presence of many friends. That 'Doc' Holliday had his faults none will attempt to deny; but who among us had not, and who shall be the judge of these things?

"He only had one correspondent among his relatives—a cousin, a Sister of Charity, in Atlanta, Georgia. She will be notified of his death, and will in turn advise any other relatives he may have living. Should there be an aged father or mother, they will be pleased to learn that kind and sympathetic hands were about their son in his last hours, and that his remains were accorded Christian burial."

His father had died, I believe, some time before. Sister Mary Melanie spent the rest of her long life working in a hospital in Atlanta.

Today all the roaring camps are towns and cities except Tombstone, and it still sits lonely under the sky almost exactly as it was when Doc knew it. The stage trails are paved highways, the Indians citizens. The fierce decade of poverty-driven progress has faded from every man's mind and the hard-won West is but countryside, mountain and desert. The men of that decade are gone as Doc is gone—and vandals have stolen the headboards that marked their graves. His monument must be the gambling games which go on forever.

FOOTNOTES TO CHAPTER 16

1. *Denver City Directory*, the Gazetteer Co., Inc. Denver, 1887.
2. Denver *Republican*, December 25, 1887.
3. Denver *Tribune-Republican*, August 5, 1885.
4. A fall required either both shoulders and one hip, or both hips and one shoulder, to touch the mat.
5. Denver *Tribune-Republican*, May 13, 1886.
6. A popular entertainer of the day, 18-year-old Blanch Curtisse was described in the Denver *Tribune-Republican* for August 3, 1886, as a vision of loveliness: "She is about 5 feet 5 and weighs about 150 pounds with a form that is seemingly perfect."
7. All these Leadville locations are from the *Leadville City Directory* for 1887.
8. Local old-timers recalled the sores on Doc's chest and I accepted them because it is a symptom of miliary tuberculosis (which the old-timers didn't know) and Doc went mighty fast, once he got started. Chronic pulmonary tuberculosis can develop overnight into the miliary form, apparently.
9. From a clipping in a scrapbook kept by James A. Riland, now in the library of the Colorado State Historical Society.
10. No record of this could be found in Glenwood Springs, and it seems unlikely that it happened any place.

Bibliography

Adams, James Truslow, and Coleman, R. V., *Atlas of American History*, Charles Scribner's Sons, New York, 1943.

Adams, Ramon, *Cowboy Lingo*, Houghton Mifflin Co., Boston, 1936.

Aikman, Donald, *The Taming of the Frontier*, Minton, Balch & Co., New York, 1925.

Aikman, Duncan, *Calamity Jane and the Lady Wildcats*, Henry Holt & Co., Inc., New York, 1927.

Appleton's *Handbook of American Travel*, D. Appleton & Co., New York, 1873.

Asbury, Herbert, *Sucker's Progress*, Dodd, Mead & Co., New York, 1938.

Avery, I. W., *History of the State of Georgia*, Brown & Derby, Publishers, New York, 1881.

Banning, Captain William, and Banning, George Hugh, *Six Horses*, Century Co., New York, 1930.

Beebe, Lucius, and Clegg, Charles, *Hear the Train Blow*, E. P. Dutton & Co., Inc., New York, 1952.

Beirne, Francis F., *The Amiable Baltimoreans*, E. P. Dutton & Co., Inc., New York, 1951.

Bennett, Estelline, *Old Deadwood Days*, J. H. Sears & Co., Inc., New York, 1928.

Blythe, T. Roger, *A Pictorial Souvenir and Historical Sketch of Tombstone, Arizona, "the town too tough to die,"* Tucson, Arizona, 1946.

Bowman, Hank Wieand, *Antique Guns*, Fawcett Publications, Greenwich, Connecticut, 1953.

Breakenridge, William, *Helldorado, Bringing the Law to the Mesquite*, Houghton, Mifflin, New York, 1928.

Bremner, M. D. K., *The Story of Dentistry*, Dental House of Interest Publishing Co., New York, 1946.

Brown, Dee, and Schmidt, Martin, *Trail Driving Days*, Charles Scribner's Sons, New York, 1952.

Burke, Emily P., *Reminiscences of Georgia*, James T. Fitch, Ohio, 1850.

Burns, Walter Noble, *Tombstone, an Iliad of the Southwest*, Double-day, Page & Co., New York, 1929.

Candler and Evans, *Cyclopedia of Georgia*, State Historical Association, Atlanta, Georgia.

Carpenter, Lewis Cass, *The Tourist's Guide to Colorado and the Carbonate Fields*, The Denver Tribune Publishing House, Denver, 1879.

Cary, Lucian, *Lucian Cary on Guns*, Fawcett Publications, Greenwich, Connecticut, 1950.

City of Dallas and Dallas County, Dallas, Texas, 1873.

Clark, Thomas D., *The Rampaging Frontier*, Bobbs-Merrill Co., Publishers, New York, 1949.

Cockrell, Frank M., *A History of Early Dallas*, Chicago, 1944.

Complete History of the Late Mexican War, by an eye-witness, F. J. Dow & Co., New York, 1850.

Connelly, William Elsey, *Wild Bill and His Era*, Press of the Pioneers, New York, 1933.

Crofutt, George A., *Crofutt's Grip-Sack Guide of Colorado*, Overland Publishing Co., Omaha, Nebraska, 1885.

Crumbine, S. J., *Frontier Doctor*, Dorrance & Co., Philadelphia, 1948.

Cunningham, Eugene, *Triggernometry*, Press of the Pioneers, New York, 1934.

Denver Directory, Gazetteer Co., Inc., Denver, 1882–1887.

DeVeny, William, *The Establishment of Law and Order on the Western Plains*, Optimist Print, The Dalles, Oregon, 1915.

Dick, Everett, *The Sod-House Frontier, 1854–1890*, D. Appleton-Century Co., Inc., New York, 1937.

Dodge, Colonel Richard Irving, *Our Wild Indians*, A. D. Worthington & Co., Hartford, Connecticut, 1883.

Downey, Fairfax, *Indian-Fighting Army*, Charles Scribner's Sons, New York, 1941.

Dreppard, Carl W., *Pioneer America, Its First Three Centuries*, Doubleday & Co., Inc., Garden City, N.Y., 1949.

Emrich, Duncan, *It's an Old Wild West Custom*, Vanguard Press, New York, 1949.

Folsom, James M., *Heroes and Martyrs of Georgia in the Revolution of 1861*, Vol. I, Burke, Boykin & Co., Macon, Georgia, 1864.

Freeman, George D., *Midnight and Noonday; or Dark Deeds Revealed*, Caldwell, Kansas, 1890.

Furber, George C., *The Twelve Months Volunteer*, J. A. and V. P. James, Cincinnati, 1848.

Gard, Wayne, *Frontier Justice*, University of Oklahoma Press, Norman, 1949.

Gardiner, Dorothy, *West of the River*, Thomas Y. Crowell Co., New York, 1941.

Gilbert, Douglas, *American Vaudeville*, McGraw-Hill Book Co., New York, 1940.

    Lost Chords, Doubleday, Doran & Co., Inc., Garden City, New York, 1942.

288

Gilpin, Laura, *Rio Grande, River of Destiny*, Duell, Sloan & Pearce, New York, 1949.

Griswold, Don L., and Griswold, Jean Harvey, *The Carbonate Camp Called Leadville*, University of Denver Press, Denver, 1951.

Hagroves, Catherine Perry, *A History of Playing Cards and a Bibliography of Cards and Gaming*, Houghton, Mifflin, Co., New York, 1930.

Hanleiter's Atlanta City Directory for 1870, William Hanleiter, Publisher, No. 1 South Broad St., Atlanta, Georgia, 1870.

Harkey, Dee, *Mean As Hell*, University of New Mexico Press, Albuquerque, 1948.

Hendricks, George D., *The Bad Man of the West*, Naylor Co., San Antonio, 1941.

History of Lowndes County, Georgia—1825-1941, published by General James Jackson Chapter, D.A.R., Valdosta, Georgia, 1942.

Hitchcock, Henry, *Marching with Sherman*, Yale University Press, New Haven, 1927.

Hough, Emerson, *The Frontier Omnibus*, Grossett & Dunlap, New York, 1936.

Huckaby, Ida Lasater, *Ninety-Four Years in Jack County*, Jacksboro, Texas, 1949.

Hunt, Frazier, *The Long Trail from Texas*, Doubleday, Doran & Co., New York, 1940.

Hunter, J. Marvin, and Rose, Noah H., *The Album of Gunfighters*, Bandera, Texas, 1951.

Hunter, Louis C., *Steamboats on the Western Rivers*, Harvard University Press, Cambridge, 1949.

Hutcheson, *A Pictorial History of Georgia*, Author's Publishing Co., Atlanta, Georgia, 1942.

Jackson, Clarence S., *Picture Maker of the Old West, William H. Jackson*, Charles Scribner's Sons, New York, 1947.

Jones, Jack, *Golden Nugget Gaming Guide*, Silver State Publishing Co., Las Vegas, Nevada, 1948.

King, Frank Marion, *Wranglin' the Past*, Hays Corp., Los Angeles, 1935.

Lake, Stuart N., *Wyatt Earp, Frontier Marshal*, Houghton Mifflin Co., New York, 1931.

Leadville City Directory, Ballenger & Richards, Leadville, 1882–1887.

Lippencott's General Guide to Settlers, J. B. Lippencott, Philadelphia, 1876.

Lockwood, Frank C., *Arizona Characters*, Times-Mirror Press, Los Angeles, 1928.

Lowther, Charles C., *Dodge City, Kansas*, Dorrance & Co., Philadelphia, 1946.

Lufkin, A. W., *History of Dentistry*, Lea & Febiger, Philadelphia, 1938.

Lynch, Denis Tilden, *The Wild Seventies*, D. Appleton-Century Co., Inc., New York, 1941.

MacRae, David, *The Americans at Home*, E. P. Dutton & Co., Inc., New York, 1952.

McKie, A. B., and Edwards, W. M., *Guide to El Paso*, El Paso, 1887.

Marshall, James, *Santa Fe, the Railroad That Built an Empire*, Random House, New York, 1945.

Martin, Douglas D., *Tombstone's Epitaph*, University of New Mexico Press, Albuquerque, 1951.

Meakins, Joseph Campbell, *The Practise of Medicine*, C. V. Mosby Co., St. Louis, 1944.

The Merck Manual of Diagnosis and Therapy, Merck & Co., Inc., Rahway, New Jersey, 1950.

Mills, W. W., *Forty Years at El Paso, 1858–1898*, privately printed, 1901.

Monaghan, Jay, *The Great Rascal, the Life and Adventures of Ned Buntline*, Little, Brown & Co., Boston, 1952.

Myers, John Myers, *The Last Chance*, E. P. Dutton & Co., New York, 1950.

Nature's Sanitarium, Las Vegas, New Mexico, Atchison, Topeka & Santa Fe Railway Co., Chicago, 1882.

Nye, Bill (Himself), *Bill Nye and Boomerang*, W. B. Conkey Co., Chicago, 1894.

Otero, Miguel Antonio, *My Life on the Frontier*, two vols., Press of the Pioneers, New York, 1935.

Owsley, Frank Lawrence, *Plain Folk of the Old South*, Louisiana State University Press, Baton Rouge, 1949.

Pangborn, J. G., *The New Rocky Mountain Tourist*, Knight & Leonard, Chicago, 1878.

Parkhill, Forbes, *The Wildest of the West*, Henry Holt & Co., New York, 1951.

Parsons, George Whitwell, *The Private Journal of George Whitwell Parsons*, Arizona Statewide Archival and Records Project, Phoenix, Arizona, 1939.

Paxon, Frederic L., *The Pacific Railroads and the Disappearance of the Frontier*, Government Printing Office, Washington, D.C., 1909.

Payne, Owen, *Lead and Likker*, Minton, Balch & Co., New York, 1932.

Perkins, J. R., *Trails, Rails, and War, the Life of General G. M. Dodge*, Bobbs-Merrill Co., Indianapolis, 1929.

Price, Goodale, *Saga of the Hills*, Cosmo Press, Hollywood, 1940.

Raine, William McLeod, *Famous Sheriffs and Western Outlaws*, Doubleday & Co., Inc., New York, 1929.

.45-Caliber Law, Row, Peterson & Co., Evanston, Illinois, 1941.

Raphael, Ralph B., *The Book of American Indians*, Fawcett Publications, Inc., Greenwich, Connecticut, 1953.

Rister, Carl Coke, *The Southwestern Frontier*, Arthur H. Clark Co., Cleveland, 1928.

Rogers, John William, *The Lusty Texans of Dallas*, E. P. Dutton & Co., Inc., New York, 1951.

Routes of Travel in Colorado, Office of the Rocky Mountain News, Denver, Colorado, 1874.

Quiett, Glenn Chesney, *Pay Dirt,* D. Appleton-Century Co., New York, 1936.

They Built the West, D. Appleton-Century Co., New York, 1934.

Sanger, Donald Bridgeman, *The Story of Fort Bliss,* privately printed, 1933.

The Santa Fe Trail, the editors of *Look,* Random House, New York, 1946.

Scarne, John, *Scarne on Cards,* Crown Publishers, New York, 1949.

Sherwood, Adiel, *A Gazeteer of Georgia,* Brawner & Putnam, Griffin, Georgia, 1860.

Siringo, Charles A., *A Texas Cowboy; or, Fifteen Years on the Hurricane Deck of a Spanish Pony,* William Sloan Associates, Inc., New York, 1950.

Sketch of the Pueblos and Pueblo County, Colorado, published by the Board of Trade, Pueblo, Colorado, 1884.

Sonnichsen, E. L., *Billy King's Tombstone,* Caxton Press, Caldwell, Idaho, 1942.

I'll Die Before I'll Run, Harper & Brothers, New York, 1951.

Souvenir of Dallas, Texas, Ward Brothers, Columbus, Ohio, 1888.

Spring, Agnes Wright, *The Cheyenne and Black Hills Stage and Express Routes,* The Arthur H. Clarke Co., Glendale, California, 1949.

Stokes, George W., and Driggs, Howard R., *Deadwood Gold,* World Book Co., New York, 1929.

Strahorn, Robert E. ("Alter Ego"), *The Handbook of Wyoming and Guide to the Black Hills and Big Horn Region,* Cheyenne, Wyoming, 1877.

Strout, Richard Lee, editor, *Maud, the Diary of Maud Rittenhouse,* The Macmillan Co., New York, 1939.

Sutton, Fred E., and MacDonald, A. B., *Hands Up! Stories of the Six-Gun Fighters of the Old West,* A. L. Burt & Co., New York, 1927.

Thomas, Edward J., *Memoirs of a Southerner, 1840–1923,* Savannah, Georgia, 1923.

Throm, Edward L., editor, *Popular Mechanic's Picture History of American Transportation,* Simon & Schuster, Inc., New York, 1952.

Triggs, J. H., *A Reliable and Correct Guide to the Black Hills, Powder River, and Big Horn Gold Fields,* Herald Steam Book and Job Printing House, Omaha, Nebraska, 1876.

Turner, Frederick Jackson, *The Frontier in American History,* Henry Holt & Co., New York, 1920.

Valdosta City Directory, R. L. Polk & Co., Jacksonville, Florida, 1908.

Van Metre, T. W., *Trains, Tracks and Travel,* Simmons-Boardman Publishing Co., New York, 1926.

Vestal, Stanley, *Dodge City, Queen of Cowtowns,* Harper & Brothers, New York, 1952.

Walters, Lorenzo D., *Tombstone's Yesterdays*, Acme Printing Co., Tucson, 1929.

Wellman, Paul S., *The Trampling Herd*, Carrick & Evans, New York, 1939.

The Westerners' Brand Book, Denver Posse, 1948.

The Westerners' Brand Book, Los Angeles Posse, 1949.

Wheeler, Colonel Homer W., *Buffalo Days*, Bobbs-Merrill Co., Indianapolis, 1923.

White, Reverend George, *Historical Collections of Georgia*, Pudney & Russell, New York, 1854.

Wilson, John Stainback, *Atlanta as It Is*, Little, Rennie & Co., Printers, New York, 1871.

Wilson, Rufus Rockwell, *Out of the West*, Press of the Pioneers, New York, 1933.

Woestemeyer, Ina Faye, and Gambrill, J. Montgomery, *The Westward Movement*, D. Appleton-Century Co., New York, 1939.

Woodbury, F. S., *Tourists' Guide Book to Denver*, Denver, 1882.

Woods' Baltimore City Directory, printed and published by John W. Woods, Baltimore, 1871.

W.P.A., *Colorado, a Guide to the Highest State*, Hastings House, New York, 1941.

    Georgia, a Guide to Its Towns and Countryside, University of Georgia Press, Athens, 1940.

    Kansas, a Guide to the Sunflower State, Viking Press, New York, 1939.

    New Mexico, a Guide to the Colorful State, Hastings House, New York, 1940.

    South Dakota, a Guide to the State, Hastings House, New York, 1952.

Wright, Robert M., *Dodge City, the Cowboy Capital*, Wichita Eagle Press, Wichita, Kansas, 1913.

Young, Edward Clarke, *Atlanta Illustrated*, J. P. Harrison & Co., Atlanta, 1881.

PERIODICALS

"The American Railroad," *Harper's New Monthly Magazine*, August, 1874.

"Beautiful and Useful Books For the Holidays Published by Harper and Brothers, Franklin Square, N.Y.," *Harper's New Monthly Magazine*, December, 1857.

"Editor's Historical Record—The Black Hills Expedition," *Harper's New Monthly Magazine*, October, 1874.

"Famous Gun Fighters of the Western Frontier, Fourth Article, 'Doc' Holliday," W. B. (Bat) Masterson, *Human Life*, May, 1907.

"The First Century of the Republic—Mechanical Progress," Edward H. Knight, *Harper's New Monthly Magazine*, December, 1874.
"The First Century of the Republic—Medical and Sanitary Progress," Austin Flint, M.D., *Harper's New Monthly Magazine*, June, 1876.
"General MacKenzie and Fort Concho," Colonel M. C. Crimmins, *West Texas Historical Association Yearbook*, Vol. X, 1934.
"New Washington," *Harper's New Monthly Magazine*, February, 1875.
"Playing Cards," Frieda Clark, *Hobbies, The Magazine for Collectors*, April, 1952.
"Single-Action Craze," R. A. Bennett, Jr., *The American Rifleman*, July, 1950.
"Smithing the Colt SA," John Lachuk, *The American Rifleman*, May, 1945.
"Tombstone's Fighting Dentist," Cleveland Amory, *Coronet*, August, 1944.

NEWSPAPERS

Atlanta Constitution, June, 1871—December, 1872.
Baltimore Sun, June, 1869—June, 1873.
Cheyenne *Wyoming Weekly Leader*, November, 1875—July, 1877.
Denver Republican, May—December, 1882; January—December, 1887.
Denver *Rocky Mountain News*, January, 1875—June, 1878; May, 1882—December, 1887.
Denver Tribune-Republican, March, 1885—December, 1886.
Dodge City Times, December, 1876—June, 1880.
Leadville Daily Herald, August 20, August 26, 1884.
Prescott *Arizona Weekly Miner*, October—December, 1879.
Pueblo Chieftain, May, 1882—December, 1882.
Tombstone Epitaph, July 31, 1880; October 9, 1880; May 30, 1881; June 4, 1881; December, 1881—June, 1882.
Tombstone *Daily Nugget*, July—December, 1881.
Tucson *Arizona Daily Star*, March—June, 1881.
Tucson *Arizona Weekly Star*, April—December, 1880; August—November, 1881.
Tucson *Daily Arizona Citizen*, March, 1882.

Index

population of, 92
saloons in, 109
and Santa Fe Railroad, 96, 124*f.*, 135
shooting affrays in, 94, 99–100, 110, 126–28
weather in, 125
Dodge City *Globe,* 99
Dodge City *Times,* 100, 101, 104, 105, 110, 111, 113, 120, 126
Dodge City trail, 52
Dodge House, 91, 105, 114, 115
Downey, Ed, Father, 283, 284–85
Driscoll, Tobe, 133, 134
Duffey, William, 120, 127
Dunbar, John, 165, 168, 172

Earp, Allie, 133, 135, 145, 155, 228
Earp, Bessie, 136, 145
Earp, Hattie, 136, 145
Earp, James, 136, 145, 148, 155, 227, 239
Earp, Mattie, 145*f.*
Earp, Morgan, 148, 153–58 *passim,* 168, 181, 204–09 *passim,* 223
  arrested at Constitution city, 225*f.*
  assassination of, 226–28, 251
  suspects implicated in, 232, 233, 234, 236
  in O. K. Corral shooting, 183, 187, 188, 190, 194–202 *passim,* 210, 211
  wound of, 185, 188, 214
Earp, Newton, 239
Earp, Virgil, 133–36 *passim,* 145, 148, 153–58 *passim,* 162, 163, 176, 179, 180, 183, 204–09 *passim*
  death of, 239
  in O. K. Corral shooting, 187–91 *passim,* 194–201, *passim,* 210, 211, 212, 213
  life threatened as aftermath of, 218*ff.,* 220–21

wound of, 185, 188, 214, 226
  Tombstone left by, 228, 230
Earp, Virgil, Mrs., 145, 146, 148
Earp, Warren, 223, 227, 228, 230, 231, 232, 234, 238, 254
  death of, 239
Earp, Wyatt B. S., 81, 106, 107, 110, 111, 120, 128
  arrested at Contention city, 225*f.*
  arrested for O. K. Corral shooting, 187, 212
  arrival in Dodge City, 101
  and Bisbee stagecoach robbery, 181
  in deal with Clanton, 173, 176*f.*
  and Holliday, John Henry, 132–35 *passim,* 148, 154, 158, 171, 178, 205, 206, 207, 219
    bailing out of, 178
    parting from, 239
  and Kinnear stagecoach robbery, 168, 171
  later years of, 239
  in O. K. Corral shooting, 183, 185, 187, 190–200 *passim,* 214
  life threatened as aftermath of, 218*ff.*
  and release by Judge Spicer, 215, 217
  testimony by, 202–12
  in posse (*1882*), 223*f.*
  in Prescott, 136, 145
  in Pueblo, 238
  and Stilwell killing, 229, 230, 231, 232, 234, 235
  wife of, 145–46, 234
Eastman, Em, 180
El Paso (Texas), 58
Elder, Katherine (Big Nosed Kate), 115, 125, 132, 136, 137, 146, 148, 149, 157, 158
  appearance of, 111

298

302

303